Software Measurement

Christof Ebert · Reiner Dumke

Software Measurement

Establish – Extract – Evaluate – Execute

With 157 Figures and 50 Tables

Springer

Authors

Christof Ebert
Vector Consulting Services
Ingersheimer Strasse 24
70499 Stuttgart, Germany
christof.ebert@vector-consulting.de

Reiner Dumke
Otto-von-Guericke Universität Magdeburg
Postfach 4120
39016 Magdeburg, Germany
dumke@ivs.cs.uni-magdeburg.de

Library of Congress Control Number: 2007929486

ACM Computing Classification (1998): D.2.8, D.2.9, G.3, H.3.4, K.4.3, K.6.1, K.6.3, K.6.4

ISBN 978-3-540-71648-8 Springer Berlin Heidelberg New York

This work is subject to copyright. All rights are reserved, whether the whole or part of the material is concerned, specifically the rights of translation, reprinting, reuse of illustrations, recitation, broadcasting, reproduction on microfilm or in any other way, and storage in data banks. Duplication of this publication or parts thereof is permitted only under the provisions of the German Copyright Law of September 9, 1965, in its current version, and permission for use must always be obtained from Springer. Violations are liable for prosecution under the German Copyright Law.

Springer is a part of Springer Science+Business Media

springer.com

© Springer-Verlag Berlin Heidelberg 2007

The use of general descriptive names, registered names, trademarks, etc. in this publication does not imply, even in the absence of a specific statement, that such names are exempt from the relevant protective laws and regulations and therefore free for general use.

Typesetting and Production: LE-TeX, Jelonek, Schmidt & Vöckler GbR, Leipzig
Coverdesign: KünkelLopka Werbeagentur, Heidelberg

Printed on acid-free paper   45/3180/YL – 5 4 3 2 1 0

Preface

> *Not everything that counts can be counted.*
> *Not everything that is counted counts.*
> Albert Einstein

Our world and our society are shaped and increasingly governed by software. We might accept it or not, but it is happening at this point and will continue further on. It is difficult to imagine our world without software. There would be no running water, food supplies, business or transportation would disrupt immediately, diseases would spread, and security would be dramatically reduced – in short, our society would disintegrate rapidly. The reason our planet can bear over six billion people is software. Since software is so ubiquitous and embedded in nearly everything we do, we need to stay in control. We have to make sure that the systems and their software run as we intend – or better. Software measurement is the discipline that ensures that we stay in control.

This is a book about software measurement from the practitioner's point of view, and it is a book for practitioners. Software measurement needs a lot of practical guidance to build upon experiences and to avoid misinterpretations and errors. This book targets exactly this need, namely to share experiences in a constructive way that can be followed. It tries to summarize experiences and knowledge about software measurement so that it is applicable and repeatable. It extracts experiences and lessons learned from the narrow context of the specific industrial situation, thus facilitating transfer to other contexts.

Software measurement applies to **products** (e.g., performance engineering), **processes** (e.g., productivity improvement), **projects** (e.g., estimation) and **people** (e.g., engineering skills). New fields have emerged in the recent years. We therefore show how software measurement applies to current application development, mobile computing, Web design, and embedded systems. Standards have emerged which we use and explain in their practical usage. We will introduce the major measurement standards such as ISO 15939, the product and service quality standards such as ISO 9001, and improvement frameworks such as the CMMI, being the very successful de facto industry standard for process improvement. Measurement theory and underlying methodologies are consolidated and ensure that the foundations of each chapter are correct with respect to mathematics and statistics.

Software measurement is not at a standstill. With the speed at which software engineering is evolving, software measurement has to keep pace. While the underlying theory and basic principles remain invariant in the true sense (after all, they are not specific to software engineering), the application of measurement to specific contexts and situations is continuously extended. This book thus serves as a reference on these invariant principles as well as a practical guide on how to make software measurement a success. It is therefore a new book and has not much in common with its "predecessor", "Best Practices in Software Measurement", that after only three years is already sold out. But, we need to remark that some contents have been taken over from this previous book.

The book summarizes the broad practical experiences of the authors in companies such as Alcatel-Lucent, Atos Origin, Axa, Bosch, Deloitte, Deutsche Telekom, Shell, Siemens, and Vector Consulting. We are learning continuously, be it while working on software projects, teaching a seminar, giving a keynote at a conference or on a consulting engagement. Companies like those we are working with are key in building knowledge and evolving a technical field because they share needs, use external advice, search for continuous improvements, and do not get trapped in the "not invented here" syndrome.

Our work as authors of such a book is built on the support, service, and knowledge of numerous experts in the field of measurement. Some should be mentioned here because they contributed with dedicated "expert boxes" to practical insight from different perspectives. These expert boxes are embedded in the text and help you to transfer technology to your own settings faster and more reliably. We want to thank these experts, namely Alain Abran, Luigi Buglione, Manfred Bundschuh, David N. Card, Ton Dekkers, Robert L. Glass, David A. Gustafson, Marek Leszak, Peter Liggesmeyer, Andreas Schmietendorf, Harry Sneed, Dieter Stoll, Jochen Scheeg, Charles Symons, Falk Uebernickel, Ruediger Zarnekow, and Horst Zuse. Many more colleagues from various measurement and process improvement communities cannot be mentioned due to space restrictions – but without them this book would have been impossible.

Special thanks go to Springer and our editor, Ralf Gerstner, for their helpful cooperation during the preparation of this book. We want to thank Volker Heine of Vector Consulting for a careful technical review and the proof readers of Springer who brought up many errors and improvement proposals which once again shows the value of technical reviews for defect containment. Thanks also to all those who mailed their feedback on the preceding book and thus helped to improve. All reading this book or attending our seminars or using our consulting are invited to provide further feedback.

The authors are available via e-mail to address specific questions that you might have when working with this book. We welcome such feedback for two reasons. First, it helps to speed up the sharing of software engineering knowledge and thus enriches the common body of knowledge. Second, since we anticipate more editions to come, such feedback ensures further improvements.

The Web site of this book is: http://metrics.cs.uni-magdeburg.de. It provides access to Internet resources on software measurement and updates.

We wish you all good success in measuring and improving with the figures. We are sure you will distinguish what counts from what can be counted. Even more, we wish you all success that what you count counts and is accountable.

Stuttgart, Magdeburg Christof Ebert
January 2007 Reiner Dumke

Contents

1. **Introduction** 1
   1.1. The Purpose of the Book 1
   1.2. Measurement Standards 4
   1.3. How this Book Is Organized 7
   1.4. Who Should Read this Book? 10
   1.5. Authors 12

2. **Making Measurement a Success – A Primer** 17
   2.1. Why Measurement? 17
   2.2. The Need for Measurement 20
   2.3. A Simple and Effective Measurement Process 23
      2.3.1 The E4–Measurement Process 23
      2.3.2 Establish 25
      2.3.3 Extract 28
      2.3.4 Evaluate 33
      2.3.5 Execute 34
   2.4. Hints for the Practitioner 37
   2.5. Summary 39

3. **Measurement Foundations** 41
   3.1. Introduction to Measurement Foundations 41
   3.2. Foundations of Software Measurement 42
   3.3. Theoretical Foundations 54
   3.4. Software Engineering with Measurement 63
   3.5. Analyzing Measurement Data 67
   3.6. Empirical Validation: Avoiding the Shotgun Approach 71
   3.7. Hints for the Practitioner 72
   3.8. Summary 72

4. **Planning the Measurement Process** 73
   4.1. Software Measurement Needs Planning 73
   4.2. Planning with Measurement Frameworks 73
   4.3. Holistic Planning of Measurement: The CAME Approach .. 84
   4.4. Hints for the Practitioner 89
   4.5. Summary 90

5. **Performing the Measurement Process** 91
   5.1. Measurement Needs Tools 91
   5.2. Instrumenting the Measurement Process 92
      5.2.1 Process Measurement and Evaluation 92
      5.2.2 Product Measurement and Evaluation 93
      5.2.3 Resource Measurement and Evaluation 95

		5.2.4	Measurement Presentation and Analysis	95

- 5.2.5 Measurement Training 96
- 5.3. Case Study: Static Code Analysis 96
- 5.4. Solutions and Directions in Software e-Measurement 102
- 5.5. A Service-Oriented Measurement Infrastructure 104
- 5.6. Hints for the Practitioner 107
- 5.7. Summary 108

6. Introducing a Measurement Program 109
- 6.1. Towards Useful and Used Measurements 109
- 6.2. The Measurement Life-Cycle 109
- 6.3. Setting up the Measurement Program 110
- 6.4. Roles and Responsibilities in a Measurement Program 113
- 6.5. Using Measurements: Success Recipes 117
  - 6.5.1 Measurement and Analysis 117
  - 6.5.2 Measurement Definition and Collection 120
  - 6.5.3 Data Quality 126
  - 6.5.4 Analyzing, Visualizing, and Presenting Measurements 129
  - 6.5.5 Statistical Traps and How to Avoid Them 133
  - 6.5.6 Performance Indicators and Scorecards 141
  - 6.5.7 Storing Measurements: The History Database 145
  - 6.5.8 The People Impact 148
  - 6.5.9 The Dark Side of Measurement 154
- 6.6. The Cost and the ROI of Software Measurement 158
- 6.7. Hints for the Practitioner 160
- 6.8. Summary 163

7. Estimation of Size, Effort and Cost 165
- 7.1. The Importance of Estimation 165
- 7.2. An Overview on Estimation Techniques 165
- 7.3. Using the COSMIC Full Function Point Approach 169
- 7.4. Case Study: Feasibility Study with COSMIC FFP 180
- 7.5. Case Study: Estimation for IT Systems 183
- 7.6. The Software Estimation Crisis 194
- 7.7. Hints for the Practitioner 197
- 7.8. Summary 198

8. Project Management 199
- 8.1. Measurement and Project Management 199
- 8.2. Software Project Management 200
- 8.3. Measurements for Project Control 205
  - 8.3.1 Basic Project Planning and Tracking 205
  - 8.3.2 Earned Value Analysis 212
  - 8.3.3 Measurements for Requirements 217
  - 8.3.4 Measurements for Testing 222
- 8.4. Agile Projects and Lean Measurement 228

8.5.	Risk Management	232
8.6.	The Project Outlook: Forecasts and Predictions	238
8.7.	Hints for the Practitioner	240
8.8.	Summary	243

9. Quality Control and Assurance 245
- 9.1. Assuring the Quality of Software Systems 245
- 9.2. Fundamental Concepts 247
  - 9.2.1 Defect Estimation 247
  - 9.2.2 Defect Detection, Quality Gates, and Reporting 251
  - 9.2.3 Case Study: Quality Gates 252
- 9.3. Early Defect Removal 258
  - 9.3.1 Reducing Cost of Non-Quality 258
  - 9.3.2 Planning Early Defect Detection Activities 260
  - 9.3.3 Identifying Error-Prone Components 262
  - 9.3.4 Defect Predictions in Embedded Systems 268
- 9.4. Validation and Testing 273
  - 9.4.1 Test Measurement 273
  - 9.4.2 Analyzing Defects 283
- 9.5. Software Reliability Prediction 287
  - 9.5.1 Practical Software Reliability Engineering 287
  - 9.5.2 Applying Reliability Growth Models 291
- 9.6. The Return on Investment from Better Quality 294
- 9.7. Hints for the Practitioner 299
- 9.8. Summary 300

10. Measuring Software Systems 301
- 10.1. Measurement Beyond the Component or Project 301
- 10.2. Performance Engineering 301
- 10.3. Measuring SOA-Based Systems 309
- 10.4. Measurement of Agent-Based Systems 317
- 10.5. Hints for the Practitioner 327
- 10.6. Summary 328

11. Improving Processes and Products 329
- 11.1. The Need for Process Excellence 329
- 11.2. Objective-Driven Process Improvement 332
  - 11.2.1 Usable and Useful Processes 332
  - 11.2.2 Managing Change 336
  - 11.2.3 CMMI for Process Improvement 342
  - 11.2.4 Setting Improvement Objectives 349
  - 11.2.5 Implementing Process Improvement 353
  - 11.2.6 Measuring Process Improvement 356
  - 11.2.7 Critical Success Factors to Process Improvement 358
- 11.3. Measurement within Process Frameworks 359
  - 11.3.1 Measurement Processes in CMMI, SPICE and ISO9000 359

Contents

    11.3.2 CMMI: Practical Measurements for each Process Area 365
11.4. Productivity, Efficiency and Effectiveness..372
11.5. Quantitative Process Management..392
    11.5.1 Process Excellence..392
    11.5.2 Techniques for Quantitative Process Management.................395
    11.5.3 Six Sigma in Software Engineering..403
    11.5.4 Case Study: Quantitative Process Management.....................410
    11.5.5 Challenges in Applying SPC to Software..............................413
11.6. Empirical and Experimental Software Engineering..............................418
11.7. The Return on Investment from Better Processes................................422
11.8. Hints for the Practitioner...428
11.9. 1Summary..432

12. Controlling for IT and Software..435
12.1. Managing Software as a Business...435
12.2. The Business Case..436
12.3. The Return on Investment (ROI)..441
12.4. Cost Controlling..443
    12.4.1 Cost Controlling in Software Projects..................................443
    12.4.2 Cost Controlling in IT Services...446
    12.4.3 Financial Analysis and Business Analysis.............................450
12.5. Strategic and Operational Management...450
    12.5.1 Portfolio Management...450
    12.5.2 Technology Management..456
    12.5.3 Product and Release Management...458
    12.5.4 Distributed Teams and Global Software Engineering 461
    12.5.5 Supplier Management...465
12.6. Hints for the Practitioner...468
12.7. Summary...469

13. Measurement Repositories..471
13.1. Access to Measurement Results..471
13.2. Building the Measurement Database 471
    13.2.1 Motivation and Requirements..471
    13.2.2 Architecture of a Measurement database..............................474
    13.2.3 Details of the Implementation...477
13.3. Benchmarking Based on the ISBSG Repository.................................478
13.4. Measurement Database Services for COTS Software 481
13.5. Hints for the Practitioner...485
13.6. Summary...486

14. Empirical Laws and Rules of Thumb...487
14.1. Applying Software Rules of Thumb..487
14.2. Project Planning..487
14.3. Global Software Engineering..490
14.4. Requirements Engineering..491

14.5. Quality 492
14.6. Software Pareto Laws 494
14.7. Productivity and Process Improvement.. 495
14.8. Hints for the Practitioner and Summary... 497

15. Getting yet more Information 499
15.1. Access to Information Beyond this Book 499
15.2. Further Reading 500
15.3. Measurement Communities 500
15.4. Internet Resources... 505
    15.4.1 Internet URLs for Software Measurement 505
    15.4.2 Internet URLs of Measurement Communities 509
15.5. Hints for the Practitioner and Summary... 510

Glossary 511

Literature.. 539

Index... 555

1. Introduction

Count what is countable.
Measure what is measurable.
And what is not measurable, make measurable.
Galileo Galilei

1.1. The Purpose of the Book

Human performance improvement is essentially unlimited. We continuously try to go beyond what is thought to be the limits. The fastest time for the mile was 4.5 minutes in 1865, 4.0 minutes in 1954, and is around 3.6 minutes today (depending on when you read this introduction). One might expect a three-minute mile during this century. Can you imagine how little runners might have improved if there were no stopwatch or measured track? Unmeasured and unchallenged performance does not improve! Moreover, it will not improve if not fostered by best practices in the discipline.

Software development is a human activity and is prone to continuous performance improvements. Software measurement is the approach to control and manage the software process and to track and improve its performance.

This book shows how to best use measurement for understanding, evaluating, controlling, and forecasting. It suggests how to improve with the numbers. To measure is simple. To give meaning to numbers and take the right decisions is the stuff this book is made of. We coined it around what we perceive as best practices in their respective domains.

Practices need time to mature towards what we perceive as best practices and they are continuously challenged by new theories and practices. Are such best practices timeless? Certainly not in this fast-changing engineering discipline, however, given the long time of maturing and the well-established foundation of software measurement since the early work during the 1970s, they face a life span which exceeds that of the availability of such a book. They certainly are mostly invariant against changes of software engineering methods, paradigms, and tools.

> Software measurements must provide answers. The needs of practitioners, managers, and scientists are not numbers but what is behind the numbers.

These answers help in understanding how a product or project is performing with respect to its objectives. They can indicate whether an organization is doing better or worse compared to a previous period.

The way software measurement is used in an organization determines how much business value that organization actually realizes. You can hardly imagine any software organization operating at its maximum performance without knowing where they are and where they should go. It would be like a fast car in the fog that needs to slow down below its capability due to not knowing where it is. Software measurements are used in the following ways:

1. **Understand and communicate**. Measurements help us understand more about software work products or underlying processes and to evaluate a specific situation or (statistical) characteristic of software artifacts for making operational decisions leading to special experiences (e.g., project management, rules of thumb, assessments, and descriptions of situations).
2. **Specify and achieve objectives**. Measurements are key in identifying and specifying objectives. They ensure we stay on course and eventually reach those objectives. They are used to estimate, predict, or forecast software characteristics in order to achieve and improve understanding leading to general experiences and guidelines (e.g., estimation formulas, development rules, and general characteristics).
3. **Identify and resolve problems**. Measurements help us evaluate work products or processes against established standards and to define and measure specific characteristics during the software life-cycle for improving quality or performance (standardized size and complexity measurements). They help to identify, analyze, and mitigate risks in order to optimize cost-benefit in an organization's business.
4. **Decide and improve**. Measurements allow monitoring, evaluating, analyzing, and controlling the business, project, product, and process attributes for operational and strategic decisions leading to improvement and evolution. This includes portfolio management, removal of root causes of problems, and process improvement.

Fig. 1.1 summarizes the measurement information model with user needs and how they relate to processes, decisions, actions, and (work) products.

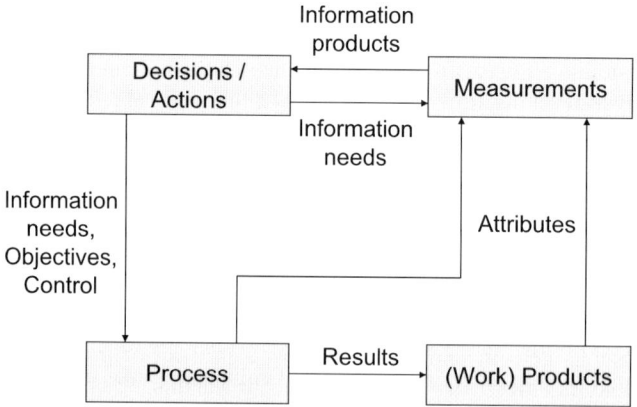

Fig. 1.1. A simplified measurement information model

Measurements exist because there are information needs. They satisfy these needs and thus ensure that the right decisions and actions are taken. The process and its resulting (work) products have certain attributes that are measured in order to provide information products to drive decisions and actions.

> The two major observations we had with several top-performing organizations were:
> (1) Measurements are deeply ingrained into the engineering and management processes and behaviors;
> (2) Measurements are fertilized by the corporate culture.
> They are not perceived as "overhead reporting", but as a useful tool to getting things done – and getting them done better.

Many measurement programs fail. Many numbers are collected but not used, and lots of data is available but without any meaning behind it. **This book tries to pinpoint common pitfalls and how to avoid them**. We target the following measurement-related risks:

- Collecting measurements without a meaning. Measurement must be goal-driven; we measure to improve. People realize quickly whether their managers and environment understand what they are doing or not, and they behave accordingly. Therefore, each single measurement must have a clear practical application or it not only is a waste of effort to collect but may also reduce morale.
- Not analyzing measurements. Measuring is easy, but working with the numbers is a real effort. Often the analysis effort is neglected. Numbers are put into charts and reports and distributed. This is insufficient, as numbers need profound analysis. They need to relate to objectives and performance. Measurements must be actionable or they distort rather than clarify matters.
- Setting unrealistic targets. Many managers, like those portrayed in the popular Dilbert cartoons become so fascinated by measurement – and the perceived accuracy and preciseness – that they pose targets that are entirely driven by the numbers. Sometimes they are not based on history and experience at all, or they drive an organization or team to their limits continuously. Dysfunctional performance and burned-out people result, just like what was seen during the dot-com bubble with the abuse of business measurements to make balance sheets and income statements shine.
- Paralysis by analysis. Measurements are used independently of underlying lifecycle and development processes. Often too much information is collected, and organizations waste time on formalisms and bureaucracy. Overkill, waste of resources and ultimately ignorance on all levels are the result. It is important to understand that measuring is a key part of engineering and project management – but not a separate activity done by accountants.

The risks all reflect cultural, behavioral, and organizational mismatches. Successful measurement programs are characterized by a deep understanding within the organization about the needs and values of measurement. Measurement in such organizations is not considered "carrot and stick" or "demand and control" but a tool similar to a craftsman's yardstick. We would never imagine a joiner, a mechanic or an architect not measuring what they are doing. Yet, many software engineers (and their managers) are in such a situation.

1.2. Measurement Standards

Why do we start with standards in the introduction of this book? Simply because we are engineers and scientists. Both "viewpoints" heavily relate to the exchange of concepts and global dissemination of knowledge and know-how. **Standards are the glue that hold the world of engineering and science together**. They ensure a lingua franca, independent whether you develop software in China, manage a product line in USA or engage into estimation research in Germany. We therefore briefly introduce the relevant standards and how they relate to measurement. We will come back to those that matter throughout the book.

Measurements work best when integrated into the organization's business. We should not think of researchers who create a measurement and users who apply it. Measurements should be selected, defined, and used with a clear goal and perspective. Therefore, measurement users must have basic knowledge about the software measurement process. They must know how to build measurements, how to use the appropriate statistics and how to prove the validity of the measurements. For that reason, the major standard organizations in the software and ICT field, under the lead of the ISO, coined a set of standards (see Fig. 1.2).

How to do	How to do better
ISO/IEC 12207: Software Life Cycle Processes	CMMI: Capability Maturity Model Integration
ISO/IEC 15288: System Life Cycle Processes	ISO 15504: Software Process Capability Determination
SWEBOK: Software Engineering Body of Knowledge	ISO 9001: Quality Management System
PMBOK: Project Management	ISO/IEC 9126: Software Product Quality
	TL 9000, AS 9100, etc.: Objectives, adaptations

 How to measure what you are doing
ISO/IEC 15939:2002
Software Measurement Process

Fig. 1.2. Standards that influence software measurement

These standards describe three perspectives, namely
- How to do things. These are so-called life-cycle processes.

1.2 Measurement Standards

- How to do things better. These standards describe management systems and process improvement frameworks.
- How to measure both. This is a dedicated standard on software measurement.

Standards ensure that the state of the practice is used and improves – on a global scale. The International Organization for Standardization (ISO) was founded in 1947 with exactly this objective and has developed and published thousands of international standards in all economic domains. The name ISO was chosen from the Greek and means *equal*. The connection of "equal" and "standard led to the choice of "ISO." ISO is independent of any government and does not belong to the United Nations Organization (UNO), although it cooperates closely with many commissions of the UNO. Expert contribution and leadership in well over 3000 working groups of the ISO is voluntary.

Fig. 1.3 gives an overview on the major software engineering related standards and how they relate to each other.

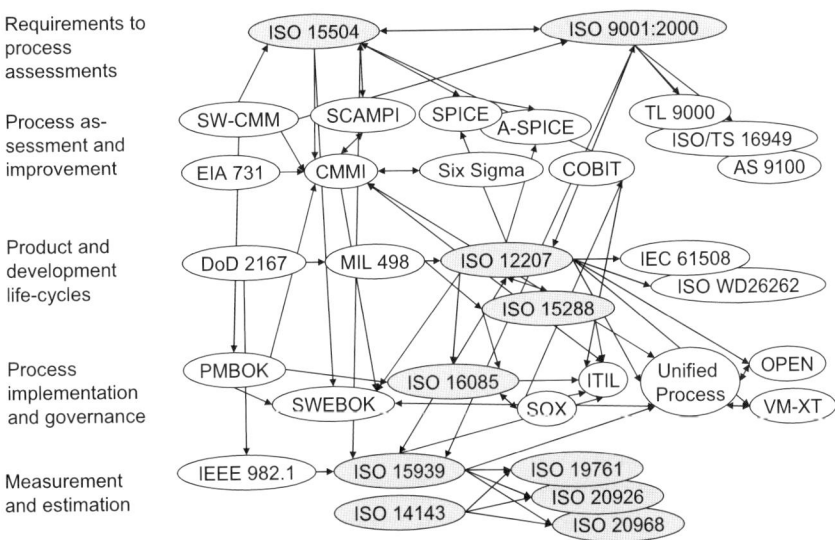

Fig. 1.3. The standards quagmire: Standards increasingly line up and cross-fertilize

Different types of software standards (both ISO and other sources including major de facto standards, such as CMMI) that we refer to in this book, are represented in that overview picture. The ISO-standards are shaded in this picture. They are grouped into categories, namely:
- Improvement standards (metamodels) such as ISO 15504 (capability maturity determination and process assessment standard [ISO04]) and ISO 9001 (quality management [ISO00])

- Improvement frameworks, such as SW-CMM [Paul95], EIA 731[GEIA02], CMMI with SCAMPI [SEI06a], SPICE, COBIT for IT organizations, Six Sigma [Harr03], TL 9000 which details requirements and measurements to telecommunication quality management systems [QuEST06], ISO/TS 16949 which provides requirements to quality management systems in automotive and thus ensures a single view on quality requirements along the supply chain on a global basis[ISO02e], or AS 9100 that enhances ISO 9001 with specific requirements for the aerospace industry .
- Process and life-cycle models, such as DoD 2167, MIL 498, ISO 15288 (system life-cycle [ISO02d]), and ISO 12207 (software life-cycle [ISO95])
- Process implementation and governance, with regulations and policies such as Sarbanes Oxley Act (SOX), standards such as ISO 16085 (risk management [ISO06b]), de facto standards such as SWEBOK [SWE01] and PMBOK [PMI04] and frameworks such as ITIL for IT service organizations, V-Model-XT for governmental contracts, Unified Process, and OPEN.
- Measurement implementation, such as IEEE 982.1 (IEEE Standard Dictionary of Measures of the Software Aspects of Dependability [IEEE05]), ISO 15939 (measurement process [ISO02a]), ISO 14143 (functional size measurements [ISO98]), ISO 20926 (Function Points Analysis according IFPUG [ISO03b]), and ISO 19761 (Full Function Points [ISO03a]).

This book explains how to practically implement a measurement process to software, IT, systems and service organizations based on proven concepts. The *ISO/IEC 15939 standard* [ISO02a, McGa01] and the *CMMI* [SEI06a, Chri06] are particularly helpful for implementing the software measurement process. They closely relate to each other when it comes to measurement and analysis. We therefore use **ISO 15939** to structure this book. Following this standard we can plan and implement a measurement process based upon best practices. We will present a structured guide for the systematic introduction and optimization of the used resources, the software development process, and the product itself. Fig. 1.4 shows the scope of ISO 15939 with the feedback and integration aspects of the software measurement application.

ISO 15939 clearly consists of two parts which are shown in the upper and lower half of the figure. First we need to establish the measurement program and prepare it within the project or organization. Then we execute measurements in each single project covering people and processes. We extract data, evaluate it and execute corrective actions – depending on the outcome of our measurement analyses.

The layout of this standard was used to structure this book for the presentation of our practical experiences and approaches in introducing the software measurement process in industrial areas. Therefore, we will start with establishing and sustaining a measurement commitment as a basic precondition for implementing a successful software measurement process in information technology. Further we will look to the execution of practical software measurement covering projects, people and processes.

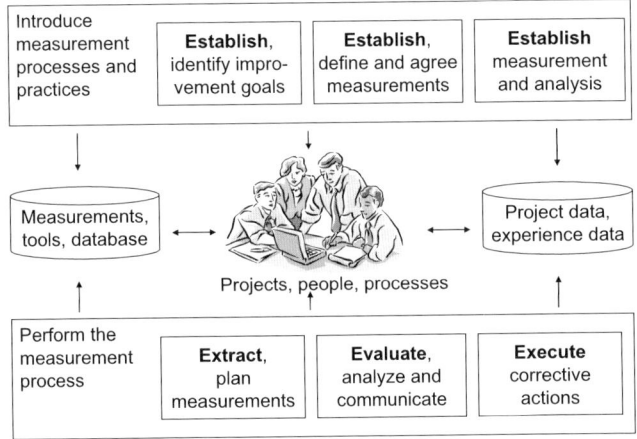

Fig. 1.4. Implementing a best practices measurement process based on ISO 15939.

1.3. How this Book Is Organized

The chapters of this book are organized to read from the general to the specific. All chapters can be grouped within the framework of the ISO 15939 software measurement standard (Fig. 1.5).

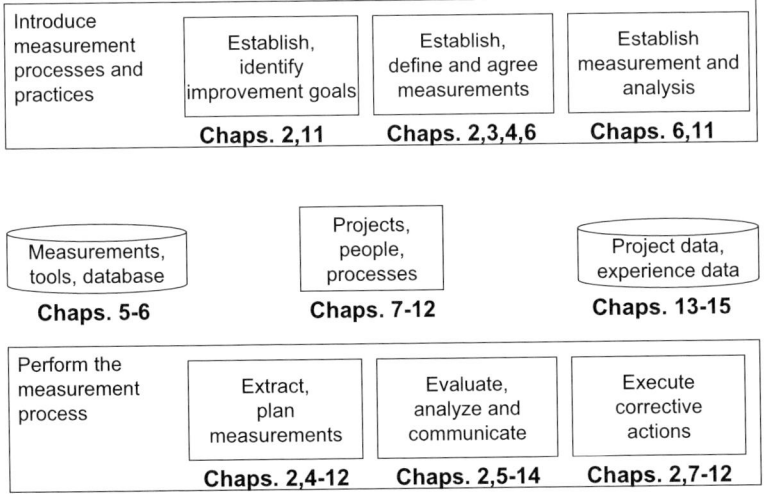

Fig. 1.5. The measurement process and the book's structure

We first introduce a simple yet effective measurement process. Chap. 2 brings measurements into the day-to-day context of your work and provides examples on the practical usage of measurements. This is driven by the need to establish improvement goals and to execute corrective actions. A four-step approach is introduced that we call **E4–measurement process** (due to the letters E that start each word). It starts with **establishing** objectives and measurement activities, then **extracting** measurements, **evaluating** the information and finally **executing** corrective actions or improvements based on the analyzed measurement data. Fig. 1.4 shows with the highlighted terms in bold characters how this E4-measurement process is used from preparation (upper part of the picture) to performance (lower part of the picture). We will use this E4–process of measurement as a reference throughout the book due to its simple yet effective set-up.

Chap. 3 introduces to the basic ingredients of software measurement. It covers measurement foundations and statistical techniques. Rather than diving into lots of mathematics, it will show what you need to know to avoid errors in your measurement processes and measurement usage. Just imagine how you distinguish outliers from trends or how you derive useful forecasts for future project performance. All this needs a sound basis or the conclusions that you or your management make will be useless.

Chaps. 4 and 5 elaborate on how the measurement process and its infrastructure are introduced. Starting a measurement program is very difficult, as it implies culture change towards visibility and accountability for results. Often measurement programs fail because middle and senior management is not capable of dealing with the visibility gained and the trust needed to make measurements successful. We show in Chap. 6 how to best handle the people aspects and cultural changes related to measurement. Anybody dealing with software measurement must consider the effects of measurements on people and the effects of the people on measurements. Often people are afraid of "being measured." Mostly this refusal has to do with a lack of knowledge about how to measure and what is in it when the numbers are used correctly. If measurements are used to threaten and punish before building a climate where targets are set realistically and are made achievable, trust will disappear and numbers will be faked. This explains the cynical behaviors we find in software management cartoons.

From here onwards, we will go into **concrete measurement application areas**. Estimation is still one area in software measurement where many users struggle mightily – right from the start. It is covered in Chap. 7. Project management, and specifically project control is at the core of Chap. 8. This chapter underlines the relationship between project success and "having the right numbers." It provides many examples for project monitoring from practical industry experience we gained over the years.

Chap. 9 deals with quality improvement and defect removal. It contains lots of practical experience on defects detection and removal, estimation and prediction, all with the objective of obtaining the right quality and of reducing the cost of non-quality. Often we tend to neglect the fact that a vast majority of our effort in software engineering goes into enhancing legacy systems. This chapter also looks into how the maintenance activities can be instrumented. It is a chapter that introduces empirical software engineering through the back door. While this will be done more systematically in Chap. 11, we thought it easier to understand if applied directly to the context of quality improvement.

Measuring software systems is described in Chap. 10. Information technology asks for measurement on performance and service availability. We cover different topics related to systems measurement, such as performance engineering and measuring the performance of a system, integrating applications with SOA-based architectures, and instrumenting agent-based systems and Web services.

Chap. 11 generalizes topics for towards the broad field of process and performance improvement. There has been a lot of misunderstanding about using measurements for process improvement. The Capability Maturity Model Integration (CMMI) has contributed in clarifying quantitative management within software engineering, including concepts such as statistical process control and Six Sigma. While many people thought that measurements for most of us are only about tracking performance, the CMMI underlines the benefits of managing organizational, project and process performance simultaneously. We will clarify and explain how to set improvement objectives and how to reach them. Quantitative management and statistical process control have gained attention and are increasingly practiced in high-maturity organizations. We will provide the basic ingredients and show how to best introduce and use quantitative management – while avoiding the traps of misusing statistics. The concepts of relevant techniques such as six sigma and statistical analyses are explained.

From here, we will go towards organizational measurement. Chap. 12 gives an overview on a variety of controlling techniques for the enterprise level. We look into managing IT and software organizations. Topics include creating and verifying the business case, portfolio management, technology management, product and release planning, strategic management, and managing global software engineering and suppliers. These are all cases where software measurement goes beyond the individual piece of code or project and ensures that the organization will be in good shape – before the financial data points to problems, which is often too late.

Measurement needs the right tools and repositories for sharing and communicating results. Though the tools are not heavy or expensive, counting, presenting, and analyzing manually is still common practice. We show in Chap. 13 what tooling should be used for different questions related to measurement. We will practically explain how measurement tools and repositories are introduced and effectively used. We will discuss which tools in the broad arena of computer-assisted measurement and evaluation (CAME) are useful. Specifically, we also look into benchmarking and into how to use external benchmarking expertise.

A book on measurement needs to provide numbers. Chap. 14 provides **facts, empirical observations, laws and rules of thumb from industry experiences**. It is about numbers and results from practical project execution in dozens of organizations worldwide. Most of these organizations are Fortune 1000 and very experienced with software and IT measurement. We are aware that any such number has to be taken with care because your own environment might be different from where we take the data. That's why we put this chapter at the end, although for many readers it will certainly become one of the most relevant chapters of the book as it helps to relate own data towards industry experiences and even fill in gaps where you do not yet have enough own data to draw conclusions.

No book is complete. Chap. 15 provides resources to get more information. It summarizes the major software measurement communities and organizations. URLs are provided for the Internet sites of these organizations. From these resources you can find even more measurement expertise, be it from communities or from repositories. There are many resources on the Internet. This chapter structures our insight and gives you concrete and useful guidance to step further. It will save you hours of surfing and not finding what you need. You will value this chapter when you need information and are under severe time pressure.

A glossary and index wrap up the book. The **glossary** should serve as a baseline reference for the many terms we use throughout this book. It draws the fine line between measurements and metrics (and why we use the first term throughout the book) and has all frequently used terms and abbreviations. An extensive literature list and index help you browse the various references made throughout the book.

Expert boxes are embedded into many chapters of the book. These subchapters are authored by a world-renowned expert on the respective domain and enrich the experience of the two authors with backgrounds from different contexts. The expert boxes highlight the many flavors of applied software measurement.

To ensure enduring value for this book, we keep information updated at its **Web site** at http://metrics.cs.uni-magdeburg.de.

1.4. Who Should Read this Book?

If you develop software for a living and if you are interested in the practical aspects of measurement, this book will show how you can better understand and control what you are doing. The book will help you in understanding what measurement means in practical terms. It will also help in selecting what counts from the perspective of understanding, evaluating, tracking, controlling, and forecasting.

If you manage software projects or organizations, this book will show you what measurement techniques to select for various needs from estimating size and effort to project and portfolio management. It will also describe the "softer" parts of measurement, such as introducing a measurement program or coping with resistance.

If you are responsible for improving quality, performance, or processes in an organization, this book will show how to set targets and how to reach them. It introduces the recent tools and environments for making measurement more efficient. We recommend in this domain using a maturity framework, such as CMMI, to stay focused and allow benchmarking with numerous organizations around the world.

If you are engaged in software engineering research, the book will show what is going on there, what is working and what is not, and how it relates to specific needs the practitioners still expect to be addressed by an improved body of knowledge.

Different persons will take different messages from using this book. We do not prescribe a "one size fits all" approach. It would contradict the above message that measurements depend on objectives and perspectives. We rather introduce measurements for different goals and provide guidelines on how to select, tailor, and best utilize them in your own situation. Measurements **without a concrete need will serve no purpose**. The following examples show what that can mean in practice:

- The engineering organization has the information at hand that they need. Information-needs result from business objectives and from observations along the way of doing business. Measurement answers two basic questions in this perspective namely: (1) are we doing good or bad, and (2) are we doing better or worse. The first is relevant for the individual team, project or department (and upwards) trying to understand progress. The second is relevant for the engineers and managers looking to improvement and to coping with ever-increasing business challenges.
- The supplier learns to implement a software measurement process to address specific project or organizational requirements. He will focus on setting realistic targets and how to track and achieve them. He will improve performance based on quantitative targets to stay competitive.
- The acquirer learns to implement a software measurement process to address specific technical and project management needs. He contracts quantitative performance targets (e.g., service level agreements, quality levels, deadlines) and periodically monitors the supplier's conformance with regard to these agreements.
- The contract between an acquirer and a supplier specifies quantitative performance targets and defines to the necessary degree the software process and product measurement information to be exchanged.

For all of you who are looking for best practices, benchmarks or simply how to get started, the book provides lots of practical hints and concrete examples. Any single entry to this book comes from practical work in industry and has been validated in the face of real-world needs.

> Practice is what matters to effectively use measurements for achieving your objectives and is therefore the lead theme throughout the book. Theory is necessary to do things right and is therefore embedded where appropriate.

1.5. Authors

Christof Ebert (christof.ebert@vector-consulting.de) is managing director and partner at Vector Consulting Services based in Stuttgart. He is helping clients worldwide to achieve sustainable improvement in systems and software engineering – end to end. His focus is on improving technologies, productivity, cycle-time, quality and on change management. Prior to that, he held engineering and management positions at Alcatel for more than a decade, most recently as Director of RD&E with global responsibilities for software technologies, engineering processes and tools. A senior member of IEEE, Dr. Ebert has authored several books, is engaged in standardization activities, lectures at the University of Stuttgart, and serves on editorial boards of several scientific journals and as a frequent keynote speaker at conferences. He is founding member and deputy chair of the German interest group on software measurement, a board member of the German GI interest group on software engineering and a distinguished visitor of the IEEE. For this book, he authored Chaps. 1, 2, 6, 8, 9, 11, 12, 14, 15, and the Glossary.

Reiner R. Dumke (dumke@ivs.cs.uni-magdeburg.de) is currently working at the Otto-von-Guericke-University of Magdeburg, Germany, as a professor with software engineering as research field. He is one of the founders of the Software Measurement Laboratory (SML@b) of the computer science department of the University of Magdeburg and co-editor of the Measurement News Journal. He is leader of the German Interest Group on software measurement and a member of the COSMIC, DASMA, MAIN, IEEE and ACM communities. He received a diploma-degree (MS) in mathematics in 1970 followed in 1980 by a Ph.D. in computer science with a dissertation on the efficiency of database projects. He is the author and editor of more than 30 books about programming techniques, software measurement, measurement tools, software engineering foundations, component-based software development, and Web engineering. For this book, he authored Chaps. 3, 4, 5, 7, 10 and 13.

Expert Contributors

The following measurement experts supported this book in several ways. First, they are authors of small embedded so-called "expert boxes" that provide concrete insight into a specific topic of software measurement. Second, they are active members of the world-wide measurement community and thus helped us and the community to advance in software measurement.

Alain Abran (aabran@ele.etsmtl.ca) is a professor and the director of the Software Engineering Research Laboratory at the École de Technologie Supérieure (ETS) – Université du Québec. He is an editor of the *Guide to the Software Engineering Body of Knowledge* project (ISO TR 19759). He is also actively involved in international software engineering standards and is Co-Chair of the Common Software Measurement International Consortium (COSMIC – ISO 19761). Dr. Abran has more than 20 years of industry experience in information systems development and software engineering.

Luigi Buglione (luigi.buglione@computer.org) is an associate professor at the École de Technologie Supérieure (ETS) at the Université du Québec and is currently working as Quality & Process Engineer at Atos Origin (formerly SchlumbergerSema). Dr. Buglione is the author of "Misurare il Software" (FrancoAngeli, 1999, 2003, 2007) and is a regular speaker at international conferences on software measurement and quality. He also serves the editorial committee of the *Journal of Software Measurement*. He received a PhD in Management Information Systems from LUISS Guido Carli University (Rome, Italy) and a degree in Economics from the University of Rome "La Sapienza", Italy. He is an IFPUG Certified Software Measurement Specialist (CSMS) Level 3.

Manfred Bundschuh (bundschuh@dasma.org) has worked in Axa Service AG in Cologne for 23 years. Since 1993, he has been appointed professor for management and project management at the University of Applied Sciences (http://www.gm.fh-koeln.de/~bundschu) in Cologne. He is president of the Deutschsprachige Anwendergruppe für Software-Metrik und Aufwandschätzung e.V. (DASMA, www.dasma.org). He is an early retiree now studying archeology. His other hobbies are traveling, trekking, geology, astronomy, reading and philosophy.

David N. Card (dca@q-labs.com) is a fellow of Q-Labs, a subsidiary of Det Norske Veritas. Previous employers include the Software Productivity Consortium, Computer Sciences Corporation, Lockheed Martin, and Litton Bionetics. Mr. Card is the author of *Measuring Software Design Quality* (Prentice Hall, 1990), co-author of *Practical Software Measurement* (Addison Wesley, 2002), and co-editor ISO/IEC Standard 15939: Software Measurement Process (International Organization for Standardization, 2002). Mr. Card also serves as editor-in-chief of the *Journal of Systems and Software*. He is a senior member of the American Society for Quality.

Ton Dekkers (Ton.Dekkers@shell.com) has been working as a practitioner, consultant and manager in the areas of project support and software measurement for over 15 years. Within these areas he specializes in estimating, performance measurement (sizing, Goal Question Metric, benchmarking) and risk analysis. His current position is Head of Centre of Excellence for Estimating & Metrics in Shell Information Technology International. He is president of the International Software

Benchmarking Standards Group (ISBSG) and director-at-large at ISBSG in the Project Management Institute (PMI) Metrics Specific Interest Group (MetSIG).

Robert L. Glass (rlglass@acm.org) is president of Computing Trends, publishers of *The Software Practitioner* newsletter, and an honorary professor of software engineering at Griffith University, Brisbane, Australia. He has been active in the field of computing and software for over 50 years. He is the author of over 25 books and 90 papers on computing subjects, editor of *The Software Practitioner*, editor emeritus of Elsevier's *Journal of Systems and Software*, and a columnist for *Communications of the ACM* ("The Practical Programmer") and *IEEE Software* ("The Loyal Opposition"). He was named a Fellow of the ACM in 1998. He received an honorary Ph.D. from Linkoping University in Sweden in 1995. He describes himself by saying, "my head is in the academic area of computing, but my heart is in its practice."

David A. Gustafson (dag@cis.ksu.edu) received his Ph.D. in Computer Science from the University of Wisconsin, Madison. He is a Professor at Kansas State University in Manhattan, Kansas and has taught software engineering for 30 years. He has over 50 publications in the software engineering, software measurement and robotics areas.

Marek Leszak (mleszak@alcatel-lucent.com) works as an R&D quality manager and CMMI coordinator for Alcatel-Lucent, Optical Networking Group in Nuremberg, Germany. He holds a M.S. (Dipl.-Inform.) degree in Computer Science from the University of Karlsruhe, and graduated as Ph.D. (Dr.-Ing.) from the Technical University of Berlin, Germany in 1986. Dr. Leszak is a member of ASQF and GI, and is in the steering committee of the German associations DASMA and the BITKOM "research funding" SIG. He authored some thirty books, conference, and journal publications.

Peter Liggesmeyer (Peter.Liggesmeyer@iese.fraunhofer.de) is a professor at the Technical University of Kaiserslautern (Chair for Software Engineering: Dependability) and director of the Fraunhofer Institute for Experimental Software Engineering, IESE. He looks back on eight years of industry experience at Siemens Corporate Technology, Munich. His Ph.D. (1992) and Habilitation (2000) are from the University of Bochum. Prof. Liggesmeyer has written several books on software quality assurance.

Andreas Schmietendorf (schmiete@fhw-berlin.de) received his Ph.D. degree in computer science from the University of Magdeburg in 2001. He is currently working at the Berlin School of Economics (FHW Berlin), Germany, as a professor doing research in systems and software engineering. Furthermore, he works as consultant for T-Systems Enterprise Services in the area of quality assurance and service oriented solutions. He is an active member in the German society of computer science (GI), the Central Europe Computer Measurement Group (CECMG) and the German interest group on software measurement and effort estimation DASMA.

Harry M. Sneed (Harry.Sneed@t-online.de) was born in Mississippi in 1940, served as a sergeant in the U.S. Army and studied public administration (MPA) and information science at the University of Maryland. Since then he has worked 35 years as a programmer, analyst, tester, project leader, labor director, researcher, consultant, instructor and university lecturer in five different countries. In addition, he has written over 200 technical articles and 17 books on all fields of software engineering. He is currently a software tester for the ANECON GmbH in Vienna and a part-time lecturer at the universities of Budapest, Passau and Regensburg as well as an instructor for the ISQI in Erlangen/Berlin.

Dieter Stoll (dieterstoll@alcatel-lucent.com) works as research project manager in the Optical Networking Division of Alcatel-Lucent in Nuremberg, Germany. He graduated from the science faculty and received a Ph.D. in theoretical physics from the University of Erlangen, Germany. After post-doctoral research positions in Tokyo University, Japan, and Erlangen, Germany, he worked in the areas of performance engineering, embedded software architecture, system definition and managed research projects in the area of intelligent multilayer networks, quality of service, and service management. Dr. Stoll is author of some thirty contributions to books, journals, and conferences.

Jochen Scheeg (jochen.scheeg@t-systems.com) is Vice President Strategic Controlling at T-Systems BPO. After studying economics and business administration, he worked as a consultant in the field of information management and IT controlling. After being awarded his PhD on IT controlling from the University of St. Gallen, he assumed responsibility for a controlling department within T-Systems ActiveBilling GmbH & Co. KG. The department deals primarily with activity based costing, cost calculations and profit center accounting.

Charles Symons (cr.symons@btinternet.com) has nearly 50 years experience in most aspects of scientific and business computing, with particular interest in recent years in IT strategic planning and in improving the performance of the IT function. He has published original work in computer use accounting, computer security, data analysis, and the measurement of software. He is currently joint project leader of COSMIC, the Common Software Measurement International Consortium.

Falk Uebernickel (falk.uebernickel@unisg.ch) holds a Master's degree in Information Management from the University of Regensburg, Germany. He has worked as consultant at Deloitte Business Consulting GmbH in Frankfurt in the area of CFO services. Since the beginning of 2005, he has been working as a research assistant and doctoral student at the Institute of Information Management at the University of St. Gallen (HSG). His main research interests are service-oriented cost accounting and control systems. He is member of the German Society of Computer Science (GI) and author of a number of research publications.

Ruediger Zarnekow (ruediger.zarnekow@ww.tu-berlin.de) holds the chair for Information and Communication Management at the Technical University of Berlin. His research focuses on the areas of IT service management, strategic IT management, and business models for the ICT industry. Previously, he worked at the Institute of Information Management at the University of St. Gallen, Switzerland, where he led the competence center "Industrialization of Information Management." Prof. Zarnekow has been working as a consultant in the area of IT management for many years. He is the author of various books and research articles.

Horst Zuse (horst.zuse@t-online.de) holds a Ph.D. degree in computer science from the Technische Universität of Berlin (TUB) in 1985. His research interests, among others, are information retrieval systems, software engineering and the measurement of software quality. In 1991 he published the book *Software Complexity – Measures and Methods* and in 1998 the book *A Framework for Software Measurement* (both DeGruyter). Today, he is a senior researcher at the TUB and a honorary professor at the University for applied sciences in Senftenberg.

2. Making Measurement a Success – A Primer

*The perception of measures and harmony
is surrounded by a peculiar magic.*
Carl Friedrich Gauss

2.1. Why Measurement?

"The answer is 42" is the popular statement around which Douglas Adams wrote a series of thought-provoking and insightful science fiction books [Adam79, Adam95]. "42" was supposedly "the answer to life, the universe, and everything" in the world, the end to all questions and the final answer that would explain all the rules and logic that make our world move. A huge computer specifically constructed to this endeavor was working for centuries to derive that answer. There was only one difficulty with that answer 42, namely that the question was unknown. The computer seemingly was only asked to provide the answer but not to explain the logic behind and what question it did really address. Therefore, another even bigger computer was built and some books later, it would come back with the question behind that answer. Well, the question was surprising and confused rather than explained anything. Yet it helped to reveal that "there is something fundamentally wrong with the universe". But that is another story.

There are many parallels to software measurement. We often measure, talk about numbers but hardly know what to do about what we measure.

Software engineering is without any doubt about measurement. IEEE's definition of the discipline is as follows:

> "Software engineering is the application of a systematic, disciplined, quantifiable approach to the development, operation, and maintenance of software; that is the application of engineering to software" [IEEE90].

Engineering requires observation, measurement, and calculation. For instance, a software engineer might be asked how long it will take to build an online game, or he might be asked how many failures will occur after the release of his embedded automation system.

> Looking to engineering disciplines, such as civil engineering or mechanical engineering, one can find that the more mature an engineering discipline, the more measurements and indicators are practically used.

The awareness of and need for measurements in software engineering, management, and ICT systems has reached a high level, yet the success rate of a measurement initiative is still poor. Everybody collects measurements, numbers can be found all over, reports look like telephone book – but hardly anyone makes use of these measurements. The answer of "42" (or other numbers for that matter) is everywhere but the questions behind and the practical use of this answer is invisible.

As industry practitioners, we are doing a poor job in using measurements for day-to-day work. Explanations which we hear when using measurements are manifold and can be summarized as follows:
- The designer: Software is an art and cannot be measured.
- The engineer: Measurements could be misinterpreted and abused by management.
- The team lead: Engineers had never been educated on using measurements.
- The project manager: There is no baseline available from previous projects.
- The product manager: Software engineering projects are highly innovative by nature and this cannot be measured.
- The department leader: Software projects are unique and thus measurements are not comparable.

These are obviously excuses for not doing what is normal behavior in any other engineering discipline. Clearly education matters, and therefore must be addressed while introducing a measurement program (see Chap. 6).

This chapter will provide a quick start to software measurement. It shows how to make use of measurements in concrete situations, such as project management and supplier management. It does not assume that you know statistics, measurement theory or goal-oriented measurement. This will be addressed later in the book. It just assumes three things, namely
- You want to know where you are;
- You want to specify where you want to go;
- You want to find out whether you are taking the right way from where you are to where you want to go.

Information theory had an answer long ago and distinguished between data and information. We need to apply the same logic and distinguish between the numbers and their meaning. We call the latter measurements. And we call the first garbage because it does not tell anything. It is much better to have few but meaningful measurements where we know baselines, trends, and how they can be explained and improved, than having many numbers and graphs but no idea what they say.

> The winners in today's competitive global economy are those who pay attention to their own and their organization's performance. They need to know the answers to two questions: "Am I doing good or bad?" and "Am I doing better or worse?"

The first question is a look into a mirror and simply tells whether performance is good enough to sustain. The second questions goes beyond performance and compares over time or across projects or organizations. Just as champions and successful athletes practice and train in order to improve their performance, so must all of us in the world of software engineering and ICT business. Success comes from tuning the process in the right direction. Trends pointing in the wrong direction and that conflict with high performance must be investigated and changed. Measurements help us focus on those things that matter and move us in the right direction. "42" is not always the answer, and even if it is the answer in a given situation, it only matters in a given environment at a given time. Furthermore it only helps if we understand the meaning of the number within that context and take appropriate actions. Let us look into how to make measurement meaningful for your own objectives. **Let us go beyond the numbers**!

During the early eighties both management guru **Peter Drucker** as well as software expert **Tom De Marco** drew attention on measurement by stating that you cannot control what you cannot measure [Druc73,DeMa82]. This statement is widely used to launch a measurement program. However it might be smart to look beyond the statement into the underlying people aspect. What does it really mean to get the expected results? It is attention, not just measurement as was pointed out by **Larry Constantine** [Cons95]. In fact, results are achieved when you monitor people. Parents know it from their children. They get what they pay attention to. If parents like pictures in red colors, they will get them. If they pay attention to singing, children will be happy to sing. The same holds for control theory and systems theory. What needs to be controlled is observed. We all know it from temperature control. Temperature can only be controlled if it is observed. To stay in control, we need to measure.

A famous example is the so-called **Hawthorne effect**. During 1925-1927 Western Electric Company, then the largest manufacturer of electric light-bulbs, wanted to evaluate the effects of lighting on productivity. They set up a series of experiments in their Hawthorne Works, located in Cicero, Illinois. In the first experiment the researchers experimented on three different departments. The striking finding was that they all showed an increase of productivity, whether the lighting increased or decreased. So the scientists extended the experiments with control groups, where in each experiment one group had stable lighting and the second either had an increase or a decrease of lighting. All groups substantially increased production during the controlled experiments. With individualized experiments it was found that if the experimenter said bright was good, the people in the experiment said they preferred the light; the brighter they believed it to be, the more they liked it. The same was true when he said dimmer was good. The series of experiments was concluded that the effects came not from lighting changes but rather from the mere attention to the people. If people receive the right attention and their work is observed and reported, productivity improves.

> You can only control what you observe and measure. The act of setting objectives and monitoring them is the guarantee to receiving the expected results.

This chapter introduces to software measurement from a very practical perspective. It is fast-pace and should help you get started. First, section 2 will look into various needs for measurement. Section 3 proceeds with a lean measurement process that we call **E4–measurement process**. We structure the entire measurement and management process into four parts, namely establishing objectives and a measurement process, extraction of information, evaluation and execution. We will not discuss here *how* measurements are selected in specific situations or environments, as this depends on the objectives and goals of a business process or an application area. We will come back to this question during the other chapters of this book. The final two sections provide hints for the practitioner and a summary on how to make measurement a success and how to be successful with measurement.

2.2. The Need for Measurement

It is eight o'clock in the morning. You are responsible for software engineering. On your way to the company building you run into your CEO. He inquires on the status of your current development projects. No small talk. He wants to find out which projects are running, about their trade-offs, the risks, and whether you have sufficient resources to implement your strategy. He is interested in whether you can deliver what he promises to the customers and shareholders – or whether you need his help. This is your chance! Five minutes for your career and success!

Sounds familiar? Maybe it is not the CEO but a key customer for a self-employed software engineer. Or perhaps you are a project manager and one of the key stakeholders wants to see how you are doing. The questions are the same as is the reaction if you have not answered precisely and concisely.

Is there sufficient insight into the development projects? If you are like the majority of those in IT and software companies, you only know the financial figures. Too many projects run in parallel, without concrete and quantitative objectives and without tracking of where they are with respect to expectations. Project proposals are evaluated in isolation from ongoing activities. Projects are started or stopped based on local criteria, not by considering the global trade-offs across all projects and opportunities. Only one third of all software engineering companies systematically utilize techniques to measure and control their product releases and development projects [CIO03, IQPC03] (for project control see also Chap. 9).

No matter what business you are in, you are also in the software business. Computer-based, software-driven systems are pervasive in today's society. Increasingly, the entire system functionality is implemented in software. Where we used to split hardware from software, we see flexible boundaries entirely driven by business cases to determine what we best package at what level in what component, be it software or silicon.

The software business has manifold challenges which range from the creation process and its inherent risks to direct balance sheet impacts. For example, the Standish Group's Chaos Report annually surveys commercial and government information technology (IT) projects. They found that only 35% of the projects finished on time and within budget, a staggering 19% were cancelled before delivery, and of the remaining projects which finished late or over budget, they only delivered a fraction of the planned functionality [Stan07].

2.2 The Need for Measurement

Measurements must be goal-oriented. Since measurements drive management decisions at various levels, they are directly linked to respective targets. Fig. 2.1 shows this goal orientation in practice. It follows the Goal Question Metric (GQM) paradigm of V. Basili [Basi94]. Starting with objectives which can be personal or company-wide it is determined what to improve. This first steps translates goals into what should be achieved in the context of a software project or process or product. A second step means identifying how the improvement should be done. Asking questions helps in clarifying how the objectives of step 1 will effectively (and efficiently) be reached. We should not leapfrog this intermediate step because it reveals whether we have fully understood the objectives in the first place. Once these questions – and the respective answers – have been addressed, the third step is to identify appropriate measurements that will indicate progress and whether the change is pointing in a good direction. As such the entire framework of questions changes. Note in this context that the GQM-paradigm is primarily looking into defining and selecting measurements and not on guiding actions to resolve issues and to implement change and direction.

> The important paradigm change in goal-driven measurement is that the primary question is not "What measurements should I use?" but rather "What do I need to improve?" It is not about having many numbers but rather about having access to exactly the information you need to understand, to manage, and to improve your business.

Fig. 2.1. Goal-oriented measurement following the GQM-paradigm

Software measurements ensure that the business is successful. They help us see what is going on, and how we are doing with respect to forecasts and plans. And they ultimately guide decisions on how to do better. Success within a software business is determined and measured by the degree the software projects and the entire product portfolio contribute to the top line (e.g., revenues) and to the bottom line (e.g., profit and loss). Late introduction of a product to market causes a loss of market share; cancellation of a product before it ever reaches the market causes an even greater loss. Not only is software increasing in size, complexity and functionality, it is also increasing in its contribution to balance sheet and P&L statements.

With the increasing application of software measurement to manage projects and business processes, it became obvious that while GQM was setting the right basis for establishing a measurement program, it failed to drive an action-oriented feedback loop from measurements to direction and change. This is where paradigms such as Establish, Extract, Evaluate, Execute (E4–Measurement Process) come into the picture.

Software measurements do not distinguish first hand between IT projects, development projects or maintenance projects. The approach is the same. Most techniques described in this book can be applied to different types of software engineering, software management and IT management activities.

Fig. 2.2 shows the relationship between different stakeholder needs and the benefits they achieve by using measurements. Each group naturally has their own objectives which are not necessarily aligned with each other, and they need visibility how they are doing with respect to their own goals. On the senior management level, certainly measurements relate to business performance. A project manager needs timely and accurate information on a project's parameters. An engineer wants to ensure she delivers good quality and concentrates on the team's objectives (see Chap. 3).

Senior Management
- Easy and reliable visibility of business performance
- Forecasts and indicators where action is needed
- Drill-down into underlying information and commitments
- Flexible resource refocus

Measurements

Project Management
- Immediate project reviews
- Status and forecasts for quality, schedule, and budget
- Follow-up action points
- Reports based on consistent raw data

Engineers
- Immediate access to team planning and progress
- Get visibility into own performance and how it can be improved
- Indicators that show weak spots in deliverables
- Focus energy on software development (instead of rework or reports)

Fig. 2.2. Measurements depend on stakeholder needs. Their goals of what to control or improve drive the selection and effective use of measurements

Measurements help us
- Characterize and understand the current way of working;
- Provide baselines against which you can compare progress or improvements;
- Evaluate status so that projects can be controlled;
- Assess the impact of technology on products and processes;

- Establish far-reaching yet achievable objectives for project cost, schedule, quality and cost;
- Predict and forecast future performance;
- Communicate progress and improvement needs.

There is some additional literature around taking a business perspective on software. Most of it looks into examples and case studies to generalize principles [Deva02, Benk03, Reme00]. Some of it look into dedicated tools and techniques and their application, such as project control and management [Royc98, McGa01] (see also Chap. 8), management of global development projects [Eber01a, Eber06b] or knowledge management in R&D projects [Auru03]. A good introduction to the topic of business cases for software projects is provided by Reifer [Reif02]. A special issue of *IEEE Software* summarizes the state of the practice of "software as a business" [Mill02].

2.3. A Simple and Effective Measurement Process

2.3.1 The E4–Measurement Process

The measurement process is an inherent part of almost any business process (Fig. 2.3). It therefore easily applies to software measurement, be it performance engineering, project control or process improvement.

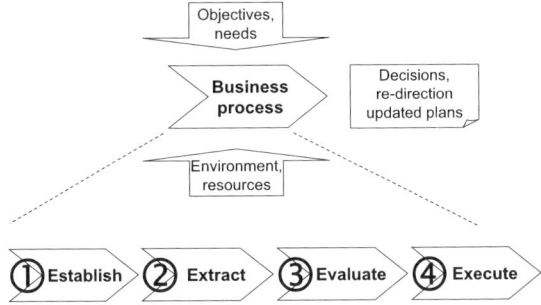

Fig. 2.3. The E4–measurement process with its four steps: Establish objectives and measurement activities, extract measurements, evaluate them, and execute subsequent decisions.

The E4–measurement process consists of four essential steps:
- **Establish** concrete objectives and the measurement and analysis scope and activities
- **Extract** measurements for the established need
- **Evaluate** this information in view of a specific background of actual status and goals
- **Execute** a decision to reduce the differences between actual status and goals

The four steps all commence with the letter "E" which explains why we call this simple process the **E4–measurement process**.

The E4–measurement process is based on the Deming-Circle (Plan, Do, Check, Act) and extends the GQM-Paradigm by adding an immediate action-focus. The Deming-Circle has the steps of setting improvement or performance objectives, executing and measuring the process, analyzing the process behaviors and improving the process. It follows the observation that to effectively and continuously improve a process it is relevant to first stabilizing it, then keeping it in its specification limits and finally continuously improving it [Jura00]. The major difference is the clear focus on goal-oriented measurement and execution of decisions at the end of the four steps. Often the Deming-Circle is seen and implemented as a process of continuous improvement and organizational learning with statistical techniques. The underlying power of Plan-Do-Check-Act had been reduced in the past years to statistical process control and continuous improvement (even if Deming had envisioned a much broader scope). We hold that the approach is the major driver for taking and implementing business decisions.

> The E4–measurement process (i.e., establish, extract, evaluate, execute) as introduced and widely used by the authors is a management paradigm and goes well beyond software measurement. It is grounded in measurement and quantitative techniques in order to achieve fact-based decision-making and sustainable impact of these decisions.

This E4–measurement process can also be portrayed as a closed control loop. We insist that it be closed by means of the last (execution) step, that is, execute decisions based on the information collected. Without the last step, we end up in collecting measurements but not using it to achieve our objectives and capitalize on concrete improvements.

Fig. 2.4 shows this closed loop where the execution is subsequently followed by a new circle of – adjusted – objectives or new questions to be resolved. We do see from the spiral-like picture that with each successfully finished circle, some improvements have been capitalized and will serve as the basis for further improvements.

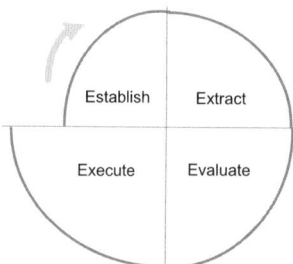

Fig. 2.4. To achieve lasting impact of decisions the E4–measurement process demands four steps in spiral-like continuous improvement circle

There is no use in extracting information and only recording it for potential further usage. If measurements are not used on the spot, if they are not analyzed and evaluated, chances are high that the underlying data is invalid. Without the pressure to have accurate measurements available, collection is done without much care. Where there is no direct use for information, the information is useless and so is the effort behind the collection.

2.3.2 Establish

The very first step in any measurement activity is to establish a scope derived from objectives that should be achieved. Measurement is not primarily about collecting numbers but rather about understanding what information is necessary to drive actions and to achieve dedicated goals. To "establish" therefore means to derive measurement needs from the objectives of the organization (which can be a company, business unit, product line, project or small team), to specify how the measurements are collected and then to extract this information from operational activities. This includes available and needed resources, skills, technologies, reusable platforms, effort, objectives, assumptions, expected benefits and market share or market growth. A consistent set of indicators must be agreed upon, especially to capture software project status.

Measurements selection is goal-oriented (see also Chap. 3). What are the best objectives? What objectives do we talk about? A good starting point is to identify how the projects or activities of an organization are viewed from the outside. Ask questions that affect the organization's and thus your own future. What is hurting most in the current business climate? Are deadlines exceeded or changed on short notice? Is the quality level so poor that customers may move to another supplier? Are projects continuously over budget? Is the amount devoted to the creation of new and innovative technology shrinking due to cost of poor quality, rework, testing and maintenance? Who feels this pain first in the company? Which direction should the product portfolio take? What exactly is a project, a product or a portfolio? Is this what sales and marketing communicate? Where does management get information? Is it reliable and timely? What targets and quarterly objectives drive R&D? Such questions point to weaknesses and challenges. In order to improve on these observations, dedicated improvements are made which need to be measured.

> The trap in most measurement programs is the disconnect between business-driven objectives and the measurement program. Too often things are measured that do not matter at all. Or, there is no clear improvement objective behind what is measured.

A simple example for a measurement need is in project management (see also Chap. 8). The goal is to master the project and to finish according to commitments. An initial set of internal project indicators for this goal can be derived from the Software Engineering Institute's (SEI) core measurements [Carl92]. They simplify the selection by reducing the focus on project tracking and oversight from a contractor and program management perspective. Obviously, additional indicators must be agreed upon to evaluate external constraints and integrate with market data.

Often the collected measurements and resulting reports are useless, and only create additional overhead (see also Chap. 6 on the misuse and abuse of measurements). In the worst case they hide useful and necessary information. We have seen reports on software programs with over 50 pages full of graphs, tables and numbers. When asked about topics such as cost to complete, expected cost of non-quality after handover or time to profit they did not show a single number. Sometimes they are even created to hide reality and attract attention to what is looking good.

> Be aware – and prepared to react where necessary – that measurements are sometimes abused to obscure and confuse reality!

To make measurements a success, more is needed than just facts. It is necessary to look at opportunistic and subjective aspects. What role and impact do you have inside the enterprise? Who benefits most from the projects, and who creates the most difficulties for the projects? Why is that? What could you do to help this person, group, or customer?

Fig. 2.5 shows this goal-driven relationship between business objectives, concrete annual targets or objectives on an operational level and to dedicated indicators or measurements. Goals cannot be reached if they are not quantified and measured. Or as the saying goes, managers without clear goals will not achieve their goals clearly. We show in Fig. 2.5 concrete instances of objectives and measurements, such as improving schedule predictability or reducing cost. Naturally, they should be selected based on the market and business situation, the maturity and certainly the priorities in the projects.

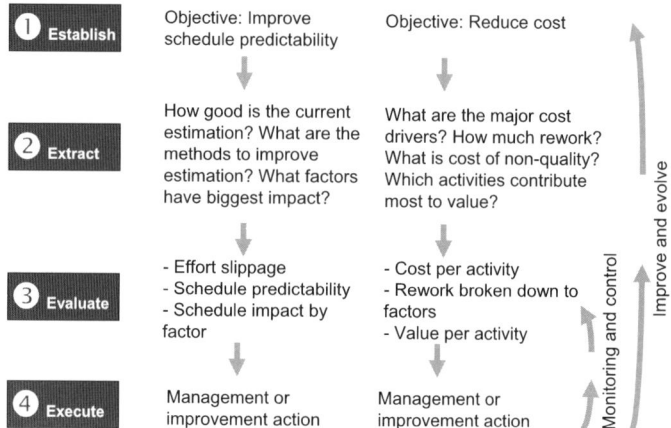

Fig. 2.5. Measurements are derived from goals. They help to achieve concrete objectives – if embedded into the E4–measurement process

To indicate measurement usage during this first step (i.e., establish), we will introduce a simplified product life-cycle as it applies to software, systems and IT projects. Fig. 2.6 shows this simplified product life-cycle in the upper part. It consists of archetypical phases as you find them in practically all product and service development, be it application software, internet software, middleware, enterprise and IT infrastructure, embedded systems, firmware, or services. For each of the life-cycle phases the lower part of the picture shows objectives or needs which are relevant for making the project and product a success. From these objectives, measurements are derived that are used in order to derive the subsequent go/no-go decisions during the life-cycle.

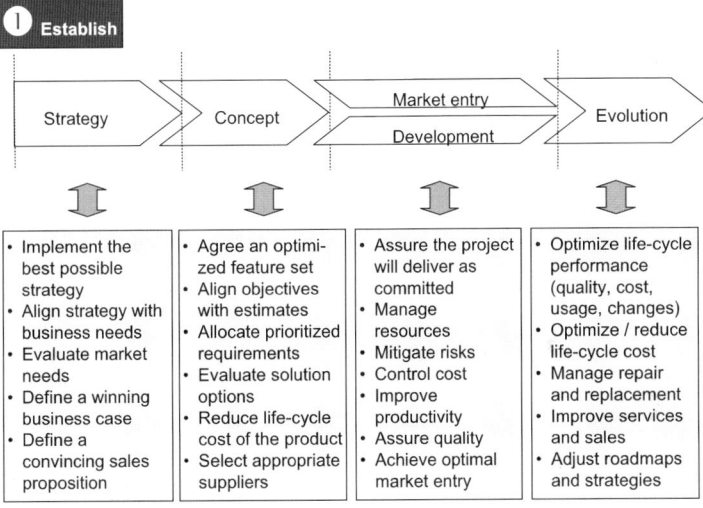

Fig. 2.6. Measurements along the product life-cycle. First the objectives and needs are established.

For instance, during the concept phase suppliers are evaluated. If the suppliers won't be able to commit to the necessary service level or content, the concept phase cannot be concluded and development would not be started. The phase depends on achieving the objectives relevant for the respective phase as stated in the diagram. Measurements help to gain sufficient insight to prepare and drive such decision.

To make the right assessments and decisions, the necessary information must be collected upfront. What factors (or targets, expectations, boundary effects) influence the investment? How did the original assumptions and performance indicators evolve in the project? Is the business case still valid? Which assets or improvements have been implemented? Which changes in constraints, requirements or boundary conditions will impact the projects and results? Are there timing constraints, such as delays until the results are available, or timeline correlations?

2.3.3 Extract

The next step of the measurement process is to extract the right information. To avoid overheads this second step must be closely linked to the first step that provides the measurement objectives. Do not collect information you will not use afterwards. Always be prepared to explain beforehand what you will do with measurements, and how you treat extracted numbers and their trends.

Assuming your objective is to reduce cost and the related action is to reduce rework. The measurements established in step 1 could be a cost measurement related to rework, such as the number of defects not found in the phase in which they are created. From your own previous product development or IT-projects the average values are known. Typically 60% of all defects are found after the phase or activity where they had been inserted. The distribution is in between 50% and 90%. The current project yields 50% at the time of release. Is this good enough? Compared to the previous distribution it looks good, and should be analyzed (next step). However it could also indicate that there were many more defects created than usual and out of this bigger amount a good part had been found immediately. This would be bad. You realize that results could vary dramatically with this one measurement. So this second step can also point to redoing the first step.

For illustration of this second step, we will go back to our simplified product life-cycle as it applies to software, systems and IT projects. Fig. 2.7 shows for each of these standard life-cycle phases some basic measurements that are necessary to steer that respective phase of the project or product release.

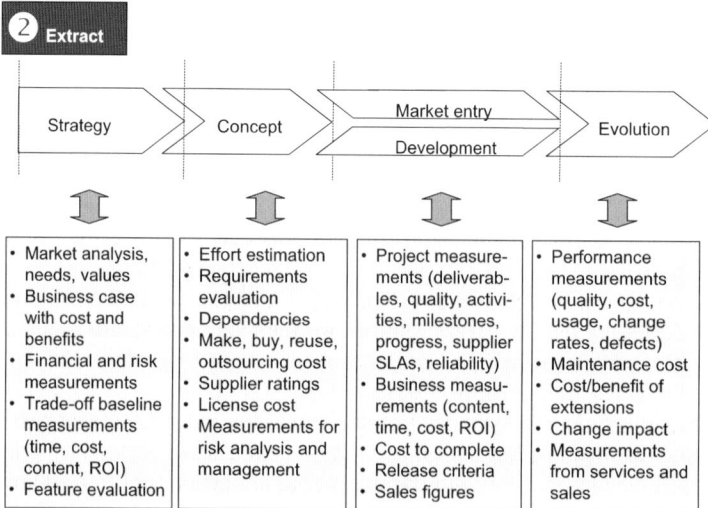

Fig. 2.7. Measurements along the product life-cycle. During each phase of the product life cycle dedicated measurements are extracted that correspond to established objectives.

These measurements are derived with a goal-driven method from the objectives which we indicated in the previous section (Fig. 2.6). Of course, the list is not comprehensive and rather serves as an example how different measurement will help along the life-cycle.

Fig. 2.8 provides an example of how the same overarching dimensions of quality, productivity, deadlines, and employees are translated into different measurements depending on the perspective taken. An internal process view necessarily looks more into how processes can be improved, while the external perspective takes more a service- or product-related perspective. Often this is underlined by the type of agreements or contracts in the different client schemes of business processes.

	Quality	Productivity	Deadlines	Employees
Internal process view	Fault rate Fault density Cost per fault Root causes	FP / Person year FP / Calendar month Tool usage	Percentage of work products within the 10% time frame	Skills Willingness Overtime Absence
External customer view	Customer satisfaction Delivered product quality Functionality	Cost per feature	Delivery accuracy of final product to contracted date	Satisfaction with contact persons (sales, after sales, engineers)

Fig. 2.8. Different stakeholder viewpoints determine how goals are translated internally and externally

Forward-looking figures need insight in order for us to be consistent in estimating cost at completion of a project or following up the earned value. Such a "dashboard" or status report compiles exactly those figures one need when comparing all projects. Try to automate the reporting, because for the project manager it is a useless – because overly aggregated – report. He should not be charged with such an effort.

Often indicators are available but are not aggregated and integrated. For instance, a quality improvement program measures only defects and root causes, but fails to look into productivity or shortened cycle times. Or in a newly created sales portal only access and performance information is known, while sales figures or new marketing mechanisms are left out of the picture. Fig. 2.9 shows how this aggregation is implemented in the various levels of an organization

Especially for software engineering projects, it is important to consider mutual dependencies between projects, organizational units, and so on. At the top is the enterprise portfolio which depicts all products within the company and their markets and respective investments. Further down a product-line or product cluster view is detailed which is aligned with platform roadmaps and technology evolution or skill building of engineers. For each product there should be a feature catalogue across the next several releases covering the vision, market, architecture and technology. From such product roadmap a technology roadmap is derived which allows one for instance to select suppliers or build partnerships. It also drives the individual roadmaps of releases and projects which typically have a horizon of a few months up to a maximum one year. On the project level, these decisions are implemented and followed through to success.

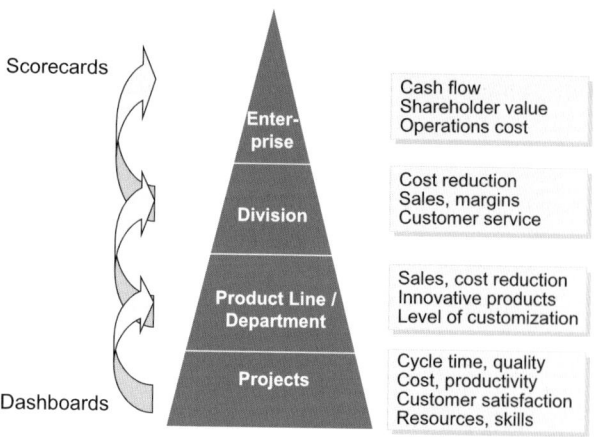

Fig. 2.9. Measurements are aggregated following the organizational needs. At project level focus is on dashboards, while at division or enterprise level it is on scorecards

Ensure that numbers are consistent across these different hierarchies. Often aggregation hides insufficient data quality which is then only revealed when it is to late to improve those underlying processes. Fig. 2.10 provides a practical example that one of the authors had established over the years for a major Fortune 100 company. The corporate scorecard was the starting point and the necessary links to distributed operational data were established stepwise with a decent effort on ensuring data quality by means of periodic reviews, governance and tool support. This small example also indicates that different processes such as corporate control, strategy management, portfolio management and project management are ultimatively related. What goes wrong on one level must be visible on the next higher level – if it is beyond the acceptable noise level.

Such aggregation is not intended for micromanagement or command and control from the top but rather to ensure that the same data is utilized across the company. This has advantages not only on the cost side due to less rework and redundant data collection mechanisms, but also to ensure that risk management is based on exactly the same insight into operational and strategic baselines and that decisions can be tracked one day in case of external investigations.

Projects typically aggregate information similar to a dashboard. Such **project dashboard** allows to have all relevant information related to project progress against commitments, including risks and other information summarized on one page, typically online accessible with periodically updated data. Examples for project dashboard information are performance of milestones against the planned

2.3 A Simple and Effective Measurement Process

dates, or showing the earned value at a given moment (for project dashboards, see also Chap. 8 and for scorecards, see Chap. 6).

Project dashboards provide information in a uniform way across all projects, thus not overloading the user with different representations and semantics that she has to wade through. They provide information at the finger tips – ready to make decisions. They help to examine those projects that underperform or that are exposed to increased risk. Project managers would look more closely and examine how they could resolve such deviation in real time within the constraints of the project. All projects must share the same set of consistent measurements presented in a unique dashboard. Lots of time is actually wasted by reinventing spreadsheets and reporting formats, where the project team should rather focus on creating value.

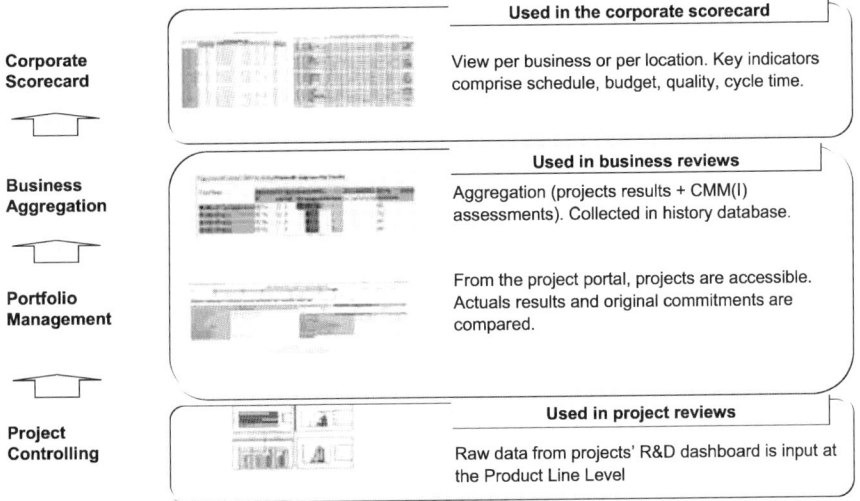

Fig. 2.10. Clearing the fog: Ensure a consistent view on all engineering projects, product lines and business units.

Fortunately, such a dashboard need not be time consuming or complex. Measurements such as schedule and budget adherence, earned value, or quality level are typical performance indicators that serve as "traffic lights" on the status of the individual project. Only those (amber and red) projects that run out of agreed variance (which, of course, depends on the maturity of the organization) would be investigated and further drilled down in the same dashboard to identify root causes. When all projects follow a defined process and utilize the same type of reporting and performance tracking, it is easy to determine status, identify risks and resolve issues, without getting buried in the details of micromanaging the project.

A standardized project dashboard is easy to set up and will not incur much operational cost. It builds on few standard measurements that are aggregated and represented typically in an intranet-accessible format to facilitate drill-down. It leverages on existing project management and collaboration tools from which it draws its raw data (e.g., schedule information, milestones, effort spent, defects detected, and so on). It is self-contained and easy to learn. Key information is collected in a single repository with access control to protect the consolidated information. Having such a dashboard in place will ensure that project issues remain on the radar screen of the stakeholders.

> By fostering early risk management by means of useful measurements and reliable predictions, it will once and for all take away the "I didn't see that coming" response. A forward-looking attitude will be established automatically when excuses are taken away.

Performance monitoring is key. Standard measurements must be collected from each project and then consolidated for all the projects to evaluate the portfolio's alignment with business objectives and performance requirements (Fig. 2.9). For the senior management levels the same information is further condensed into a scorecard that relates different businesses to the annual objectives. Scorecards should be balanced [Kapl93] in order to avoid local optimization of only one target.

Combining and aggregating the raw data creates useful management information. For instance, a product with a new technology should be looked at from different angles. By using Linux instead of a proprietary operating system one might not only look into skills and introduction costs, but also into financial health of the packaging company or liability aspects in the medium-term. It is necessary to extract indicators from all operational areas and assess them in combination [Kapl93, Hitt95].

As an example, let us look at different ways to measure success or returns from software engineering activities. Obviously there are operational figures that benefit calculation, such as phase durations in the product life-cycle, time to profit, time to market, cycle time for single processes, maintenance cost, cost of non-quality, cycle time for defect corrections, reuse rate, and license cost and revenues. Another dimension that is often neglected is improvements in productivity or people, such as cost per engineer, learning curves, cost per employee (in different countries), cost evolution, output rates per engineer or capital expenses per seat.

From these indicators one can select the few that reflect the assumptions of the original business case for the underlying products. They will help to further trace and predict costs and benefits. Indicators should be translated into the "language" of the projects or stakeholders to allow seamless extraction from regular project reviews without much overhead.

Once the necessary indicators are aggregated and available in one central repository or from a single portal, it is easy to generate reports covering the entire set of activities, projects, products or departments. Frequently asked queries are accessible online to save time and effort. Such reports, for instance, provide a list of product releases sorted to their availability. They can show average delays or budget overheads. One can single out projects with above-average cost and compare with their earned value, or one can portray products according to revenues, market shares and life-cycle positioning. This reduces the effort to identify outliers which need special treatment.

2.3.4 Evaluate

After indicators and relevant project and marketing tracking information have been agreed upon and are available, evaluation of this information starts. This includes the evaluation of cost against benefits, business case, usefulness of the results from projects, and market readiness – all as future scenarios in terms of opportunities and risks. Such evaluation happens continuously and for the totality of projects. Even if product lines are not related technically or perhaps they even address fully different markets, it makes sense to evaluate mutual dependencies or synergies, such as resource consumption or asset generation.

For illustration of this third step, we will go back to our simplified product life-cycle as it applies to software, systems and IT projects. Fig. 2.11 shows for each of these standard life-cycle phases typical analyses that are necessary to steer that respective phase of the development. They are based on the extracted measurements (Fig. 2.7) and correspond to the objectives which were agreed during the first step (Fig. 2.6).

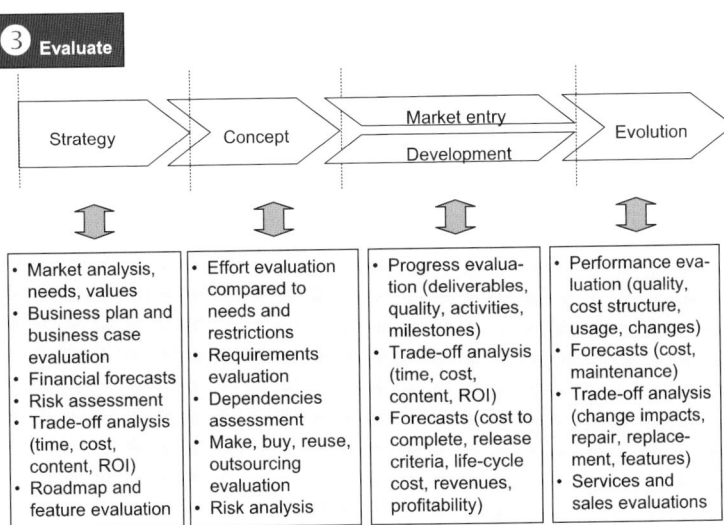

Fig. 2.11. Measurements along the product life-cycle. During each phase of the product life-cycle measurements are evaluated to ensure progress towards established objectives.

Certainly a monthly exercise for projects and products or a yearly exercise for portfolios as was done historically in many companies is far too coarse and falls behind the facts. Even the monthly or quarterly exercises preceding budget cycles and agreements turn out to be illustrative rather than guiding. On the project-level a weekly reassessment of assumptions should be an ideal balance of effort and benefits. On the level of products and portfolios, a monthly reassessment still allows one to actively steer the evolution reflecting market changes. If projects change or deviate from the agreed objectives or if the risk level gets higher and the chances that the project manager can recuperate within the project get smaller, it is time to reevaluate and realign the project and portfolio with reality.

It is crucial to simultaneously evaluate *cost and benefits* or *trade-offs* between objectives. Regarding cost, the following questions could be addressed: Where are the individual elements of the portfolio (i.e., the products, product releases or projects) with respect to cost and cost structure? Is cost evolution following the approved plans and expectations? Is cost structure competitive (e.g., the share of test effort of the total development cost)? How is the evolution of the entire cost structure (e.g., is the trend going in a direction that allows sustainable growth)? Are the different elements of engineering cost under your control or are they determined from outside? Are all operational cost elements appropriately budgeted (e.g., covering maintenance, service, product evolution, corrections)?

We do the same for the benefits. Do the components of the portfolio follow the original assumptions? Is one investment better than others? Why is this the case? Which factors impact benefits? Which revenue growth relates to certain decisions or changes that have been implemented? What are the stakeholders' benefits from the IT or the R&D, both financially (e.g., return on assets (ROA), return on capital employed (ROCE)) as well as operationally (e.g., value generation for customers' businesses, market expectations, competitive situation)? What are the major impacts on performance and capacity to grow? How do internal processes and interfaces influence innovativeness, capability to learn or improvements?

Today "time to profit" is more relevant than "time to market" when evaluating benefits from different software projects. A delayed market entry in the world of Internet applications as well as other software solutions immediately reduces ROI dramatically. Entry levels for newcomers are so low and the global workforce is growing so fast that the market position is never stable. Even giants like Microsoft feel this in times of open source development and usage and an overwhelming number of companies who all want to have their own piece of the pie. As a rule of thumb one can consider that in a fast-changing market – as is the case for many software applications and services – a delay of only three months impacts revenues by 20% because of being late and the related opportunistic effects such as delays of subsequent releases.

2.3.5 Execute

After having extracted the necessary information and having evaluated the projects comprehensively, it is time to decide and to execute the decisions. Management means to actively take decisions and implement changes. The implications on different managerial levels are comparable. Whether it is on the project or the portfolio level, decisions need to suit the proposed scenarios. For instance, if risks grow beyond what the project can handle, it is time to reconsider features and project scope. Maybe incremental deliveries can help with coping too big a scope and unmanageable size or duration.

If the value and benefits from a product release turn out to be below the standard expected return on the investments (e.g., the current interest rates for this risk level), they should be cancelled. Only those projects and products should remain in the portfolio that represent the biggest value and shortest time to returns. A certain percentage of the software budget should always be reserved for new projects and new technology to avoid being consumed by the legacy projects and products and becoming incumbent.

Different alternatives for decisions result from the previous two steps (extraction and evaluation). You decide only on this basis, as you otherwise invalidate your carefully built tools. Decisions should be transparent in order to influence behaviors and maintain trust and accountability. Particularly if projects are going to be cancelled it is important to follow an obvious rule set so that future projects can learn from it. For instance, if there is insufficient budget, a project is immediately stopped or changed instead of dragging on while everybody knows that sooner or later it will fail. Basic decision alternatives include doing nothing, canceling the project or changing the project or the scope of the project.

Do not neglect or rule out any of these three basic options too early. Different options should be further broken down in order to separate decisions which have nothing to do with each other. For instance, whether and which new technology is used in a project should not depend on the supplier. Each decision brings along new risks and assumptions that one need to factor into the next iteration of the evaluations. If one of the key assumptions turns out to be wrong or a major risk materializes, it is the time to implement the respective alternative scenario.

To ensure effective execution on project and product level, software measurement should be closely linked and integrated in the company's product life-cycle management (PLM). Typical software life-cycles might follow ISO 15288 (systems life-cycle [ISO02d]) or ISO 12207 (software life-cycle [ISO95]). They have in common a gating process between major phases based on defined criteria. These gates enforce evaluating the overall status (both commercial and technical) and deciding on whether and how to proceed with the project [Wall02]. PLM is the overall business process that governs a product or service from its inception to the end of its life in order to achieve the best possible value for the business of the enterprise and its customers and partners.

For illustration of this last (and most relevant) step, we will go back to our simplified product life-cycle as it applies to software, systems and IT projects. Fig. 2.12 shows for each of these standard life-cycle phases a sample of decisions and actions that are taken to ensure progress against commitments and objectives. They are based on the underlying measurements (Fig. 2.7) which are evaluated (Fig. 2.11) and correspond to the objectives which were agreed during the first step (Fig. 2.6).

Let us look at the scenario of deciding whether a project should be stopped before its planned end. This is typically a difficult situation, not only for the project manager and for the people working on the project, but because many organizations consider a stopped project a failure. Well, it might be from a financial perspective, but it will be an even bigger failure if it is not finished. Only few deal with such "failure" constructively, learn their lessons, and work on the next project. We will look at the decision from a higher-level perspective. There are costs after the decision to stop, such as ongoing infrastructure write-offs, leasing contracts and relocation costs. Often these costs are close to the cost of bringing the project to the intended end which implies a delivery. On the other hand, opportunistic factors should be considered, because the engineers could work on other projects that generate more sales.

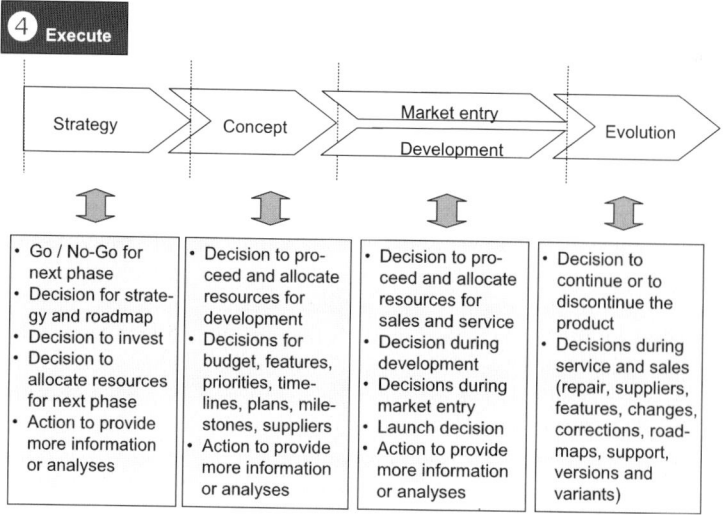

Fig. 2.12. Measurements along the product life-cycle. During each phase of the product life-cycle specific actions must be implemented to ensure that objectives and commitments will be achieved.

Especially for software engineering projects, it is important to consider mutual dependencies (see also Fig. 2.9). At the top is the enterprise portfolio which depicts all products within the company and their markets and respective investments. Further down a product-line or product cluster view is detailed which is aligned with platform roadmaps and technology evolution or skill building of engineers. For each product there should be a feature catalogue across the next several releases covering the vision, market, architecture and technology. From such product roadmap a technology roadmap is derived which allows one for instance to select suppliers or build partnerships. It also drives the individual roadmaps of releases and projects which typically have a horizon of a few months up to a maximum one year. On the project level, these decisions are implemented and followed through to success.

2.4. Hints for the Practitioner

Measurements should satisfy some simple criteria:
- Goal-oriented. Measurements must be goal-oriented to address concrete objectives. They are only created and reported if there is a specific need and decision you want to take based on these measurements. Measurements should drive informed decision-making. They must be used for effectively communicating status and progress against the objectives set for the business, process or project. Measurements, both direct and indirect, should be periodically evaluated in conjunction with the driving objectives and to identify problems or derive decisions.
- Sustainable. The measurements must be valid and useful over some period. Data integrity and consistency must be maintained at all times. This can be achieved if the operational measurement process is supported by tools. Measurements should be portrayed and compared over time. Often markets show cyclical behaviors which can only be assessed if the same indicators are followed up for several years.
- Timely. The indicators must be available literally on a push button approach. They must be valid and consistent with each other. If market data is one month old and quality reports arrive only half-yearly, this makes no sense. If cost to complete is derived monthly and you have project reviews on weekly basis, decisions are not consistent.
- Meaningful. The indicators should provide exactly the information you ask for. They should be aggregated to the level useful to make decisions. To avoid overloading occasional readers there should be few numbers with concise explanations. Further details should be drilled down from your portals and warehouses.
- Balanced. Look at measurement results from an overall perspective and do not focus on isolated measurements. They might signal something which can only be interpreted with further sources – or they might direct attention to the wrong issues. For instance, looking only at the number of defects or delays will not help if the impact behind these defects or delays from a business perspective is not considered. Look into all directions that are or will be relevant for your business. Most reporting has some blind spots. Often they appear at interfaces between processes, such as cost of an engineering activity or net present value of a platform with its evolution. Knowing about them is a first step to removing them. Starting from goals, it is easy to see why goals and measurements cannot and must not be separated.
- Action-focused. Measurements that result in reports and data cemeteries are good for statisticians but not to improve your business. As a practitioner help your management that they take decisions on the basis of measurements. Give them the necessary information before and after the decision so that they can follow the effects and compare to goals. As a manager ensure that you decide based on facts and analyses. Always consider the fourth E-letter in the E4–

measurement process, namely to execute. Make sure that your decisions move your business towards agreed objectives.

> Good objectives or goals should be "smart." Smart goals are (and the first letters obviously show why we call them "smart"):
> - **S**pecific (or precise)
> - **M**easurable (or tangible)
> - **A**ccountable (or in line with individual responsibilities)
> - **R**ealistic (or achievable)
> - **T**imely (or suitable for the current needs)

Objectives should always be reviewed and approved by upper-level managers before proceeding further. This ensures that priorities are appropriate and that nothing relevant had been overlooked or misunderstood.

Here are some practical reporting hints:
- First, summarize in your reports all your results from a business perspective (an "executive summary"). Keep it short and to the point. Indicate conclusions and actions to be taken. Do not talk in this summary about the technology, as everybody trusts your technological competence – and they will probe further anyway once they go to the details.
- Always distill the value proposition to monetary numbers. Your management normally does not like what is not tangible and not traceable. They want to see the impact of a decision in money values.
- Distinguish clearly between capital expenses (e.g., licenses, hardware within your products) and project costs (e.g., persons, infrastructure). Often these means come from different sources or budgets; sometimes they are taxed differently. Certainly they appear in different sections in your profit and loss statement (P&L) and balance sheet.
- Review figures carefully and repeatedly. Many good ideas were killed too early because their presentation was superficial and included obvious errors. A small error in calculating measurements or a wrong underlying assumption will make all your efforts invalid.
- The measurements and numbers will mean different things to different persons. If you provide numbers, ensure that they are accompanied with precise definitions. That is simple with today's online intranet technology, however, equally necessary for your presentations. Have a short definition in small letters on the same sheet, if the numbers are not well known in your company. Frequently presentations are distributed further or even beyond your reach. Often something is copied or sent out of context, and thus having the explanations on one sheet avoids unnecessary questions.
- Use industry standards as far as possible. Today many figures have standards and agreed-upon definitions that can easily be reused [McGa01, Reif02, Kapl93].

2.5. Summary

> The four steps of the measurement process (establish, extract, evaluate, execute) should be introduced in that order.

First, look into the available data and how to achieve or improve visibility. Set up an inventory of all the projects, assets and proposals for changes or investments. Add to this list, and following the same structure break down, the major status measurements per project or proposal and the respective targets in terms of quality, effort, total cost, deadlines, sales and profit expectations. Then evaluate compared to your upfront agreed objectives. Drive actions from the evaluations and monitor the actions to closure. Be fast in suggesting and taking corrective actions where you risk missing objectives.

> The two major observations we had over the past years with top-performing organizations were that
> (1) measurements are deeply ingrained into the engineering and management processes and
> (2) measurements are fertilized by the corporate culture.

What does this mean for the company? Measurement is a cultural change. Too often software engineers and management only realize the value of measurement when some unfortunate event has occurred. Projects are failing, product quality is below all expectations, deliveries are delayed, or teams realize that they will never meet the objectives. The culture change means building upon visibility and accountability (see also Chap. 6 for details on these cultural aspects).

People should make realistic commitments and are later held accountable for achieving them. Visibility means trust. The figures are not "made up" for reports, they are a normal (self-) management tool. Not providing visibility or not delivering committed results is the failure. Deviations that are out of a team's or a project's own control are flagged in due time to allow resolution on the next higher level.

Accountability also means to set realistic and measurable objectives. Objectives like "reduce errors" or "improve quality by 50%" are pointless. The objective should be clear and tangible, such as "reduce the number of late projects by 50% for this year compared to the previous year." These objectives must end up in a manager's key performance indicators. Goals that are measured will be achieved!

3. Measurement Foundations

There is no sense being precise about something when you do not even know what you are talking about.
John von Neumann

3.1. Introduction to Measurement Foundations

Software measurement as an essential part of the software engineering discipline does not consider the *measurement process* only. In order to support the decision findings in any aspect of software systems or products, software processes and software resources would involve plenty of approaches and methodologies for analysis, understanding and evaluation of software in general. This point of view motivates the consideration of measurement as "software measurement *and evaluation*" and involves the statistical methods supporting the tasks of the measurement processes themselves.

The state of theory in software measurement is as follows:

- We do not have any general *system of measurements* in software engineering as in physics. Hence, we must consider in software development *rules of thumb, statements of trends, analogue conclusions, expertise, estimations* and *predictions* ([Dumk02c, Endr03]).
- We also do not have any *standardized measurement system* that implements the system of measurements. Therefore, we must use the general techniques of *assessment (continuous, periodic* or *certified), general evaluation, experiences* and *experimentation*. Sometimes, the experimentation is not immediately used for decision support, improvement or control. We also use the experimentation for understanding new paradigms or for cognition of new kinds of problems ([Basi86, Wohl00]).
- Software measurement instruments are mostly not based on a physical analogy such as the column of mercury to measure temperature. In most cases, *software measurement is counting* [Kitc95].
- Software measurement has a context and is not finished with measurement values or thresholds. Software measurement can be a *generic measurement and analysis process* ([Card00b, Jacq97]).
- Empirical techniques are divided into *informal observation, formal experiments, industrial case studies* and *benchmarking exercises or surveys* ([Juri01, Kitc96]).
- "In software engineering measurements area, should place more emphasis on the validity of the mathematical (and ***statistical***) tools which have been (and are currently being) used in their development and use. Areas which give cause for concern in the past include the use of dimensionally incorrect equations, incorrect plotting of equations and consequent incorrect inferences, the sloppy use of mathematical notation and of calculated values and the lack of underpinning mathematical models." [Hend96b]

42   3 Measurement Foundations

This chapter will introduce you to measurement foundations from a mathematical and statistical perspective. It will formally define several important terms, such as measurement or scale, and help translate them into day-to-day operational measurement work. Specifically it introduces to measurement analysis. An expert box shows how misuse of statistical techniques can yield wrong conclusions (i.e., the so-called shotgun approach).

In providing these measurement foundations we want to achieve that you *first* state what you want to know and *then* get precise to find out the answers to what you need to know. Getting precise could still mean that you get the answer "42" (see Chap. 2, [Adam79]) but instead of mere numerology it will be a useful measurement. It will have a meaning that is useful to you because it addresses your information needs and questions, be it the effort estimate of your next project, the answer to all questions in the world or simply this paragraph's page number.

3.2. Foundations of Software Measurement

In order to consider most of the measurement issues we characterize a *software measurement system* as follows [Card00b, Dumk94, Dumk01, Jacq97, Kitc95, Pott00, Skyt05, Zuse94, Zuse98] :

MS = *(measurement_elements, relation_about_measurement_elements)*
    = (M_{MS}, R_{MS})

    = $(\{G, A, M, Q, V, U, E, T, P\}, R_{MS})$

where G is the set of the measurement goals, A IS the set of measured artifacts or measurement objects, M is the set of measurement methods, objects or entities, Q is the set of measurement quantities (normally we use $\mathbb{R}$ as the set of real numbers), V is the set of measurement values (especially when we have the situation $Q = V$), U is the set of measurement units, E is the set of measurement-based experience, T is the set of measurement CASE tools (i.e., CAME tools), and P is the set of the measurement personnel. Considering this kind of formalization we can describe the following elements of the presented sets of the measurement system ([Muns03, Offe97]). The general measurement aspects are described in Fig. 3.1.

The *measurement goals* G are the main intention of the software measurement. The elements of G can be summarized as follows (see also [Basi86, Fent97, Muns03, Schm02])

G = *{understanding, comprehension, learning, proving, validation, improvement, falsification, investigation, exploration, management, controlling, certification)*

The different measurement goals can be described briefly as follows ([Dumk04, Fent93, Muns03, Whit97, Zuse98]):

- The measurement goal of *understanding* considers the essential knowledge about the measured artifacts of products, processes and resources and is related mainly to the software user [Wein92].
- The goal of *comprehension* describes the effort to understand some characteristics of the software artifacts by the developer [Hump00].
- In our context, *learning* is the extension of the software engineering knowledge based on different measurement or experimentation methods related to personnel resources or communities [Hump97].
- The measurement goal of *proving* considers the confirmation of any assumptions or hypotheses about the measured artifacts [Sing99].
- The "*validation* of a software measurement is the process of ensuring that the measurement is a proper numerical characterization of the claimed attribute; this means showing that the representation condition is satisfied." ([Fent97], see also [Muns03, Zuse94]):

validation ∈ *{criterionOrientedValidation, contentValidation, constructValidation, empiricalValidation}*

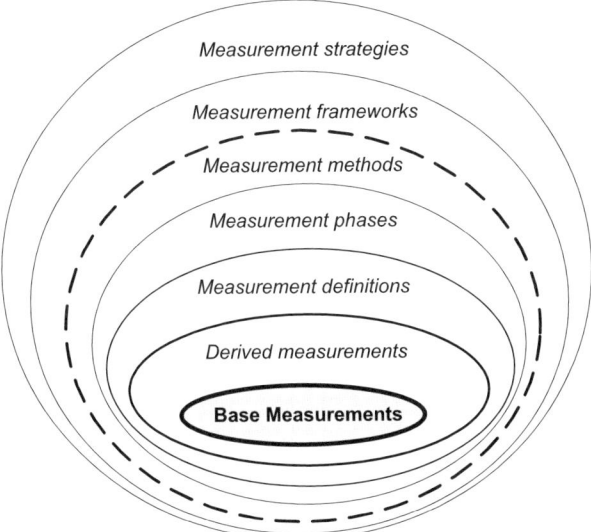

Fig. 3.1. General aspects of software measurement

- The *improvement* is based on the artifacts' evaluation and describes the improved characteristics of these artifacts [Kulp03]. The improvement could be one-dimensional or multi-dimensional oriented. Note, that the improvement is only valid for the considered aspect or attribute of a measurement object.
- The goal of *investigation* leads to the analysis of the given artifacts in the direction of assumed laws, rules and hypothesis' [Armo04]

- The *exploration* considers the artifacts under a special point of view in order to recognize some of meaningful new measurement goals and interesting artifacts [Pand04].
- The *management* involves the activities of planning, assigning, coordination, assessment and correction of the software processes including the appropriate resources [Wein92].
- The *controlling* considers the interactions of components that will provide a desired component or system response as time progresses [Erdo02].
- The measurement goal of *certification* considers the evaluation of the artifact by a special institutional community and by standardized assessment rules [Kene99].

The *measurement process* MP, as one of the instantiations of the software measurement system, could be explained by the following sequence of relations

$$MP: (G \times A \times MD)_{T,P} \rightarrow (Q \times E)_{T,P} \rightarrow (V \times U)_{T,P} \rightarrow E' \times A'$$

The *measured artifacts* A can be characterized briefly as ([McGa01, Muns03, Schm03b, Zuse98])

$$A = \{SP, SD, SR\},$$

where SP is software product that was developed by the software process SD and is based on the supporting resources SR. In order to demonstrate the complexity of these potential artifacts of measurement we will give some general views of their involvement in software development and use.

The *measurement methods* M are derived from their intentions, roles and benefits in the software measurement and evaluation process. Fig. 3.2 shows the measurement phases, methods and supportive elements. Otherwise, the detailed measurement activities are embedded in the different layers in order to build a measurement. Fig. 3.3 provides a classification of the measurement methods called as measurement operations.

A raw clustering of these operations can be defined as follows. Note that we have used the naming convention of the object-oriented paradigm (i.e., combined words) for the measurement operations.

- *artefactBasedOperation* ⊆ *{modeling, measurement, experimentation, assessment}*

- *quantificationBasedOperation* ⊆ *{transformation, regression, factorAnalysis, calibration}*

- *valueBasedOperation* ⊆ *{unitTransformation, correlation, visualization, analysis, adjustment, prediction}*

- *experienceBasedOperation* ⊆ *{trendAnalysis, expertise, estimation, simulation, interpretation, evaluation, application}*

3.2 Foundations of Software Measurement 45

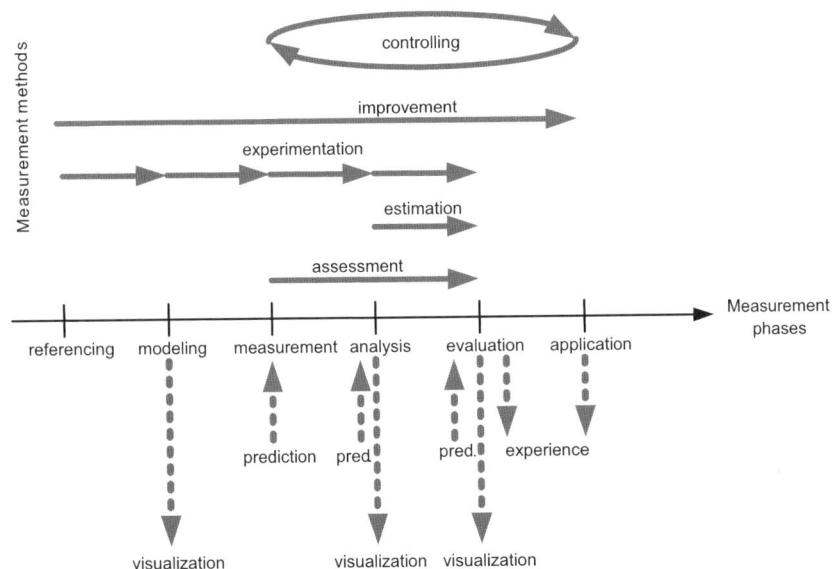

Fig. 3.2. Software measurement phases and methods

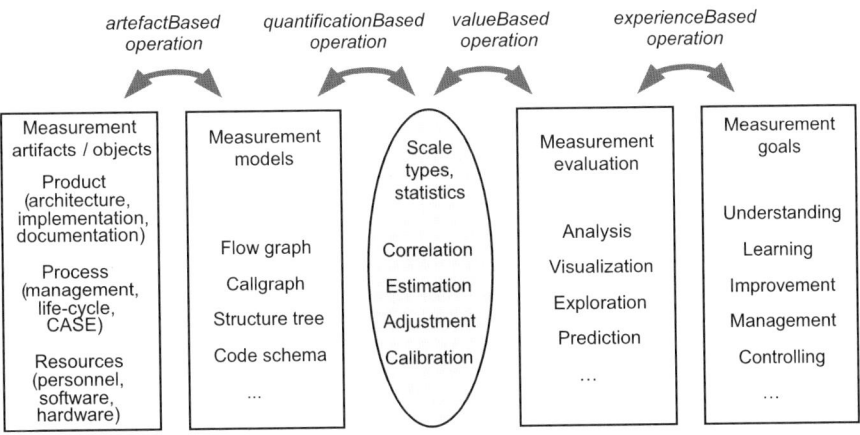

Fig. 3.3. Software measurement operations

In the following we will characterize these measurement activities very briefly. For more details see the references given at each activity description.

"Modeling is the reflection of the properties of a theory and, thereby of some reality of which that theory is an abstract description." [Marc94] We consider the process of abstraction from the (software) artifact to the special kinds of measurement-related models ([Endr03, Fent93, Gome04, Niel99]).

modeling ⊆ *{graphicalModeling, statisticalModeling, FSMmodeling}*

For modeling we describe different kinds of models which are the result of the respective modeling techniques.
- *graphicalModeling* ∈ *{callGraph, controlflowGraph, dataflowGraph, componentDiagram, processChart, mindMap, layerDiagram}*
- *statisticalModeling* ⊆ *{probabilityModeling, reliabilityModeling, deterministicModeling, strategicalModeling}*
- *FSMmodeling* ⊆ *{paradigmRelatedModeling, operationalModeling}*
- *paradigmRelatedModeling* ⊆ *{setBasedModeling, algebraicModeling, logicalModeling}*
- *operationalModeling* ⊆ *{sequentialModeling, concurrentModeling dynamicalModeling}*

"*Software measurement* is a technique or method that applies software measurements to a (class of) software engineering object(s) to achieve a predefined goal" [Marc94]. The phase of measurement is the kernel element of the software measurement system. We can establish the following general characteristics ([Fent97, Muns03, Pott00, Zuse98]). We differentiate between direct and indirect software measurement depending upon the use of measurements as cascades or only the artifact measurement itself.

The *software measurement* implies a (functional) relation or operation called a *software measurement* or – exceptionally when it comes to a distance function – a *software metric* ([Whit97, Zuse94]).

The triple (**A, B, μ**) is called a *scale* and we can distinguish the following scale types based on special transformation rules:

- *nominal scale:* $((A, \approx), (\mathbb{R}, =), \mu)$,
  where ≈ stands for an equivalence relation and = for a numerical relation (two objects are equivalent or not). Pandian considers a *typological scale* if there are identified types or categories [Pand04]. The nominal scale and the typological scale are summarized to the *linguistic scales*.

- *ordinal scale:* $((A, \bullet \geq), (\mathbb{R}, \geq), \mu)$,
  where •≥ describes ranking properties

- *interval scale:* $((A \times A, \bullet \geq), (\mathbb{R} \times \mathbb{R}, \geq), \mu)$,
  where •≥ is a preference relation about the measured objects, entities or artifacts,

- *ratio scale:* $((A, \bullet \geq, \circ), (\mathbb{R}, \geq, \otimes), \mu)$,
  where the described axioms of an extensive structure above are valid.

For detailed mathematical background see our expert box in this chapter.

3.2 Foundations of Software Measurement 47

Experimentation is one of the empirical strategies for analysis and investigation. "Experiments are launched when we want control over the situation and want to manipulate behaviors directly, precisely, and systematically" [Wohl00]. In experimentation we can distinguish the survey, the case study and the controlled experiment. The controlled experiment can be explained as follows ([Basi86, Juri01, Prec01, Shel97, Wohl00]):

controlledExperiment = {definition, planning, operation, interpretation}

The *Assessment* can involve all kinds of measurement but the results are defined on a special time point or moment. The main function of the assessment is to consider a special time point or interval which is the *valid moment* for the assessment. ([Kene99, Pfle98, Putn92]). We describe the different kinds of the assessment as follows:

assessment ∈ *{certifiedAssessment, frequentlyAssessment}*

frequentlyAssessment ∈ *{periodicAssessment, continuedAssessment}*

The *transformation* includes all operations about the numbers produced by the measurement and achieving special measurement goals and intentions [Pand04]:

transformation ⊆ *{ initialization, modification, tuning}*

The "*regression analysis* is the process of determining how a variable, y, is related to one or more other variables, $x_1, x_2, \ldots, x_n$. The y variable is usually called the *response* by statisticians; the x_i's are usually called the *regressor* or simply the *explanatory variables.*" [Bert03] We can write

regression ∈ *{linearRegression, logisticRegression, non-linearRegression}*

The *factor analysis* considers reducing a large number of response variables to a smaller set of uncorrelated variables and interpreting these newly created variables [Hane03]:

factorAnalysis ∈ *{exploratorialFactorAnalysis, confirmatoricalFactorAnalysis, LISREL}*

The *calibration* of measurement data is the modification of the numerical relational system without modifying the empirical relational system [Zuse98].

The *unit transformation* is the modification of the measured value from one unit to another [Juri03]. It could be based on *conversion rules* describing the transformation of one measurement to another [Zuse 97].

The *correlation* considers the relationship between different variables and is usually based on the correlation coefficient, which characterizes the dependency between the variables [Kan95].

The *visualization* is a process of data analysis using graphical, optical and other kinds of viewing techniques [Gero03]. The measurement values are presented by a special kind of visualization object.

visualizationObject ∈ *{barDiagram, kiviatDiagram, tieDiagram, cycleDiagram, scatterPlot, paretoDiagram, histogram, topicMap, checkTable, clusterMap, tileBar, treeMap, coneTree}*

The *Analysis* is "the process of integrating measures, decision criteria, and project context information to evaluate a defined information need" [McGa01].

The *adjustment* is the modification of the empirical relational system without modifying the numerical relational system based on (new) experience [Dumk99a]. Typical kinds of analysis are the data analysis in frequency domain, in time domain and in the relationship domain including general approaches like the Six Sigma approach [Harr03, McCa04, Pyzd03] (see Chap. 11).

"A *prediction system* consists of a mathematical model together with a set of prediction procedures for determining unknown variables and parameters. The purpose of prediction is to provide managers with a forecast of the quality of the operational software early in the development process so that corrective actions can be taken, if necessary, when the cost is low" [Zuse98].

The *trend analysis* is a special kind of prediction considering a large future-directed time period and involving the artifacts [Kene99].

The *expertise* or *expert review* is a kind of evaluation of software artifacts involving the (defined) experts [Boeh00].

"*Estimation* is a process that uses prediction systems and intuition for cost and resource planning. ... It is concerned about assumptions regarding the future and the relevance of history." [Pand04]

We can define the following methods of estimation [Boeh00]:

estimationMethod ∈ *{topDownEstimation, bottomUpEstimation, parkinsonEstimation, expertOpinionEstimation, analogicalEstimation, algorithmicEstimation}*

The *simulation* considers a model-based execution of the considered artifacts or systems and leads to approximated system characteristics and (simulated) system behavior [Erdo02].

simulationMethod ∈ *{discreteSimulation, continuousSimulation stochasticSimulation, deterministicSimulation}*

The *interpretation* includes the extrapolation of the results from a particular sample to other environments and it should be visible in professional forums for feedbacks ([Basi86, Juri01]). Methods of interpretation are

interpretationMethod ⊆ *{contingenceAnalysis, discriminanceAnalysis, varianceAnalysis, regressionAnalysis, factorAnalysis, clusterAnalysis}*

This activity is one of the sources for *experience building* for the different types of IT knowledge.

The purpose of *evaluation* is to provide an interested party with quantitative results concerning a software artifact that is comprehensible, acceptable and trustworthy [Kitc96]. Some essential evaluation methods are

evaluation ∈ *{heuristicEvaluation, prospectiveEvaluation, empiricalEvaluation, roundRobinEvaluation, snowballEvaluation, educationalEvaluation}*

The measurement *application* includes the different types of presentation, distribution, operation and reaction ([Dumk99a, Kene99, Will02]). The presentation and distribution extend the existing experience in the software engineering area. Especially applications such as *operation* or *reaction* represent a form of *online measurement* [Pand04].

The **measurement quantities** Q are derived from the measured artifacts and have no empirical meaning ([Fent93, Whit97, Zuse98]). Note that the measurement scale type depends on the characteristics of Q. We can formulate them as the first step in the measurement process. The set of Q does not fulfill the scale characteristic. But it determines the essential basis for the potential scale type [Dumk99a]. Referring to the numerical relative as $(\mathbb{R}, \geq, \otimes)$ we can distinguish the following terms:

- Potentially nominal scaled: $(Q, =)$
- Potentially ordinal scaled: $(Q, \geq)$
- Potentially interval scaled: $(Q \times Q, \geq)$
- Potentially ratio scaled: $(Q, \geq, \otimes)$

The *qualified measurement* (nominal scale and ordinal scale in the potential manner) leads to

$q \in \{nomination_1, \ldots, nomination_n\}$

where $nomination_i$ consists of the different kinds of string values depending on the kind of nomination. For the *quantified measurement* (interval scale and ratio scale

in the potential manner) it is held that q ∈ Q: q ∈ $\mathbb{N}$ ∨ q ∈ $\mathbb{Z}$ ∨ q ∈ $\mathbb{Q}$ ∨ q ∈ $\mathbb{R}$.
Furthermore, we can summarize the following structures of ***Q*** ([Dumk04, Juri01, Pand04, Sing99])

$\boldsymbol{Q} = [\ (\{number\})_{structure}\ ]_{aggregation}$

$\boldsymbol{Q} \in \{vector, matrix, tensor\}$

$\boldsymbol{Q} \in \{pair, Eigenvalue, residual, adaptive, randomized, predictive\}$

$\boldsymbol{Q} \in \{uniform, rated, normative, harmonic, orthogonal\}$

The ***measurement values*** ***V*** lead to an (unit-based) measurement by mapping the measurement quantities to an empirical meaning. Relating to the empirical relative as (A, •≥, ○) we can derive the following forms of scale types (see [Denv92, Zuse98])

- *Nominal scale*: $((A, \approx), (\boldsymbol{Q}, =), \mu)$
- *Ordinal scale*: $((A, \bullet\geq), (\boldsymbol{Q}, \geq), \mu)$
- *Interval scale*: $((A \times A, \bullet\geq), (\boldsymbol{Q}\times \boldsymbol{Q}, \geq), \mu)$
- *Ratio scale*: $((A, \bullet\geq, \circ), (\boldsymbol{Q}, \geq, \otimes), \mu)$

The measurement values themselves could be structured as follows ([Bach94, Kitc96, Pfle98, Pott00])

$V = [\ (\{value\})_{valueStructure}\ ]_{valueRelation}$

values ∈ *{classificator, nominator, naturalNumber, ratioNumber, realNumber}*

valueStructures ⊆ *{interval, tuple, set, list}*

valueRelations ∈ *{nominalScale, ordinalScale, intervalScale, ratioScale}*

The ***measurement units*** ***U*** is only given in the case of *quantified measurement*. The meaning of these measurement units is the following: "The standardized quantitative amount that will be counted to derive the value of the base measurement, such as an hour or line of code. A unit is a particular quantity, defined and adopted by convention, with which other quantities of the same kind are compared in order to express their magnitude relative to that quantity." [McGa01] In the context of software measurement, we can define the following parts of the measurement units

U = *measurementUnits* = *{physicalMeasureUnits, economicalMeasureUnits, sociologicalMeasureUnits, softwareMeasureUnits, hardwareMeasureUnits}*

3.2 Foundations of Software Measurement

For different sets of measurement units we will only describe some examples without the claim of completeness.

physicalMeasureUnits ∈ *{Fahrenheit, gallon, gram, hertz, horsepower, hour, joule, karat, lux, meter, mile, millisecond, parsec, pound, watt, yard}*

economicalMeasureUnits ∈ *{Euro, GNP, hurdleRate, MBI, ROI, $, shareIndex, uninflatedCost, VAT}*, where *GNP* means (gross national product), *MBI* means (manpower buildup index), *ROI* means (return on investment), *VAT* means (value added tax);

sociologicalMeasureUnits ∈ *{IQ, Mfactor, StroudNumber, Ufactor}*, where *IQ* means (intelligence quotient), *Mfactor* means (ordinal scaled part of motivation), *Ufactor* means (part of unbroken working hours per day);

softwareMeasureUnits ∈ *{$FFP^{(COSMIC)}$, FP, KDSI, $L^{(Halstead)}$, $N^{(Halstead)}$, PM, RSI, SLOC, $t_{operation}$, $t_{projectDuration}$, $t_{response}$, $V^{(McCabe)}$}*, where *FFP* means (full function points by the COSMIC community), *FP* means (function points), *KDSI* means (kilo delivered source instruction), $L^{(Halstead)}$ means (program level by Halstead), $N^{(Halstead)}$ means (program length by Halstead), *PM* means (personnel (effort in) month), *RSI* means (reused source instruction), *SLOC* means (source lines of code), $V^{(Halstead)}$ means (program volume by Halstead), $V^{(McCabe)}$ means (cyclomatic number by McCabe) [McCa76, Eber95];

hardwareMeasureUnits ∈ *{MTFD, MTDD, MTDR, MTFR, MTBF, MTTD, MTTF}*, where *MTFD* means (mean time between failure and disclosure); *MTDD* (mean time between disclosure and diagnosis), *MTDR* (mean time between diagnosis and repair), *MTFR* (mean time between failure and repair), *MTBF* (mean time between failures), *MTTD* (mean time to defect), and *MTTF* (mean time to failure).

The measurement unit plays an important role in the operations of calibration, adjustment and unit transformation or conversion.

The **measurement experience** *E* summarizes the general aspects of the concrete measurement results in different forms of aggregation, correlation, interpretation and conclusion based on a context-dependent interpretation. Note that the measurement experience is divided into the experiences of the measurement results and the (evaluated-based) experience of the measurement itself. In the following we only consider the first aspect. Some kinds of measurement experience are ([Armo04, Davi95, Endr03, Kene99])

E ⊆ *{analogies, axioms, correlations, criterions, intuitions, laws, lemmas, formulas, methodologies, principles, relations, ruleOfThumbs, theories}*

Some examples of these experiences are (see also [Basi01, Boeh89, Dumk03b, Hals77, Putn03])
- *analogies* ∈ *{analogicalEstimation, systemAnalogy, hardwareSoftwareAnalogy}*
- *criteria* ∈ *{fulfilCondition, qualityAspect, minimality, maximality}*
- *laws* ∈ *{BrooksLaw, DijkstraMillsWirthLaw, FagansLaw, GlassLaw, GraySerlinLaw, McIlroysLaw, MooresLaw, SimonsLaw}*
- *lemmas* ∈ *{'any system can be tuned', 'installability must be designed in', 'human-based methods can only be studied empirically'}*
- *methodologies* ∈ *{agileMethodology, cleanroomMethodology, empiricalBasedMethodology}*
- *principles* ∈ *{'don't set unrealistic deadlines', 'evalvate alternatives', 'manage by variance', 'regression test after every change'}*
- *rulesOfThumb* ∈ *{'one dollar in development leads to two dollars maintenance', '1 KLOC professionally developed programs implies 3 errors', 'more than 99 percent of all executing computer instructions come from COTS', 'more than the half of the COTS features go unused'}*

Fig. 3.4 shows the variety of intentions of such laws applied to the different parts of software development (see also Chap. 14 for such laws and how they are used in practice; [Endr03] also details many such laws).

The **measurement tools** T are also called *Computer Assisted Measurement and Evaluation* (CAME) tools [Dumk96a]. Some typical kinds of CASE tools are summarized as follows:

T = *{modelingTool, measurementTool, (statistical) analysisTool, visualizationTool, metricsRepositoryTool}*

We distinguish between the following characteristics of measurement tools by using special notations:
- in the case of the special measured artifact by CAME tools we use the index notation, e.g., $T_{sourceCode}$ or $T_{process}$.,
- in the case of the application of a special measurement method by the measurement tool we prefer the exponential notation, e.g., $T^{(modeling)}$ or $T^{(estimation)}$,
- in the case of different characteristics of a measurement tool we use the same notation, e.g., $T^{(open)}$ or $T^{(flexible)}$.

The tool operations such as *composition, combination* and *integration* are essential aspects for effective application of CAME tools. For more details about CAME tools see the Chap. 5.

The **measurement personnel** P includes all the personnel resources in a creative, motivated and active manner in order to
- define measurements, measurement processes, measurement strategies, validation techniques, and measurement methodologies,

3.2 Foundations of Software Measurement   53

- carry out the measurement process installation and realization in a practical environment for software (process) improvement and controlling.

The personnel resources themselves could be divided into two kinds of measurement application:
- the original measurement staff like ([Dumk03, Pand04, Pfle98]) as

  $P \subseteq \{measurementAnalyst, certificator, librarian, metricsCreator, user, validator\}$

- the IT staff which use the software measurement additionally as

  $P \subseteq \{administrator, analyst, auditor, designer, developer, expert, maintainer, programmer, reviewer, tester, customer\}$

The measurement personnel of the second class is one of the developers which uses technologies as the personal software process (PSP) or the team software process (TSP) ([Hump97, Hump00]).

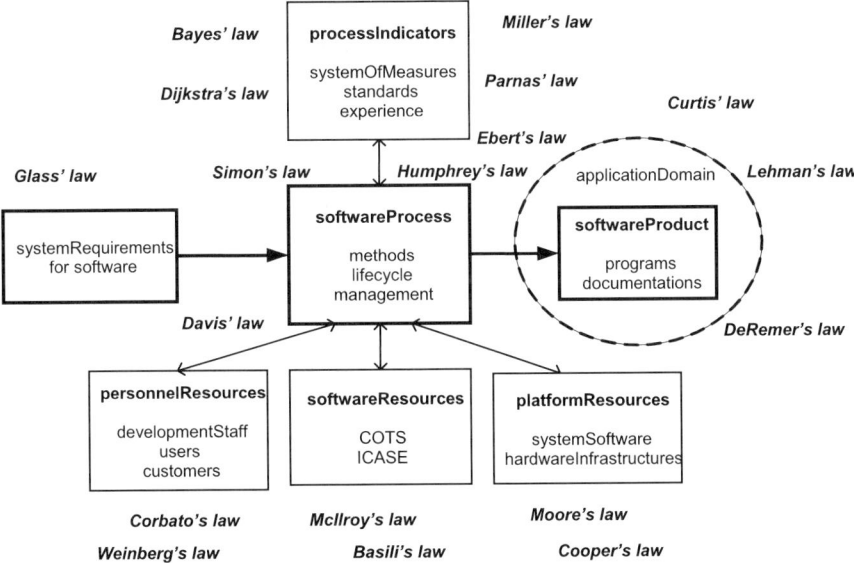

Fig. 3.4. Intentions of chosen software engineering laws

3.3. Theoretical Foundations

Expert Box. Author: Horst Zuse

Software measurement has no well-established theoretical framework. In physics measurement has a long tradition. Two hundred years ago, the measurement of temperature was created. However, measurement in physics and in software engineering is differently. Qualitative attributes, like portability, understandability, and so on have something to do with humans, they depend on human views. Different views of humans are possible and the consequence is that we have hundreds of software measurements that correspond to those. In physics, more the quantitative than the qualitative aspects of measurement are considered.

We think, it is a fact, that software measurement or software engineering measurement is not a mature science, today. The word engineering implies a mature science. Engineering means the application of solid methods, like reliability engineering, structured analysis, structured design, formal methods, configuration management, measurement theory, and so on. Sometimes, practitioners are ahead the theory, and sometimes, the theory is ahead practical applications. These statements are very true in the area of software measurement. A discussion of measurement scales (nominal, ordinal, interval, ratio, absolute scale) is mostly ahead practical applications. Mostly, people do not consider measurement scales in practice. Validation of software measurements by correlation coefficients or regression analysis is ahead the theory. People say that software measurements are validated. But, it is not clear what validation exactly means. The use of the Function-Point Method is another example, that people are ahead of the theory. The Function-Point Method was created pragmatically. Today, some research projects investigate with measurement theory the idea of the size of software systems behind the Function-Point method.

We think, it is necessary to present a theoretical framework for software measurement. This framework should not only be helpful for people who are interested in the theory of software measurement, it should also be helpful for practitioners. It should help to create a uniform terminology of software measurement, to give a clear interpretation of software measurements, and show the limits of software measurement. The final goal is to get hypotheses of reality and to build empirical theories of software quality attributes, like understandability, maintainability or cost estimation.

Measurement theory is appropriate to give answers to many questions of software measurement, like properties of measurements, measurement scales, qualitative models behind measurements, validation of measurements and prediction models. From our view, the major advantage of measurement theory is not the description of scales, it is the representational approach, that allows the translation of numerical conditions back to empirical conditions. We follow the research of Roberts, Krantz and Luce et al. (all discussed in [Zuse98]) with some extensions for special needs in the software measurement area. The axiom systems in measurement theory are not formulated for a direct transfer to software measurement.

Behind measurements, for example a complexity measurement, a model of complexity is hidden. Using axiom systems, the model of complexity behind a measurement is characterized. In order to do that we use axiom systems from measurement theory and weaker axioms from the function of belief. It is important to mention, that we do not require or reject axioms. We use them in order to make clear what the measurement actually measures.

What is measurement? At an early stage of scientific development, measurement is usually performed at only the crudest level, that is classification. However, what are the advantages of performing measurement that goes beyond simple classification? Roberts [Zuse98], p.2, describes some of the advantages: if we can measure things, we can begin to differentiate more than we can by simply classifying them. For example, we can do more than simply distinguishing between warm objects and cold ones; we can assign degrees of warmth. Greater descriptive flexibility leads to greater flexibility in the formulation of general laws. Assigning of numbers makes possible the application of the concepts and theories of mathematics. Thus, the existence of experience with centuries of mathematical reasoning is a large part of the reason we find it useful to measure things.

In software engineering, the stage of software measurement today is mostly on the crudest level, that is ranking of objects. However, people want to predict, for example, costs of maintenance. Doing this, they assume much stronger laws than only ranking of objects. This shows that software measurement differentiates more and more. That is a further reason to get more clearness of hypotheses about reality.

Measurement bases on the **comparison** of objects. This is very important. We compare the objects a and b and say a is warmer than b and write this as a $\bullet >$ b. We also say a is equally warm than b, and we write this as: a $\approx$ b. And, we say a is as warm as or warmer than b and write this as a $\bullet \geq$ b.

The sign $\bullet >$ is an empirical relation. We compare the efforts of changes of Modules a and b and say that Module a is easier to change than Module b (a $< \bullet$ b). The idea of comparisons of objects is widely spread. For example, if we today have 20°C and tomorrow 40°C, then we can say tomorrow it is warmer than today. The same statement holds for Fahrenheit units. But, we cannot say that 40°C is twice as warm as 20°C. It is not meaningful for Fahrenheit or Celsius. Such statements can only be made with Kelvin units.

Measurement is more than creating some numbers. Measurement can be seen as a *detour* (or redirection). This detour is necessary because humans mostly are not able to make clear and objective decisions or judgments. Kriz [Zuse98] gives a good explanation of the benefits of measurement in general. Fig. 3.5 is a slight extension of the measurement Model of Kriz by the author.

The measurement model of Kriz describes very intuitively that measurement is more than producing numbers. It shows that measurement is the combination of empirical entities with numerical entities. The measurement process starts with the real world.

Real World: Users want to have relevant empirical results of problems in reality. For example, users want to have relevant empirical statements about the understandability of programs or software systems. The real world contains the objects that should be measured such as objects of daily life, like potatoes, cars, and so on, and objects of software engineering. For example, people want to know whether the software System D-B1 is easier to understand or to maintain than software System D-B2. This is a question of the real world. It is an empirical statement and we can discuss it without using a measurement. Other examples are related to the ISO9126 standard. There relevant empirical statements are the following: Module a is more reliable than Module b or Module a is easier to maintain than Module b.

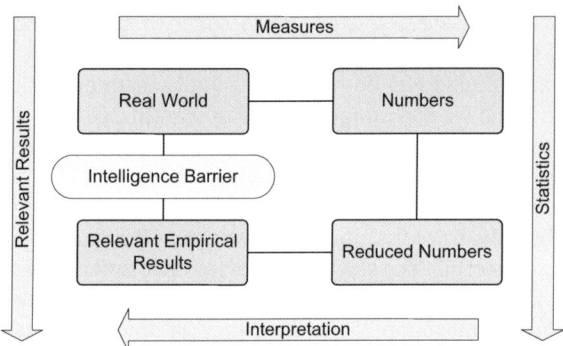

Fig. 3.5. The measurement process based on Kriz

Intelligence Barrier: However, our human brain, in many of the cases, is not able to produce directly relevant empirical results. An exception is, for example, the length of wooden boards. In this case humans can make clear relevant empirical statements. However, considering the understandability of programs, the human brain very often is not able to make relevant empirical statements. The relevant empirical statements related to software understandability can change over the time and people have different ideas of understandability. In many cases the human brain is unable to make relevant empirical decisions. Kriz calls this problem the *intelligence barrier*. That means, in many cases, the human brain is not able to reduce information without certain help.

Measurements: One way to by-pass the intelligence barrier is the aid of mathematical and statistical models. A very important prerequisite is that the empirical information which consists of objects and the empirical relationship between them, has to be translated properly in numerical objects and relationships. This is called measurement. Measurement is a mapping of empirical objects to numerical (mathematical) objects, in our case the real numbers, by a homomorphism. The problem of the selection of appropriate software measurements exists. The variety of software measurements shows the confusion.

Statistics: Mathematics and statistics are used to process the information. Doing this we get reduced numeric results (reduced numbers). The numerical data created by measurements are reduced by certain rules. The result of a statistical reduction of data should be certain statistical results, like means, variances, corre-

3.3 Theoretical Foundations

lation coefficient, and so on. The reduction of information is very often impossible. The goal is to reduce the information of the empirical world to adequately address some important questions. The human brain is mostly not able to make such empirical reductions in a proper way.

Interpretation: Now, the important step is to give the reduced numerical results an empirical meaning (interpretation). Without an interpretation of numbers it is not possible to make relevant empirical statements. Measurement theory gives conditions for the translation of numerical statements back to empirical statements.

Measurement theory considers, among other things, the qualitative attributes of the considered objects or the qualitative (empirical) relations between the objects. Using measurement structures, different homomorphisms are defined in order to connect the qualitative attributes with the numerical representations. These homomorphisms also are called the representational theorem and lead to scales. We introduce here basics of measurement theory and the concept of the extensive structure.

Firstly, we introduce the empirical and numerical relational systems. Relational systems consist of a set of objects, relations between them and concatenation operations.

Empirical Relational System. Let $\mathbf{A} = (A, \bullet \geq, o)$ be an empirical relational system, where A is a non-empty set of objects, $\bullet \geq$ is an empirical relation on A and o is a closed binary operation on A (of course, there is more than one relation and binary operation possible). According to Luce et al. [Zuse98], p.270, we assume for an empirical relational system $\mathbf{A}$ *that there is a well-established empirical interpretation for the elements of A and for each relation $\bullet \geq$ of A*. We also assume the same for binary / concatenation operations. "Binary" and "concatenation" are used synonymously.

Numerical Relational System. Let $\mathbf{B} = (\Re, \geq, \otimes)$ be a numerical (formal) relational system, where $\Re$ are the real numbers, $\geq$ a relation on $\Re$, and $\otimes$ a closed binary operation on $\Re$ (of course, there are more than one relation and binary operations possible). We also include the case that there are no relations or no operations. We call $\otimes$ a combination rule defined as $u(a \circ b) = g(u(a), u(b))$, where g is a function and u is a measurement. If we have an additive combination rule, like $u(a \circ b) = u(a) + u(b)$, then we can replace the sign $\otimes$ with $+$ and we have $\mathbf{B} = (\Re, \geq, +)$. Combination rules give important characteristics of software measurements.

Definitions of Measurements. We now introduce the basic definition of a measurement. Firstly, we do not consider a concatenation operation and a combination rule. For this reason we have the both relational systems $\mathbf{A} = (A, \bullet \geq)$ and $\mathbf{B} = (\Re, \geq)$ and a Measurement u. We also write this as

$((A, \bullet \geq), (\Re, \geq), u)$.

The operations o and $+$ have been left out because we only consider ranking structures. Then a measurement based on ranking is defined as

Definition 1: A **measurement** is a mapping: u, $A \; \varepsilon \; \Re$ such that the following holds for all $a,b \in A$:
$$a \bullet \geq b \iff u(a) \geq u(b).$$
Then the Triple (A, B, u) is called a **scale (not scale type!)**.

The definition of a measurement u above only considers ranking orders. It says that the empirical ranking order has to be preserved by the numerical ranking order or vice versa. It shows that the basic idea of **measurement is the comparison of objects and numbers**. A scale here is denoted as
$$(A, B, u) = ((A, \bullet\geq), (\Re, \geq), u).$$

A scale is a homomorphism between the two relational systems **A** and **B** by a Measurement u. It is very important to mention, that scale types are not scales. Scale types are defined by admissible transformations. One more important aspect has to be mentioned: The definitions above do not deal with units. The discussion of units is a subject after the determination of the measurement structures and scales.

Additivity. We actually demand more from a measurement. We want to have something above poor ranking or comparing of objects. We want to be additive in the sense that the combination of two objects is the sum of their measurement values. We want to consider the combination rule: $u(a \circ b) = u(a) + u(b)$. Considering length of wooden boards that is a reasonable requirement. The sign o characterizes, for example, a concatenation of two wooden boards. In software measurement an additive property of the numerical relational system can be found very often [Zuse98]. Additivity has an important impact on the relational systems. Formally, we need to speak of a binary operation o on the set A of objects – think of a o b as a combination of two objects (below, we will discuss this in detail). We want a real-valued function u on A that does not only satisfy
$$a \bullet\geq b \iff u(a) \geq u(b),$$
but also preserves the binary operation o, in sense that for all $a, b \in A$
$$u(a \circ b) = u(a) + u(b).$$

We now introduce an extended definition of a measurement which includes the additive property. Suppose we have the both relational Systems $\mathbf{A} = (A, \bullet\geq, o)$ and $\mathbf{B} = (\Re, \geq, +)$ and a Measurement u. We write this as:
$$(A, B, u) = ((A, \bullet\geq, o), (\Re, \geq, +), u).$$
Then an additive measurement is defined as

Definition 2 (Measurement based on an additive homomorphism): An **additive measurement** is a mapping: $u: A \; \varepsilon \; \Re$ such that the following holds for all $a,b \in A$:
$$a \bullet\geq b \iff u(a) \geq u(b),$$
and
$$u(a \circ b) = u(a) + u(b).$$

Then the triple (**A**, **B**, u) is called a **scale (not scale type!)**.

Both definitions of measurements show that scales (not scale types) are not uniquely defined. They depend on the relational system. According to this definition we see that measurement assumes, among others, a ranking or an additive homomorphism. The homomorphism describes rules for the mapping u: A ε ℜ. The first rule says that the ranking properties have to be preserved, and the second rule – called an additive homomorphism – considers the additive operations of measurement values and the assigned empirical concatenation operation o. Again, the definitions of measurements do not consider units. We consider units after the determination of the measurement structures and the scales. We now define the extensive structure [Zuse98].

Definition 3 (Extensive Structure). Let A be a non-empty set, •≥ a binary relation on A, and o a closed binary operation on A. The relational system (A, •≥, o) is a positive extensive structure if and only if (<=>) the following axioms hold for all a, b ∈ A:

A1: (A,•≥)   is a weak order
A2: a o (b o c) ≈ (a o b o c,   axiom of weak associativity
A3: a •≥ b <=> a o c •≥ b o c <=> c o a •≥ c o b
     axiom of monotonicity
A4: If c •> d then for any a, b, there exists a natural number n, such that a o nc •≥ b o nd,   Archimedean Axiom

The extensive structure consists of empirical and qualitative conditions. The theorem of the extensive structure connects the extensive structure with an additive measurement u. In [Zuse98] we introduce the theorem of the extensive structure.

Theorem (Extensive Structure). Let A be a non empty set, •≥ is a binary relation on A, and o a closed binary operation on A. Then (A, •≥, o) is a closed extensive structure if there exists a real-valued function u on A such that for all a,b∈ A:
  a •≥ b <=> u (a) ≥ u (b)
and
  u (a o b) = u (a) + u (b)
Another function u' satisfies the both statements iff there exists α>0 such that
  u' (a) = α u (a).

Fig. 3.6 illustrates the connections of the empirical and numerical relational systems.

The empirical relational system (A, •≥, o) consists of the considered objects A, the empirical relation •≥ between the objects (a •≥ b) and the (empirical) concatenation operation o between two objects (a o b) with a, b ε A. The measurement u maps the empirical properties to the numerical ones with **B** = (ℜ, ≥, +) and the measurement u maps to the numerical relational system (ℜ, ≥, ⊗). The mapping from (A, •≥, o) to ($\Re$, ≥, +) is described by the theorem of the extensive structure. Applying a strictly increasing monotonic function f to ($\Re$, ≥, +) leads to the numerical relational system ($\Re$, ≥, ⊗). It holds: u' = f(u). The measurement u' assumes the same extensive structure as the measurement u. However, the measurement u' cannot be used as a ratio scale, anymore. The numerical transformation with f does not change the ranking order. The consequence is that non-additive measurements assume an extensive structure, too. Since the function f is a strictly monotonic function the inverse function f^{-1} also is strictly monotonic function and it holds: u=f^{-1}u'. This shows, that non-additive measurements which assume an extensive structure can be transformed to additive measurements by f or f^{-1}.

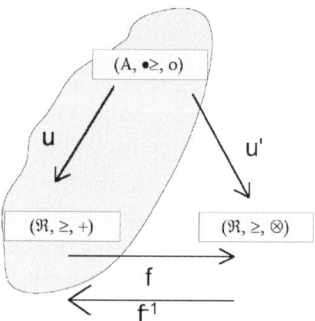

Fig. 3.6. The mappings of the empirical and numerical relational systems by the measurements u and u' and the functions f and f^{-1}

Application of Measurement Theory to Measurements. We now apply the measurement theoretic concepts to one of the Halstead measurements [Hals77]. The measurements of Halstead are based on the quadruple (n1, n2, N1, N2), where n1 are the number of distinct operators, n2 are the number of distinct operands, N1 are the total number of used operators and N2 are the total number of used operands. It generally holds that operands are variables and constants, and operators are the other elements of programs. A clear definition of n1 and n2 is still missing, however, for our investigation this lack of a clear definition is without any relevance. The Halstead measurement N is defined as follows:

Measurement N (length of a program): N = N1 + N2.

We will discuss whether the Halstead measurement N assume an extensive structure or not. Using the extensive structure a concatenation operation based on the model of the Halstead measurements has to be defined. The model of the Halstead measurements is H= (n1, n2, N1, N2). A concatenation operation is defined as: g(a, b) = a o b: AxA ε A, where A is a set of objects with a, b, aob∈ A. g is a function which concatenates two objects to a new one. The model for a program is: P = {S1, S2,...,Sn), where S1, S2, and so on are statements in the programming language. We introduce the following notation for programs: P_{si} = {Si) is a program with one statement Si. P_{arbi}= {S1, S2,...,Sn) is an arbitrary program. We use the following concatenation operations: $P = P_{arb1} \circ P_{arb2}$. Fig. 3.7 will serve as an illustration of this example.

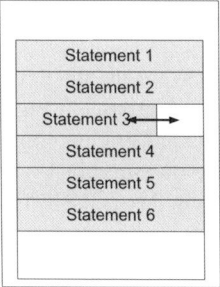

Fig. 3.7. A program P consists of statements Si

We assume, that a program, module, class, and so on consists of a set of statements Si. For example, we have Statement S1. We can add statement S2 writing it below S1. We can do this in an editor. Adding S2 below S1 is a concatenation operation $P = P_{s1} \circ P_{s2}$. Then, we can add Statement S3 to S1 o S2 and we get (S1 o S2) o S3. This is a concatenation operation, too. Adding statements are typical operations in the editor. We also can change the length of a statement Si. Let us consider the first two statements S1 and S2. Let us add statement S3. However, we can add Statement S3 in different lengths and we always have a concatenation operation (S1 o S2) o S3.

Working with an editor implies automatically concatenating operations on the statement level Si. The described concatenation operations are always there, it is not necessary to define one artificially. It is no artificial definition of a concatenation operation, it is simply there.

We consider the concatenation operation of two arbitrary programs $P = P_{arb1} \circ P_{arb2}$. For the measurement N holds the following combination rule: $N(P_{arb1} \circ P_{arb2}) = N1(P_{arb1}) + N2(P_{arb2})$. It is easy to see that the measurement N assumes additivity which includes the assumption of the extensive structure via the theorem of the extensive structure. The consequence is that the measurement N can be used as an additive ratio scale. This result is consistent with our intuitive understanding of length. In physics, length also assumes an extensive structure and a measurement for length, like a ruler, assumes an extensive structure and can be used as a ratio scale. In short [Zuse05]:

The measurement N has very nice and clear properties and can be used to analyze the length of programs based on the source code. The resulting numbers are clear (additive ratio scale). Assume that an extensive structure implies the condition of consistency (axiom of monotonicity) means that changes in one or more statements cause consistent changes in the measurement of the whole module. In [Zuse98] measurement theory is applied to hundreds of software measurements.

Conclusions

Measurement structures are theories, that assume empirical and numerical models, and between them exists a homomorphic mapping. The existence and the uniqueness of these homomorphisms are derived from the axioms of a measurement structure. Measurement structures are prerequisites to figuring out quantitative and empirical laws and they are the origin for the development of complete empirical theories. The axiomatic building of theories is possible in social sciences, but it is also possible in the area of software engineering and especially software measurement. In the area of software measurement, we can build theories of costs of software, for example by analyzing the COCOMO model with measurement theoretic axioms. The empirical study of measurement theoretic axioms can lead to the discovery of new qualitative and quantitative laws. As mentioned above, the major advantages of measurement theory are the hypotheses about reality and theory building.

- Measurement theory gives a clear definition of a measurement with a homomorphism between the empirical world and the world of numbers.
- Measurement theory explains the meaning of numbers by the empirical and numerical relational systems.
- Measurement theory allows a translation of numerical properties of measurements back to empirical properties and vice versa under the assumption of a homomorphism. This helps to easier understand the properties of measurements.
- Measurement theory shows that the extensive structure plays a central role in software measurement.
- The independence conditions characterize essential properties of measurements related to teamwork and substitution operations.
- Measurement theory gives conditions for the use of measurements on certain scale levels, like nominal, ordinal, interval, ratio and absolute scale. This is important for the proper use of statistics. It also shows, that counting is not an absolute or ratio scale per se.
- Measurement theory gives conditions for the internal and external validation of software measurements. It shows the limits of the validation of software measurements or prediction models.
- Measurement theory gives conditions for prediction models. Here the independence conditions are playing an important role. There it is the question whether a software quality attribute of a whole software system can be determined by the components of the system.
- Measurement theory shows, that we can have additive and non-additive ratio scales.
- Measurement theory discusses combination rules between concatenated objects. They give a deeper understanding of the meaning of numbers and give criteria for normalization rules of measurement values.
- Measurement theory gives clear conditions for verbally formulated (desirable) properties of software measurements. By doing so it will also pinpoint to contradictions of desired properties. Not every combination of desirable properties is measurable.

- Measurement theory shows, that the basic COCOMO model is the only one which can be used for prediction if a ratio scale for the predicted variable is assumed.
- Measurement theory derives hypotheses about reality. This is essential, because deriving hypotheses about reality is one of the major goals in science.
- Measurement theory explains the idea of size measurement behind the Function-Point Method and the assumed scale type.
- Measurement theory gives conditions for hybrid measurements.
- Measurement theory shows that wholeness (The whole is greater than the sum of the parts) is only a numerical modification without changing the empirical evidence of a measurement.
- Measurement theory gives a clear definition of calibration of software measurements.
- Measurement theory gives clear conditions for the usage of units. Units are only compatible with higher scale levels, like interval and ratio scales.

Again, it should be made clear, that measurement theory cannot solve the question: what software quality is or what program understandability is. However, measurement theory can give qualitative criteria in order to understand, for example, cost estimation models or software measurements.

3.4. Software Engineering with Measurement

We should formulate the general background on software measurement as the software engineering itself. We already mentioned that *"software engineering is the application of a systematic, disciplined, quantifiable approach to the development, operation, and maintenance of software; that is, the application of engineering to software"* [IEEE 90]. This definition leads us to the simple visualization of the software engineering components in the following manner ([Dumk03b, Marc94, Pfle98]) given in Fig. 3.8.

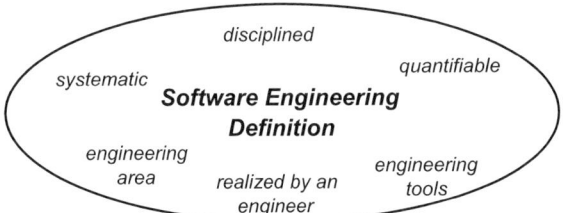

Fig. 3.8. Basic characteristics of software engineering

We will briefly characterize experiences in software engineering with measurement ([Basi01, Boeh00, Clar02, Davi95, Dumk03b, Eber04, Endr03, Herb03, Jone91, Kitc02, Pfle98, Putn03, Zuse98]).

Software management and application
- *#(development method)$_{IT\ area}$ >> 1*: leads to the problem in managing the software process including the software personnel and CASE. But, we do not know the thresholds for the acceptability.
- More than 99 percent of all executing computer instructions come from COTS products. And, the average COTS software product undergoes a new release every eight to nine months, with active vendor support for only its latest three releases.
- Non-development costs, such as licensing fees, are significant, and projects must plan for and optimize them.
- The complexity of IT projects is divided in *organizational complexity* (structural and dynamic) and in *technological complexity* (structural and dynamic) [Xia04] and must be considered in this context.
- Note that the software product depends on the different development aspects such as the kind of the development method m, the product class p, the variant of the process f, the type of (basic) platform b, and the kind of the development team e. Hence, we can formulate the software product elements in the following detailed form:

$$M_{SP}(p,m,b,e,f) = \bigcup_i \{program_i(p,m,b,e,f)\} \cup \bigcup_j \{documentation_j(p,m,b,e,f)\}$$

Probabilities in software development
- *Product specification → formal product implementation:* would be achieved with little or more effort as *verification*. But the principles of customer-satisfying development expressed by the implication *product requirements → product implementation* are not addressed automatically. That means that the probability $p(validation) \ll 1$ should be the usual situation.
- *Applied test cases ≪ all possible/necessary test cases:* this well-known situation implies an effect of probability as $p(correctness) \ll 1$.
- *Probability of errors in programs:* Halstead estimates that professional software includes three errors per 1 KLOC source code (see [Hals77]).
- *Schedule probability curve:* "The basic idea is to use the probability curves to let us back off from the planned schedule for enough to provide the risk protection we need. Our work plan must always be located on the time-effort trade-off line" [Putn03].
- *Limitations of direct model checking:* "Model checking and verification are usually performed on a model of the verified system, rather than being applied directly. One reason for this is that without introducing some abstraction, the amount of detail we need to consider quickly becomes extremely large" [Pele01].
- *Process modeling by Bayesian networks:* The characteristics of probabilistic networks like Bayesian networks are helpful in order to model software quality aspects and process-related structures [Fent02].

Causalities in software engineering [Davi95]
- *General principles*: "Productivity and quality are inseparable. ... Communicate with the customers/users. ... Change during development is inevitable. ... Technique before tools. ... Most cost estimates tend to be low. ... What applies to small systems does not apply to large ones. ... A system that is used will be changed."
- *Software specification:* "Prototypes reduce risk in selecting user interfaces. ... Requirement deficiencies are the prime source of project failures."
- *Software design:* "Design for change, maintenance, and errors. ... Hierarchical structures reduce complexity. ... Architecture wins over technology. ... Software reuse reduces cycle time and increases productivity and quality."
- *Software coding and testing:* "Don't test your own software. ... Do not integrate before unit testing. ... Instrument your software. ... Do not cause errors personally. ... Online debugging is more efficient than offline debugging."
- *Software measurement:* "Measurements are always based on actually used models rather than on desired ones. ... Empirical results are transferable only if abstracted and packaged with context. ... Measurement requires both goals and models."

Thus, the software measurement application based on different methodologies or frameworks requires *statistical methods* ([Muns03, Sing99, Zuse98]). We will describe two directions of empirical software engineering in the following: *software experimentation* and *statistical process control*.

Software experiments are usually performed in an environment resembling a laboratory to ensure a high amount of control while carrying out the experiment ([Wohl00, Pand04]). One of the main tasks of an experiment is to calibrate variables and to evaluate the effects they cause. This measurement data is the basis for the statistical analysis that is performed afterwards. Experiments are used for instance to confirm existing theories, to validate measurements or to evaluate the accuracy of models. In software engineering several aspects are rather difficult to establish. These are [Juri03]:
- Finding variable definitions that are accepted by everyone
- Proving that the measurements are nominal or ordinal scale
- Validating of indirect measurements: models and direct measurements have to be validated

The experiment definition is the basis for the whole experiment. It is crucial that this definition be performed with some caution. When the definition is not well founded and interpreted, the whole effort spent could have been done in vain and one worse thing to happen is that the result of the experiment is not displaying what was intended. The definition sets up the objective of the experiment. Following a framework can support this definition step. The GQM templates could supply such a framework for example [VanS99]. After finishing the definition the planning step has to be performed. While the previous step was to answer the question why the experiment is performed, this step answers the question how the

experiment will be carried out. Six different stages will be needed to complete the planning phase cited from [Wohl00].
- *"Context selection*: The environment in which the experiment will be carried out is selected.
- *Hypothesis formulation and variable selection*: Hypothesis testing is the main aspect for statistical analysis when carrying out experiments. The goal is to reject the hypothesis with the help of the collected data acquired through the experiment. In the case that the hypothesis is rejected it is possible to draw conclusion out of it. More details about hypothesis testing can be read in the following sections. The selection of variables is a difficult task. Two kinds of variables have to be identified: dependent and independent ones. This also includes the choice of scale type and range of the different variables. The section above also contains more information about dependent and independent variables.
- *Subject selection*: It is performed through sampling methods. Different kinds of sampling can be found at the end of this chapter. This step is fundamental for the later generalization. Therefore, the selection chosen here has to be representative for the whole population. The act of sampling the population can be performed in two ways either probabilistically or non-probabilistically. The difference between those two methods is that in the latter the probability of choosing a sample of the selection is not known. Simple random sampling and systematic sampling, just to name two, are probability-sampling techniques. Those and other methods can be found at the end of this chapter. The size of the sample also has influence on the generalization. A rule of thumb is that the larger the sample is the smaller the error in generalizing the results will be. There are some general principles described in [Juri03]: If there is large variability in the population, a large sample size is needed. The analysis of the data may influence the choice of the sample size. We therefore need to consider how the data be analyzed at the design stage of the experiment.
- *Experiment design*: The design tells how the tests are being organized and performed. An experiment is so to speak a series of tests. A close relationship between the design and the statistical analysis exists and they have effect on each other. The choices taken before (measurement scale, and so on) and a closer look at the null-hypothesis help to find the appropriate statistical method to be able to reject the hypothesis. The following sections provide a deeper view into the subject described briefly above.
- *Instrumentation:* In this step the instruments needed for the experiment are developed. Therefore three different aspects have to be addressed: experiment objects (i.e., specification and code documents), guidelines (i.e., process description and checklists) and measurement. Using instrumentation does not affect the outcome of the experiment. It is only used to provide means for performing and to monitor experiments [Wohl00].
- *Validity evaluation*: After the experiments are carried out the question arises how much valid the results are. Therefore, it is necessary to think of ways to check the validity."

Controlled experiments imply that the experiment follows the steps as mentioned above (Basi86, Zelk97]):
1. Experiment definition. It should provide answers to the following questions : "what is studied?" (object of study), "what is the intention?" (purpose), "which effect is studied?" (quality focus), "whose view is represented?" (perspective) and "where is the study conducted?" (context).
2. Experiment planning. Null hypothesis and alternative hypothesis is formulated. The details (personnel, environment, measuring scale, and so on) are determined and the dependent and independent variables are chosen. First think about the validity of the results.
3. Experiment realization. The experiment is carried out according to the baselines established in the design and planning step. The data is collected and validated.
4. Experiment analysis. The data collection gathered during the realization is the basis for this step. First descriptive statistics are applied to gain an understanding of the submitted data. The data is informally interpreted. Now the decision has to be made how the data can be reduced. After the reduction the hypothesis test is performed. More about hypothesis testing can be found in the following sections.
5. Experiment report: Presentation of the results and conclusion about the hypothesis: the analysis provides the information that is needed to decide whether the hypothesis was rejected or accepted. These conclusions are collected and documented.

Statistical Process Control (SPC) quantitatively considers all elements contributing to process control and process improvement ([Juri01, Wohl00, Pand04, Kulp03], see also Chap. 11). Because it involves numbers, and then scrutinizing the numbers to determine whether the numbers are correctly collected, reported, and used throughout the organization. Many organizations will collect measurements to summarize the best practices we can find in other organizations. So we will describe different types of charts and discuss reasons for using the charts and reasons for collecting data.

SPC consists of techniques used to help individuals understand, analyze, and interpret numerical information. SPC is used to identify and track variation in processes. All processes will have some natural variation. Due to the normal variation in any process, the numbers can change when the process has not. Therefore, we need to understand both the *numbers* relating to our processes and the *changes* that occur in our processes so that we may respond appropriately. SPC and process improvement are further detailed in Chap. 11.

3.5. Analyzing Measurement Data

The general background of statistical methods is described at the beginning of this chapter. Here we will give a short summary about some helpful statistical methods and techniques for analysis and exploration of measurement data ([Kitc97, Juri01,

Pand04, Pfle98, Sing99, Wohl00]). The following seven questions are a beginning in order to reviewing one's measurement data stored in charts [Kulp03]:
1. Who collected these data? (Hopefully people who are trained in proper data collection techniques.)
2. How were the data collected? (Hopefully by automated means and at the same phase of the process.)
3. When were the data collected? (Hopefully all at the same time on the same day or at the same time in the process – very important for accounting data dealing with month-end or year-end closings.)
4. What do the values presented mean? (Have you changed the process recently? Do these values really tell you what you want or need to know?)
5. How were these values computed from raw inputs? (Have you computed the data to arrive at the results you want, or to accurately depict the true voice of the process?)
6. What formulas were used? (Are they measuring what we need to measure? Are they working? Are they still relevant?)
7. Are we collecting the right data, and are we collecting the data right? (The data collected should be consistent, and the way data are collected should be consistent. Do the data contain the correct information for analysis? In our peer review example, this information would be size, complexity, and programming language.)

The seven main analytical diagrams for presenting measurement data and preparing first explorations are as follows. They are further detailed and shown with practical examples in Chap. 11.
- *Check Sheet:* The check sheet is used for counting and accumulating data in a general or special context.
- *Run Chart:* The run chart tracks trends over a period. Points are tracked in the order in which they occur. Each point represents an observation. You can often see interesting trends in the data by simply plotting data on a run chart. A danger in using run charts is that you might overreact to normal variations, but it is often useful to put your data on a run chart to get a feeling for process behaviors.
- *Histogram:* The histogram is a bar chart that presents data that have been collected over a period, and graphically presents these data by frequency. Each bar represents the number of observations that fit within the indicated range. Histograms are useful because they can be used to observe the amount of variation in a process. Using the histogram, you get a different perspective on the data. You see how often similar values occur and get a quick idea of how the data are distributed.
- *Pareto Chart***:** The Pareto chart is a bar chart that presents data prioritized in some fashion, usually either in descending or ascending order of importance. Pareto diagrams are used to show attribute data. Attributes are qualitative data that can he counted for recording and analysis; for example, counting the number of each type of defect. Pareto charts are often used to analyze the most often occurring aspect of some phenomenon.

- *Scatter Diagram/Chart:* The scatter diagram is a diagram that plots data points, allowing trends to be observed between one variable and another. The scatter diagram is used to test for possible cause-and-effect relationships. A danger is that a scatter diagram does not prove the cause-and-effect relationship and can be misused. A common error in statistical analysis is seeing a relationship and concluding cause-and-effect without additional analysis.
- *Cause-and-Effect/Fishbone Diagram:* The cause-and-effect/fishbone diagram is a graphical display of problems and causes. This is a good way to capture team input from a brainstorming meeting, from a set of defect data, or from a check sheet.
- *Control Chart:* The control chart is a run chart with upper and lower limits that allows an organization to track process performance variation. Control charts are also called process behavior charts. Control charts are used to identify process variation over time. All processes vary. The degree of variance, and the causes of the variance, can be determined using control charting techniques. While there are many types of control charts, the ones we have seen the most often are [Kulp03]
  - *c-chart:* This chart uses a constant sample size of attribute data, where the average sample size is greater than five. It is used to visualize the number of defects (such as "12" or "15" defects per thousand lines of code). c stands for the number of nonconformities within a constant sample size.
  - *u-chart:* This chart uses a variable sample size of attribute data. This chart is used to chart the number of defects in a sample or set of samples (such as "20 out of 50" design flaws were a result of requirements errors). u stands for the number of nonconformities with varying sample sizes.
  - *np-chart:* This chart uses a constant sample size of attribute data, usually greater than or equal to 50. This chart is used to chart the number of defects in a group. For example, a hardware component might he considered defective, regardless of the total number of defects in it. np stands for the number defective.
  - *p-chart:* This chart uses a variable sample size of attribute data, usually greater than or equal to 50. This chart is used to visualize the fraction of defects found in a group. p stands for the proportion defective.
  - *X* and *mR charts:* These charts use variable data where the sample size is one.
  - *X-bar* and *R charts: These* charts use variable data where the sample size is small. They can also be based on a large sample size greater than or equal to ten. X-bar stands for the average of the data collected. R stands for the range (distribution) of the data collected.
  - *X-bar* and *s charts:* These charts use variable data where the sample size is large, usually greater than or equal to ten.

These seven graphical displays can be used together or separately to help gather data, accumulate clam, and present the data for different functions associated with SPC. These charts and their practical usage are further detailed in Chap. 11.

Test methods to evaluate hypotheses with measurement data are summarized in the following Table 3.1. We distinguish parametric and non-parametric tests depending on the format and distribution of the underlying raw data.

Table 3.1. Overview of parametric and non-parametric test methods

Experiment type	Parametric tests	Nonparametric tests
One factor, one treatment	Correlations, regression analysis	Rank correlations, Binomial test, chi-square
One factor, two treatments completely randomized	t-test, F-test	Mann-Whitney, chi-square
One factor, two treatments paired comparison	Paired t-test	Wilcoxon, Sign test
One factor, more than two treatments	ANOVA	Kruskal-Wallis, chi-square
More than two factors	ANOVA	

The main characteristic of the parametric tests consists in the fact that the analyzed models have a specific distribution. The main characteristic of the non-parametric is that only a very general assumption is made, more general than parametric test. A listing of the statistical testing methods needed for the different design types is given in alphabetical order in the following. More details about them can be found in [Juri01].

- *ANOVA:* This test is an analysis of variance between groups of artifacts.
- *Binomial test*: This test analyses the differences among dichotomy variables.
- *Chi-square:* This type of test is used when frequencies are involved. This means that the data has the form of frequencies.
- *F-test:* The F-test compares the variance of two (independent) samples.
- *Kruskal-Wallis*: In this case one-way analysis of variance by ranks is performed.
- *Mann-Whitney*: When the assumption made in the t-test is uncertain it is possible to use the Mann- Whitney test instead. Similar to the Wilcox test this method is based on ranks.
- *Paired t-test*: This method compares two samples, collected through repeated measurements.
- *Sign test:* It depends on the sign of the difference of the values of the examined pairs.
- *t-test*: This test compares two (independent) samples.
- *Wilcoxon*: For this method it is important that it is possible to determine the greater value of the examined pair and that the difference can be ranked because the ranks are the basis of the Wilcoxon test.

Finally, the context of any data analysis must be considered in order to keep the appropriateness of any chosen test method. Pandian differentiates three kinds of the analysis domains [Pand04] as measurement data analysis in *frequency domain*, measurement data analysis in *time domain*, and measurement data analysis in the *relationship domain*.

3.6. Empirical Validation: Avoiding the Shotgun Approach

Expert Box. Author: Dave A. Gustafson

It is normal to validate a prediction system by using a proposed measurement to predict a performance measurement such as effort. Two measurements that are often used are the Pearson linear correlation and mean standard error (MSE). The Pearson correlation is very effective at showing that there is a relationship between the estimated value and the actual value. The possible values of the Pearson correlation are from -1 to +1. +1 indicates a perfectly positive correlation; a 0 indicates that there is no relationship between the values of the performance measurement and the value of the proposed measurement; and -1 indicates a perfectly negative correlation. That is, when the proposed measurement is high, the performance measurement is low, and vice versa. Normally, we want a high positive correlation.

The mean standard error is a measurement of how far off the predictions are on the average. For example, if the prediction system gave estimates exactly twice the actual value, the correlation would be +1 while the MSE would be 200%. It is desirable to have as low an MSE as possible. MSE values are useful as estimates of the accuracy of the predictions.

However, correlations and MSE are not a good way to develop prediction systems or to look for relationships. Shotgun correlations [1] are those that use a large number of possible measurements in a correlation analysis to find one measurement that correlates most closely with the desired dependent variable. From a study using random values, we found that when the number of variables being tested as possible predictors was close to the number of samples (e.g., checking 10 variables as possible predictors using data from 10 projects), at least one of the pairs of random numbers would have a high correlation (greater than 0.73) [Cour93].

An additional problem with using correlations as search techniques is that the two possible measurements may actually be related to a third unmeasured measurement. For example, many negative performance measurements are influenced by the size of the program. Thus, errors reports may correlate highly with the number of decisions in a program. However, both of these measurements are probably most related to the size of the program. If a potential relationship exists between a possible measurement and a performance measurement, then using correlations and MSE to validate that relationship is good.

> Do not start with correlations for finding the relationships. The simple rule is to use statistics to validate, not to explore.

3.7. Hints for the Practitioner

We will summarize some basic rules for handling measurement data and using measurements:
- There is not the single best measurement. A single measurement is not sufficient because software systems possess many different properties. Depending on your objectives, environment and processes, measurements will vary.
- There is no preferred set of measurements that fits to each organization. You need to apply the E4-measurement process to identify appropriate measurements suitable for your environment and objectives.
- Just one single measurement is not sufficient to express software quality. Software quality is multi-facetted and needs different measurements, such as reliability, maintainability, error-rate, and so on.
- The properties of the used measurement should be well known. Some measurements are not applicable in certain situations. Sometimes they do not allow the requested statistical analyses.
- A measurement index, combining many measurements, has to be analyzed carefully to ensure that it delivers the requested properties and will not oversimplify.
- A measurement that is validated in one environment is not automatically a validated measurement for other environments.
- Non-validated measurements can be useful too, if for instance used to benchmark across two similar environments.
- A measurement that has a strong correlation with a validated measurement is not automatically validated itself.

3.8. Summary

This chapter provided foundations for software measurement and defined some basics of measurement in order to address their proper use in different fields of software measurement and evaluations. We have shown a general background of measurement demonstrating the high complexity of the measurement artifacts grounded in the product, process and resource areas.

The explanations about the statistical background should be helpful in order to consider the results of measurement and evaluations carefully and appropriately in different software environments.

4. Planning the Measurement Process

*In physical science a first essential step
in the direction of learning any subject
is to find principles of numerical reckoning
and methods for practicably measuring
some quality connected with it.*
Lord Kelvin

4.1. Software Measurement Needs Planning

Usually the software measurement process is embedded in software engineering processes and depends on the environmental characteristics such as
- the *estimation* of the next or future product components, process aspects and resource levels for keeping a successful continuous project in the software development ([Chri06, Dumk02b, NASA95]);
- the *analysis* of artifacts, technologies and methods in order to understand the appropriate resources for the software process ([Dumk99b, Dumk02a, Wang00]);
- the *structuring* of the software process for planning the next steps including the resource characteristics ([Dumk97, Dumk03b, Kene99]);
- the *improvement* of techniques and methodologies for software development as software process improvement ([Chri06, Dumk01, Eber03b, Emam98, Garm95, Muta03a, Warb94]);
- the *control* of the software process, including the analysis of the product quality aspects and their relationships ([Dumk01, Eber03b, Eber97b], and [Kitc96]).

This chapter will introduce to planning software measurement. It will first explain the rationales for measurement planning. Then it will detail frameworks for measurement planning and finally it will lay out how computer assisted measurement and evaluation can help in getting measurement done.

4.2. Planning with Measurement Frameworks

Software measurement needs planning like any other project activity. Otherwise the risk is high that resources are not available or skills and tools are insufficient. At first the analysis of a specific project needs the identification of the measurement goals, from which it derives the measurement aspects and finally the usable measurements and evaluation methods. Interviews with project members assisted in that matter. To derive the specific benchmark goals we used *goal-oriented measurement approaches* which are explained, in the next section.

74   4 Planning the Measurement Process

Furthermore, software measurement is embedded in process improvement concepts and methodologies. As a fundamental basis for measurement planning we will explain the measurement intentions of general process improvement approaches CMMI and ITIL in more detail. These improvement frameworks will be further detailed in Chap. 11.

Measurement in Process Standards

We will start with the *ISO 15939 measurement standard* that include the phases of establishing and sustaining measurement commitment, planning the measurement process, performing the measurement process, and evaluating the resulting measurements [ISO02a]. Fig. 4.1 shows essential components of this standard. Note that this layout is fully consistent with the CMMI process area of measurement and analysis [Chris06]. Aside that you will recall that this structure is the structure of the book in your hands (see Chap. 1).

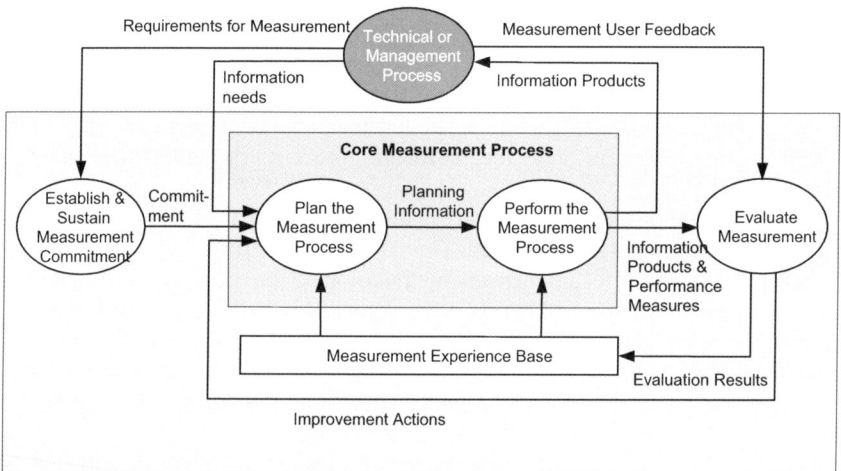

Fig. 4.1. The ISO 15939 measurement standard

Table 4.1 describes the basic tasks and artifacts or objects of this approach with the seven steps of the measurement planning.

Table 4.1. Activities to implement a measurement process based on ISO/IEC15939

Process	Scope
Establish and Sustain Measurement Commitment:	
Accept the requirements for measurement	Identify the scope of measurement. Establish a commitment of management and staff to measurement. Communicate the commitment to the organizational unit.

Assign competent resources	The measurement process should be assigned by competent experts.
	Provide resources to plan the measurement process.
Plan the Measurement Process:	
Characterize organizational unit	Characterize the organizational units that are relevant to selecting measurements.
Identify information needs	Identify the information needed for measurement and prioritize it.
	Information needs shall be selected, documented, and communicated.
Select measurements	Identify the candidate measurements that satisfy the selected information.
	The measurements shall be documented by name, unit of measurement, formal definition, method of data collection, and their link to the information needs.
Define data collection, analysis, and reporting procedures	Define procedures for data collection, data storage, and data verification.
	Define procedures for data analysis, information reporting, and configuration management procedures.
Define criteria for evaluating the information products and the measurement process	Define criteria for evaluating information and the measurement process.
Review, approve, and staff measurement task	Plan the review and approve of the measurement results.
	Resources shall be made available for implementing the planed measurement tasks.
Acquire and deploy supporting technologies	Available supporting technologies shall be evaluated and appropriate ones selected.
	The selected supporting technologies shall be acquired and deployed.
Perform the Measurement Process:	
Integrate procedures	Integration of data generation and collection into relevant processes.
	The integrated data collection procedures shall be communicated to the data provider.
	Integration of data analysis and reporting into the relevant processes.
Collect data	Collect data and store them, including any context information necessary to verify, understand, or evaluate the data.
	Verify the collected data.
Analyze data and develop information products	Analyze of collected data with interpretation of the results.
	Review of information products.
Communicate results	Documentation of the information products.
	Communication of the information products to the measurement users.

Evaluate measurements:	
Evaluate information products and the measurement process	Evaluate the information products against the specified evaluation criteria. Evaluate the measurement process against the specified evaluation criteria. Store lessons learned from the evaluation in "Measurement Experience Base."
Identify potential improvements	Identify potential improvements to the information products. Identify potential improvements to the measurement process. Communicate the improvements.

CMMI stands for *Capability Maturity Model Integration* and provides a process improvement framework for software and systems development, services and acquisition [Chri06]. It is explained and detailed in Chap. 11. The CMMI is driven by measurement to know process performance and being able to improve processes. In the planning of measurement the current process maturity level must be considered in order to continuously improve. Some of these appropriate software measurement intentions are as follows (see Chap. 11, [Chri06]):

- **Quality and process performance attributes** for which needs and priorities might be identified: Functionality, reliability, maintainability, usability, duration, predictability, timeliness, and accuracy [ISO01];
- **Quality attributes for which objectives might be written**: Mean time between failures, critical resource utilization, number and severity of defects in the released product, number and severity of customer complaints concerning the provided service;
- **Process-performance attributes for which objectives might be written**: Percentage of defects removed by product verification activities (perhaps by type of verification, such as peer reviews and testing), defect escape rates, number and density of defects (by severity) found during the first year following product delivery (or start of service), cycle time, percentage of rework time;
- **Sources for improvement objectives**: Requirements, organization's quality and process-performance objectives, customer's quality and process-performance objectives, business objectives, discussions with customers and potential customers, market surveys;
- **Criteria used in selecting subprocesses for quantitative management**: Customer requirements related to quality and process performance, quality and process-performance objectives established by the customer, quality and process-performance objectives established by the organization, organization's performance baselines and models, stable performance of the subprocess on other projects, laws and regulations;
- **Sources of risks**: Inadequate stability and capability data in the organization's measurement repository, sub processes having inadequate performance or capability, suppliers not achieving their quality and process-performance objectives, lack of visibility into supplier capability, inaccuracies in the organization's process performance models for predicting future performance, deficien-

cies in predicted process performance (estimated progress), other identified risks associated with identified deficiencies;
- **Actions to be taken to address deficiencies in achieving the project's objectives**: Changing quality or process performance objectives so that they are within the expected range of the project's defined process, improving the implementation of the project's defined process so as to reduce its normal variability (reducing variability may bring the project's performance within the objectives without having to move the mean), adopting new subprocesses and technologies that have the potential for satisfying the objectives and managing the associated risks, identifying the risk and risk mitigation strategies for the deficiencies, terminating the project;
- **Subprocess measurements**: Requirements volatility, ratios of estimated to measured values of the planning parameters (e.g., size, cost, and schedule), coverage and efficiency of peer reviews, test coverage and efficiency, effectiveness of training (e.g., percentage of planned training completed and test scores), reliability, percentage of the total defects inserted or found in the different phases of the project life-cycle, percentage of the total effort expended in the different phases of the project life-cycle;
- **Anomalous patterns of process variation**: lack of process compliance, undistinguished influences of multiple underlying subprocesses on the data, ordering or timing of activities within the subprocess, uncontrolled inputs to the subprocess, environmental changes during subprocess execution, schedule pressure, inappropriate sampling or grouping of data;
- **Criteria for determining whether data are comparable**: Product lines, organizational structures, application domain, work product and task attributes (e.g., size of product), size of project;
- **Process boundaries and control limits**: Control charts, confidence intervals (for parameters of distributions), prediction intervals (for future outcomes);
- **Techniques for analyzing the reasons for special causes of variation**: Cause-and-effect (fishbone) diagrams, designed experiments, control charts (applied to subprocess inputs or to lower level subprocesses), sub grouping (analyzing the same data segregated into smaller groups based on an understanding of how the subprocess was implemented facilitates isolation of special causes);
- **Needs for recalculating process boundaries and control limits**: There are incremental improvements to the subprocess, new tools are deployed for the subprocess, a new subprocess is deployed, the collected measurements suggest that the subprocess mean has permanently shifted or the subprocess variation has permanently changed;
- **Actions to be taken when a selected subprocess' performance does not satisfy its objectives**: Changing quality and process-performance objectives so that they are within the subprocess' process capability, improving the implementation of the existing subprocess so as to reduce its normal variability (reducing variability may bring the natural bounds within the objectives without having to move the mean), adopting new process elements and subprocesses and technologies that have the potential for satisfying the objectives and man-

aging the associated risks, identifying risks and risk mitigation strategies for each subprocess' process capability deficiency;
- **Work products placed under configuration management**: Subprocesses to be included in the project's defined process, operational definitions of the measurements, their collection points in the subprocesses, and how the integrity of the measurements will be determined, and collected measurements;
- **Stakeholder involvement**: Establishing project objectives, resolving issues among the project's quality and process-performance objectives, appraising performance of the selected subprocesses, identifying and managing the risks in achieving the project's quality and process-performance objectives, identifying what corrective action should be taken;
- **Monitoring and controlling within projects**: Profile of subprocesses under statistical management (e.g., number planned to be under statistical management, number currently being statistically managed, and number that are statistically stable), number of special causes of variation identified.

Based on these quantifications according to the CMMI: "a `managed process` is a performed process that is planned and executed in accordance with policy; employs skilled people having adequate resources to produce controlled outputs; involves relevant stakeholders; is monitored, controlled, and reviewed; and is evaluated for adherence to its process description." The CMMI (maturity and capability) level four emphasizes a measurement-based management of all parts and elements of software product, processes and resources.

ITIL (the *IT Infrastructure Library*) is a set of documents used to aid the implementation of a framework for *IT Service Management* [ITIL06]. This framework characterizes how *Service Management* is applied within an organization. ITIL was originally created by the CCTA, a UK Government agency, it is now being adopted and used across the world as the de facto standard for best practice in providing IT services.

ITIL is organized into a series of sets as a ***best practice approach*** which themselves are divided into eight main areas
1. *Service Support* is the practice of those disciplines that enable IT Services to be provided effectively (service-desk, incident management, problem management, change management, configuration management, release management).
2. *Service Delivery* covers the management of the IT services themselves (service level management, financial management for IT services, capacity management, service continuity management, availability management).
3. *Security Management* considers the installation and realization of a security level for the IT environment (trust, integrity, availability, customer requirements, risk analysis, authority, and authenticity).
4. *ICT Infrastructure Management* describes four management areas: design and planning, deployment, operations, technical support.
5. *Application Management* describes the service life-cycle as requirements – design – build- deploy – operate – optimize.

6. *Planning to Implement Service Management* defines a guide in order to deploy the ITIL approach in a concrete IT environment.
7. *The Business Perspective* describes the relationships of the IT to the customers and users.
8. *Software Asset Management* defines the processes and the life-cycles for managing the software assets.

Fig. 4.2 shows a *triangle* characterizing the different relationships between the service management standards and ITIL. BS 15000 is the service management standard, ISO 20000 describes the specification for service management, and PD 0005 stands for code of practice for the IT service management (ITSM). Usually, the implementation of the ITIL approach is supported by any *ITIL toolkits*.

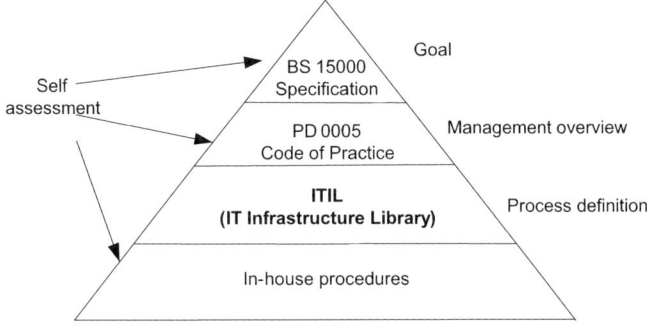

Fig. 4.2. The relationship between the service standards and ITIL

The measurement planning based on ITIL must consider the different standard levels by using case studies that are correlated to the best practices.

Measurement frameworks help in planning the software measurement process. They can be divided in general in two classes: the declarative and the operational measurement frameworks [Dumk05a]. *Declarative software measurement frameworks* describe *what* we achieve based on the software measurement methods and activities. *Operational software measurement frameworks* characterize *how* we achieve the measurement goals and levels.

There are plenty of measurement frameworks but we only consider two of both kinds of frameworks in this paper.

Declarative Measurement Frameworks

First we will consider the ***Zuse Measurement Framework*** which includes the largest and profoundest investigations of existing measurement approaches [Zuse98]. In following we will only characterize some of the essential intentions of this measurement framework.

The following kinds of *requirements for software measurements* are defined by Zuse:

$requirementsForMeasures = \{req_{general}, req_{rankingProperties}, req_{units}, req_{substitutionOperation}, req_{additiveRatioScale}, req_{non-additive}, req_{densityMeasures}, req_{wholeness}, req_{predictionModels}, req_{sizeMeasures}, req_{simpleMeasures}, req_{componentIndependence}\}$

The *types of measurements* based on the measurement theory are the following:

typesOfMeasures = {TM-CNT, TM-ADD, TM-HYA, TM-HYAS, TM-DEN, TM-DENM, TM-NADDR, TM-BSA, TM-HYM, TM-ORD, TM-PC, TM-FB, TM-MIMA, TM-IND, TM-NGEXT}, with *TM-CNT* (counting on attribute), *TM-ADD* (additive measurement), *TM-HYA* (hybrid measurement by additivity), *TM-HYAS* (hybrid measurement additive plus a constant), *TM-DEN* (density measurements), *TM-DENM* (density measurement with an additional condition), *TM-NADDR* (non-additive ratio scale), *TM-BSA* (two concatenation operations), *TM-HYM* (hybrid measurement by multiplication), *TM-ORD* (purely ordinal measurement), *TM-PC* (percentage measurement), *TM-FB* (modified function of belief), *TM-MIMA* (minimum – maximum), *TM-IND* (independence conditions), *TM-NGEXT* (negative extension structure and non-additive ratio scale).

The following kinds of measurements of *artifacts* are considered in detail in the Zuse framework:

$A_{framework} = \{ A_{ISO9000-3}, A_{functionPoints}, A_{COCOMO}, A_{maintainability}, A_{structureCharts}, A_{informationFlow}, A_{measuresOfBowles}, A_{coding}, A_{testing}, A_{cohesion}, A_{maintenance}, A_{documentQuality}, A_{OOmeasures}, A_{life-cycle}\}$

In the *scale analysis*, the following operations about the components of the measured artifact are helpful:

$M_{modeling} \in \{BALT, BSEQ, CINT, CUNI, DSEQ, HAGG, HGEN, LSEQ, RALT, RSEQ, SBSEQ\}$, with *BALT* (parallel concatenation), *BSEQ* (sequential concatenation), *CINT* (object-oriented concatenation), *CUNI* (object-oriented unification), *DSEQ* (charts sequential concatenation), *HAGG* (object-oriented hierarchical concatenation), *HGEN* (object-oriented generalizing concatenation), *LSEQ* (boards sequential concatenation), *RALT* (resistors parallel concatenation), *RSEQ* (resistors sequential concatenation), *SBSEQ* (source code sequential concatenation);

The application of the *viewpoint principle* for using measurements. The viewpoint and the empirical system are identical. The word viewpoint is more intuitive for the user and well known from the conventional usage.

The application of the software measurement framework by Zuse ensures that measurement theoretical aspects for achieving useful measurements and their correct use in the software evaluation are maintained.

Operational Measurement Frameworks
We will consider the GQM and the Six Sigma approach as examples of operational measurement frameworks in following.

The **Goal Question Metric (GQM) approach** is a concept of how to proceed during measurement and was published by Basili and Weiss in 1984 [Basi94] (note that in the context of the GQM paradigm and abbreviation we keep the authors' original notion of "metric" meaning the same as "measurement"). The GQM-paradigm also helped in defining the E4–measurement process.

Measurement is necessary to control the software development process and the software product. The basic idea of GQM is to derive software measurements from measurement questions and goals. Today, GQM has proven its quality in the problems of measurement selection and implementation (see especially [VanS00]). Measurement's main task is making understanding of the specific process or product easier for the user. Successful improvement of software development is impossible without knowing what your improvement goals are and how they relate to your business goals. The most difficult question is how to define particular improvement goals in terms of business goals or with respect to particular project needs. Measurement provides the means to identify improvement goals. By applying measurement to a specific part of the process, problems within the process can be identified for which improvement goals can be defined. Currently, process improvement is broadly approached across the software and IT industries in order to become and stay competitive on a global scale. People have realized that without continuous process improvement, others will take the lead and clients move away.

Several improvement models, methods and techniques are available, divided into two major classes.

- *Top-down approaches* which are based on assessment and benchmarking. For example: the Capability Maturity Model Integration (CMMI), the Software Process Improvement and Capability detErmination (SPICE), (see [Chri06, Emam98, Muta03]),
- *Bottom-up approaches*, mainly apply measurement as their basic guide for improvement; an example of this type of approach is GQM. They are called bottom-up because they apply for single processes and can scale up to achieving organizational improvement needs.

It is possible, and often very useful, to combine two approaches, for example, GQM with the CMMI. A capability maturity model (such as the CMMI) helps organizations to improve the maturity of their software process and in that way decrease the level of risk in performance. *Process maturity suggests that you can measure only what is visible.* Using both CMMI and GQM thus gives a more comprehensive and complete picture of what measurements will be the most useful. GQM tells us why we measure an attribute, and CMMI tells us if we are capable of measuring it in a meaningful way.

Goal-oriented measurement points out that the existence of explicitly stated goals is of the highest importance for improvement programs. GQM presents a systematic approach for integrating goals to models of the software processes, products and quality perspectives of interest, based upon the specific needs of the project and the organization. In order to improve a process you have to define measurement goals which will be, after applying the GQM method, refined into questions and then into measurements that will supply all the necessary information for answering those questions. The GQM method provides a measurement plan that deals with the particular set of problems and the set of rules for interpre-

tation of the obtained data. The interpretation answers whether the project goals were attained. The GQM approach provides a framework involving three steps [VanS00]:
1. Set concrete goals for your change, performance improvement, project behaviors, or visibility (e.g., to improve customer satisfaction or productivity).
2. Ask questions how goals would be achieved (e.g., specific changes), or what effect you would see when the goals are achieved (e.g., concrete operational results).
3. Determine measurements that show that goals are achieved (e.g., defects after handover, effort for a standardized maintenance requirement).

Fig. 4.3 shows the different aspects and intentions used in the application during the three steps of the GQM approach.

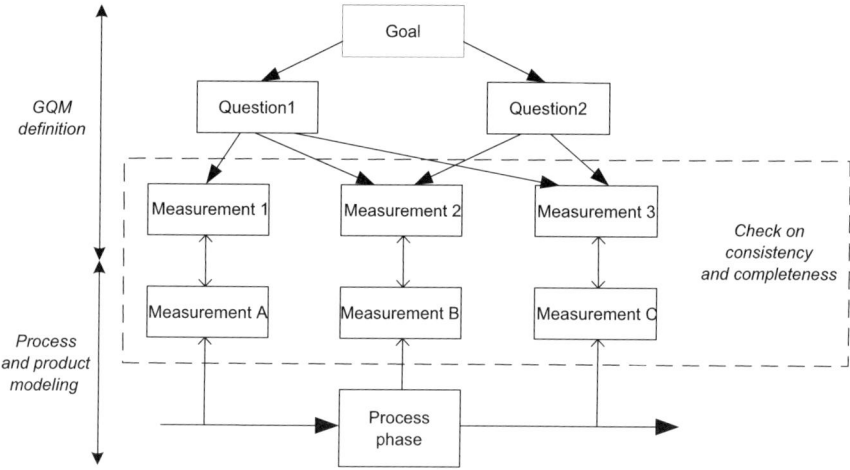

Fig. 4.3. The GQM approach

The GQM methodology contains four phases:
- The *planning phase*, during which the project for measurement application is selected, defined, characterized and planned, resulting in a project plan.
- The *definition phase*, during which the measurement program is defined (goal, questions, measurements and hypotheses are defined) and documented.
- The *data collection phase*, during which the actual data collection takes place, resulting in collected data.
- The *interpretation phase*, during which the collected data is processed with respect to the defined measurements into measurement results which provide answers to the defined questions, after which goal attainment can be evaluated.

Fig. 4.4 shows the topology of the GQM components considering the intentions of the ISO 15939 standard. Table 4.2 shows an example of a GQM hierarchy adapted from [Fent97].

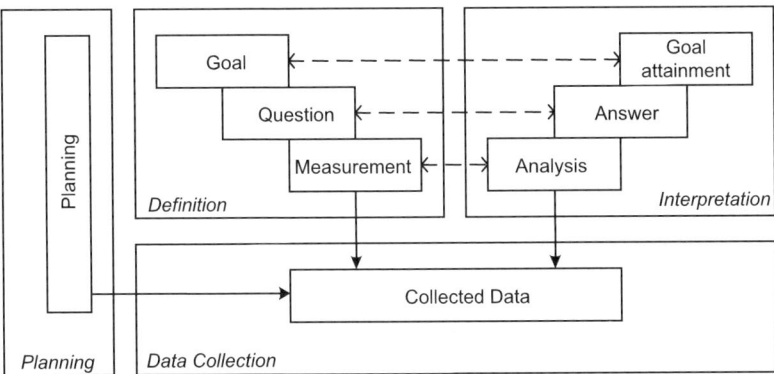

Fig. 4.4. The GQM methodology

Table 4.2. GQM example

Goal	Questions	Measurements
Plan	How much does the inspection process cost?	Average effort per KLOC Percentage of reinspections
	How much calendar time does the inspection process take?	Average effort per KLOC Total KLOC inspected
Monitor and control	What is the quality of the inspected software?	Average faults detected per KLOC Average inspection rate Average preparation rate
	To what degree did the staff conform to the procedures? What is the status of the inspection process?	Average inspection rate Average preparation rate Average lines of code inspected Total KLOC inspected
Improve	How effective is the inspection process?	Defect removal percentage Average faults detected per KLOC
	What is the productivity of the inspection process?	Average effort per fault detected Average inspection rate Average preparation rate Average lines of code inspected

Measurement planning should be based on the clear definition of the goals and the details in order to achieve these goals primarily.

The *Six Sigma approach* has its origins in statistics using the symbol for standard deviation [McCa04, Harr03, Pyzd03]. For details in Six Sigma, see Chap. 11. Is has also become a management philosophy that includes the need for fact-based decisions, customer focus, and teamwork. The focus is related to error deviation with different levels of considerations (usually from 3σ to 6σ). Six Sigma is based on the *DMAIC model* which involves the cyclical phases *define, measure, analyze, improve,* and *control.* Considering the measurement process involvements we can establish the following characteristic steps in the general Six Sigma phases:

- The key steps within the *definition phase* are: define the problem, form a team, establish a project charter, develop a project plan, identify the customers, identify key outputs, identify and prioritize requirements, and document the current process.
- The key steps within the *measurement phase* are: determine what to measure, conduct the measurements, calculate the current sigma level, determine the process capability, and benchmark the process leaders.
- The key steps within the *analysis phase* are: determine what caused the variation, brainstorm ideas for process improvements, determine which improvements would have the greatest impact on meeting customer requirements, develop a proposed process map, and assess the risks associated with the revised process.
- The key steps within the *improvement phase* are: gain approval for the proposed changes, finalize the implementation plan, and implement the approved changes.
- The key steps within the *control phase* are: institutionalize the process improvements so that the changes are permanent and gains are sustained, develop and communicate measurements that continue to reinforce the value of the improvements, and establish mechanisms for dealing with out-of-control situations.

Addressing measurement planning, the Six Sigma approach is available for [Tayn03] traditional software development life-cycles, legacy systems, package software implementations, and outsourcing.

Otherwise, there are a lot of formal approaches for software measurement including operational or framework aspects. Fig. 4.5 shows these approaches without any further discussion (see the details in [Dumk05c]).

4.3. Holistic Planning of Measurement: The CAME Approach

We will use the acronym CAME with three meanings to meet the requirements of software measurement. CAME is defined in a layer model which consists of a kernel CAME tools, a general CAME strategy with an embedded CAME framework. The *CAME strategy* stands for [Dumk99a]

4.3 Holistic Planning of Measurement: The CAME Approach 85

- *Community:* the necessity of a group or a team that is motivated and has the knowledge of software measurement to install software measurements. In general, the members of these groups are organized in measurement communities such as our German Interest Group on Software Measurement (http://ivs.cs.uni-magdeburg.de/sw-eng/us/giak/).
- *Acceptance:* the agreement of the (top) management to install a measurement program in the (IT) business area. This aspect is strong connected with the knowledge about required budgets and personnel resources.
- *Motivation:* the production of measurement and evaluation results in a first measurement application which demonstrates the convincing benefits of the measurement application. This very important aspect can be achieved by the application of essential results in the (world-wide) practice which are easy to understand and should motivate the management. One of the problem of this aspect is the fact that the management wants to obtain *one single (quality) number* as a summary of all measured characteristics.
- *Engagement:* the acceptance of spending effort to implement the software measurement as a permanent measurement system (with continued measurement, different statistical analysis, measurement set updates etc.). This aspect includes also the requirement to dedicate personnel resources such as measurement teams etc.

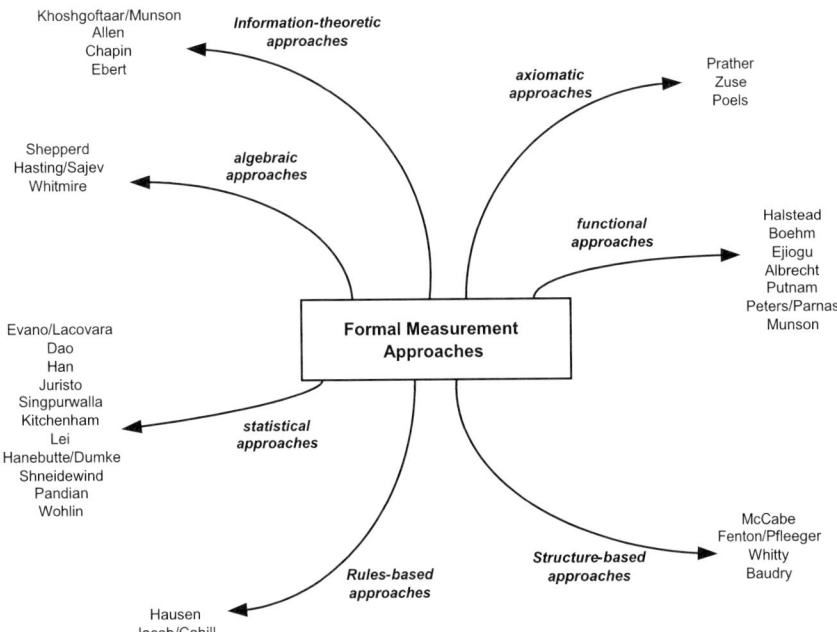

Fig. 4.5. Overview of formal software measurement approaches

The *CAME framework* itself consists of the following four phases:
- *Choice:* the selection of measurements based on a special or general measurement view on the kind of measurement and the related measurement goals – as *measurement areas*,
- *Adjustment:* the characteristics of the measurements for the specific application field – as *measurement levels*,
- *Migration:* the semantic relations between the measurements along the whole life-cycle and along the system architecture – as *characteristics of the measurement methods and their integration level*,
- *Efficiency:* the automation level as construction of a tool-based measurement – as *implementation of the measurement methods* by *CAME tools (computer assisted measurement and evaluation tools)*.

Choice characteristics help to decide about the *coverage* of our measurement areas relating to the product, process and resources, i.e., we decide which areas (components, artifacts) are "out of control." Dividing the measured artifacts in *design, description* and *working* we can define the following **choice levels** of measurement:
- *No measurement:* no kinds of measurement and evaluation are applied and used for the considered IT area
- *Aspect-oriented measurement*: only some characteristics, criteria or entities were considered
- *Capability-oriented measurement*: some sub-areas or sub-domains were considered in the IT area
- *Total measurement*: in the sense of full/total quantitative analysis and management of the IT area.

Fig. 4.6 shows a compact presentation of the choice level from our point of view adapted and extended from Wille [Will05] considering the declarative part of the CAME framework. Note that the measured artifacts are derived in three components/states: *design* (modeling, architecture), *description* (documentation, characterization), and *working* (interpretation, runtime) – which does not mean any reduction in information content.

The quality of the chosen measurements was determined by their scale characteristics which mean that we can establish the situation of *qualitative measurement* (achieving a nominal or ordinal scale) or of *quantitative measurement* (achieving an interval or ratio scale). On the other hand, the used measurement characteristics like thresholds could be applied from another technology (as *approximation*) or from another product of the same technology (as *tuning*). Both characteristics determine the **adjustment level**.

In the case of *missing thresholds* empirical values could be taken from another experience like analogies, expertise or rules of thumb. The situation of *undetermined scale characteristics* could be improved by the initial use of the lower level scale type such as qualitative measurement with nominal and ordinal scales.

In order to achieve a full measurement process is a complex never ending task. Software measurement ontology is a meaningful point of view of the detailed measurement process components and involvements.

4.3 Holistic Planning of Measurement: The CAME Approach

Measurement migration involves the principles of integration of the measurement in the given IT area. That means it should be integrated in the general process improvements and evaluations. Let us consider these aspects in special context. Process improvement based on a model is defined by Wang and King as [Wang00]: *"A **process improvement model (PIM)** is an operational model that provides guidance for improving a process system's capability by changing, updating, or enhancing existing processes based on the findings provided in a process assessment."*

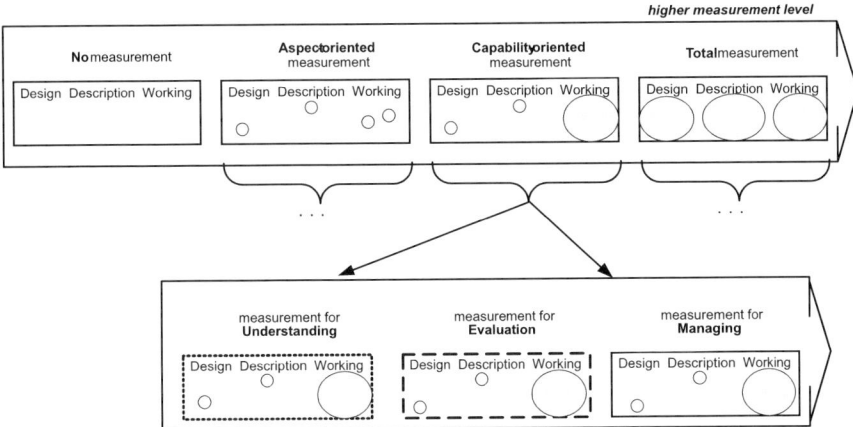

Fig. 4.6. The CAME levels choosing/selecting the measurement areas

In a concrete IT area it is necessary to consider the relationships between the chosen/selected improvement approaches. Assuming that the general software process is divided in the components of (system) *requirements*, *process* (as methodology, life-cycle and management), *product* (as programs and documentation), *resources* (as personnel, software (COTS and CASE) and platforms), and *application domain* (as society, organization and IT area) we can construct the relationships (Fig. 4.7) [Dumk06].

On the other hand, we can build an analogical presentation considering the chosen or selected measurements. We will use a definition of the process measurement model by [Wang00] again as: *"**Software process measurement model (SPM)** is a model that defines an organized and benchmarked software process system and applies process measurements with quantitative measurement characteristics."* The relationships could be presented in a semantic network (Fig. 4.8).

These kinds of visualization can be very helpful to demonstrate the involved components and the chosen measurements in the measurement planning.

The CAME approach can also been used to analyze the general measurement situation in different IT areas, development paradigms and certain kinds of software systems and can establish necessary research activities and missing measurement field applications.

4 Planning the Measurement Process

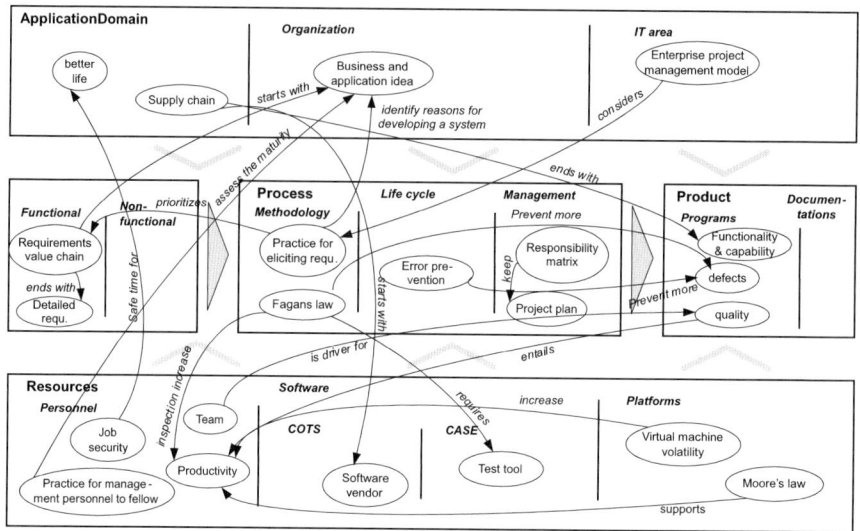

Fig. 4.7. The PIM based process related semantic network

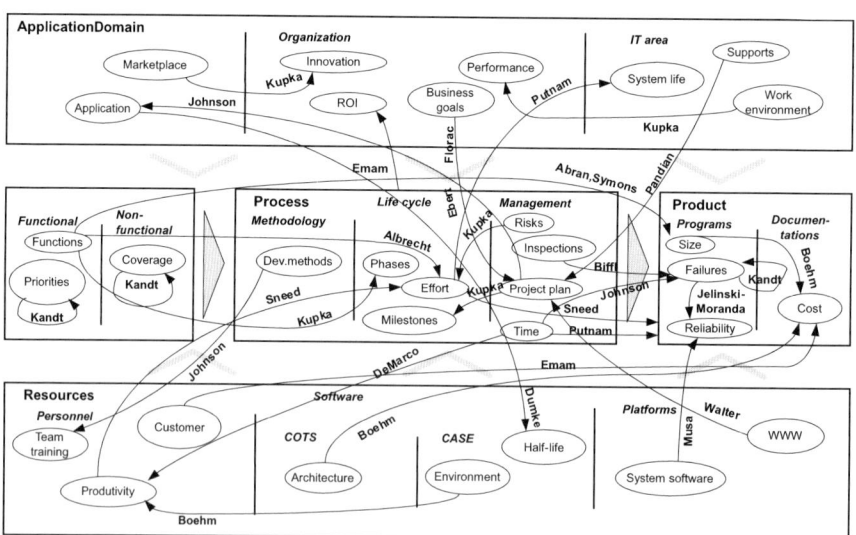

Fig. 4.8. The software process measurement model based semantic network

4.4. Hints for the Practitioner

In the planning of measurement we must consider the current process maturity carefully in order to manage the software process quantitatively. Different maturity means that quantitative management must be adjusted. For instance, a defined process can be measured and then stabilized in its performance. A not-defined process needs first process definition before it can be stabilized.

The measurement planning based on ITIL must consider the different standard levels by using case studies which are correlated to the best practices. In the planning of software measurement should be considered the measurement approaches or standards themselves of course. Addressing to the measurement planning, the Six Sigma approach is available for traditional software development life-cycle, legacy systems, package software implementation, and outsourcing.

Goal-oriented measurement approaches should look to following practical experiences:
- Goal-oriented approaches address special aspects, characteristics or intentions to the software process, product or resources. Typical examples in software engineering are usability engineering, performance engineering or security engineering.
- GQM presents a systematic approach for integrating goals to models of the software processes, products and quality perspectives of interest based upon the specific needs of the project and the organization.
- The E4–measurement process extends goal-oriented measurement with a closed feedback loop on actions and decisions to be taken and executed until the goal is reached.

Since process maturity suggests that you can measure only what is visible, using any goal-oriented methodology (e.g., GQM, E4–measurement process or measurement and analysis process area of CMMI) provides tailored and useful software measurements. Furthermore, the CAME approach helps to determine your software measurement level and appropriate tooling. The main intentions and experience of the CAME approach for the practitioners are:
- The CAME approach considers both sides of software measurement: the detailed measurement process (methods, measurements and scales) and the measurement process environment (strategy, motivation and installation).
- Considering also the both sides of software measurement application, that is, the numerical measurement side and the empirical goal side.
- Investigating the scale characteristics of the measurements carefully in order to obtain the correct answers of the goal-based questions.
- Integrating the different kinds of measurement methods in the process that should be managed.
- Aggregating the different intentions and measurement tools in your measurement concept or approach.
- Constructing a profound architecture of measurement databases or repositories.

4.5. Summary

Goal-oriented approaches are well-established methods of achieving constructive and successful improvements in the IT area and addressing special needs, characteristics or intentions of the software process, product or resources. They can be used in different granularities: as a small aspect of product or process improvement or as a complex set of criteria for managing and controlling some of the IT processes themselves.

The CAME framework description showed the step-by-step planning of the installation of a software measurement process in the chosen environment of customer relationships including a prototypical implementation of this approach. The structure of the measurement selection and analysis should be helpful for appropriate adaptation in chosen process areas.

In general, the CAME approach supports the characterization of the measurements or measurement level and helps to understand the necessary steps or activities for improving, managing or controlling the different IT processes. Some levels of the measurement characterization are the following:

- the measurement of only few product artifacts
- the consideration of basic product and process aspects
- the orientation of resource efficiency
- the dominance of the ordinal measurement as a simple kinds of ranking

Most of all, goal-oriented approaches are a meaningful way in order to achieve measurable success and quality in the IT area.

5. Performing the Measurement Process

*A science is as mature
as its measurement tools.*
Louis Pasteur

5.1. Measurement Needs Tools

We will look into the "performing" of the measurement process from a systematic tools-oriented perspective here. The remaining part of the book will detail the practical process-oriented aspects of the measurement process.

> The efficiency of the software measurement process depends on the level of automation by tools.

The importance of measurement tools is as obvious as the tool support in other disciplines of software engineering. The purpose of determining the performance of the software process is to produce and collect the measurement data supported by so-called *measurement tools*. Therefore, in this chapter we describe the current situation in the area of measurement tools and an outlook on future evolution. The first section includes an overview of some measurement tools and the current situation in the area of software e-measurement.

We choose the notion of computer assisted software measurement and evaluation (CAME) tools for identifying all the kinds of measurement tools in the software life-cycle [Dumk97]. CAME tools are tools for modeling and determining the measurements of software development components referring to the process, the product and the resource. Presently, the CAME tool area also includes the tools for model-based software components analysis, measurement application, presentation of measurement results, statistical analysis and evaluation.

In general, we can establish CAME tools for classification, for component measurement, for process or product measurement and evaluation, as well as for training in software measurement. The application of CAME tools is based on the given measurement framework (see [Dumk96a, Dumk96b, Dumk96c, Oman97, Zuse98], Chap. 4). On the other hand, CAME tools can be classified according to the degree of integration in software development environments such as integrated forms, external coupling forms and stand-alone measurement tools.

We will describe some classes of CAME tools based on the tool investigations in the Software Measurement Laboratory at the University of Magdeburg (SML@b) during the last ten years. CAME tools are useful in all areas of software engineering such as software product evaluation, process level determination and the measurement of the quality of the resources. We provide here a list of measurement tools for these different aspects in software development and maintenance (for the detailed description of these tools see [Dumk96a, Smla06] and http://ivs.cs.uni-magdeburg.de/sw-eng/us/CAME/). Naturally such selection of tools is subjective and non-exhaustive.

5.2. Instrumenting the Measurement Process

5.2.1 Process Measurement and Evaluation

The following CAME tools are used and tested in the SML@b [Smla06]. They are helpful for application during the measurement of the software process phases, components and activities.
- Knowledge PLAN (USA). This estimation/feasibility tool uses a lot of experience implicitly. One of the used size measure is function points. A lot of helpful project information is executed and printed based on many input parameters such as product, process and resource characteristics.
- COSTAR (USA). The COSTAR tool supports the software estimation based on the COCOMO II approach. The execution is based on different variants of components and size measurements.
- SLIM Palm Tool (University of Magdeburg, Germany). This CAME tool implements the software life-cycle management (SLIM) formula for the Palm computer. It is an example of the appropriateness of handhelds for the application of useful CAME tools.
- SOFT-ORG (Germany). This tool helps to define a general enterprise-based measurement model as the essential basic for a successful measurement application.

Fig. 5.1 shows the layout of the *COSTAR tool which* supported the cost estimation during the earlier phases of software development based on the COCOMO II approach. Other cost estimation tools are discussed in Chaps. 7 and 9.

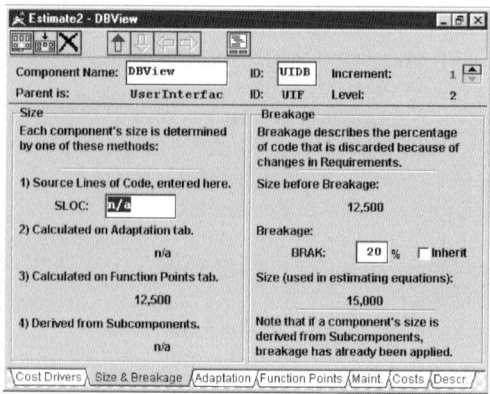

Fig. 5.1. Layout of COSTAR cost estimation based on COCOMO II

5.2.2 Product Measurement and Evaluation

In this section we consider the different phases during the software development relating to efficient CAME tool support. We will choose only a few examples to demonstrate the essential aspects.

Requirements engineering
- RMS (Germany). The reading measuring system (RMS) supports the analysis of the quality of documentation by using some of the text quality and readability measurements.
- Function Point Workbench (Australia). The FPW supports all the steps of the IFPUG 4.x evaluation [ISO03b] and can be considered as the primarily used FP tool with a large background of measurement experience.
- SOFT-CALC (Germany). This CAME tool supports the cost estimation for different point-based approaches such as function points, data points and object points. The SOFT-CALC tool is compatible to SOFT-ORG.
- COSMOS (Netherlands). COSMOS stands for cost management with measurements of specification and realizes an evaluation of different programming and formal specification languages such as LOTOS, Z, and so on. The tool has a good variance in measurement definition, adjustment and calibration.

Software design
- MOOD (Portugal). The MOOD concept as measurements for object-oriented design implements an evaluation of object-oriented class libraries based on the well-established object-oriented software measurements.
- Metrics One (USA). This Rational tool supports the measurements of unified modeling language (UML) diagrams by counting a lot of aspects from and between the basic charts and components of an UML-based software specification.
- SmallCritic (Germany). This Smalltalk measurement and evaluation tool supports essential object-oriented measurements during the software development itself.

Program evaluation
- CodeCheck (USA). CodeCheck implements code measurement based on language parsing. The price for this high flexibility is the greater effort for learning its application.
- QUALMS (UK). This quality analysis and measurement tool supports the code measurement including varieties of statistical data exploration.
- DATRIX (Canada). This CAME tool implements code measurement for C, C++, and so on and is based on a large experience in practice.
- LOGISCOPE (USA). LOGISCOPE supports code measurement including quality evaluation of large-scale software. In contrast with the static measurement-based evaluation, this tool supports the dynamic testing including the essential coverage measurements.

- PC-METRIC (USA). This small tool is very helpful for code measurement based on the Halstead and McCabe measurements and has a high stability in the measurement results. [McCa76, Eber95]
- PMT (University of Magdeburg, Germany). (This Prolog measurement tool supports the software measurement of Prolog programs by using new kinds of descriptive measurements.
- OOMJ (University of Magdeburg, Germany). This CAME tool implements the object-oriented measurement of Java-based measurements including Chidamber-Kemerer and MOOD measurements as a Web service.

Fig. 5.2 shows one of the methods of code evaluation by the *LOGISCOPE tool* using the Kiviat diagram. This tool includes variants of code visualization (flow graph, call graph, and so on), Furthermore LOGISCOPE evaluates software systems based on a complex quality model which must be carefully considered in order to keep the correct or appropriate intentions of the tool customer.

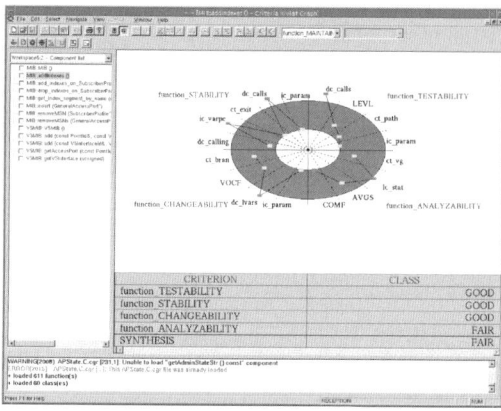

Fig. 5.2. Code evaluation by the LOGISCOPE measurement tool

Software testing
- LDRA (UK). This testbed includes a complex test environment applicable for different programming languages and supports the user by flexible program visualization.
- STW-METRIC (USA). The software test workbench implements a concept of statistical analysis and test support and is a component of general software analyzing and evaluation system.

Software maintenance
- Smalltalk Measure (University of Magdeburg, Germany). This Smalltalk extension by code measurements executes the size and complexity measurements for every class, application or system level in the Smalltalk system.

- COMET (University of Magdeburg, Germany). The CORBA measurement tool supports the measurement of object-oriented Java applications including CORBA components.
- Measurement Aglets (University of Magdeburg, Germany). This set of measurement agents supports the measurement of distributed Java code by Java agents as aglets.

5.2.3 Resource Measurement and Evaluation

The following CAME tools are helpful during the measurement of the software resources components and activities.

Productivity
- SPQR/20 (USA). The software productivity and quality research tool estimates the size based productivity from twenty parameters.
- Estimation tools such as those mentioned above also offer possibilities to rate productivity changes over time or across different volume within a closely defined context.

Performance
- Foundation Manager (USA). This tool addresses the testing of network performance and availability with a comfortable visualization.
- SPEC JVM Benchmark (USA). This CAME tool uses the technique of simulation of the performance characteristics of chosen resource configurations.

Usability
- COSAM (University of Magdeburg, Germany). This customer satisfaction tool supports the evaluation of the customer satisfaction based on process, product and resource measurements.
- DOCTOR HTML (USA). This Web measurements tool produces an evaluation of Web sites including the appropriateness of the resources like the Web browser acceptability.

5.2.4 Measurement Presentation and Analysis

In order to analyze and evaluate the software measurement results, the following CAME tools are helpful for application during these activities.
- Excel (USA) and other similar spreadsheet programs (e.g., from StarOffice or OpenOffice). This well-established spreadsheet tool can be used for data presentations and analysis. Other common office spreadsheet tools work equally well.
- SPSS (USA). This statistical package for the social science is a data exploration tool including the essential statistical methods and should be used for careful data analysis and exploration.

5.2.5 Measurement Training

The following CAME tools are helpful for learning and understanding the phases, components and activities of software measurement including their theoretical background.
- METKIT (UK). The measurement tool kit represents a European initiative for measurement education and training. The most components are tutorials for learning the software measurement theory and practice.
- ZD-MIS (Germany). This Zuse Drabe measurement information system is addressed to the measurement education based on the measurement theory including more the 1500 analyzed software measurements and references.

5.3. Case Study: Static Code Analysis

Expert Box. Author: Andreas Schmietendorf

The following example of industrial measurement is based on an application of the Logiscope tool in order to evaluate the maintainability of a telecommunication system at the German Telekom. The software in this application is increasingly reused. New software is built from reused components, frameworks or libraries. Most software however is built on top or by changing existing software. Especially for legacy systems, it is often difficult to get information on software quality, since these systems have grown to complex structures over time, and often the documentation is no longer up to date.

Because of the size and complexity of software it is usually impossible to evaluate it manually; for this reason methods and tools are needed to support this task. With help of a static software analysis tool the previously explained theoretical foundations are applied to a large software system, and evaluation examples from the project quality report are presented. The underlying quality model is explained in detail as are the experiences made (e.g., tool handling, surplus value).

Note that there are several tools available for static code analysis with comparable functionality (e.g., Logiscope, Klocwork, LDRA, Splint, QAC). We focus here on Logiscope in this context to provide in-depth examples how such tools are used. Other tools could also have been also used with similar results.

The software system under investigation is a large telecommunication system. It supports the realization of administration tasks for digital operator interfaces. The tasks are realized with an OSI-compatible Common Management Information Protocol (CMIP) by a so-called Q3 interface providing the functionality of the operator interface. With the help of Common Management Information Service Element (CMISE) operations it is possible to administrate analog and digital telephone connections.

Because of the OSI-compatible protocol approach, systems of different suppliers (e.g., Alcatel-Lucent) can be administered inside a single application. Furthermore, the system has a customer relationship management (CRM) system interface for the handling of customer jobs as well as additional interfaces, e.g., for the automatic transmission of e-mails. The system has existed for about ten years and is implemented as object-oriented with C++. The reason for this analysis was the desire to replace the object-oriented database management system in use by a relational database management system. Since the system was developed over such a long time, among other things a general overview of the whole system quality was desired and the critical components were to be identified. We focused on investigating some critical parts of the telecommunication system. For that reason one component out of over 30,000 classes was chosen that is especially involved in the changes caused by the database replacement. Since there was no well-defined persistence layer, the analyzed component realizes parts of such a layer for the reengineered system.

The analysis presented here comprises a prototype of the database access component. Ninety-six files were investigated, some of them in a quite unspecified state. The Logiscope tool could extract 45 classes and 773 functions, but because of the state of the prototype some identified components contained only rough information.

The Logiscope tool can be used for different purposes in the area of software quality management/assurance, such as software quality and structure analyses, tool-based generation of quality reports, and so on [Tele06]. It contains three main components, an Audit component (quality and structure analyses), a RuleChecker component (control of programming rules) and a TestChecker component (test coverage), and among other languages it supports Java, C++, C and ADA. The basic tools are static analysis (Fig. 5.3) and dynamic analysis (Fig. 5.4).

The static analysis performs a syntactic and semantic analysis of the source code, is programming language-dependent and delivers the input for complexity measurements, call graphs, control graphs, quality reports, and so on. With help of the dynamic analysis, test coverage analysis can be realized. In contrast to the static analysis, the running program is investigated. Before compiling the program the source code is instrumented, and the program structure statements are marked. When the program is running after the compilation process it permanently writes information to an execution result file. This file can be used to observe the test coverage, and thus the test case generation is supported as well as a statement about the status of the tests can be derived. In our case only static analyses were used because the software system under investigation is an embedded system on a certain platform and the effort to arrange a running environment seemed to be too demanding.

The quality models are built according to commonly used principles, including the GQM approach (see [VanS00]). First, the model of the application level will be shown. To clarify: The factor maintainability is defined on the application level. The maintainability is broken down by analyzability, changeability, stability and testability. The other attributes and criteria at the different levels are composed in the same manner. For each measurement there is an upper and a lower limit, and during the static analysis it is determined whether the measurement value for the component is within the limits or outside. This information is used to derive a statement for the criteria (e.g., analyzability and changeability), and the criteria statements are composed to the factor statements (e.g., for the maintainability).

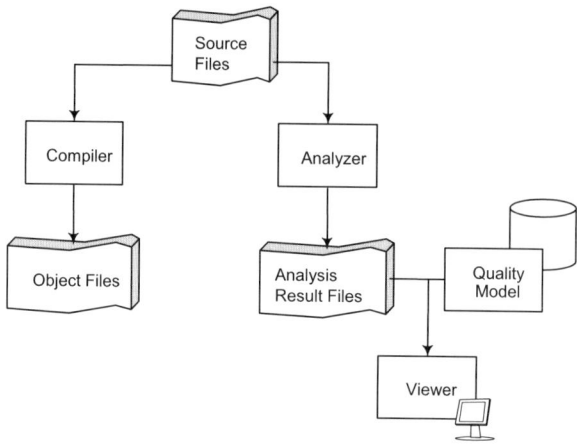

Fig. 5.3. Principle of static code analysis

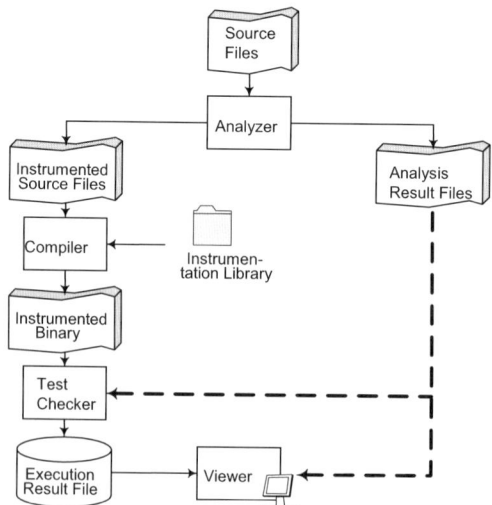

Fig. 5.4. Principle of dynamic code analysis

Let us look into the results and analyze findings for the three levels: the application level, the class level and the function level.

Function level. At their function level the functions are the components of interest, including their size, complexity and dependability on other functions. Different visualizations give an overview of the function distribution according to the factor maintainability (Fig. 5.5) and the criteria (e.g., analyzability, Fig. 5.6) as well as a precise mapping of the functions to the factor/criteria ranges from excellent to poor (e.g., the listing of functions that rate fair according to the analyzability).

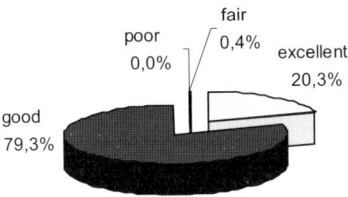

Fig. 5.5. Function distribution for the maintainability factor

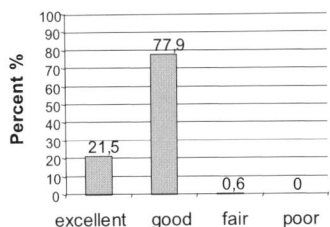

Fig. 5.6. Function distribution for the analyzability criteria

With help of these visualizations a general overview of the functions can be obtained and critical components can be identified (e.g., functions that score fair or poor). Obviously, in our analysis the functions rate quite well for the factor maintainability and the chosen criteria analyzability; there are only a few outliers. Another very powerful view into the functions dependability can be obtained with help of a call graph showing the call relations between the functions.

With help of the different views on the software, basically the source code, the criteria Kiviat diagram (see Fig. 5.7) and the control flow graph (not shown) a good overview of the functions can be obtained, and thus the software decisions (acceptance, redesign etc.) are supported by the tool. With help of the control flow statements, conditions and loops can be identified as well as jumps, dead code and exceptions. This graph is a very good view to control, if the function visits the parts as expected.

The criteria Kiviat diagram (Fig. 5.7) provides the measurement results for the chosen function Object3::functionC mapped to the criteria. Thus, problem areas can be identified (e.g., complexity that is too high or a high number of calls), and this knowledge can be included in following recoding or redesign steps. The synthesis gives the overall result for the function.

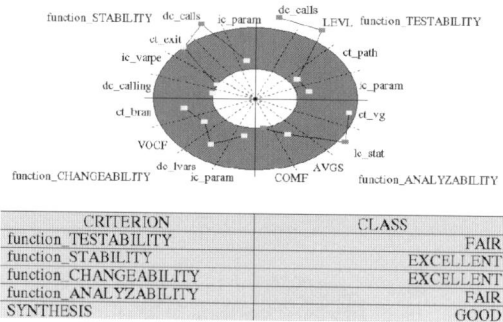

CRITERION	CLASS
function_TESTABILITY	FAIR
function_STABILITY	EXCELLENT
function_CHANGEABILITY	EXCELLENT
function_ANALYZABILITY	FAIR
SYNTHESIS	GOOD

Fig. 5.7. Object3::functionC criteria Kiviat diagram

Class level. At the class level the classes are of major interest, including their size, complexity and dependability on other classes. In the reference quality model the two factors maintainability and reusability are investigated. As an example Fig. 5.8 provides the class distribution for the analyzability in order to enable a comparison between function and class level.

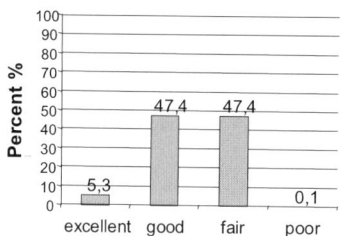

Fig. 5.8. Class distribution for criteria analyzability

Another very helpful view on the software system at the class level is the inheritance tree visualizing the static structure of the developed system. With the help of the available Logiscope results at the class level, design decisions are supported, as well as the identification of critical classes.

To sum up, Logiscope provides three granular evaluation levels, the application level, the class level and the function level. The different granularities provide different views on the software, and in our opinion this distinction is very helpful and appropriate.

Usually, measurement tools are applied to selected source code artifacts or components and produce some diagrams for the software evaluation. For large-scale software systems, the following aspects have to be taken into consideration:
- the effort (time) for the preparation (collecting and making available the software elements that have to be included in the measurements or analyses);

- the effort for the information mining (gathering of knowledge about the software system in order to understand the measurement levels and results);
- the effort for the tool understanding (handling of features, characteristics and particularities);
- the effort for measurement.

In our project the *preparation effort* was negligible, because the software under investigation was available as a package. Since this package was a prototype it was known that certain parts of the software were not fully specified or possibly were missing.

The *information mining* was supported by project reports, in particular the so-called cookbook (which contained information about the database substitution) and software models (e.g., Rational Rose models). For the generation of the Logiscope analysis project special emphasis had to be given to the source file suffixes, because they differed from the familiar notation.

The applied methodology shows a practicable way for the quality evaluation of large software systems. With help of the Logiscope tool it was possible to get an overview of the system quality as well as to identify critical components (classes or functions, respectively) and thus to take these components under further investigation. In this way, the software maintenance as well as the software development itself can be supported and test priorities can be set. For the participated software developer it was the first time to get another system view than through source code or Rational Rose models. Therefore the applied methodology was considered very helpful for the developer's purposes. Furthermore, it was possible to trace the project progress (important information for the customer) and the training period into the software system was shortened.

An important question for the software developer was whether statements in accordance with the database replacement effort could be derived. Unfortunately, only quality and structure statements could be deduced, because no exact persistence criteria were available, and furthermore, the old and the reengineered components were too different to be comparable. For that reason, no direct statement could be obtained, but at least information about the coupling between classes/functions could be extracted because of the integrated coupling measurements. In spite of this lack of information the developer was satisfied with the results, because he received a new, very helpful perspective on the software.

Altogether the system under investigation rates quite well, even if the application level result is only fair. We found one reason for this result in the unspecified state of some classes. On the other hand, a strength of the Logiscope tool is its capability to extract information from the source code, even if not all system information is available. The different results for the different granularities (application, class and function level) were interesting. Obviously, it is not enough to program small, high-quality functions but also the composition of these functions to classes and later on to the whole system is very important for the overall quality results.

Even though a couple of hurdles (e.g., tool understanding, measurement effort) have to be overcome, we can strongly recommend the use of a source code analysis tool like Logiscope for quality evaluations of large-scale software systems, because without tool support quality analyses of such systems are nearly impossible. In this context the following statement is very important (from our own experience and as often mentioned in the literature): measurement programs are more (or, possibly, only) likely to be successful if the measurements can be tool-based and at least semi-automated.

The applied methodology and tool should be used to continually control the progress of prototype development (also of final system development), thus enabling compliance to certain quality goals, rules and restrictions (e.g., design requirements, complexity limits). Only with continued quality control will the quality of the code improve permanently and significantly.

5.4. Solutions and Directions in Software e-Measurement

Software e-measurement means the application of the World-Wide Web in order to support software measurement processes, activities, and communities. In the following we describe some first solutions and potential. Basic e-measurement principles are
- the *ubiquitous characteristics* (including availability and mobility) of the resources as measurement artifacts, methods or services;
- the possibility of *external supports* by the use of different kinds of shoring (outsourcing, off shoring etc.);
- the effects of the *pervasiveness* in the Web considering the knowledge and application resources;
- the future principles of *self-management* and *adaptation* of Web-based solutions and infrastructures.

The realization of e-measurement on the World-Wide Web leads to many kinds of infrastructures that combine the application, the consulting, the communication and the information ([Dumk01, Dumk03a, Loth02b, Wink03]). The following e-measurement areas are intended:
- The application of software measurement in the IT area does not have an appropriate implementation in many companies. Therefore, the creation and the hosting of *e-measurement communities* should be helpful in order to improve this current situation.
- Services or measurement realization and the presentation of the measurement results are meaningful supports and could be provided by special companies on the Web. Furthermore, the collaboration on the Web between companies could produce some new kinds or levels of *e-measurement services*.
- Based on the incremental Web use and the technologies of mobility, software quality assurance can be supported by *e-quality services*. This means that the software quality process would be divided in subprocesses and subcomponents that are available in the Web.
- In order to support the implementation of measurement processes, *e-measurement consulting* could be helpful. These kinds of services include con-

sulting during the measurement planning, the measurement performance and the measurement exploration processes.
- The comparison of measurement results between companies or the discussion about measurement results could be supported by some kinds of *e-experience* or *e-repositories* in the World-Wide Web.
- Fundamental knowledge about software measurement is an essential part of a successful software measurement process. Hence, some kinds of *measurement e-learning* would be helpful in managing these tasks.
- Finally, services for certifying the quality or performance of IT areas in the Web could lead to *e-certification* on the Web.

Web-based measurement frameworks must be ***living systems*** like the World-Wide Web. Therefore, the creation and the hosting of *e-measurement communities* should be helpful in order to improve this current situation (see Chap. 15).

Services or measurement realization and the presentation of the measurement results are meaningful supports and could be provided by special companies on the Web. Furthermore, the collaboration on the Web between companies could produce some new kinds or levels of *e-measurement services*. Fig. 5.9 shows online services for Functional Size Measurement Portal (FSeMP) [Loth04] and a Web Service Trust Center (WSTC) [Schm04] with a service of continuous performance measurement of real Web services (see http://ws-trust.cs.uni-magdeburg.de/).

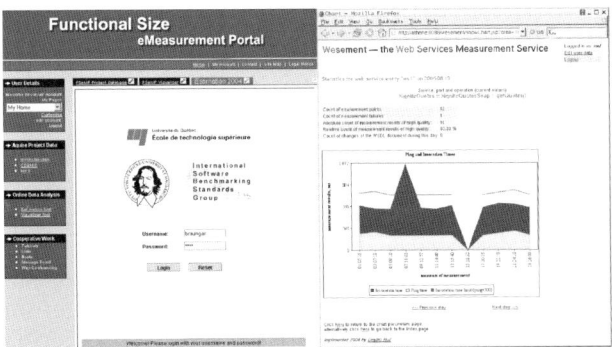

Fig. 5.9. Examples of e-measurement services

These kinds of services include consulting during the measurement planning, the measurement performance and the measurement exploration processes. Especially, the comparison of measurement results between companies or the discussion about measurement results could be supported by some kinds of *e-experience* or *e-repositories* in the World-Wide Web. Fundamental knowledge about software measurement is an essential part of a successful software measurement process.

Hence, some kinds of *measurement e-learning* would be helpful managing these tasks. Fig. 5.10 shows the e-learning services of the Software Measurement Laboratory of the University of Magdeburg (SML@b) [Smla06] (on the left side the overview and on the right side the COSMIC Full Function Point tutorial). An OWL-based presentation of the ISO 15939 approach is founded in [Dumk05b] and can be used for semantic Web-based measurement infrastructures.

Fig. 5.10. Examples of measurement e-learning

5.5. A Service-Oriented Measurement Infrastructure

Measurement, in general, is the process by which numbers or symbols are assigned to attributes of entities in the real world in such a way as to describe them according to clearly defined unambiguous rules. Software measurement applies to a software engineering process thereby measuring numerous entities encountered along the way.

Multi-step measurement automation, being in most instances embedded in corporate measurement programs or quality assurance initiatives, turns out to be a key factor [ISO01] for cost effectiveness and developer's commitment to the measurement process. Fig. 5.11 shows a dynamic composition of software measurement services. That procedure enables a service consumer to flexibly tailor a measurement environment at runtime according to its instantaneous needs in terms of the four service areas previously mentioned and cover all aspects by leasing services with SOA characteristics from a service provider via a registry as long as needed and combining them with the aid of a contract in contrast to investing in inappropriate and expensive conventional, hardwired measurement software suites [Kunz06].

The SOA capability depends predominantly on import potential of measurement data, export potentiality of results, and the facilities implemented to control the tool. Fig. 5.12 shows three Web services that support such approach.

Since the most important thing for the usage of a distinct tool is the occurrence of interfaces for the export of measurement results, we focused our analysis on this. By considering 37 tools we have analyzed, one can see that over half of all

5.5 A Service-Oriented Measurement Infrastructure

tools just have a proprietary interface with a medium up to high adoption effort. Based on the results one can reason that the majority of existing measurement tools have a medium or high effort for embedding them into an SOA. Only one third (34%) need just marginal or low effort.

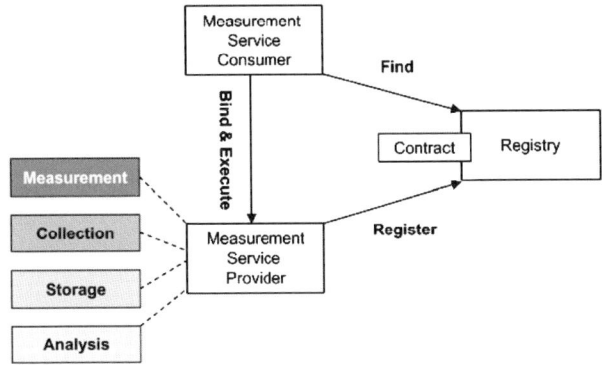

Fig. 5.11. Service-oriented measurement architecture

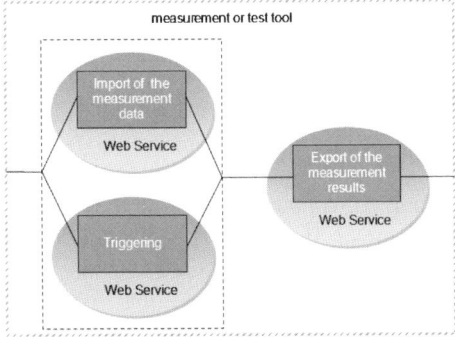

Fig. 5.12. Basic measurement functionality enabled by a service-oriented architecture

The second focus in the survey was on the combination of the functionality of different tools or the possibility to control the tool by an interface. This is important for the SOA idea of measurement tools because the main goal is to create a tailored measurement tool out of the functionality from different independent tools [McGa01].

The results in this area are very uneven. Over half of all the tools provide just proprietary interfaces and no ways exist to access functionality or control the tool via the interface. Another 10% use database connections to transfer data in the first instance. These connections also do not have the precondition to either control or to access tool functionality. Even if the other 34% do not provide options for controlling or accessing functionalities, the usage of XML at least allows enhancements in this direction in the near future.

Seemingly the functionality of the interfaces presented does not deliver the requirements needed for service oriented architectures. In this way the realization of a software measurement tool as a Web service [Pelt03] offer is the exception.

Therefore, our second step was to survey measurement tool manufactures how far their products are applicable for creating service-oriented measurement infrastructures [Erl05], and if they are available as a service offer. Another aspect was to find out if there are any planed ideas for SOA´s in future releases, if at the moment there is no service-oriented functionality.

As an outcome of our survey, we received over 30 replies. Some of the tools were part of our first assessment and, in general, we can assume that the answers give a representative view on software measurement tools from the manufactures point of view. The first look is again on export interfaces. Every tool has an export possibility but the effort to integrate them into SOA´s is not marginal due to non service-able connection type.

The next questions target another important fact for service-oriented Measurement Architectures: the combination of different tools according to distinct functionalities. The results can be that for every distinct information need, different functionalities from different tools were combined to a new service [McGa01].

The results point out an optimistic view to this issue: over 80% of all manufactures say that their tool can be combined with other tools, and nearly 80% say that single functionality of their tools can be used independently.

As we pointed out we can not approve this appraisal. The first reason is that tool manufactures often understand combining opportunities as the option to combine tools from their product portfolio and not to other tools e.g., by using open or standardized interfaces or connections. Because of the fact that we implicate more features into the concept of tool combination, we see our assessment not as rebut.

Especially for commercial software, the question about the different type of license models is very important. If a software measurement tool provides functionality as a Web-service, the license model should provide pay-per-use to avoid high acquisition cost and therewith open up new possible users.

Unfortunately, this aspect is not considered by tool manufactures today. Only 3% provide a pay-per-use option, and just a quarter provide the possibility to purchase a single module/component.

To clarify how measurement services work, two examples of measurement services are presented in the following.

The Open Office Activity Sensor [Ullw06] is intended to measure different functionalities (e.g., open a file, save a file) that a user can use within Open Office [Open06]. This type of measurement tool can measure all activities of a development process using Open Office as an integrated development environment (IDE). To realize the implementation the HackyStat framework [John05] was used to create this measurement service, thereby using the Simple Object Access Protocol (SOAP) which facilitates a simple integration into a service-oriented software measurement architecture. Fig. 5.13 shows this example. The implementation using SOAP does not mean that a resource has to be implemented with SOAP. Distinct interface specifications make it possible to use for example .NET.

5.6 Hints for the Practitioner   107

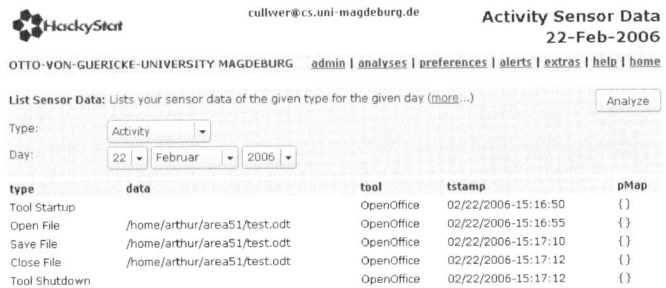

Fig. 5.13. OpenOffice Activity Sensor

Besides this process-oriented measurement products can also be measured with distinct resources. An example is the "Object-oriented measurement of Java Technologies" (OOMJ) [Faro05]. OOMJ is a software measurement Web service designed to reliably compute Chidamber-Kemerer and MOOD measurements of Abreu for any Java library or application and provides an efficient graphical analysis of the obtained results. It is unique in being freely available online and providing the measurement results in portable XML format for further customized analysis or otherwise used [Faro05]. Fig. 5.14 shows an example.

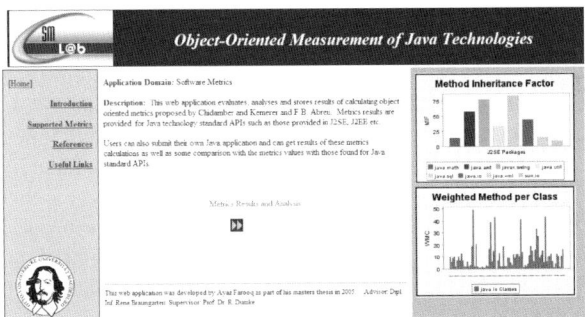

Fig. 5.14. Object-oriented measurement of Java Technologies

For further description of this measurement service and some of the possible applications see Chap. 13.

5.6. Hints for the Practitioner

Measurement tool applications should be guided by the following reasoning and goals:
- The efficiency of the software measurement process depends on the level of automation of the tools. That means that you should try to achieve a complete tool-based solution for your measurement process. But, you must consider the

different methodological and platform-related requirements of these CAME tools carefully.
- Measurement tools should cover the whole software measurement process, starting with establishing measurement, and continuing with planning, performing the measurement and exploring the results for process, product and resource evaluation. These help you embed the measurement into software development environments for assessing, improving and controlling the original IT processes.
- The philosophy of the measurements or CAME tool should be applied in the proper order. The applied CAME tools should be embedded in a compatible software measurement framework
- Specific parameters of the software development environment should be known to ensure correct and complete input information for the CAME tool. A profound analysis of the empirical aspects such as effort and cost is an imperative precondition for proper use of a selected CAME tool (for the *right use* of the *right measurement tool*).

The use of the features of e-measurement should be arranged in the following manner:
- Software e-measurement means the application of the World-Wide Web in order to support software measurement processes, activities and communities. Therefore, future applications include the software measurement combined with new technologies such as pervasive, mobile and ubiquitous computing. Inform you in a timely way about the actual trends and perspectives.
- e-measurement leads to integrated architectures including e-learning, the e-community and measurement activities and services themselves. You should be oriented to other partners, companies and coworkers for the conception, installation and using these new kinds of measurement systems based on different roles in the Web.
- e-measurement implies a great deal of potential for initiatives and successful cooperation in the area of software measurement.

5.7. Summary

Performing the measurement process includes using effective measurement tools. The efficiency of the software measurement process depends on the level of automation by tools. This chapter has given a short description about these CAME tools.

We primarily addressed new technologies and concepts for measurement tools based on the World-Wide Web and considered service-oriented paradigms. Our overview of e-measurement includes visions and existing solutions and should motivate further activities in this area.

6. Introducing a Measurement Program

You may forget some critical factors,
but they will not forget you.
Alwin Toffler

6.1. Towards Useful and Used Measurements

Better, faster, cheaper! Practically all enterprises work towards one or more of those slogans. They have often dedicated programs in place to reduce cost, improve productivity or simply adjust towards the ever-changing business in which they operate. While such objectives and the related bold management statements are on each company website, the same companies do not know where they are and how to measure progress towards these objectives. Measurements not only must be technically defined, repeatable or reliable.

> Measurements must be useful (i.e., perceived as helping to achieve an objective) and used (i.e., operationally applied in order to achieve their stated objective).

To make your measurement program useful and used, we need to look beyond technology and processes and consider the human side. It is important to realize that measurement success is also determined by soft factors. This chapter will look into the entire measurement life-cycle from planning, selecting, defining and introducing measurement to the analysis, communication and storage. It describes the underlying roles and responsibilities in a measurement program. Many examples are inserted to explain typical success factors, lessons learned and traps during the measurement introduction. We will investigate about positive and negative aspects of software measurement – and will not hide the "dark side of measurement." It is important to be alerted on risks and traps in order to mitigate in due time. The ROI of measurement is calculated to help you in defining and defending your measurement program. We conclude with practical guidance for a stepwise introduction of a measurement program, describing also the time horizons to consider.

6.2. The Measurement Life-Cycle

Measurements have a life-cycle. Fig. 6.1 shows the typical **measurement life cycle**. It identifies four major steps that characterize the introduction of a measurement program. They are mapped to the E4–measurement process to show the relevance of the "establish" step in such measurement life-cycle.

The measurement life-cycle applies recursively to both the individual measurement (i.e., introduction, usage, optimization) as well as the entire measurement program (i.e., introduction and continuous improvement of measurement activities).

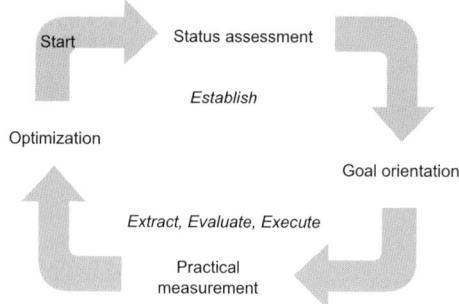

Fig. 6.1. The measurement life-cycle: A continuous improvement process

The four phases of the measurement life-cycle can be characterized as follows:
- Status assessment. This first step looks into the different projects, roadmaps, processes, needs, and improvement goals of the enterprise. It helps to identify what matters and focus on exactly that need.
- Goal orientation. This is the practical implementation of goal-oriented measurement. It takes results from the previous assessment phase and underlines the improvement objectives. Then the questions are asked and hypotheses built which would help in identifying the right measurements to monitor progress against the improvement goals.
- Project execution. This is the operational work where software engineering or IT projects are executed. It is here where the major part of the E4–measurement process (extract, evaluate, execute) comes into the picture (see Chap. 2). Measurements are collected, analyzed and communicated in order to achieve operationally the improvement objectives identified in the previous steps.
- Optimizing and feedback. This last step closes the loop and ensures that the right measurements and analysis techniques are included to the organizational process assets. Those measurements which have proven effective and efficient would become institutionalized (upper left exit from the cycle). Others might only be relevant for a while (e.g., during an improvement project) and need further tuning. Or some are not yet mature and need another cycle to prove effective and eventually become institutionalized.

6.3. Setting up the Measurement Program

Independent whether your intended measurement program is big or small, independent whether you target a more plan-driven or a rather agile and lean set of processes, for a successful measurement program you ought to ensure that your measurements follow the basic E4–process which we introduced in Chap. 2.

6.3 Setting up the Measurement Program

There are four phases to be followed during the introduction (or evaluation) of a measurement program, namely understanding the environment in which the measurement program will be introduced, establishing measurement objectives and the concrete measurements, performing the practical measurement (i.e., extracting measurements, evaluating them in front of the objectives, and executing decisions on the basis of the evaluation), and optimizing the measurement program.

> A measurement program must be introduced like a project. And like any successful project, it should be done in iterations and not as a waterfall! Start small and let it grow with growing success.

Measurements should not be extracted and collected in a vacuum but need to be aligned with objectives and they need thorough analysis in order to trigger the right decisions. Fig. 6.2 provides details to the measurement life-cycle showed in Fig. 6.1.

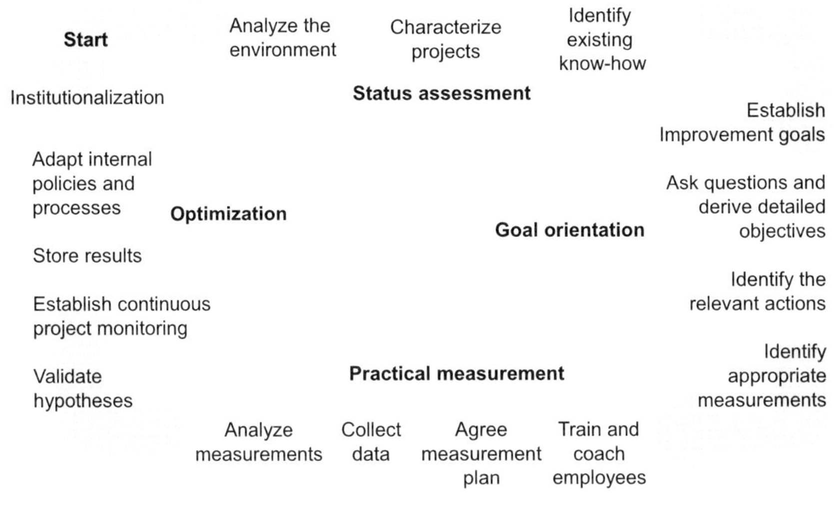

```
                                                       Identify
        Start      Analyze the      Characterize       existing
                   environment         projects        know-how

Institutionalization              Status assessment
                                                              Establish
Adapt internal                                        Improvement goals
policies and
processes                                             Ask questions and
              Optimization                             derive detailed
                                     Goal orientation      objectives
Store results
                                                          Identify the
Establish continuous                                   relevant actions
project monitoring
                                                             Identify
Validate           Practical measurement                  appropriate
hypotheses                                               measurements

              Analyze    Collect    Agree       Train and
           measurements    data   measurement    coach
                                     plan     employees
```

Fig. 6.2. Detailed view on the measurement life-cycle

The introduction of software measurement to projects has to follow a stepwise approach that must be carefully coached. Each new measurement that needs tools support must be piloted first in order to find out whether definitions and tools descriptions are sufficient for the collection. Then the institutionalization must be planned and coached in order to obtain valid data.

An initial timetable is provided in Table 6.1. Absolute timing is applicable for small and large companies. We practiced this approach in many different settings – and it worked all over. After latest eight weeks you should have the measurement program up and running, when starting from zero. If you already have defined measurements agreed or can reuse a dashboard from another part in your company it should take not more than four weeks to launch and have the first reviews. Clearly we should not expect after the first collection high quality data or even statistical analyses. To go too fast will demotivate your project managers and other persons involved in this measurement program. Initially what counts is that the definitions are understood and bought by the audience and that they stop debating about their own reporting approach repeatedly.

Table 6.1. Timetable for setting up a measurement program

Activity	Elapsed time	Duration
Initial targets set-up	0	2 weeks
Creation and kick-off of measurement team	2 weeks	1 day
Goal determination for projects and processes	3 weeks	2 weeks
Identifying impact factors	4 weeks	2 weeks
Selection of initial suite of measurements	5 weeks	1 week
Report definition	6 weeks	1 week
Kick-off with management	6 weeks	2 hours
Initial tool selection and tuning	6 weeks	3 weeks
Selection of projects and set-up of measurement plan	6 weeks	1 week
Kick-off with project teams/managers	7 weeks	2 hours
Collection of measurement baselines	7 weeks	2 weeks
Measurement reports, tool application	8 weeks	Continuous
Review and tuning of reports	10 weeks	1 week
Monthly measurement-based status reports within projects	12 weeks	Continuous
Application of measurements for project tracking and process improvement	16 weeks	Continuous
Control of and feedback on measurement program	24 weeks	2 hours
Enhancements of measurement program	1 year	Continuous

This timetable indicates that setting up a measurement program consists of a lot of communication and training. Kick-off meetings with management, project teams or practitioners ensure that measurements are understood and used consistently. Especially senior management needs good training to avoid they abuse measurements for penalizing – before understanding what to effectively gain with this new visibility. It is definitely not enough only to select goals and measurements. Tools and reporting must be in line, and all of this takes its time. It must however be clearly determined what needs to be measured instead deciding based on what can be measured.

6.4. Roles and Responsibilities in a Measurement Program

Measurement roles and responsibilities in an enterprise depend on the scope and focus of the respective organizational unit. Fig. 6.3 introduces a simplified organizational hierarchy which is applicable to almost any software enterprise. It depicts three tiers with very different scopes and responsibilities. The top-level holds accountable for the enterprise management and thus looks into strategic goals, how they translate into operational targets and where the company is with respect to those targets. This is the top level of any scorecard mechanism which aggregates the performance of the next lower level which is a business unit.

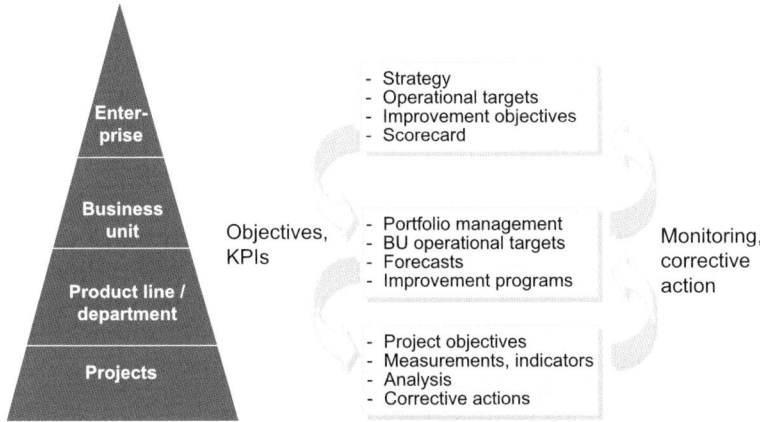

Fig. 6.3. Measurement responsibilities in the enterprise

The business unit level sets operational targets, looks into forecasts and monitors the performance against the agreed performance targets. It needs visibility on the portfolio level and demands aggregated measurements with drill-down functionality to individual portfolio elements. Given the operational responsibility and profit and loss accountability, this level also has different improvement projects which demand close follow-up to achieve the cost reductions or quality improvements necessary for reaching the annual performance targets.

Projects are shown on the lowest level of the pyramid. There are many of them and they all have their own project objectives against which they monitor performance. They will take immediate corrective action of project objectives that are missed. This control loop is the fastest and most focused across the enterprise. If it is not working, none of the upper tiers will work.

Regardless of its goals, a measurement program will only be taken seriously if the right people are given responsibility for it [McGa01, Fent97] (see Chap. 7 for roles in the estimation process). For that reason two roles are recommended for a successful measurement program, namely the project manager and the measurement responsible (Fig. 6.4).

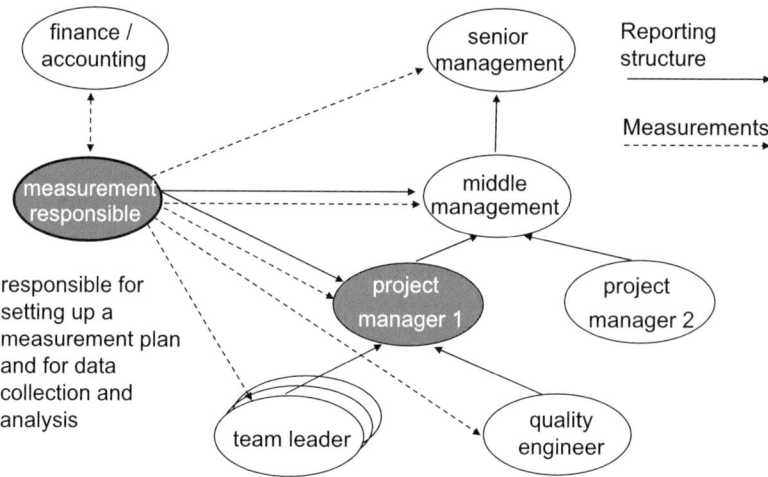

Fig. 6.4. Roles and responsibilities within a measurement program

The **project manager** ensures that information and measurement needs are articulated and actions are taken from measurements. He closely works with the measurement responsible. It is always the project manager who has to ensure that the right actions are taken. measurement responsibles only serve as a support role.

The **measurement responsible** serves as a focal point for engineers and the project management of the project. She ensures that the measurement program is uniformly implemented and understood. The role includes support for data collection across functions and analysis of the project measurements. The latter is most relevant for project managers because they must be well aware of progress, deviations and risks with respect to quality or delivery targets. Note that this role is not necessarily a stand-alone role (except in larger organizations), but one which could be handled by a program office, an engineering process group or by the individual project and program managers. It would be extremely dysfunctional having such role working in isolation. Measurements are here to be used – not to be collected and reported.

A measurement team can be established if there are several measurement responsibles in an organization. It coordinates measurements and project control across organizational and location boundaries. It ensures that rationalization and standardization of a common set of measurements and the related tools and charts is accelerated. A key role of such measurement team is consistent education across the company. This includes training to project managers and project teams on effectively using measurements. They serve as focal points for all measurement-related questions, to synchronize measurement activities, to emphasize commonality and to collect local requirements from the different projects. Upon building a

6.4 Roles and Responsibilities in a Measurement Program 115

company-wide measurement program and aligning processes within the process improvement activities, the creation of a history database for the entire organization is important to improve estimates. It also maintains measurement definitions and related tools. High-maturity organizations and those embarking on Six Sigma and related quantitative management should have a measurement team to ensure consistent and continuous learning across the organization.

This structure guarantees that each single change or refinement of measurements and the underlying tools as well as changes from projects can be easily communicated from a single project to the whole organization. The use of teams should, however, be done cautiously. While a team has the capability to take advantage of diverse backgrounds and expertise, the effort is most effective when there are not more than three people involved in a distinct task. Larger teams spend too much time backtracking on measurement choices.

We also found that when potential users worked jointly to develop the measurement set with the measurement support staff, the program was more readily accepted.

The related measurement process is applicable in the day-to-day project environment. Fig. 6.5 provides an overview on the measurement process seen from a project perspective. Four steps are visible in each project, namely selecting measurements, collecting and analyzing them and finally implementing decisions derived from the measurement analysis. Each of the boxes describes one process step. The responsible for executing the respective process is identified in the upper part of the box. A measurement team that is active across all different projects ensures coherence of the measurement program.

The operational measurement process as described in Fig. 6.5 is based on a set of defined measurements and supports the setting up and tracking of project targets and improvement goals:

1. Based on a set of predefined corporate measurements, the first step is to select measurements suitable for the project.
2. The raw data is collected to calculate measurements. Be aware of the operational systems that people work with that need to supply data. If the data is not available easily chances are high that the measurement is inaccurate and people tend to ignore further measurement requests. People might then comply with the letter of the definition but not with the spirit of the measurement.
3. Measurements are analyzed and reported through the appropriate channels. Analysis includes two steps. First, data is validated to make sure it is complete, correct, and consistent with the goals it addresses. Do not assume that automatic measurements are always trustworthy; at least perform sample checks. The real challenge is the second step which investigates what is behind the measurements. Some conclusions are straightforward, while others require an in-depth understanding of how the measurements relate with each other. Consolidating measurements and aggregating results must be done with great caution, even if apples and apples might fit neatly, so to speak. Results are useless unless reported back to the people who make improvements or decisions.
4. Finally, the necessary decisions and actions are made based on the results of the analysis. The same measurements might trigger different decisions based on the

target audience. While senior management may want to get just an indication how well the improvement program is doing, a process improvement team will carefully study project and process measurements to eliminate deficiencies and counteract negative trends.

The measurement team is instrumental in communicating and training on software measurement. In less mature organizations it helps in collecting and analyzing measurements. In more mature organizations it helps spread best practices and advance in new analysis methods and statistical techniques. It should however never get trapped into "outsourcing" measurement activities. Implementing effective project control is the key responsibility of each single project manager.

Several repetitive stages can be identified in project control and the related measurement and improvement processes (see Fig. 6.5).

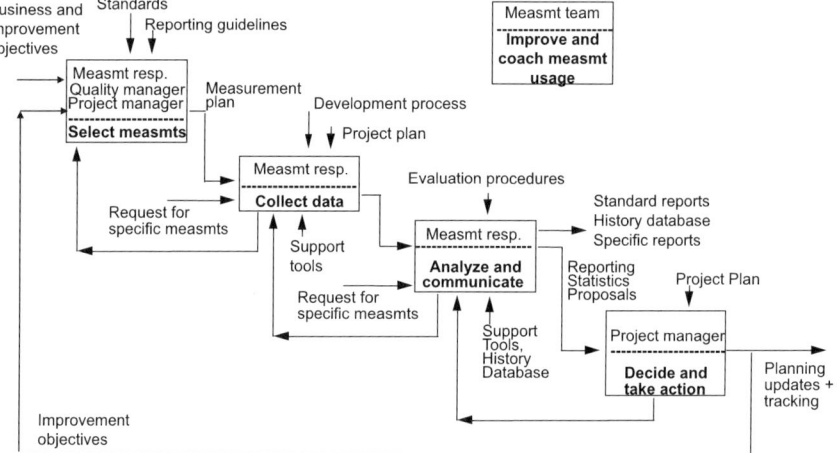

Fig. 6.5. Process overview for an integrated measurement program covering project control and process improvements

- Set objectives, both short- and long-term for products and process
- Forecast and develop plans both for projects and for departments
- Compare actual measurements with original objectives
- Communicate measurements and measurement analyses
- Coordinate and implement plans
- Understand and agree to commitments and their changes
- Motivate people to accomplish plans
- Measure achievement in projects and budget centers
- Predict the development direction of process and product relative to goals and control limits
- Identify and analyze potential risks
- Evaluate project and process performance
- Investigate significant deviations

- Determine if the project is under control and whether the plan is still valid
- Identify corrective actions and reward or penalize performance
- Implement corrective actions

Different control objectives request different levels of measurement aggregation. Individual designers or testers need progress measurements on their level of deliverable work products and contribution to the project. Group leaders and functional coordinators need the same information on the level of their work area. Department heads request measurements that relate to time, effort and budget within their departments. Project managers on the other hand look much more at their projects' individual budgets, schedule and deliverables to have insight into overall performance and progress. Clearly all users of measurements need immediate insight into the lower and more detailed levels as soon as performance targets are missed or the projects drift away from schedule or budget. Easy access to the different levels of information is thus of high importance.

6.5. Using Measurements: Success Recipes

6.5.1 Measurement and Analysis

Measurement and analysis belong together and cannot be separated. The moment we embark on defining measurements derived from our (improvement) goals, we should also think about how they will be used. A number is information only if it has a meaning (linguistically speaking, it should offer more than a mere syntax which is the definition and describe semantics and pragmatics). The meaning of measurements comes from their analysis (i.e., semantics) and usage (i.e., pragmatics).

Typical questions of such analyses include
- Is the measurement valid with respect to its definition?
- What does the measurement tell?
- Is it consistent with other measurements or does it point to an outlier or trend?
- How can we distinguish a trend from an outlier?
- Which other measurements can be explained with this measurement?
- Are there further information needs?
- What potential decisions can be derived from the measurement?
- What conclusion should be reported to management?

> The CMMI (being the most widely used process improvement framework) demands from an organization to develop and sustain a measurement capability that is used to support management information needs.

This is explicitly stated in the respective process area on measurement and analysis [SEI06a, Chri06]. And it also resembles the already mentioned ISO

118   6 Introducing a Measurement Program

15939 standard on software measurement [ISO02a] (compare the two overview pictures in Fig. 1.4 and Fig. 6.6).

A small note for the advanced reader: We look here only to the measurement and analysis process area within the CMMI. Higher maturity process areas around quantitative management will be discussed further in Chap. 11.

> There are two specific goals specified in the CMMI for the process area of measurement and analysis:
> Specific Goal 1: Align Measurement and Analysis Activities. Measurement objectives and activities are aligned with identified information needs and objectives.
> Specific Goal 2: Provide Measurement Results. Measurement results that address identified information needs and objectives are provided.

These two specific goals are further broken down into specific practices with four of them detailed for each of the two specific goals (see upper and lower boxes in Fig. 6.6). The first specific goal with its specific practices describes the preparation phase of measurement and analysis. Goal-driven measurement drives this preparation which is underlined with the very first specific practice, namely to establish measurement goals. Aside from that, measurements, storage and analysis procedures are prepared. This being done, measurement execution is detailed in the second specific goal. Measurements are collected, analyzed and the results stored and communicated.

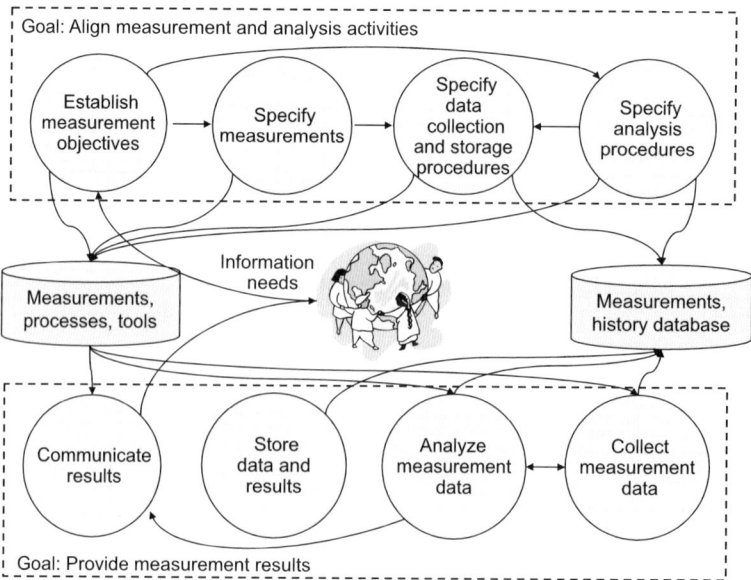

Fig. 6.6. Measurement and analysis as described in the CMMI

It is important to note that emphasis is given to the analysis of measurements. The CMMI describes this analysis: "The measurement data are analyzed as planned, additional analyses are conducted as necessary, results are reviewed with relevant stakeholders, and necessary revisions for future analyses are noted" [SEI06a]. Measurements are not published after collection. They are analyzed and reviewed before being communicated.

> Measurement is not about periodically publishing numbers but about communicating useful information that is actually used.

Our recommendation is to position measurements from the beginning as a tool for process improvement (to be used by both engineers and management) and to explicitly state that one of their purposes is to improve efficiency in the competitive environment. Make explicit what the results will be used for. When used for competition and benchmarking, first stimulate that people work with their measurements and start improving. For instance if faults are counted for the first time over the life-cycle, establish a task force with representatives from different levels to investigate results from the viewpoint of root cause analysis and criticality reduction. Educate your senior management. Uneducated managers tend to use measurements without reasoning about context. If there were many defects in a software component, they would conclude that the designer does not know his job. More often, however, the valid conclusion is that a specific piece of software is error-prone because of high complexity or many changes in the past.

Restricted visibility and access to measurements helps in creating credibility among practitioners especially in the beginning. For instance, the skills or number of delivered defects of an individual engineer is not the type of information to be propagated across the enterprise. It is often helpful to change perspective to the one providing raw data: is the activity adding value to her daily work? Statistical issues might not automatically align with emotional priorities. Remember especially with measurements that their perception is their reality.

Good communication is necessary in every business for it to be successful and to reduce friction, whether it is from engineer to manager, manager to engineer, or engineer to engineer. It is easy for software to be relegated to a low priority in a company focused on other technologies in its products. Software engineers need to speak out clearly and be heard and understood by management. Both sides need to learn how to address each other's real needs. Management does not care for techno-babble, while engineers are easily bored with capitalization or depreciation questions regarding their software.

Success with software measurement demands that project leaders and project team members get frequent and timely information about the goals and the effects of the implementation of measurement. For this reason a department, product line or competence center can for instance publish its own periodic reports to show what is measured, analyzed and decided in order to improve performance. It can also use the estimation training sessions to inform the participants about actual measurements. All-hands meetings of the department should be used to address questions related to usage of measurements.

6.5.2 Measurement Definition and Collection

Measurement collection, reporting and progress monitoring must be standardized across the company.

> Standardized templates and counting rules are necessary for fast evaluation of measurements, their comparison, benchmarking, storing in repositories, understanding, and driving the right actions.

Outliers can not be detected if the representation formats, colors, measurement units and even underlying definitions (e.g., what is counted as a defect or what is counted as a person week) vary from project to project. If somebody talks about progress in his project it must be the one and same definition for all projects.

The following small example shows that precise measurement definitions are necessary (Fig. 6.7). Assume that you are interested in knowing the volume of your code. As a small test try to count the lines of code (LOC) of this segment using your own definition.

```
#define LOLIMIT      0      /* lower limit of table */
#define UPLIMIT      300    /* upper limit of table */
#define STEPSIZE     10     /* step size */

/* print a conversion table from Fahrenheit to Celsius */
main()
{
    int Cels, Fahr;
    for (Fahr=LOLIMIT; Fahr<=UPLIMIT; Fahr=Fahr+STEPSIZE)
        Cels=(Fahr-32)*(5.0/9.0); printf("%4d %6f\n",Fahr,Cels);
}
```

Fig. 6.7. A small code fragment

The author asks this example to each of his measurement classes and found an interesting distribution. Some people would count 10 or 11 LOC depending whether they count the empty line. Essentially their definition of LOC is simply each printed line. The question appears what if the printer has different output depending on paper size or what if different printers are used. The definition lacks repeatability. A further group of people would count 9 LOC because they do not care for comment lines. Others would count 6 because they only count for executed program lines and not the include files at the beginning. Finally the extreme accounting delivers 3 or even 1 LOC, for those who try to put one statement in one line or count only the for-loop because it is the only functionally relevant statement. Such a large distribution of answers and opinions which the author practically observed again and again for such a simple question! The conclusion is to agree a single counting standard in the company no matter what it is and to practice it. Clearly this standard should be goal-driven. For instance if the goal is to minimize paper output or screen size, then you ought to count all lines regard-

6.5 Using Measurements: Success Recipes

less whether they are code, comment or blank. If the goal is to build a predictor for defects (see Chap. 9) then only executable code should be counted because it contributes to the defects.

> The very first step of selecting and introducing appropriate measurements must start with a useful and accurate definition.

A measurement is no end in itself, but a way to achieve and to monitor achieving an objective. Any measurement definition must therefore explicitly state the objective, directly linked to external business objectives, and the attribute of the entity being measured. The problem with many software measurements is that they are typically not described in business terms and are not linked or aligned to the needs of the business. While traditional business indicators look on revenue, productivity or order cycle time, their counterparts in software development measure size, faults or effort. Clearly both sides must be aligned to identify software product or process measurements that support business decisions.

Relating the current actual project situation (e.g., project duration, delivered quality or project cost for an average set of requirements) to the best-of-practice values in most cases motivates a process improvement program. Keeping these relationships from business objectives towards critical success factors to operational management and finally to software processes in mind ensures that customer-reported defects are not seen as yet another fault category and percentage to be found earlier, but within the broader scope of customer satisfaction and sustained growth.

A project-specific measurement plan links the generic measurement definitions to concrete projects with their individual goals and responsibilities. Additional measurements to be used only in that project are referred to in the measurement plan. The measurement plan is linked to the quality plan to facilitate alignment of targets.

Often terminology must be reworked and agreed upon with different parties to ensure proper usage of terminology. The good news with measurement definitions is that they ask for precision. It is impossible to sustain a "fluffy definition", and many past improvement programs indicated that with the measurement program a lot of other terminology and process imprecision could be cleaned up [Grad92].

> In introducing and communicating measurements use *one* consistent measurement template that provides the measurement goal, the measurement definition, tools support where appropriate and concrete usage in typical project situations.

Table 6.2 shows the template for specifying a measurement. Table 6.3 shows a concrete example of how to use the template.

Each measurement definition should ensure consistent interpretation and collection across the organization. Capturing precise measurement information not only helps with communicating the rationale behind the figures but also builds the requirements for automatic tools support and provides basic material for training course development.

Most tracking measurements cover work product completion, open corrective action requests, and review coverage to identify and track the extent to which development and quality activities have been applied and completed on individual software deliverables (see also Chaps. 8 and 9). These measurements provide visibility to buyers and vendors about the progress of software development and can indicate difficulties or problems that might hamper the accomplishment of quality targets.

Table 6.2. Measurement template

Unique identifier	Name and identifier of the measurement
Description	Brief description of the measurement
Value, measurement goals	Relationships to business objectives or improvement targets, such as quality factors, schedule performance, cost reduction and tracking distinct improvement activities; every measurement should be traced to business objectives at organizational level and to the goals and risks at program level
Definition	A concise and precise calculation and extraction algorithm
Measurement scale	The underlying scale (e.g., normal, ordinal, rank, interval, absolute)
Underlying raw data	Raw data and other measurements used to calculate this measurement (e.g., measurements primitives used for calculating the measurement or derived measurements)
Tools support	Links and references to the supporting tools, such as databases, spreadsheets, and so on
Presentation and visualization	References to report templates; e.g., chart or table type, combination with other measurements, visualization of goals or planning curves
Reporting frequency	Describes how often the measurement is extracted, evaluated and reported
Cost of the measurement	Covering one-time introduction and continuous collection effort
Analysis methods	Proposed/allowed statistical tests and analyses (including a validation history if applicable). Show with a concrete example how the measurement will be used practically in business.
Target, control limits and alarm levels for interpretation	Control limits for quantitative process management (e.g., release criteria, interpretation of trends)
Configuration control	Links to storage of (periodically collected) measurements
Access rights and visibility	Determines visibility and how a valid report is accessible (e.g., availability date, audience, access control)
Training	In case dedicated training is available or necessary for using this measurement
Example	A real project case showing how the measurement and the presentation look in practice

Table 6.3. Measurement template with a concrete example

Unique identifier	Early defect removal
Description	The measurement shows the percentage of defects found before code completion and before start of validation activities.
Value, measurement goals	The detection rate of defects before code completion should be around 50-70% of all defects. Defects remaining for testing that could be found before testing create unnecessary delays and cost extra effort in testing. A dedicated business case has been done that indicates that each 10% of defects found in a business unit before validation would reduce overall engineering cost by 3%.
Definition	All defects that are reported are classified according to detection / removal activity. There are 5 such activities: - Defects found during requirements and specification reviews - Defects found during design reviews and code verification activities (including unit testing) - Defects found during validation activities - Defects found during beta test - Defects found after start of deployment to an external customer A percentage is calculated for the first two categories compared to all defects. For verification activities all those defects are considered which would contribute to malfunctions. Editorials and improvement proposals are not considered. For validation and field performance all accepted defects are considered, including high and low priority. Duplicate identical defects are not considered. Activities are considered for reporting and NOT the current project phase. This means that defects found during code verification of a correction release are counted as design defects and NOT as defects found after deployment. Internal deliveries of a product as a component to be used to build a solution product follow the same scheme of external customer. Defects found during system testing of that solution product are counted as defects found during validation activities for BOTH products, i.e., the component and the solution.
Measurement scale	Relational scale
Underlying raw data	Defects from the different defect detection databases for each of the five mentioned activities.
Tools support	- Defects found during requirements and specification reviews: Bugzilla tool - Defects found during design reviews and code verification activities (including unit testing): Bugzilla tool - Defects found during validation activities: Bugzilla tool - Defects found during beta testing: Sugar CRM - Defects found after start of deployment: Sugar CRM

Presentation and visualization	Defects are reported as percentage per project, per module and per class. They are aggregated to product lines and business units. A list of percentages per module for a project can be generated automatically from the project portal entry level.
Reporting frequency	The measurement is reported on monthly basis for the product line / business unit level. Project managers and development team leaders might look ton their own data more frequently.
Cost of the measurement	Raw data is automatically retrieved from the defect databases. No manual collection effort is necessary.
Analysis methods	Distribution of defects across detection activities and percentage Trend analysis for sets of projects over time The analysis should first relate the current project (including the forecasts for not yet finished activities) towards the history. If there are deviations in both directions (too many defects found or too few defects found), the root cause must be evaluated starting with a deviation of 5% or more. Data quality should also be analyzed, such as a brief sanity check about how many defects one would expect in this type of product.
Target, control limits and alarm levels for interpretation	The corporate target is 60% (individual KPI's might change that target) Modules below 50% are flagged red automatically. Projects with over 70% should justify the business case, because too many defects found before test can create extra effort.
Configuration control	The measurements are stored in the project portal database and time stamped like all project data.
Access rights and visibility	Module and project data is classified confidential and will not be reported beyond development manager and team leaders. Measurements on product line level and higher are visible to entire company.
Training	Training on early defect removal is available in three formats: - E-learning for all prominent verification techniques - Review and inspection training in classroom - Quality control training for team leaders, project managers and senior managers is available upon request.
Example	Project A: overall early defect removal: 60% Module A: 55% Module B: 65% Module C: 60% No alarm level.

Measurement collection can be done with different tools (see also Chap. 5). Low cost tools include a spreadsheet program which you typically have already installed on your PC or an open source tool, such as the Software Process Dashboard [Proc06]. We will briefly comment on the latter. Compared to a

6.5 Using Measurements: Success Recipes

spreadsheet program, this tool runs in stand-alone mode on the PC. Once installed, set-up and configured for proper usage a simple menu will appear as is shown on the top of Fig. 6.8. Values can be entered, such as time or effort. A simple effort reporting tool is available that starts counting time on pressing a button which is very helpful if we are working on several tasks. The tool also offers some analysis and reporting functions as shown in Fig. 6.9. The most interesting analysis for the individual designer is the earned value which can scale up towards a full project recording if for instance a project manager in an agile project set-up is using this dashboard tool. Data can be filtered, put into different analysis views and even exported. Since the tool is open source, it is possible to build interfaces to operational databases, such as the corporate defect tracking tool which would then directly read the number of defects found by the individual designer.

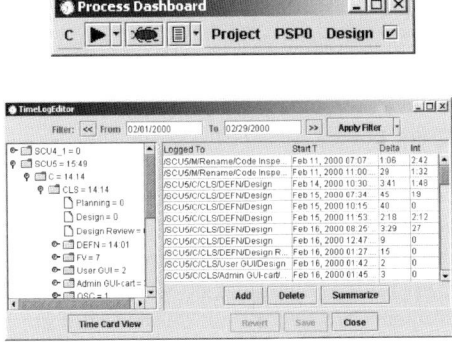

Fig. 6.8. Software Process Dashboard [Proc06]: The reporting tools

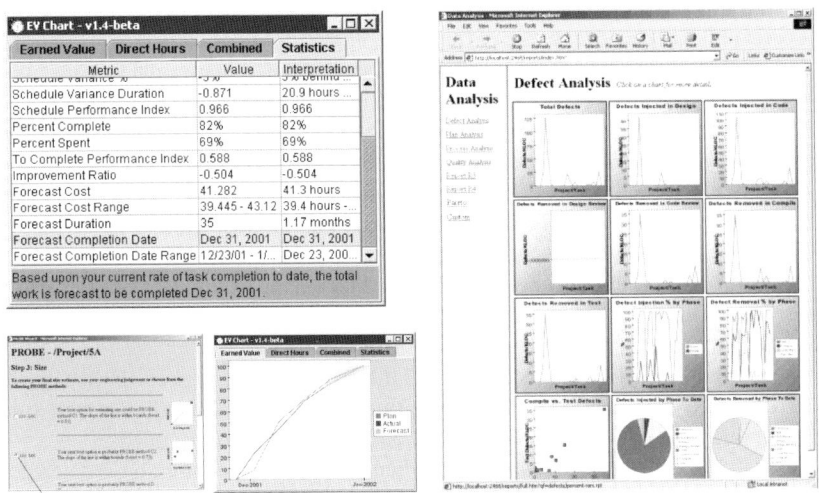

Fig. 6.9. Software Process Dashboard [Proc06]: The analysis tools

Progress during design activities can be tracked based on the effort spent for the respective processes on the one side and defects found on the other hand. Especially defect-based tracking is very helpful for reaching high-level management's attention because this is the kind of decision driver that accompanies all major release decisions.

When the effort is less than planned, the project will typically be behind schedule because the work simply is not getting done. On the other hand, design might have progressed but without the level of detail necessary to move to the next development phase. Both measurements should be reported weekly and can easily be compared with a planning curve related to the overall estimated effort and defects for the two phases. Of course, any design deliverables might also be tracked (e.g., UML descriptions); however, these come often late in the design process and are thus not a good indicator for focusing management's attention.

6.5.3 Data Quality

A measurement program is only successful if the underlying software measurements bear a sufficient data quality. Data quality refers to the quality of data as it is provided by measurements (e.g., the correctness of calculations and statistical analyses, the completeness of project reports, and so on). Data are deemed of high quality if they correctly represent the mapping from the empirical system (i.e., the real world where we operate) to the numeric system. Data quality is a necessary condition that measurements are fit for their intended use in planning, monitoring, controlling and management. It is the totality of features and characteristics of data that bears on their ability to satisfy a given need or objective. Such characteristics include accuracy, availability, completeness, consistency, repeatability, timeliness and validity:

- **Accuracy**. Recorded values conform to actual values. They accurately express the mapping from the empirical system to the intended numerical system, while complying to underlying goals and constraints.
- **Availability**. The data is available to those who need it. The same data points are used for all different operational and managerial needs. A single source ensures availability of data. Measurements that have been used to justify a decision must be accessible in exactly the format and content used to make that decision – long after it has been taken. This holds specifically if the decision related to risk taking and management or had financial impact. But is also ensures that certain analyses of your measurement data can be repeated when arriving at a higher maturity where more insight is possible
- **Completeness**. Information comprises all projects and sources. If data points are removed from the collection, it is done based on clear policies and rules. Data points are not collected to a set to only justify temporary needs.
- **Consistency**. Recorded information when compared does not show discrepancies or errors.

- **Repeatability**. Data collected today by one person must be the same if another person would collect the data at another time or another place – if following the same measurement and collection process.
- **Timeliness**. Measurements and history data are available on the spot when needed for decision-making.
- **Validity**. Data points and measurements must be validated against their underlying requirements and operational needs. This is done before any further analysis is performed and communicated.

Data quality depends on the actual usage of the measurements and history information. What may be considered "good data" in one case for a specific project or process need may not be sufficient in another case. While an effort estimate in person-weeks is sufficient for a feasibility study of a new project or evaluation of a portfolio, it is clearly not enough for tracking the project internally.

A word of warning on data quality. With individual and ad-hoc project measurements, people might get along for a while with lousy data quality. Their decisions might be wrong and they might mislead their management, but it has only personal consequences if there are any consequences at all. Assembling measurements to a corporate scorecard brings in the information quality requirements we are used from the financial communities. Each single element must be auditable, reviewed and following a consistent definition.

> Attention: Data quality is one of those measurement requirements governed by laws and regulations! For instance, Sarbanes-Oxley Act and related financial reporting requirements demand clean internal control and risk management, approved by C-level (i.e., corporate executives) for effectiveness.

Often we are asked by companies to analyze measurement programs and to help them in achieving performance improvements, such as cost reduction or cycle time improvements. Of course they would have project data available, but we realize while looking to the data that it cannot be used to drive decisions across projects and thus help in detecting inefficiencies or else. We then have to sit down and start cleaning up the measurement repository (which often is a set of Excel files) to assess the quality of the data before moving on. In many cases it means to start again, because what was labeled effort included net hours spent on the project including overtime in one case, gross hours including holidays and absence in another case, and only regular work hours without overtime in a third case. Such experiences – across companies – showed us that it was a real problem area, one that needs being addressed by the measurement program.

Data quality is a major flaw in almost any measurement program. Practically all software and IT organizations are struggling with this. In fact, the only reason that an organization may not yet be struggling with data quality is that they have not really started to reflect on this question. When we go into to help clients with their process improvement and look to measurements and how to use them, we inevitably discover problems with their measurement and analysis infrastructure. Then

before we can move on with the real work, we must first clean up the data. Here a few examples which underline on what you should look to improve data quality:
- Overtime is not completely reported.
- Asset capitalization for software products is done ad-hoc.
- R&D investment is misstated to achieve optimal tax benefits.
- Customer support, defect corrections or cost of non-quality is sometimes classified as R&D.
- Future R&D investments are understated (e.g., due to insufficient project management culture and practices).
- Inaccurate tracking and allocation of resources (people, infrastructure) to projects.
- Informal and invisible R&D investment approvals.

Data quality can be improved. Let us look to a few concrete guidelines that you can apply in your own organization.

Establish measurement policies. The first an most crucial need is on clear rules what is measured, for what purpose, by whom with what algorithms and tools and how measurements are accessible, secured and ensured over time. Mostly this will be communicated within the measurement definitions. However governance is necessary across the organization to ensure this is actually done. Often companies have rock solid measurement definitions and huge data collections, but nobody ever cared that this was done consistently. Data quality is a management task and has to be driven top-down. Do not engage into measurement analysis, if the quality of those measurements is not guaranteed for the scope you want to analyze. Obviously project management needs less governance and has a smaller scope than a productivity improvement program across the organization.

Agree on measurement definitions that are used consistently – across the organization. Even if processes vary, the measurements must be collected based on one algorithm with defined accuracy. For instance defects need to be reported together with attributes characterizing their content, such as severity, origin, or applicability. Effort must be reported as a net effort spent on a specific activity including overtime. Activities can be aggregated later, but initially some basic activities, such as design, test, error corrections should be distinguished.

Agree on measurement formats and storage. Often the same measurements are stored in different formats which can later not be compared or which would create errors when being aggregated. Typographical errors play a role here, such as spelling the project names correctly and consistently. Use defined referentials for all such global data points, such as project names, people names, company names, measurement attributes or project activities. Agree which format to be used for dates and time, and what precision within your data formats. Formats also include how to transform measurements such as effort to cost. Although this might be impossible across countries and different accounting systems, it is frequently demanded by management to allow evaluations and benchmarks. Having some sound rules with average work hours, and so on at the least ensures consistency and reverse calculations if definitions would change.

Ensure that the same information is only collected once. For instance, accuracy can always be aligned to needs, but storing the accuracy of the original data certainly helps to reuse history data in the future when your needs may have evolved. While defect tracking in a CMMI Maturity level 1 organization might only look into avoiding critical defects after delivery to a customer, more mature organizations follow through the totality of defects created per phase or detected per verification and validation activity. Having gained such experiences these organizations start to address deviations from targets early in the development process thus effectively moving defect detection towards the phase that generated the defect. At the end of this growth is effective defect prevention.

Automate your data collection. A process that is defined and automated will yield consistent measurements – over time and across regions and impacted projects. Invest into process automation and product life-cycle management. Data quality comes at a cost. Automation is inevitable to save on this effort. In many enterprises R&D or engineering reporting and accounting is way below expectations. In fact some CFOs will be surprised on the lousy data quality in their R&D shops. They will typically agree to improving data quality because it is their major decision-making tool – across the company.

Data quality was the major reason why the SEI decided to moving measurement and analysis already to a maturity level 2 process area. What they realized with their industrial partners was that improving data quality ex post is close to impossible.

> Data quality is a life insurance for software measurement. A good measurement program must consider the needs for data quality right from its beginning.

6.5.4 Analyzing, Visualizing, and Presenting Measurements

Analyzing and presenting measurements is at least of the same relevance than collecting the raw data. Reliable data quality, clear understanding of what the measurements show, and a thorough basis for further execution all depend on good analysis, visualization and presentation. We should not neglect the presentation because understanding is much easier if the right graphical techniques are chosen. While in the past most information gained from measurement had been displayed as tables, today graphical methods must be utilized that are well-suited to human communication [Eber92]. The advantages are numerous, however a few should be mentioned:
- Well-designed charts are more effective in creating interest and in appealing to the viewer's attention than huge textual tables.
- Visual relationships are more easily grasped and remembered.
- Graphical displays concentrate information and reduce overheads, thus providing a comprehensive picture of a problem.
- Different data sets are compared simultaneously.

Be careful though with the underlying statistical analysis and graphical techniques. Normalization and information reduction might be used to distort unbiased

viewers. Excellence in analysis and presentation consists of complex ideas communicated with clarity, precision and efficiency. Analysis methods therefore should:
- show the data and its meaning – not the interpretation
- being as "unbiased" as possible
- make the viewer think about the measurements and the underlying relations rather than about the analysis and statistical techniques
- be self-explanatory.

The most common approach for data analysis in software measurement is one-dimensional statistical analysis. They are offered in all spreadsheet programs and can typically be mastered without much statistical knowledge (see also Chap. 3). They include Pareto analysis, correlation measurement, ranking, or sensitivity analysis. Such one-dimensional statistical methods of scaling have been developed and employed to present a distinct subjective criterion that is related to a measurable aspect of a software process or product.

Simple analyses checks are the first thing to do with any data set. The target is to determine relationships, detect outliers, and identify what further analyses need to be performed. The first thing to ask is about **data quality**. Can the data be trusted? Is each of the data points valid or should some of them be verified before continuing the analysis. For instance, it could easily happen that you have project data from 20 projects but five of them had insufficient reporting. Speaking with the project managers you might realize that the data is not valid and would better be removed from the study. Ensure in such cases to mention this decision along with your analysis.

A next check is on **outliers**. Are there data points that are measured accurately and thus possess the right data quality but do not fit to the overall scheme? An example is field defects across a set of projects and over time. One of these data points might show a much higher defect number than all of the others. Looking to the measurement you find out that this was a contract where the client tried to make many late changes – far more than what had been agreed. On top the acceptance of the product was delayed due to the client's inability to integrate the product. This all contributed to a high defect number being reported – but maybe not comparable to typical acceptance and release procedures of all the other projects in the data set. Identify and carefully remove such outliers. Make sure you report why and what you removed.

Another simple check is on underlying **dependencies to different factors**. Classifying the data into quartiles can reveal behaviors resulting from yet unknown relationships. For example, project duration could be grouped according to size. Are the trends equal in the four groups of smallest to biggest projects? Is the trend the same if calendar years are used for grouping? What other factors could influence cycle time? Maybe markets or regional areas.

A next analysis is to draw **time series** and simply see how data evolved from past to present. Have there been sudden disrupts in an otherwise smooth curve? What is the reason of such disrupts? Are there groups of outliers in specific time-frames? Is the trend stable or does it show different slopes according to season?

For instance defect rates in software products depend on release cycles. Showing defects over time will usually show a zigzag-pattern with a small increase when a new release is distributed. Be sure that what you call a trend is really a trend and not determined by some unknown relationship!

Pareto analysis is used for fast quality or problem analyses. The goal of a Pareto analysis is to identify those 20% (could be also a range, but certainly the smaller part of the data set) of all components that contribute heavily to all troubles. The principle is called '80:20 rule' because it assumes that the 20% share is responsible for 80% of the problems. It is amazing that this simple approach holds in most application domains. Software quality management methods, such as root cause analysis, typically also start by applying a Pareto analysis and identify the small number of problems (20%) that provide the biggest return on effort when resolved. A typical application of Pareto analysis is software size (i.e., the top 20% of all modules ranked according to module size are selected for verification) or defects (the top 20% of all components with errors must be regression tested with a fully new test strategy). We suggest applying Pareto classification as a quick rule of thumb to decide on further analysis methods.

This is where **statistical tests** come into the picture. Often we assume relationships but need to make sure that we know before taking further decisions. There are many such tests around such as correlations, **chi-square tests**, and so on. We will only look towards correlation analysis, since any good statistical book will have much more background to explain the methods and applicability.

Correlation analyses are used to verify the relationships of two data sets. A high correlation coefficient which is close to 1 shows a strong relationship. One variable depends on the other. Weak correlation with a value close to zero shows no relationship between the two data sets. Before using a specific correlation analysis, especially those offered in spreadsheet programs, it is of utmost importance to analyze the distribution of the data (there are also dedicated tests available to identify the distribution type) and potential underlying factors which influence correlations. If the distribution is close to normal the regular parametric correlation analysis can be performed. It will show whether there is a linear relationship between two data sets. If the distribution is unknown or not normal, non-parametric or robust analysis techniques should be applied, such as rank correlation. The rank correlation assumes only rank scales and compares the order of the values in the data pairs. It is more robust than the parametric correlation because any type of data distribution can be used and still relationships will be indicated. Make sure for any type of correlation analysis to know the significance level (or α-factor) of the analysis. This significance level shows the trust you can have in the measured relationship. A significance of 95% or $\alpha = 5\%$ tell that with the given number of data points, you have a reliability of 95% that the measured correlation is the actual relationship.

The most important – yet difficult – task in finding such a relationship is to use controlled experiments where just one measurable aspect of the design process is varied, while all the other aspects are kept unchanged. The result of scaling measurements is an ordered set of measurements according to the one and distinct quantified property being under consideration. The obvious disadvantage of this process is the need of an almost clean room-development environment that permits the variation of just one design aspect.

A small example will illustrate this aspect. If we investigate productivity, we might find that effort is increasing almost in parallel to delivered size of code. The resulting productivity measurement which our management is keen to see growing to reduce cost (the underlying goal of the entire exercise) is almost flat over time and across projects. The explanation is simple: there are other variables which had not been considered and which both impact effort and size. One such underlying parameter is complexity of the delivered code. If it increases over time with all other parameters kept stable, it is obvious that the productivity will not improve while measuring the ratio of delivered code and effort, because both are directly influenced by complexity.

> Before looking to simple ratios and normalized measurements, ensure that no information is distorted.

Being aware of this problem, regression analysis on the one hand and correlation analysis on the other hand have been introduced. Both deal with relations among different sets of measurements of the same set of objects. The ultimate goal is to find independent sets of measurements, thus reducing the effort of measuring by eliminating redundant sets, or to find relations among sets of product measurements and process measurements, hence establishing the basis of a model for quality aspects being related to the design process.

Multivariate statistics are used for the analysis of measurements with a priori unknown relations. There are a lot of methods, mainly from the field of psychology and sociology, that allow to deal with such data situations, e.g., the statistical preparation, the tools for finding relations between the data elements and finally means for graphical visualization [Dill84, Eber92, Gibb76]. These techniques typically derive a – smaller – set of new variables from the original variables. This reduced set of variables is intended to focus on certain aspects of the original data without losing relevant information from the original data. Especially multidimensional methods for graphical representation permit a brief but thorough view of complex relations and interactions of different measurements from many objects, thus allowing a comprehensive analysis and interpretation. These techniques help to find unknown structures and dependencies among measurements, to represent and visualize different data sets, to improve communication and comparability of distinct analyses and to improve the comprehensibility of theoretic quality models. The two most important techniques for multidimensional statistical analysis in software measurement and experimentation are actor analysis and cluster analysis.

Factor analysis is the transformation of interrelationships among measured values for software components to a new set of variables, fewer in number than the original set of variables, that express what is common among the original variables. Complex and diverse relationships existing among a set of observed variables are simplified by uncovering common dimensions or factors that link together seemingly unrelated data sets. For example, the effort spent on a project in person weeks and the delivered size from that project in lines of code or function points are often highly correlated as already mentioned. This correlation is resulting from common factors such as complexity, environment, programming languages, and so on. The underlying goal of factor analysis thus is to reduce large sets of relationships to a small yet intuitive set of factors describing all relationships.

Cluster analysis is an instrument to identify structures and relations in a set of objects. The underlying assumption is that objects under investigation may be grouped such that elements residing in a particular group or cluster are, in some sense, more similar to each other than to elements belonging to other groups. Clusters can be obtained for measurements and for software components or projects. The construction of homogeneous subclasses is generally based on a similarity matrix of objects and measured attributes. The fundamental description of hierarchical clustering of n measurements consists of (n-1) steps of successively merging clusters. At each step two objects or clusters that are already merged are combined by the clustering algorithm (e.g., single or complete linkage). This algorithm is based on the measurement of dissimilarity between all pairs of objects in the separate clusters as already described. Using cluster analysis the criticality of a set of modules can be identified by showing the similarities in terms of code complexity, number of changes, change history of the code, defect history, exposure to critical functionality, experience of the designers, or previous verification activities.

6.5.5 Statistical Traps and How to Avoid Them

Measurement helps in understanding the real world. It is not primarily about numbers that are collected but rather about understanding the real world which is in its complexity difficult to comprehend. Measurement from a psychological perspective is a cognitive process that depends on the people involved in it. Cognition or cognitive processes can be natural and artificial, conscious and not conscious. There are many influences along the way from a real world or empirical system to the state where a person would draw its own conclusions. Many of those influences trade back to our own objectives (how we want to see the world) and our social and scientific formation (how we interpret what we are seeing).

Fig. 6.10 shows this flow of data or information from the real world to the person trying to get an understanding and trying to influence. We have so far looked primarily to the upper half and defined measurement as a transformation from an empirical system to a numerical system (see Chap. 3). In fact it is not only a transformation but rather a selection of what we want to distill from the empirical system. By applying a goal-oriented measurement process, such as the E4–process of measurement or the goal question metric paradigm, we deliberately select a transformation which we consider most helpful to achieve our objectives. It is not necessarily the right transformation, but hopefully you learned throughout the book so far what to consider to select the right measurements (see also Chap. 2).

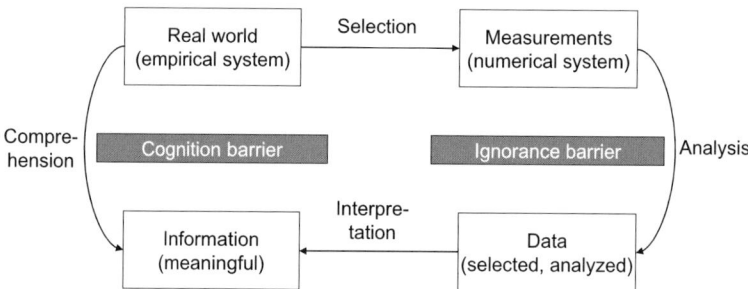

Fig. 6.10. Measurement helps to comprehend the real world

The difficulty comes from barriers which impact the cognition process. Fig. 6.10 shows the two most relevant barriers that influence our perception of reality. The one of the left side is essential to any perception and won't be removed. Cognition theory has it that there is no "neutral" reality which is independent of the observer. We all build our own picture of reality and live in it, as Plato already remarked in his famous allegory of the cave [Plat03]. We call this gap between the real world and what we comprehend of it the "cognition barrier." A second barrier is rather accidental and is shown on the right side of the figure. It is our ignorance that makes us interpret things in very different ways. Ignorance might sound strange but it trades back to the above mentioned allegory of the cave, where people inside the cave and only seeing shadows on the wall will interpret those shadows as two-dimensional beings. Measurement helps us to comprehend the real world, but we must be careful to acknowledge these two barriers and have to consciously cope with them.

In measurement theory and statistics this picture will show us the typical traps with measuring, analyzing, interpreting and communicating data. Let us discuss some of the traps and how to cope with them. Fig. 6.11 portrays the three major traps throughout the measurement process. They follow the three steps of selection, analysis and interpretation by which we get our understanding (or perception) of the real world.

Trap 1: We measure only according to stated objectives (i.e., manipulating the measurement).
It might seem odd that we call our leading paradigm a trap. Our reasoning is simple. At the moment where we state a goal, we want to achieve it. This is human, and it is intended in goal-oriented measurement. The trap is to measure only what shows the changes and moves towards this goal and perhaps neglecting that the goal is wrong or that there are better ways to achieve the goal. If the objective of an improvement program is cost reduction we will necessarily measure some aspect of cost. Let us assume that we measure the cost of software development. Looking to it, we will find that it is high and could be reduced by outsourcing to a low-cost country. We will do it and we will initially reduce labor cost. Additional cost will be created because of the transactional complexity and frictions in working across regions. Due to our objective to reduce cost, we might simply continue

6.5 Using Measurements: Success Recipes

in measuring the mere engineering cost and compare hours and cost per hour without looking to overall productivity which in fact might be hampered by outsourcing. Our measurement is insufficient because we looked too much to the goal and not to the environment.

Our guidance:
- Always measure several dimensions and never take only the one obvious indicator for what is the direct objective.
- Balance your objectives and measurements. Avoid the blind spot.
- Review the selection process of measurements thoroughly. There are always alternative measurements. Why were the measures selected? Are these measures broadly used in industry for that purpose? What other measures are used to look to influences on the primary measures?
- Revisit how the measurement could be manipulated.

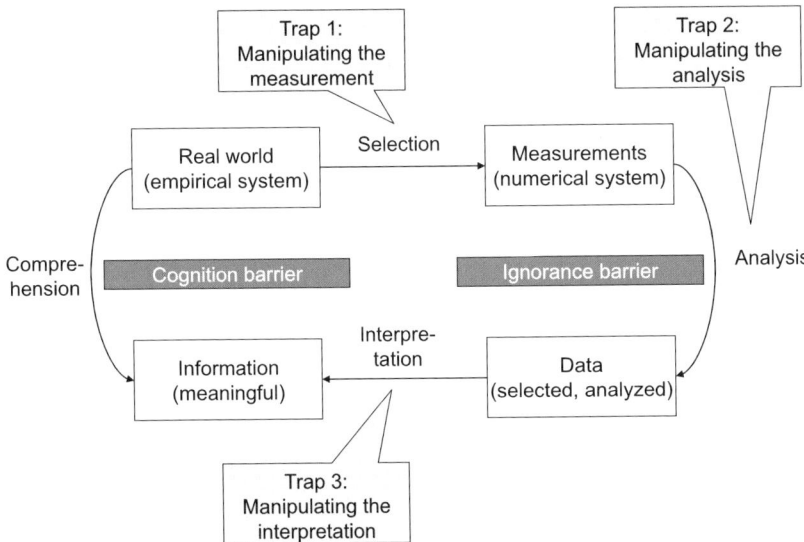

Fig. 6.11. Three traps along the measurement process

Trap 2: We need to achieve objectives (i.e., manipulating the analysis).
This second trap is a consequence from the first. By being responsible to achieve an objective we start finding ways to at least create the perception that we are on the right way. Often measurements are normalized to volume or effort or time without clarifying upfront what this normalization might achieve or distort. Defect rates are a classic example how measurements are tuned to show that objectives are achieved. If defects per new or changed statement are measured, this defect rate naturally depends on both quality and output volume. Having many defects can be camouflaged by restating how volume is measured. During analysis an increasing defect rate can be interpreted as bad (i.e., more defects in the code) or

good (i.e., better quality control and less defects in the field). What is right or wrong? There is no clear answer as long as environmental factors are not analyzed in parallel.

This trap clearly results from what we call the ignorance barrier. We interpret measurements in a way showing that things are moving. A project manager might show progress in terms of simple requirements that are implemented, while the real big ones are stagnating. A middle manager might show productivity improvement by showing that his staff has produced more code with same effort, while in fact the software won't satisfy its customers due to having unnecessary features and being designed way to complex. Another "expert" analyzing measurement data might remove outliers and therefore polish the data set to point in the right direction. Or, take the following example. A senior manager wants to evaluate the results of a process improvement initiative. He demands to his engineering process group to provide a benchmark of successful and failed projects over the past three years. Fig. 6.12 shows what they measured and what they analyzed. For two departments A and B the success rate clearly decreased. However when normalizing it to the entire company with two departments they would suddenly point to an improvement. Even worse they might simply say that the share of successful projects improved by over 13 percentage points (from 58% to 71%), by 22 percent (taking the difference of 13 percentage points and normalize with the 58%) or even by 36 percent (taking the 2o failed projects and normalize it with 55 failed projects in 2003). You will realize with this simple story what Benjamin Disraeli meant when talking about lies, damned lies and statistics.

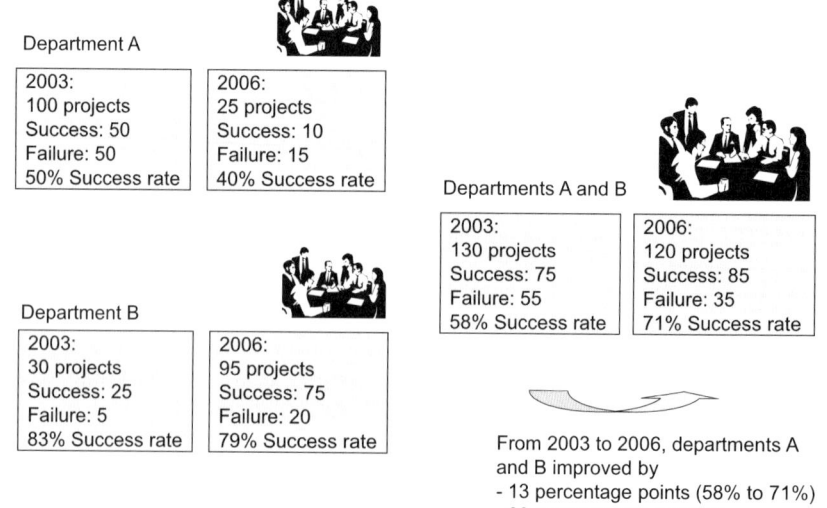

Fig. 6.12. Be careful with normalization and aggregating sub-sets

Our guidance:
- Always show all data and have somebody independent review the measurement process and the results drawn from interpreting the data.
- Start with looking to the base set of all data points and interpret variances before investigating correlations.
- Avoid any type of internal parameterization of measurements which is not transparent to the observer. For instance, function points or productivity metrics are based on many impact factors which characterize the environment. These factors need to be carefully adjusted (if at all) and should follow industry best practices and experiences. There is no use to have complex formulas with many parameters that aggregate standard measurement to the one company indicator for productivity, defect rate or effort. Better to work with raw data and store it to always trace back conclusions to that data.
- Revisit measurements which are normalized. It might be necessary to benchmark but it should be equally clear that there are limits to normalization. For instance, often defect densities are compared. A designer might create more code with the same absolute number of defects and thus reduce his defect density – although the created code has less value than before. If defects were normalized to value of the code, the programmer would have decreased his productivity.
- To ensure that a statistical analysis is meaningful, it should have a significance level of 5%. This translates into a confidence level of 95% that results are not obtained by pure random chance. This 5% significance level has been established in statistics for a while across disciplines and is considered sufficient to draw conclusions that would not be merely accidental. The necessary sample size can be calculated with statistical tests which depend on the distribution. Alternatively they are estimated with Monte Carlo simulation. Determine and then collect adequate sizes of samples based on this 5% significance threshold before analyzing any measurements.

A simple test for the confidence that a result is not by random chance is given by Sackett's formula [Sack01]:

confidence = signal / noise x sample size$^{1/2}$

The signal is typically the changes in values that are observed. It could be the arithmetic difference between values under investigation. The noise level is all type of errors that are introduced from other influences which are not observed in the study. The sample size finally is the number of data points being investigated. It is a simplification, but effective as a first rule of thumb test.

- Before removing outliers during statistical analysis we recommend defining strict criteria for what are outliers, and why they are removed.
- Data quality must be checked during analysis. If data is not trustworthy, the measurement needs to be repeated.
- We recommend a dedicated measurement team which is doing this analysis across the company – not being measured on the same goals as their internal

clients. Or you should demand external consulting to review your measurement process and what conclusions are drawn.

Trap 3: We need to show results (i.e., manipulating the interpretation).
This last trap is the most frequent and mostly results that we want to please our audience when presenting measurements. Assuming that measurement selection and analysis was done correctly by an independent team or external consultant, this third trap can still occur because the data generated before needs to be presented. Such presentations are done by those who are responsible for a project, process or product, to their line management who is responsible that budgets are allocated where there is most value for the enterprise. Here the pressure is to keep things going or show that value will be reached. Measurement pointing in that direction are amplified, others are ignored or explained as irrelevant. The product manager might receive feedback from his projects that defects are high, failure rates in the field are increasing and cost of service is beyond what she has foreseen and budgeted. Now she demands more resources to increase staffing for test and service. Would she state that quality (i.e., her own responsibility) has deteriorated? Often she would rather try to point neutrally to the demand for service by clients and that this is part of her strong customer and quality focus. She might even go as far as stating that defect measurements are too high because some defect severities are shown which do not impact her clients.

Fig. 6.13 shows an interesting example of how regression lines can show a non-existing trend. The data is from a survey that was published to indicate the relationship of defect density and maturity level. The weakness is the fact that a single data point (i.e., the one in the upper left corner) determines the regression line (regression line 1). Maybe it was an outlier and should have been removed. The regression without such data point (regression line 2) would look very different. Line 1 was selected to prove a non-existing relationship based on insufficient data (probably it exists in reality, but the raw data does not allow such conclusion).

Another almost classic example from another study is on productivity evolution. Fig. 6.14 provides the raw data. It shows starting from a normalized value of 100 how productivity evolved over time. Fig. 6.15 shows the segment where the change happens and thus amplifies the trend dramatically. Fig. 6.16 goes one step further and removes an "outlier" without any explanation (at least they left the product release 8 empty and did not remove it fully). A trend line is introduced and put to the foreground, while the data points start to disappear. Fig. 6.17 finally provides the forecast for subsequent product releases with a continued strong evolution. The given sequence of four individual presentations with the same data immediately shows where the defects are, in reality you would only see one of these charts, which makes it very difficult to find out what is not presented ands what is hidden by the visualization.

These small examples support Tom DeMarco who once stated that studies which prove what they intended to prove are suspicious.

6.5 Using Measurements: Success Recipes   139

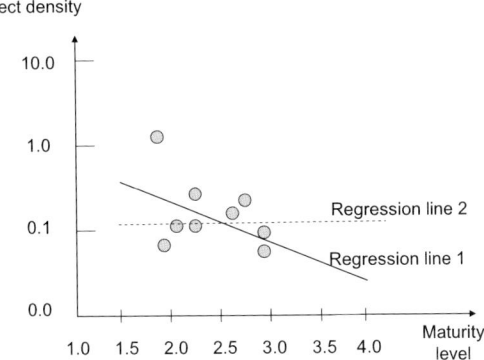

Fig. 6.13. Regression lines and regression lies

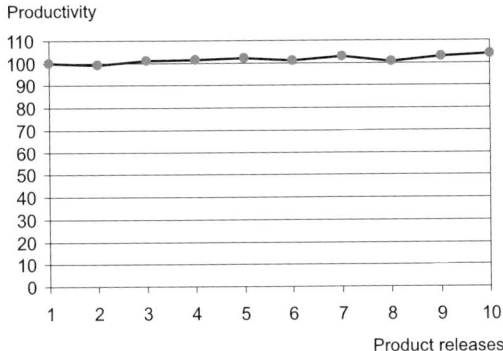

Fig. 6.14. Visualization traps: The raw data

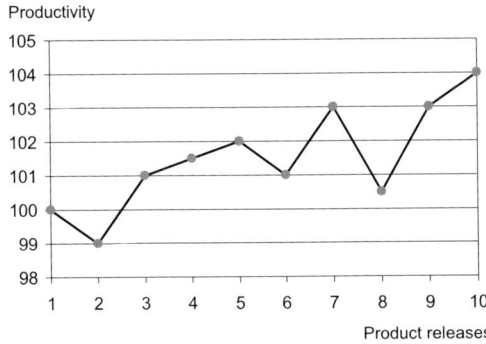

Fig. 6.15. Visualization traps: Show the relevant segment and thus amplify the trend

140   6 Introducing a Measurement Program

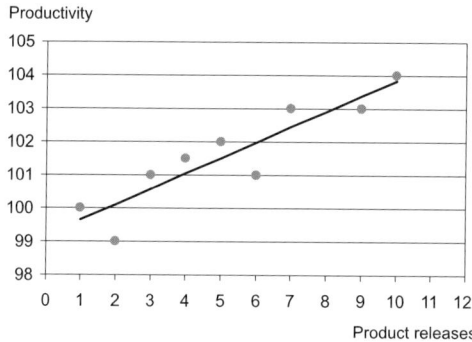

Fig. 6.16. Visualization traps: Remove outliers and highlight the trend

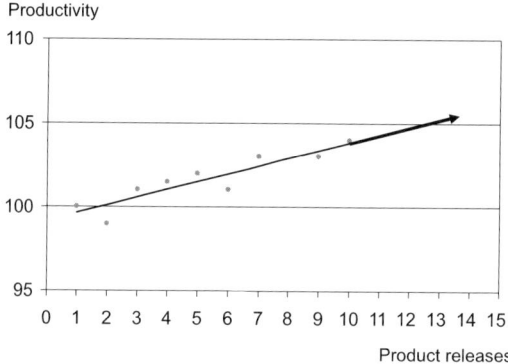

Fig. 6.17. Visualization traps: Let the dots disappear and present a strong outlook

Our guidance:
- Establish rigorous rules and policies how results are presented in management reviews.
- Rigorously apply visualization guidance and governance to avoid exaggerations and misleading presentations.
- Be careful with showing regression lines within your data. Make sure that the shape of the line and its positioning is checked with tests such as least square distances. Excel offers a multitude of such regression lines, from linear to polynomial, logarithmic, exponential and even splines. It all depends on the underlying data, and should not just be selected to present nice results. Test what would happen to the curve if a single data point would change. Is it sufficiently robust?
- When forecasting, make sure that the method has credibility. For instance defects or cost predictions can be based on various methods that had been used before. Right and wrong depend on your data set and its inherent rules. For example, defect predictions depend of mechanisms used for verification, valida-

tion, test case selection, coverage, debugging, and many more. There is not the single best method for such forecasts.
- When groups are used to show improvements, evolutions or evaluations, make sure that the groups are comparable. Often groups are aggregated in a way to simply show improvement. For instance if you have two programmer teams with different productivity, it is sufficient to move a few of below average programmers from the higher ranking team to the other team and overall productivity with increase for both teams – without any real change.
- As a measurement user, check diagrams and presentations whether there are effects highlighted which result from changing scales, cutting out segments of scales, including trend lines or arrows, using alerting color schemes. Ask for the complete set of raw data and allow yourself some time to draw your own conclusions – specifically if there are extrapolations and forecasts. Demand mean and median values for data sets and ask for the distribution or variance of the raw data. Is it a cloud of dots or is the highlighted trend really visible? Which data points are labeled outliers and why?
- Standard templates avoid that each presentation selects its own spreadsheets, tables, color schemes, and so on. These templates should be governed across the company for project reviews, funding decisions, business cases, and so on. Only with such standards based on common measurement definitions and using appropriate measurement tools, the right level of data quality and visibility can be ensured.
- On reports with quantitative data, the measurement constraints and environmental conditions should be mentioned. This can be easily done based on a common automatic measurement system from which the data is distilled. In such case only the filter criteria (i.e., how date was selected from the base data) need to be reported.
- Where there is no automatic measurement tooling covering both extraction and presentation, the constraints must be explicitly mentioned.
- If in doubt on the validity of reporting and conclusions, ask for external help to audit your measurement and reporting system. The cost of using wrong information or drawing conclusions from insufficient baselines is certainly much higher and might collapse your reporting system – leaving aside legal impacts from a finance reporting and risk management perspective.

6.5.6 Performance Indicators and Scorecards

Measurements must be goal-oriented to be useful and used. This is a lesson we learned in Chaps. 1 and 2. Goal-oriented measurement needs to have the right goals to start from. These goals are derived from different sources and can have several dimensions:
- Business objectives of the enterprise (e.g., improve productivity by 10% or reduce defects in the field by 20% per year or improve market share towards 7%).

- Policies and business processes that apply to the entire company (e.g., visibility on expenses and risks following Sarbanes-Oxley Act or capital expenses and software capitalization following the internal controlling rules).
- Process goals and policies which people have to follow in the software department (e.g., a project manager must provide periodic visibility by using the standard report template or effort is reported on weekly base in standard work hours including overtime).
- Project-specific objectives and commitments to be reached (e.g., project progress against committed requirements or project cost against allowed budget).

These different objectives can easily result in a multitude of measurements and measurement databases or reports which are creating overheads and cost unnecessary effort. It is therefore important to relate all the different dimensions above into one picture and agree for the company which standard measurements are to be reported.

Often information is collected and presented in only one dimension. For instance, a quality improvement program looks only to defects. Or for the new sales portal the only measurement is the page hits. Or your sales representatives are judged on revenues and not on cost of sales. There are many such examples of dysfunctional objectives and measurements due to locally optimizing and forgetting on the other impacts.

> There are always side effects which you do not know yet – and which you do not want. Therefore you have to extract few indicators from all operational areas which can be simultaneously evaluated.

One of the first steps towards relating the many dimensions of business indicators was the **Balanced Scorecard** concept [Kapl92, Kapl93, Hitt95]. A balanced scorecard applicable to all IT and software companies is provided in Fig. 6.18. The link to software measurements is given by investigating the operational view and the improvement view of the balanced scorecard. Questioning how the operational business can stay competitive yields critical success factors (e.g., cost per new or changed functionality, field performance, maturity level).

The **finance indicators** are typically selected from the following set of measurements:
- Profitability: Return on Investment (ROI), Return on Assets (ROA), Discounted Cash-Flow (DCF) or Net Present Value (NPV), operating profit over revenues, operating profit per customer, Earnings Before Interest and Tax (EBIT) for products in first year, risk-adjusted EBIT and risk-adjusted NPV.
- Strategic impact: share price or financial analyst rating.
- Cost: revenue created per employee, cost per employee (in various regions), cost per engineering seat, project cost structure, product cost structure (depending on place in life-cycle), employed working capital, cost of quality, cost of non-quality, revenue turnover, reduced organization costs (e.g., total cost of ownership (TCO), capital investments, effort cost).

Fig. 6.18. Balanced scorecard basic layout

Indicators for the **process dimension** are selected from the following sectors:
- Productivity: cycle time for key phases, time from inception to market, time to profit, productivity per engineer, cost of rework.
- Quality: maintenance cost, defect rates, correction time, license cost, cost of non-quality, customer satisfaction, critical customer issues (according to priority), early defect detection and removal before start of test or death on arrival (for embedded software systems).
- Project management: success rate of projects. Predictability, budget adherence, or a combined schedule and cost variance index to show project performance.

The **employee and human resource dimension** can choose from the following parameters:
- Engineering capability and learning: experience profiles, competence profiles, skills needs and variance profiles, training (provided, needed) or certificates.
- Innovativeness: patents created per full-time equivalent or license income per full-time equivalent.
- Availability: demographic evolution, absence, average tenure for certain roles, offshoring and outsourcing rates compared to market, and increased retention rates for staff.
- Strategic and operational fitness: understanding and execution of company values, availability and execution of role-specific missions, improved employee satisfaction ratings.

Finally the **customer dimension** looks into the following:
- Competitiveness: market evolution, market share or market positioning.
- Products: average age of products, innovation degree, maintenance share, cost of defects or changes, license income or product and service quality parameters (see above).
- Customers: demographical evolution, customer satisfaction or total customer experience, reduced support effort (e.g., support hours charged to the customer), improvement to specific customer concerns (e.g., call center response time, defect closure time).

- Quality: reduced number of problem reports, less service calls, fewer high-priority defects after delivery, faster installation cycles, reduced outage duration for repair or service.

Based on these aggregated scorecard profiles senior management can proactively take decisions – as opposed to the individual product manager or project manager who can only react because he has no broad overview.

> Whatever the level on which the scorecard is introduced we recommend the following guidelines:
> - Take firm decisions and execute them in the weeks after.
> - Do not delay the cancellation of a project or product, if there is no longer a belief in its success. Not all accounts are equally profitable and not all products will achieve their initial assumptions.
> - Always execute what brings the company closer to its targets, such as maximizing the value of the assets, improving the ROI from all investments, reducing the age of products, decreasing maintenance efforts or improving quality and customer satisfaction.
> - Hold the project managers accountable for achieving their commitments.
> - Hold the product managers accountable to achieving the business case and underlying assumptions. Even if you are not successful in the first attempt, reassess the assumptions of the business case after the project is finished in order to learn from it.
> - Ensure good and consistent data quality across all the measurements you report. What is lousy should be improved or personnel changed if they fail to help and support.

Feedback is the key to benefiting from measurements. Measurements being only collected in so-called data cemeteries are of no use. They result in useless overheads. If there is one single message from this chapter, than it is to actually **use** measurements. Using measurements means to analyze and evaluate them, to draw conclusions, to base decisions on facts and to communicate the measurements and the consequences resulting from measurements. Pro-active usage of course is better than analyzing after the facts. Good measurement programs result in good estimation and planning. They result in good predictions. And they drive sound decision-making – away from the chaotic fire-fighting behaviors of so many managers.

The described measurement-based management approach asks for a close link from engineering tasks and expenses to business objectives and the overall strategy of the company. Cost, benefits, technologies or capital investments are assessed and decided in combination. The R&D portfolio and investment is part of the overall portfolio and is thus subject to the same rules for evaluation. It is certainly helpful and ensures transparency if the portfolio information is closely linked with the product catalogues and product release information. Do not establish a full new reporting scheme and instead ensure that appropriate security mechanisms and access rights are established to control who gets visibility.

Someone who is able to generate numbers on the spot and off the top of his head might be a genius, but they are rare. Typically he has just invented them and has so far been lucky enough not to get burned. As a consumer, do not accept such figures; ask for the context. Do not just quote them, as you will suddenly be the source.

Managing with measurements consists of four individual steps, namely establishing concrete objectives, extracting information, evaluating this information and executing decisions to drive change or ensure progress. These four steps need to be done continuously. To facilitate smooth and continuous data collection and aggregation without generating huge overheads extraction should be highly automated and accessible from intranet portals (Fig. 6.20). If constraints or assumptions are changing, the evaluation must be changed.

Measurements properly applied first help to set objectives and to provide a mechanism to track progress towards these objectives. They will help the company or software department or business manager to obtain visibility and to improve, not only for the CEO or analyst or customer, but also for oneself.

6.5.7 Storing Measurements: The History Database

Project management as well as tracking portfolio information or improvement projects needs a wealth of historic data. Only what has been collected in the past projects can be utilized to draw conclusions for the current and new projects. Having an accurate history database of past projects helps to identify risks during launch and along the project, thereby improving estimations, assessing feasibility of project proposals and identifying which processes are suboptimal.

Building history data is time consuming. It takes many projects to complete in order to have a sufficiently comprehensive set of key performance measurements from finished projects in order to make valid judgments on new projects. Different needs require different amounts of history data. Simple project tracking can actually be done without much own history data. It is just necessary to accurately track the progress against commitments. Project tracking thus is the first step in building history data. Agree on standard measurements and set up a dashboard for the ongoing projects. After some ten finished projects you will obtain the first set of history data to use for the second step.

Estimating future work builds upon this initial history data. Naturally, the confidence and granularity of the estimates depends on the accuracy and details collected in the first step. If only project size and effort are collected, do not expect to estimate quality or cost. There are ways to predict quality based on incomplete raw data such as size information which we explain in Chap. 7.

A third step comprises managing projects and processes quantitatively. This includes activities such as statistical process control (SPC) as well as empowering every engineer towards resolving process issues on the spot. Measurement, like process maturity, grows first from chaotic ad hoc behaviors to organizational competence and further on back to projects and individuals.

Data quality is a major need while building the history database. It comprises dimensions such as accuracy (i.e., recorded values conform to actual values), completeness (i.e., information comprises all projects and sources), consistency (i.e., recorded information when compared does not show discrepancies or errors) and timeliness (i.e., measurements and history data are available on the spot when needed).

A simple yet effective architecture for measurement collection, storage and presentation is shown in Fig. 6.19. The bottom part shows operational tools which typically contain raw data (or base measurements). Examples are the project management tools that contain original plans, progress against these plans, budget and consumed resources or actual against planned effort.

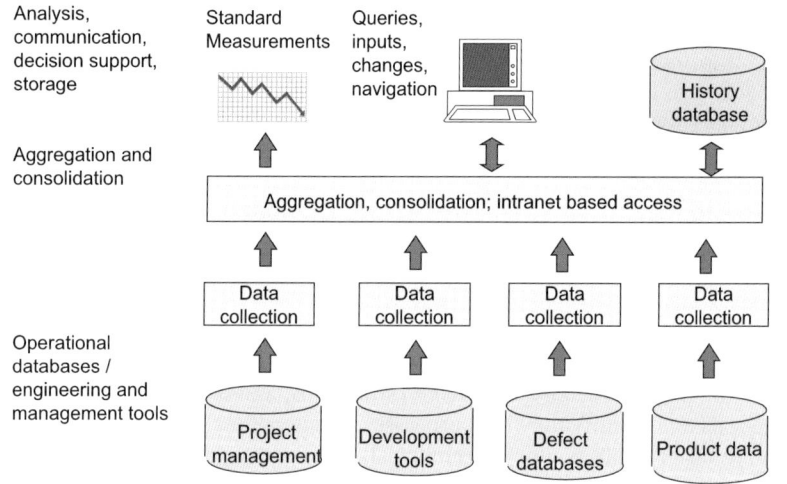

Fig. 6.19. Aggregating and storing measurement results

Defect tracking tools contain defect data from internal quality control and from external releases to the customer. They are used for calculating quality measurements. Development tools such as design or testing tools help in forecasting quality or the remaining effort to complete the project. All these tools remain as they are and simply get an interface access to their respective data storage. This information is then consolidated and stored in a central history database that is used for measurement and analysis purposes (upper right corner). A variety of query mechanisms allow selecting the appropriate view or graph and digging deeper into the raw data.

A typical query would be to show the quality of all current projects. A specific project would be identified as having found fewer defects during design than the others. So the analyst would dig into the project and look how many defects had been reported per defect removal activity and how they are distributed across the software. He might find out that some modules had no defects reported and finally detect that reviews were not completed due to insufficient estimation and re-

6.5 Using Measurements: Success Recipes

sources. In consequence he would trigger the inspection of one critical module and static code analysis of all modules that had no reviews completed. Finally he would also rework the estimation and planning guidelines to allow a project manager to earlier see if resources are available to do these important quality control activities.

Such reporting together with intranet-based navigation is shown in the example portfolio view in Fig. 6.20. The example shows in a simple yet effective intranet portal how a drill-down would start from the enterprise level to the individual portfolios (e.g., business areas, product lines) to the level of project management with specific progress tracking and details on content, responsibilities, plans and so on.

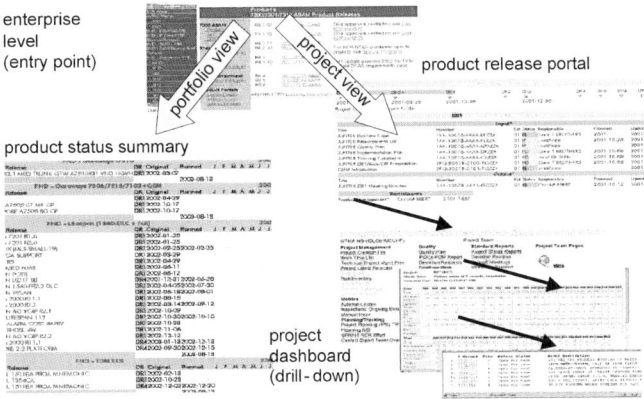

Fig. 6.20. Example of a project and portfolio portal which allows zooming from a product summary into single engineering projects and their respective project status information

The numbers which are utilized, will be questioned from all angles, because so much depends on them. Often (and unfortunately) software management will be reduced to the numbers alone. As this is normal given the relevance of well-founded decisions, this should be accepted and any figures that are provided must be provided with utmost care.

> Be careful! What is released is public. Numbers are quoted right away when they are out – independent on the many footnotes you might have included as warnings. There is no way back once reports have been presented. This holds especially for measurement interpretations and analyses.

Having more data recorded than presented helps in adjusting reports to the stakeholders' and users' specific needs. The project manager is interested to see all his milestones and how they are with respect to original commitments. A senior executive might be interested in seeing how much *anticipated* delays or budget overruns there are in her portfolio. A process manager might want to know how well estimates and predictions correlate with actually achieved reality.

To improve data quality and ensure that measurement usage is evolving, we recommend frequent reviews of the contents of the history database. This should be done before each major reporting cycle, as well as when a project is finished. The owner of the raw data per project should be the project manager. Her role comprises having accurate project information. She is in the best position to judge the quality of all reported information of her own project. The project manager can trigger dedicated corrective actions at any point during her project if some information is missing or invalid. This is hardly possible after the end of the project.

Too often, measurement is used to record the past, instead of anticipating the future. A history database is a means to stimulate forward looking. It is not supposed to be a measurement graveyard or repository for the sake of audits. One way to ensure forward-looking measurement is to make strategy reviews, performance indicators and annual objectives depend directly on actual measurements. This will stimulate the question: do we have measurements in place that will serve as early warning indicators of future problems? Measurements will be asked to indicate whether projects are doing well or not, or whether organizations are doing better or not. From a portfolio management perspective measurements will be asked that can signal future opportunities.

Once management perceives the dashboard and project measurements as reliable, there is a natural transition towards using measurements in the daily decision-making processes. We found in industrial settings that, depending on the education of management and maturity of the organization (if not management), it can take months until they would use the measurements. Basing key performance indicators on the measurements and setting up annual targets in line with business needs will accelerate usage. No reasonable manager will agree to objectives without a baseline. If it takes several months and still no progress is seen, the failure is due to either wrong attitude or incompetence which must change from the top.

6.5.8 The People Impact

Expert Box. Author: Manfred Bundschuh

An effect often overlooked in establishing a measurement program is its impact on the people involved. Software is developed by engineers, and not entirely by machines. Although introducing measurements means a cultural change to typically all involved parties, the focus is too often only on tools and definitions. If faults, efficiency or task completion are measured, it is not some abstract product that is involved, it is the practitioners who know that they will be evaluated and compared. Staff at all levels is sufficiently experienced to know when the truth is being obscured.

> As a rule, we can state that the more detailed and fine-grained the measurements, the more people need education to ensure use and usefulness.

Tracy Hall et al. [Hall01] document in an interesting empirical study of 13 groups of developers, 12 groups of project managers and 4 groups of senior managers in 11 enterprises positive and negative opinions of these interviewed relating to the use of IT measurements. Their joint result is that many of the positive aspects are more beneficial for the project mangers than for the developers, manifest in the declaration of a developer: "if any of us came up with a workable approach to measurement we'd become very rich."

Table 6.4 shows that the overwhelmingly positive perception of measurement cited by developer groups was that measurement data allows progress to be tracked (69%) and that it improves planning and estimation (38%).

Table 6.4. Perceived general positive aspects of software measurement

Benefits of software measurement		Percentage of groups		
		Developers	Project managers	Senior managers
P1	Know whether the right things are being done	23	25	50
P2	Find out what is good and what is bad	23	58	50
P3	Identify problems	8	42	25
P4	Support and improve planning and estimating	38	25	25
P7	Track progress	69	58	50
P8	Make what you are saying more substantial	15	8	50
P9	Provide feedback to people	8	25	25

Project managers and senior manager have a more positive view of IT measurements (Table 6.5). Project managers favor the use of IT measurements for estimation purposes (P1, P2, P7) and for the identification of specific problems (P3).

Table 6.5. Favorite aspects of software measurement

Favorite aspects of software measurement		Percentage of groups		
		Developer	Project managers	Senior managers
B1	Can target effort into things (that are) not doing so well	8	8	25
B4	A check that what you are doing is right	15	17	50
B5	People cannot argue	8	25	0
B6	The confidence they give	8	17	50

Three negative aspects of software measurement were mentioned by 38% of the developers:
- Developers are often not informed or do not know if and how the measured data are used.
- There is no feedback about the measured data

- Data collection is time consuming for developers (something that was also confirmed by 67% of the project managers). It is interesting that this insight did not lead to the requirement for automatic measurement.

Tables 6.3 and 6.4 demonstrate that 23% of the developers dislike the extra effort for data collection and the rather sparse presentation of the results. About 60% of the project managers said that they had difficulties in identifying and collecting data for the correct software measurement. A quarter of them added that software measurements do not always measure what you want them to measure. Senior mangers mostly found the following negative aspects (Table 6.6):
- Data collection detracts from the main engineering job.
- It is difficult to collect, analyze and use the right measurements.
- Software measurement must be used for the right reason.

Table 6.6. Perceived general negative aspects of software measurement

	General negative aspects of software measurement	Percentage of groups		
		Developers	Project managers	Senior managers
N3	Hard to measure what you want to measure	15	25	0
N6	Do not know how or if the data is being used	38	8	0
N7	No feedback from the data	38	8	0
N8	Detracts from the main engineering job	8	8	50
N10	Difficult to collect, analyze and use the right measurements	23	58	50
N11	Time consuming to collect the data	38	67	25
N12	They must be used fort the right reason	15	33	50
N13	There must be integrity in the data	15	17	25
N17	They can be used against people	0	0	25

A quarter of them commented that measurement should not be used against people. It is interesting that none of the other two groups identified this issue. We can speculate on a variety of reasons for this. Maybe developers and project managers had not experienced measurement being abused and so it did not occur to them as a problem. Or – most often the case – senior managers have not been educated on practical measurement (i.e., not being exposed to this book) and fear measurements as a pointer to previous decisions, thus creating an accountability that they do not like.

The least favorite rated aspects were (Table 6.5)
- Poorly presented data (50% of senior managers and 23% of developers)
- Difficult to compare data across systems or projects (25% of project leaders)
- Poor quality data (25% of project leaders)
- Data that can be misunderstood (25% of senior managers)
- Data not used enough (25% of senior managers)

All positive aspects fell into the following three categories:
- Assessment (P1, P2, P3)

- Planning (P4, P7)
- Decision support (P8)

All negative aspects fell into the following three categories:
- Implementation (N6, N7, N12, N13)
- Time and effort (N8, N11)
- Measurement-immanent difficulties (N10)

This book practically explains how the disadvantages mentioned or risks perceived with the use of measurements can be best handled and mitigated in order to make your measurement program a success.

Table 6.7. Least favorite aspects of software measurement

Least favorite aspects of software measurement		Percentage of groups		
		Developers	Project managers	Senior managers
L1	Extra work	23	8	0
L3	Difficult to compare data across systems or projects	0	25	0
L4	Can be misunderstood	15	8	25
L5	Not used enough	8	17	25
L6	Poorly presented data	23	17	50
L7	Data too abstract to use easily	15	17	0
L8	Poor quality data	15	25	0

Introducing measurement and analysis will change behavior – potentially in dysfunctional ways. Knowing the benefits of measurements for better project management or for steering the course of improvement initiatives does not at all imply that people will readily buy into the decision to be measured. To clearly explain the motivation from the beginning and to provide the whole picture is better than superficial statements about project benefits.

The result of lacking acceptance can lead to a general behavior of resistance in different forms, such as
- passive resistance
- work (only) on order
- active resistance

We thus recommend collecting several behavioral arguments in addition to some slogans that can readily help you to oppose resistance, as e.g., in Table 6.8.

It must be said explicitly that there is an immense interdependency between motivation and acceptance. Hence a major success factor for the implementation of measurement and estimation is the construction of a motivational system. It should have the goal to positively influence the staff for active cooperation and, last but not least, to identify the individual processes or techniques. The three most important pillars of such a motivational system are information, training and participation – the so-called king's road for introduction of innovations. This recommendation cannot be stressed enough.

Table 6.8. Fighting resistance

Resistance ...	Fighting resistance:
is natural and unavoidable!	expect resistance!
can often not be seen at a glance!	find resistance!
has many causes!	understand resistance!
discuss the hesitations, not the arguments!	confront resistance!
there is not just one way to fight resistance!	manage resistance!

A typical killer argument is "lack of time" ("we have to do more important things" or "we must reach the deadline"). The answer to this is threefold [Bund00a].

1. In our experience, even for larger IT projects, an estimate can be made in a couple of days. Medium and smaller projects can normally be estimated within half a day or a day (with the aid of a competence center). This is a small effort compared to the whole project size. Only for large IT projects (more than 100 person years), might this effort be double or triple. Normally, an IT project should have the necessary and current information for measurement and estimation readily available. If this is not the case see point 3. In any case compared to the overall project effort the effort for the estimation is negligible.
2. If there is truly a lack of time, it has to be stated that there are (time) problems in a very early stage of that project. Thus the project leader should be asked if he should not stop the project before starting it, since experience shows that time will become scarcer during the project progress. It is a high risk to not quantify the project size.
3. The effort for the measurement and estimation increases significantly when the project team has to search for the necessary documentation or they cannot find it since it does not exist. The detection of such deficits allows management to bring the quality of projects to an acceptable level. This is much the same as the statement that the necessary documentation is not up to date or is not complete. This shows that measurement and estimation have a quality assurance function as a side effect. The effort for fixing such deficits is erroneously accounted as estimation effort. In reality it is a neglected documentation task. This again fosters the prejudice that estimation takes too much effort.

Further obstacles for the dissemination of software measurement and estimation are deficits in usability, relevance, end user efficiency and the poor presentation of software measurements. Other obstacles are lack of discipline and the chaotic nature of many IT organizations.

In many organizations the dissemination of estimation methods that are used in one department fails in other departments because of the "not invented here" syndrome. This syndrome exists internationally and leads to the habit where nobody is responsive, or that valuable ideas are ignored or repulsed in order to use politically correct but less valuable estimations.

6.5 Using Measurements: Success Recipes

On the other hand, the newest trends in software development are copied, and the newest propagated innovation is blindly adapted. The existence of a realistic and positive effect on the performance, however, is not evaluated. The demand to deliver software solutions faster and cheaper also leads to a tendency to start with a "quick and dirty" programming approach before the requirements of the end users are understood correctly. This again leads to lower product quality.

Acceptance problems can also be solved by experts in the domain who have done it before (i.e., *consultants*). At the beginning their assistance is a *conditio sine qua non* to start quickly and effectively with the right concept for estimation. On the other hand, problems will arise if their assistance is too great: the staff might feel that the management does not have enough confidence in their staff. The good thing is that management listens more readily to consultants (gurus) than to their own staff. There is the additional danger that too much knowledge will be lost to the organization if it is not transferred to the employees before the consultants leave. This is mostly neglected for time- and cost-saving reasons.

It is also important that experiences be exchanged with other organizations in order not to become mired in one's own problems. Participation in conferences like the annual SEPG conferences, local SPIN meetings, or those organized by DASMA or the MAIN Network – the joint European IT measurement organizations – offers the opportunity to learn from other organizations that face the same problems or that are a step ahead. This allows us to benefit from other experiences, see positive examples or help to avoid errors reported from third parties. Often useful contacts can be made that might lead to an exchange of experiences with partners between such conferences.

The next logical step on the way to acceptance is participation. The goal of participation is the creation of widespread cooperation of all involved persons leading to active teamwork. Hence it is of immense importance to not blindly import existing processes. Instead, elaborate an adaptation according to the requirements of the own organization and in dialogue with the involved staff. This can typically be done with a neutral (external) consultant together with the staff in a pilot project. These staff members will be the promoters of the new methods in one's organizations. Fig. 6.21 presents some highlights of problems during the implementation of a measurement program.

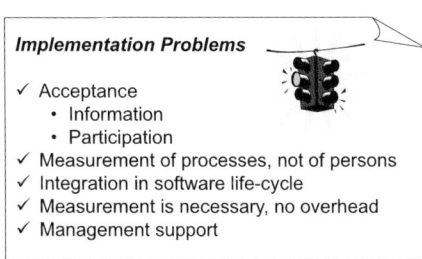

Fig. 6.21. Implementation problems

Besides acceptance problems there are a number of other challenges associated with the implementation of measurement. The focus should be that processes are measured, not persons. If one does not follow this rule the motivation of the staff will be undermined and honesty of measurements cannot be fostered. Measurement should be integrated into the software life-cycle. Otherwise the necessary tasks will be regarded as overhead. The most important of all measurements is support from management. Lack of support from managers will allow the project leaders to neglect the necessary tasks for measurement. It will thus help to delay the implementation process.

6.5.9 The Dark Side of Measurement

There is a dark side of measurement, no doubt. People might report numbers that manipulate others. If this is not addressed in a professional way, the entire measurement program is at stake!

Sometimes measurements are misused or abused. Examples are manifold and we all have read extremely bad accounts in our newspapers, such as the faked balance sheets used in companies to continue getting credits for illegal or insufficient business. "Do not trust statistics that you did not manipulate yourself" is an old saying, and there is some truth in the belief that opinions can be "guided" or manipulated by the way how measurements are described. While we do not want to provide recipes how to mislead your audience, it is clear that **the line is thin between malpractice and misinformation**. While the first deserves training and coaching, the second calls for a manager to be replaced.

A famous example of such wrong-doing with measurements and reporting is the Challenger disaster in 1986. The information provided here is drawn from the original Challenger report and some background to the root cause analysis [Chil02]. The foreground story is rather simple. It was a cold January day in 1986 and the Space Shuttle Challenger was supposed to launch for another mission to orbit. It was in the true sense "supposed" to be launched because the mission would bring in the long-awaited money which was paid to the main contractors per Shuttle launch. Management had the mission to get the thing off the ground. Engineers had repeatedly pointed to the risk of failing O-rings used to insulate the booster rocket. They found that these O-rings seem to fail more with colder temperature. They brought this finding in front of their management because today was a very cold day. The full statistic looked like the lower part of Fig. 6.22. It shows the number of O-ring failures over temperature in degrees Fahrenheit (for those being not familiar with conversion, we recommend passing back to the algorithm showed in Fig. 6.7). Obviously there was a tendency that these failures increase with lower temperature. Launches at higher temperature have a lower risk of failing O-rings, just looking to the history. On top it has only 31 degrees Fahrenheit that January day – a temperature never ever observed during the entire Shuttle program. Engineering management clearly had a conflict of interest and decided to warn their executives but keep it low profile. So they used the table showed in the upper part of Fig. 6.22. They pointed only to those incidents where

O-rings failed. It was not often the case and the table indeed is useless due to the few dots which can mean anything. The launch was decided positively for lack of evidence of risk – and the rest is history. Too big a challenge for the Challenger.

> The first Challenger lesson: Frequently statistics are manipulated to serve – perceived – management needs.

The worst is that such needs are rarely explicit but only assumed or perceived. There was clearly no need to launch the Shuttle if there was such big exposure. However along the command line this risk was reduced systematically until it was below the threshold.

> The second Challenger lesson: A long command line reduces accountability and visibility.

Nobody was anymore fully accountable for these O-rings and their correct functioning. Both errors happen day to day in software projects and reports created for management. Engineers point to risks. Engineering managers who used to be engineers claim that engineers are risk-adverse and see only the negative things and so decide to stick to the truth but manipulate the communication. Their management is used to look to the really big things and has the tendency not to care for engineering inputs, especially if it is a product in maintenance, and therefore decide for whatever means the fastest return of their investment. They would care if they knew that down the line their company is at stake. But nobody would tell them ...

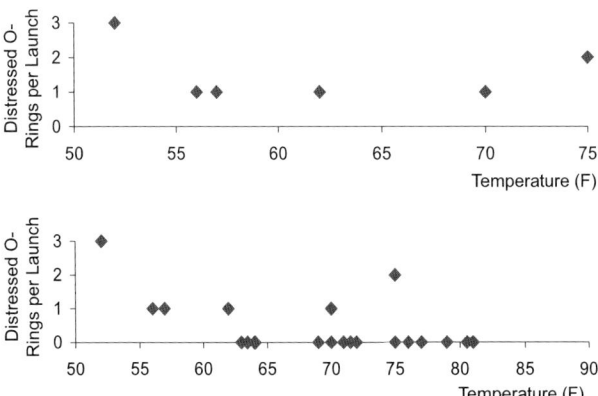

Fig. 6.22. Example for wrong measurement usage: Space Shuttle Challenger accident 1986

Wherever where numbers are used to manage, there will be all type of hypes around these numbers. These can be too low estimates to make sure a project will be approved, overly high sales figures and valuation of the project in order to push an investment decision or inaccurate reporting to reduce management pressure. We observed the following typical sources of such misuse of measurements:

- **Sales forecasts**. A major source of inaccuracy or bluntly wrong information is sales. While at times this might be wrong assumptions, we found many situations where they exaggerated and faked in order to get their short-term targets. Sales are measured on revenues and those revenues can best be achieved if the product or project is exactly aligned with short-term needs. Customer needs are tweaked and if there are changes, they are pushed in the loudest voice – independent whether it is valid a month or year later.
- **Estimation**. Planning is often tweaked in order to get approval for the project. A pet project with unclear business impact is polished in order to be approved. Costly yet interesting features are underestimated to avoid them being removed. Often insufficient estimates result from not taking the time to find out the reality and details behind the needs. Or, calculation formulas and methods are wrong. Or, certain cost types are not known.
- **Project monitoring**. If pressure is high or assumptions are impossible to achieve, software engineers and their managers might be tempted to show progress that is not yet achieved. A frequent example is to show progress on the basis of percentages which cannot be verified. This even has its own name, the "90%-complete syndrome." It means that 90% of the time a project is 90% complete. Obviously it was not 90% complete at the beginning but who would be able to find out?
- **Performance measurement**. Where there are quantitative KPI's linked with bonus, salary, reputation and ultimately the job in the company, the pressure is high to achieve those KPI's. Management by objectives makes sense and ensures that objectives are reached – but if they are not reachable or if accidents prohibit reaching those objectives, some people might start polishing results or changing raw data. It happened in the biggest companies and several senior executives ended up in prison for such faking. But it also happens on smaller scales. Risks are overlooked and later camouflaged when they materialize. Projects are sized down without approval in order to keep a deadline with lots of rework later on. Quality control activities such as reviews are skipped to win time which costs later extra money, not to mention opportunistic impacts.

How can this be avoided? A simple answer is to reduce pressure. But that's short-sighted because pressure is mostly not created inside the enterprise but externally. Reducing it would mean to give up and let competitors take over. The pressure is necessary. So we need to look into other ways.

> There are four concrete success factors for making your measurement program a success, namely value, culture, data quality and training.

- **Value**. Addressing the question "what's in it for me?" is the single most important instrument towards a sustainable measurement program. Measurement collection and analysis is overhead for many in the company. They are a burden to satisfy management's need for numbers. That is what engineers and many middle managers think. One can argue whether this attitude is helpful, professional or future-safe. But it simply is what they think. Have a look to Dilbert cartoons and you know why. On the other hand, there are many organizations with excellent measurement programs that manage statistically and achieve outstanding performance. What is different? It is the benefits visible from using measurements. Many managers and engineers first learn about measurement when there is a policy or directive. This is a perceived burden. Those who learn from measurement because it helps to get their work done better and faster, see it differently. Managers on all levels from the team lead to the project manager and her line hierarchy benefit from measurements because they have visibility and less surprises. They are in control of their own responsibility and destiny. Measurements are a tool for them with direct value. Engineers will see the benefit when they can use measurements for their own improvement, estimates and making realistic commitments. They feel the value when their direct management and "those guys up there" are more pro-active and trust to engineers' estimates and thus plan and commit more realistically to customers and the financial world.

- **Culture**. The value system of the company is crucial in achieving honest and professional behaviors. Is the truth really a value? Are people held accountable for what they claim? Are business cases and sales forecasts validated after the facts or is it just the "number exercise"? What will happen to somebody who obviously faked to improve his image or position? Is management walking the talk with its own values? Insisting on such values will typically yield big improvements as we have seen in our companies. Measurements provide most value and have most effect in an organization that encourages taking controlled risk and pro-actively articulating problems. For many companies this can be a major culture change.
- **Data quality**. Verify all measurement data and therefore improve and ensure data quality. There are numerous ways, such as audits of an independent party, establishing ways to verify estimates based on history or expert judgments, asking external consultants to probe assumptions or contribute to estimates, or using independent estimation and forecasting techniques which are in a second step assembled, such as using the Delphi-method.
- **Training**. Measurements and analysis are not trivial. Most engineers and their management have never learned in school how to manage quantitatively. Insufficient data quality is not often caused by insufficient preparation, unprofessional working or misunderstanding of underlying definitions and rules. This is where training comes into the picture. Due to the big culture impact, organizations should periodically train their staff in utilizing measurements. Management and engineering teams should frequently review their progress against objectives and question what measurements tell them.

Companies that are good at managing with measurements will use all four approaches, value, culture, data quality and training. Good organizations we have worked with not only demand periodic training but have in each single meeting and review some data points evaluated in order to base decisions on facts. For those organizations it is not anymore the question what and how to measure but rather how to get even more out of quantitative management.

6.6. The Cost and the ROI of Software Measurement

Measurements cost money and effort which needs to be controlled itself. We will briefly look towards what is the cost of a measurement program and how it is justified.

> Software measurement like any other activity must be cost-effective and it must deliver immediate tangible value.

Tom DeMarco is often quoted in measurement literature with his statement from the early eighties that "You can't control what you can't measure" [DeMa82]. A decade later when people started to measure like crazy and rarely thought about how to properly analyze measurements and draw the right conclusions he added another thought to it. In the essay "Mad about Measurement" [DeMa95], he underlines: "Metrics cost a ton of money. It costs a lot to collect them badly and a lot more to collect them well...Sure, measurement costs money, but it does have the potential to help us work more effectively. At its best, the use of software measurements can inform and guide developers, and help organizations to improve. At its worst, it can do actual harm. And there is an entire range between the two extremes, varying all the way from function to dysfunction." DeMarco draws our attention to measuring those things we really need – and not creating data cemeteries.

If done properly, there are many benefits to measurements, such as
- visibility of project and process performance
- improved predictability
- accountability for results due to verifiable commitments
- maximized value generation of the engineering investments
- transparent, fair and repeatable decisions on funding of projects
- optimized balance of content, technology, risk and funding
- improved interfaces and communication between engineering and business/sales/marketing management
- harmonized decision-making of product technology and content with business needs
- efficient and effective resource allocation
- fewer redundant projects and fewer overlaps
- outsourcing and supplier monitoring
- simplified and transparent cancellation of projects.

On the cost side we found that a fully operational measurement program – similarly to other controlling activitiess – costs some 0.3-1% of related engineering (or

6.6 The Cost and the ROI of Software Measurement

IT) effort. If the size of the organizational unit where measurements are introduced is 100 persons, one should budget approximately a half person-year for measurement collection and analysis. During the introduction phase the effort needed may almost double, due to training and communication needs and due to the introduction of templates, collection mechanisms or tools. Where there are intranet portals, access to measurements and project information can be provided with low effort which will over time further reduce the running cost of measurements collection. The effort for evaluation and execution naturally will not decrease, as this is a management responsibility, starting from the level of an individual engineer who, for instance, wants to improve her own performance and thus looks into her productivity or the quality of her deliverables.

Measurements have a positive business case. Let us summarize the reasoning.
- The introduction cost (for the first year) can account for 1-2% of the total engineering or IT effort. This cost assumes that no experiences are available and that the measurement program has to be set up from scratch. It also assumes that people do not set it up in isolation but take consulting and inputs from sources like this book. Otherwise there could be many dead-ends and not even any return because the measurement program would fail along this first year.
- So we have to also account for a probability of success which is in the range of 50-70%. This is the percentage of programs that succeed after the first year. The number is drawn from many own and external references, such as C. Jones [Jone01, Jone95] or Putnam [Putn03].
- Running measurement operations will account for 0.3-1% of the respective IT or engineering effort. This effort is primarily due to evaluating the measurements. Collection should be automated.
- Tangible benefits arrive from different directions. Due to better visibility and estimations that are more accurate and thus less delays, the immediate savings can be in the range of more than 5% of the R&D or IT spending. Some companies reported up to 10-20% savings due to introducing technical control and a software measurement program [Kütz03, Jone95]. Our own experiences in a variety of companies see the tangible value in visibility which drive both predictability (i.e., honoring of customer or contract commitments) and a focus on the things that matter (i.e., reducing overhead cost, improving cycle time, increasing field quality, stopping projects or products with low margin-to-risk ratio).
- All these inputs bring up a ROI of close to 2 for the first year, and well beyond 5 for the following year.

What value can one achieve for the customers? First, they are offered more choices and better-tailored solutions from the different product lines or business units. Having aligned product life-cycle processes and consistent visibility of status and results of all products inside the portfolio, sales and marketing initiatives are more pro-active. Milestones and gating decisions are feasible and visible. The effects of underlying assumptions are known and can be adjusted to changing business needs. New applications are faster to market once they have been developed before for another market.

Measurement clearly has a value which not only justifies the cost but also puts rationales towards visibility and accountability across the company – like controlling does for the business figures. This value can be picked like apples because during the past twenty years the industry has learned a lot from the successes and failures in measurement. This book provides insight and guidance how to make your measurements valuable and how to pick those fruits that matter for your objectives.

6.7. Hints for the Practitioner

Measurements are the vehicle to facilitate and reinforce visibility and accountability. The following key success factors could be identified during the introduction of .
- Always start with concrete improvement objectives. Measurements must relate towards something meaningful, something worth fighting for. Improvement objectives clearly fulfill this prerequisite. Such goals must be in line with each other and on various levels. The business strategy and the related business goals must be clear before discussing lower-level improvement targets. From the overall business strategy those strategies and goals must be extracted that depend on successful software development, use and support. Size or defect measurements alone do not give much information; they become meaningful only as an input to a decision process. This is where the balanced scorecard approach comes in and helps in relating the measurement program to specific corporate goals. Business goals must be broken down to project goals and these must be aligned with department goals and contents of quality plans.
- Motivate measurements and project control with concrete and achievable improvement goals. Measurements are not accepted because they are automated or reported in the intranet. They must relate to objectives people want to reach. The more concrete these objectives the more useful are measurements because they serve the same function like the dashboard in the car: They tell how far you got and how much is still to be done. Unless targets are achievable and are clearly communicated to middle management and practitioners, they will clearly feel measurements as yet another instrument of management control. Clearly communicated priorities might help with individual decisions. The value of measurement comes from the value of the underlying improvement goal.
- Start small and immediately. People often claim that measurement takes long because you first need to define lots of measurements, then train people, automate collection, and so on. This approach indeed is heavy and too long. It is much more efficient to launch the measurement program on the fast track with the clear ambition to achieve success within four to eight weeks. Go with a few measurements that address the improvement or visibility objectives you have.

6.7 Hints for the Practitioner

Start measuring right away to see how they work and what needs to be improved or automated. Then use these measurements in decision making and show the progress on your improvement program so people buy into the measurements. Let it grow afterwards once these initial measurements have proven useful and are actually used.
- Actively use measurements for daily decision making (e.g., for project control). Data collected at phase end or on monthly basis is too late for real-time control. Utilize the measurements on each level of the hierarchy. Explain the usage (including analysis and communication) to your senior management to ensure consistent usage. It is the senior managers who are looked to and who have to be the change in behaviors they want to see. They must walk the talk and use measurements for reaching their improvement targets – not abuse them.
- Avoid statistical traps. Measurements have individual scales and distributions that determine their usage and usefulness. Almost by nature, measurements in software and IT are skewed. Rarely they follow a normal (or Gaussian) distribution. Avoid showing average values which often compensate the good, the bad and the ugly. For instance, making an average across all delivery dates necessarily balances nicely the ugly delays with those that were severely overestimated. Both is bad from a performance management perspective. In such case showing quartiles makes much more sense. In other cases we advice showing not only a mean value but also the maximum and minimum values. Often a scatter plot already reveals the real message behind the numbers. Be careful with correlations and use preferably robust non-parametric statistical techniques such as rank correlations or chi square tests.
- Determine the critical success factors of the underlying improvement program. The targets of any improvement program must be clearly communicated and perceived by all levels as realistic enough to fight for. Each single process change must be accompanied with the respective goals and supportive measurements that are aligned. Those affected need to feel that they have some role in setting targets. Where goals are not shared and the climate is dominated by threats and frustration, the measurement program is more likely to fail.
- Provide training both for practitioners, who after all have to deliver the accurate raw data, and for management who will use the measurements. The cost and effort of training often stops its effective delivery. Any training takes time, money and personnel to prepare, update, deliver or receive it. Good training is worth the effort. If measurements are not used for decision-making or wrong decisions are taken, the cost is higher than that of training. Training can be class-room or e-learning. In any case it should include lots of concrete project examples preferably from your own projects. Use external consultants where needed to get additional experience and authority.
- Establish focal points for measurements in each project and department. Individual roles and responsibilities must be made clear to ensure a sustainable measurement program. This is small effort but very helpful to achieve consistent use of measurements and related analysis.
- Define and align the software processes to enable comparison of measurements. While improving processes or setting up new processes, ensure that the related

measurements are maintained at the same time. Once estimation moves from effort to size to functionality, clearly the related product measurements must follow.
- Collect objective and reproducible data. Ensure that the chosen measurements are relevant for the selected goals (e.g., tracking to reduce milestone delay) and acceptable for the target community (e.g., it is not wise to start with productivity measurements). If measurements are only considering what is measurable but do not stimulate improvements they will be used for hiding issues and creating fog.
- Get support from management. The enduring buy-in of management can only be achieved if the responsibility for improvements and the span of necessary control are aligned with realistic targets. Since in many cases measurements beyond test tracking and faults are new instruments for parts of management, management must be provided with the necessary training.
- Avoid by any means abuse of measurements. The objective is to get control on project performance, not to assign blame. Measurements must be "politically correct" in a sense that they should not immediately target persons or satisfy needs for personal blame. Measurements might hurt but should not blame.
- Ensure data quality and avoid "measurement lies." There are three cures, namely values, training and verification. Apply all of them to ensure that people understand usage of measurement and the consequences of wrong usage. Ensure that action is taken if malpractice occurs. It is about professional ethics!
- Communicate success stories where measurements enabled better monitoring or cost control. This includes identifying measurements advocates that help in selling the measurement program. Champions must be identified at all levels of management, especially at senior levels, that really use measurements and thus help to support the program. Measurements can even tie in an individual's work to the bigger picture if communicated adequately. When practitioners get feedback on the data they collect and see that it is analyzed for decision-making, it gives them a clear indication that the data is being used rather than going into a data cemetery.
- Slowly enhance the measurement program. This includes defining "success criteria" to be used to judge the results of the program. Since there is no perfect measurement program, it is necessary to determine something like an "80% available" acceptance limit that allows declaring success when those measurements are available. Measurements should not be frozen so that over years always the same measurements are collected and reported. After a while measurement needs and improvement objectives change – and so must the measurements. Even organizations with well-established measurement programs should on an annual basis step back and review which measurements they would need in the following year. They should ask which of the measurements still bring value and which are rather rarely looked at. What measurements have insufficient data quality and need improvement? Which improvement targets need more information – such as efficiency figures per activity? This is typically achieved on a calendar year basis in the same intervals as the quality management system and the annual targets are updated.

Do not overemphasize the numbers. Having lots of numbers and no reasoning will not keep you in business; it is useless overhead. It is much more relevant what they bring to light, such as emerging trends or patterns. After all, the focus is on successful projects and efficiency improvement and not on measurements. A well-defined and implemented measurement program allows an enterprise to identify, standardize and continuously improve their best practices.

6.8. Summary

There are a number of positive and negative aspects of measurement and estimation. Considering these can help to motivate the employees for better acceptance. Management support and clear guidelines are a prerequisite for a positive estimation culture and estimation honesty. A roadmap for successful implementation of measurement and estimation should start with building the foundations followed by strategic planning for implementation and establishment of the processes. The strategic plan should comprise frequently asked questions about the effort and the right moment for estimation as well as the pros and cons for centralized and decentralized measurement and estimation.

The implementation of measurement and estimation faces many acceptance problems. There are a lot of killer arguments to be countered, e.g., lack of time and too much effort for estimation. Additionally there are a lot of accompanying obstacles hindering the implementation process. The "not invented here" syndrome is a well known example. The advice from the experts is to solve all these problems using the king's road for introduction of innovations: overall information, sound training and participation of all involved persons. An alternative would be the counsel of experts.

Lack of acceptance fosters all kind of resistance damaging the process of implementation. This resistance has to be expected, found, understood, confronted and managed. Acceptance can be gained via correct information policy and exchange of experiences with measurement organizations or business partners. Participation creates cooperation and motivation. Many measurement organizations and experts offer trainings and certifications. Awareness has to be fostered for the insight that measurement and estimation are necessary and no overhead. Management assistance plays an important role for the success of the implementation process. There exist a lot of known positive and negative aspects of measurement that can be used for setting up measurements to support the measurement and estimation program. Estimation conferences are not only beneficial for team-building but also give useful hints for risk-management. Estimation honesty can be fostered by motivation and stressing the benefits of measurement and estimation. Given all this positive prerequisites supported by clear goals an estimation culture can evolve. This is a time-consuming process.

164   6 Introducing a Measurement Program

> Success factors for your measurement program comprise value, culture, data quality and training. Our experience is that there are some technical issues impacting successful implementation of measurement and estimation (which you should be able to resolve after having read this book), but the major risk are psychological and managerial challenges.

The crucial part of a measurement and estimation program is the process of implementation. It starts with the definition of the goals and information. A standard process has to be defined and pilot projects have to be found. Training and motivation have to be organized, awareness and expertise to be created. Planning, budgeting, scheduling and resource coordination have to be performed and structures, processes, methods and tools have to be defined in order to establish precedence. Accompanying measurements for support of the implementation process are the subjects of frequently asked questions, e.g., effort, cost and timing, centralized or decentralized measurement and estimation.

7. Estimation of Size, Effort and Cost

What you see is what you see.
Frank Stella

7.1. The Importance of Estimation

Estimating size and cost is one of the most important topics in the area of project management. You cannot plan if you don't know these basic parameters. The dynamics of the software market with increasing usage of external components and adapting code instead of writing it from scratch has lead to extended or new kinds of methods for the estimation of product size or development effort in the background of *cost estimation*. Gradually estimation moves away from mere volume- or size-based estimation towards functional and component estimation.

This chapter is an overview of estimations. It covers both technical aspects (i.e., specific estimation methods and their use), as well as the estimation process and its introduction. The *COSMIC Full Function Points* (COSMIC FFP) standard ISO 19761 is described by including the basic intentions and activities in order to use it in different kinds of software systems – especially in *embedded systems*. We will give a short overview about this approach and demonstrate the steps in order to consider the feasibility of the FFP application in an industrial environment. Soft factors are also captured, since especially estimations are subject to lots of "political" influences, be it during bidding (i.e., the customer wants the project at lowest cost, while the supplier wants the best match of effort and duration) or internally during the feasibility study and inception of a project.

7.2. An Overview on Estimation Techniques

The dynamics of the software market lead to a variety of methods for the estimation of product size or development effort in the background of *cost estimation*. We will list some of the key estimation techniques.

The **general relationship** between different indicators of quality, quantity, effort and productivity are defined by Sneed in the following manner [Snee05]:
- quantity = (productivity × effort) / quality
- quality = (productivity × effort) / quantity
- productivity = (quantity × quality) / effort
- effort = (quantity × quality) / productivity

Different kinds of effort estimation use the *functional sizing approach*. The major point-measurements are described here. Fig. 7.1 provides an overview about the history of function points [Fetc99, Loth01, Dumk05b].

166   7 Estimation of Size, Effort and Cost

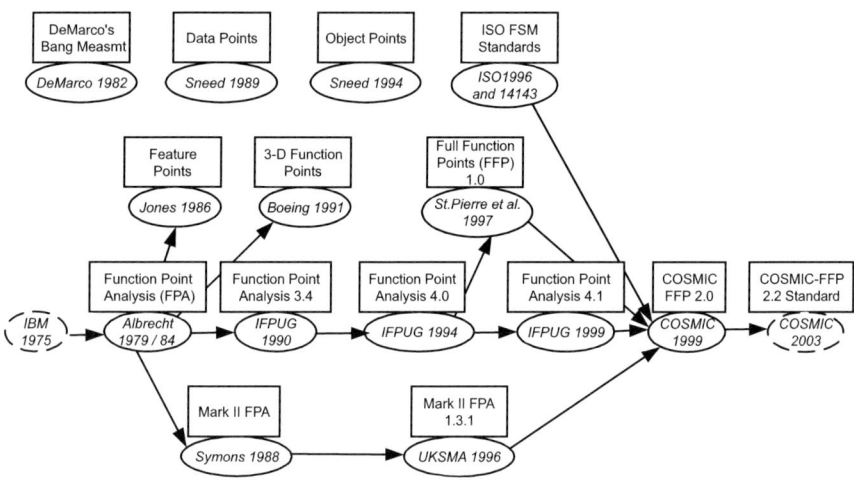

Fig. 7.1. The history of function point methods development

(IFPUG) Function Points

The function point method is based on counting system components relating to their functionality such as *input, output, inquiries, files,* and *interfaces* ([Albr83, Dreg89]). These characteristics are weighted by a classification of *simple, average* and *complex* (s, a, c) and leads to the (unadjusted) function points (UFP):

   $UFP = a \times inputs + b \times outputs + c \times requires + d \times files + e \times interfaces$

with the (s, a, c) for a = (3,4,6), b = (4,5,7), c = (3,4,6), d = (7,10,15), and e = (5,7,10). The *adjusted function points* (FP) are executed by application of a weighted number (0-5) for each of the 14 factors (cost drivers) as *data communication, distributed functions, performance requirement, hardware configuration, high transaction rate, online data entry, end user efficiency, online update, complex processing, reusable requirements, ease of installation, operational ease, multiple sites,* and *ease of modification.* The special kind of execution is

   $FP = 0.65 + 0.01 \times cost\ drivers$

The effort estimation is based on experience data and could be executed by [Bund00a]

   $Person\ month \approx 0.015216\ FP^{1.29}$

The IFPUG function point method is well-established and is supported by the *International Function Point User Group* (IFPUG). It is standardized by ISO [ISO03b].

Mark II Function Points

This method is modification of the function point method described above by changing the viewpoint to the database system approach [Symo91]. The counting characteristics are *input, entities referenced,* and *output.* The weight factors are quite different from the FP method (0.58 for inputs, 1.66 for entities referenced and 0.26 for outputs).

$FP = 0.58\ W_i + 1.66\ W_e + 0.26\ W_o$

The 14 FP adjustment factors were extended by six other factors considering actual system aspects and leads to the possibility of effort estimation. It is standardized by ISO [ISO02c].

Use Case Points

The use case point measurement addresses UML-based software modeling and implementation (see [Snee05]). The use case points (UCP) are computed as

$UCP = TCP \times ECF \times UUCP \times PF$

where TCP stands for the technical complexity factors which evaluate by weights the technological type of the system such as distributed system, reusability, concurrent etc., ECF the environmental complexity factors which characterize the system background like stability of the requirements, experience in OO and UML etc., UUCP the unadjusted use case points which counts the different use case diagram components, PF the productivity factors which weight the UCP considering person hours per use case.

COSMIC FFP

The COSMIC Full Function Point (FFP) method was developed in the Common Software Measurement International Consortium (COSMIC) and is established as ISO/IEC 19761 (see [Abra04]). A full function point only considers a *data movement* which means that there are no (weighted) difference between inputs, outputs etc. The Cfsu (COSMIC functional size unit) is the FFP measurement unit. The basic formula for COSMIC FFP counting is

$FFP = counting(((entry, exits),(reads, writes))_{archictureLevel\ i})\ [Cfsu]$

The COSMIC FFP measurement method is designed to be independent of the implementation decisions embedded in the operational artifacts of the software to be measured. To achieve this characteristic, measurement is applied to the FUR (functional user requirement) of the software to be measured expressed in the form of the COSMIC FFP *generic software model*. This form of the FUR is obtained by a mapping process from the FUR as supplied in or implied in the actual artifacts of the software. The architectural reasoning of boundaries is given through the *software layers* such as tiers, service structures or component deployments. The functional size of software is directly proportional to the number of its *data transactions*. All data movement subprocesses move data contained in exactly one data group. Entries move data from the users across the boundary to the inside of the functional process; exits move data from the inside of the functional process across the boundary to the users; reads and writes move data from and to persistent storage.

Full function points are standardized by ISO [ISO03a].

Further methods of estimation are based on the *size* of the developed software system. Examples of these estimation methods are (see also [Biel00, Boeh00, Hale00, Lair06]):

COCOMO and COCOMO II

The Constructive Cost Model (COCOMO) was defined by Boehm [Boeh99] and is based on the formula

$Personal\ effort = scale\_factors \times KDSI^{type\_of\_project}$ [PM]

where KDSI means *Kilo Delivered Source Instruction* that must be estimated at the beginning. The scale factors define the *cost drivers* Boehm classify three types of projects: organic, semidetached, and embedded.

The COCOMO II approach extends the set of cost drivers and considers the different/new aspects of software systems like code adaptation, reuse and maintenance. Furthermore, it is possible to execute/estimate the development time TDEV as

$TDEV = scale\_factors \times PM^{calibration}$

Helpful variants of COCOMO II are *COPSEMO* (Constructive Phased Schedule and Effort Model), *CORADMO* (Constructive Rapid Application Development cost Model), *COCOTS* (Constructive COTS cost model), *COQUALMO* (Constructive Quality cost Model) and *COPROMO* (Constructive Productivity cost Model). A special kind of COCOMO is called as *early design model equation* and was executed by (see also [Keye03])

$Effort = KLOC \times adjustment\_factor$

SLIM

Considering the Software Life-cycle Management (SLIM) Putnam adapted the Raleigh curve for the software development area in the following manner [Putn92]

$Current\_effort = (Total\_effort/duration) \times t \times e^{(-t \times t/2 \times duration)}$

where *duration* stands for the square of total duration of the development and *t* means the time point of evaluation. The current effort was measured in *personal years*. Another kind of estimation based on the Raleigh formula is known as **software equation** (see also [Keye03]) as

$System\_size = technology\_constant \times Total\_effort^{1/3} \times duration^{2/3}$

where the *technology_constant* depends on the development methodology.

Further relationships

The **customer cost of a software** product was calculated by Emam [Emam05] in the following manner:

$Customer\ Cost = Defect\_density \times Kilo\_Lines\_of\_Code \times Cost\_per\_defect \times Defects\_found\_by\_customer$

The **return on investment (ROI)** was executed by Emam as [Emam05] as

$ROI_1 = (Cost\ saved - Investment) / Investment$
$ROI_2 = (Cost\ saved - Investment) / Original\ cost$
$New\ cost = Original\ cost \times (1 - ROI_2)$

$Schedule\ reduction = (Original\ schedule - New\ schedule) / Original\ schedule$ [personal month]

7.3. Using the COSMIC Full Function Point Approach

Expert Box. Authors: Alain Abran, Charles Symons
Part of this work is based on the COSMIC Guide to ISO 19761. Used with permission.

COSMIC, the COmmon Software Measurement International Consortium, is a voluntary initiative of a truly international group of software measurement experts, both practitioners and academics, from Asia/Pacific, Europe and North America. The principles of the COSMIC-FFP method of measuring a functional size of software were laid down in 1999. Field trials were successfully conducted in 2000/01 with several international companies and academic institutions. The process of developing an International Standard for the COSMIC-FFP method was started in 2001 and adopted and published by ISO in 2003. For further information about COSMIC visit www.cosmicon.com, or www.gelog.etsmtl.ca/cosmic-ffp, including for a free download of the COSMIC Implementation Guide to ISO 19761, measurement bulletin updates, case studies, certification, and so on (see also [Abra01a, Abra01b, Abra05, Abra03]).

The COSMIC-FFP measurement method is designed to be applicable to software from the following domains:

Business application software which is typically needed in support of business administration, such as banking, insurance, accounting, personnel, purchasing, distribution or manufacturing. Such software is often characterized as "data rich", as its complexity is dominated largely by the need to manage large numbers of data about events in the real world.

Real-time software, the task of which is to keep up with or control events happening in the real world. Examples are software for telephone exchanges and message switching, software embedded in devices to control machines such as domestic appliances, lifts and car engines, for process control and automatic data acquisition, and within the operating system of computers. Hybrids of the above, are used for example in real-time reservation systems for airlines or hotels.

It is possible, to define extensions to the COSMIC-FFP measurement method, such as for software which is characterized by complex mathematical algorithms or other specialized and complex rules (such as may be found in expert systems, simulation software, self-learning software, weather forecasting systems, and so on), and for software processing continuous variables such as audio sounds or video images (such as found, for instance, in computer game software, musical instruments and the like).

COSMIC-FFP measurement process model
The derivation of the functional size of the software being measured is independent of the effort required to develop or maintain the software, of the method used to develop or maintain the software and of any physical or technological components of the software.

The COSMIC-FFP measurement method is also designed to be independent of the implementation decisions embedded in the operational artifacts of the software to be measured. To achieve this characteristic, measurement is applied to the functional user requirements (or 'FUR') of the software to be measured (see Fig. 7.2).

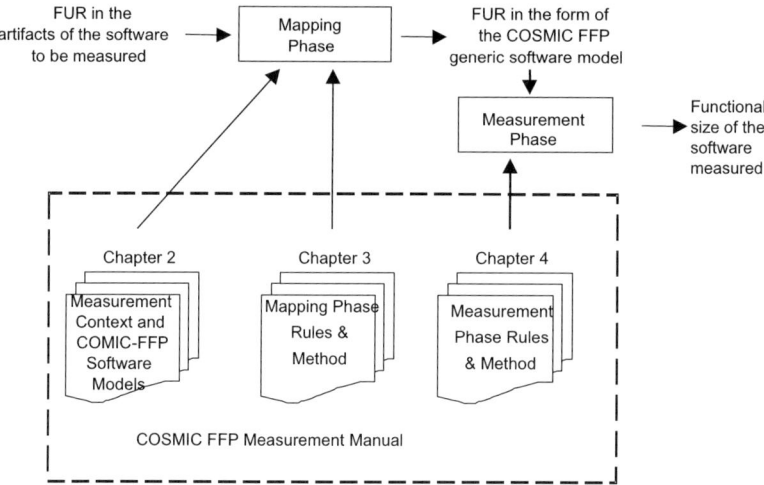

Fig. 7.2. The COSMIC-FFP measurement process model version 2.2 (January 2003)

Extracting functional user requirements

The functionality delivered by software to its users is described through the *functional user requirements (FUR)*. These state what the software must do for the users and exclude any technical or quality requirements that say 'how' the software must perform. In practice, FUR sometimes exist in the form of a specific document (requirements specifications, for instance), but often they have to be derived from other software engineering artifacts. As illustrated in Fig. 7.3, FUR can be derived from software engineering artifacts that are produced before the software exists (typically from architecture and design artifacts). Thus, the functional size of software can be measured prior to its implementation on a computer system.

In other circumstances, software might be used without there being any, or with only a few, architecture or design artifacts available, and the FUR might not be documented (as in legacy software, for instance). In such circumstances, it is still possible to derive the software FUR from the artifacts installed on the computer system even after it has been implemented, as illustrated in Fig. 7.4.

COSMIC-FFP Mapping phase

The COSMIC-FFP mapping phase takes as input a statement of functional user requirements (FUR) of a piece of software and, using a defined set of rules and procedures, produces a specific software model suitable for measuring functional size. The software model produced corresponds to the set of the FUR to be included in the specific FSM measurement exercise, as determined by the purpose, scope and measurement viewpoint of the measurement.

A key function of software functional size measurement is the establishment of what is considered part of the software and what is considered part of the software's operating environment. Fig. 7.5 illustrates the generic flow of data from a functional perspective from which the following can be observed:

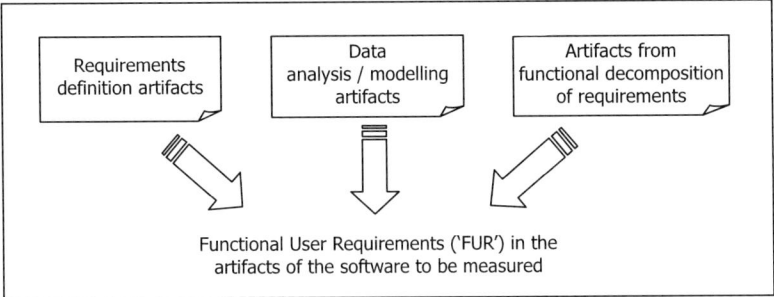

Fig. 7.3. COSMIC-FFP pre-implementation functional user requirements (FUR) model

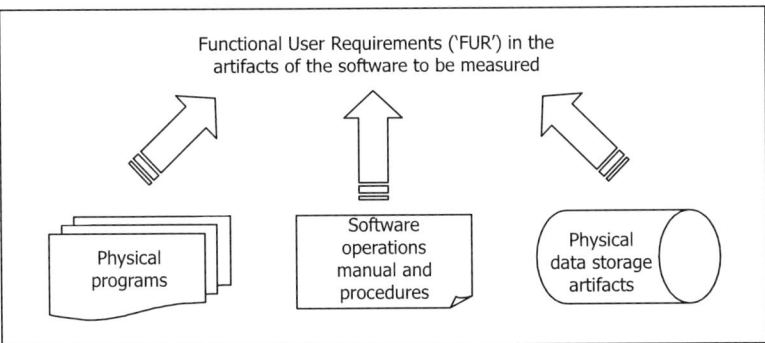

Fig. 7.4. COSMIC-FFP post-implementation functional user requirements (FUR) model

Software is bounded by hardware. In the "front-end" direction, software used by a human user is bounded by I/O hardware such as a mouse, a keyboard, a printer or a display, or by engineered devices such as sensors or relays. In the so-called "back-end" direction, software is bounded by persistent storage hardware like a hard disk and RAM and ROM.

The functional flow of data attributes can be characterized by four distinct types of movement. In the "front end" direction, two types of movement (ENTRIES and EXITS) allow the exchange of data with the users across a 'boundary'. In the "back end" direction, two types of movement (READS and WRITES) allow the exchange of data attributes with persistent storage hardware.

Different abstractions are typically used for different measurement purposes. For business application software, the abstraction commonly assumes that the users are one or more humans who interact directly with the business application software across the boundary; the 'I/O hardware' is ignored. In contrast for real-time software, the users are typically the engineered devices that interact directly with the software, that is the users ARE the 'I/O hardware'.

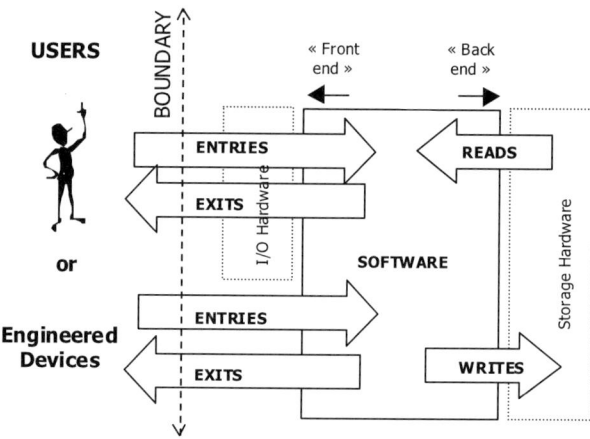

Fig. 7.5. Generic flow of data through software from a functional perspective

The generic COSMIC-FFP model asserts that all software functional user requirements can be expressed in terms of a set of 'functional processes', each triggered by an event in the world of the user. (See below for more on functional processes.) The model further distinguishes four types of data movements: entry, exit, read and write, as defined by this measurement method. All data movements move data contained in exactly one data group. Entries move data from the users across the boundary to inside the functional process; exits move data from inside the functional process across the boundary to the users; reads and writes move data from and to persistent storage.

Of course, as shown in Fig. 7.6, software manipulates data as well as moving it. However, given that (1) the COSMIC-FFP method is aimed at software from domains that are data movement-rich, rather than algorithm-rich and (2) that how to measure the functional size of data manipulation is not at all clear, the method makes the simplifying assumption that each data movement type also accounts for the data manipulation associated with it.

COSMIC-FFP measurement phase
The COSMIC-FFP measurement phase takes as input an instance of the COSMIC-FFP generic software model and, using a defined set of rules and procedures, produces a size based on the following principle: The functional size of software is directly proportional to the number of its data movements. Therefore:
- Each instance of a data movement is assigned 1 Cfsu (Cosmic functional size unit).

- The functional size of a functional process is defined as the arithmetic sum of the values of the measurement function, as applied to each of its data movements.
- The functional size of any required functional *change* to a piece of software is by convention the arithmetic sum of the functional sizes of all the added, changed and deleted functional data movements of that piece of software.

There is no upper limit to the functional size of a piece of software and, notably, to the functional size of any of its functional processes.

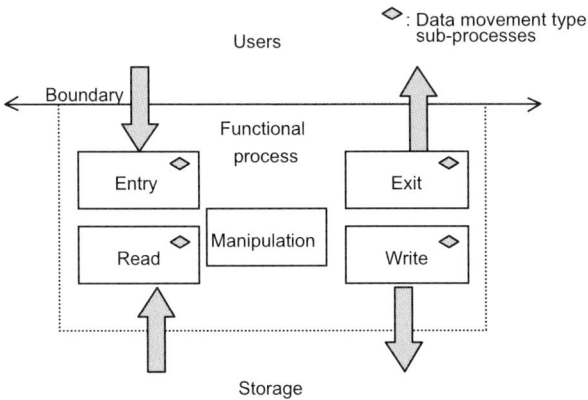

Fig. 7.6. The data movement types and some of their relationships

Functional size measurement context
Before starting a measurement using the COSMIC-FFP method it is imperative to carefully define the purpose, the scope and the measurement viewpoint. This may be considered as the first step of the measurement process

There are many reasons to measure the functional size of software, just as there are many reasons to measure the surface areas of a house. In a particular context, it might be necessary to measure the functional size of software prior to its development, just as it might be necessary to measure the surface areas of a house prior to its construction. In a different context, it will be useful to measure the functional size of software some time after it has been put into production, just as it might be useful to measure the surface area of a house after it has been delivered and the owner has moved in.

Likewise, measuring the functional size of software after it has been put into production entails a somewhat different measurement procedure when the required dimensions are extracted from the various artifacts. Although the nature of these artifacts differs, the dimensions, the unit of measurement and the measurement principles remain the same. Equally, it is important to define the Scope of the measurement which is derived from the purpose, before commencing a particular measurement exercise. Example: if the purpose is to measure the functional size of software delivered by a particular project team, it will first be necessary to define the functional user requirements of all the various components to be delivered by the team. These might include the FUR of software which was used once only to convert data from software which is being replaced. If then the purpose is changed to measure the size which the users have available once the new software is operational, this would be smaller, as the FUR of the software used for conversion would not be included in the scope of the measured size.

Finally, it is essential to define the measurement viewpoint which again may follow from the Purpose. The measurement viewpoint, in general terms, determines the level of detail that can be seen and therefore measured, within the Scope. The measurement viewpoint is highly significant, because in general measurements taken from different measurement viewpoints cannot meaningfully be compared or added together.

Purpose of a measurement.
Examples:
- To measure the size of the FURs as they evolve, as input to an estimating process
- To measure the size of changes to the FUR after they have been initially agreed, in order to manage project 'scope creep'
- To measure the size of the FUR of the total software delivered, and also the size of the FUR of the software which was developed, in order to obtain a measure of functional reuse
- To measure the size of the FUR of the existing software as input to the measurement of the performance of those responsible for maintaining and supporting the software.

Scope of a measurement.
Examples:
- A contractually-agreed statement of FUR
- A project team's *delivered* work-output (i.e., including that obtained by exploiting existing software parameters and re-usable code, software used for data conversion and subsequently discarded, and utilities and testing software developed specifically for this project)
- A project team's *developed* work-output (i.e., including software used for data conversion and subsequently discarded, and utilities and testing software developed specifically for this project, but *excluding* all new functionality obtained by changing parameters and exploiting re-usable code)
- A layer
- A reusable object
- A software package
- An application
- An enterprise portfolio

In practice a Scope statement needs to be explicit rather than generic, e.g., the developed work-output of project team 'A', or Application 'B', or the portfolio of Enterprise 'C'. The scope statement should also, for clarity, state what is excluded.

Specific measurement viewpoints
As outlined above, for consistent measurement, their users need to define and use consistently a very limited number of measurement viewpoints. The two measurement viewpoints that most obviously need to be standardized are the measurement viewpoint of the 'End Users' of an item of application software and the measurement viewpoint of the Developer of the software to be provided to meet the FUR.

End user measurement viewpoint
A measurement viewpoint that reveals only the functionality of application software that has to be developed or delivered to meet a particular statement of FUR. It is the viewpoint of users who are either human who are aware only of the application functionality that they can interact with, or of peer application software that is required to exchange or share data with the software being measured. It ignores the functionality of all other software needed to enable these Users to interact with the application software being measured.

Developer measurement viewpoint
A measurement viewpoint that reveals all the functionality of each separate part of the software that has to be developed or delivered to meet a particular statement of FUR. For this definition, the 'U' of 'FUR' strictly means 'user' as referred to in Note 1 of the definition of user in the glossary of this measurement manual

The developer may see that a statement of FUR implies that more than one separate 'major component' has to be developed or delivered. This can arise if, due to the requirements, parts of the software have to be developed using different technologies, or will execute on different processors or belong to different layers of a given architecture, or are to be realized as separate peer items in the same layer. Note also, that for any one such major component, this measurement viewpoint is also that of all Users (as defined in the COSMIC-FFP method) of that major component.

Identifying functional processes
This step consists of identifying the set of functional processes of the software to be measured, from its functional user requirements. A functional process is an elementary component of a set of functional user requirements comprising a uniquely cohesive and independently executable set of data movements. It is triggered by one or more triggering events either directly, or indirectly via an 'actor'. It is complete when it has executed all that is required in response to the triggering event (-type). An 'actor' is a user of the system being measured, acting as an intermediary to convey data about a triggering event to the functional process that has to respond to that event.

Once identified, candidate functional processes must comply with the following principles:
- A functional process is derived from at least one identifiable Functional User Requirement,

- A functional process is performed when an identifiable triggering event occurs,
- A functional process comprises at least two data movements, an entry plus either an exit or a write,
- A functional process belongs to one, and only one, layer
- A functional process terminates when a point of asynchronous timing is reached. A point of asynchronous timing is reached when the final (terminating) data movement in a sequence of data movements is not synchronized with any other data movement.

Identifying data groups

This step consists in identifying the data groups referenced by the software to be measured. A data group is a distinct, non-empty, non-ordered and non-redundant set of data attributes where each included data attribute describes a complementary aspect of the same object of interest. A data group is characterized by its persistence. Data persistence is a characteristic used to help distinguish between the four types of subprocesses. Once identified, each candidate data group must comply with the following principles:

- A data group must be materialized within the computer system supporting the software.
- Each identified data group must be unique and distinguishable through its unique collection of data attributes.
- Each data group must be directly related to one object of interest described in the software's functional user requirements.

The data group definition and principles are intentionally broad in order to be applicable to the widest possible range of software. This quality has a drawback in the fact that their application to the measurement of a specific piece of software might be difficult. Therefore, the following rules, drawn from Functional Size Measurement practice, might assist in the application of the principles to specific cases.

Application to business and application software. Measurement practice has established that, in business application software, a data group is identified for each 'entity-type'. In COSMIC-FFP, the term 'object of interest' is used instead of 'entity-type' or 'TNF relation' in order to avoid using terms related to specific software engineering methods.

For example, in the domain of management information software, an object of interest could be 'employee' (physical) or 'order' (conceptual) – the software is required to store data about employees or orders. Furthermore, data groups showing transient persistence are formed whenever there is an ad hoc enquiry which asks for data about some 'thing' about which data is not stored with indefinite persistence, but which can be derived from data stored with indefinite persistence. In such cases the transient object of interest is the subject of the entry data movement in the ad hoc enquiry (the selection parameters to derive the required data) and of the exit data movement containing the desired attributes of the transient object of interest.

Example: we form an ad hoc enquiry against a personnel database to extract a list of names of all employees aged over 35. This group is a transient object of interest. The entry is a data group containing the selection parameters. The exit is a data group containing the list of names.

Application to real-time software. Real-time software measurement practice has established that data groups for this type of software often take the following forms:
- Data movements which are entries from physical devices typically contain data about the state of a single object of interest, such as whether a valve is open or closed, or indicate a time at which data in short-term, volatile storage is valid or invalid, or contain data that indicates a critical event has occurred and which causes an interrupt.
- A message-switch may receive a message data group as an Entry and route it forward unchanged as an exit. The attributes of the message data group could be, for example, 'sender, recipient, route_code and message_content', and its object of interest is 'message'.
- A common data structure, representing objects of interest that are mentioned in the functional user requirements held in volatile memory and accessible to most of the functional processes found in the measured software,
- Reference data structure, representing graphs or tables of values found in the functional user requirements held in permanent memory (ROM memory, for instance) and accessible to most of the functional processes found in the measured software,
- Files, commonly designated as "flat files", representing objects of interest mentioned in the functional user requirements held in a persistent storage device.

Identifying the data movements

This step consists of identifying the data movements (entry, exit, read, and write-types) of each functional process. A COSMIC-FFP data movement is a component of a functional process that moves one or more data attributes belonging to a single data group. There are four types of COSMIC-FFP data movement: entry, exit, read, and write, each of which includes specific associated data manipulation.

Applying the measurement function

This step consists of applying the COSMIC-FFP measurement standard to each of the data movements identified in each functional process.

According to this measurement function, each instance of a data movement (entry, exit, read or write) receives a numerical size of *1 Cfsu* (Cosmic functional size unit). The last step consists of aggregating the results of the measurement function, as applied to all identified data movements, into a single functional size value.

For each functional process, the functional sizes of individual data movements are aggregated into a single functional size value by arithmetically adding them together.

$Size_{Cfsu}$ *(functional process$_i$)* $= \Box\ size(entries_i) + \Box\ size(exits_i) + \Box\ size(reads_i) + \Box\ size(writes_i)$

Note that the minimum size of a functional process is 2 Cfsu (there must always be one entry and either a write or an exit) and there is no upper limit to the size of any one functional process. For any functional process, the functional size of changes to the functional user requirements is aggregated from the sizes of the corresponding modified data movements according to the following formula.

$Size_{Cfsu}$ (Change(functional process$_i$)) = □ size(added data movements) + □ size(modified data movements) + □ size(deleted data movements)

The size of each piece of software to be measured within a layer shall be obtained by aggregating the size of the new and any changed functional processes within the identified FUR for each piece

Sizes of layers or of pieces of software within layers may be added together only if measured from the same measurement viewpoint.

Furthermore, sizes of pieces of software within any one layer or from different layers may be added together only if it makes sense to do so, for the purpose of the measurement. (For example, if various major components are developed using different technologies, by different project sub-teams, then there may be no practical value in adding their sizes together.)

An example: A requested change to a piece of software might be: "add one new functional process of size 6 Cfsu, and in another functional process add one data Movement, make changes to three other data movements and delete two data movements." The total size of the requested change is 6 + 1 + 3 + 2 = 12 Cfsu.

Using COSMIC FFP early in the life-cycle

It may be necessary in practice to determine a COSMIC-FFP size early in a project life-cycle before all detailed information has become available to produce a size according to the detailed rules given in the Measurement Manual.

In these circumstances we can use a locally calibrated approximate version of the COSMIC-FFP method to obtain the early size estimate. Any approximate COSMIC-FFP method relies on finding a concept at a higher level of abstraction than the data movement, that can be assigned a size in Cfsu.

The first higher level concept above the data movement is the functional process. The simplest process for obtaining an approximate size of a new piece of software is therefore as follows. For the new piece of software:

1. Identify a sample of other pieces of software with similar characteristics to the new piece
2. Identify their functional processes
3. Measure the sizes of the functional processes of these other pieces with COSMIC-FFP
4. Determine the average size, in Cfsu, of the functional processes of these other pieces (e.g., = 8 Cfsu)
5. Identify all the functional processes of the new piece of software (e.g., = 40)
6. Based on the sample the early estimated size of the new piece of software is 8 x 40 = 320 Cfsu.

Such a process can be refined to give a more accurate result if instead, before step 4 above, the functional processes are sorted into categories giving equal contributions to the total size. In a real example for one component of a major real-time avionics system, it was decided to divide the functional processes into four

quartiles of equal contribution to size. The average sizes of the functional processes in each quartile (and the names given to these quartiles) was:
'Small'   3.9 Cfsu
'Medium'   6.9 Cfsu
'Large'   10.5 Cfsu
'Very Large' 23.7 Cfsu
(To interpret these figures, for example, 25% of the total size of the component was accounted for by 'Small' functional processes whose average size was 3.9 Cfsu, another 25% of the total size by 'Medium' functional processes of average size 6.9 Cfsu, and so on).

In step 5 of the above process, the functional processes of the new piece of software are identified and also classified as 'Small', 'Medium', 'Large' or 'Very Large'.

In step 6, the average sizes listed above are then used to multiply the number of functional processes of the new piece of software, in each quartile respectively to get the total early estimated size.

Anyone wishing to adopt this process is strongly advised to calibrate his average sizes with local data relevant to the piece of software to be sized (and NOT to use the above averages). Much further research and measurement is needed before it will be possible to give 'industry average' sizes of functional processes for various circumstances.

Measurement worksheet example

The matrix below (Fig. 7.7) can be used as a repository to hold each identified component of the specific software measured. It is designed to facilitate the use of the measurement process.
- Each identified data group is registered in a column,
- Each functional process is registered on a specific line, grouped by identified layer.
- For each identified functional process, the identified data movements are noted in the corresponding cell using the following convention: "E" for an entry, "X" for an exit, "R" for a read and "W" for a write;
- For each identified functional process, the data movements are then summed up by type and each total is registered in the appropriate column at the far right of the matrix;
- The measurement summary can then be calculated and registered in the boxed cells of each layer, on the "TOTAL" line.

The increasing number of COSMIC-FFP method applications show the usability of this approach for size measurement in several functional domains and thus as fundamental for effort and cost estimation [Abra01a, Dumk01, Dumk03b, Loth03a].

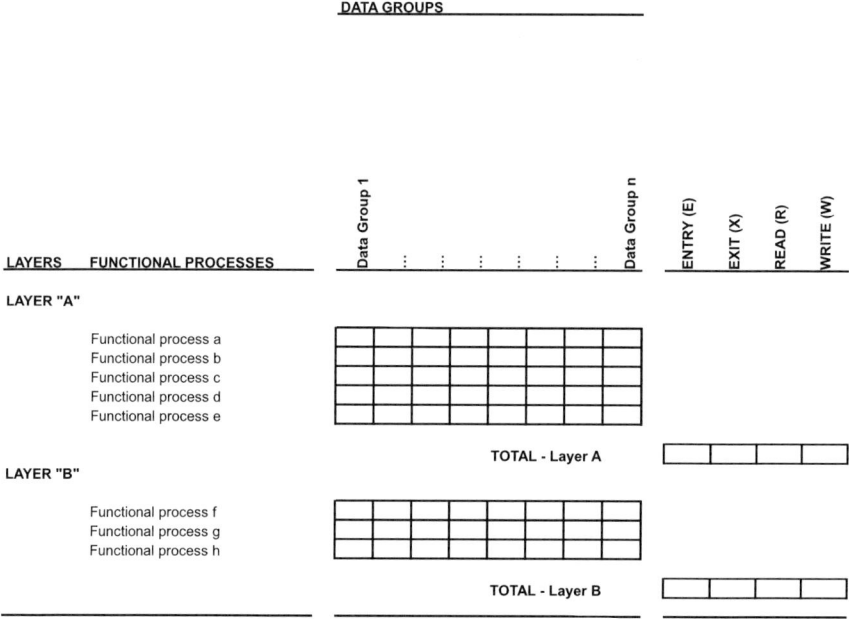

Fig. 7.7. COSMIC FFP worksheet example

7.4. Case Study: Feasibility Study with COSMIC FFP

In the following we describe a *feasibility study* in order to evaluate the appropriateness of the COSMIC-FFP method in an industrial environment at Bosch [Loth03a]. The project results described in a feasibility study arose from the ambition to continually improve the software development processes (in efforts towards a CMMI maturity level 3 or 4), adding new ideas, measurements and thus new value to the processes. In order to obtain business data, e.g., effort estimation, critical computer resources, market value and productivity measurements, the need for a software size measurement was recognized.

Lines of code (LOC) have been proven to be insufficient for several reasons, e.g., because of the late point of LOC measurements and because they are counterproductive (especially when software has to be very efficient in order to fit into the electronic control unit memory). For that reason, another applicable software size measurement approach to replace LOC had to be identified and tested. The main project goal was the determination of a functional size measurement as a basis for the improvement of existing effort estimation techniques, for estimation of the software market value as well as for other business considerations.

The selection of an Functional Size Measurement (FSM) method is affected by several influencing factors such as the software's functional domain and the par-

7.4 Case Study: Feasibility Study with COSMIC FFP

ticularities of the software development process. The typical automotive software as considered here can be characterized as real-time, embedded control software. A high ratio of the developed software results from variant development (where existing software is modified/extended or the development is continued in different ways/branches at a certain point of time) and has a high algorithmic complexity. The measurement/counting automation, the general tool support and the convertibility between different sizing methods have not been subject of these selection considerations. The objectivity and repeatability of the measurements in the homogeneous target environment is assumed.

Now, we present the main results of the feasibility study (see [Loth03a] for more details). We assume that the measurement is divided into a mapping phase and a measurement phase.

Mapping Phase – Layer (proof of the appropriateness of the (functional) domain). Since the analyzed piece of software is not characterized by a client/server structure and no different levels of abstraction can be identified, the layer concept cannot be applied. Because of the manner of the software, for single software components layers are not expected at all within the given application area. Only if a whole system with several components (client/server) is under investigation, can layers possibly play a role.

Mapping Phase – Boundary (evidence of suitable structuredness). For single software components the boundary can be identified very easily, because the software under investigation is a self-contained control process. The boundary is right around the software component. Three areas for data exchange have been identified: input signals from the CAN bus, output signals to the CAN bus and influencing parameters from the ROM. Since the value of the parameters directly influences the functionality of the software under investigation, this part was explicitly integrated in the measurements. Fig. 7.8 shows the typical boundary model for the measured software components in the application area.

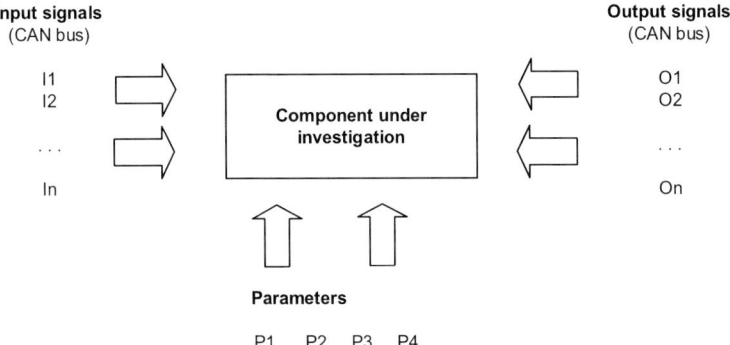

Fig. 7.8. Typical boundary model

Mapping Phase – functional processes / trigger / data groups (examination of the necessary scalability). The software component under investigation has only one functional process that is triggered when the CAN bus contains the appropriate message. This behavior is symptomatic for nearly all components in the application area, and so most of the components contain only one functional process. The grouping of data attributes into data groups will be shown in the measurement phase (Fig. 7.9).

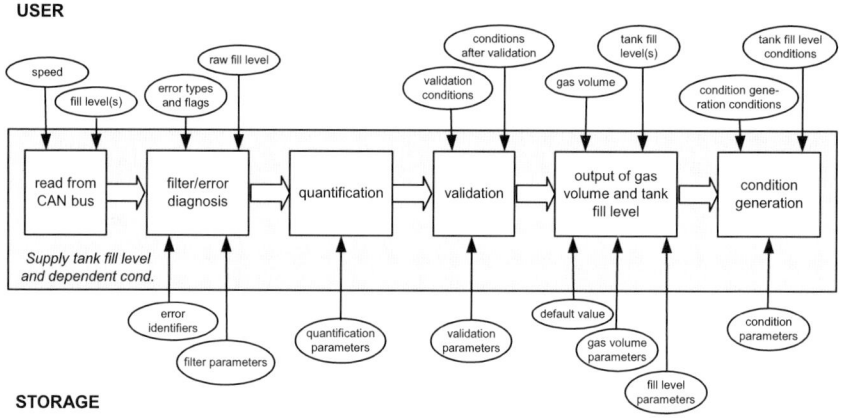

Fig. 7.9. Schematic diagram

Measurement Phase – subprocess identification and counting (proof of efficient (tool-based) countability). The available functional description mainly consists of a hierarchical ordered set of block diagrams. Because of the representation style of the information in the beginning it is difficult to extract the needed information for the subprocess identification. The subsequent calculation revealed 26% entry data, 32% exit data, 42% read data and no write data.

Measurement Phase – measurement summary (evidence of empirical-based explorability). One functional process has been identified within the component under investigation; the final COSMIC FFP size is 19 C_{FSU}.

Summary: All of the considered components under investigation could be transferred to such a schematic diagram easily. Because of the described properties and the similarities of the components under investigation, a procedure has been identified that easily allows the application of the FFP measurement for the given specifications. According to widely accepted statements, for a successful FSM certain conditions must be met, thus knowledge of the functional domain and the measurement domain is required as well as an adequate source of information.

Once again, particularly the understanding of the functional descriptions was difficult and a lot of effort had to be spent on this task. An FFP counter who is familiar with the block diagram notation should be able to extract the required information very quickly (expected mean value: less than one hour per functional description). The effort will decrease with an increasing number of measurements (e.g., because of growing experience, trust in necessary decisions, and so on), as can be seen from our effort data.

7.5. Case Study: Estimation for IT Systems

Expert Box. Author: Manfred Bundschuh

Project estimations are required as early as possible – not only from the contractors but also from every project leader. Because of the importance of early estimation methods Meli and Santillo [Meli99] published a comparative overview of function point estimation methods that shows a valuable collection of worldwide efforts in this direction. Since function point counts are based on the requirements documentation, so-called function point prognoses or approximations proved in practice to aid early estimations.

Our experience shows, that the necessary information for such approximations can be gained very early, at the beginning of a project (or, in stable environments, even before) in discussions with the project leader. In a few cases we used this function point estimation a year before project start. Of course, we added large percentages for each error, uncertainty, early estimation and risk.

We will in this chapter describe a case study about introducing and increasingly improving an estimation and measurement program inside an IT organization.

In 1995 the IT department of the Axa Service AG in Cologne (the non-insurance part of Axa Germany) started a measurement program with function point (FP) measurements, the introduction of a handbook for measurement and estimation, and the evaluation of tools. In 2001 the IT department completed the total counts of all 78 application systems (excluding Enterprise Resource Planning (ERP) applications, e.g., SAP, Peoplesoft) totaling about 100,000 unadjusted function points (FPs). By 2003 the portfolio increased to 98 application systems with about 150,000 unadjusted function points. Actually, more than 100 staff members are trained in FP counts and project estimation. In each group of developers there is at least one FP and estimation "expert." The competence center consists of two persons. In 2002 productivity Measurements were developed, and a baseline for productivity measurement was completed. In 2003 the measurement database was introduced as Version 1.0. Some of the enterprise embedded solutions are presented in this chapter.

The IT organization
The IT department of Axa Service AG includes about 500 IT professionals with approximately 50 project leaders. In addition, there is an outsourced computing center with about 250 staff members. The insurance branches deliver about 160 IT coordinators supporting the IT projects. IT development is mostly host-based with COBOL programming. There exist about 2,700 databases (1,600 CICS, 1,100 IMS), 2,500 DB2 tables (1,600 production, 900 disposition), and about 7,800,000 transactions per day (5,600,000 CICS and 2,200,000 IMS). PC projects use Optima++, a C++ shell, for programming and Internet programming is done with Java.

FP counts are obligatory at Axa Service AG, at least at the end of the requirements analysis and at the project post mortem. function point estimation, – as described here – instead of only FP count is mandatory during the feasibility study and at the start of a project. The counts and their details are documented centrally. Throughout this chapter function points mean IFPUG 4.0 unadjusted FPs.

To get access to history data, we use a project register database (Excel) which shows detailed information (extracted from the Function Point Workbench) for each FP count. It contains the quantity as well as the function points of EIs (External Inputs), EOs (External Outputs), EQs (External Inquiries), ILFs (Internal Logical Files) and EIFs (External Interface Files) for each of these components and some additional information (platform, VAF (Value Adjustment Factor), adjusted function points). When a project was counted repeatedly only the most recent count is shown and older counts are kept in a history table. There are sums of the quantity of EIs and EOs, of ILFs and EIFs which were needed for our research. IO means throughout this chapter the sum of the number (quantities) of EI and EO.

We started in 1997 with 20 application counts which increased to 39 counts a year later [Bund99]. A balanced scorecard was introduced for the department leaders, combining their success in counting all of their application systems with 20% of their financial bonus. This was essential management support for the success of the measurement program.

Function point project baseline
In addition to the investigation of the formulae for estimation we also investigated the FP proportions and average function complexity of our FP counts and compared it, e.g., with the International Software Benchmarking Standards Group (ISBSG) data. The ISBSG (http://www.isbsg.org) publishes every year a collection of measurements. The actual Release 8 is based on more than 2,040 projects worldwide. Since we did this research several times over the last few years, we now have at least three historical annual measurements of our own data for comparison, as can be seen in the following parts of the chapter.

Value adjustment factor.
One of the first results of our data collection was the perception that the value adjustment factor (VAF) of our counts is typically in the range 0.73-1.22, with an average of 0.95 in the 2001 data (0.93 in 1998), and an average of 0.94 for the host and 0.96 for the PC environment. The average for migrations is 0.73. We have used this measurement for quality assurance of our function point counts since 1998.

Function component proportions
Table 7.1 shows the historic development of the function component proportions in Axa Service AG. Of course, the first two years are not very representative. The figures from 1998 and 2001 are similar, and the division into host and PC development shows differences that should be carefully observed in future. The domination of the EIs and EOs (61% together) seems to be the reason for the strong correlation between IOs and the unadjusted FPs – the main result of this research.

Table 7.1. Function component proportions

2001		Percent of Function Points				
Platform	Number of Application Systems	EI	EO	EQ	ILF	EIF
Total	78	22	39	8	16	14
Host	69	21	40	8	16	15
PC	9	28	31	12	19	10
ISBSG Rel. 6	238 New development projects	33.5	23.5	16	22	5
Metricviews		26–39	22–24	12–14	24	4–12
Checkpoint		20	24	10	43	3
1998 Total	39	25	39	14	17	6
1996/97 Total	20	27	39	11	18	5
1997 Total	12	18	43	12	18	9
1996 Total	8	34	35	11	18	2

It can be seen that EOs dominate in Axa Service AG (39%) compared with the results obtained by Morris and Desharnais [Morr96] (22%-24%), and the quick estimation mode of Checkpoint for Windows (CKWIN), the estimation tool from SPR (Software Productivity Research) in Burlington, MA, (20%), whereas ILFs are of minor importance (16% versus 24% and 43%, respectively). Because of this peculiarity one conclusion was not to use Checkpoint for Windows (EIF + ILF = 46% versus 23% in Axa Service AG) in Quick Estimate mode for the estimation of FPs. The reason for the major importance of EOs may be that Axa Service AG has much centralized management information.

In 2000 we accomplished an error calculation with the 1998 data by using the percentage of each component to calculate 100% and compared the result with the actual function point count. Errors range from 37% (EOs) to 48% (EQs) [Bund00b]. Hence we use the percentages of the components only as a rule of thumb for the quality assurance of our function point counts.

Average function complexity

We used the Excel problem solver to calculate from the project register database the average function complexity of the five components, i.e., how many FPs a "typical" EI, EO, EQ, ILF or EIF has in our environment. It is widely agreed that this measurement is stable and can be used as a rule of thumb for quick estimation of counts, since the components need not be classified as low, average or high. SPR function points, e.g., use the average IFPUG classification for function point estimation.

Table 7.2 shows that that the average function points increased over time which may be caused by growing complexity in application development environment. In 1998 we tested the applicability of the typical FPs for estimation purposes by multiplying it with the quantities of the EIs, EOs, EQs, ILFs and EIs, respectively, and compared the results with the unadjusted function points of the counts. The error was less than 13%.

Table 7.2. Average Function Complexity

2001		Average Function Points				
Platform	Number of application systems	EI	EO	EQ	ILF	EIF
Total	78	4.7	5.9	4.4	8.6	6.5
Host	69	4.7	5.9	4.6	8.7	6.5
PC	9	4.3	5.7	3.8	7.6	6.5
IFPUG		4	5	4	10	7
ISBSG	Release 5	4.3	5.4	3.8	7.4	5.5
	Release 5 Europe	4.2	4.9	3.8	7.2	5.3
1998	Number of application systems	EI	EO	EQ	ILF	EIF
Total	39	4.6	5.7	4.3	8.2	6.1
Host	28	4.8	5.7	4.5	8.5	6.2
PC	11	4.0	5.7	3.9	7.3	5.4
1997	Number of application systems	EI	EO	EQ	ILF	EIF
Total	20	4.6	5.5	4.3	8.1	5.7

Table 7.3. Ratios of components

Application systems	Axa Service AG			ISBSG Rel. 5	
	2001	1998	1997	Europe	Total
Quantity	78	39	20	32	238
EI per ILF	2.6	2.7	2.7	3.8	2.9
EO per ILF	3.6	3.3	3.7	2.6	1.5
EQ per ILF	0.9	1.4	1.2	1.9	1.1
EIF per ILF	0.6	0.5	0.4	-	-
Ratios per input and ratios per output					
78 Application systems	2001		78 Application systems	2001	
EO per EI	1.3		EI per EO	0.7	
EQ per EI	0.3		EQ per EO	0.3	
ILF per EI	0.4		ILF per EO	0.3	
EIF per EI	0.2		EIF per EO	0.2	

Table 7.4. Ratios of Functions Points per component

78 AS	2001	78 AS	2001	78 AS	2001
EI FPs per ILF	12.2	EO FPs per EI	8.0	EI FPs per EO	3.4
EO FPs per ILF	21.0	EQ FPs per EI	1.5	EQ FPs per EO	1.1
EQ FPs per ILF	4.0	ILF FPs per EI	3.3	ILF FPs per EO	2.4
EIF FPs per ILF	4.2	EIF FPs per EI	1.6	EIF FPs per EO	1.2

Function point ratios
One would expect three inputs (add, change, and delete) at least, one output and one EQ for maintenance of a file. The following results show the averages in Axa Service AG (Table 7.3).

Ratios of components
There are remarkable differences between the afore-mentioned expectations and some differences between the ratios in our application systems (AS) and the ISBSG findings [ISBS06, ISBS02], as can be seen from Table 7.6.

Ratios of function points per component
The ratios of function points per ILF, input and output were also calculated (Table 7.4).

Function point prediction
Regression analysis on our project register database was used to find correlations between the number of components and the unadjusted Functions Points of the counts [Gaff94]. The result of the research was that the sum of the quantities of EIs and EOs (IOs in our terminology) is correlated with about $R^2 \geq 0.95$ ($R \geq 0.97$) to the total number of FPs of a count and can thus be used as a Rule of thumb for the estimation of FPs when the FPs of EQs, ILFs and EIFs are not known.

An interesting result was that the correlation was not as reliable (R^2 mostly less than 0.9) for other components as for data subsets of small, medium and large counts, and it was not better with polynomial regression. Of course, the use of FPs instead of the IOs for the estimation gives a stronger correlation, but the higher effort for classification of the components instead of only counting the inputs and outputs is not adequate for the higher precision. One should always keep in mind that estimation has to do with uncertainty.

The 1998 data were analyzed independently by Noel [Noel98] in joint research with the Software Engineering Management Research Laboratory, Department Informatique, Universite du Quebec a Montreal (UQAM), Canada, who obtained the same results. He applied the same method to seven projects with COSMIC Full Function Points (FFPs), in order to find a similar correlation for FFPs, but the sample seemed to be too small for reliable results. He reported in his thesis an error margin of 20%. Table 7.5 gives a historical overview of the estimation formulae.

Table 7.5. Function point estimation formulae

2001	Number of counts	R^2	Error in%	Formula for Estimation
Total	78	0.9483	13	FP = 7.8 × IO + 43
Host	69	0.9498	12	FP = 7.9 × IO + 40
PC	9	0.9503	21	FP = 6.4 × IO + 172
1998	39	0.9589	20	FP = 7.6 × IO + 50
Host	28	0.9580		FP = 7.9 × IO + 11
PC	11	0.9760		FP = 6.5 × IO + 134

Fig. 7.10 visualizes the regression analysis result for all counts.

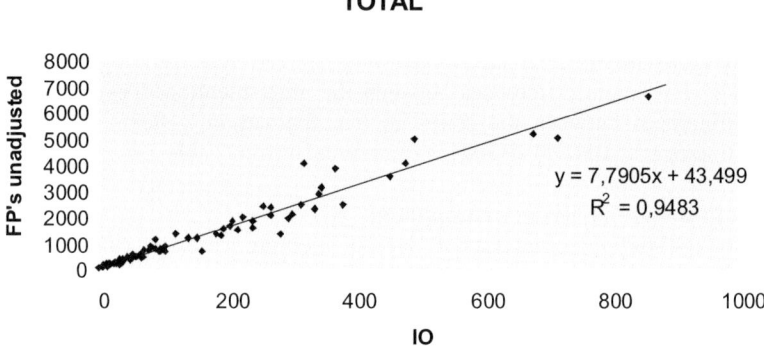

Fig. 7.10. Typical boundary model

Conclusions: Counting and accounting

Good documentation of counting and estimation data is a treasure for measurement programs. Our investigations show that valuable measurements can be gained from the collected data. A surplus benefit was finding (via regression analysis) a prediction that helped us to estimate FPs very early in the process. Since FPs is an important measurement for the estimation of effort, we thus gained the synergetic benefit to be able to do reliable estimations very early in the lifecycle of our IT projects. Of course, a complete count of FPs at the end of the requirements analysis is obligatory, as well as an improved estimation.

There is strong evidence that different environments will lead to different results, thus each organization should develop its own heuristic solutions. Nevertheless, comparisons with other measurements are valuable for the enterprise.

From the start of the introduction of our measurement program in 1996 it has been a long road to arrive at these results of application counting. The success could only have been achieved with sufficient management support. The year 2002 was devoted to introducing project FP counting and estimation as well as productivity measurements.

The quality of a software product is measured by the degree of how well it fits the requirements of the end users. The increasing diffusion of IT in private life leads to increasing requirements and quality of software systems. This consciousness of increased quality made it one of the most important goals of software development. There exist a lot of relevant and validated measurements, methods and techniques for improvement of quality of software and software development.

Quality today is no coincidence, but can and must be exactly planned. For this reason quality assurance in IT projects consists of at least the following functionality:
- quality planning
- quality measurements

- quality control
- quality assurance

The first three functions are secured by so-called constructive quality assurance measurements, which have to be performed systematically in order to define quality a priori. Constructive quality assurance measurements are, e.g., the systematic use of methods, development tools or standardized processes. Quality control is performed by analytical quality assurance measurements in order to measure quality or deviations and to correct them.

The focus of these tasks is directed to constructive quality assurance measurements, since prevention is better than error correction, or, in a metaphor: fire prevention is better than fire fighting.

This is accompanied by the requirement for the definition of quality goals for the software development process, from which the quality goals of the software can be deducted. Quality is then measured by comparison of the goals and the obtained quality features of the developed software. In IT projects, as part of the requirements, the quality measurements are defined at the start of the project. This is a direct link to estimation.

Distribution of estimated effort to project phases
With the help of an Excel chart the distribution of the estimated effort of the project phases can be done with the percentage method. A corporate solution, e.g., would ask for following input:
1. Effort as estimated
2. Effort for interfaces (e.g., computing center, other projects) as individually estimated, or from estimation tool
3. Team size of IT staff for each phase
4. Team size of end users and specialists for each phase

Fig. 7.11 demonstrates this standard. In the first folder the estimated effort for development and users is divided into the three partial efforts for IT department, user and IT Organization. After input of the effort for interfaces the estimation relevant effort will be calculated and the project category is determined (estimation class C in this case). The effort is shown in person hours (PH), person days (PD) person months (PM) .
The explanation of terms is as follows:
- *IT department*. Effort as estimated with estimation tool. This effort comprises effort for development of the application by the project team: effort for IT staff, users and specialists, but not the effort for interfaces.
- User effort by users.
- *IT organization*. Effort by other departments, specialists, project management, quality assurance and consultancy.
- *Effort 1*. Effort by the IT team, comprising all conceptional tasks, programming and test relevant tasks as well as effort for project management and quality assurance.

- *Interfaces*. Effort for interfaces required in other applications or departments that have to change their systems or processes for the integration of the new project.
- *Effort according to estimation class*. Dimension relevant effort is the sum of effort by the IT team and effort for interfaces. It determines the project category that is used for planning the organizational structure of the project.
- *Effort 2*. This is the sum of Effort 1 and interface effort.

Effort Distribution						
				Project Class C		
				PH	PD	PM
IT-Department	55,75%	85,98%	51,10%	9.812	1.226,5	61,3
User	29,25%		26,81%	5.148	643,5	32,2
IT-Organization	15,00%		13,75%	2.640	330,0	16,5
Effort 1	100,00%		91,67%	17.600	2.200,0	110,0
Interfaces		14,02%	8,33%	1.600	200,0	10,0
Effort according to Proj.Class		100,00%		11.412	1.426,5	71,3
Effort 2			100,00%	19.200	2.400,0	120,0

Fig. 7.11. Effort distribution

Fig. 7.12 is used to determine the phase relevant effort for the IT staff and users. The project duration is computed from effort and team size. The percentages shown in both tables were ascertained from the competence center in a large organization which documented and maintained project data centrally.

	Project		IT-Core Project				User				
Phase	Percent. Phase	Effort (PM)	Percent. Phase	FTE	Effort (PM)	Duration (Month)	Percent. Phase	FTE	Effort (PM)	Duration (Month)	Duration (Month)
Req. Anal.	24,0%	26,4	11,0%	5	12,1	3,23	10,5%	7	11,55	2,2	3,67
Design	21,5%	23,65	15,05%	6	16,56	3,68	3,05%	5	3,36	0,89	3,68
Coding	25,5%	28,05	19,5%	7	21,45	4,09	3,3%	3	3,63	1,61	4,09
Test	14,5%	15,95	6,8%	4	7,48	2,49	5,7%	2	6,27	4,18	4,18
Integr. Test	14,5%	15,95	3,4%	3	3,74	1,66	6,7%	3	7,37	3,28	3,28
Sum	100,0%	110,0	55,75%	25	61,33	15,15	29,25%	20	32,18	12,16	18,89

Fig. 7.12. Phase relevant effort distribution

It is important to mention the work of Jeffrey [Jeff97] which states that the effort in IT projects grows linearly up to a project size of about 10 person years (about 125 to 300 FPs) and exponentially above. The distribution of the estimated effort to the project phases and involved teams is a necessary prerequisite for resource planning. In addition, information about costs, effort, schedule and staff are needed.

Estimation of maintenance tasks
Project estimation often does not include the maintenance effort during the lifetime of an application system, but it usually exceeds the other application development costs. Software maintenance is often defined as the modification of a software product after delivery to correct faults, improve performance or other attributes, or to adapt the product to a changed environment. Practical experience shows that IT systems live longer than expected. It is a common practice that the costs for maintenance are accumulated during the lifetime of a system without controlling the amounts and without differentiating between the different kinds of costs as when in a supermarket when the shopper is afterwards astonished that the many cheap goods in the basket (i.e., comparably maintenance requirements) accumulate to a large sum at the register. It is only a pity that in software maintenance nothing can be removed from the basket afterwards.

The analogy with the supermarket directs our attention to measurements for the estimation of maintenance effort. The aim is to develop measurements and threshold figures to find out when the service effort will exceed the costs of a new development. Often it is not considered that software – like other products or goods – ages with time and that preventive planning of maintenance or redevelopment is necessary.

Productivity and maintenance effort depend on software size and some other parameters. The COCOMO-M(aintenance) model and SLIM both use only one parameter related to maintenance, while PRICE-S, SEER-SEM and Jones' estimation tool Checkpoint [Jone02] use several such parameters. Parameters related to maintenance may be found in a publication by Abran et al. [Abra02], e.g., type of application system, programming language, age of software, quality of existing documentation, necessity of a complete system test, restrictions in availability of resources, functional complexity, technical complexity, degree of reuse.

This field study was done in two organizations; it concerns 15 maintenance projects with functional changes in one organization, and 19 maintenance projects in the other organization. The result was that there exists a positive but weak relationship between size and effort. The regression analysis gave evidence of other parameters influencing the effort. The introduction of a second free parameter increased the significance ($R^2 = 0.85$ to $R^2 = 0.87$, respectively). The average size of the maintenance tasks in the organization with the Web-based environment was four times as large as in the military organization, but the average effort was only two times as much. Thus the average cost per maintenance task in the Web-based environment was only half as much (about 115 person-hours) as in the military environment (221 person-hours).

Zuse [Zuse98] collected the following measurements which can be used for estimation of maintenance tasks:
- Number of errors occurring after delivery. Often the measurements are performed during six months after delivery.
- Number of changes or change requests.
- Effort for error search and correction.
- Error quote recorded as errors per function point.
- Mean time until error occurrence.

Estimation for (single) maintenance tasks
Single maintenance tasks are necessary due to legal, technical and organizational requirements as well as for error correction. Often the effort of such tasks is less than 3 person months and therefore the effort for a function point count cannot be economically justified.

The estimation competence center of the Axa Service AG developed with some project leaders an Excel chart with typical tasks and parameters which were considered influential for maintenance tasks [Bund02b]. Each of these factors was correlated with an estimated effort for estimation which could be changed by plus/minus 100%. The actual effort was also documented. During two years five of the application development departments performed more than 220 estimations using these spreadsheets. More than 90 of this estimations contained actual efforts.

The estimations were changed according to the actual averages. In average the reduction of the former estimated efforts was about 44%. Table 7.6 shows the new Excel estimation sheet for host maintenance tasks.

Table 7.6. Estimation sheet for host maintenance tasks

Parameters:		Effort in person days (PD), 1 PD = 8 person hours
Project Management	Planning, coordination, controlling, management	10% from total effort
Discussions	Number of involved IT persons	0,2 PD
	Number of involved users of insurance branches	0,3 PD
	Number of involved interfaces	0,4 PD
Databases	Number of new tables and databases	3 PD
	Number of concerned tables and databases	2,5 PD
Programs	Number of peanuts program changes	0,1 PD
	Number of small program changes	0,3 PD
	Number of "normal" program changes	3,0 PD
	Number of large program changes	5,0 PD
	Number of all programs to be changed	0,1 PD
Other elements	Number of concerned program status Blocks (PSB's)	0,2 PD

Documentation	Number of new or to be changed jobs	0,7 PD
	Number of concerned formats	0,3 PD
	Number of concerned pages of system documentation	0,3 PD
	Number of pages of system documentation to be written new	0,3 PD
Test	Number of new test cases to be defined	0,1 PD
	Number of old test cases to be verified or adapted	0,05 PD
	IT test effort	0,8 PD
	Number of test cycles for end user test	2,8 PD

Simulations for estimation

One of the most best-known estimation tools is Checkpoint for Windows (CKWIN). Note that since we don't want to promote a specific tool, you also might want to look into QSM or COCOMO tools which are roughly equivalent. The follow-up product is KnowledgePlan. CKWIN is a knowledge-based expert system developed by Software Productivity Research (SPR) from Burlington, MA, USA. It uses about 220 project parameters and a large knowledge base for estimation and planning of IT projects. The database consists of about 6,700 IT projects. The difference between KnowledgePlan and CKWIN can roughly be described as: KnowledgePlan uses fewer parameters than CKWIN, i.e., the estimations can be done quicker. It can be integrated with MS Project, i.e., MS Project plans can be imported into KnowledgePlan, and vice versa. Estimations from KnowledgePlan can be used in MS Project plans as work breakdown structures. A very useful application of Checkpoint KnowledgePlan (or any other estimation tool that has this feature) is simulations in order to answer questions for process improvement. Questions such as how project durations can be reduced by reduction of requirements creep and project complexity can be investigated.

Checkpoint/KnowledgePlan (and similar tools, such as SLIM or COCOMO) support simulations by variation of its input parameters. Hence the concrete goal for the simulations is to find out the most effective parameters affecting project duration using the estimation of a typical IT project. The following steps were followed in the simulation project.

We started the simulation project with sensitivity analysis in order to see from Checkpoint/KnowledgePlan the parameters that have the greatest influence on project duration. With the sensitivity analysis Checkpoint/KnowledgePlan shows the 16 strongest parameters for the project goals: duration, effort, productivity and quality. Hence we got a hit list of parameters mostly influencing the matching goal, independent of the actual parameter value. For our investigations only the goal project duration was of relevance.

Next these parameters were improved successively by about one unit at a time, documented in tables and reset afterwards. For the evaluation of the parameters Checkpoint/KnowledgePlan uses a scale off 1 to 5. On this scale a value between 1.0 and 2.99 gives a positive, and between 3.0 and 5.0 a negative influence for the estimation results. The default is N/A (Not Applicable), and the value 3.00 is the industry (database) average. The values can be set in hundredths. But this precision makes no sense since one cannot explain e.g., the difference between 2.75 and 2.76, and the difference in the results would also be marginal. In some cases we used halves, e.g., 3.5 in cases when we could not decide between say, 2.0 and 3.0.

Sensitivity analysis
When modifying the parameters, according to the hit list of the sensitivity analysis we found that three of the 16 parameters could not be used for shorter durations since they had the best values (1.0) from the start.

The hit list of parameters is sorted in decreasing order. The first parameter has the most effect for shorter duration. The last parameter, delivered a three-day longer duration for some reason. The next step was the summation of the parameters, followed by step-by-step improvement to 1.0. All simulations were documented in analogous tables which are not shown here.

Checkpoint/KnowledgePlan shows an alternative for the improvement of an IT project with the report on weaknesses. In this case the weaknesses are the parameters with values between 3.5 and 5.0. Again, these parameters were modified step-by-step and in sum.

The simulations clearly demonstrated that there are a large number of ways to finish projects earlier. But not all parameters can be influenced by senior managers, project mangers or the project team, as e.g., the involvement of the users. Based on the modification of only one parameter, the project duration could improved by 32.60% with equal quality and more staff (138 instead of 86).

The lesson learned is that tools should be used more frequently for simulations. This rule is also valid for project planning tools. We found in daily project life that this rule is almost neglected by project leaders, leaving them without an essential aid for project survival.

7.6. The Software Estimation Crisis

Expert Box. Author: Bob Glass

A lot of people think we have a software crisis. They say that software projects are "always over budget, behind schedule, and unreliable." I do not agree with that assessment. We live in what I would call the "computing era," an era that could only exist through the creation of successful software. Most software projects, like most people, are mostly good, I would assert. I can write my articles (like this one), do my banking, interact with my government, search for information, and make my travel reservations successfully through the use of software that works quite reliably.

But we do have a "**software estimation crisis**." We do an abysmal job of estimating how long it will take, and how much it will cost, to build a successful software product.

Note that this software estimation crisis is very different from the software crisis I described above. This one is about measurement processes (that is why it is in this book!), not the technical processes of building software. It is about something very separable from the act of actually building the software product. A software product can have excellent quality and do exactly what the customer or user wants it to, for example, but still not meet its estimation criteria. In fact, I believe that is commonly the case.

So my point here is that what most people are calling a "software crisis" is really yet another instance of my "software estimation crisis." It is extremely important to decouple these two very different ideas. Otherwise, we end up blaming the software developers for doing a faulty job, when we should really be faulting the software estimators for doing that faulty job.

Let me lay out for you how I see software estimation happening in our field. I do not think you will find my "estimation life-cycle" different from your own beliefs.
1. The concept of a problem to be solved by software is brought to the attention of software developers by the potential customers/users.
2. An estimate of the cost and schedule for producing that software is developed.
3. The software life-cycle process itself begins – the requirements are analyzed and specified, a solution is designed, the design is coded, the code is tested, and the software product is put into production status.
4. The product is used by its customers/users. Feedback is given to the developers on how satisfactory the solution is.

Fairly straightforward and generally acknowledged, right? But there are three important things wrong in that estimation life-cycle:
1. The estimation is done before the software product life-cycle begins. In particular, the estimate is developed before the requirements are analyzed, before the problem is really understood. Let me repeat that in another way, because what we are saying is that there is some insanity in how we currently do estimation: Estimation is done at the wrong time in the life-cycle.
2. There is no place in the life-cycle where the estimate is redone. Software people live or die by an estimate that is extremely unlikely ever to have been correct. There is no mechanism for fixing estimation errors in the life-cycle.
3. Research study after research study has shown that software estimation is not done by technically knowledgeable people, as you might expect. It is done, these studies find, by upper management and marketing. People who have little or no basis for making legitimate estimates, people who think in terms of "wishes" rather than "expectations." Estimation is done by the wrong people.

So there you have it. Estimation is done at the wrong time, by the wrong people, with no mechanism in place to correct the problem. Given all of that, would not we be surprised if there were NOT a software estimation crisis?

Now, why is this happening, and what can be done about it? I will answer the second question first, because it is an easy one. I believe it is clear that we need to redo software estimates once the problem is thoroughly understood (say, as part of the beginning of the design phase of the life-cycle), that we need to provide a place in the life-cycle where estimates are yet again re-analyzed (say, at the beginning of each subsequent life-cycle phase), and that we need to make sure that technically knowledgeable people have at least a strong input into the estimation process (say, the project manager has veto power over, or at least equal power with, those managerial estimates). That is so straightforward that I find myself astonished, 50 years into the history of software development, that we have not fixed the problem long ago.

Which brings us back to the question "why is this happening?" The straightforward answer to the question is "because software is the new kid on the block." Compared to the older disciplines whose problems we are solving and whose business thrusts we are in some sense competing with, we have not been around very long. How, specifically, does that cause the estimation crisis?

- The new kid on the block has little political clout. While we should be elbowing aside those upper managers and marketers who are doing our estimation job for us, we do not have the power to do so.
- The new kid on the block is troubled by uncertainty and lack of self-confidence. While we know we should overrule those "wishtimates" with our own sense of estimation reality, we really are not certain in our own minds that our estimation answer is a better one.
- The new kid on the block rarely has time for retrospection. While we should be learning the lessons of last year's project (and death march), we are instead rushed into next year's project. Study after study analyzes software project events, and scolds software people for failing to learn from their past mistakes.

> There is a software estimation crisis, characterized by the wrong people making the wrong estimates at the wrong time, with no mechanism to fix it.

It is obvious what needs to be done to fix it, but the process necessary to do so has not yet been put in place. There is a reason for that lack of process, stemming from the "new kid on the block" status of software people.

I would like to believe that, having described the crisis, its symptoms, its causes, and its solutions, we would soon find a solution in place. But that would be naïve of me. It will take concerted and dedicated effort to alleviate the software estimation crisis. It is time we began that effort.

> What is the message to software managers? Strengthen your political and negotiating clout, so that you can:
> - Play a key role in the original estimation process
> - Revisit and update your estimates at well-defined times during the course of the project
> - Institute retrospections as a normal part of your software process

- Insist that a proper process be followed on software projects no matter how acute the schedule pressure
Not the least, educate your estimators in the best ways of performing their crucial task, so that when the time comes you can back their findings to the hilt.

7.7. Hints for the Practitioner

The following questions are frequently discussed in organizations in the context of implementation of estimation
- The effort for implementation
- The right moment for implementation
- The pros and cons for a competence center

The implementation of estimation in a large organization may take about two years. To gain estimation experience and integrate estimation into the project management processes and the consequent introduction of IT measurements for continuing improvement may need another two years.

The cost of an implementation program is often cited as an argument against systematic and professional estimation. Considering the effort for large projects in service organizations and administrations it can be said that only one failed IT project will cost more than all the effort that is necessary to implement and support sound methods for estimation and software measurement [Jone96].

The right moment for implementing estimation is always too late in practical life. A favorable moment is when project management processes or the development environment change. At this moment the estimation tasks can be integrated directly. If the quality of software development is to be guaranteed the motto must be: start any time. Gaining experience and the accompanying learning cycles can thus be started any time.

The selection of the appropriate method of cost estimation based on size or effort prediction depends on different aspects and motivations:
- Carefully investigate your own background in software sizing. Your experience in code size or design elements motivates the appropriateness of cost estimation method. Different sizing techniques are around, such as lines of code, function points, use cases, and so on.
- FSM methods are successful if they are defined by the functional system model or the system architecture. But, the quality of estimation was determined through the experience background for mapping the "points" to the effort or size unit.
- COSMIC-FFP applicability depends on the following experience for a successful migration like considering the domain of software systems (e.g., embedded), using the given experience in FFP application for some well-known application domains, and defining the strategic process for the stepwise use of the FFP method based on the handbook.

- A helpful strategy is given by designing tool-based support for FP counting, aggregation and exploration.
- Finally, it also depends on your own empirical background for use of the FFP method in decision making in different areas of management.

7.8. Summary

In this chapter we presented some recent approaches to estimation including size and effort estimation. The selection of a FSM method is influenced by several influencing factors such as the software's functional domain and the particularities of the software development process.

A functional size measurement standard COSMIC FFP is described and discussed in the application of embedded system development. Functional definitions (at the end of design phase) are the source of information for the measurement. The recognized, typical measurement scheme helps to reduce the training time required for new FFP counters. The essential characteristic of the COSMIC FFP is the simplicity and flexibility of the application. The success in using this method is supported by extending the experience base in further industrial applications.

The essential context and aspects of software estimation are described in order to demonstrate the appropriateness of chosen estimation methods.

> A final guidance: Always consider the difference between an objective, an estimate and a commitment. You can start with either one, but should follow through to get the other two parameters. Optimal results are achieved when you commit what you can deliver and set stretching yet feasible objectives.

8. Project Management

*Without the right information,
you're just another person with an opinion.*
Tracy O'Rourke

8.1. Measurement and Project Management

Project management is the major application of software measurement. And still, measurement is not sufficiently used to keep projects on track. Whether it's software engineering for a new embedded automation product, or the development of a software application or the introduction of a managed IT-service, demand outstrips the capacity of an organization. As a result we see two things. First the acceptance of impossible constraints in time, content and cost. Second and a direct consequence of the first is an increase in churn and turmoil, as well as budget overruns, canceled projects and delays.

In this chapter we show how software measurements are used to reinforce and support project control for software projects. Our motivation for building such a corporate software measurement program is to embed it within the engineering control activities in order to align the different levels of target setting and tracking activities. The close link of corporate strategy with clearly specified business goals and with the operational project management ensures the achievement of overall improvements. We therefore recommend coordinating the measurement program with a parallel process improvement initiative to ensure that goals on all levels correspond with each other. Often though, the measurement program is actually stimulated by an ongoing process improvement program. Improvement programs absolutely need underlying and consistent project measurements to follow up progress of the improvement activities.

The chapter is organized as follows. Section 2 introduces software project management and explains the use of measurement for planning and control. Section 3 looks into concrete measurement activities during the project life-cycle. Section 4 demystifies measurement for agile projects. It provides hints how to establish lean measurements without simply saying measurement applies only for complex situations.

Measurements should not only look into the rearview mirror. They ought to provide insight how to decide today for tomorrow's challenges. Section 5 gives guidance on how to instrument risk management to go beyond guessing and guts feeling in the assessment and mitigation of risks. Forecasts and predictions are addressed in section 6. Hints for the practitioner and experiences with software measurements introduction that hold especially from the perspective of organizational learning are provided in Section 7. Finally Section 8 summarizes this chapter.

8.2. Software Project Management

Many software projects are out of control and do not reach their targets. Both Gartner and Standish report from their periodic surveys [Gart02, Stan07] that three fourths of all projects fail to deliver according to agreed commitments. For each project, there is an average sum of roughly one million Euro that is spent in excess before the project is terminated – for good or bad. On average a project that is cancelled takes 14 weeks of the 27 weeks of average project duration. Only half way through a flawed project is it decided to cancel it. The interesting aspect is, that by six weeks before that termination it is clear to all participants that the problem cannot be cured. That is, in the average cancelled project 20% of time and resources are completely wasted because people do not acknowledge facts.

Only 25% of all companies periodically review their project progress. Often projects are even trapped in a vicious circle that the management involved (including sales or marketing) are aware of this, and in anticipation keep requirements overly volatile to negotiate further trade-offs with customers.

We need a way to determine if a project is on track or not. There is a saying that "you cannot control what you cannot measure." Because there is little or no visibility into the status and forecast of projects, it is apparent that some common baseline measurements need to be implemented for all projects in an organization. Such core measurements would provide visibility into the current against planned status of engineering projects, allowing for early detection of variances and time for taking corrective action. Measurements reduce "surprises" by giving us insight into when a project is heading towards trouble, instead of our discovering it when it is already there. Standardized measurements provide management with indicators to control projects and evaluate performance in the bigger picture.

> Project control answers few simple questions derived from the following management activities:
> - Decision-making. What should I do?
> - Attention directing. What should I look at?
> - Performance evaluation. Am I doing good or bad?
> - Improvement tracking. Am I doing better or worse than the last period?
> - Target setting. What can we realistically achieve in a given period?
> - Planning. What is the best way to achieve our targets?

The **basic activities within software project management** can be clustered as
- tendering and requirements management
- estimation and costing
- resource management
- planning and scheduling
- monitoring and reviews
- product control

Much has been written on the parts related to classic project management, however the monitoring aspect is often neglected. We will therefore focus on this part and call it "*project control*" to distinguish from other financial control activities (e.g., corporate budgeting) [DeMa82]. Often software managers have all technical background but lack the exposure to management techniques. We will thus look here to some basic techniques to track and control projects. Most key techniques in software project control were driven by classical management.

Many organizations that consider software development as their core business often have too much separation between business performance monitoring and evaluation and what is labeled as low-level software measurements [Gart02, Royc98, Pfle97, McGa01]. As with a financial profit and loss (P&L) statement, it is necessary to implement a few core measurements to generate reports from different projects that can easily be understood by non-experts. If you maintain consistency across projects, you can easily aggregate data to assess business performance and to assist with estimating, culminating in a kind of engineering balance sheet. This allows for better predictability of future projects and quantification of the impact of changes to existing ones.

The project manager is the single point of responsibility within the project. It is the project manager's role to implement a management structure which meets the needs of his company, his project and the project's stakeholders. He determines how to best execute a project or contract. He ensures the project is executed as defined. He is accountable for business and customer success within a contract project. He manages the project plan and its execution and asks: How do we get all this done? Seasoned project managers claim: "When I see how your project starts I can tell you how it ends." They set the rules for their team to follow. If a project manager is not used to work with measurements it is difficult to get quantitative techniques utilized in the different teams.

The project manager determines the appropriate **project life-cycle**. Mostly these life-cycles are defined at the corporate level to avoid ad-hoc process changes in each single project. The four basic project life-cycle phases are shown in Fig. 8.1.

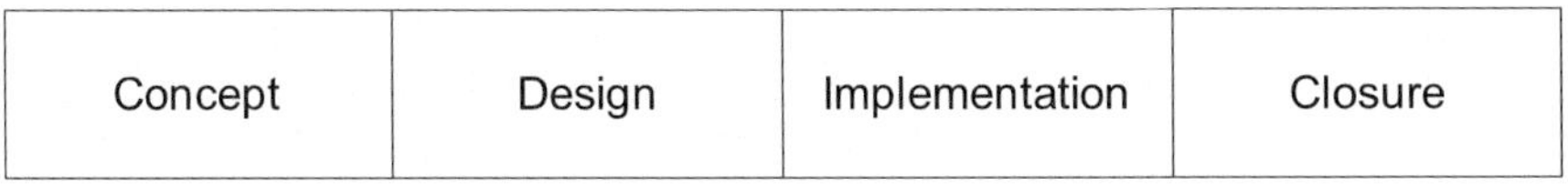

Concept	Design	Implementation	Closure

Fig. 8.1. The project life-cycle and its four phases

Basically, each project can be broken down into these four phases
- **Concept**: The project is initiated and defined in terms of basic scope and set-up.
- **Design**: The project is detailed and an exact plan is determined and agreed. The phase is critical as it includes negotiation and finalization of the project's contract with its clients. Such contracting applies for both external and internal projects.

- **Implementation**: The project's major deliveries are built. Deliveries are verified and validated to confirm to the project's quality objectives. This is the most important project phase and consumes the most resources.
- **Closure**: The finished results of the project are handed over to the respective client and the project is terminated. This phase is critical in contract projects, as it must ensure payment based on deliverables.

The implementation phase should especially be adjusted for specific project situations, such as incremental, iterative or evolutionary project development.

The project life-cycle is subordinate to the **product life-cycle** (Fig. 8.2). While the product life-cycle shows the major product phases from inception to delivery and service, the project life-cycles are embedded into these phases [Burk03]. Can be are projects for the software development, software maintenance, installation or consulting.

Different types of projects benefit from the same basic underlying project management techniques. While the content and targets of each project are (usually) unique, the approach for establishing a project plan and for monitoring and control can be very much aligned. Having such standard techniques and templates in place for project planning and control allows us to compare projects and to immediately find out how each project in the enterprise is doing. A development project for a new product or service is mostly challenged by unclear requirements or insufficient resources. Both must be tracked very closely. Risk management must set threshold levels from which corrective actions are triggered.

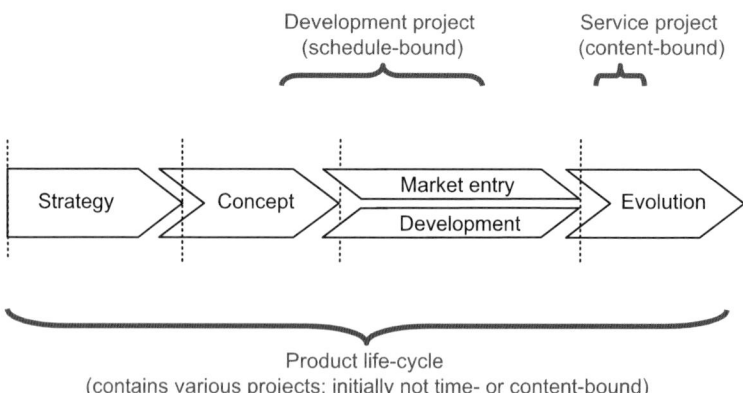

Fig. 8.2. The product life-cycle consists of several projects that utilize similar project management techniques and measurements

The maintenance projects might deliver upgrade releases or corrections. They are often hampered by too many defects being detected, configuration inconsistencies across variants and versions and – again – insufficient resources. Especially maintenance projects need close supervision from a portfolio and product management perspective to avoid releases from proliferating without delivering value. We have seen many such projects that had insufficient margins and were done simply because defects were corrected or small feature upgrades were sold within a frame contract.

> It is the product manager's task (and not that of the project manager) to decide which releases and corrections are done and which are not done. The project manager decides only within the space of her project.

Often project reviews are distorted by too many numbers or they lack facts because almost no data is shown. Both is wrong! A project plan needs concrete quantitative targets for deadlines, quality and performance. It needs to define when a work package will be delivered and what value it will add to the overall project targets. The project control will compare these initial commitments (sic!) with the actual performance.

> Project managers are accountable for their commitments. It is their duty and role to not overcommit and not to get into continuous changes during the project and later being unable to deliver.

Obviously project content and sometimes customer needs change during project execution. What matters is that the project manager is able to cope with these changes without endangering his original commitments. To all experience are project delays home-made and not the consequence of the "bad customer." It is mostly management errors, either senior management and sales who overcommit without knowing what they can deliver or project managers (the majority of failures) who do not know the basic techniques of their business.

> The single best technology for getting control over deadlines and other resource constraints is to set formal objectives for content, schedule, budget and quality in a measurable way and then monitor periodically.

Most of the techniques we describe here and that we use today were developed during the 1950s and 1960s by the defense and aerospace industries in the US. This includes planning techniques such as WBS and PERT, configuration management and earned value analysis. They were adopted later almost unchanged in software and IT projects.

Planning and control activities cannot be separated. Managers control by tracking actuals against plans and acting on observed deviations. Controls should focus on significant deviations from standards and at the same time suggest appropriate ways for fixing the problems. Typically these standards are schedules, budgets, and quality targets established by the project plan. The project manager should set plans and formally track
- Schedule against committed deadlines
- Actual expenses and effort against committed budget
- Progress against planned value (i.e., earned value analysis)

- Quality of his software product against the agreed quality objectives (i.e., defect distribution, residual defects, and so on)
- Scope and requirements changes (e.g., is the change rate manageable?)

All critical attributes should be established both measurable and testable to ensure effective tracking. The acceptance criteria should be clear although the internal target is in most cases higher. Project progress is the value achieved at a given moment compared to the initial commitments to the external stakeholders. Value exists only in the beholders' eyes and therefore the project measurements have to show the value accordingly.

The use of measurements from project start (e.g., estimation, target setting and planning) to steering (e.g., tracking and budget control, quality management) to maintenance (e.g., failure rates, operations planning) is detailed in the following Chaps. 7, 8 and 9. The IEEE Standard for Developing Software Life-cycle Processes [IEEE06] helps in defining the different processes that constitute the entire development process including relationships to management activities. The IEEE Standard for Software Project Management Plans details the steps towards establishing a project management plan, specifically topics such as work breakdown structure, estimation and relating different activities with each other [IEEE98].

Measurement insights for project management:
As a professional in today's fast-paced and ever-changing business environment, you need to understand how to manage projects on the basis of measurements and forecasts. You need to know which measurements are important and how to use them effectively. Here are some success factors for your projects:
- Estimate project time and effort and realistically set deadlines.
- Check feasibility on the basis of given requirements and needs and past project
- performance (productivity, quality, schedule, and so on).
- Manage your requirements and keep track of changes. Measure requirements changes and set thresholds of what is allowed.
- Understand what is behind delays and defects. Do not let delays accumulate.
- Be decisive and communicate with a fact-based approach.
- Avoid disputes with management, clients and users.
- Deliver what matters and keep commitments.
- Know what is value in the beholders' eyes and track the earned value of your project.

Project monitoring and control is defined as a control activity concerned with identifying, measuring, accumulating, analyzing and interpreting project information for strategy formulation, planning and tracking activities, decision-making and cost accounting. As such, it is the basic method for gaining insight into project performance and is more than only ensuring the overall technical correctness of a project [PMI04, ISO02a, Burk03, DeMa82].

Project control is a classic control process as we see it in many control systems. Most important is the existence of a closed loop between the object being controlled, the actual performance measurements and a comparison of targets against actuals. Fig. 8.3 shows this control loop. The project with its underlying engineering processes delivers results, such as work products. It is influenced and steered by the project targets. Project control captures the observed measurements and risks and relates them to the targets. By analyzing these differences specific actions can be taken to get back on track or to ensure that the project remains on track. These actions serve as an additional input to the project besides the original project targets. To make the actions effective is the role of the project manager.

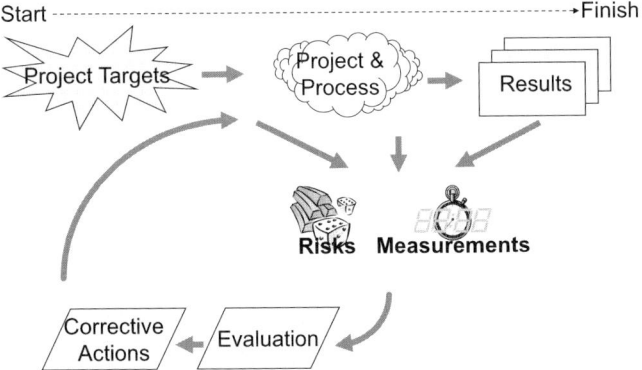

Fig. 8.3. Project control starts with project targets. It evaluates measurements and risks and ensures that corrective actions are taken

8.3. Measurements for Project Control

8.3.1 Basic Project Planning and Tracking

Software projects do not fail because of incompetent project managers or engineers working on these projects; nor do they fail because of insufficient technology. Primarily they fail because of the use of wrong management techniques. Management techniques derived and built on experience from small projects that often do not even stem from software projects are inadequate for professional software development. As a result, the delivered software is late, of low quality and of much higher cost than originally estimated [Gart02].

Project control of software projects is a control activity concerned with identifying, measuring, accumulating, analyzing and interpreting project information for strategy formulation, planning and tracking activities, decision-making, and cost accounting. Further (perhaps even better known) control activities within software projects, such as configuration or change control of deliveries and intermediate working products are not included in this definition.

It is obvious that dedicated management techniques are needed because software projects yield intangible products, and often the underlying processes for creating the products are not entirely understood. Unlike other engineering disciplines at universities, software engineering education until recently meant primarily design and programming techniques instead of proper project management.

The single best technology for getting some control over deadlines and other resource constraints is to **set formal objectives for quality and resources in a measurable way** [Royc98, Fent97, Eber96, Star94]. Planning and control activities cannot be separated. Managers control by tracking actual results against plans and acting on observed deviations. Controls should focus on significant deviations from standards and at the same time suggest appropriate ways for fixing the problems. Typically these standards are schedules, budgets and quality targets established by the project plan. All critical attributes established should be both measurable and testable to ensure effective tracking. The worst acceptable level should be clear although the internal target is in most cases higher.

Control is only achievable if measurements of performance have been defined and implemented, objectives have been defined and agreed, predictive models have been established for the entire life-cycle, and the ability to act is given. The remainder of this section will investigate examples for each of these conditions (Table 8.1).

Table 8.1. Appropriate measurements are selected depending on the process maturity (CMMI maturity level).

CMMI Maturity level	Maturity description	What it means for measurement
5	Continuous improvements are institutionalized	Control of process changes; assess process innovations and manage process change; analysis of process and product measurements; follow through of defect prevention and technology or process changes
4	Products and processes are quantitatively managed	Process measurements to control individual processes; quantitative objectives are continuously followed; statistical process control; control limit charts over time. Objectives are followed at process level; control is within projects to immediately take action if limits are crossed
3	Appropriate techniques are institutionalized	Measurements are standardized and evaluated; formal records for retrieving project measurements (intranet, history database); automatic measurement collection; maintain process database across projects. Objectives are followed on organizational level
2	Project management is established	Few reproducible project measurements for planning and tracking (contents, requirements, defects, effort, size, progress); profiles over time for these measurements; few process measurements for process improvement progress tracking. Objectives are followed on project basis
1	Process is informal and ad hoc	Ad hoc project measurements (size, effort, faults); however, measurements are inconsistent and not reproducible.

The influence of measurements definition and application from project start (e.g., estimation, target setting and planning) to steering (e.g., tracking and budget control, quality management) to maintenance (e.g., failure rates, operations planning) is very well described in the related IEEE Standard for Developing Software Life-cycle Processes [ISO06a, ISO02a]. This standard helps also in defining the different processes that constitute the entire development process including relationships to management activities.

One of the main targets of any kind of measurement is that it should provide an objective way of expressing information, free of value judgments. This is particularly important when the information concerned is "bad news", for instance related to productivity or cost, and thus may not necessarily be well received. Often the observed human tendency is to ignore any criticism related to one's own area and direct attention to somebody else's. Testing articulates "the design is badly structured", while operations emphasize "software has not been adequately tested." Any improvement activities must therefore be based on hard numerical evidence. The first use of measurements is most often to investigate the current state of the software process. On CMMI Maturity levels 1 and 2, basically any application of measurements is mainly restricted due to non-repeatable processes and thus a limited degree of consistency across projects.

A selection of the most relevant project tracking measurements is provided in Fig. 8.4, Fig. 8.5 and Fig. 8.6. Projects typically aggregate and provide information similar to a dashboard. Such a **project dashboard** allows to have all relevant information related to project progress against commitments, including risks and other information summarized on one page, typically online accessible with periodically updated data. Example for dashboard measurements include milestone tracking, cost evolution, a selection of process measurements, work product deliveries and faults with status information. There can be both direct measurements (e.g., cost) as well as indirect measurements and predictions (e.g., cost to complete).

We distinguish three views on project measurements with different underlying goals, namely:

- **Aggregated view**. This is the typical dashboard with all relevant information on one page (see Fig. 8.4). It is standardized for an organization or enterprise to ensure that information is presented uniformly with same measurement definitions and visualization semantics – thus ensuring that no time is lost in answering questions around scope, content or data quality.
- **Work product progress**. This are the typical bar charts indicating how much progress is visible from looking to work products, requirements, increments or detected defects (see Fig. 8.5).
- **In-process measurements**. This is the most sophisticated view that is typically only used in organizations with sufficiently mature processes in order to control and optimize processes within the project. Such measurements vary very much depending on the current focus and process improvement activities (sere Fig. 8.6).

Fig. 8.4 shows a simplified dashboard it is used to track projects. It covers the major dimensions of milestone control, budget and cost control, quality level and earned value. These four dimensions give a fast insight into progress in contrast to commitments and allowed resources. You realize in this dashboard the mixture of plan-driven tracking as we are used to from techniques such as PERT and the forecasting trends with defect predictions or earned value evolution.

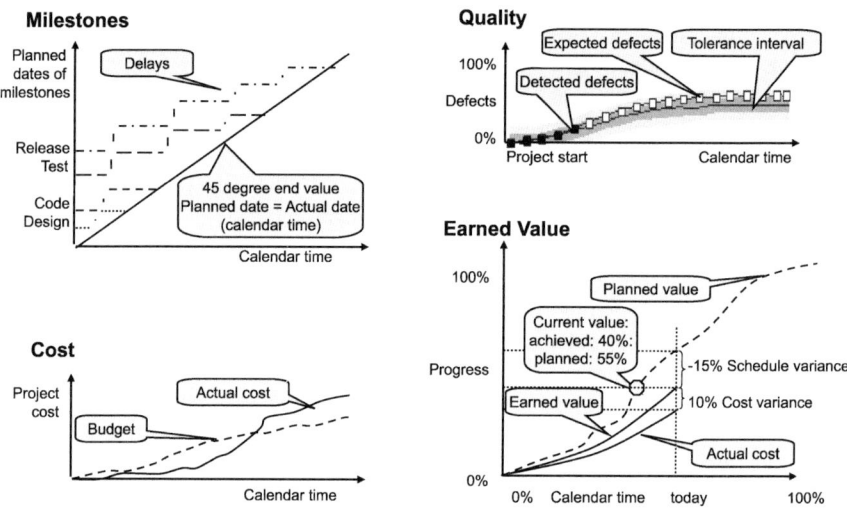

Fig. 8.4. Measurement dashboard (part 1): Overview measurements for schedule, cost, quality and earned value

Fig. 8.5 expands this project view towards a more WBS and work-product driven perspective. Do not get lost in such work products tracking as long as the overall project perspective is not established. Fig. 8.6 is more advanced and links process performance with project performance. Different core measurements and process indicators are combined to get a view into how the project is doing and how it performs against the estimated process behaviors. It not only reveals underperforming projects easily, but it also helps to see risks much earlier than with after the fact tracking alone. In-process checks are always better than waiting until it is too late for corrections.

These project control measurements are periodically updated and provide an easy overview on the project status, even for very small projects. Based on this set of measurements few measurements can be selected for weekly tracking work products' status and progress (e.g., increment availability, requirements progress, code delivery, defect detection), while others are reported periodically to build up a history database (e.g., size, effort). Most of these measurements are actually by-products from automatic collection tools related to planning and software configuration management (SCM) databases.

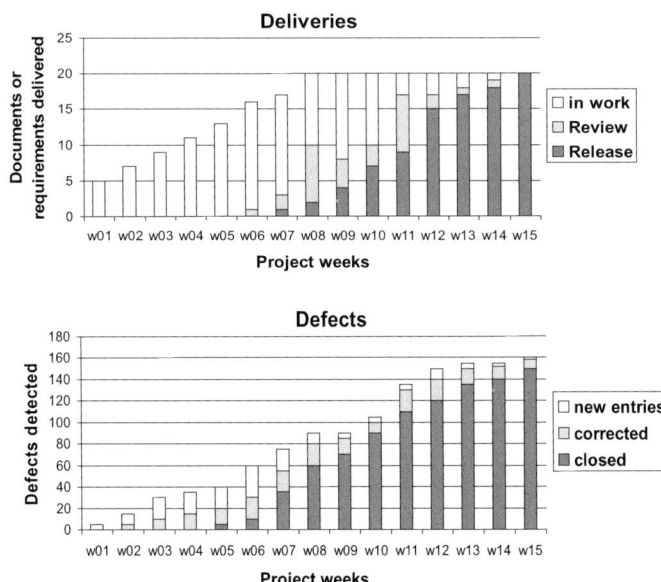

Fig. 8.5. Measurement dashboard (part 2): Work product measurements on delivery and quality for a project over project time. Status information is indicated with different shades

Metrics	targets	actuals	comment
size [KLOC]			
effort [PY]			
time to market [months]			
tested requirements [%]			
design progress [% of est. effort]			
code progress [% of est. size]			
test progress [% test cases]			
inspection efficiency [LOC/h]			
effort per defect in peer reviews [Ph/defect]			
effort per defect in module test [Ph/ defect]			
effort per defect in test [Ph/ defect]			
defects detected before integration [%]			
number of defects in design			
number of defects in peer reviews			
number of defects in module test			
number of defects in test			
number of defects in the field			

Fig. 8.6. Measurement dashboard (part 3): In-process measurements comparing actuals with targets

Fig. 8.7 shows a tailorable project dashboard that has all necessary information in one sheet, namely risks and open issues, budget and expense control, milestone control, earned value tracking, requirements and their respective implementation

210   8 Project Management

status, test planning and tracking, and defects status. Built into the commercial eASEE PLM tools suite, it receives parts of its data from operational databases and others from the internal data backbone [eASE06]. This ensures sufficient data quality to compare project status across all projects of a portfolio.

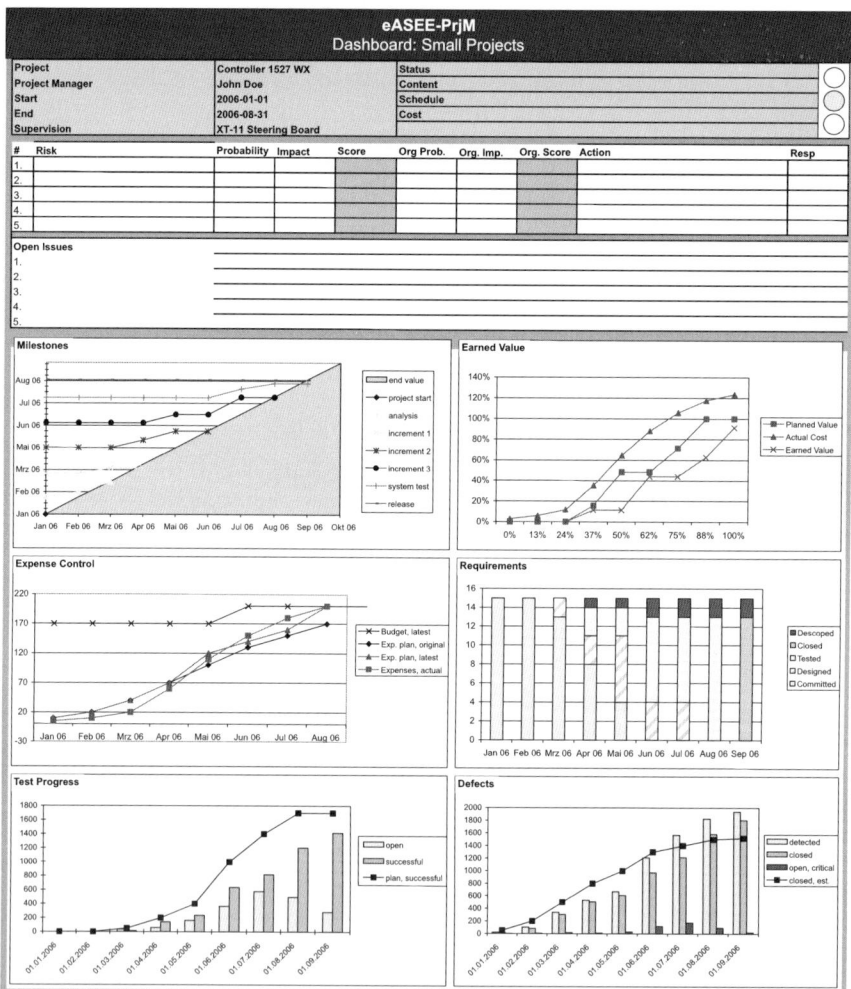

Fig. 8.7. A tailorable project dashboard view with eASEE combining the most relevant information

Fig. 8.8 shows the navigation in the eASEE PLM tools suite starting from an entry level with selected projects or releases and then browsing to details such as release planning with requirements or defect tracking with different status information. Needless to say that such environments scale up with the number of projects and provide strong workflow management along the agreed product and project life-cycles.

> Effective project tracking and implementation of immediate corrective actions requires a strong project organization, not just a single project manager in front of classic line and command organizations.

As long as department heads and line managers interfere with project managers, decisions can be misleading or even contradictory. Frequent task and priority changes on the practitioner level with all related drawbacks are the consequence. Demotivation and inefficiency are the concrete results. A project or matrix organization with dedicated project teams clearly shows better performance than the classic line organization with far too much influence of department leaders.

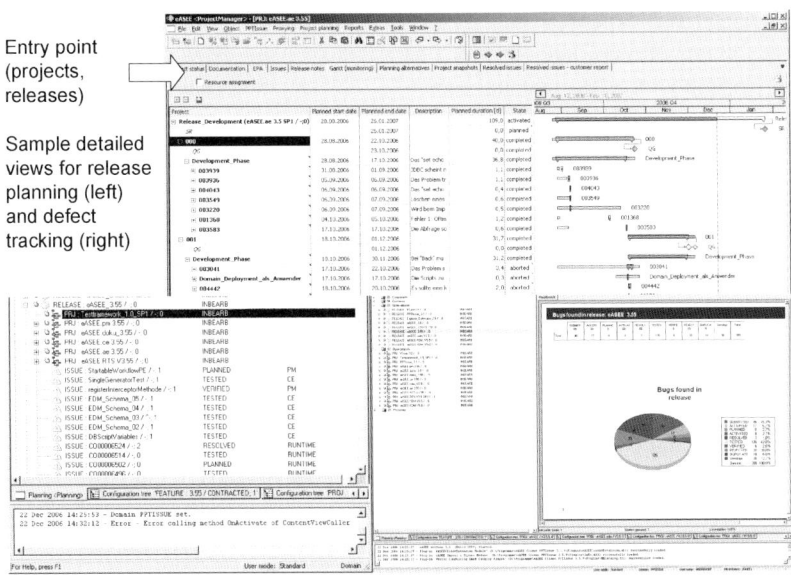

Entry point (projects, releases)

Sample detailed views for release planning (left) and defect tracking (right)

Fig. 8.8. Project planning and tracking with eASEE

Project managers must work based on defined roles and responsibilities. They are required to develop plans and objectives. Measurable performance and quality targets are defined within the project (quality) plans and later tracked through the entire project life-cycle. Project managers report project and quality progress using standardized reporting mechanisms, such as fault removal efficiency or progress against schedule in terms of deliverables (similar to the curves and completeness status in Fig. 8.4, Fig. 8.5, Fig. 8.6).

Committing to such targets and being forced to track them over the development process ensures that project managers and therefore the entire project organization carefully observe and implement process improvement activities.

Test tracking is a good example of how to make use of tracking measurements. Test results can be used to suggest an appropriate course of action to take either during testing activities or towards their completion. Based on a test plan all testing activities should be seen in the context of the full test schedule, rather than as independent actions. If the goal is, for instance, how well an integration test detects faults then models of both test progress and defects must be available. Information that supports interpretation (e.g., fault density per subsystem, relationships to feature stability) must be collected and integrated.

8.3.2 Earned Value Analysis

Often, projects are monitored primarily on the basis of expenses compared to planned cost. This however does not allow to easily forecast how the project is doing with respect to value and schedule. Fig. 8.9 shows this dilemma in project monitoring. The expenses sum up rather fast, however the delivered value increases comparatively late. In fact this value delivers depends very much how work packages are structured and how well they can be closed independently.

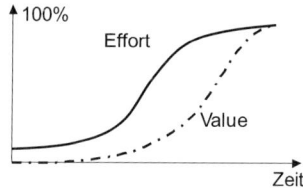

Fig. 8.9. Value-oriented progress tracking

Earned value analysis is a project monitoring technique that combines schedule performance and cost performance to address the question: "how much value die we get for the effort we spent?" The concept is detailed within the PMBOK [PMI04] and in standard project management literature [Burk03]. It is based on a few basic assumptions:
- All project steps (or work packages) "earn" value as work is completed.
- Progress of the project is measured as monetary value (e.g., Euros), so schedule performance and cost performance can be analyzed in the same terms.
- The Earned Value (EV) of these completed work packages can be compared to actual costs and planned costs to determine project performance and predict future performance trends.

As an example imagine a project planned with a budget of 25,000 € to be spent by today (Fig. 8.10; column called planned value). The actual expenses to date accumulate to 20,000 € (Fig. 8.10; column called actual cost). You present this progress in a project review and people would be initially delighted to see that to date you have spent only 80% of the planned resources. But they would ask immediately what you achieved with this money. After all, there could be the risk that

80% spent might already point to a delay. Looking to the completion of the 10 work packages planned to date, you admit that only one is finished. These percentages can be used to calculate what has actually been earned with the effort spent. You will find a meager 10,000 € of value generated (Fig. 8.10; column called earned value).

Date: TODAY	Planned Value	Actual Cost	Completion	Earned Value
Work Package 1	1.000 €	1.000 €	100%	1.000 €
Work Package 2	1.500 €	2.000 €	50%	750 €
Work Package 3	2.000 €	2.500 €	10%	200 €
Work Package 4	3.000 €	3.000 €	50%	1.500 €
Work Package 5	10.000 €	8.000 €	50%	5.000 €
Work Package 6	1.500 €	1.000 €	50%	750 €
Work Package 7	1.000 €	1.000 €	50%	500 €
Work Package 8	2.000 €	1.000 €	10%	200 €
Work Package 9	1.000 €	500 €	10%	100 €
Work Package 10	2.000 €	0 €	0%	0 €
Total	25.000 €	20.000 €		10.000 €

Completion of a work package: 100%: ready, 50%: in progress, 10%: started

Schedule variance = earned value - planned value	-15.000 €
Cost variance = earned value - actual cost	-10.000 €

Fig. 8.10. Example: Progress tracking in a project

It is common practice for tracking work packages to only consider three different values for completion, namely 10% for work that started, 50% for work in progress and 100% for work completed. This avoids the common trap of 90% complete which can take forever.

Comparing the earned value (i.e., what your project delivered so far on the basis of work packages) you find that only 40% of the planned work had been completed pointing towards a substantial delay, and the cost is 10,000 € more than what was expected. The project is late and has cost overrun.

> Earned value analysis is a project monitoring method as well as a forecasting approach. It is used to
> - Measure work accomplished
> - Quantify the impact of known issues (e.g., delays)
> - Use this data to forecast estimates at completion

In addition to more accurate project status assessment, the earned value analysis allows the project manager to analyze both schedule and cost performance in different ways. Using a limited set of basic work package information, it is possible not only to determine how a project has been performing, but also to predict future performance trends as well.

Our example project above shows expenses of 20,000 € to accomplish 10,000 € worth of work. If this trend continues, this project will cost 50,000 € to complete 25,000 € worth of work. The schedule variance is a little more complicated but suffice to say we are significantly behind schedule as we planned on doing 25,000 € worth of work and only 10,000 € of work was accomplished. We can say today we are 60% behind what we had planned to accomplish.

Another example shows how these techniques are used for a real project. Fig. 8.11 provides an outline of the finished project with 11 major work packages (left column). The project was planned to run between 01. January and 20. June. It actually finished on 31. August. The planned value (or budget) was 500,000 €. The actual cost accumulated to 695,000 €. The last two columns in the table show how cost variance and schedule variance evolved over time. Note that due to the delays of work packages, the earned value must be adjusted to the delays to allow a schedule performance index at any given moment. This picture is therefore not ideal to track variances and performance. It only provides the summary data after project closure. To monitor status at a given moment we recommend using a format like in Fig. 8.10 with individual tasks and their completion.

Earned Value Report							
Milestone WBS Element	Planned finish date	Achieved finish date	Planned value PV	Actual cost AC	Earned value EV	CV = (EV-AC)/EV	SV = (EV-PV)/PV
0. Start	1-Jan-06	1-Jan-06	0 €	0 €	0 €	0%	0%
1. Analysis	15-Jan-06	1-Mrz-06	50.000 €	105.000 €	50.000 €	-110%	-76%
2. Architecture design	7-Feb-06	28-Mrz-06	45.000 €	60.000 €	45.000 €	-74%	-57%
3. Stable build available	28-Feb-06	24-Apr-06	70.000 €	100.000 €	70.000 €	-61%	-49%
4. Increment 1	10-Mrz-06	10-Mai-06	55.000 €	85.000 €	55.000 €	-59%	-47%
5. Increment 2	27-Mrz-06	30-Mai-06	40.000 €	60.000 €	40.000 €	-58%	-43%
6. Increment 3	11-Apr-06	15-Jun-06	50.000 €	50.000 €	50.000 €	-48%	-39%
7. Increment 4	29-Apr-06	27-Jun-06	35.000 €	25.000 €	35.000 €	-41%	-33%
8. System test	6-Mai-06	10-Jul-06	40.000 €	65.000 €	40.000 €	-43%	-34%
9. Packaging / qualification	28-Mai-06	1-Aug-06	30.000 €	40.000 €	30.000 €	-42%	-31%
10. Limited release	1-Jun-06	10-Aug-06	40.000 €	60.000 €	40.000 €	-43%	-32%
11. General availability	20-Jun-06	31-Aug-06	45.000 €	45.000 €	45.000 €	-39%	-30%
Sum			500.000 €	695.000 €			

Fig. 8.11. Earned value analysis (example): Summary of raw data of finished project. Schedule delay is considered in comparing earned value and planned value at a given timestamp.

Fig. 8.12 brings this information into one chart which allows a graphical earned value analysis. The top line shows the planned value over time. Note that all the data is normalized to percentages to facilitate our comparing the values in a single chart. While actual cost is below the planned value, it continues to increase even after the planned end date (the 100% value for time) until the actual end date was reached.

Fig. 8.13 shows the same picture at the completion of increment 1. The cost variance at that moment was already -59% and the schedule variance was -47%. Both indicate the overruns at the project's end. In fact, the project manager knew about these issues from the very beginning of the mentioned project. The very first work package took far too long. Engineers seemingly did not get started with the project, maybe because requirements were not known or not sufficiently specified. He should have reacted much earlier. This early visibility and forecasting capacity shows the immense power of earned value analysis. The project manager can react much earlier and force changes to the project if it is obvious that he will not finish according to commitments.

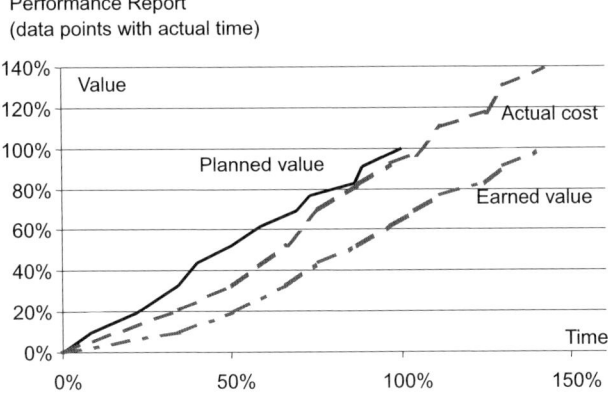

Fig. 8.12. Earned value analysis (example): Graphical format with planned value, actual cost and earned value

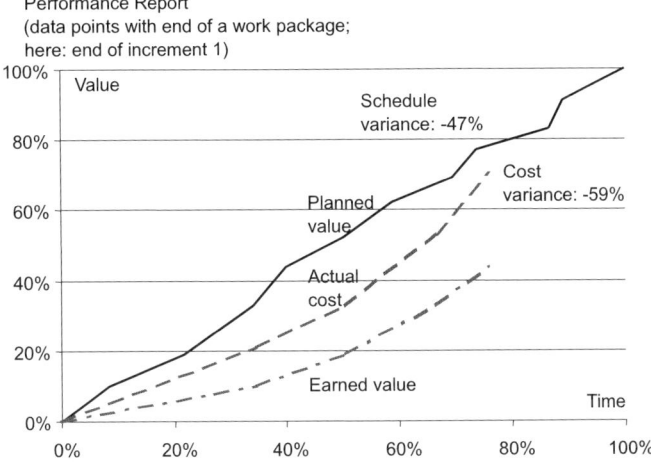

Fig. 8.13. Earned value analysis (example): Progress at the delivery of increment 1

A few indicators in fact allow analyzing project performance, namely:
- Cost variance (CV) is the algebraic difference between earned value (EV) and actual cost (AC). CV = EV - AC. A positive value indicates a favorable condition and a negative value indicates an unfavorable condition.

- The cost performance index (CPI) is the measurement of cost efficiency on a project. It is the ratio of earned value (EV) to actual costs (AC). CPI = EV / AC. A value equal to or greater than one indicates a favorable condition and a value less than one indicates an unfavorable condition.
- Schedule variance (SV) is defined as the algebraic difference between the earned value (EV) and the planned value (PV). SV = EV - PV.
- The schedule performance index (SPI) is a measurement of schedule efficiency on a project. It is the ratio of earned value (EV) to planned value (PV). The SPI = EV / PV. An SPI equal to or greater than 1 indicates a favorable condition and a value of less than 1 indicates an unfavorable condition.

If both SPI and CPI are greater than 1, i.e., the respective variance values are positive, the project is faster and cheaper than what was planned. This is a desirable state. If both SPI and CPI are below 1, i.e., the respective variance values are negative, the project will be delayed and cost more than what was planned. For CPI < 1 < SPI, the project will be faster than what was planned but at a higher cost. With SPI < 1 < CPI the project will be delayed but deliver below expected cost. These latter two scenarios are often used to adjust projects in case of strong demands to accelerate or deliver at lowest possible cost. They both mean to tweak the standard planning in order to achieve these changes.

Task or work package completion must relate to the actual value that stakeholders will see in the project. It is of not much use to introduce artificial work packages that are close to complete but will not show value. An example is the document progress, such as having specifications and architecture ready. Even if this is documented and reviewed with a lot of lead time and effort (see the example in Fig. 8.12) the progress in fact is close to zero.

We therefore recommend a few practical rules for task completion:

- Define project tasks and work packages as close as possible to the actually delivered value. Validated and integrated requirements are better than documents without clear marginal value. Incremental development with requirements mapped to work packages is certainly the best possible way of tracking earned value. Having completed requirements that relate to a tangible market or user value implies that progress has been achieved. This does not mean not to document your design or test. But it demands inserting or linking the document completion into the progress of the single requirement. The latter allows to trace each single fulfilled requirement to its related work products and make sure they are consistent and therefore delivering a progress in terms of the requirement.
- Avoid the *90% complete syndrome*. Ensure that tasks are only signed off as complete if they have no open issues. A 100% completion of a work package should indicate that the related requirements had been successfully implemented. Unfinished tasks should be "far away" from the 100%. We recommend using the value of 10% for work that just started in order to see those work packages on which engineers are currently working. Work in progress should not exceed the 50% value. These three values of 10%, 50% and 100% are sufficient for progress tracking. Do not go into more detail.

- When working incrementally with requirements as the basis for work packages, those requirements can be weighted with the actual value or priority they have for the product or for the market. This approach allows earned value analysis in terms of market value which is better than only linking it to the estimated effort.

A final word on all cost-based tracking schemes. You need to look at more than just the cost and quantity of outputs. Quality matters as well as environmental factors. If for instance the project is estimated conservatively, the earned value will almost certainly beat the planned value and actual cost. This however is pointless if down the road the product is overly expensive.

> A reminder in all this formal tracking of what is accomplished: In parallel to cost tracking and earned value analysis, you need to measure how work is done and not just what is completed. Combine your project measurements with insight into product and processes.

8.3.3 Measurements for Requirements

Properly expressed requirements form a high-level abstraction of the functional and non-functional behaviors of the product. Formalizing such a description helps in tracking progress at a level independent of any particular solution or component structure. Requirements measurement thus starts with a standardized specification that captures both the functional and non-functional content and the business reasoning.

> The basis for all requirements measurement (and thus project monitoring) is the set of formalized and baselined requirements which should at least provide a short description of content, a clear identification, the effort for implementing this requirement and the value it would deliver. Estimated effort and proposed value can be provided on an ordinary scale, i.e., with a simple 1-5 scale.

Fig. 8.14 shows an example how objective-driven requirements measurements are introduced following the E4–measurement process. We have selected two quite frequent objectives in order to show how requirements related measurements are established. On the left side, we see the objective of productivity improvement and on the right side the objective of improving schedule accuracy. These two objectives are further broken down into questions (following the GQM paradigm) which extract background information how the improvement objectives could be reached. From here we evaluate dedicated measurements depending on the detailed focus. Finally the execution step is pushing for concrete change and improvement which then should be measurable with the selected measurements.

Fig. 8.14. The E4–Measurement process for requirements management

Requirements are evaluated by different stakeholders (e.g., product manager, project manager, engineering, marketing, sales) to ensure that different perspectives are considered. Each single requirement must be justified to support the business case and to allow the managing of changes and priorities. Impact analysis is based on requirements, as well as priority setting and portfolio management. Often a business case is done and impact analysis is done for the entire project. If some requirements start changing later on, it is very difficult to assess what is necessary and what was a lower priority or maybe only an enhancement to existing features. Therefore the breakdown to individual requirements is the starting point.

Should requirements drive schedule and resource allocation? The clear answer is no.

> Products should be designed to value proposition, cost and schedule – not based on a set of requirements. After all, rarely a customer or market comes with a precise shopping list of features but with desires and ideas.

Requirements are evaluated – one by one – in line with these business needs, but should not drive them. Do not start with the long list of potential requirements but rather find out which few key requirements uniquely characterize the product (release). Evaluation looks into several dimensions: What are the requirements? How do they relate between markets and correlate with each other? What is their impact? What markets have asked for it and for what reason? Are they necessary for a solution or just inherited from an incumbent approach perhaps becoming obsolete in meantime? To address these questions requirements must be documented

8.3 Measurements for Project Control

in a structured and disciplined way. They must be expressed allowing both technical as well as business judgment. Any incoming requirement should be reviewed with the product catalogue and global product evolution in mind to also evaluate marginal value versus marginal costs. If changes cannot be met move them to the next release, instead of making the current project overly late and thus delay the entire roadmap.

There are risks and uncertainties, especially in very dynamic markets like software products and services. It is the product manager to anticipate risks and deal with uncertainty. Several techniques have been explained which of course depend on environmental constraints. A key success factor is to manage requirements with their underlying business case. Often we find a lack of commitment amongst stakeholders.

> To achieve commitment and shared objectives beyond engineering, we strongly recommend installing a product core team with product management, marketing (or sales) and engineering – lead by the product manager.

They use the product life-cycle and specific planning and tracking tools in order to ensure visibility, agreement and commitment as a team. By doing so, they reduce requirements changes and together with strong project management in this team of empowered stakeholder representatives improve predictions, schedule performance and quality at handover.

> Requirements almost by definition (because we talk about desires and ideas) are uncertain, sometimes vague, unclear and evolving, and therefore need to be tightly controlled in order to keep risks within accepted limits.

Fig. 8.15 shows how requirements change in a typical project. Before project start, the change rate is high, and the measurements should look towards stabilizing the key requirements so that the project can start with a defined baseline of requirements. Later there is a change rate of typically 1-3% per month (normalized to project effort) which of course in specific situations can be much higher [Eber06a]. This volatility has to be tracked to ensure that changes are mastered and that the point is communicated from which no changes are accepted anymore.

The goal is not to freeze requirements too early because this would reduce business opportunities. The goal is to know how much change can be coped with and then to manage that change professionally. A number of solid techniques exist to deal with requirements uncertainty and master project risks (e.g., prioritizing requirements and designing them according to value, time-boxing to ensure that high-priority requirements are developed first; see also the later chapters on risk management). They deal with requirements elicitation, communication, analysis and planning. Projects must be planned to handle risks coming from uncertain customer needs, supplier commitments or technology evolution. Prioritizing requirements and planning incremental stabilization, measured by the earned value achieved in the project is a key success factor.

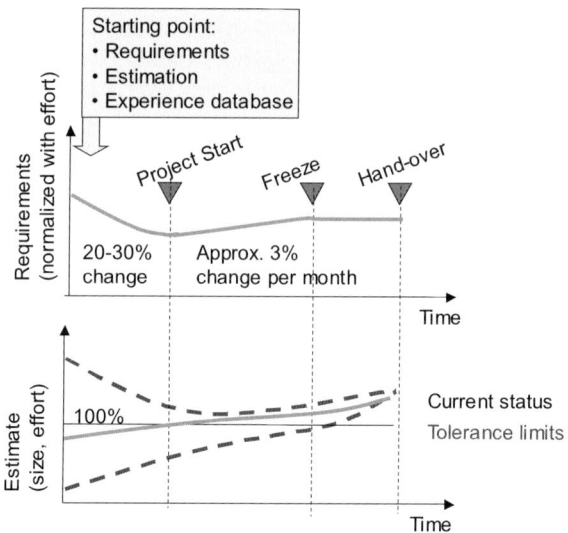

Fig. 8.15. Controlling requirements evolution during the project

Measuring requirements quality

A good requirement describes something (function, characteristic, attribute), that is valuable, verifiable and achievable. To measure requirements quality we must look into these three dimensions.

- **Valuable**: Typically we should ask at the beginning of requirements elicitation and analysis the following questions: What will happen if the requirement is not taken into account? What other requirements determine this requirement? What marginal utility does this requirement deliver? There is often no answer and the requirement can be deleted or prioritized. The related measurement should therefore always compare the proposed value of the requirement compared to its cost.
- **Verifiable**: When the requirement is documented it must be clear how it will be tested and accepted at a later stage. The related measurement looks into the percentage of requirements that have test cases associated.
- **Achievable**: Requirements must be technically feasible. They should not conflict with other requirements or constraints such as budget or handover date. The measurement provides the percentage of requirements that had been verified and signed off by all stakeholders. Do not start with requirements that have not yet been signed off.

Measuring requirement status and progress.

A few measurements are sufficient to manage requirements:
- Number of total requirements for the project. Typically this measurement indicates value and thus should be as close as possible to what is meaningful from a

customer perspective. To allow tracking of requirements, it might be helpful to weight the requirements according to priority, valuation, business case or similar. Weighting according to implementation effort is dangerous, because this is an internal view, and rarely customers pay for internal effort.
- Requirement status (e.g., analyzed, agreed, tested). Fig. 8.16 provides an example how this tracking can be easily achieved. Only three statuses are distinguished which is sufficient for most projects. The status information is derived directly from the requirements spreadsheet or database. The initial state is that the requirement is identified and elicited. The next state is that the requirements is agreed and committed for the project or release. The final state relates to successful integration or delivery of the requirement. This tracking sheet is much more powerful than many other project tracking mechanisms because it shows actual achieved value on the basis of integrated requirements.

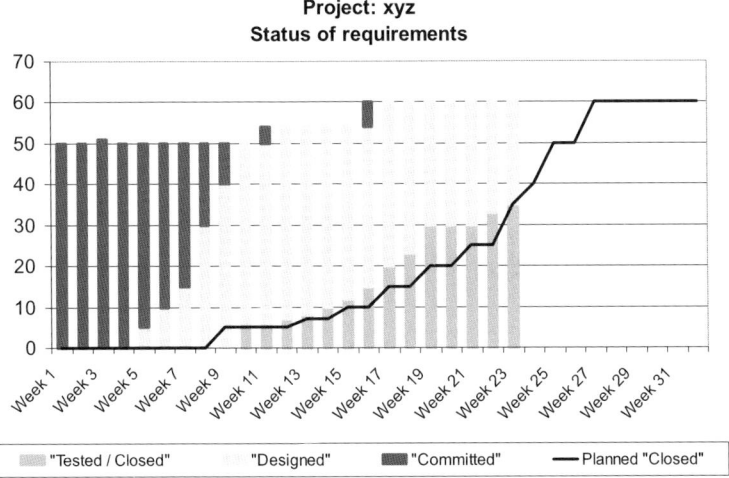

Fig. 8.16. Status tracking of requirements in a project

- Project progress (e.g., percentage of integrated requirements after successful test, earned value)
- Percentage of requirements changes after start of project. Some call this measurement "feature churn", but this name is misleading. "Feature" is a colorful word as it could mean an external or internal or combined view. This is typically pointless, because external value is what counts in requirements management. We should thus take the change of customer or system requirements to measure feature churn. To measure requirements change, you baseline requirements at project start and then measure change rate over time in terms of new, changed, deleted. The easiest is to simply add all those 3 factors and calculate it as a percentage of the original set of requirements. Note that a single requirement can change several times in the course of a project. If there are a hundred requirements and 5 are changing once and one additional requirement is chang-

ing five times, we have a total change rate of 10%. Depending on size, complexity and impact of requirements, weights should be put on the requirements because one single heavy requirement that is changing five times close to the end of the project obviously means more trouble than few low-priority small requirements each changing once at the beginning of the project. Fig. 8.17 provides an example from a project which had too many requirements changes and that was subsequently cancelled. Due to not measuring and evaluating requirements changes and their reasons during regular project reviews there was no visibility (and of course no action taken) until it was too late. The example shows that the problem was with changing customer needs. Most probably the project was started without clear understanding of what the market demands. In fact the causal analysis afterwards highlighted severe deficiencies in product management.

- Causes of changes in requirements
- Defect density in requirements
- Defect types in requirements (unclear, incorrect contents, and so on)

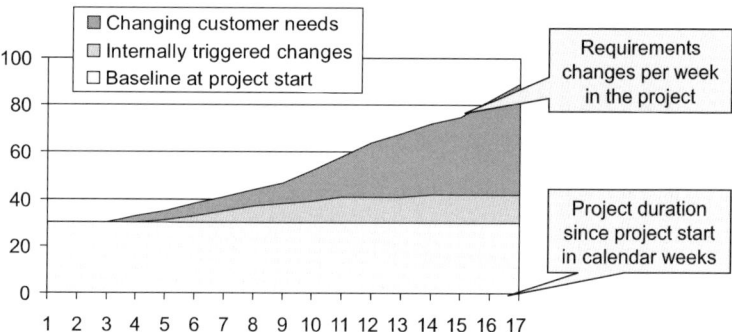

Fig. 8.17. Measuring the evolution of requirements

8.3.4 Measurements for Testing

In looking for optimized product development an organization needs to balance quality, cost and schedule. The key activity within the product life-cycle is testing! Typically testing consumes more than 40% of the resources and – depending on the project life-cycle (sequential or incremental) – a lead-time of 15-50% compared to total project duration. The minimum 15% lead-time is achieved when test strongly overlaps with development, such as in incremental development with a stable build which is continuously regression tested. In such case, there is only the system test at the end contributing to lead-time on the critical project path. On the other hand 50% (and more) stem from testing practiced in a classic waterfall approach with lots of overheads due to components that won't integrate.

The overall life-cycle cost of the product is further influenced by test in the cost of non-quality. The more defects are detected late, the higher the cost of non-quality. Defects released to the customer due to schedule pressure and shortened test could mean additional rework and maintenance releases. Obviously any organization trying to improve the cost, schedule and quality needs to optimize test activities against business objectives.

A test activity is typically planned (and executed) following an S-shaped curve (Fig. 8.18). The shape results from the difficulty of getting started which has a slow progress over time. When in steady progress mode, test cases are approached and successfully closed in a very predictable speed. Practically all testers have experiences on that speed and would for instance know whether they close 1 or 10 test cases per day. Finally, testing comes into saturation because fewer defects are found with the specific test strategy being applied to this test activity.

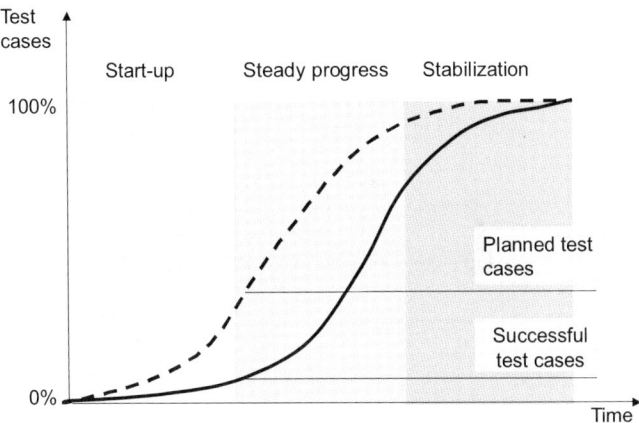

Fig. 8.18. Basic test planning and tracking based on test plans and progress

The speed and shape depends on several parameters:
- Test automation. If test is automated then progress will be faster compared to fully manually executed test cases. Projects with high repetition factor will have many reusable test cases which are running routinely to see the stability of the code basis. Their start-up will still be S-shaped, however speed can improve towards thousands of test cases per hour.
- Incremental project life-cycle. Typically code is developed by using an incremental approach with some architecture decisions taken in the beginning and then features implemented according to their value and architecture dependencies. The entry to the steady-progress phase can be accelerated if a stable code basis is available. In such case, the code basis will be taken and new or changed code is added stepwise. Previously running test cases are repeated to ensure a stable build with determined quality. Code which breaks the build is rejected and has to be improved to be tried again. This certainly is the optimal approach

to reducing testing cost and improving cycle time. It makes projects highly predictable, especially if the requirements with most value are available early.
• Sequential project life-cycle. A sequential life-cycle such as the waterfall model will create first the design and code and then start up with testing where different components are integrated. This approach especially applies towards integration projects, where different (mostly external) components are developed and then integrated to one specific customer solution. This approach will face a difficult to predict entry to the steady progress phase due to stabilization problems of the component assembly. Note that sequential life-cycles are still most popular in software and IT systems. While components are developed incrementally, the systems are integrated sequentially following the waterfall approach.

Test planning based on test cases alone makes no sense. After all, who decides how many test cases are necessary and when results are good enough? Test planning and tracking therefore must primarily monitor achieved quality. Fig. 8.19 shows such integrated test progress tracking combing the test cases with the defects. The thinner lines relate to test case planning and tracking, while the thicker lines relate to defect detection and removal.

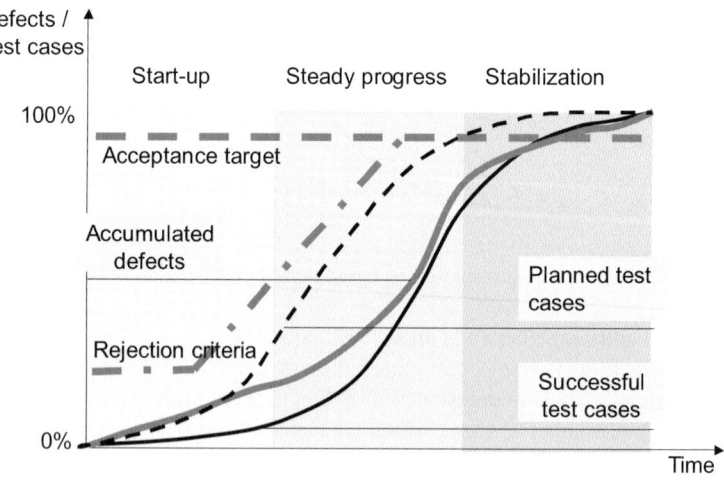

Fig. 8.19. Integrated test progress tracking looking at test cases and detected defects and various criteria for acceptance and rejection of the test object

Fig. 8.19 indicates that effective tracking combines original plans with actual evolution, outlooks, updated plans and decision guidance, such as curves for early rejection if delivered quality is below expectations. Such previously agreed-upon limits or boundaries avoid inefficient and time-consuming fights between departments when delivery occurred with unsatisfactory quality. Transparent decision criteria followed up with respective measurements certainly serve as a more effective decision support for management.

A major question for any project manager is how effective his test activities are. Test – though necessary to judge quality – essentially is a waste of resources, because the longer it takes the more value is destroyed. The project manager therefore tries to optimize test effectiveness (do the test activities find defects?) and efficiency (what is the cost per defect or per test case?). Besides the typical S-shaped appearance, several questions must be answered before being able to judge progress or efficiency. For example, how effectively was the specific test method applied? What is the coverage in terms of code, data relations or features during regression testing? How many faults occurred during similar projects with similar test case suites over time?

A final question to ask is about the optimal release timing. How stable is the system being tested? Fig. 8.20 shows a typical project situation with resource planning in the lower part and defects in the upper part. A reliability threshold (horizontal line) shows which level of defects over time are allowed in order to release the product. Such a line is typically determined by the project manager and product manager (or sales representative) by weighting customer (or market) needs with the cost to deliver and maintain such expectations. It will always be a trade-off because late delivery might improve quality but reduce the profit margins due to a shorter window of opportunity. On the other hand both insufficient quality and later delivery will dissatisfy clients. More test demands more effort (see the dark boxes in the picture) which eats the marginal value of the product.

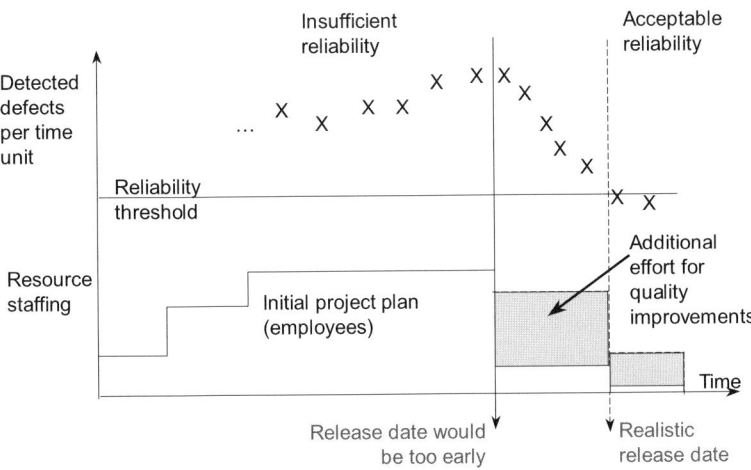

Fig. 8.20. Integrated test progress tracking looking to test cases and detected defects and various criteria for acceptance and rejection of the test object

Based on such a premise, it is feasible to set up not only release-oriented phase end targets but also phase entry criteria that allow for rejection to module testing or inspections if the system quality is inadequate. Related test process measurements include test coverage, number of open fault reports by severity, closure delay of fault reports, and other product-related quality, reliability and stability measurements. Such measurements allow judgments in situations when, because of difficulties in testing, decisions on the nature and sequence of alternative paths through the testing task should be made, while considering both the entire testing plan and the present project priorities. For example, there are circumstances in which full testing of a limited set of features will be preferred to an incomplete level of testing across full (contracted) functionality.

What are typical measurements used for testing? We distinguish different categories of topics being addressed by testing and thus being relevant for the project manager to know and to control.

Test planning and test strategy
Appropriate test approaches are selected depending on effort and cost per defect and other efficiency measurements. Typically test execution runs into a saturation as we have seen in Fig. 8.19. Different test approaches are therefore combined starting with unit test and moving to feature test, integration test and finally system test. Additional test activities include qualification test and acceptance test. Test automation is judged in comparing the total cost of testing given that the goal of test is to achieve distinct release criteria. Automation typically costs more during preparation, test set-up and configuration and maintenance of test cases. It saves effort in execution. Ensure that you compare apples and apples when judging the business case of test automation.

Test progress
Test progress is tracked by comparing planned test cases and planned defect detection with reality (see also Fig. 8.19). Efficiency in terms of cost or effort per test case and per defect is compared with the planning parameters. This is when the project manager has to be alerted if too much time is used to detect defects (is the system highly unstable or is the quality already better than assumed?) or if defect detection is not moving towards more stability (are too many new defects inserted or is the system highly unstable and would be better move backwards towards code verification activities?).

Test effectiveness
Effectiveness will establish how many defects are detected by different test strategies. If for instance black box testing stagnates at a low effectiveness and efficiency, the project manager might decide to move backwards to white box testing and try to find out code segments with insufficient quality. Test coverage measurements are used to judge progress in terms of code (white box coverage criteria) or functionality (black box coverage criteria). There are different such coverage measurements being used in practice (see also Chap. 9). C0 coverage is the most frequent coverage measurement. It relates test progress towards the coverage of all executable source code. 100% would mean that all statements have at least passed one test case. Typically, projects target beyond 90%, where it can well happen that

100% is not reachable due to design reasons. C1 coverage measures how many paths or segments of the code are hit by test cases. C1 coverage should be well beyond 70% to have covered the most frequently used paths executed by test cases. A warning on coverage measurement: It needs instrumentation of the code which impacts timing behaviors. Real-time systems need dedicated instrumentation to get an idea about coverage.

Product or component release
Instead of looking at individual defects and how they are distributed across the system and its various architectural entities, release is determined based ion overall quality. Defects are only grouped into severities which are compared over execution time with the allowed margins. To judge the optimal release date, the project manager together with his test engineers has to ensure that the right usage profile is being tested based on operational scenarios which had been determined during requirements analysis. It is of no value to waste test effort on a high white box coverage, while a majority of issues and risk would be centered in one component.

Test improvement
The test activity needs improvement based on lessons learned from each project. The typical indicators are effectiveness and efficiency of each single test activity. The baseline against which all test activities are compared is the code review due to its low cost per defect removal. If test cases have overly low effectiveness, test cases and the coverage criteria need to be improved. If the cost per defect is too high, maybe there are too many test cases which overlap or the system is not robust enough to be tested with the respective strategy. It is helpful to benchmark across projects and products (and even across companies or product lines within the same company) to learn about how others are doing and maybe share best practices.

In determining which test cases should be chosen and thus improving the test strategy it should be noted that defects are not distributed equally across code. We found two relevant parameters to be considered, namely criticality of code segments and their complexity.

As a rule of thumb you can assume that 70% of defects are clustered within 30% of code – which is critical or complex. Focus your attention on these complex parts with high defect densities.

Criticality determines those code segments which have key functionality related towards successful customer business case performance. In a communication system it is billing. In a gaming console it is graphics performance. Critical components or segments need to be tested more thoroughly than others. Complexity relates to the "artificial" attributes that make code or designs error-prone. Complex structures are difficult to design and verify because hardly anybody really understands them. We find such overly complex code segments often in code which had been changed frequently by different people. Defects tend to cluster in these complex segments. Once you start detecting defects it might be smart to test the neighborhood of that code, especially if it lies within a critical area.

A major project risk is that testing is insufficiently planned and later poorly executed. This sounds as if everything in testing is done wrong. But remember that testing typically consumes 30-40% (and more) of the resources and therefore poor planning and execution will have dramatic impacts on project performance. Typical failure points are that test is started with instable and premature code, rather than introducing quality gates which any code has to pass before being added to the build (so-called smoke tests). Test cases are selected on the basis of what was used in the past or what are the required functionalities, rather than determining critical functionality and misuse cases to select appropriate test cases. How do you defend your test plan and schedule if you do not have measurements at hand for coverage, efficiency and effectiveness which justify your test planning. How would you improve test and reduce project cost if there are no measurements on test effectiveness based on residual defects after test.

> It is business-critical to reduce your test expenses by a certain percentage per year in order to boost productivity. Saved test effort directly impacts your bottom line as long as your early defect removal and defect avoidance grow at the same speed. It is smart to so only on the basis of solid measurement and thorough understanding of defect distribution.

Often testing has lousy progress and due to schedule needs it is cut short – both adding to insufficient quality after release. This chapter has shown a variety of measurement-driven techniques to improve your testing activities.

8.4. Agile Projects and Lean Measurement

With the everlasting pressure to deliver more in less time to markets with volatile needs, development processes during the past years adapted to a more agile approach. The underlying paradigms for agile project management can be summarized as follows [Soft05, Beck00, Cock02, Schw04]:
- Human-centric working
- Small teams, preferably at one place
- Coping with fast changing requirements and goals
- Continuous communication with the customer
- Simple, minimalistic design and code
- Fast turn-around for new or changing code and features
- Proactive, risk-oriented management

Most of these principles are best practices for any development project and known for a long time – regardless of whether or not they are called "agile development." Especially the focus on requirements and small increments which show the earned value of the project at any time make lots of sense and had been emphasized in this book repeatedly. Other principles are more difficult to implement and thus point to the fine line between rigorous agility and intelligent agility. For instance, the customer is not always interested of being on board – even if he is aware, that he does not know the requirements to the product, he demands. But such a customer expects that the supplier is able to deliver according to the needs. Insisting on planning games and continuous change reviews with the customer, as is demanded in extreme programming does not make much sense [Beck00]. The same holds for simple, minimalistic design and code. While it is appropriate for internet software, most other software projects (e.g., embedded software with a life-time of several years or decades) will have difficulties with the mentality that "the code is the design" [Beck00, Cock04]. We will later explain how appropriate – or intelligent – agile practices are best used for successfully managing projects and how this would be measured without overhead.

The more a project moves towards incremental development the more of the total project effort is spent on management activities (see Table 8.2). This sounds like a paradox, given that agility is supposed to reduce overheads. However, we talk here only about the shares of effort. The total effort for doing the same is typically lower in an incremental set-up. Management tasks as referred to in the table should also be seen in light of the decentral approach. Autonomous feature teams need some synchronization and internal planning which contributes to project management effort.

Table 8.2. Effort distribution of projects following sequential and incremental paradigms

Project activities	Sequential approach (e.g., conventional waterfall, big iterations)	Incremental approach (e.g., agile, small features being continuously integrated)
Management activities (project management, quality management)	5%	10%
Infrastructure management	5%	10%
Requirements management	5%	10%
Design	10%	15%
Construction (incl. reviews and unit test)	30%	25%
Test	40%	25%
Transition, deployment	5%	5%
Sum	100%	100%

Agile projects are relatively straightforward for measurement. They give excellent visibility on progress – much better than those projects with big increments. The more a project plans according to single requirements, the easier it is to track. Good project management – and this holds regardless of how the project is set up – should ensure that all of the project's activities and work products should stay aligned with the requirements. If they are not aligned this should be fixed – at any time. If they are aligned and a requirement changes, it is time to realign.

> All your planning and engineering should be continuously aligned with the actual committed set of requirements!

To ease project management, some activities are only done if "trigger events" point to risks, deviations or challenges. For instance a project manager would check requirements traceability (or for that matter consistency with downstream work products) only if there is a change to requirements – not maintaining traceability per se. The same holds even for project reviews which are only triggered if projects reach out-of-boundary criteria. Otherwise project tracking is done electronically to have records and see evolution. The only meeting typically is the daily Scrum which facilitates a fast round of status and daily work plan.

With this alignment of all project contents with requirements a **lean measurement set for agile projects looks as follows**.

Progress
Project progress in agile projects is directly derived from integrated requirements. All code is linked to requirements. Once the code of a specific requirement is unit tested and inserted to the continuous build, this requirement would be checked as "closed" or "tested", and the progress would move one step forward. This step can be linear (one step per requirement) or weighted by the value of the requirement.

Quality
The single most useful quality measurement in agile projects is the defect rate during regression test of the continuous build. Assuming that each night regression test is running, the quality level can be derived from the number of successful test cases. A second quality measurement is code coverage with successful unit test cases. With these two measurements which can be both easily automated, you have sufficient insight into achieved quality.

Project management
As in all projects, software project management quality is measured with schedule and budget adherence. Schedule adherence is the ratio of overrun in schedule compared to committed schedule (e.g., two weeks overrun in a ten-week projects means 120% total duration or 20% overrun). The same formula is used for budget overrun. The target is to deliver within a defined interval of schedule and budget deviation. If engineers claim that delays and overruns were caused by too much requirements changes, then a third measurement is necessary, namely requirements volatility. This is the ratio of new and changed requirements divided by the number of all requirements. Targets should be determined from market and customer needs.

Business success
The success of the project is determined by the market. The standard measurement for business success is the business case accuracy. It is calculated as the ratio of achieved value by forecasted value (e.g., if the requirements were assumed to gen-

erate a first year revenue of 100 K€ and finally deliver after one year only 80 K€, the business success is only 80%). Different types of mapping are feasible, such as looking to the benefit (i.e., revenues minus cost) and relate that towards what was predicted.

Agile projects allow us to detect issues and remove them faster. Fig. 8.21 shows an example which we found in our own agile projects when comparing the same project type and contents done with agile project life-cycle or done with sequential development. The defect curve increases almost linearly in the agile approach, while for a sequential development with late validation activities, visibility is limited. In the extreme of a pure waterfall, it is hard to see any progress until the last 20-30% of project time – which is definitely not enough to adequately manage a project.

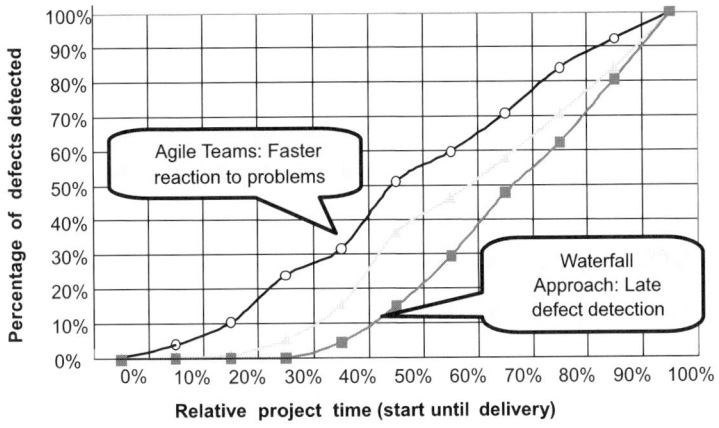

Fig. 8.21. Agile development accelerates reaction time in projects

When working agile it is important to not try to reinvent all development practices but rather to cut out overheads.

> Many engineers or organizations who claim that *processes* are heavy and create bureaucracy and overheads typically mean that *their own specific* processes are old-fashioned and dysfunctional. Process per se is not heavy or agile. It is the way you are doing things – and it should be the best possible way.

Looking into such behaviors frequently showed us in our consulting activities with many companies that there are lots of unnecessary documents and tasks which can easily be carved out with an immediate improvement of cost and cycle time.

> Agile development is not about rigorous and bureaucratic versus lean and simple, but rather about selecting and implementing the most efficient and suitable process for a given scenario.

This was underlined in several studies which investigated the usage of so-called agile methods and paradigms [Hans06]. These surveys show that software companies typically are adapting their own processes very much to needs – rather than pursuing a defined set of practices such as those in extreme Programming. If the requirements are flexible and highly volatile practically all companies use respective life-cycles and development methods that range from incremental to explorative design. If a customer is available for direct interaction, this is used – if the risk of too much day-to-day interaction is not getting too high.

On the other hand, companies also are aware that some mandated agile principles can cause confusion or unnecessary challenges to a project. If a customer is not interested in participating despite all the perceived benefits, than a proxy (such as marketing or sales) must serve this need. If deadlines are critical, a 40-hour week as demanded by extreme programming makes no sense. If the development is distributed across time-zones than an overly light-weight design approach creates too much rework and the design will be the design rather than only the code. Each of the agile paradigms and requested methods has somewhere limits of applicability – and this is utilized in modern software engineering. Being rigorous with agility just because it is written in theoretical books showing toy examples is of no business value. True agile projects need rigor in micro-planning and team planning and for that matter reliable processes. The measurements which we described here for agile project management are capable to help in agile projects of any type – and they can scale up from the small 5-person collocated team to the distributed offshore development in an 18-month project.

8.5. Risk Management

What if the quality of the software in our airplanes or automobiles would be as poor as many desktop and office applications? What if the medical systems that control life support or radiation devices would be on the same quality level as what we are used to from operating systems and office software? What if our internet portal or that of our bank would be as bad as …? We all had at moments panicked on such thoughts knowing exactly how lousy most of the software is with which we have to deal. Each year over a billion US$ are sunk with delayed, canceled or dysfunctional software [Char05]. This does not seem a lot given the overall amount of software revenues per year, but still it could be your project or the airplane you are currently sitting in.

Software can be late, have defects, and cause your product screw up. No doubt on that. The difficulty here is that we do not know for sure where we are. There a so many uncertainties in the entire software project and life-cycle that it is hard to judge what the impacts are.

8.5 Risk Management

This is where risk management and measurement come into the picture. Simply speaking a risk describes an event with consequences. Consequences could be positive but western tradition typically portrays risks as something negative. We can therefore precise our definition and state that a risk is the function of a probability of an undesired event and the size or impact of its outcome. Mostly a risk is defined as the product of the probability of an event and the outcome.

Fig. 8.22 shows this calculation with a small example. There is the risk (right side) of a 10 person week rework which will occur with the probability of 30%. This gives an exposure of 3 person weeks per project in average. Alternatively this event can be mitigated (left side) by spending in each project an additional person week. Since this is done in each project, its "probability" is 100% and therefore the exposure 1 person week. Comparing these two possible outcomes, we see that there is a clear ROI, even if additional opportunistic cost is neglected. This looks like mathematics and indeed we need to understand a bit of statistics to professionally understand and manage risks.

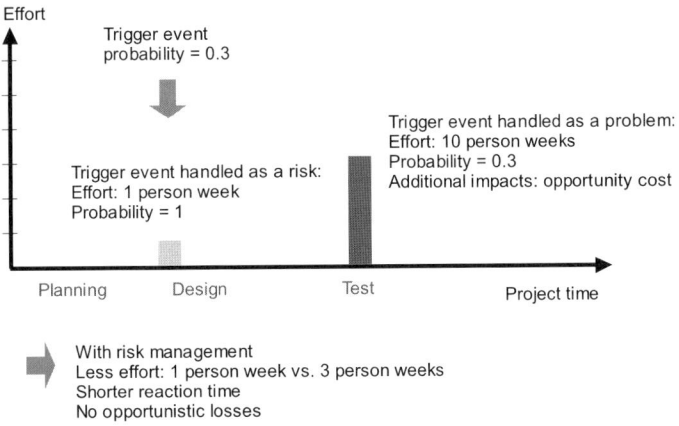

Fig. 8.22. Risks and risk management

The word "**professional**" is a key word in risk management. Customers expect the software product to be fit for purpose. If not they might sue you for a variety of reasons. Laws like product liability were created to protect the customer and are today used to sue suppliers if their products are not fit for purpose. Most of these laws demand that **state-of-the-practice techniques** be used for engineering and managing the software. Knowing and using such techniques is what is also labeled professional. Other laws look into the financial health of companies and try to protect banks and other sources of money. The Sarbanes-Oxley Act and other related laws demand that risks are professionally managed. They expect visibility, control and clear responsibilities. An example is that you as a senior executive of such company need to know about risks and how they are managed. These risks in a software or IT company include insufficient quality or delays because both will impact income which has immediate consequences on shareholders. These two examples underline that risk management in software and IT projects have to be taken seriously.

> Risk management is the systematic application of management policies, procedures and practices to the tasks of identifying, analyzing, evaluating, treating and monitoring risk.

Risk management evaluates the effects of today decisions on the future. Is used in project management, product management and portfolio management. It is not the problem management after a risk had materialized. The CMMI specifies: "The purpose of Risk Management is to identify potential problems before they occur, so that risk-handling activities may be planned and invoked as needed across the life of the product or project to mitigate adverse impacts on achieving objectives." [Chri06].

What are the risks you need to look into? Essentially it is all with negative impact on your business. A risk could be that you have unexpectedly high cost or revenues below expectations. These risks are triggered by numerous sources, so we will walk a little bit backwards. What could cause unexpected cost or reduced revenues? For most projects and products these trigger events could be along the following lines:

- Trigger event: Project is late. Consequence: Unexpected cost and reduced revenues.
- Trigger event: Project is over budget. Consequence: Unexpected cost.
- Trigger event: Product has insufficient quality. Consequence: Unexpected cost or reduced revenues.
- Trigger event: Initial market and business case assumptions do not hold in reality. Consequence: Reduced revenues.

The problem with risk management especially in the world of software is that too often we do not work professionally. Here are few examples that could immediately backfire:

- Projects are started without clear understanding of their objectives, contents and constraints.
- Requirements are insufficiently specified and change continuously.
- The real heroes and thus people to be promoted are those that first set fire due to ad-hoc management and then help to fight the fires they set.
- Projects are not systematically planned and managed.

Imagine any of these examples in other risk business such as medicine or aviation. Would you go into a surgery if the objectives and constraints were unclear? Would we like to have a pilot who never looks at his dashboard and instead tries to fly higher than any pilot before him? We try to avoid that. Yet, we do not hesitate to use software which is build on top of such malpractices. Lawyers start understanding this and increasingly use product liability and shareholder protection laws to sue software and IT companies. Where there is no risk management, a company will have difficulties to defend their case.

What can we learn from these other high-risk businesses? First they always base their projects on repeatable factors and well-funded estimates. Then, they plan and track deliverables and base progress on what had been agreed as deliverables and value. An activity is only started after checks had been thoroughly performed. Controlling instruments and measurements are used extensively to determine the current position against what is planned and to implement focused corrective actions where appropriate.

Fig. 8.22 helps us understand several aspects of measurement and risk management. First the two input factors need to be known. Probability and outcome need to be quantified. We recommend using a simple scale such as an ordinary scale to avoid dealing with unnecessary precision. For instance if a supplier is late it will not matter for practical risk management whether he is late with a probability of 20% or 30%. Use for both factors scales from 1-5 to simplify the initial risk analysis. This will give you a range of 25 possible risk values which is sufficient to sort risks. Only in a second step when you determine more precisely the risks and exposures for the top five or top ten risks (never more!), you should move towards real cost or delays to characterize the outcome. Together with a probability you can easily calculate the exposure in a currency or time unit.

An example for using such risk analysis in a real project situation is provided in Fig. 8.23. It shows a typical project control question related to managing project risks. Time is running, and the project manager wonders whether he should still spend extra effort on regression testing of some late deliveries. Naturally this can and must be decided based on facts. There are two alternatives, namely doing regression test or not doing it. Each alternative can have three possible outcomes, namely that a critical defect is detected by regression test, a critical defect would be found by the customer, and that there is no critical defect remaining. The respective probabilities are different and are illustrated in the figure. Clearly the probability of detecting a critical defect when no regression test is run is small compared to the scenario with regression testing. If the probabilities are mapped to the expected outcome or loss (or cost of the outcome), one can calculate a forecasted risk value. The decision is finally rather simple to make, given the big differences in the accumulated cost (or risk) functions.

Project assumptions are mostly uncertain, especially when it comes to requirements and estimation. Risk management helps in setting up meaningful plans. Let us assume you are the product manager or sales person who needs some insight into the next project and its schedule. It is November and the project should start on 01. January. You pass the requirements and constraints to your development team and receive the following feedback from the designated project manager: "before May it is impossible", "if all runs well the second quarter should be feasible" and "for July / August timeframe there is a realistic chance for delivery." You are a bit worried with all this insecurity and fuzziness and ask the project manager when it will be ready for sure (the upper estimation limit). The reply is – as you were probably afraid already: "you have to wait until March the year after to be really sure." No doubt this includes a lot of margin, but what can you do?

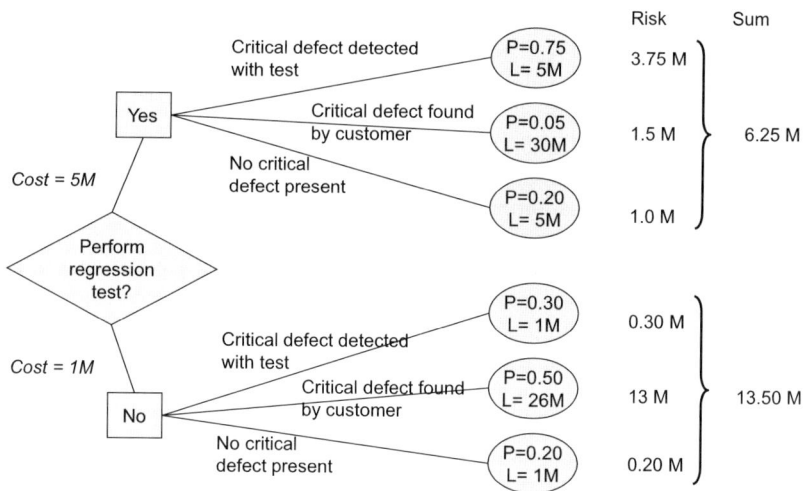

Fig. 8.23. Practical risk management: Should regression test be performed or can the effort be saved?

Since this is a normal reaction of a project manager when asked such question, there are techniques to deal with it. As a product manager the normal approach is to first ensure that the guesses are in an acceptable limit. If that is confirmed you use the rule of thumb for estimations, namely

Estimated value = (lower limit + 4 x most realistic value + upper limit) / 6

In above example this yields the timeframe of end August

Risk managers sit down and approach the uncertainty graphically to get a picture of probability [Chap03]. Fig. 8.24 shows this approach. The upper curve shows the probability density and the lower curve the probability of finishing at a given date. With this picture you avoid the common trap in which most of your colleagues will run, namely to use the date of May because that is seemingly the first which looks "realistic." The curve will show you that in fact for May the probability is zero, and even for July it is still way below 50%. That means if you chose August to commit to your client, he would not see anything in one out of two cases. That is bad for a lasting customer relationship – except it should be resolved in court.

The curve allows another judgment which we call the uncertainty width. It is the ratio of the uncertain range and the impossible range. In our example this would be 10 months / 5 months = 2.0. Typically, you would expect for simple projects such an uncertainty width of 0.2. A normal risk should be well below 1.0. And high-risk projects are > 1.5. A value of 2.0 immediately shows that either the requirements are highly unclear (which is your fault) or the project management processes are very immature (ask for the maturity level).

8.5 Risk Management 237

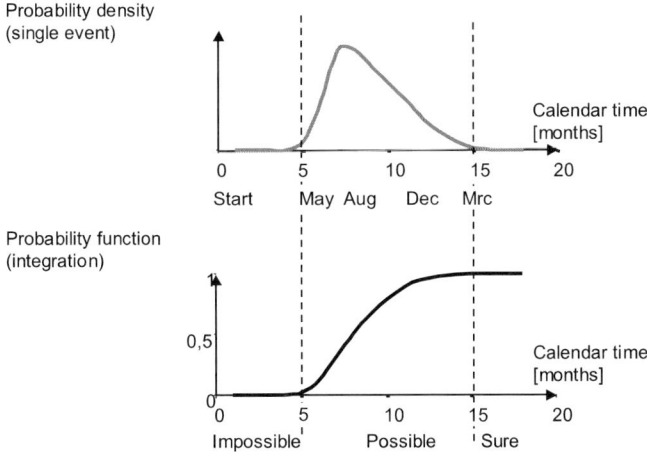

Fig. 8.24. Project uncertainties and how to practically cope with them

After you have clarified this initial picture and have asked for a more thorough requirements analysis you demand from the project manager again an assessment of the project feasibility. This time he is in a much better shape and immediately comes back with his measurement database where similar projects are stored. Fig. 8.25 shows how such feasibility analysis looks like.

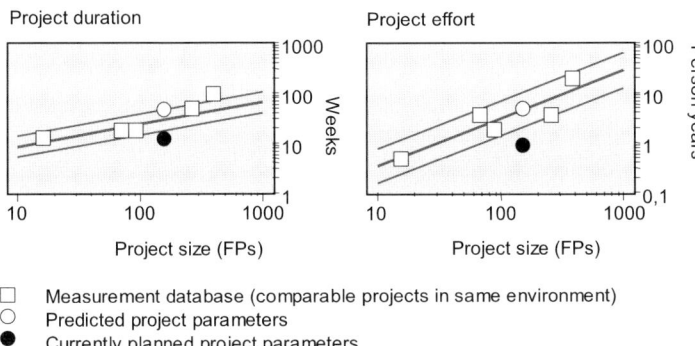

Fig. 8.25. Using the measurement database to assess the feasibility of a project

The size seemingly is 35 function points (or 4 KLOC in C language). While the project manager demands some 50 weeks lead-time, your proposal to the customer with 3 months was far too optimistic. The same is true for the effort which you overly optimistically assumed as 1 person year, while the history database points in the direction of 6 person years. This approach is very helpful before impossible commitments are made. To our experience both product managers and project managers like such studies because this takes out feelings and guesses and allows

238   8 Project Management

to "play" with constraints (such as staffing, duration or content) in order to identify win-win-situations with customers.

To complement regular project monitoring we recommend using a few selected risk indicators depending on the currently active project activities (see Table 8.3). These risk indicators highlight if trigger events for new risks occur. For instance during test the risk indicators look into residual defects or reliability prediction which both determine when the product can be released.

Table 8.3. Risk tracking and risk indicators

Project phase	Risk monitoring	New risk indicators
Project management	Project progress (earned value, completeness and coverage of requirements, risk status), availability of skilled resources, supplier SLA performance, supplier	Effort and budget expenses against planning, earned value
Quality management	Quality progress (stability of components, open defects, quality audits)	Residual defects, incoming field defects, customer satisfaction
Requirements management	Analysis progress (specifications, test strategy generation)	Availability of all requirements, requirement volatility
Construction	Design progress (documents, code, verification, efficiency, detected defects)	Development effort compared to plan, cost to complete, current delays, achieved quality level
Test	Test progress (effort, coverage, efficiency, detected defects, closed defects)	Residual defects, reliability, cost to complete, time to complete
Transition, deployment	Field performance (defects, corrections, outages, downtime, maintenance and service cost)	Residual defects, reliability

8.6. The Project Outlook: Forecasts and Predictions

While measurement-based decision making is more accurate and reproducible for managing software projects than intuitive and ad hoc approaches, it should be clear that there will always be components of uncertainty that ask for dedicated techniques of forecasting:
- Requirements are volatile in order to achieve shorter lead times and faster reaction to changing markets. The risk is that the project is built on a moving baseline which is one of the most often-quoted reasons for project failure.
- Plans are based on average performance indicators and historical data. The smaller the project and the more the critical paths that are established due to requested expert knowledge, the higher the risk of having a reasonable plan from a macroscopic viewpoint that never achieves the targets on the microscopic level of individual experts' availability, effectiveness and skills. It was shown

in several studies that individual experience and performance contributes up to 70% to overall productivity ranges (see Chaps. 2 and 10) [Hump89, Jone01].
- Estimations are based on individual judgment and as such are highly subjective. Any estimation model expresses first the experience and judgment of the assigned expert. Even simple models such as function points are reported as yielding reproducibility inaccuracy of >30% [Fent97, Jone01]. To reduce the risk related to decision making based on such estimates a Delphi-style approach can be applied that focuses multiple expert inputs to one estimate.
- Most reported software measurements are based on manual input of the raw data to operational databases. Faults, changes, effort, even the task break down are recorded by individuals that often do not necessarily care for such things, especially when it comes to delivery and time pressure. Software measurements, even if perceived as accurate (after all, they are numbers), must be related to a certain number of error limits which as experience shows is in the range of 10–20% [Fent97, Jone01].
- Earned value based techniques might change with requirements being taken out of the package or market value of requirements (or increments) being changed.

Forecasts are today an inherent part of any project control. Traditional project tracking looked to actual results against plans, where the plans would be adjusted after the facts indicate that they are not reachable. This method creates too many delays and is not sufficiently precise to drive concrete corrective actions on the spot. Therefore, predictions are used to relate actual constraints and performance to historical performance results.

Table 8.4 gives an overview on the use of measurements for forecasting. It is important to note that typically the very same underlying raw data is used for both tracking current performance and predicting future results. For instance, for the project management activities, effort and budget are tracked as well as requirements status and task or increment status. This information can also be used to determine risk exposure or cost to complete which relates to forecasting. The same holds for the other phases. In particular, defects and test tracking have a long tradition in forecasting a variety of performance parameters, such as maintenance cost of customer satisfaction.

Good forecasts allow adjusting plans and mitigating risks long before the actual performance monitoring measurements visualize such results. For instance, knowing the average mean time to defect allows planning for maintenance staff, help desk and support centers, or service level agreements.

Table 8.4. Measurements are selected based on the objective and suitability to the respective project phase. Measurements of status (progress) are distinguished from forecasting measurements (outlook).

Project phase	Project progress measurements	Measurements for predictions/outlook
Project management	Effort and budget tracking; requirements status; task/increment status, earned value	Top ten risks and mitigation outlook; cost to complete; schedule evolution, earned

		value
Quality management	Code stability; open defects; in-process checks; review status and follow-up	Residual defects; open defects; reliability; customer satisfaction
Requirements management	Analysis status; specification progress, earned value	Requirements volatility/completeness, earned value
Construction	Status of documents, code, change requests; review status; efficiency	Design progress of requirements; cost to complete; time to complete
Test	Test progress (defects, coverage, efficiency, stability)	Residual defects; reliability; cost to complete
Transition, deployment	Field performance (failures, corrections); maintenance effort	Reliability; maintenance effort

8.7. Hints for the Practitioner

Define project tasks and work packages as closely as possible to the actually delivered value. Validated and integrated requirements are better than documents. Incremental development with requirements mapped to work packages is certainly the best possible way of tracking earned value. This does not mean not to document the design, but it demands inserting the document completion into the progress of the single requirement.

Plan projects based on work breakdown and with actual skills. Plans are based on average performance indicators and historical data. The smaller the project and the more the critical paths are established due to requested expert knowledge, the higher the risk of having a reasonable plan from a macroscopic viewpoint that never achieves the targets on the microscopic level of individual experts' availability, effectiveness and skills. It was shown in several studies that individual experience and performance contributes up to 70% to overall productivity ranges [Jone01, McCo03].

Avoid the 90% complete syndrome. Ensure that tasks are only signed off as complete if they have no open issues. A 100% completion of a work package should indicate that the related requirements had been successfully implemented. Unfinished tasks should be "far away" from the 100%. We recommend using the value of 10% for work that just started in order to see those work packages on which engineers are currently working. Work in progress should not exceed the 50% value. These three values of 10%, 50% and 100% are sufficient for progress tracking. Do not go into more detail.

Measure on the basis of project requirements. Requirements are the cornerstone of any project. They speak the voice of the customer and thus can be communicated to your management. The most effective measurement is the simple status tracking of requirements as it was introduced in Fig. 8.16. Project progress exists only in the eyes of the stakeholders. The most relevant indicator is the percentage of already integrated requirements. Try to time-box and work incrementally so that the most relevant requirements are implanted and "closed" first. Ensure in the project that development effort is never spent on requirements that are not yet agreed and committed. Make sure that your engineers know that rule. Another important measurement is the change rate of requirements. Too many changes mean that the project is out of control. Determine breakpoints that alert you that the change rate in a given project phase are exorbitantly.

Verify estimates and perform a feasibility analysis. Estimations are based on individual judgment and as such are highly subjective. Any estimation model expresses first the experience and judgment of the assigned expert. Even simple models such as function points are reported as yielding reproducibility inaccuracy of greater than 30% [Jone01]. To reduce the risk related to decision-making based on such estimates a Delphi-style approach can be applied that focuses multiple expert inputs to one estimate. Feasibility can be evaluated in simulating a project plan or relating it to previous experiences with tools such as QSM.

Measure actual results and periodically update your estimation rules. Most estimates are based on historical data and formulae from operational databases. Faults, changes, effort, even the task break-down are recorded by individuals who often do not necessarily care for data quality, especially when it comes to delivery and time pressure. Measurements must be verified and upon finished analysis fed back to the estimation tool.

Start with few meaningful measurements that are mandatory for all projects. This will help to ramp up fast and educate others on usage and analysis of the measurements in a variety of project situations. Some five to ten different measurements should be reported and evaluated. They should be standardized across all projects to allow benchmarking, automation and usability. A typical suite of project measurements or common measurements with examples for practical usage is summarized in Table 8.5.

Table 8.5. Core measurements for project control

Measurement type	Examples
Project size	- New, changed, reused, and total size of code; in KLOC or KStmt
	- Functional measurement such as function points
Schedule	- Estimated end date with respect to committed milestones
	- Increment or work package deliveries compared with planning data
	- Schedule accuracy (total duration divided to originally committed duration)
Effort and budget	- Total effort in project
	- Cost to complete
	- Cost at completion
	- Budget accuracy (final cost compared to originally committed cost)

Productivity	- Efficiency in important processes (e.g., defects per person week, function points per person year) - Cost structure (cost break-down per activity compared to estimates or benchmarks) - Cost of non-quality (effort spent on detecting and removing defects across all phases) - Test effectiveness (defects detected per test case)
Progress	- Requirements status (percentage of requirements in different status, such as open, designed, verified, validated, integrated) - Completed requirements (percentage of requirements that have already been successfully validated and integrated compared to total; can be weighted with requirements value) - Test progress (test cases completed against planned) - Earned value (effort spent so far normalized with the delivered requirements and their planned effort or value)
Quality	- Effectiveness of defect detection during project life-cycle (percentage of defects removed per development activity compared to total number of defects in project) - Defect leakage (total number of post release defects * weight of defects) divided by project size) - Total defects per project size in new or changed software - Failures per execution time during test and in the field - Reliability estimate (e.g., critical failures per month, downtime per month, service and maintenance effort) - Requirements volatility (new and changed requirements divided by number of all originally committed requirements)
Business success	- Business case validity (i.e., achieved benefits divided by predicted benefits) - Forecast validity (i.e., achieved revenues divided by forecasted revenues)

Agile projects and development processes demand lean measurement processes. A minimum set of measurements for agile development should include:
- Requirements with their status
- Increment planning with schedule, effort and mapping of requirements
- Stability with few quality measurements, such as stability of automated regression test

When working agile it is important to not try to reinvent all development practices but rather to cut out overheads. Agile development is not about rigorous and bureaucratic versus lean and simple, but rather about selecting and implementing the most efficient and suitable process for a given scenario. True agile projects need a lot of rigor and for that matter reliable processes.

For maintenance projects with small new development rates, and for projects that primarily need to continue delivering services without new development, the measurement suite might need to be adjusted to focus on service level agreements and quality. Measurements could include: the SLAs' adherence; mean time between failures (MTBF) of different severity (critical, major, minor) which helps to predict the occurrence of customer maintenance requests; average time and effort taken to resolve a defect; maintainability measurements; or load of project resources which helps in resource allocation.

Risk management is a key activity within project management and depends very much on useful measurements. It will not prevent problems but it will reduce the surprise factor. It allows anticipating in due time what would be reactions to the top five or top ten risks which are expected. Risk management allows distinguishing between estimates and objectives. It provides techniques to mathematically handle probabilities and outcome of risks and therefore to determine exposure to find the most appropriate answers. It demands processes, such as escalation or change management in order to avoid ad-hoc crisis management once a risk materializes. Finally risk management like any other project management activity also needs effort and time to be performed. This additional effort is small and negligible for the risk controlling but might take some effort for dedicated mitigation actions.

Project monitoring and control must make sense to everybody within the organization. It should be simple and insightful without lots of measurements. Earned value analysis is a technique with few measurements that allows monitoring and forecasting project performance easily. Therefore, measurements should be piloted and evaluated after some time. Potential evaluation questions include:

- Are the selected measurements consistent with the original improvement targets? Do the measurements provide added value? Do they make sense from different angles and can that meaning be communicated simply and easily? If measurements consider what is measurable but do not support improvement tracking they are perfect for hiding issues but should not be called measurements.
- Do the chosen measurements send the right message about what the organization considers relevant? Measurements should spotlight by default and without cumbersome investigations of what might be behind. Are the right things being spotlighted?
- Do the measurements clearly follow a perspective that allows comparisons? If measurements include ambiguities or heterogeneous viewpoints they cannot be used as history data.

8.8. Summary

We have presented the introduction and application of a software measurement program for project control. The targets of project control in software engineering are as follows:
- setting process and product goals
- quantitatively tracking project performance during development
- analyzing measurement data to discover any existing or anticipated problems
- determining risk
- making available early release criteria for all work products
- creating an experience database for improved project management

Most benefits that we recorded since establishing a comprehensive software measurement program are indeed related to project control and project management:
- improved tracking and control of each development project based on standardized mechanisms
- earlier identification of deviations from the given targets and plans
- accumulation of historical data from all different types of projects that are re-used for improving estimations and planning of further projects
- motivating and triggering improvements
- tracking process improvements and deviations from processes

Many small and independent measurement initiatives had been started before within various groups and departments. Our experience shows that project control of software projects is most likely to succeed as a part of a larger software process improvement initiative (e.g., CMMI Maturity level 2 demands basic project control as we explained in this chapter, while CMMI Maturity level 4 and Six Sigma initiatives explicitly ask for statistical process control and process measurement). In that case, the control program benefits from an aligned engineering improvement and business improvement spirit that encourages continuous and focused improvement with support of quantitative methods.

A measurement program must evolve along with the organization: it is not frozen. The measurement process and underlying data will change with growing maturity of management and organization. Measurements must always be aligned with the organization's goals and serve its needs. While raw data definitions can remain unchanged for long periods, the usage of the measurements will definitely evolve. What used to be project tracking information will grow into process measurements. Estimation of effort and size will evolve into statistical process control. Setting annual objectives by the senior management level will grow into continuous improvements based on and tracked with flexibly used software measurements.

The good news is that measurement is a one-way street. Once managers and engineers get used to measuring and building decisions on quantitative facts instead of gut feelings, they will not go backwards. This in turn will justify the effort necessary for introducing and maintaining a measurement program which is around 0.25-2% of the total R&D or IT budget. The higher numbers occur during introduction, later the effort is much less.

> We measured benefits in the range of over 5% just by having measurements and thus being able to pinpoint weaknesses and introduce dedicated changes, thus improving project plans and their delivery dates. What gets measured gets done!

Senior managers who are used to measurement will drive hard to get trustworthy data which they will increasingly use to base their decisions upon and show to customers, analysts or at trade shows.

9. Quality Control and Assurance

> *Quality is not an act.*
> *It is a habit.*
> *Aristotle*

9.1. Assuring the Quality of Software Systems

Customer-perceived quality is among the three factors with the strongest influence on long-term profitability of a company [Buzz87]. Customers view achieving the right balance of reliability, market window of a product and cost as having the greatest effect on their long-term link to a company. This has been long articulated, and applies in different economies and circumstances. Even in restricted competitive situations, such as a market with few dominant players (e.g., the operating system market of today or the database market of few years ago), the principle applies and has given rise to open source development. With the competitor being often only a mouse-click away, today quality has even higher relevance. This applies to Web sites as well as to commodity goods with either embedded or dedicated software deliveries. And the principle certainly applies to investment goods, where suppliers are evaluated by a long list of different quality attributes.

Methodological approaches to guarantee quality products have lead to international guidelines (e.g., ISO 9001 [ISO00]) and widely applied methods to assess the development processes of software providers (e.g., SEI CMMI [SEI06a, Chri06]). In addition, most companies apply certain techniques of criticality prediction that focus on identifying and reducing release risks [Khos96, Musa87, Lyu95]. Unfortunately, many efforts usually concentrate on testing and reworking instead of proactive quality management [McCo03].

Yet there is a problem with quality in the software industry. By quality we mean the bigger picture, such as delivering according to commitments. The industry's maturity level with respect to "numbers" is known to be poor. What is published in terms of success stories is what few excellent companies deliver. We will help you with this book to build upon such success stories.

While solutions abound, knowing which solutions work is the big question. What are the most fundamental underlying principles in successful projects? What can be done right now? What actually is good or better? What is good enough – considering the immense market pressure and competition across the globe? The first step is to recognize that all your quality requirements can and should be specified numerically. This does not mean "counting defects." It means quantifying quality attributes such as security, portability, adaptability, maintainability, robustness, usability, reliability and performance [Eber97b]. Defects are not just information about something wrong in a software system or about the progress in building up quality.

> Defects are information about problems in the process that created this software. The three questions to address are:
> 1. How many defects are there?
> 2. How can they be removed most effectively and efficiently?
> 3. How can the process be changed to avoid the from reoccurring?
> Defect measurement is not about assigning blame but about building better quality and improving the processes to ensure quality.

In this chapter we look into how quality of software systems can be measured, estimated, and improved. Among the many dimensions of quality we look into defects and defect detection. We use several abbreviations and terms that might need some explanation. CMMI is the Capability Maturity Model Integration. ROI is return on investment; KStmt is thousand delivered executable statements of code (we use statements instead of lines, because statements are naturally the smallest unit designers deal with conceptually); PY is person-years and PH is person-hours.

A failure is the departure of system operation from requirements, for instance, the non-availability of a channel in an exchange. A defect or fault is the reason in the software that causes the failure when it is executed, for instance, the wrong populating of a database. The concept of a fault is developer-oriented. Defects and faults are used with the same meaning. Furthermore, $\lambda(t)$ is the failure intensity, and $\mu(t)$ is the number of cumulative failures that we use in reliability models.

Reliability is the probability of failure-free execution of a program for a specified period, use and environment. We distinguish between execution time which is the actual time that the system is executing the programs, and calendar time which is the time such a system is in service. A small number of faults that occur in software that is heavily used can cause a large number of failures and thus great user dissatisfaction. The number of faults over time or remaining faults is therefore not a good indicator of reliability. The term "system" is used in a generic sense to refer to all software components of the product being developed. These components include operating systems, databases, or embedded control elements, however, they do not include hardware (which would show different reliability behaviors), as we emphasize on software development in this chapter.

The chapter is organized as follows. Section 2 summarizes some fundamental concepts of achieving quality improvements and estimating quality parameters. Section 3 describes the basic techniques for early defect detection. Knowing that inspections and module tests are most effective if they are applied in depth to the components with high defect density and criticality for the system, we look at approaches for identifying such components. This section introduces to empirical software engineering. It shows that solid rules and concrete guidance with reproducible results can only be achieved with good underlying historical data from a defined context. Section 4 looks to measurement during the validation and test activities. Reliability modeling and thus predicting release time and field performance is introduced in Sect. 5. Section 6 looks into how the return on investment is calculated for quality improvement initiatives. Section 7 provides some hints for practitioners. It summarizes several rules of thumb for quick calculation of quality levels, defect estimation, and so on. Finally, Sect. 8 summarizes the chapter.

9.2. Fundamental Concepts

9.2.1 Defect Estimation

Reliability improvement always needs measurements on effectiveness (i.e., percentage of removed defects for a given activity) compared to efficiency (i.e., effort spent for detecting and removing a defect in the respective activity). Such measurement asks for the number of residual defects at a given point in time or within the development process.

But how is the number of defects in a piece of software or in a product estimated? We will outline the approach we follow for up-front estimation of residual defects in any software that may be merged from various sources with different degrees of stability. We distinguish between upfront defect estimation which is static by nature as it looks only on the different components of the system and their inherent quality before the start of validation activities, and reliability models which look more dynamically during validation activities at residual defects and failure rates.

Only a few studies have been published that typically relate static defect estimation to the number of already detected defects independently of the activity that resulted in defects [Cai98], or the famous error seeding which is well known but is rarely used due to the belief of most software engineers that it is of no use to add errors to software when there are still far too many defects in, and when it is known that defect detection costs several person hours (PH) per defect [Mill72].

Defects can be easily estimated based on the stability of the underlying software. All software in a product can be separated into four parts according to its origin:
- Software that is new or changed.
- Software to be tested (i.e., reused from another project that was never integrated and therefore still contains lots of malfunctions; this includes ported functionality).
- Software reused from another project that is in testing (almost) at the same time. This software might be partially tested, and therefore the overlapping of the two test phases of the parallel projects must be accounted for to estimate remaining malfunctions.
- Software completely reused from a stable project. This software is considered stable and therefore it has a rather low number of malfunctions.

The base of the calculation of new or changed software is the list of modules to be used in the complete project (i.e., the description of the entire build with all its components). A defect correction in one of these components typically results in a new version, while a modification in functionality (in the context of the new project) results in a new variant. Configuration management tools such as *CVS* or *Clearcase* are used to distinguish the one from the other while still maintaining a single source.

To statically estimate the number of residual defects in software at the time it is delivered by the author (i.e., after the author has done all verification activities, she can execute herself), we distinguish four different levels of stability of the software that are treated independently:

$$f = a \times x + b \times y + c \times z + d \times (w - x - y - z)$$

with

- x: the number of new or changed KStmt designed and to be tested within this project. This software was specifically designed for that respective project. All other parts of the software are reused with varying stability.
- y: the number of KStmt that are reused but are unstable and not yet tested (based on functionality that was designed in a previous project or release, but was never externally delivered; this includes ported functionality from other projects).
- z: the number of KStmt that are tested in parallel in another project. This software is new or changed for the other project and is entirely reused in the project under consideration.
- w: the number of KStmt in the total software – i.e., the size of this product in its totality.

The factors a-d relate defects in software to size. They depend heavily on the development environment, project size, maintainability degree and so on. Our starting point comes from psychology. Any person makes roughly one (non-editorial) defect in ten written lines of work. This applies to code as well as a design document or e-mail, as was observed by the personal software process (PSP) and many other sources [Jone97, Hump97]. The estimation of remaining malfunctions is language independent because malfunctions are introduced per thinking and editing activity of the programmer, i.e., visible by written statements. We could prove in our own environment this independency of programming language and code defects per statement when looking to languages such as Assembler, C and CHILL.

This translates into 100 defects per KStmt. Half of these defects are found by careful checking by the author which leaves some 50 defects per KStmt delivered at code completion. Training, maturity and coding tools can further reduce the number substantially. We found some 10-50 defects per KStmt depending on the maturity level of the respective organization. This is based only on new or changed code, not including any code that is reused or automatically generated.

Most of these original defects are detected by the author before the respective work product is released. Depending on the underlying personal software process (PSP), 40–80% of these defects are removed by the author immediately. We have experienced in software that around 10–50 defects per KStmt remain. For the following calculation we will assume that 30 defects/KStmt are remaining (which is a common value [Jone96]. Thus, the following factors can be used:

9.2 Fundamental Concepts 249

- *a*: 30 defects per KStmt (depending on the engineering methods; should be based on own data)
- *b*: 30 × 60% defects per KStmt, if defect detection before the start of testing is 60%
- *c*: 30 × 60% × (overlapping degree) × 25% defects per KStmt (depending on overlapping degree of resources)
- *d*: 30 × 0.1–1% defects per KStmt depending on the number of defects remaining in a product at the time when it is reused

The percentages are, of course, related to the specific defect detection distribution in one's own historical database (Fig. 9.1). A careful investigation of stability of reused software is necessary to better substantiate the assumed percentages.

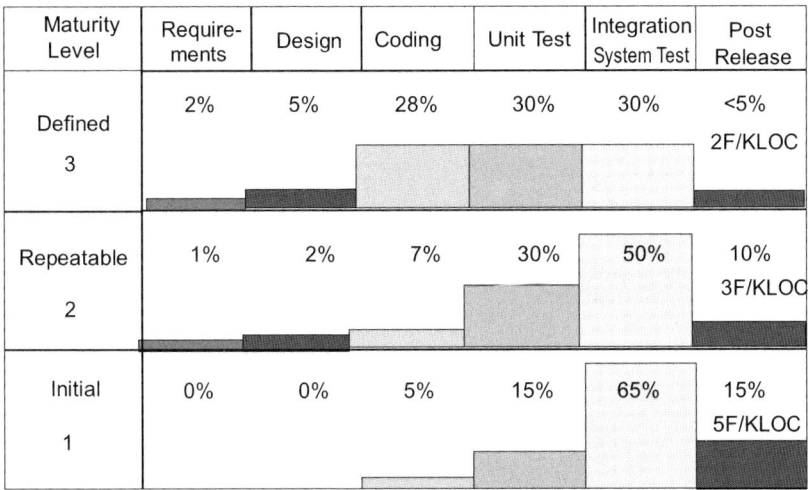

Sources: Siemens '95, Jones '96, Alcatel '98

Fig. 9.1. Typical benchmark effects of detecting faults earlier in the life-cycle

How good are predictions ? Obviously a defect prediction is only good and useful if the relevant defects have been identified, while at the same time not too many irrelevant defects are in that very set. Predictions or critical components from a software system demand the same quality, namely to identify those few which would otherwise contribute to quality issues, while the number of those that actually have no defects would not be selected in order to reduce overhead. Unfortunately getting everything which is relevant while avoiding "junk" is difficult, if not impossible, to accomplish. The two needs contradict each other.

There are two aspects to this question on predictive quality:
- **Precision**: How many irrelevant items have been characterized as relevant? Including an irrelevant item to the set of positives is what we call a (prediction) error of type 1. We define precision as the ratio of the number of relevant re-

cords retrieved to the total number of irrelevant and relevant records retrieved. It is usually expressed as a percentage. It can be tuned towards 100% by removing irrelevant items (i.e., no type 1 errors). However such tuning might increase another error, namely that of leaving out relevant items from the set.

- **Recall**: Have all relevant items been identified? Leaving out a relevant item is what we call a (prediction) error of type 2. We define recall as the ratio of the number of relevant records retrieved to the total number of relevant records in the database. It is usually expressed as a percentage. It forms a natural pair with the first measurement, precision.

Fig. 9.2 shows this relationship of precision and recall in information retrieval or prediction. Any search or prediction of specific elements from a bigger data set needs to optimize both in a direction that is governed by principles of precision and recall. Labeling the entire data set as critical would certainly improve recall to 100% of hit rate, but at the cost of precision or effort. Recall and precision ignore the concepts of true and false negatives. False positives (i.e., irrelevant elements identified as relevant) correspond to type 1 errors and false negatives (i.e., relevant entries identified as irrelevant) correspond to type 2 errors.

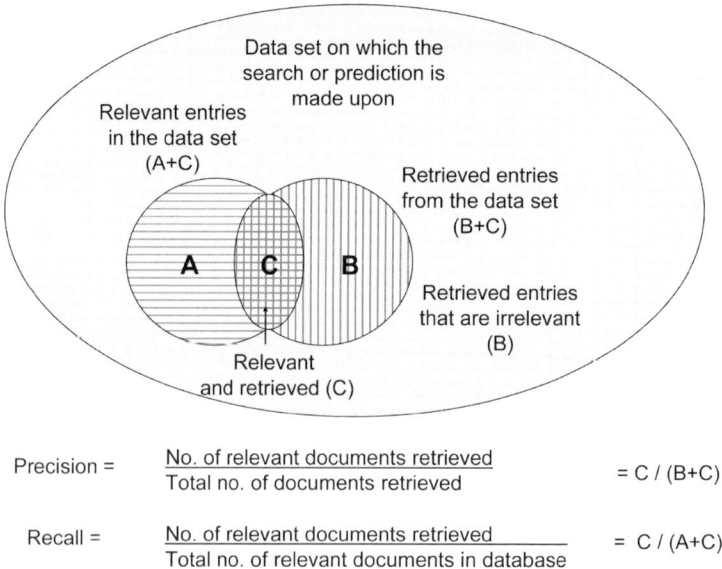

Fig. 9.2. Precision and recall in predictions

For instance, let us assume a data set of 100 software components of which 20 are error-prone (set A + C). Our prediction might result in a set labeled relevant or positive with 30 entries (set B + C). Those being correctly identified as positive (i.e., error-prone components that are actually containing many defects) is set C which we assume has 17 elements. Then we have a precision (i.e., relevant entries retrieved compared to all retrieved elements) of 17 / 30 = 57%. The recall (i.e., relevant being retrieved as a share of total relevant) is 17 / 20 = 85%. False positives (i.e., error type 1) is 13 / 30 = 43% and false negatives (i.e., error type 2) is 3 / 20 = 15%.

As a quality measurement, recall and precision are invaluable to predictions. Knowing the goal of the search, such as to find all critical components, just a few but very key error-prone components, or something in between, determines what strategies the prediction will use. There are a variety of techniques which may be used to affect the level recall and precision. A good searcher must be adept at using them. Many of these techniques are discussed in the following sections.

9.2.2 Defect Detection, Quality Gates, and Reporting

Since defects can never be entirely avoided, several quality control techniques have been suggested for detecting defects early in the development life-cycle:
- design reviews
- code inspections with checklists based on typical fault situations or critical areas in the software
- enforced reviews and testing of critical areas (in terms of complexity, former failures, expected fault density, individual change history, customer's risk and occurrence probability)
- tracking the effort spent for analyses, reviews, and inspections and separating according to requirements to find out areas not sufficiently covered
- test coverage measurements (e.g., C0 and C1 coverage)
- dynamic execution already applied during integration testing
- application of protocol testing machines to increase level of automatic testing
- application of operational profiles and usage specifications from the start of system testing.

We will further focus on several selected approaches that are applied for improved defect detection before starting with integration and system test. The starting point for effectively reducing defects and improving reliability is to track all faults that are detected. Faults must be recorded for each defect detection activity.

Counting faults and deriving the reliability (that is failures over time) is the most widely applied and accepted method used to determine software quality. Counting faults during the complete project helps to estimate the duration of distinct activities (e.g., module testing or subsystem testing) and improves the underlying processes. Typically, software engineer view quality based on faults, while it is failures that reflect the customer's satisfaction with a product. Failure prediction is used to manage release time of software. This ensures that neither too much time or money is spent on unnecessary testing that could possibly result in late delivery, nor that an early release occurs which might jeopardize customer satisfaction because of undetected faults. More advanced techniques in failure prediction focus on typical user operations and therefore avoid wasting time and effort on wrong test strategies. Failures reported during system testing or field application must be traced back to their primary causes and specific faults in the design (e.g., design decisions or lack of design reviews).

The quality of defect reporting during the entire development process determines the validity of quality predictions. Based on fault reports starting with first delivery of software code by the author to the configuration management system, predictive models can be developed on the basis of complexity measurements (see Sect. 4) and on the basis of reliability prediction models (see Sect. 5). As a result, it is possible to determine defective modules or classes during design and field failure rates during testing. This in turn can be used as exit criteria to balance cost of quality with cost of non-quality and with project duration.

Fig. 9.1 shows that in organizations with rather low maturity (i.e., ranked according to the CMMI) defects are often detected at the end of the development process despite the fact that they were present since the design phase. Late fault detection results in costly and time-consuming correction efforts, especially when the requirements were misunderstood or a design flaw occurred. Organizations with higher maturity obviously move defect detection towards the phases where they were introduced.

9.2.3 Case Study: Quality Gates

Expert Box. Authors: Marek Leszak and Dieter Stoll

This section introduces the concept of **quality gates** as a successful approach for quality control. It demonstrates quantitative and empirical evidence for its practical value to sustain or even increase software product quality. Originally quality gates have been applied in very large projects especially in the automotive and aerospace domains, but meanwhile also many IT and telecommunications companies apply quality gates as inherent part of process-driven project control, thereby also fulfilling process adherence requirements of maturity models like the CMMI or SPICE.

> A quality gate is a significant project event, characterized by a set of quality-related conditions when finishing a development phase or certain work products resulting from one or more phases. As soon as all relevant conditions are declared as fulfilled in a formal (management) review, the quality gate is determined to be accomplished.

Product Life-cycle Management applied for large-scale projects include synchronous milestones guarded by quality gates, leading to GO/NO-GO decisions on project continuation, or to certain corrective actions or improvements in case of partial fulfillment only. All concurrent phases of various functions like R&D, service, and supply chain are checked if certain exit conditions are fulfilled, e.g., if all plans are available to start the development project. In some product divisions of Alcatel-Lucent this concept has been extended to a mix of synchronous and asynchronous gate reviews. It has been applied exhaustively on all major system and software components within each development project, following an iterative / evolutionary paradigm to systems and software development. An example of using quality in an evolutionary system & software development process is outlined in Fig. 9.3.

Development is embedded into the synchronous product life-cycle (PLC) gates "PL" and "GA." (Synchronous gate means that by one gate review, readiness for continuation is checked not only for R&D but also for other functions like service, supply chain, customer documentation, and so on.) The R&D gates "SE" and "SWA" are performed once major parts of Systems Engineering (SE) and Software Architecture (SWA) work products are available, as main input for subsequent software domain development. A domain is a unit of software structure, configuration, and team organization, and can be considered synonymous with software subsystem or software component. Several domain teams work concurrently on implementing new features and fixing reported defects, in a time box-driven delivery model where each week "some" delivery towards software integration is to be accomplished. Close to the last incremental feature delivery, a domain development ("DD") gate review is conducted per domain team. The last integrated feature load towards system testing is guarded by a "SWI" gate. Note that Fig. 9.3 depicts the principle phase hand-over products and the associated flow, but the iterative nature of several phases, and also some overlap in time, is not shown.

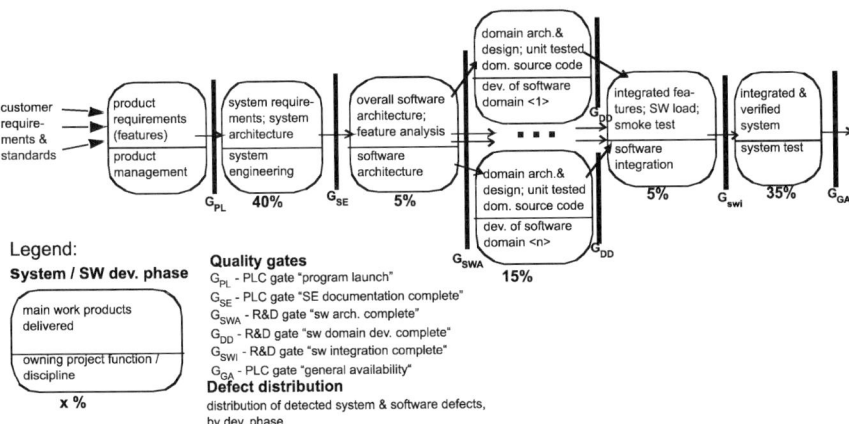

Fig. 9.3. Embedding quality gates into the system and software development process

This figure contains also a typical distribution of defects per phase, detected by verification activities, i.e., by document and code reviews, and by testing. This defect distribution has been collected from a certain release of a large telecommunication multiplexer. Note that the high portion of defects in the system engineering phase comes from the large effort to refine customer features for a new product release into system requirements; all resulting documents are reviewed thoroughly by a cross-functional team. The low portion of defects found by reviewing software architecture documents is due to the incremental, rather small architecture change for a new release of a mature product. Only 0.1% of all defects in the release life-cycle are found by customers of the product (portion not shown in figure) – a necessarily low amount, considering the ultra-high availability requirements of five minutes per year per delivered system of this particular product category. For more details of this development model applied in our product division since many years, see [Lesz04].

Quality-related conditions checked by a gate review include for example portion of deliverables specified and reviewed, achieved code coverage and so on, to reveal quality issues. Quite often, gate reviews are performed for checking maturity of hand-over deliveries between functions participating in a project. In higher maturity organization, phase exit conditions are defined quantitatively by "SMART" process and product measurements, and measurement targets are controlled by the quality management organization. Such conditions are related to activities, work products, and defined quality milestones of the "organizational process" applied, thus checking *process conformance*.

This concept should be contrasted to assessments or appraisals based on a process maturity model like CMMI or SPICE which results in a process capability statement, whereas a quality gate review determines to which extent a certain life-cycle process or development process has been applied. Quality gate reviews differ also from classical quality assurance activities like audits or project retrospectives (lessons learned). Audits are applied more in an ad-hoc manner and often apply sampling both on the work products checked and the criteria checked, whereas quality gates are applied more systematically and check well-defined and pre-determined criteria. A quality checklist is applied, based for example on the defined software development process, as a structured tool used to verify that a set of required steps has been performed, as required by the PMBOK. Thus, quality gate reviews can be seen as "rigorous" quality audits. This concept can be applied not only for software projects, but also to the development of any kind of large system including hardware.

If several criteria (or process measurements) contribute to a quality gate then these criteria can be combined into a process measurement called *process quality index*, by mapping the measurement to a uniform (e.g., 0-1) scale, possibly assigning weights per measurement, and then relating the resulting data to a risk exposure classification, e.g., based on traffic light colors.

Does the additional effort of performing extensive quality gate reviews pays off, as opposed to less frequent and sample based quality audits? Such classical audits also can reveal non-conformances to process standards which should be used for corrective and preventive improvement actions. It is the purpose of this brief praxis report to provide evidence for the additional benefit quality gate reviews can provide. Recent results show a strong correlation between process compliance measured by gate reviews, to product quality data measured e.g., by defects found downstream. Thus, one key improvement goal from findings from quality gate reviews is to increase conformance to the defined software process in subsequent releases or projects, thereby influencing resulting product quality positively and significantly. In contrast to audits performed usually "after-the-fact", the findings in gate reviews can be used in-process, with corrective actions to push the actual project back in line with the quality targets.

The following two examples are based on two empirical studies, carried out in large-scale telecommunications development projects at Lucent Technologies [Lesz00, Lesz02, Ruff06]. Both examples demonstrate the high benefit of applying quality gate reviews systematically within a development project, showing strong evidence that software process compliance (in the sense defined above and checked by quality gate reviews) has a high positive impact on resulting product quality, measured by the number of defects found "downstream", i.e., after software delivery through system integration and testing. Fig. 9.4 shows the principle flow of detected and corrected defects. Applied for each software component, this method can also be used to identify critical components (see also the following section). The evidence found in the projects analyzed has high internal validity: an organizational software development process is defined and consistently deployed for all projects in the particular organization, supported by independent "quality coordinators" who e.g., take care of moderating quality gate reviews with all relevant stakeholders in the project. Furthermore, there is an organizational change request management process and toolset applied, i.e., defect data figures are valid. So the input data to the statistical analyses performed can be considered as highly reliable.

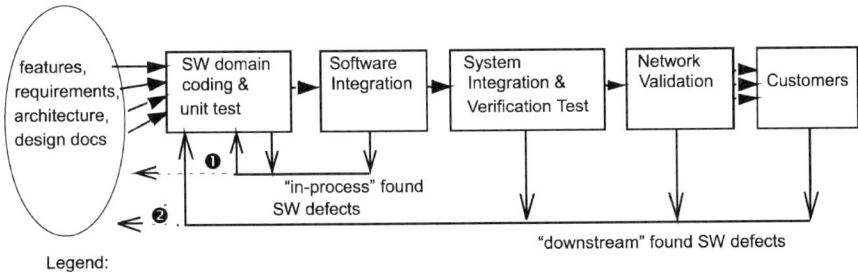

Fig. 9.4. Software defect detection and correction flow

The first example is based on a classification scheme for quality-related activities, applied to the software development process from design to component delivery. Attributes considered included the execution of design and code reviews, the specification and execution of test cases, and the existence of known defects when SW was delivered to the integration team (see Fig. 9.4). The result of the quality gate is determined per SW component. Per component, the overall traffic-light is determined from the combined results of all contributing factors (see Fig. 9.5), according the following rules:
- If all factors are green then the component is labeled green.
- If at least one factor is red then the component is red.
- In all other cases, the component's label is yellow.

Since the exploratory data analysis reveals a distribution function for the (ordinal variable) number of defects which is different from normal and the fact that the quality label is a factor variable, the data set is best analyzed using rank test methods. Applying the Mann-Whitney (U-Test) with the hypothesis that red labeled SW components show a higher number of defects, results in a p-value of 0.0671, which means that the hypothesis is correct at a 93.3% significance level.

Since it is well known that the number of defects needs to be appropriately normalized by the size of the respective component, it is better to perform tests using defect density, i.e., the number of defects per 1000 non-comment source lines (defects/KNCSL) or per new or changed NCSL (defects/KCNCSL) as a quality measurement. The resulting p-values are presented in Table 9.1.

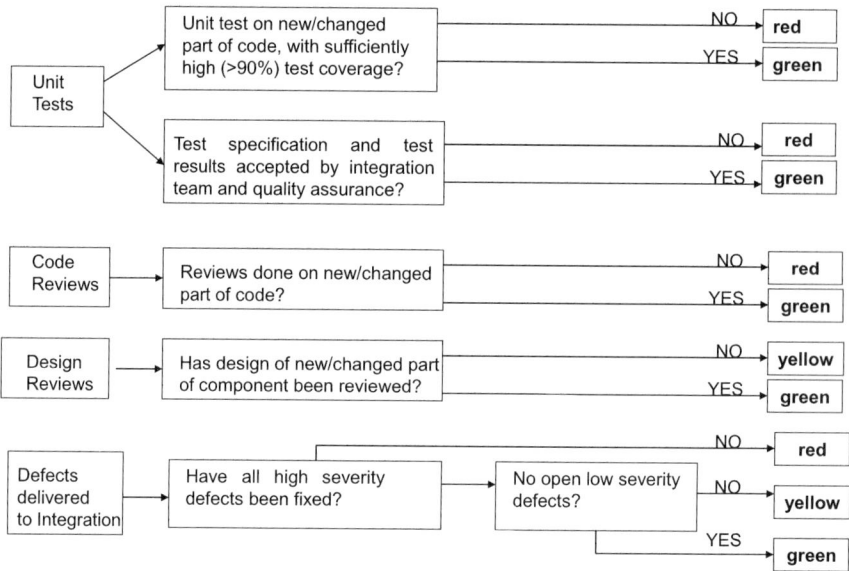

Fig. 9.5. Scheme for qualitative assessment of software component maturity

Table 9.1. Defect distribution and significance levels in the case study

All defects	All defects/KNCSL	All defects/KCNCSL	Severity 1 and 2 defects/KNCSL	Severity 1 and 2 defects/KCNCSL
p = 0.0671	p = 0.0167	p = 0.0272	p = 0.0146	p = 0.0173

Thus using the normalized defect measurement all tests are significant on a 95% level. The same test can also be applied to the difference between green and yellow classification with the results not being significant.

Although this analysis is statistically sound, a more intuitive understanding is achieved, when looking at the cumulative distribution function for each quality class. This distribution approaches 100% the faster the more likely its components are located at small numbers of defect (or defects/NCSL etc.). This is shown in Fig. 9.6, where obviously the red classified components follow a distribution which stretches out to larger values compared to green and yellow classified components. Note that an additional data set is plotted consisting of modules not classified. These modules were not subject to the QA procedures since they have been reused unchanged from previous releases. They show highest quality, as expected from a quality process perspective. For more details see [Stoll99, Lesz02].

The second example contains an enhanced statistical analysis of the same hypothesis (higher process compliance leads to fewer defects found downstream), i.e., instead of accumulating all quality gate observables into a single measurement, we focus on one explicit example of such an investigation, i.e., on "software documentation maturity." This is determined during a quality gate review for each significantly changed component within a project. For each component it is checked 1) if certain documents required by the software process are available and have been baselined, and 2) and if they are complete as determined by associated peer reviews of such documents.

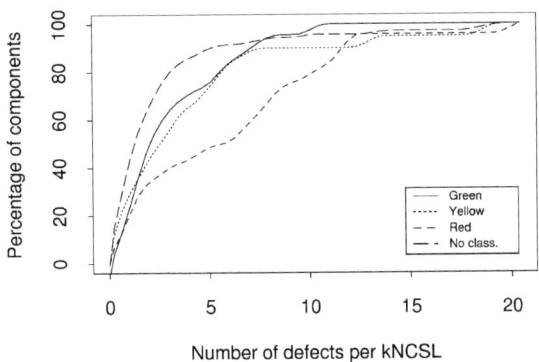

Fig. 9.6. Cumulative distribution function of SW component maturity vs. defect density

According the software process applied, the required documents include behavior and interface specifications (called domain architecture documents, DAD) and software unit test specifications (called domain integration test specification documents, DITS) For each component developed or enhanced within one project, all SW artifacts have been grouped according to the following criteria:
- G1 = "Both, DAD and DITS not available"
- G2 = "One document partially available"
- G3 = "One document completely available, or both partially"
- G4 = "One document completely available, the other partially"
- G5 = "DAD and DITS completely available"

As in the first example the interesting question studied has been whether this classification correlates significantly with the number of defects in the respective components. Fisher's analysis of the variance method with the null-hypothesis, i.e., that all group expectation values are the same, can be rejected at the 5% confidence level.

While this method provides the statistically sound result which has also been verified using alternate means, it is again beneficial to look into exploratory data analysis to get a visual impression of the differences. The ANOVA test method reveals that at least one mean value significantly differs from the remaining mean values. A simple plotting of the data underlying the statistics, as shown in Fig. 9.7, identifies easily that G1 is the critical criterion.

Summarizing it can be stated that the determination of quality attributes can be used to classify software into criticality classes (see next section). If this classification is well tailored to the respective development process it provides the opportunity to identify problematic components on a statistical level. Since this can be done at various levels in the development process, it is in particular applicable before expensive test execution is started, thus offering a means for highly effective process control.

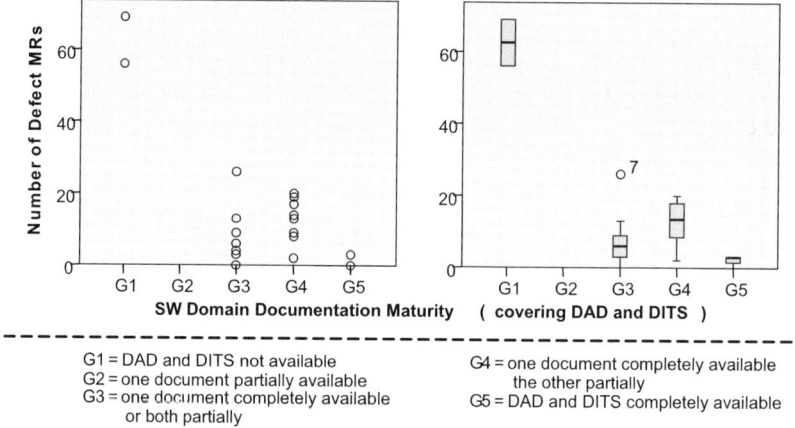

Fig. 9.7. Box plot of impact of SW documentation maturity on downstream defects

9.3. Early Defect Removal

9.3.1 Reducing Cost of Non-Quality

Quality improvement activities must be driven by a careful look into what they mean for the bottom line of the overall product cost. It means to continuously investigate what this best level of quality really means, both for the customers and for the engineering teams who want to deliver it.

9.3 Early Defect Removal 259

> One does not build a sustainable customer relationship by delivering bad quality and ruining his reputation just to achieve a specific delivery date. And it is useless to spend an extra amount on improving quality to a level nobody wants to pay for. The optimum seemingly is in between. It means to achieve the right level of quality and to deliver in time. Most important yet is to know from the begin of the project what is actually relevant for the customer or market and set up the project accordingly. Objectives will be met if they are driven from the beginning.

We look primarily at factors such as cost of non-quality to follow through this business reasoning of quality improvements. For this purpose we measure all cost related to error detection and removal (cost of non-quality) and normalize by the size of the product (normalize fault costs). We take a conservative approach in only considering those effects that appear inside our engineering activities, i.e., not considering opportunistic effects or any penalties for delivering insufficient quality. To identify the respective measurements we followed a goal-driven approach [VanS00].

Reducing total cost of non-quality is driven by the fault detection distribution (see Fig. 9.1 again). Assuming a distinct cost for fault detection and repair (which includes regression testing, production, and so on) per detection activity allows one to calculate the total cost of non-quality for a distinct project. Obviously the activities of fault detection are taken into consideration and not necessarily the achieved milestone. Milestones in today's incremental development might completely mislead the picture because a distinct milestone could be achieved early, while major portions of the software are still in an earlier development phase. Cost of non-quality in terms of average cost per fault is then calculated based on the respective detection activity. This also supports using a fixed value per fault and activity in a distinct timeframe, because finding a fault with module test including the correction takes a rather stable effort, as well as for instance the detection, correction, regression test, production and delivery during system test.

Three key drivers for achieving the downstream targets were singled out and periodically measured in all projects to improve defect detection during the lifecycle. They later coined the underlying engineering rules to establish consistent defect detection processes.

1. Reading or checking speed in inspections or peer reviews. Reducing reading speed during code inspections improves design defect detection effectiveness and thus reduces normalized fault cost and customer-detected faults.
2. Faults found per new or changed statement with module testing. Increasing faults found per new or changed statement with module testing improves design defect detection effectiveness and thus reduce normalized fault cost and customer detected faults.
3. Test defect detection effectiveness. Increasing test defect detection effectiveness (i.e., percentage of remaining faults detected during integration) reduces normalized fault cost and customer-detected faults.

Our contribution to research in this domain is that we validate several key relationships in real settings with projects based on legacy software [Eber99a]. Our contribution for practical development projects is that we propose meaningful and valid approaches to achieve quantitative field performance improvement.

9.3.2 Planning Early Defect Detection Activities

The most cost-effective techniques for defect detection are code reviews and inspections and module test. Detecting faults in architecture and design documents has considerable benefit from a cost perspective, because these defects are expensive to correct. Major yields in terms of reliability, however, can be attributed to better code, for the simple reason that there are many more defects residing in code that were inserted during the coding activity. We therefore provide more depth on techniques that help to improve the quality of code, namely code reviews (i.e., code reviews and formal code inspections) and module test (which might include static and dynamic code analysis).

There are six possible paths in the delivery of a piece of software from design until the start of integration test (Fig. 9.8). They indicate the permutations of doing code reading alone, performing code inspections and applying module test. Although the best approach from a mere defect detection perspective is to apply inspections and module test, cost considerations and the objective to reduce elapsed time and thus improve throughput suggest carefully evaluating which path to follow in order to most efficiently and effectively detect and remove faults. In our experience code reading is the cheapest detection technique, while module test is the most expensive. Code inspections lie somewhere in between.

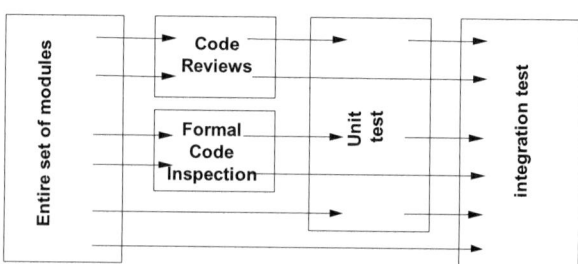

Fig. 9.8. Six possible paths for modules between end of coding and start of integration test

Unit tests, however, combined with C0 coverage targets, have the highest effectiveness for regression testing of existing functionality. Inspections, on the other hand, help in detecting distinct fault classes that can only be found under real load (or even stress) in the field.

The target is to find the right balance between efficiency (time spent per item) and effectiveness (ratio of detected faults to remaining faults) by making the right decisions to spend the budget for the most appropriate quality assurance methods.

In addition overall efficiency and effectiveness have to be optimized. It must therefore be carefully decided which method should be applied on which work product to guarantee high efficiency and effectiveness of code reading (i.e., done by one checker) and code inspections (i.e., done by multiple checkers in a controlled setting). Wrong decisions can mainly have two impacts:
- The proposed method to be performed is too "weak." Faults which could have been found with a stronger method, are not detected in the early phase. Too little effort is spend in the early phase. Typically in this case efficiency is high, and effectiveness is low.
- The proposed method to be performed is too "strong" or overly heavy. If the fault density is low from the very beginning, even an effective method will not discover many faults. This leads to a low efficiency, compared to the average effort that has to be spent to detect one fault. This holds especially for small changes in legacy code.

Faults are not distributed homogeneously through new or changed code [Wayn93, Eber97a]. By concentrating on fault-prone modules both effectiveness and efficiency are improved. Our main approach to identify fault-prone software-modules is a criticality prediction taking into account several criteria. One criterion is the analysis of module complexity based on complexity measurements. Other criteria concern the number of new or changed code in a module, and the number of field faults a module had in the preceding project.

The main input parameters for planning code inspections are:
- **General availability of an inspection leader**. Only a trained and internally certified inspection leader is allowed to plan and perform inspections to ensure adherence to the formal rules and achievement of efficiency targets. The number of certified inspection leaders and their availability limits the number of performed inspections for a particular project.
- **Module design effort (planned/actually spent).** The actual design effort per module (or class) can give an early impression on how much code will be new or changed. This indicates the effort that will be necessary for verification tasks like inspections.
- **Expertise of the checker.** If specific know-how is necessary to check particular parts of the software, the availability of correspondingly skilled persons will have an impact on the planning of code reviews and code inspections.
- **Checking rate.** Based on the programming language and historic experiences in previous projects the optimal checking rate determines the necessary effort to be planned.
- **Size of new or changed statements.** With regard to the checking rate, the total amount of the target size to be inspected defines the necessary effort.
- **Quality targets.** If high-risk areas are identified (e.g., unexpected changes to previously stable components or unstable inputs from a previous project) exhaustive inspections must be considered.
- **Achieving the entry criteria.** The inspection or review can start earliest if entry criteria for these procedures can be matched. Typically at least error-free compileable sources have to be available.

The intention is to apply code inspections to heavily changed modules first, in order to optimize payback of the additional effort that has to be spent compared to the lower effort for code reading. Formal code reviews are recommended by the author even for very small changes with a checking time shorter than two hours in order to profit from a good efficiency of code reading. The effort for know-how transfer to another designer can be saved.

For unit testing some additional parameters have to be considered:

- **Optimal sequence of modules to be tested before start of integration testing**. Start-up tests typically can start without having the entire set of new features implemented for all modules. Therefore the schedule for unit testing has to consider individual participation of modules in start-up tests. Later increments of the new design are added to integration testing related to their respective functionalities.
- **Availability of reusable unit test environments**. The effort for setting up sophisticated testing environments for the unit test must be considered during planning. This holds especially for legacy code, where often the unit test environments and test cases for the necessary high C0 coverage are not available.
- **Distribution of code changes over all modules of one project**. The number of items to be tested has a heavy impact on the whole planning process and on the time that has to be planned for performing unit testing. The same amount of code to be tested can be distributed over a small number of modules (small initialization effort) or over a wide distribution of small changes throughout a lot of modules (high initialization effort).
- **Achieving the entry criteria**. The readiness of validated test lists is a mandatory prerequisite for starting unit testing.

9.3.3 Identifying Error-Prone Components

The distribution of defects among modules in a software system is not even. An analysis of many projects revealed the applicability of the Pareto rule: 20-30% of the modules are responsible for 70-80% of the malfunctions of the whole project [Eber97a, Eber01c]. These critical components need to be identified as early as possible, i.e., in the case of legacy systems at start of detailed design, and for new software during coding. By concentrating on these components the effectiveness of code inspections and unit testing is increased and fewer faults have to be found during test phases.

It is of great benefit for improved quality management to be able to predict early on in the development process those components of a software system that are likely to have a high fault rate or those requiring additional development effort. Criticality prediction is based on selecting a distinct small share of modules that incorporate sets of properties that would typically cause defects to be introduced during design more often than in modules that do not possess such attributes. Criticality prediction is thus a technique for risk analysis during the design process.

9.3 Early Defect Removal

Criticality prediction addresses typical questions often asked in software engineering projects:
- How can I early identify the relatively small number of critical components that make significant contribution to faults identified later in the life-cycle?
- Which modules should be redesigned because their maintainability is bad and their overall criticality to the project's success is high?
- Are there structural properties that can be measured early in the code to predict quality attributes?
- If so, what is the benefit of introducing a measurement program that investigates structural properties of software?
- Can I use the often heuristic design and test know-how on trouble identification and risk assessment to build up a knowledge base to identify critical components early in the development process?

Criticality prediction is a multifaceted approach taking into account several criteria [Eber95]. Complexity is a key influence on quality and productivity. Having uncontrolled accidental complexity in the product will definitely decrease productivity (e.g., gold plating, additional rework, more test effort) and quality (more defects).

> A key to controlling accidental complexity from creeping into the project is the measurement and analysis of complexity throughout in the life-cycle.

There is no common agreement among psychologists what complexity is and what makes some things more complicated than others. Of course, volume, structure, order or the connections of different objects contribute to complexity. However, do they all account for it equally? The clear answer is no, because different people with different skills assign complexity subjectively, according to their experience in the area.

Certainly criticality must be predicted early in the life-cycle to effectively serve as a managerial instrument for quality improvement, quality control effort estimation and resource planning as soon as possible in a project. Tracing *comparable* complexity metrics for different products throughout the life-cycle is advisable to find out when essential complexity is overruled by accidental complexity (see also Chap. 12). Care must be used that the complexity metrics are comparable, that is they should measure the same factors of complexity. Measuring and tracing complexity factors results in the following observations:
- Same pragmatic approach in different techniques. Distinct complexity metrics can be traced easily because the underlying factors are identical. An example is cyclomatic complexity or the number of decisions in a software product. It actually does not matter what formal notation is used for describing this product because almost all notations used in software engineering permit the formulation of control flow decisions. The syntax of such formulations might differ but the pragmatic approach is the same: selecting a distinct control flow path out of a group of several paths dependent on a set of data.

- Different notations for different techniques. It is not that easy to trace length or volume because its definition varies widely. Graphical notations that are used in the early phases of the software development process have another volume in terms of number of patterns than textual notations.
- Method dependent appearance. There are some forms of complexity that appear only during distinct phases of the life-cycle dependent on the underlying method and technique used. For example, in a design language with lots of redundancy for analysis reasons the length is much larger than that of the final source code.
- Human interpretation. There is no common agreement among psychologists what complexity is and what makes things more complicated than others. Of course volume, structure, order, hierarchy, or the connections of different objects contribute to complexity. However, do they account evenly? The clear answer is no, because different people with different skills assign complexity subjectively according to their experience in the area. Some see a well-structured image where others see just patterns and yet others see mere characters (or nonsense). This results in different interpretations of visual complexity of graphical representations.
- Finding overly complex components. Results of analyzing several projects, including industrial projects in telecommunication, show that the *80:20 rule* holds even in this area. Most projects consist of few parts that contribute heavily towards all problems being reported. It is only a relatively small group of modules with outlying complexity measurement vectors that forms these trouble group. Some factors of complexity clearly indicate problem components already during the analysis phase. It is hence worth investigating all outlying parts or modules of a project more closely in order to use complexity traces as quality-control procedures. Early analysis of such overly complex components allow corrective actions being performed early in the life-cycle, hence improving cost-effectiveness.
- Tracing steep complexity changes. One of the advantages of tracing complexity over several phases including their specific delivered products is to find out rapid changes or peaks in measurement data. Steep increases of a distinct complexity factor may be caused by methods and supporting tools (e.g., design languages with high redundancy in interface descriptions cause volume peaks). However, such increases can also be indicators of problem components. For example, rapidly increasing data complexity or decision complexity are caused by insufficient predecessor products (i.e., incomplete analysis or design). These changes are a clear indicator that accidental complexity is not sufficiently managed.

An example for such complexity is the structural complexity of software source code as measured by **McCabe's cyclomatic complexity**.[McCa76, Eber95] Fig. 9.9 provides a small example for calculating the cyclomatic complexity.

Control flow complexity is caused by control flow decisions and their individual levels of nesting. Cyclomatic complexity is a direct software measurement for the number of linearly independent paths through a program's source code. The higher the cyclomatic complexity, the more linearly independent paths exist in the control flow and therefore more test effort is necessary to achieve code coverage. Higher complexity also means that source code is more difficult to understand and therefore to design and debug. Cyclomatic complexity thus highly correlates with poor software quality [Eber97a, Eber99a]. Typically (and in combination with other complexity measurements) it is used as an indirect measurement for complexity, criticality, understandability, testability and so on

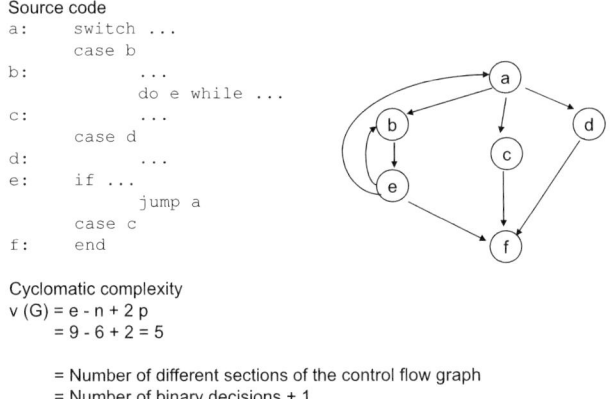

```
Source code
    a:    switch ...
              case b
    b:        ...
              do e while ...
    c:        ...
              case d
    d:        ...
    e:    if ...
              jump a
              case c
    f:    end
```

Cyclomatic complexity
$v(G) = e - n + 2p$
$= 9 - 6 + 2 = 5$

= Number of different sections of the control flow graph
= Number of binary decisions + 1

Fig. 9.9. Cyclomatic complexity

Other criteria concern the amount of new or changed code in a module, and the number of field faults a module had in the predecessor project and so on. All these criteria are used to build a complete criticality prediction model. Based on a ranking list of criticality of all modules used in a build, different mechanisms can be applied to improving quality, namely redesign, code inspections or unit test with high coverage.

Instead of predicting the number of faults or changes (i.e., algorithmic relationships) we consider assignments to groups (e.g., "fault-prone"). While the first goal can be achieved more or less exactly with regression models or neural networks predominantly for finished projects, the latter goal seems to be adequate for predicting potential outliers in running projects, where preciseness is too expensive and is unnecessary for decision support.

Training and test data were taken from previous projects. All modules selected for this experiment were from completed projects. They had been placed under configuration control since the start of coding. Software defects or faults are all deviations from functional requirements that are observed after the specific module had been delivered by the designer as having full functionality. They are recorded within the configuration control system for each module together with several complexity measurements. At this point we do not distinguish faults in terms of potential downstream impact (e.g., cost or performance), as this is difficult to judge during coding. Soft factors, such as designers' experiences are recorded during the design process; however, for privacy reasons they were only temporarily recorded and not for public access.

Having identified such overly critical modules, risk management must be applied. The most critical and most complex, for instance, the top 5%, of the analyzed modules are candidates for a redesign. For cost reasons mitigation is not only achieved with redesign. The top 20% should have a code inspection instead of the usual code reading, and the top 80% should be at least entirely (C0 coverage of 100%) unit tested. By concentrating on these components the effectiveness of code inspections and unit test is increased and fewer faults have to be found during test phases. To achieve feedback for improving predictions the approach is integrated into the development process end-to-end (requirements, design, code, system test, deployment).

Evaluation of the classification approaches is based on [Wads90]:
- low chi-square values, which is equal to reduced misclassification errors
- comparing the two types of misclassification errors, namely type-I errors ("fault-prone components" classified as "uncritical components") and type-II errors ("uncritical components" classified as "fault-prone components").

The goal obviously must be to reduce type-I errors at the cost of type-II errors because it is less expensive to investigate some components despite the fact that they are not critical compared to labeling critical components as harmless without probing further.

Fuzzy classification proved to be especially effective in the early identification of critical components. This was underlined in some studies we performed. If software engineering expert knowledge is available we recommend fuzzy classification before using learning strategies that are only result-driven (e.g., classification trees or mere neural network approaches). However, we see the necessity of such approaches when only a few guiding principles are available and sufficient project data can be utilized for supervised learning. Fuzzy classification was combined with genetic algorithms to improve type-I misclassifications, while preserving the maximum chi-square. A natural limit of prediction correctness was detected as the two data sets belonged to two entirely different populations.

It must be emphasized that using criticality prediction techniques does not mean attempting to detect all faults. Instead, they belong to the set of managerial instruments that try to optimize resource allocation by focusing them on areas with many faults that would affect the utility of the delivered product. The trade-off of applying complexity-based predictive quality models is estimated based on
- limited resources are assigned to high-risk jobs or components
- impact analysis and risk assessment of changes is feasible based on affected or changed complexity
- gray-box testing strategies are applied to identified high-risk components
- fewer customers reported failures

The process for criticality classification and validation is shown graphically in Fig. 9.10. It consists of several steps which we will briefly outline.

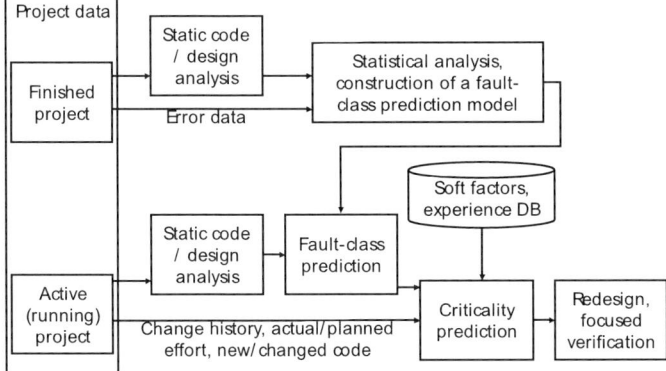

Fig. 9.10. Criticality prediction for source code based on static code analysis and code history

1. Provide a list of all modules (or classes in object-oriented languages) at the start of the project, during design and at the end of unit testing.
2. Provide a fault history classification for each module on the lists. A root cause analysis might be added for high-ranking faults that allows for a Pareto-based mitigation list.
3. Provide a change history classification (i.e., number of compiles or number of deliveries).
4. Provide a complexity classification as indicated in previous sections.
5. Finalize a comprehensive criticality list that takes into account the different inputs from steps 2-4 mapped on the appropriate input list. Before the final rankings are presented to decide on further actions, the validity of the lists must be evaluated (e.g., screening on reasonable modules, outliers, potential misleading effects and so on). The goal of screening is not to filter out what is thought to be unchangeable, but rather to question undesired influences from history. Of course, screening and ranking must primarily ensure that type I prediction errors are at the lowest feasible levels.
6. Prepare suggestions based on ranked critical modules. Typical approaches include redesign of a few highest ranked modules according to a simultaneous classification (i.e., the top modules must rank high in all three lists simultaneously). Redesign includes reduction of size, improved modularity and so on. Application of thorough unit testing with high C0 coverage should be applied to high runners according to independent classification (i.e., the top modules of all three approaches are grouped). Details of complexity measurements must be investigated for the selected modules to determine the redesign approach. In all cases it is typically the different complexity measurements that indicate which approach in redesign or test should be followed.
7. Validate and improve the prediction model based on post mortem studies with all collected faults and the population of a "real" criticality list. Then the actual fault ranking is compared with the predicted ranking. The reasons for deviations are investigated and the automatic classification approaches used are

tuned. The rules for screening are improved to ensure that type-II prediction errors will be reduced the next time.

Our experiences show that, in accordance with other literature [Evan94b] corrections of faults in early phases is more efficient, because the designer is still familiar with the problem and the correction delay during testing is reduced.

The effect and business case for applying complexity-based criticality prediction to a new project can be summarized based on results from Alcatel projects (taking a very conservative ration of only 40% defects in critical components):
- 20% of all modules in the project were predicted as most critical (after coding);
- these modules contained over 40% of all faults (up to release time).

Knowing from these and many other projects that
- 60% of all faults can theoretically be detected until the end of module test and
- fault correction during module test and code reading costs less than 10% compared to fault correction during system test,

it can be calculated that 24% of all faults can be detected early by investigating 20% of all modules more intensively with 10% of effort compared to late fault correction during test, therefore yielding a 20% total cost reduction for fault correction. Additional costs for providing the statistical analysis are in the range of two person days per project. Necessary tools are off the shelf and account for even less per project. There are numerous other benefits from these criticality analyses, such as the removal of specific defect types that otherwise are hard to identify (e.g., security).

9.3.4 Defect Predictions in Embedded Systems

Expert Box. Author: Peter Liggesmeyer

Software development is facing an ever-growing demand for dependable reliability figures. This is particularly important for embedded software which drive safety critical systems. In such applications software reliability influences the availability, reliability and safety of the system. In non-safety critical applications quantified software reliability is necessary to estimate the availability and life-cycle costs.

Safety is usually addressed by applying modeling approaches, e.g., fault tree analysis. Although these techniques may also be used to analyze reliability, a measurement-based approach may also be used in addition. Fault prediction techniques based on measurements can pinpoint fault-prone software components. Testing can focus on these components. If the fault-content is not equally distributed over software components, identification of fault-prone components in advance would be beneficial from a technical and economic perspective. Focusing the test effort on potentially fault-prone components, would reduce the number of residual faults after testing and raise the number of revealed faults per test case. Reliability measurement techniques can be used to guarantee that the reliability goals of the customers are met.

Statistical software reliability measurement and prediction

Software reliability models first appeared in the literature almost 25 years ago. An overview of software reliability engineering is given in [Lyu95]. The initial idea that some reliability models would be universally useful, has not been realized. It became clear, that no single model can be trusted to perform well in all contexts because every model is based on different specific assumptions, e.g., about development environments, the nature of software failures, or the probability of individual failures occurring. Furthermore, it does not seem possible to analyze the particular context in which reliability measurement is to take place, thereby deciding a priori which model is likely to be trustworthy. Techniques have been developed for comparing the validity of software reliability models with respect to certain criteria (e.g., predictive quality). These facilitate the identification of good models for a specific set of failure data.

In spite of the theoretical maturity of the field there is a lack of easy-to-use tools that allow application of the techniques. A mature tool in this field is RATplus (Fig. 9.11). The practical application of reliability growth model requires appropriate tools that provide assistance for selecting adequate models, calibrating models, and applying them in order to predict failure count, MTBF and failure rate. It is necessary that the prediction is provided alongside confidence intervals, since these define the horizon of predictability, i.e., the maximum forecast interval.

Reliability growth models are the statistically sound way to apply statistics to observed failures in order to measure and predict reliability.

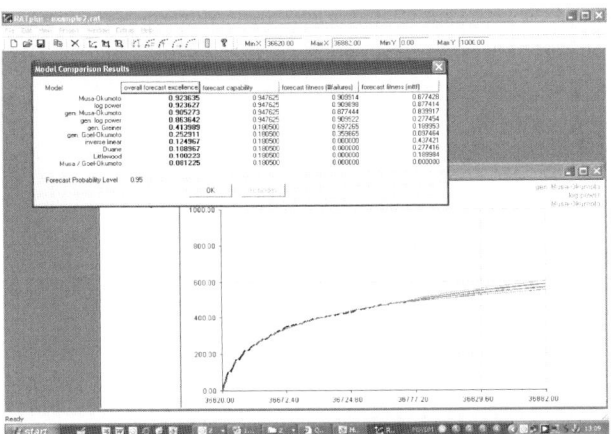

Fig. 9.11. User interface of RATplus

Identifying fault-prone components with software measurements

Software fault content is not directly measurable. But it might be correlated with measurable properties, e.g., software complexity. One approach for predicting the potential fault content of software components are correlation models, these are based on measurements and predict the fault content. This information may be used to focus test effort on fault-prone components. There are accepted methods to identify appropriate measurements for certain defined goals, e.g., the GQM approach (see Chap. 3). Usually, hypotheses are used within the process of identifying adequate measurements. A commonly used hypothesis is: "Complicated software is likely to be fault-prone." This assumption is based on plausibility and requires additional empirical evidence. If the hypothesis is valid, prediction models can be generated based on data from previous projects. Fig. 9.12 shows the conclusions chain behind this approach.

The approach is only valid, if its core hypothesis is true. It is thus necessary to validate the hypothesis empirically. In the following, some empirical evidence from published studies will be presented.

Table 9.2 presents empirical data which address the distribution of faults over software components. The symbols mean as follows: ++: strong confirmation; +: weak confirmation; 0: no statement; -: weak rejection; - -: strong rejection; /: not evaluated; ?: unclear. There is compelling evidence, that fault distribution follows the Pareto principle, i.e., faults are not equally distributed over software modules. The majority of faults are contained in few modules. These modules cause the majority of problems. Large modules are not necessarily more fault-prone than small modules.

Detecting many defects during test does not mean many defects during field use. The rules, with respect to fault distribution, seem to be stable between releases. On the one hand, these empirical data underline, that the idea of identifying fault-prone components makes sense. On the other hand, the simple way to focus on large modules is misleading. But since the rules are stable, extracting prediction models from previous projects and applying them to present projects is likely to be a fruitful approach.

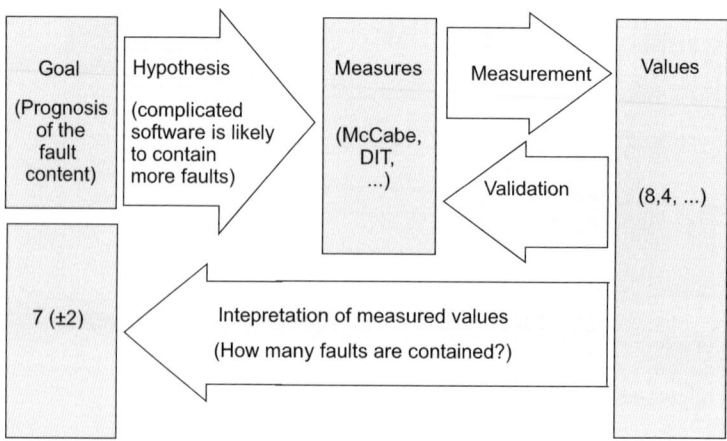

Fig. 9.12. The conclusions chain behind measurement-based fault prediction

Table 9.3 shows empirical data on the correlation between software complexity and fault content. The abbreviations mean as follows: WMC: Weighted Methods per Class; DIT: Depth of Inheritance Tree; NOC: Number Of Children; CBO: Coupling Between Object-classes; RFC: Response For a Class; LCOM: Lack of Cohesion on Methods; MHF: Method Hiding Factor; AHF: Attribute Hiding Factor; MIF: Method Inheritance Factor; AIF: Attribute Inheritance Factor; POF: Polymorphism Factor; COF: Coupling Factor.

Table 9.2. Hypotheses on fault distribution

	[Fent00]	[Basi96]	[Cart00]	[Basi84]	[Abre96]
Few modules contain the majority of faults.	++	++	(+)	++	/
Few modules cause most failures.	++	/	/	/	/
Many faults in unit testing means many faults in system testing.	+	/	/	/	/
Many faults during testing means many failures during field use.	--	/	/	/	/
Fault densities of corresponding process phases remain constant	+	/	/	/	/
Size measurements are appropriate for fault estimation.	+	/	+	-	/

Table 9.3. Correlation between code complexity and fault content

	[Fent00]	[Basi96]	[Cart00]	[Basi84]	[Abre96]
Code complexity measurements are appropriate means for fault prediction.	More appropriate than size measurements: -	WMC: + DIT: ++ RFC: ++ NOC: ? CBO: ++ LCOM: 0	WMC: / DIT: ++ RFC: / NOC: ? CBO: / LCOM: /	More appropriate than size measurements: -	MHF: + AHF: 0 MIF: + AIF: (+) POF: + COF: ++

Individual complexity measurements, e.g., McCabe's cyclomatic complexity, can be combined with size measurements but are typically correlated and thus do not provide more insight for estimation. But a combination of specific complexity measurements provide appropriate prediction quality. Identification of fault-prone modules seems to be possible, if a specific combination of well-suited complexity measurements is used. [McCa76, Eber95]

Cartwright and Shepperd investigated whether fault prediction is also possible during early development phases. They identified a high correlation between number of events in Shlaer-Mellor models and fault content, whereas the number of states was correlated with software size. Thus, design measurements may be appropriate for size and fault prediction at an early development stage.

Using fault prediction and reliability measurement to improve safety
The reliability of embedded software influences, e.g., the safety and availability of technical systems. In many application domains customers increasingly define quantified availability targets that are usually protected by fines. In some application domains (e.g., public transportation) systems need third-party certification. It is thus required to quantify the reliability of embedded software, because it is necessary to combine the results concerning software with results concerning hardware component into a valid result for hybrid systems.

Safety integrity of a system in quantifiable terms is required more and more by customers, assessors and licensing bodies. Fault tree analysis (FTA) is a commonly used method to derive and analyze potential failures, and their potential influence on system reliability and safety. They are proven and accepted methods in reliability and safety engineering. FTA is used, for example, in the chemical industry, for aviation and space systems, nuclear plants, and transportation systems. By means of Boolean logic, fault trees represent the relationship between causes (failures for example) and undesired or hazardous events. The root of a fault tree represents the undesired event; its leaves represent causes. The Boolean logic is given in a graphical representation. It is therefore suitable for communication and discussion. Fault tree analysis can be started very early in the design process. Typical questions are: Does the chosen design meet the reliability and safety requirements? What are the most critical components? Alternative designs can be judged reasonably. Design errors can be detected early.

Fault trees are usually generated manually. Highly skilled and experienced engineers analyze the system based on existing documents that describe the system. Typically, such documents are design and architecture specifications, configuration descriptions and so forth. Considerable knowledge, system insight and overview are necessary to consider many failure modes, possible consequences and dependencies between system components and their functionality at a time. Due to the complexity, this manual work is error-prone, costly, and usually incomplete.

A critical point is usually the consideration of software components. Software faults cause failures during runtime. Software reliability influences the safety of systems. Software failures may cause safety-critical behavior. The estimation of these effects requires quantified reliability estimates of software components, that are an input to a fault tree. Fault trees accept those failure rates as an input, that are calculated by statistical software reliability growth models. These models are the sound way to provide input on software influence on system safety.

It is possible to construct a fault tree for the hardware components of a system that accepts software reliability measurements as an input. Statistical software reliability models and fault trees may be composed to build a valid model for a hybrid system.

Conclusions

Reliability growth models are mature, but their practical application requires appropriate tools. Software reliability measurements can be propagated into safety models, e.g., fault trees, in order to model system properties, e.g., safety.

Some common hypotheses with respect to quality measurement have been empirically falsified, but there is evidence, that faults accumulate in few modules and that these modules may be identified using code complexity measurements and design measurements. Single measurements do not provide appropriate fault prediction capabilities, but a combination of measurements may be used to generate reliable predictions. The rules which connect subsequent projects seem to be very stable. It is thus possible to extract prediction models from completed projects and to apply them to new projects in order to predict properties.

9.4. Validation and Testing

9.4.1 Test Measurement

Expert Box. Author: Harry Sneed

As with software development, for software testing measurements serve to evaluate the product, to calculate the project, to measure the progress and to assess the process. So we can distinguish between four types of test measurements – the four "P's"
- Product measurements
- Project measurements
- Progress measurements
- Process measurements.

Product measurements
Let us begin with product measurements. In testing we are concerned with the testability of the product. A product is testable when it requires a minimum quantity of test cases and test data to demonstrate its correctness and when its results are maximally visible. The goals then are
- minimize the number of test cases required
- maximize visibility

Minimizing the number of test cases means different things at different semantic levels. In testing there are at least three such levels
- the unit test level
- the integration test level
- the system test level

At the unit test level, having less test cases is equivalent to having less paths thru the code to test. The number of logical paths is determined by the number of methods and logical conditions as well as the structure of the classes. Thus, the less methods and conditional branches there are relative to the size of the code in statements, the greater will be the testability. On the other hand, the fewer levels there are in the class hierarchy relative to the number of classes, the greater will be the testability.

In addition to that, we have data coming in and out of the classes. Much of the input data is just used to set or compute results. However, some of it serves to control the logic in the classes. The more control data we have, the harder it is to test the classes since the control data can not be randomly generated. It has to be explicitly set. Thus, the more control parameters there are the less is the testability.

Taking on these different views of the units under test, we will come up with at least three measurements for unit testability

$$1 - \frac{Methods + Branches}{Statements}$$

$$1 - \frac{ClassLevels}{Classes}$$

$$1 - \frac{ControlParameters}{AllParameters}$$

To demonstrate the measurement of unit testability, assume we have a component of 1500 statements with 7 classes at 3 levels. Each class has 10 methods each with 5 logical branches. Then, each method has three parameters of which one is a control parameter. That would lead to the following unit testability measurements

$$1 - \frac{70 methods + 350 branches}{1500 statements} = 0.72$$

$$1 - \frac{3 levels}{7 classes} = 0.57$$

$$1 - \frac{70 ControlParameters}{210 Parameters} = 0.67$$

Assuming that all of the measurements are assigned an equal weighting, the average testability of this particular component would be

$$(0.72 + 0.57 + 0.67)/3 = 0.65$$

Its testability could be improved by reducing the number of logical branches, by having less class levels and by decreasing the number of control parameters.

At the integration test level having less test cases is equivalent to having less interactions between the components and having fewer data interfaces. Interactions between components occur when a method within one component calls a method within another component. These calls are referred to as foreign calls, i.e., long distance calls, as opposed to the local calls of methods within the same component.

Components can also be coupled by sharing the same data. If two separate components access the same database table or use the same file, i.e., one produces the file and the other consumes that file, then they have a data coupling. The relation of the shared database tables and files to the total number of database tables and files is an indicator of testability.

Finally, we have the number of system and user interfaces as opposed to the total number of components. The more interfaces there are the more we have to test. Having fewer interfaces reduces the testing burden thus the relation between external interfaces and components is another indicator of integration testability.

From these three views of component integration we derive three measurements for integration testability.

$$1 - \frac{ForeignCalls}{AllCalls}$$

$$1 - \frac{SharedFiles\ \&\ DatabaseTables}{AllFiles\ \&\ DatabaseTables}$$

$$1 - \frac{ExternalInterfaces}{Components}$$

To demonstrate the measurement of integration testability, assume we have 16 components. Within these 16 components there are some 540 method calls of which 96 are foreign calls. These 16 components also process 40 database tables and 10 files. Of the 40 database tables 12 are accessed by two or more components and of the 10 files, 6 are used to pass data between components. The other 4 files are external interfaces. There are 8 user interfaces giving a total of 12 external interfaces. This results in the following measurements of testability

$$1 - \frac{96\ ForeignCalls}{640\ Calls} = 0.85$$

$$1 - \frac{18 SharedDataStores}{30 DataStores} = 0.40$$

$$1 - \frac{12 ExternalInterfaces}{16 Components} = 0.25$$

Assuming that all of the measurements are assigned an equal weighting, the average integration testability of this particular set of components would be

$$(0.85 + 0.40 + 0.25)/3 = 0.50$$

It is low because of the high number of shared data stores and external interfaces relative to the number of components.

At the system testing level having less test cases is a function of the number of database attributes one has to generate, the number of objects in the user interfaces one has to test and the number of system interfaces one has to deal with.

First, the number of database tables can be viewed in relation to the number of attributes contained within those tables. The more attributes the tables have, the harder it is to populate them. It is easier to deal with many small tables than fewer larger ones. Since any database table will have at least 2 to 4 attributes as a minimum we must adjust it by at least a factor of 4, thus giving the measurement

$$\frac{Tables}{Attributes} \times 4$$

Secondly, systems have user interfaces and user interfaces contain objects. Their number drives the effort required to test those user interfaces. The more objects the tester has to manipulate, the more the test effort. As is the case with the database tables, it is easier to test many user interfaces with few objects than a few interfaces with many objects. Thus, the user interface testability is the relationship of user interfaces to objects contained therein, whereby it is assumed that each user interface has at least two objects, giving the measurement

$$\frac{UserInterfaces}{Objects} \times 2$$

Thirdly, there are the system interfaces to deal with. These can be import / export files, remote procedure calls or messages sent and received. Each such interface contains a set of parameters. The number of parameters determines the width of the interface. The more there are, the wider the interface, thus increasing the number of potential data combinations and the required number of test cases. A system with many narrow interfaces requires less effort to test than one with fewer wider interfaces. Thus, we derive the ratio of parameters to interfaces as another measurement of system testability. Since an interface will have as a rule at least parameters, we must adjust the interface ratio by multiplying it by 3.

9.4 Validation and Testing

$$\frac{SystemInterfaces}{SystemParameters} \times 3$$

To demonstrate the measurement of system testability, let us assume a system has 400 data attributes in 32 tables, that it has 92 widgets or objects in 36 user interfaces and that it has 240 parameters in 24 system interfaces. To measure the testability of this system we use the measurements

$$\frac{32 Tables}{400 Attributes} \times 4 = 0.08 \times 4 = 0.32$$

$$\frac{36 UserInterfaces}{92 Objects} \times 2 = 0.39 \times 2 = 0.78$$

$$\frac{24 Interfaces}{240 Parameters} \times 3 = 0.10 \times 3 = 0.30$$

The average of these three measurements gives us a system testability ratio of 0.46. To obtain a maximum rating of 1, the database tables could have no more than 4 attributes, the user interfaces no more than 2 objects and the system interfaces no more than 3 parameters on average [Snee06a, Snee06b].

Project measurements
Project measurements are used to estimate the effort and the time required for a test project. As with other cost estimations, the key parameters are the size of the task and the productivity of the workers. Size and productivity in testing are expressed in terms of the number of test cases required to test a system. This number can be derived from an analysis of the requirements, by counting each action, state and rule as well as each acceptance criterion to be tested. The productivity in test cases per time unit can only be gained from experience or by copying someone else's experience which is always risky to do.

For estimating test effort and time a modified version of the COCOMO II method is recommended. The system type and the scaling exponent are the same as in COCOCO II [Boeh99]. The units of productivity are, instead of statements or function points, test cases. The quality adjustment factor is replaced by the testability factor. That results in the equation

$$TestEffort = SystemType \times \left\{ \frac{TestCase^{SE}}{Testproductivity} \right\} \times Testability$$

To demonstrate the use of that equation, we will assume that we have counted 400 test cases and that our previous productivity was 4 test cases per person day or 1 for every 2 hours worked on testing, including test design, test case specification, test data preparation, test execution and test evaluation, but not including test planning. This would give us an unadjusted effort of 100 person days.

Now this has to be adjusted by the testing scaling exponent which ranges from 0.91 to 1.23 depending on five influence factors.
- degree of reuse of previous tests
- testing environment
- target architecture
- test team cohesion
- test process maturity

Each of these factors is evaluated on the scale of 0.91 to 1.23 with 0.91 being the highest fulfillment and 1.23 being the lowest fulfillment. Then the average is taken. In the case where
- degree of reuse = low = 1.10
- testing environment = medium = 1.00
- target architecture = highly known = 0.96
- team cohesion = low = 1.10
- process maturity = medium = 1.00

we arrive at a scaling exponent of 1.03.

Our raw effort of 100 person days is adjusted by this scaling factor to 115 person days.

Now we must adjust this effort further by multiplying it by the testability factor. To obtain this factor we take the measured system testability of 0.46 which we obtained from the analysis of the databases, user interfaces and system interfaces. To convert it into a multiplication factor we divide it into the median testability grade of 0.5. A testability ratio higher than the median will reduce the testing effort. A testability ratio lower than the median will increase the testing effort. Here the test effort will be increased by 8% due to the below average testability.

$$0.5\% / 0.46 \times 115 \text{ PD} = 1.08 \times 115 \text{ PD} = 124 \text{ person days}$$

The last step is to multiply the adjusted effort by the system type. In COCOMO II there are four system types each with another multiplication factor
- Stand alone Application = 0.5
- Integrated Application = 1
- Distributed Application = 2
- Embedded Application = 4

Assuming that we are developing a distributed Web application we would multiply the 124 person days by 2 giving a final effort of 248 person days or 12 person months for testing.

To estimate the calendar time required we proceed to use the COCOMO II time equation

$$Time = \left(C \times Effort^F\right)_{PMs} \times (1 - SCED\%/100)$$

where C is a constant depending on the project type. In the case of a new development it is 3.67

F is the time-scaling exponent, not to be confused with the effort scaling exponent. It is computed as follows:

$$F = D + (0.2 \times (SE - LB))$$

where SE is the effort-scaling exponent from the effort equation, in our case 1.03. LB is the lower bound of the scaling exponent which is 0.93; D is a time base coefficient, depending on the project type. For a new development, it is 0.28.

That leaves us with a time scaling factor of

$$(0.28 + (0.2 \times (0.03 - 0.93))) = 0.3$$

The normal time to complete this particular testing project would be

$$(3.67 \times 12^{0.3}) = 8 \quad \text{months using one tester}$$

The SCED% is referred to by Boehm as the schedule compression factor. It is the percentage to which to project time can be reduced by adding more persons to the project. In development it is seldom more than 50% per person, however in testing it can go up to 75% per person. Adding more testers to a testing project will not necessarily make it last longer, provided the testers are familiar with the project and know what to do.

So for our project assume we can add an additional two testers thus compressing the project time by 0.75 x 0.75 = 56% and giving a compression factor of

$$1 - (56/100) = 0.44$$

With the two testers we would need only 8 x 0.44 = 3.5 calendar months. Using the modified COCOMO II method, we have calculated an effort of 12 person months and a duration of 3.5 calendar months for this testing project.

Progress Measurements
Test progress can be measured in terms of test coverage and errors found. Test coverage is measured in many ways. One is the conventional code coverage which could be measured at the
- method,
- statement, or
- branch level.

It is expressed as the number of code units traversed by the test relative to the total number of code units, e.g.

$$\frac{BranchesTested}{TotalBranches}$$

Since the advent of frameworks, reuse and code generation this form of coverage has become to mean less. In fact, it has become meaningless unless it is possible to establish a profile of which code units belong to the application under test.

For this reason functional and architectural coverage have become more important. Architectural coverage captures the methods affected by the application, the interactions between those methods and the object types created. What remains to be done is instrumenting the code in such a way that these methods, interactions and state transitions are marked. Then the architectural coverage would be

$$\frac{Methods, Calls\ \&\ StatesTested}{All\ RelevantMethods, Calls\ \&\ States}$$

Functional coverage is the easiest to measure provided all of the functions are documented. A static analysis of the functional requirements will tell us how many test cases are required to test all of the functions. The functional test coverage is then

$$\frac{TestCasesExecuted}{TestCases\ Required}$$

Measuring the error detection rate presupposes that the testing team has the error statistics on previous projects or versions, since that is necessary in order to compute the expected error density and to project the number of errors.

There are here two key measurements
- the system size and
- the error count.

The system size can be measured in statements, function points, object points or any other size measurement provided it can be extracted from the source code of a system. The error count is the number of errors found by the testers in that particular system. To project the error count on to a future system we need the error density. This is computed by dividing the error count by the system size.

Having completed a system and put it into production the code is analyzed and found to contain 18,000 statements. When testing that system 120 errors were discovered. That gives an error density of

$$\frac{120}{18,000} = 0.007$$

or 7 errors per 1000 statements.

The new system to be developed is estimated to have 1200 function points. From previous measurements we have a ratio of Function – Points to statements in this particular language of 1 to 33. From that ratio we can predict that the new system will have some 39.600 statements. Multiplying that by the previous error density of 0.007 tells us that we should find at least 277 errors in the new system, as it is more than 2 times larger than the previous one.

Of course the more systems we have for comparison, the more reliable will be our error projection. The error density rate projected on to the new system could be the median error density of all the comparable systems. In any case, once we have a predicted error count, we can use this as a reference point for the number of errors we should be able to find.

Tracing the test coverage rate and the error discovery rate are the primary means of measuring the progress of a test project. Both measurements can be compared with the rates to be achieved as well as with the expended test effort in person days to locate where the project is (see Fig. 9.13).

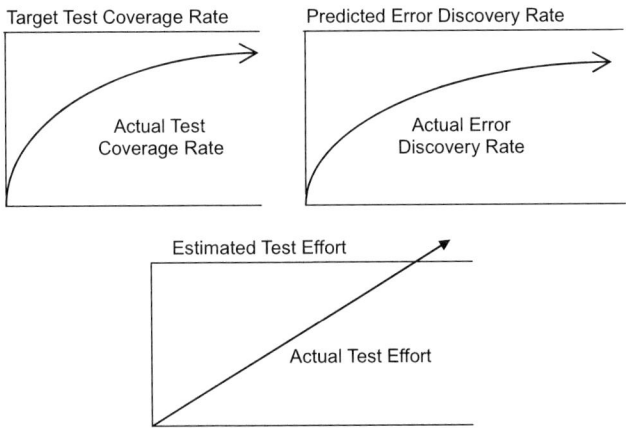

Fig. 9.13. Test measurements

Process measurements

In the end, every process must be evaluated. To this end, we need process measurements to assess the efficiency and effectiveness of the process. Effectiveness is measured in terms of how close the process comes to achieving the goals set for it. Efficiency is measured in terms of the cost incurred in achieving those goals.

The two primary goals of testing are to uncover errors and to achieve confidence in the system to be released [Spil06]. The first goal can be measured by comparing the number of errors uncovered by the testers before the system is released to the number of errors reported by the users after the system is released. The error discovery measurement is

$$\frac{TestreportedErrors}{AllreportedErrors}$$

According to the pertinent literature on testing this should be at least 0.85. If in our case 260 errors were found by the testers and another 40 reported by the users, the test efficiency would be 0.86 which is sufficient.

The second goal, that achieving confidence, is a function of the errors found in the final test compared to the number of test cases run and the test coverage achieved. The user wants to know that the remaining error probability is very low and that the test coverage is very high. When both factors come together, his confidence in the system is ensured. Thus, confidence can be expressed in the following measurement

$$TestConfidence = \left\{1 - \frac{ErrorsFoundInLastTest}{TestCasesRun}\right\} \times TestCoverage$$

Assuming that we have run all 400 test cases in the last test and only discovered 3 errors and that the functional test coverage was 95% then the test confidence would be

$$\left\{1 - \frac{3}{400}\right\} \times 0.95 = 0.94$$

The final test measurement is the efficiency measurement. Efficiency in testing can be expressed in terms of the test cases run and the errors found per person day, smoothed by the achieved test coverage rate.

$$Efficiency = \left\{1 - \frac{Tester\_days}{Errors + TestCases}\right\} \times TestCoverage$$

Assuming we have executed all 400 test cases and found 260 errors with 180 person days of effort and that the final test coverage rate was 0.95 then the test efficiency would be

$$\left\{1 - \frac{180}{260 + 400}\right\} \times 0.95 = 0.69$$

If we would have required 300 person days to run the same number of test cases while only finding 220 errors and achieving a test coverage of only 75%, then the test efficiency would be significantly less.

$$\left\{1 - \frac{300}{220 + 400}\right\} \times 0.75 = 0.39$$

This ends this short discourse on the subject of test measurements. The reader has learned the four main classes of test measurements for measuring
- product testability,
- project time and costs,
- progress of the test and
- process effectiveness and efficiency.

In addition, we have demonstrated how these measurements can be applied. One final remark is that errors are not equivalent. Critical errors weigh more than major errors and major errors weigh more thane minor errors. Therefore, rather than simply counting errors, the reader should consider counting weighted errors. The IEEE Standard 1044 proposes 5 classes of errors [IEEE93]
- critical,
- severe,
- major,
- minor and
- disturbing.

The critical errors could be weighted by 8, the severe by 4, the major by 2, the minor by 1, and the disturbing by 0.5. This would help to make the error discovery rate more meaningful in terms of the service rendered. And that is what business is all about, namely the return on investment or as Tom DeMarco once put it – the bang for your bucks [DeMa82].

9.4.2 Analyzing Defects

Expert Box. Author: Luigi Buglione

As stated in the introduction to this chapter, quality does not mean simply "*counting defects*" but means quantifying and evaluating by a series of attributes (and sub-attributes) as proposed for instance by the ISO/IEC 9126 series of standards (now incorporated into the new 25000 series). But it is fundamental to remember that measurement is a tool, not the goal itself in the management of an entity of interest, in this case a software project. And in order to achieve a continuous improvement of the project, it is fundamental to ask continuously the reason why a certain effect (no matter if positive or negative) occurred, until arriving to a satisfactory answer from the analysis. That's the "5 why's game" learned and applied from children when growing.

Because process improvement needs quality tools, the motto for the near future should be "*back to TQM!*", retrieving those quality tools (where old tools are more quantitative-oriented, while the new ones are more qualitatively oriented), very useful for realizing a valuable and real continuous improvement, whatever the application domain.

In particular, the **Ishikawa diagram** (also known as the "Fishbone" or "Cause-Effect" diagram), is a powerful tool for helping in the elicitation of possible causes for a certain effect to analyze (usually, even if it can be used also for positive effects, the logic is to take into account negative effects to be removed) when the final goal is to remove mainly causes more than the solely emerging errors. Fig. 9.14 shows an example Ishikawa diagram for an analysis of software defects [Lesz00].

The typical application of those diagrams was from a qualitative perspective, detecting possible causes and using them for the creation of an action plan, in order to put in place corrective or improvement actions. But there are few applications from a quantitative perspective, determining "how much" we should bring into those actions.

In Fig. 9.14, when the analysis arrives at its final stage and the final leafs (or bones) have been determined, it will be possible to "metricate" each low-level cause with the **GQM** (Goal-Question-Metric) approach or retrieve the measurements yet defined for the related processes of your BPM (Business Process Model) [Bugl06]. The Quality Management System (QMS) can be referred as a sub-set of the more comprehensive BPM, where the boundary is typically theme-delimited by ISO 9001:2000 clauses.

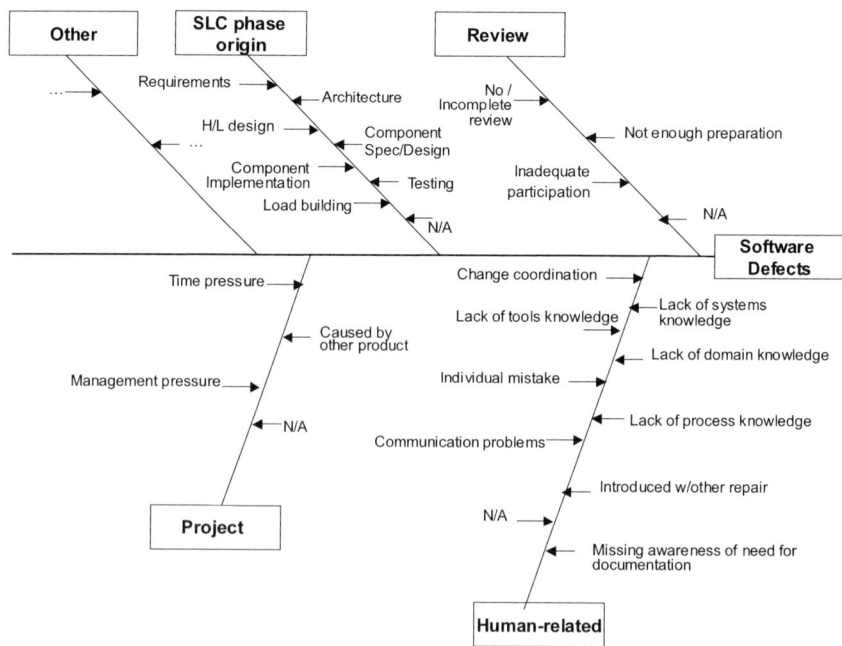

Fig. 9.14. Ishikawa Diagram: an example showing the qualitative usage [Lesz00]

In order to properly use retrieved values from measurements for the decision-making process and the creation of a well-established and balanced action plan, it is advisable to create and maintain a "definition table" for each measurement used (see chapter 6). A fundamental point for successfully applying measurements for making valuable action plans as response to a finished cause-effect analysis is the establishment (and maintenance) of thresholds, possibly both an Upper and a Lower Control Level (respectively, UCL and LCL), as in control charts, or at least some reference values that can help the decision-maker in determining the right *intensity* of the action to be taken. Fig. 9.15 proposes this shift from the qualitative to the quantitative usage of this tool.

The good news is that the application of Ishikawa diagrams in this way can surely bring an added value to an organization, moving people towards a more quantitative perspective on management practices, not only those related to the software production and making easier the data gathering for creating and maintaining historical databases for estimation purposes, at all levels.

The bad news is that the original diagram implies a brainstorming and – therefore – open and original solutions to each problems to analyze and the output from such analysis will lead to the identification of (possibly) different "bones" (or "leaves", using the *tree* metaphor) that cannot allow a comparability among analyses with a similar background.

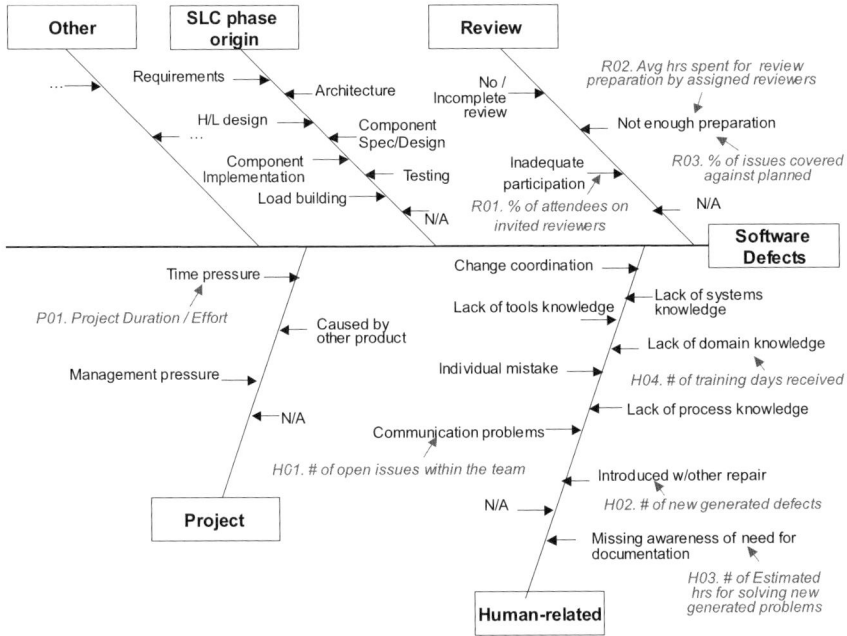

Fig. 9.15. Ishikawa Diagram: an example (quantitative usage)

In order to partly solve this problem, a specific instantiation of the Ishikawa diagram for defect management in the software engineering domain was proposed, called **ODC** (*Orthogonal Defect Classification*) by Ram Chillarege [Chil92], at that time an IBM scientist. ODC introduced a standard taxonomy of causes with quantitative elements that allows to compare during time gathered data with the defects historical databases, providing also tips on causes removal and speaking about *in-process measurement* for the software development process.

In fact, ODC proposed the usage of two main attributes: the defect *type* and the defect *trigger*. *Type* is needed in order to classify the kind of defect detected: function, interface, checking, assignment, timing/serialization, build/package/merge, documentation, algorithm where the eight types initially foreseen, to be associated to the related SLC phase. The *trigger*, defined as the condition that allows a defect to surface, helps in the verification process to understand where the defect has been originated. An intensive usage of the trigger concept allow to know more and more in detail a certain process and to detect new possible triggers when the process will evolve. For both attributes, it is possible to analyze and take into account several views on data, allowing to understand more and more the mechanics of processes and possible ways to improve them. Possible views to consider could be

- Age vs. activity in uncovering defects in code
- Frequency of a component within activity
- Trigger classification of field defects over time
- Frequency of activities with triggers
- Frequency of defect type with qualifiers in previous (or current) releases
- Defect frequency for triggers within a certain defect type

Over the years, ODC has been widely adopted in many software organizations as IBM, Bellcore (now Telcordia Technologies), Motorola, NASA, among others. The main advantage using this technique is a powerful combination of cause-effect analysis through standard defects taxonomy by a quantitative approach. As usual, there are good and bad news. The good news is that ODC overcomes some limitations provided by a quantitative usage of Ishikawa diagrams. The bad news is that the implementation of ODC could be not possible in those organizations with a certain maturity level. A confirmation of this point comes from a 2002 SEI report: it emerged that ODC was applied by two large organizations out of 27 examined, both rated at maturity level 5 of the CMM. From a CMMI perspective [SEI06a, Chri06], that kind of practices is expected at ML3 in the CAR (Causal Analysis and Resolution) process area, where SP1.2-1 practice asks for the need to "*analyze causes*", developing solutions by action proposals for implementations.

Therefore, even if it seems a common sense mechanism, there is room (and time) to apply consistently such techniques to small and medium enterprises (SMEs). A possible path towards this goal within the boundary of defect management can be:

Table 9.4. Examples of possible transformation forms

#	Technique	Variant	Goal
1	Ishikawa diagram	Qualitative	Learning and applying the basics about cause-effect analysis
2	Ishikawa diagram	Quantitative	Refining its usage, introducing a quantitative management
3	ODC	Standard	Introducing standard defect taxonomies for external benchmarking
4	ODC	Tailored	Tailoring ODC to your own BPM/QMS processes and procedures

In conclusion, only by moving in this direction, ICT companies will achieve consistent improvements from several perspectives. There is a lot to work for quantitatively managing defects and their causes which represents a "new frontier" for ICT companies. But more than techniques, a fundamental *enabler* to achieve that goal (and consequently also financial results), still remain people, as also formulated in excellence models and frameworks such as the Balanced Scorecard (BSC) and EFQM models.

9.5. Software Reliability Prediction

9.5.1 Practical Software Reliability Engineering

Software reliability engineering is a statistical procedure associated with test and correction activities during development. It is further used after delivery, based on field data, to validate prediction models. Users of such prediction models and the resulting reliability values are development managers who apply them to determine the best suitable defect detection techniques and to find the optimum delivery time. Operations managers use the data for deciding when to include new functionality in a delivered product that is already performing in the field. Maintenance managers use the reliability figures to plan the allocation of resources they need to deliver corrections in due time according to contracted deadlines.

The current approach to software reliability modeling focuses on the testing and rework activities of the development process. On the basis of data on the time intervals between occurrences of failures, collected during testing, we attempt to make inferences about how additional testing and rework would improve the reliability of the product and about how reliable the product would be once it is released to the user.

Software reliability engineering includes the following activities [Musa87, Lyu95, Musa91]:

- selecting a mixture of quality factors oriented towards maximizing customer satisfaction
- determining a reliability objective (i.e., exit criteria for subsequent test and release activities)
- predicting reliability based on models of the development process and its impact on fault introduction, recognition and correction
- supporting test strategies based on realization (e.g., white box testing, control flow branch coverage) or usage (e.g., black box testing, operational profiles)
- providing insight to the development process and its influence on software reliability
- improving the software development process in order to obtain higher quality reliability
- defining and validating measurements and models for reliability prediction

The above list of activities is mainly from the customer's point of view. When making the distinction between failures and defects, the customer is interested in the reduction of failures. Emphasis on reducing failures means that development and testing is centered towards functions in normal and extraordinary operational modes (e.g., usage coverage instead of branch coverage during system testing, or operational profiles instead of functional profiles during reliability assessment). In this section we will focus on the aspect of reliability modeling that is used for measuring and estimating (predicting) the reliability of a software release during testing as well as in the field.

Fig. 9.16 shows the usage of reliability models in a software project. The reliability model is primarily used to help in project management (e.g., to determine release dates, service effort or test effort) and in engineering support (e.g., to provide insight on stability of the system under test, to predict residual defects, to relate defects to test cases and test effectiveness). It is also used for critical management decisions, such as evaluating the trade-off of releasing the product with a certain number of expected failures or to determine the necessary service resources after release. The reliability model is based upon a standard model that is selected by the quality engineer from the literature of such models and their applicability and scope [Lyu95]. Then it is adapted and tailored to the actual situation of test and defect correction. Detected defects are reported into the model together with underlying execution time. More sophisticated models also take into consideration the criticality of software components, such as components with a long defect history or those that had been changed several times during the current or previous releases.

Test strategies must closely reflect operational scenarios and usage in order to predict reliability after release. The model then will forecast the defects or failures to expect during test or after release. Accuracy of such models should be in the range of 20-30 percent to ensure meaningful decisions. If they are far off, the wrong model had been selected (e.g., not considering defects inserted during correction cycles) or the test strategy is not reflecting operational usage.

Such models use an appropriate statistical model which requires accurate test or field failure data related to the occurrences in terms of execution time. Execution time in reliability engineering is the accumulated time a system is executed under real usage conditions. It is used for reliability measurement and predictions to relate individual test time and defect occurrence towards the would-be performance under real usage conditions.

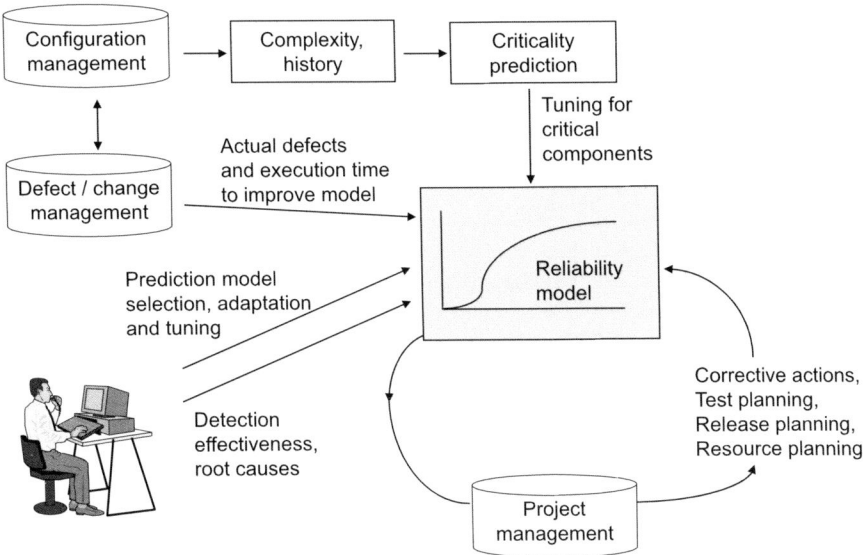

Fig. 9.16. Reliability models in software engineering

Fig. 9.17 shows the execution time approach to determine the optimal release time. Compared to the standard project tracking charts (e.g., defect tracking like in Fig. 8.19), here the horizontal axis shows the combined execution time of the system under test. It allows comparing actual performance of system test to the defined acceptance or release criteria in terms of failure rates. If for instance the specification demands less then 5 defects of severity 2 and less then 2 defects of severity 1 per 20 days, you can set up these thresholds and relate actual test performance to this acceptance level. This is shown with the thick horizontal lines in the graph. Only after these lines are not anymore reached, the system can be released without expecting immediate rejection or severe customer dissatisfaction. Obviously the test conditions must reflect realistic usage conditions to approximate the usage behaviors once released.

Several models should be considered and assessed for their predictive accuracy, in order to select the most accurate and reliable model for reliability prediction. It is of no use to switch models after the facts to achieve best fit, because then you would have no clue about how accurate the model would be in a predictive scenario. Unlike many research papers on that subject, our main interest is to select a model that would provide in very different settings (i.e., project sizes) of the type of software we are developing a good fit that can be used for project management.

Reliability prediction thus should be performed at intermediate points and at the end of system testing.

At intermediate points, reliability predictions will provide a measurement of the product's current reliability and its growth, and thus serve as an instrument for estimating the time still required for test. They also help in assessing the trade-off between extensive testing and potential loss of market share (or penalties in case of investment goods) because of late delivery. At the end of development which is the decision review before releasing the product to the customer, reliability estimations facilitate an evaluation of reliability against the committed targets. Especially in communication, banking and defense businesses, such reliability targets are often contracted and therefore are a very concrete exit criterion. It is common to have multiple failure rate objectives.

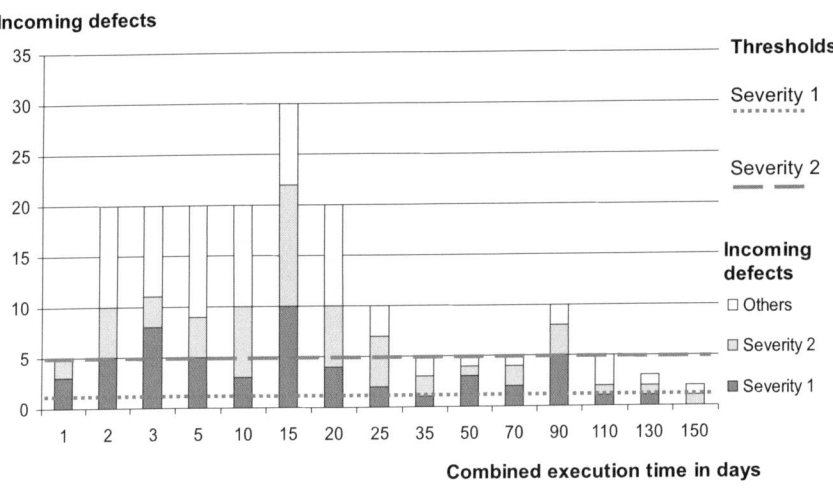

Fig. 9.17. Defects during system testing are tracked following combined execution time

For instance, failure rate objectives will generally be lower (more stringent) for high failure severity classes. The factors involved in setting failure rate objectives comprise the market and competitive situation, user satisfaction targets and risks related to malfunctions of the system. Life-cycle costs related to development, test and deployment in a competitive situation must be carefully evaluated, to avoid setting reliability objectives too high.

Reliability models are worthless if they are not continuously validated against the actually observed failure rates. We thus also include in our models which will be presented later in this section, a plot of predicted against actually observed data.

The application of reliability models to reliability prediction is based on a generic algorithm for model selection and tuning:
1. Establish goals according to the most critical process areas or products (e.g., by following the quality improvement paradigm or by applying a Pareto analysis).

2. Identify the appropriate data for analyzing faults and failures (i.e., with classifications according to severity, time between failures, reasons for faults, test cases that helped in detection and so on).
3. Collect data relevant for models that help to gain insight into how to achieve the identified goals. Data collection is cumbersome and exhaustive: Tools may change, processes change as well, development staff are often unwilling to provide additional effort for data collection and – worst of all – management often does not wish for changes that affect it personally.
4. Recover historical data that was available at given time stamps in the software development process (for example, fault rates of testing phases); the latter of these will serve as starting points of the predictive models.
5. Model the development process and select a fault introduction model, a testing model and a correction model that suit the observed processes best.
6. Select a reliability prediction model that suits the given fault introduction, testing and correction models best.
7. Estimate the parameters for the reliability model using only data that were available at the original time stamps.
8. Extrapolate the function at some point in time later than the point in time given for forecasting. If historical data is available after the given time stamps it is possible to predict failures.
9. Compare the predicted fault or failure rates with the actual number of such incidents and compute the forecast's relative error.

This process can be repeated for all releases and analyzed to determine the "best" model.

9.5.2 Applying Reliability Growth Models

Reliability growth models assume that when a failure occurs there is an attempt to remove the design fault that caused the failure. After the correction the software is set running again, to eventually fail yet again because of another fault. When the defect is removed without causing a new fault, and under the assumption that the number of defects is limited, reliability will grow over time. The successive times of failure-free working are the input to probabilistic reliability growth models which use these data to estimate the current reliability of the software under study, and to predict how the reliability will further improve in the future.

Many software reliability prediction models are based on some kind of Poisson processes [Musa87, Lyu95, Musa91]. Poisson processes are well known in all fields that deal with events that occur at random and independently from each other. Applications include the occurrence of phone calls in a switching system or their individual length. Both situations have been extensively investigated in traffic theory with the result that they follow typical (Poisson) distributions that are not normal but skewed, and which depend on several parameters. Naturally, the occurrence of failures and of phone calls can be compared, providing a basis for the definition of reliability models. Poisson models are based on a set of assump-

tions that are as follows (with time t, failure intensity $\lambda(t)$ and cumulative failures $\mu(t)$):
- Cumulative number of failures at the beginning is $\mu(t) = 0$.
- Failures are independent of other events or of history.
- The probability of occurrence of a failure in a given small time interval is negligible and is the same for a second occurrence in the same small time interval.

An important property of the Poisson process is its additivity which states that mutually independent Poisson processes with intensities λ_i can be superimposed to create an overall Poisson process with intensity λ, where λ is the sum of all λ_i. Formally both the failure intensity $\lambda(t)$ and the collection of all failures at time t, $\mu(t)$, are Poisson distributed random variables.

A model with constant failure intensity, a homogeneous Poisson process, is applicable during field operations without fault corrections. On the other hand, if corrections are made in response to failures, such as during testing or when new releases are introduced to the field, then a non-homogeneous Poisson process (NHPP) is appropriate. In the latter case the failure rate decreases over time with corrections being provided (including the consideration of defective corrections). The second approach to a decreasing failure rate is divided into two basic models [Musa87, Lyu95].

- Infinite failure models like the logarithmic non-homogeneous Poisson execution time model (LNHPP):

$$\lambda(\mu) = \lambda_0 \exp(-\theta\mu)$$

Other representatives are the Littlewood-Verrall model and the Weibull process model.

- Finite failure models like the basic exponential non-homogeneous Poisson execution time model (ENHPP):

$$\lambda(\mu) = \theta(\mu_0 - \mu)$$

This function assumes a linear decrease in intensity with each detection (and correction) of a failure. Other representatives are the expanded exponential S-shaped Yamada-Osaki model and the Crow model.

For a distinct subset of tests during subsystem and system testing, an ENHPP model can approximate the reported fault rates with good accuracy. In order to validate forecasts made in the past, rates reported after the time that the forecast was made can be compared with the ones that were extrapolated (Fig. 9.18).

The reality of software development and operation lies somewhere between the two formal models. Failures may occur because of interaction between several faults (e.g., two fatal faults are in immediate sequence, leaving the correction of only one of them without any effect on the failure rate). Another phenomenon that we observed within communication systems is load-dependent failures that typically occur after the same parts of the code have been executed several times. In this case the individual fault processes are not Poisson distributed as long as the

9.5 Software Reliability Prediction 293

execution or load sequence by itself is not a Poisson process. This pattern often causes communications software to fail once the environment changes (e.g., workload or equipment changes), although the software seemed to operate fault-free during test.

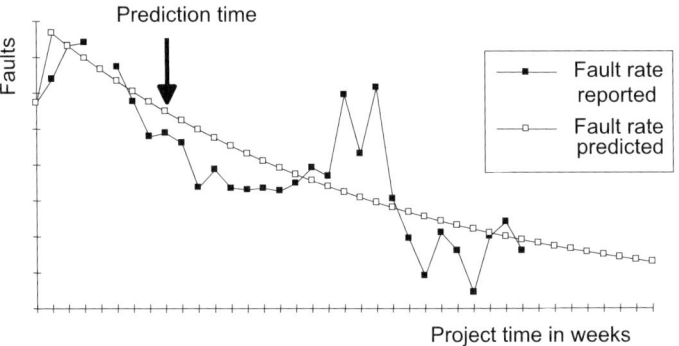

Fig. 9.18. Application of ENHPP model to predict fault rates

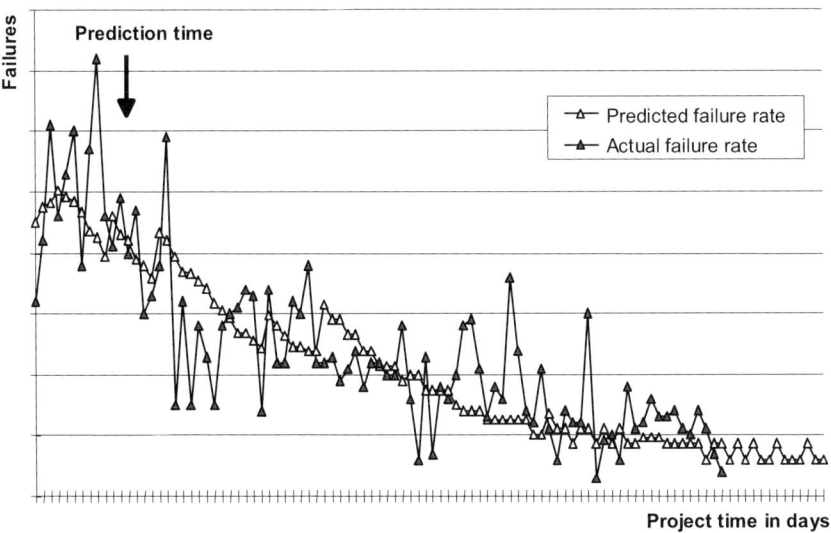

Fig. 9.19. Predicted field failure rate of several increments

Software failures are gathered and faults are detected from time to time based on an analysis of accumulated failure descriptions, resulting in the detection of faults that have caused between none and several different failures. Delayed fault detection and correction or cumulative corrections of software (which is common in huge systems with several million statements) are, of course, non-Poisson distributed. To make things easier, theory provides a law of large numbers: as time and thus failures approach infinity in such a way that the arrival of any failure is very unlikely (i.e., in the field), superimposed occurrences $\mu(t)$ converge to a Poisson process.

The overall goal is, of course, not to accurately predict the failure rate but to be as close as possible to a distinct margin that is allowed by customer contracts or available maintenance capacity. An example for a practically used combined reliability profile summarized from various models is shown in Fig. 9.19.

9.6. The Return on Investment from Better Quality

Quality improvement is driven by two overarching business objectives, both contributing to increased returns on engineering investments.
- Improve the customer-perceived quality. This impacts the top line because sales are increased with satisfied customers.
- Reduce the total cost of non-quality. This improves the bottom line, because reduced cost of non-quality means less engineering cost with same output, therefore improved productivity.

Improving customer-perceived quality can be broken down to one major improvement target, to systematically reduce customer detected faults. Reducing field defects and improving customer-perceived quality almost naturally improves the cost-benefit values along the product life-cycle. Investments are made to improve quality which later improves customer satisfaction. Therefore the second objective of reducing the cost of non-quality comes into the picture: this is the cost of activities related to detecting defects too late.

Return on investment (ROI) is a critical, but often misleading expression when it comes to development cost (for ROI and business case related information, see also Chap. 12). Too often heterogeneous cost elements with different meaning and unclear accounting relationships are combined into one figure that is then optimized. For instance, reducing the "cost of quality" that includes appraisal cost and prevention cost is misleading when compared with cost of nonconformance because certain appraisal costs (e.g., unit test) are components of regular development. Cost of nonconformance (cost of non-quality) on the other hand is incomplete if we only consider internal cost for fault detection, correction and redelivery because we must include opportunity cost due to rework at the customer site, late deliveries or simply binding resources that otherwise might have been used for a new project.

> Not all ROI calculations need to be are based immediately on monetary benefits from accounting. Depending on the business goals, they can as well be directly presented in terms of improved delivery accuracy, reduced lead time or higher efficiency and productivity. The latter have a meaning for the market or customer, and thus clearly serve as a ROI basis.

9.6 The Return on Investment from Better Quality

One of the typical improvement objectives (and thus measurements) related to process improvement is reduced cost of non-quality. Reducing cost is for many companies a key business concern and they look for ways how to effectively address sources of cost. Philip Crosby's **cost of quality model** provides a useful tool for measuring the impacts of process improvement in this domain [Cros79]. We have extended his model to cover the quality-related cost in software and IT projects. Our model segments cost of building a product and is applicable to all kinds of software and IT products, services and so on. Fig. 9.20 shows the quality related cost and its elements following four categories.

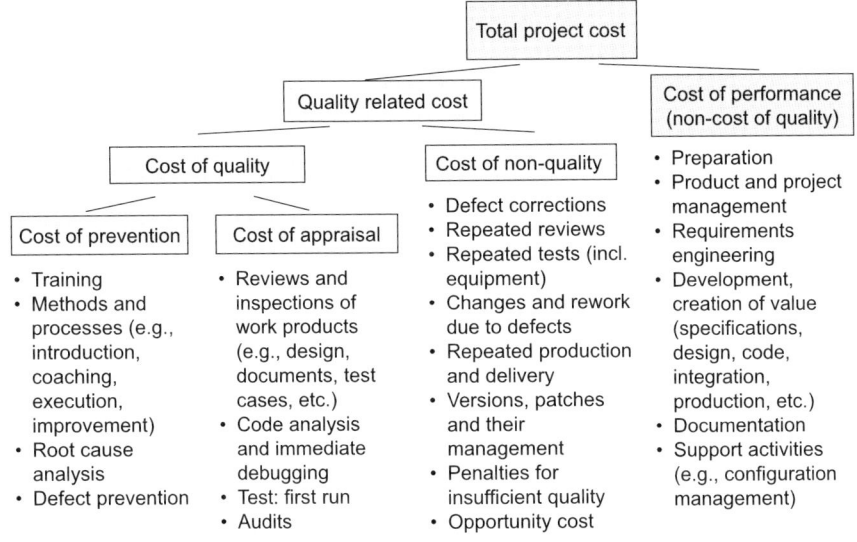

Fig. 9.20. Quality related cost and its elements

- **Cost of performance** or **non-cost of quality**. These are any regular cost related to developing and producing the software, such as requirements management, design, documentation or deployment environments. It includes project management, configuration management, tools and so on. It excludes only the following segments which have been defined to distinguish quality-related activities.
- **Cost of prevention**. These are the cost to establish, perform and maintain processes to avoid or reduce the number of defects during the project. It includes dedicated techniques and methods for defect prevention and the related measurement, change management, training and tools.
- **Cost of appraisal**. These are the cost related to detecting and removing defects close to the activity where they had been introduced. This cost typically includes activities such as reviews, unit test, inspections, but also training in these techniques.
- **Cost of nonconformance** or **cost of non-quality**. These are the cost attributable to not having prevented or removed defects in due time. They can be dis-

tinguished towards cost of internal defects (found in testing) and cost of external defects (found after release of the product). Specifically the latter have huge overheads due to providing corrections or even paying penalties. Regression testing, building and deploying patches and corrections, staffing the help desk (for the share of corrective maintenance and service) and re-developing a product or release that misses customer needs are included to cost of non-quality. For conservative reasons (i.e., to not overestimate ROI and savings) they do not include opportunistic cost, such as bad reputation or loosing a contract.

Let us look to a **concrete example with empirical evidence**. For early defect detection, we will try to provide detailed insight in an ROI calculation based on empirical data from Alcatel which was collected during the late nineties in numerous studies from a variety of projects of different size and scope (Table 9.5, Fig. 9.21) [Eber99a, Eber01c]. The data that are used for calculations result from average values that have been gathered in Alcatel's global project history database. We will compare the effect of increased effort for combined code reading and code inspection activities as a key result of our improvement program. The summary shows that by reducing the amount of code to be inspected per hour by more than a factor of three, the efficiency in terms of faults detected increased significantly. As a result the percentage of faults detected during coding increased dramatically. While reading speed reflects only the actual effort spent for fault detection, the effort per KStmt includes both detection and correction, thus resulting in around 3 PH/fault which seems stable.

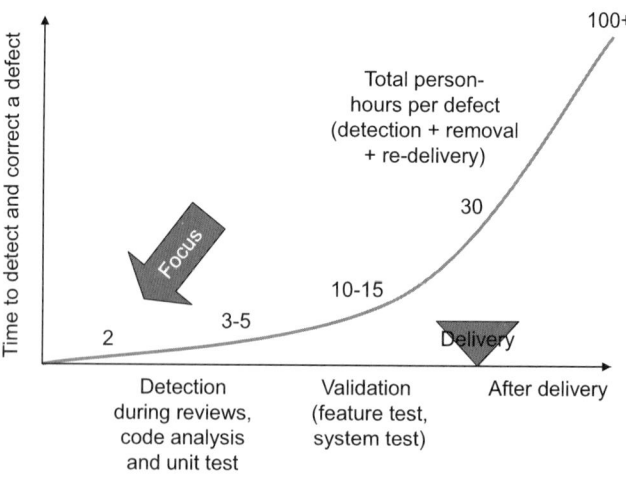

Fig. 9.21. The effort per defect depends on the activity where it is found

Given an average-sized development project and only focusing on the new and changed software without considering any effects of defect-preventive activities over time, the following calculation can be derived. The effort spent for code reading and inspection activities increases by 1470 PH. Assuming a constant average combined appraisal cost and cost of nonperformance (i.e., detection and correction effort) after coding of 15 PH/fault (the value at the time of this analysis in the respective product-line), the total effect is 9030 PH less spent in year 2. This results in a ROI value of 6.1 (i.e., each additional hour spent on code reading and inspections yields 6.1 saved hours of appraisal and nonperformance activities afterwards).

The effects of applying complexity-based criticality prediction to a new project can be summarized as follows: 20% of all modules in the project were predicted as most critical (after coding). and these modules contained over 40% of all faults (up to release time). Knowing that at least 60% of all faults can be detected until the end of unit test and fault correction during unit test and code reading costs less than 10% compared to fault correction during system test, 24% of all faults can be detected early by investigating 20% of all modules more intensively with 10% of the effort compared to fault correction during system test, therefore yielding a 20% total cost reduction for fault correction.

Table 9.5. ROI calculation of process improvements with focus on code reading / inspections (defect prevention activities are not considered for this example)

	baseline	year 1	year 2
Reading speed [Stmt/PH]	183	57	44
Effort per KStmt	15	24	36
Effort per Defect in code reviews	7.5	3	3
Defects per KStmt	2	8	12
Effectiveness [% of all]	2	18	29
Project: 70 KStmts. 2100 faults estimated based on 30 defects per KStmt			
Effort for code reading or inspections [PH]	1050		2520
Defects found in code reading/inspections	140		840
Residual defects after code reading/inspections	1960		1260
Correction effort after code reading/inspections [PH] (based on 15 PH/F average correction effort)	29400		18900
Total correction effort [PH]	30450		21420
ROI = saved total effort/additional detection effort			6.1

Additional costs for providing the static code analysis and the related statistical analysis are in the range of few person hours per project. The tools used for this exercise are off-the-shelf and readily available (e.g., static code analysis, spreadsheet programs).

The business impact of early defect removal and thus less rework is dramatic. Taking above observations, we can generalize towards a simple rule of thumb. Moving 10% of defects from test activities (with 10-15 PH/defect) to reviews and phase-contained defect removal activities (with 2-3 PH/defect) brings a yield of 3% of total engineering cost reduction.

The calculation is as follows. We assume that an engineer is working for 90% on projects. Of this project work, 40% is for testing (which includes all effort related to test activities) and another 40% is for constructive activities (including requirements analysis, specification, design, coding, together with direct phase-contained defect removal). The rest is assumed as overheads related to project management, configuration management, training and so on. So the totality of engineering effort on design and test is 32%, respectively. Obviously the design and test could be done by one or different persons or teams without changing the calculation.

We assume the design engineer delivers a net amount of 15 KStmt verified code per person year. This amount of code consists only of manually written code, independently whether it is done by means of a programming language or of design languages that would later be translated automatically into code. It does not include reused code or automatically generated code.

Let us assume the person year as 1500 PH. This code contains 20 defects per KStmt of which 50% are found by the designer and 50% by test. So the designer delivers 150 defects per year to test, which cost 10 person hours per defect to remove and re-deliver. This results in an effort of 1.500 PH for testing, which is roughly one person year. Detecting 10% of these defects already during design would number to 150 PH of saved test effort assuming that test cases would be decreased, which is normally the case once the input stability is improving. These 10% of defects would cost 2 person hours each for additional verification effort, totaling to 30 PH. The savings would be 120 PH which we can compare to our engineering cost for the 15 delivered KStmt.

Original cost of the 15 delivered KStmt of code is one person year of design and one person year of test. This accumulates to 3000 PH. With the change, the total cost would be 1530 PH (design plus additional verification) plus 1350 PH (new test effort), which equals 2880 person hours. The 10% move of defects from test to verification total a saving of 120 PH which is 4% of the respective workload being saved. We have reduced net engineering cost by 4% by detecting an additional 10% of defects before test!

Taking into consideration the gross cost of engineering, which allows only 90% of engineering time spent on project work and only 80% of that time spent for design and test within the project-related effort means that 72% of engineering time is directly attributable to code and test. 72% multiplied with the 4% savings above results in a gross saving of 2.9%.

> This means that from a total engineering expense perspective, moving 10% of defects from test to design yields a benefit of 3% to overall engineering cost. Early defect removal is a key element of any efficiency improvement – much more reliable than offshoring.

Note that we took a conservative approach to this savings calculation, by for instance leaving out any cost of defects found after delivery to the customer or opportunistic effects from a not so satisfied customer or from additional service cost. You should certainly make a similar calculation in your own environment to judge the business impact of your change and improvement initiatives.

There are many similar observations in software engineering that the author has observed throughout many years of working with very different engineering teams, working on all types of software [Shul02, Eber01b, Eber06b, Eber99a, Eber06a]. Generally it pays off to remove defects close to the phase where they are inserted. Or more generally to remove accidental activities and outcome, while controlling essential activities.

We assert this observation and the impacts of early defect removal to **Ebert's law** which states in simple words:

> Productivity is improved by reducing accidents and controlling essence.

This law can be abbreviated with the first letters of the four words to a simple, yet powerful word: RACE (**R**educe **A**ccidents, **C**ontrol **E**ssence; see also Chaps. 11, 14). Those who succeed with RACE will have not only cost savings but also be in time and thus win the race on market share. Early defect removal (reduced accidents) and focus on what matters (control essence) means productivity and time to profit!

9.7. Hints for the Practitioner

Know about defects, where they origin, how to best detect them and how to remove them most effectively and efficiently. Do not be satisfied with removing defects. Testing is a big waste of effort and should be reduced as much as possible. With each defect found think about how to change the process to avoid the defect from reoccurring.

Implement the combination of "built-in" and "bolt-on" attributes of quality. The approach of combination of prevention and early detection of defects will cut the risk of defects found by the customer.

Leverage management and staff with previous quality assurance experience to accelerate change management.

Measure and monitor quality consistently from requirement definition to deployment. This will help in keeping the efforts focused across the full life-cycle of the product development. Use measurements for effectiveness (i.e., how many defects are found or what percentage of defects are found or what type of defects are found with a distinct defect removal activity) and efficiency (i.e., how much effort per defect removal or how much effort per test case, cost of non-quality) to show the value of early defect removal. Convince your senior management of the business case and they will be your best friends in pushing enough resources into development to contain defect removal to the phase where defects are introduced. Only old-fashioned managers like test (because they think it is the way to see the software working), modern managers just hate test due to its high cost, insufficient controllability and poor effectiveness.

Defects should be removed in the phase where they are created. Being successful with defect phase containment needs few practical prerequisites:

- Ensure right level of "formalism" (discipline). This includes planning, preparation, training, checklists, monitoring. Too much formalism can cause inefficiencies, not enough formalism will reduce effectiveness. Reporting of defects and effort per defect is key to optimize the process and forecast residual defects. Without reporting, reviews are not worth the effort.
- Different types of early defect correction are applied. Requirements inspections are mandatory for all projects (done by testers). Hardware is analyzed by tools and inspected with specific guidelines. GUI design (e.g., Web pages) are reviewed for usability and so on. Software design and code are statically analyzed plus inspected.
- Verification techniques should find 50-60% of the residual defects. They are typically cascaded to detect different defect types. Detecting 10% more defects in design or code reviews and therefore reducing test effort and long rework cycles yields a savings potential of 3% of engineering cost.
- Inspections should focus on critical areas with more defects than average. Critical areas can be identified based on complexity, change history and so on.

Follow the structured methodology as defined in CMMI, Six Sigma, ISO 9001 etc. as the basis for process improvement. Once the processes are in place, measure their performance, reduce variation and define strategy for continuous improvement.

Include training and development on quality control and quality assurance procedures for every employee as a part of their role and incentives.

9.8. Summary

Quality improvement, such as increased reliability and maintainability is of utmost importance in software development. In this field which was previously ad hoc and unpredictable rather than customer-oriented, increasing competition and decreasing customer satisfaction have motivated many companies to put more emphasis on quality. The software industry's problem is that maturity with respect to "numbers" is poor. While solutions abound, knowing which solutions work is the big question.

We have introduced you in this chapter to several practical techniques for analyzing and improving software quality. They are based on ideas of measurement, quantification, and feedback. All your quality requirements can and should be specified numerically. This means quantifying qualities such as security, portability, adaptability, maintainability, robustness, usability, reliability, and performance. Based on experiences in our projects as well as external benchmarking studies we have summarized some rules of thumb for practitioners. They allow introducing quality measurements without exhaustive upfront internal data collection. Of course, these rules of thumb do not relieve us of using our own measurements for improving accuracy.

10. Measuring Software Systems

*Measurement is an excellent
abstraction mechanism
for learning what works
and what doesn't.*
Victor Basili

10.1. Measurement Beyond the Component or Project

Software measurement of different systems are related to the different kinds of systems (information-based, embedded, Web-based, decision support, knowledge-based etc) and to the different kinds of software development paradigms such as object-oriented software engineering (OOSE), aspect-oriented programming (AOP), component-based software engineering (CBSE), feature-oriented development (FOD), service-oriented software engineering (SOSE), event-based design (EBD) and agent-oriented software engineering (AOSE). On the other hand, general characteristics of software systems are meaningful in different IT environments such as performance, security and usability or context-dependent as outsourcing and offshoring. Finally, measurement artifacts can depend from the different kinds of systems such as embedded systems, information systems, and so on.

This chapter describes software measurement of systems with few concrete views (performance engineering, service-oriented systems, agent-based systems) to show how to apply the techniques we introduced earlier.

10.2. Performance Engineering

Software performance engineering is defined as a collection of methods for the support of performance-oriented software development of application systems along the entire software development process to ensure appropriate performance-related product quality. It uses a systems engineering perspective to ensure a comprehensive view on performance requirements. It extensively uses software measurements to define, implement and monitor performance objectives. Software performance engineering often uses *aspect-oriented software development* techniques.

In the systems analysis, software developers, customers and users define performance characteristics as service level objectives in addition to functional specifications (Fig. 10.1).

Concrete application functions and interfaces can be evaluated at this time. The software development process should allow a cyclical verification of the performance characteristics. They will be analyzed in the respective phase of the software life-cycle in the available granularity. In the first phases estimations have to be used that are often based on rules of thumb. In further development phases analytical and simulative models can be used. If prototypical implementations of individual program components are already available, measurements can be executed.

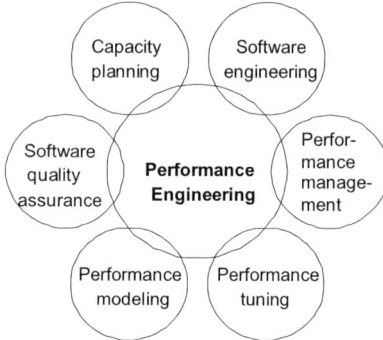

Fig. 10.1. Performance Engineering: Use of existing concepts from other disciplines

The quantified measurements should be continuously compared with the required performance characteristics. Deviations lead to an immediate decision process. Performance engineering uses existing methods and concepts from the areas of performance management, performance modeling, software engineering, capacity planning, and performance tuning as well as from software quality assurance. It enlarges and modifies them by performance-related analysis functions (see Fig. 10.2). However, the performance measurements are only as exact as the basis data of the models. In order that the calculations be concrete and realistic as possible, the setting up of a performance database is imperative.

Since a lot of performance data can be collected in the productive operation of a software system by benchmarking and monitoring, it should be ensured that these data are stored in the database for other performance engineering tasks in future development projects. The quality of the performance evaluation depends decisively on the maturity of the development process.

If prototypical implementations were not used within the design and implementation phase, the fulfillment of the performance requirements can be verified with the help of load drivers, e.g., by synthetic workload, in the system test phase. The real production system is available in the system operation phase. Often performance analyses are performed again in pilot installations over a certain period, since the analysis is now based on real workloads conditions. Thereby, an existing system concept can be modified again. The workload of the system often increases with a higher acceptance. That is why reserves should be considered within the system concept. The proposed procedure has to be adapted to domain-specific environments. Because of the scope of the tasks, specialists should support performance engineering.

The efficient operation of business processes depends on the support of IT systems. Delays in these systems can have fatal effects for the business. The following examples clarify the explosive nature of this problem:
- The planned development budget for the luggage processing system of the Denver, Colorado airport increased by about US $ 2 billion because of inadequate performance characteristics. The system was only planned for the terminal of United Airlines. However, the system was enlarged for all terminals of the airport within the development without considering the effects on the system's workload. The system had to manage more data and functions than any comparable system at any other airport in the world at the time. In addition to faulty project management, inadequate performance characteristics delayed the opening of the airport by 16 months. A loss of US $ 160,000 per day was recorded.
- An IBM information system was used for the evaluation of individual competition results at the Olympic Games in Atlanta, Georgia. The performance characteristics of the system were tested in advance with approximately 150 users. However, more than 1,000 people used the system in the production phase, and the system collapsed under this workload. Some competitions were delayed and IBM suffered temporary image damage. These examples show that the evaluation of the performance characteristics of IT systems is important, especially in highly heterogeneous system environments.

The performance characteristics of a system have to be considered within the whole software development process [Scho99]. Performance has to be given the same priority as other quality factors like functionality or maintainability. However, a practicable development method is necessary to ensure sufficient performance characteristics. Extensive and cost-intensive tuning measurements which are a major part of most development projects, can be consequently avoided. The operation of highly critical systems, e.g., complex production planning and control solutions, depends on specific performance characteristics, since inefficient system interactions are comparable to a system breakdown because the subsequent processes are affected. However, the system users' work efficiency is impaired with inadequate response times, causing frustration. Additionally, software ergonomic analyses show that users who have to wait longer than five seconds for a system response initiate new thought processes. Controlled cancellations of the new thought processes and the resumption of the old condition take time and lead to lower user productivity.

In order to take both software and hardware properties into account, a combined software and hardware model is needed. Whereas software models are currently usually created based on rather informal notation such as Unified Modeling Language (UML), hardware systems in the environment of performance assessment are traditionally modeled using queue models or Petri nets.

The first step is to identify performance-critical scenarios that pinpoint the interaction or exchange of messages between the objects in the software system and that are involved in executing a specific user function [Smit90]. Assuming that UML notation is used, these should be represented in detail using sequence diagrams (isolated message sequence charts can be used too). The next step is to transform the diagrams into "execution graphs" which, amongst other things, may be made up of elementary nodes, branch nodes, repetition nodes, apportionment nodes or nodes that represent parallel processes (Fig. 10.2).

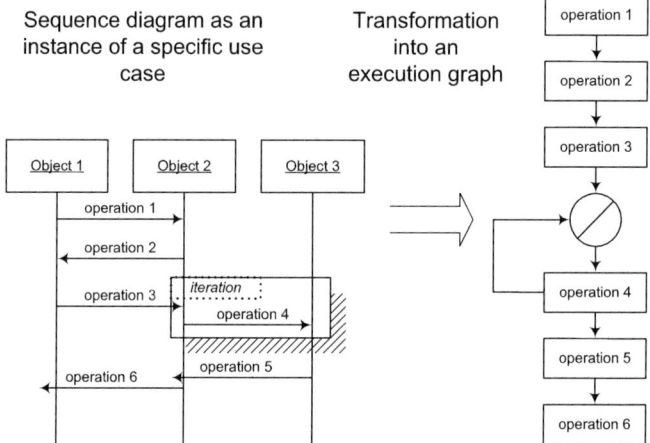

Fig. 10.2. Transformation of sequence diagrams into execution graphs

Once the execution graphs have been created, the nodes contained in the model must be quantified with regard to their resource consumption. What must be specified may include the CPU instructions needed for the nodes or the number of input and output operations performed to transfer data from and to the hard disk system or network (Fig. 10.3).

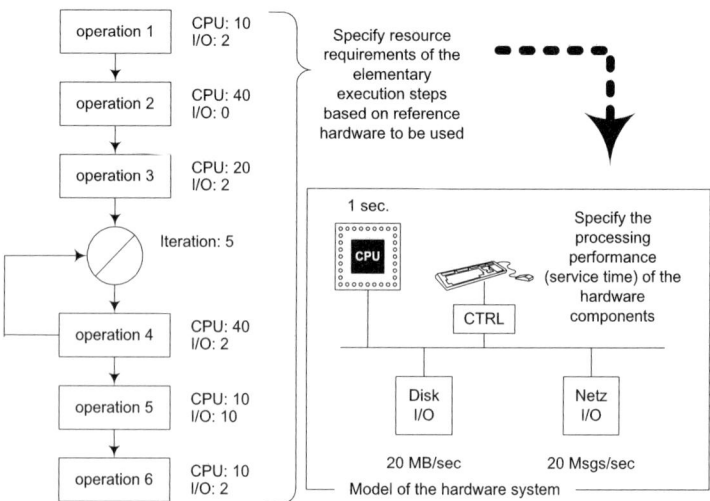

Fig. 10.3. Defining resource requirements based on reference hardware

The specified sequence of resources is based on the hardware system used in the model in each case. This must also be specified in terms of the achievable operating times (service time) for resources such as the CPU, the available throughputs for hard disks used and the network capacity.

Another step to be performed is to specify the load model. This entails defining job details – such as the number of jobs per second, arrival time distributions (e.g., exponential) and the number of users – for the model.

Regardless of the specific models, methods and tools used for performance modeling, it is necessary to access information and modeling variables that are able to describe the system – made up of hardware and software – with regard to its performance properties. In the context of performance models, the following basic information that is needed can be determined [Schm01].

Workload (classes of elementary jobs)
- number and type of job classes (online, interface, batch)
- load profiles over periods of time (frequency of execution of job classes)
- job volumes (data quantity that is submitted to the system for each job)
- output volumes (quantity of data returned to the user)
- complexity of and relationships between read and write job classes
- proximity of accesses to the database (cache vs. synchronization)
- response time and throughput demands for each job class

Description of the software architecture
- operating system and network protocols
- standard services (e.g., Web, file, database, and application servers)
- middleware used (e.g., DCE, ODBC, JDBC, RMI, CORBA)
- design models of client and server components (e.g., in UML)
- aspects regarding the implementation of client and server components
- mapping job classes to application processes

Description of the hardware architecture
- hardware systems used (representation of the CPU, HD, RAM, structure and so on)
- network systems used (sketch of the LAN or WAN properties)
- I/O controllers and network controllers used
- special controllers (e.g., audio and video cards)

Description of the performance capability
Once the load and the hardware and software architecture have been described, it is still necessary to quantify the performance of the hardware and software components used, for instance, in the form of "service rates" or possible throughput rates. Modeling tools, such as SES-Strategizer, contain templates allowing entire server systems to be mapped with regard to essential resources (CPU, I/O, memory, network). In the case of the processor, for instance, performance is often described in terms of the number of instructions that can be executed per time unit or

in terms of results of standard benchmarks such as SPECint95 or tpmC (TPC-C, by the Transaction Processing Council).

Description of the load behavior
The next step is to assign resource requirements to specific model elements or application system processes that are met via jobs submitted for processing. For a specific component in the design model or a server process, therefore, it must be determined how many CPU instructions, I/O activities or network accesses are needed in order to provide the functionality necessary. These steps require fairly detailed knowledge of the operating system concerned because such variables can only be determined with the help of monitoring systems (e.g., system activity reporter or *sar*).

We will now provide a summary of the sources from which model variables can be obtained.

Model variables from operational systems
It is possible to obtain model variables from systems that have already been implemented. Typically, this is done as part of performance management tasks. These tasks are only of interest for software development if the recorded consumption of resources such as CPU, main memory, hard disk requirements, I/O system, and network bandwidths can also be assigned to technical application functions. In addition, it is also necessary to know the load parameters mentioned in the previous section as well as the hardware and software architecture.

Model variables based on prototypes (individual benchmarks)
In the case of new technologies, such as applications servers, models cannot be used until sufficient experience of generating meaningful performance model variables has been gained. In order to build up experience with regard to the performance of new technologies, therefore, it is necessary to carry out measurements on real systems or appropriate prototypes. This task especially lends itself to using load driver systems in order to gather suitable data with prototypical implementations. Only in this way can reproducible performance data be obtained based on a defined load profile.

Model variables based on standard benchmarks
In the area of server systems you can usually obtain performance specifications from benchmark organizations. In addition to allowing you to conduct a relative comparison of computer systems, these allow you to estimate the necessary resources based on your own application, provided these resources and the load used can be largely compared with the benchmark application. Corresponding measurements are used in performance modeling, for instance, with BEST/1 as model variables, especially for the task of characterizing CPU performance. Manufacturer-independent benchmarks are offered by organizations such as TPC, SPEC and BAPCo. Information on the results of these benchmarks can be found in [Idea00].

Model variables based on datasheets for hardware systems
Using datasheets is a particularly good idea when it comes to describing the performance properties of network controllers (data throughput), bus systems or hard disk systems being used. In the case of a hard disk system, for instance, the following performance attributes play a role:
- Properties of the disk controller (e.g., typical available bandwidth in MB/s, cache hit rates for any available read and write cache)
- Properties of the connected disk drives (e.g., search times – positioning of the R/W head above the required track, rotation delay – positioning of the R/W head within the track, transfer rate – transmission of data between the controller and disk drive, memory capacity of the hard disk systems).

Because new information systems are becoming more and more complex, the empirical assessment of architectures and software systems is becoming increasingly important. In order to allow the entire life-cycle of an information system to be evaluated in terms of quality and quantity and be iteratively optimized, software engineering makes use of measurements. The process of quantifying the attributes of software engineering objects and components in relation to specific measurement goals, possibly by using measurement tools, is referred to as "software measurement." The basic idea behind software measurement is to record valid measurements in order to achieve an empirical assessment of the process, the resources used, and the actual product.

To formalize this approach, Norton [Nort00] has suggested using an adapted spiral model as defined by Boehm [Boeh88]. The spiral model processes which should be iterated, are planning, development, evaluation and presentation.

The spiral model for performance measurement introduction which should be iterated, consists of following steps:
- Planning. Implementing the goals with the least effort
- Development. Deriving suitable performance data
- Evaluation. Verifying and validating the results
- Presentation. Evaluating whether customer requirements have been met
---

Empirical data relating to the performance properties of an IT system may be obtained, for instance, by applying the empirical layer model specified as
- Level 1 (strongest): original measurement (PO)
- Level 2: counterpart measurement (PP)
- Level 3: model-based analysis (PM)
- Level 4: model-based estimation (PS)
- Level 5: analogy conclusion (PA)
- Level 6 (weakest): trend analysis, expertise (PE)

Emulating the work in [Dumk00], we have extended this model, putting it into concrete terms. In order to draw empirical conclusions about the "next level in" (the i-1th level), the following general connection can be deduced based on a software system or software component k:

$(performance\ behavior\ (k))_i =$

$(\text{correction factor} \times \text{performance determined}^{\text{correction exponent}})_{i+1}$

The accuracy of the "performance determined" decreases as the number of layers increases because of the abstracting from the underlying original system. Existing comparative data often has to be used for subcomponents of a software system in the early development stages due to a lack of alternatives (Table 10.1).

Table 10.1. Examples of possible transformation forms

Transformation	Description
PP → PO	Performance Counterpart – The application of data regarding the performance behavior of a network-based application under laboratory conditions through monitoring as an initial assessment for real practical implementation
PM → PO	Performance Model – The model-based performance analysis, based on analytical or simulated resolution procedures, of a client/server application as the starting point for assessing the performance of distributed systems
PS → PO	Performance Estimate – The use of an estimation model (rules of thumb) for characterizing the performance properties of a generally known technology such as file or database server systems
PA → PO	Performance Analogy – Application of the key performance figures of a LAN for estimating the application characteristics in a WLAN
PE → PO	Performance Expertise – The application of general trend data regarding performance development for network-based platforms as a basis for estimating the performance of the software system to be developed

The main point of interest in software performance engineering is to find or generate manageable relationships between the layers in order to support appropriate error rectification. If the transformations that have been presented are carried out step by step, this corresponds to the successive accumulation of performance experience relating to a new system to be developed that Norton [Nort00] proposed in the context of his spiral model. We do not intend to look any further here at other time-based, multivariate or reflexive aspects.

In order to establish such dependencies, we need statistical evaluations (such as correlation analyses) that are able to take both performance and software measurements into account. Both at universities and in the industrial environment, software measurements and performance measurements are usually stored separately and are partially redundant, making it difficult for complex connections between these measurements to be proven. The aim, however, should be to set up a control loop covering the entire software life-cycle. On the one hand, this means that software developers should be given access to performance data for live information systems so that such practical knowledge regarding the performance engineering process can be taken into account. On the other hand, potential operators of new information systems should be given access to performance measurements relating to software development, for instance, to allow them to conduct forward-looking system planning (e.g., regarding necessary network expansion for the implementation of new application types). It goes without saying that each of these groups of users is only interested in a limited section of the data available. For example, application developers are only interested in measurements regarding application types that can be compared to a certain degree with the applications that they are developing.

10.3. Measuring SOA-Based Systems

Expert Box. Author: Andreas Schmietendorf

A service-oriented architecture (SOA) is a modern approach to building distributed applications which can cross organizational boundaries. "Building blocks" for this kind of applications are services – independent software entities, whose functionalities and metadata are uniformly accessible throughout the network. These platform independent loosely coupled service offerings encapsulate internal or external business functionalities of involved parties. Every service is described with help of a standardized interface and can be found by potential consumers so. Actually many technologies can be used to implement service offerings – almost any type of distributed components, e.g., Web services, CORBA, DCOM, EJB, and so on can build the basis for SOA. Nevertheless, the technology of Web Services in connection with the implementation of a SOA is discussed mostly.

Web services are network-based applications that use the WSDL protocol (Web Service Description Language) to describe the functions they offer on the Internet, XML documents (eXtensible Markup Language) to exchange information, and the SOAP protocol (Simple Object Access Protocol) for calling remote methods and transferring data. The data and function calls that are packaged into XML documents are typically transferred using the http protocol which means communication can also take place across firewalls. It is this property in particular that opens up the possibility of developing genuine Business to Business (B2B) applications. UDDI directory services (Universal Description, Discovery, and Integration) are used to localize the Web services provided on the Internet.

The properties inherent in such architectures and the disadvantages associated with traditional technologies explain poor usage of measurements:
- Web service-based applications are designed for use across various companies, whereas previous applications were primarily used within a single company.

- Current pressure on costs is giving rise to customer demand for transparent costs for service provision, and Web service-based applications support this goal.
- Until recently, SLAs have been primarily based on resource-related measurement variables that were generally incomprehensible to the customers view.
- In the case of Web service-based applications, the main focus is on the interaction chain involving measurement variables that are based on functions or business processes and that take the actual customer benefit into account.
- Commercial application systems based on integrated Web services urgently require the services used to be subject to quality assurance (efficiency, security, availability, and so on).

The following representation shows different measurement and evaluation aspects in context of a service-oriented architecture. After a short introduction of general measurement aspects it shows examples from related works and overviews from evaluations of real service offerings.

The use of measurements supports the quality assurance of software development projects. The question is what kind of measurements should be used within development and integration projects for service oriented architectures.

For the identification of measurement possibilities it is useful to know the relationships of several SOA-related aspects. For this task, the application of a reference model can be helpful. Fig. 10.4 shows a first suggestion of the OASIS standardization committee for such a model.

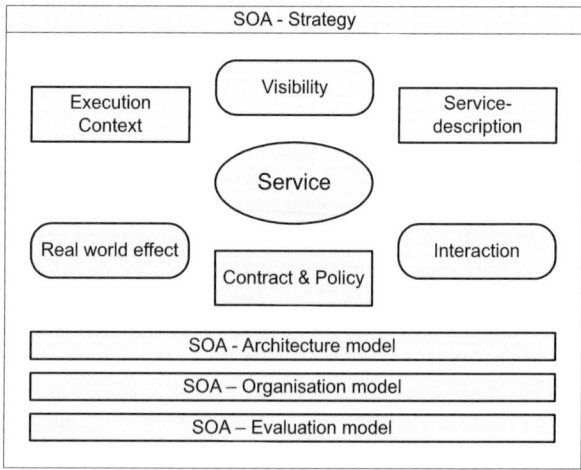

Fig. 10.4. SOA reference model

In the model, potential measurements should consider statically and dynamically aspects of service offerings and service compositions. Furthermore it requires measurements for the evaluation of the overall architecture and the organizational prerequisites. The SOA scorecard consists of a set of measurements and

will vary by organizations. Typical measurements in the context of a SOA scorecard could refer to the following areas ([Mark06]):
- SOA – Business Measurements: *Market penetration, time to market, customer satisfaction, turnover increase, …*
- SOA – Process Measurements: *Process terms, process mistakes, number of process-referential events, …*
- SOA – Financial measurements: *Return of Investment, cost savings, project costs, …*
- SOA – Usage measurements: *Number of used service offerings, number of service customers, …*
- SOA – Performance measurements: *Performance of basic and orchestrated Services and availability, …*
- SOA – IT efficiency measurements: *Productivity, development time, quality behavior, …*
- SOA – Optimization measurements: *Number of services in conception, development and production, …*
- SOA – Governance measurements: *Standard conformity, potential exceptions, …*

From the software engineering point of view, these approaches resemble some features of formerly known component-based and object-oriented software systems and Web applications, but the differences are substantial enough to make it impossible to simply reuse existing measurements.

Quality of service offerings

To derive performance measurements (e.g., to check SLA constraints) of a basic or composite service offering it is necessary to use measurement tools. One example of such a tool is a measurement service. The use of a measurement service allows the measurement of different attributes (e.g., performance, availability) of several Web services. The Web Services to be measured can be selected freely within the Internet. Furthermore, the functionalities of the measurement service can be used through a Web services-based interface (see also Fig. 10.5).

The components of the agent perform the following tasks:
- Measurement probes. Executes the measurements by the use of one or more methods from the Web service. For the isolation of the processing time of the Web services from the needed time within the network we simply used a "ping" in addition. The "ping" is a simple measurement. This is executed briefly before the actual measurement runs.
- Configuration of the Web Service access. Gives the possibilities for the configuration of the measurement agent by the use of an XML file. Adaptation to the particular shaping of the WSDL description from a specific Web Service, selection of the method for measuring, definition of corresponding parameter, establishing of intervals for the measurements.
- Load driver component. It allows the simulation of the expected workload. The required performance behavior of the Web Service can be tested on this virtual basis. In detail this component provides the definition of the load mix, definition of response time goals and the necessary substitution of parameters.

- User configuration and access. It offers the possibility to administer users of the measurement service with different access rights. That means rights to read available measurements, rights to configure the measurement of new Web Services.
- Prediction component. It is based on existing measurements, forecast models can be developed. These models can be developed by the use of mathematical calculations like the operational analysis.
- Measurement storage and export component. For deeper analysis it is necessary to use separate statistical tools like Microsoft Excel or SPSS. The current version offers a comma-separated file which contains all measurements.
- WSDL-based access layer. Provides all functions of the measurement agent as service-oriented interface (this means the agent is even a Web service). On the base of this function the agent can be used to control "service level agreements" for a specific Web service.
- Web based GUI. It provides a simple graphical control interface. Provides the configuration of the measurements time interval and measurement goals and generates simple graphical reports too.

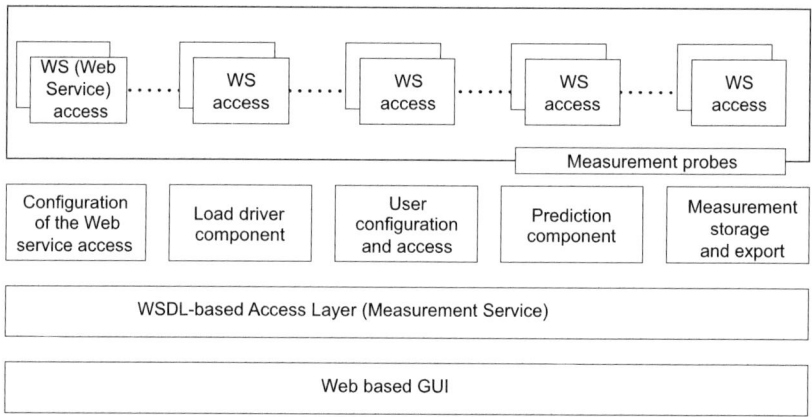

Fig. 10.5. Architecture of a measurement service

A measurement service based on the shown architecture was first implemented under [Schm03]. It has the possibility to measure the availability, the performance, the functionality and the complexity of a specific Web service from the users (or better integrators) point of view.

Web services offered on the Internet usually only have a rudimentary description of their functional and non-functional properties which means that determined properties can usually not be assumed for the Web services offered. Numerous offerings are only available temporarily and do not have a commercial character.

From the viewpoint of the authors, it is vital that the opportunities provided by a SLA management in the environment of Web service-based applications are taken into consideration during development. The generic Web Service Level Agreements (WSLA) framework supports the implementation of a service level management solution. However, the WSLA approach only addresses selected problems (primarily issues regarding performance) when it comes to guaranteeing a defined service level. [Kell02]

The vast majority of problems has to be taken into account during software development. In the process, development should be based not only on the tasks related to process modeling and analysis but also on the actual software development. Web services that take both functional behavior and non-functional properties into account and, what is most important, guarantee these during execution need to be positioned successfully on the Internet before commercial solutions can be implemented based on this technology.

The task for software development is to create Web services with determined properties. From the viewpoint of the authors, this requires the use of agent technology or, in an initial approach, the instrumentation of technically founded user functions.

Granularity of service offerings
The right granularity of corresponding service offers is crucial for the successful implementation of a SOA. Object-oriented, component-based and service-oriented software engineering paradigms have many resembling features – modularity, encapsulation of functionality and data, separation of interface and implementation, and so on. Therefore it could be possible to derive experiences from this field.

The literature proposes the following set of measurements to measure the granularity indirectly:
- Size of the service interface (operations, parameter, ...)
- Share of the service of the complete business application (supported business processes)
- Size of the effective source code (lines of code, number of classes, ...)

Nevertheless, these measurements can give only one indication of the granularity. Whether it is about a good or bad granularity cannot be derived directly from it. The number of arguments of a method (of a function, of an operation, and so on) is a classic design measurement in the object-oriented and component-based software engineering domains. But it is not always applicable to service operations because under the document interaction style all values (e.g., name, address and phone number of a customer) will be "packed" into one coarse-grained data structure which can also be weak, i.e., its some parts/elements may be optional.

The right granularity of the offered functions of a service can be assessed only on the basis of the successful uses within different application scenarios. Therefore, the frequency of the application of a specific service as well as individual service functions should be prepared as measurement.

The depth of the implementations lying behind a service interface can be considered as another indirect measurement for the evaluation of the granularity. In certain respects, this measurement can be compared with the inheritance depth of the object-oriented programming. However, the block box view of a service offering is injured in this case.

Evaluation of Internet services

Diverse service offers can be found within the internet currently. To discover service offerings you can use directories like XMethods (http://www.xmethods.com) or the service marketplace StrikeIron (http://www.strikeiron.com). They provide in general functionalities for the service registration and for searching a specific service offering. The search is supported with the help of defined classifications and categories. Furthermore, there are assessments about the qualitative behavior of a service offering and developer support (e.g., programming interfaces, tutorials, test tools) for the implementation of a service based solution. Until to the beginning of the year 2006, there were also the UBR (UDDI business registry) in the internet. This solution was operated by SAP, IBM, Microsoft and NTT.

The use of these registries is not much. There were primarily the following causes for it.
- Insufficient support management
- Low functionalities of provided services
- Poor quality statements about service offers
- Insufficient version management

Fig. 10.6 shows the entry dialog of StrikeIron; this marketplace is available since the beginning of 2006.

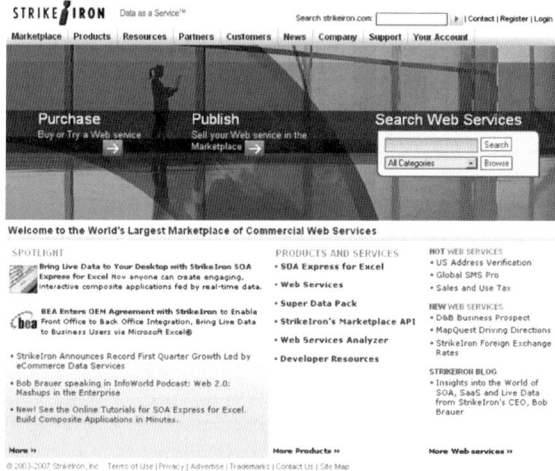

Fig. 10.6. Web services market place: Entry dialog of StrikeIron

In order to gain experience with deposited service offers, an empirical analysis was done. The analysis used 10 randomly selected service offerings. The investigated services provided between 2 and 8 operations. In average, 4.1 operations were offered. In all cases of the investigated Web services the http-protocol were used for the data transmission. The processing of the SOAP-messages took place in a document oriented way (SOAP-style DOC). Given several XML-related constraints usability and thus use was low.

Another aspect of the executed analysis referred to an overall evaluation of the offered services. The goal was to forgive ordinal scaling evaluations. Under consideration of the "factor – criteria – measurement" approach, the assessment was executed with help of the following simple evaluation model. For every criterion, a corresponding measurement (mostly yes or no) were defined.

Service description:
- Availability of a WSDL-based service description
- Semantic representation of used data and functions
- Examples for the service-integration
- Experience reports from known service users

Service quality aspects:
- Availability information
- Performance under workload
- Scalability information (changed requirements)
- Test possibilities

Further important aspects:
- Payment possibilities
- Support possibilities
- Use of service-level agreements (SLA)
- Legal conditions

To represent the fulfillment degree, the following 6 evaluation levels were defined. The defined criteria were integrated into the evaluation model by the use of different weights (represented not here).

1. *very good* (the requirements were met completely – SLA compliant)
2. *good* (security and trustworthiness are guaranteed)
3. *satisfactory* (different price models are available)
4. *defective* (basic support, maintenance and test possibilities are available)
5. *poor* (semantic interpretations of offered functions and data)
6. *not industrial usable* (only WSDL is available, the service can be used under risks)

Not one of the offered services reached the evaluations of "very good" or "good." With half of the investigated services, a "satisfactory" evaluation could be forgiven. Four analyzed services were assessed as "poor" and one as "not industrially usable."

The current basic specifications (e.g., SOAP, WSDL, and UDDI) in Web service technology only support the description of qualitative aspects in a very limited manner. Correspondingly, most Web service offerings provide no indication of the qualitative behavior. Furthermore Service offerings provided through the internet are limited by a small number of functionalities. This means that these services are primarily technically oriented and not business oriented.

Case study: Evaluation of an industrial service
The development of an industrial service offer will be analyzed with a concrete case. The service will be analyzed from the "black box" perspective and from the "white box" perspective too. The service development must consider the existing SOA infrastructure from the customer side. That means the service should be usable within the established runtime-environment. The investigated SOA project deals with the wrapping of existing information systems. With the service-oriented solution, the provisioning process of a complex telecommunications product should be supported.

The functionalities of the legacy applications are accessed by XML-specific messages. These messages are processed within EJB-based wrapper applications (wrapper A-C). This kind of architecture requires the use of an EJB container (application server) as run-time environment. Between the wrapper applications and the service controller the Java Remote Methods Invocation Interface (RMI) technology is used. A controller application works as mediation device. It provides the following functionalities:
- A Web service based interface
- Business process execution control
- Message-based event- and notification-handling
- Logging, recovery and error handling.

The Web service supports 13 business oriented subprocesses. For the support of these subprocesses the Web service divided 30 direct operations (size of the corresponding wsdl-file 2117 LOC) and 38 indirect operations (size of the corresponding wsdl-file 1820 LOC). Fig. 10.7 shows the coarse architecture of the investigated SOA-application.

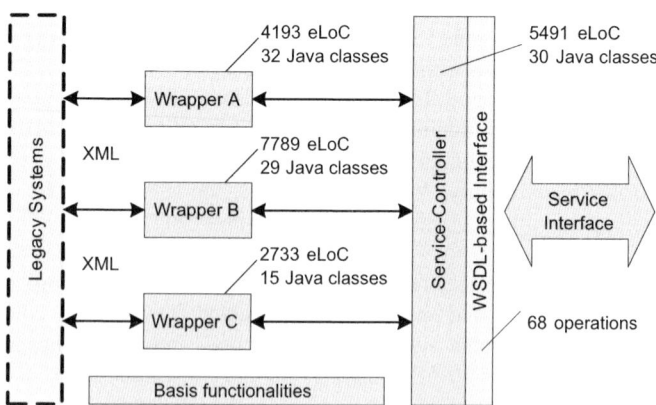

Fig. 10.7. Architecture of an industrial SOA service

Altogether we can count 68 business-related operations which require at least 136 SOAP messages. The most complex SOAP message consists of 29 parameters (simple and complex data types are involved). Within each SOAP-message it is necessary to provide meta-information to support specific error handling, transactions, time stamps, authentication and authorization.

Currently, diverse measurement and evaluation approaches are required in the context of the implementation of a SOA. The approaches shown here consider not all aspects. It was important to show the different qualities of internet provided services in comparison to real industrial SOA services. Especially the number of provided functionalities is much higher in context of industrial SOA service offerings, than in the context of service offerings provided through the internet. The causes of it lie in the immediate consideration of business related functions through the service implementation. Still, the implementation of service market places stands at the beginning. As shown the service offerings available at present in the internet cannot help with the implementation of an SOA. Therefore, measurement and evaluation approaches should concentrate on internal business questions in the context of an SOA.

10.4. Measurement of Agent-Based Systems

Agent-oriented software technology as the engineering of software agents, multi-agent systems (MAS), agent development tools and methodologies is an active research area. Software agents have high potential to become more and more a part of the mainstream software development process. Autonomy, high availability and fault tolerance are some of the features supported by software agents. To reach the goal of industrial acceptance quality criteria have to be fulfilled. This section introduces a software measurement approach to evaluate software agents and MAS. Based on existing object-oriented measurement experiences the Agent Academy as a multi-agent based expert system has been evaluated. The given examples introduce a quality model which includes measurements based measurement for the analysis of agent maintainability on different levels. The shown results explain how measurements based software measurement can help to detect potentially critical areas. The future work will be focused on an agent measurement framework which includes all facilities of software agents and MAS.

To talk about agents and to use them it is necessary to understand what they are. Often for outstanding people the differences between agent orientation and the well known object orientation are not clear. Wooldridge et al. describe the difference between objects and agents in the following manner [Wool01]:

- Agents embody a stronger notion of autonomy than objects, and in particular, they decide for themselves whether or not to perform an action or request from another agent.
- Agents are capable of flexible (reactive, pro-active, social) behavior; and the standard object model has nothing to say about such types of behavior.
- A multi-agent system (MAS) is inherently multi-threaded, in that each agent is assumed to have at least one thread of control.

There are many measurements for the measurement of object-oriented implementations, but the analysis of agent-oriented systems is still a topic of on ongoing research [Will05]. Based on a classic definition of agents we define agents as software components with certain properties [JeWo94]. Autonomy, social competencies, reactivity and pro-activity are indispensable. Additional properties can be mobility, collaboration and the ability to learn. Agents are situated in a certain environment which they are part of. Those agent platforms supply the needed infrastructure. A service directory, an agent directory, message transport and agent communication languages are those infrastructural elements as defined in the FIPA-Standard (Foundation for Intelligent Physical Agents) [FIPA06]. To ease the development of agent-based systems, frameworks are provided. They include the necessary packages for the infrastructure as well as for the implementation of agents and multi-agent systems. The later ones are collections of agents working together to perform the given tasks.

Measurement within the area of software development is of high concern in the industrial domain as well as for scientific institutions. Its main goals are the improvement of the software development process and its continuous assistance. Therefore certain measurements exist. Examples are the measurement sets of Chidamber and Kemerer and MOOD (Measurements for Object Oriented Design) of F. B. Abreu. Chidamber and Kemerer proposed six structural design measurements [Chid94]:

- *Weighted Method per Class* (WMC): It is the sum of complexities of all methods in a class.
- *Depth of Inheritance Tree* (DIT): For this paper, DIT is taken as the maximum length of the inheritance tree up to the root.
- *Number of Children* (NOC): All direct sub-classes subordinated to a class in the class hierarchy are counted for this measurement.
- *Coupling between Objects* (CBO): Here direct coupling of objects is observed. The usage of methods or instance variables of the other class is counted.
- *Response for a Class* (RFC): RFC describes the size of the response set of a class. This set of methods can be potentially executed in response to a message received by an object of this class.
- *Lack of Cohesion in Methods* (LCOM): This measurement is a count of the number of method pairs whose similarity is 0 minus the count of method pairs whose similarity is not 0. The degree of similarity for two methods M_1 and M_2 in class C_1 is given by: $\sigma() = \{I_1\} \cap \{I_2\}$ where $\{I_1\}$ and $\{I_2\}$ are the sets of instance variables used by M_1 and M_2.

Abreu presented a revised set of system-level measurements in [Abre96]. It quantifies the use of main mechanisms of object-oriented design. The following descriptions include a Java-based interpretation.

- *Method Hiding Factor*: MHF is the quotient of private methods and the number of existing methods.
- *Attribute Hiding Factor*: AHF is the quotient of private attributes and the number of existing attributes.
- *Method Inheritance Factor*: MIF is the quotient of inherited methods and the number of existing methods.

- *Attribute Inheritance Factor*: AIF is the quotient of inherited attributes and the number of existing attributes.
- *Polymorphism Factor*: POF specifies the usage of polymorphism.
- *Coupling Factor*: CF describes the message passing but was not measured.

The core of these measurements was implemented in a Java Measurement Service [Faro05] that was used to perform the analysis of chosen agent frameworks. The results are presented in the following paragraphs.

Due to interoperability many agent systems are implemented in Java. The evaluation of chosen representative frameworks is focus of this work. Therefore, we analyzed the Aglet technology of IBM research, the JADE system of the Telecom Italia Lab and MadKit, an open source project.

Aglets are Java-based mobile agents. The provided framework of the analyzed version 1.0.3 consists of three parts: an API for the development of agents, a server API for the development of agent platforms and the agent platform Tahiti [Agle06]. Basic Aglet functionalities are described in the following Fig. 10.8.

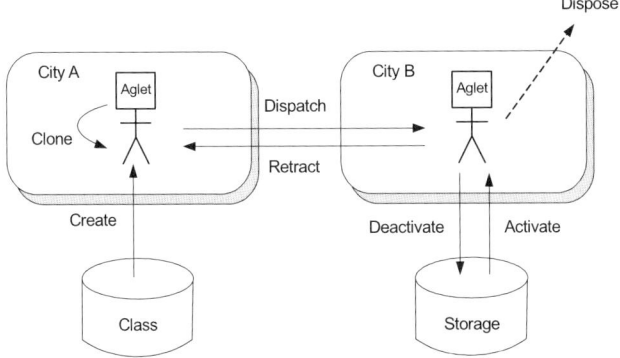

Fig. 10.8. Basic Aglet functionalities [Lang98]

Table 10.2 shows the Chidamber-Kemerer measurements for Aglets. Standard deviation (std. dev.) is included to measure variation of scores about the mean.

The results indicate that the *depth of inheritance tree* (DIT) is quite small for the Aglet classes. A high complexity value often is observed in deeper classes and refers to an increased possibility of maintainability problems.

Higher reuse but also improper class abstraction is indicated by the *number of children* (NOC) measurement (see Fig. 10.9). The mean value for Aglets is 0.222 because of many zero-values. Most extreme outlier values are 6 (com.ibm.aglet.AgletException) and 12 (com.ibm.aglets.tahiti.TahitiDialog).

Table 10.2. Chidamber and Kemerer measurements for Aglets

	Min.	Max.	Mean	Std. Dev.
DIT	0	2	0.239	0.465
NOC	0	12	0.222	1.091

WMC	0	74	10.35	11.355
CBO	0	52	5.022	6.716
RFC	0	236	25.05	30.388
LCOM	0	2250	80.011	253.186

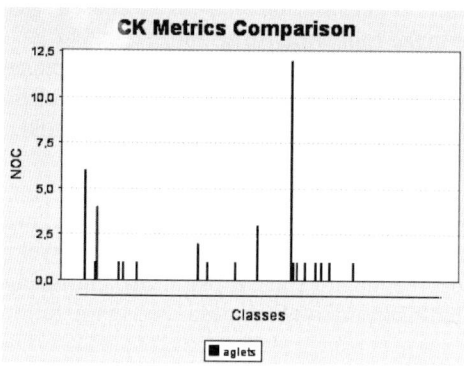

Fig. 10.9. Chidamber-Kemerer measurements for sample set of aglets: NOC

Weighted method per class (WMC) affects class complexity and thereby time and effort for maintenance and testing. Classes with large number of methods are likely to be more application specific, limiting the possibility of reuse. The mean value is observed to be 10.35, but several extreme values occurred. Six percent of all classes show a value above 31. Most noticeable are com.ibm.aglets.LocalAgletRef (74), com.ibm.atp.agentsystem. aglets. AgletsSecurity (64) and com.ibm.atp.agentsystem.aglets.NullAgletsSecurity (56). The outliers are the reason for the standard deviation of 11.355.

Coupling between Objects (CBO) describes the dependency of a class on others and vice versa. Our result shows CBO close to 5. Most extreme values are 52 (com.ibm.aglets. AgletContextImpl) and 51 (com.ibm.aglets.LocalAgletRef).

Response for a class (RFC) is a similar coupling value which focuses on coupling between classes. Mean value is 25.05 with a standard deviation of 30.388.

According to Chidamber et al. [Chid98] high values of *lack of cohesion between methods* (LCOM) are associated with lower productivity, greater rework and greater design effort. The mean value is 80.11 with a standard deviation of 253.186 due to several outliers yet the values ranges from 665 to 2250. The measurement goal of the MOOD measurements *Method hiding factor* (MHF) and *attribute hiding factor* (AHF) is the level of encapsulation of a system. High values indicate maintainable and reusable software. Aglets show values of above 99%.*Method inheritance factor* (MIF) and *attribute inheritance factor* (AIF) are aimed to measure inheritance that results in reuse but also added design complexity. Values are ranging from 17.7% to 29%.Polymorphism allows simplicity by providing dynamic binding but may also complicate tracing control flow. For the measurement *polymorphism factor* (POF) a low value of 4.3% was obtained.

10.4 Measurement of Agent-Based Systems

JADE (Java Agent Development Environment) provides an agent platform and packages for FIPA-compliant agent development [JADE06]. A basic set of functionalities is given instead of a specific agent architecture. The actual available version 3.4 is analyzed in the following paragraphs (Fig. 10.10).

The Chidamber-Kemerer measurements present similar results for the JADE system as for Aglets. DIT measurement presents a mean value of 0.745 and a standard deviation of 1.261. Extreme values range from 4 to 6 for several classes like jade.proto.ContractNetResponder and jade.proto.IteratedAchieveREInitiator. The values for the NOC measurement are higher (up to 11 for class jade.onto.Ontology). The mean value is 0.535 with a standard deviation of 1.223. The other measurement values are presented in Table 10.3.

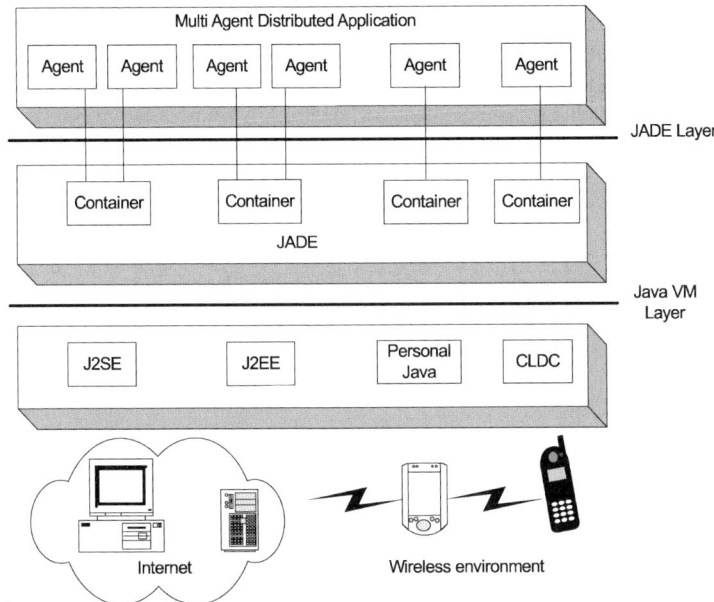

Fig. 10.10. The JADE architecture

The MOOD measurements MHF and AHF show a very high level of encapsulation. Both values are close to 99.8%. The values for measured inheritance at the method and attribute level are in the middle with around 40% and 50%. The *polymorphism factor* is 4.128%.

MadKit is a modular and scalable multi-agent platform written in Java and built upon the AGR (Agent/Group/Role) organizational model: agents are situated in groups and play roles. MadKit is intended to allow high heterogeneity in agent architectures and communication languages and various customizations [MadK06] (see Fig. 10.11).

Table 10.3. Chidamber and Kemerer measurements for JADE

	Min.	Max.	Mean	Std. Dev.
DIT	0	6	0.745	1.261
NOC	0	11	0.353	1.223
WMC	0	102	9.552	11.6
CBO	0	94	6.951	9.218
RFC	0	220	15.871	27.065
LCOM	0	4052	55.585	230.222

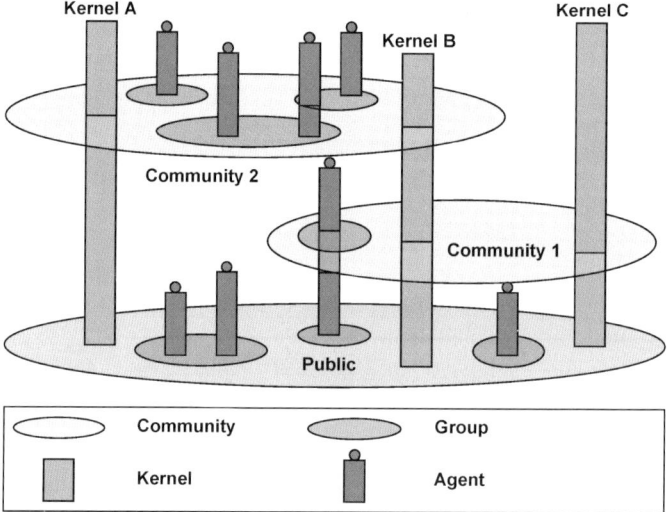

Fig. 10.11. Possible architecture of MadKit multi-agent system

An overview of the measured results for Chidamber- Kemerer measurements of primary MadKit packages is presented in Table 10.4.

Table 10.4. Chidamber-Kemerer measurements for primary packages of MadKit

	Min.	Max.	Mean	Std. Dev.
DIT	0	5	0.685	1.062
NOC	0	38	0.387	2.568
WMC	0	413	8.690	18.539
CBO	0	49	5.331	5.436
RFC	0	482	21.931	32.437
LCOM	0	4934	50.144	271.002

The MOOD measurement to measure method-related encapsulation shows a high value of 99.7% as well as the attributed-related one is 99.9%. The result of MIF is 59.4% and of AIF 48.5%. The *polymorphism factor* is 3.7%.

10.4 Measurement of Agent-Based Systems

In the following paragraphs we present the most important results of our analysis. Table 10.5 visualizes simple size measurements for Aglets, JADE and MadKit.

Table 10.5. Size measurements for measured AOSE technologies

System	# Classes	# Methods	LOC/Class	Methods/Class
Aglets	180	1863	67.61	10.35
JADE	487	4652	99.18	9.55
MadKit	683	5929	109.0	8.68

Despite the differences in the size of the agent platforms the results for the Chidamber-Kemerer measurements are quite similar. Only a few values need to be further analyzed. Standard deviation measures the variation of scores about the mean. The analyzed packages inherit similar standard deviation values for the particular measurements, except the standard deviation of the DIT value for Aglets and the standard deviation of WMC value for MadKit. The first one is 0.465 for Aglets compared to 1.261 (JADE) and 1.062 (MadKit). That is a possible indication that maintenance problems may occur for few classes of JADE and MadKit despite the fact of a small DIT mean value. A similar argumentation can be applied to the standard deviation of the WMC measurement results. Complexity and thereby time and effort for maintenance and testing are varying more between the classes of the MadKit system. The standard deviation value for the WMC measurement is 18.539. Some classes seem to be more application specific, limiting the possibility of reuse. Particular values for Aglets and JADE are 11.355 and 11.600.

Interesting results can be found while analyzing measurements heuristics. All Aglet classes have DIT values up to 2, meanwhile JADE and MadKit classes have some higher values. According to the DIT measurement and compared with the other systems Aglets are less complicated and easier to maintain. This may also be an indication for additional and more complex functionalities provided by JADE and MadKit.

Another similar result is about the NOC value. As shown in Fig. 10.12 only very few classes have NOC values above 2. So almost all classes are almost never reused, but do not need increased attention during testing, too. Few outliers of JADE and MadKit may show improper class abstraction that is related to a high NOC value.

A high CBO value affects change proneness and higher inter-object class coupling calls for rigorous testing. Smaller values are advocated. Results of Aglets and MadKit are quite similar but values above 21 are observed for 6% of JADE classes.

Another significant difference can be observed between the values for *Lack of Cohesion in Methods* measurement. The Aglet package tends to be associated with lower productivity, greater rework and greater design effort because of its higher LCOM mean value of 80.011 compared with JADE and MadKit. Their values are in middle with 55.585 and 50.144, respectively. Another mentionable result is outliers in LCOM measurement of Aglets. No values of JADE and MadKit classes are above 1500, but there are 2% outliers of Aglets.

Similar results of increased maintenance effort and system complexity were derived in [Kern04], where Grasshopper technology was analyzed in a case study which is another example of the AOSE-paradigm.

Table 10.6 presents values of the MOOD measurements. Small standard deviations for MHF and AHF are obvious. In combination with high mean values above 99.8% an overall high level of encapsulation is observed. It indicates maintainable and reusable software. AHF is close to the optimal value, because ideally all attributes should be hidden. The very high MHF value might be an indication for little functionality.

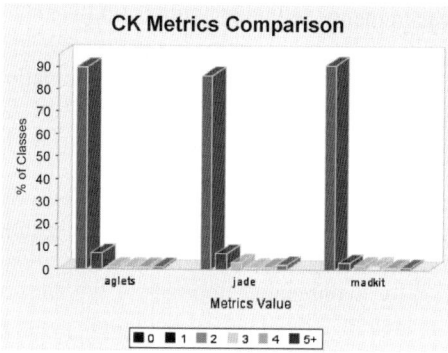

Fig. 10.12. NOC value comparison

Table 10.6. MOOD values and associated mean and std. dev. values

	Aglets	JADE	MadKit	Mean	Std. dev.
MHF (%)	99.87	99.84	99.75	99.82	0.062
AHF (%)	99.88	99.79	99.88	99.85	0.052
MIF (%)	17.71	40.69	59.35	39.25	20.857
AIF (%)	29.06	80.84	48.53	52.81	26.154
POF (%)	4.30	4.13	3.66	4.03	0.333

The *polymorphism factor* does not show high variations, either. Observed results tend to be typical for AOSE paradigm.

The other two MOOD measurements, *method inheritance factor* and *attribute inheritance factor* are varying more. So MadKit has the highest MIF with 59.35% compared to Aglets (17.71%) and JADE (40.69%). MadKit is making increased use of inheritance and reuse. In one way, it can be an efficient approach while on the other side it can cause more effort on class design and raise understandability issues. The value related to JADE is quite high, too.

For AIF similar conclusion can be made in case of JADE. Compared to Aglets and MadKit (although for MadKit, value is quite high, too) it shows extensive use of attribute inheritance. Although there are no empirical results that connect high AIF values with complexity but intuition and interpretation of attribute inheritance indicates such a possible relationship.

At the first glance size of measured AOSE and OOSE classes obviously differ. There were 1,320 AOSE classes measured and compared with 10,213 OOSE classes. That is one possible reason for smaller standard deviation values of AOSE classes. Other differences in the comparison of the particular value sets for Chidamber and Kemerer measurements are the mean values of CBO and LCOM measurements (see Table 10.7). DIT, NOC, WMC and RFC differences are because of few outliers and show no significant interpretable difference to OOSE values. The significant differences of the *coupling between objects* measurement cannot be justified by outliers. 30% of AOSE classes have values from 6 to 20. One possible conclusion is higher complexity within agent platforms. That directly refers to higher testing and maintenance efforts for those systems. The LCOM value has only little significance because around 10% of classes have higher values of 100 to 500. A very high value indicates improper use of OO-design. A question of further research is whether AOSE classes should be redesigned or accepted as having a slightly higher LCOM value.

Table 10.7. Chidamber and Kemerer measurements for OOSE and AOSE technologies

	Aglets	JADE	MadKit	Mean of AOSE	Std. dev. of AOSE	Mean of OOSE	Std. dev. of OOSE
DIT	0.239	0.745	0.685	0.556	0.276	0.59	0.82
NOC	0.222	0.353	0.387	0.321	0.087	0.15	0.45
WMC	10.35	9.552	8.69	9.531	0.830	8.69	7.90
CBO	5.022	6.951	5.331	5.768	1.036	3.00	4.22
RFC	25.05	15.871	21.931	20.951	4.667	14.78	16.35
LCOM	80.011	55.585	50.144	61.913	15.907	37.51	82.82

Similar analysis was made for the MOOD measurements set of Abreu (see Table 10.8). Significant results were observed for MHF measurements as well as for inheritance measurements. MHF value is close to maximum for OOSE and AOSE technologies. It seems anomalous for both and the value is even higher for agent platforms and less varying. A possible reason might be an indicated lack of functionality but more probable reasons are:

- The value is actually not indicating encapsulation: Following a critical analysis of MOOD measurements in [Maye99] the value is numerically true and is calculating ratio between visible and total available methods in the system but is not an indication of the level of encapsulation.
- Incorrect definition of Java bindings: As described in [Faro05], the actual view of Java binding in the tool used might not be appropriate.

Table 10.8. MOOD measurements for OOSE and AOSE technologies

	Aglets	JADE	MadKit	Mean of AOSE	Std. dev. of AOSE	Mean of OOSE	Std. dev. of OOSE

MHF (%)	99.87	99.84	99.75	99.82	0.062	98.77	2.92
AHF (%)	99.88	99.79	99.88	99.85	0.052	98.70	3.77
MIF (%)	17.71	40.69	59.35	39.25	20.86	25.35	22.37
AIF (%)	29.06	80.84	48.53	52.81	26.15	24.75	25.70
POF (%)	4.30	4.13	3.66	4.03	0.33	4.60	7.48

Significant differences for inheritance measurements were already observed between different AOSE representatives. Compared to OOSE results there are mentionable aspects, too. The *method inheritance factor* ranges from 25.35% (OOSE) to 39.25% (AOSE). The higher value indicates a more efficient approach but it also refers to increased effort on class design. AOSE representatives are making increased use of inheritance and reuse. The attribute related measurement differs in 28.02% (AOSE: 52.82%, OOSE: 24.75%). This proves an extensive use of attribute inheritance for AOSE systems. We interpret this value as an indication for increased complexity of those systems.

In general an analysis based on measurements highlights features and supports anticipation of effects of design on external quality factors. In this paper we analyzed three representatives of AOSE technologies using the Chidamber-Kemerer measurements set and the MOOD measurements set of Abreu. Basic results in comparison to JADE and MadKit present Aglets as less complicated, easier to maintain but less productive, too. These other two agent platforms seem to be further developed. Indications are higher MIF values that are related to increased efficiency. MadKit itself contains more application specific classes that is limiting the possibility of reuse and may cause maintenance problems. Outliers are mainly much specialized agent classes in *madkit.designer* package. That tends to be technology specific. Comparisons of AOSE and OOSE results prove representatives of following the first paradigm to be more complex. There are indications for higher testing and maintenance efforts. The higher LCOM value may lead to a focus on future research. Normally it indicates improper use of paradigms of OO-design. Being a normal attribute of AOSE is another possibility and should be further analyzed. As a summary following aspects of AOSE technology were deduced:

- AOSE is developing, that is shown by increased size, complexity and efficiency of particular frameworks over time.
- Agent technology is more complex than standard object-oriented packages. Higher testing and maintenance efforts are expected to be usual.
- AOSE makes an increased use of inheritance and reuse. That indicates a more efficient approach but leads to higher effort on class design, too.
- There are indications that OO-design is not as usual for AOSE as for OOSE.

The derived result presents an initial view on AOSE technology. In the future, it is necessary to analyze more agent frameworks to get statements that are more substantial.

10.5. Hints for the Practitioner

The measurement of software systems is influenced by architectural and development-oriented aspects. These influences are
- The kind of *software technology or paradigm* such as OOSE, AOP, CBSE, SOSE and AOSE. In this case it is helpful to use the measurement experience from the previous paradigm in order to approximate the evaluation at the beginning. In the first measurement of agent-based system the use of the object-oriented measurements including their thresholds could be meaningful.
- The different *kind of systems* such as information systems, embedded systems and knowledge-based systems. This is one of the reasons for choosing the appropriate measurement method, e.g., IFPUG function points or information systems and COSMIC FFP for embedded systems. Furthermore, experience of existing systems can play an essential role for the start of measurement and evaluation activities of new (kinds of) software systems.
- The evidence of the considered *system attributes* such as performance and usability on the one hand and *process attributes* such as distributing and offshoring on the other hand are important involvements for the strategy and methodology for the applied measurement and evaluation approach.

When the full software life-cycle is considered, a performance management tool chain (tools for measurement, short term analysis, long term analysis, performance prediction) should be implemented immediately before and during operational use to address the following performance-relevant issues:
- generation of performance-relevant information concerning software components/architectures through prototype benchmarks
- verification of required service levels based on the whole IT system using performance benchmarks
- definition of tuning measurements for efficient production, consideration all software and hardware components of the system
- support in capacity planning for changing load profiles.

The performance measurements gathered from production systems can then be used as input parameters for modeling tools, when the same software components are to be used for newly developed software systems. We recommend a stepwise approach for building a performance risk model:
1. Provide a project-specific checklist (i.e., a tailoring activity). This includes determination of potential risk categories in dependence on affected fields and specialization of the risk categories through the actual risk criteria
2. Carry out interviews with representatives of the customer, developer and operator side to identify the corresponding performance risk measurements. This includes identification of organizational information (participants, date, project-phase), Information for all participants about the used PRM valuation model, contents-related introduction of the project to be analyzed, common analysis of the validity of potential risk criteria and summarizing remarks about performance-related project experience

3. Statistically analyze the registered data for the identification of primary risk problems. This includes identification of cluster frequencies via the evaluated projects, derivation of the corresponding monetary performance risks and determination of the corresponding SPE activities for minimization of performance-related risks
4. Verify the valuation model and identify potential improvements both of the valuation model and of the employed checklist procedure.

The application of performance models for a particular technology is only possible if there is sufficient performance experience. For new technologies, this can only be gained by running prototypical performance tests and successively building up empirical results from information systems in active operation.

The described principles of system performance can also been applied for the other aspects like security, usability or reliability.

10.6. Summary

This chapter has provided an overview of a practical way for system measurement considering the different involvements such as kind of systems, kind of development methods and variance of the system or process attributes.

The ideas proposed in this chapter in order to measure new kinds of software technologies and system characteristics should be helpful in order to qualify the decisions for project management and software quality assurance.

11. Improving Processes and Products

*They always say
time changes things,
but you actually have
to change them yourself.*
Andy Warhol

11.1. The Need for Process Excellence

Today, software is a major asset of many companies. Engineering investments are primarily spent for software development for the majority of applications and products. In our fast changing world, a company will only succeed if it continually challenges and optimizes its own performance. Engineering of technical products is currently undergoing a dramatic change. Ever more complex systems with high quality must be developed at decreasing cost and shortened time to market. At the same time, competition is growing and the entry barriers to established markets are diminishing. The result is more competitors claiming that they can achieve better performance than established companies. An increasing number of companies are aware of these challenges and are pro-actively looking at ways to improve their development processes.

Development processes along the product life-cycle determine how things are done – end to end. They provide guidance to those who do and focus on what to do. Guidance means understanding and ensures repeatability. Focus means achieving targets both effectively and efficiently, without overheads, frictions and rework. Good processes are as lean and agile as possible, while still ensuring visibility, accountability and commitment to results. Insufficient processes reduce business opportunities and performance due to not keeping commitments and delivering below expectations.

Fig. 11.1 summarizes the results of insufficient development processes. Inadequate assumptions, ad-hoc processes, a lack of strategy and poor management together contribute towards insufficient results. Many companies fail for one or several of those reasons.

To stay competitive with their software development, many companies are putting in place orchestrated improvement programs of their engineering processes. Process improvement in today business is crucial to improve competitiveness (productivity), to expand markets, to extend market penetration, to better support customers and address their real needs more effectively, to better manage the increasing variety of software assets and to be more profitable. If your processes do not demand continuous improvement, you will not stay in business for long. Suppose a competitor systematically improves productivity at a relatively modest annual rate of 5% (as we can see in many software and IT companies specifically in India). After only 3 years, the productivity difference is $(1.05)^3 = 1.16$, a 16% advantage which directly translates into more capacity for innovation, higher margins and improved market positioning.

> Processes exist whether we acknowledge it or not. The major question is: Do we allow them to develop organically and drive our organizations with uncontrolled results – or do we take a systematic approach to manage their evolution according to our needs and goals.

Process and product improvement must be combined with a strong focus on business objectives and measurements for follow-up of change implementation. Otherwise, the risk is high that too much attention is focused on processes and not enough on what is essential for customers and shareholders.

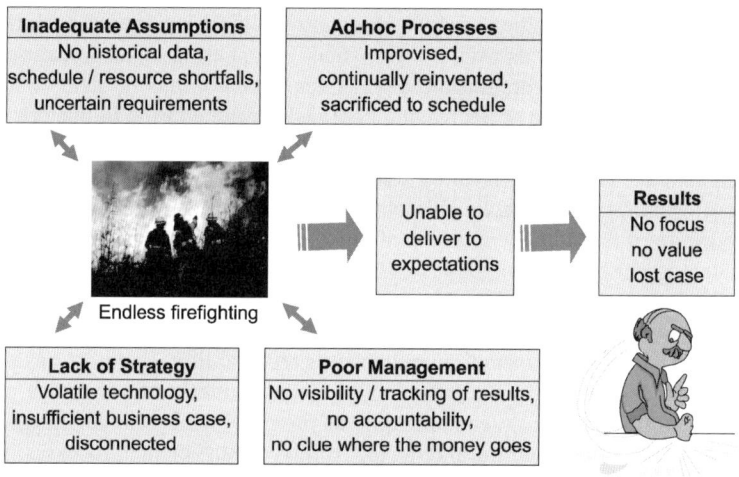

Fig. 11.1. The need for good processes. Crisis mode is miserable and attracts competitors

Good processes should not result in bureaucracy or overheads because those working with these processes ensure continuous improvement. Risks and challenges are manifold as is shown in Fig. 11.2. Continuous improvements of processes and products can be grouped into four dimensions, namely
- Innovation of solutions, products, services and technologies
- Consolidation of products, solutions, architectures, components and suppliers
- Industrialization of projects, processes, knowledge and skills
- Globalization of customers, markets and employees

Improvement needs change in highly dynamic markets such as software and IT. For instance, several years ago, Alcatel's voice networks business unit primarily focused on field quality improvement in order to achieve outstanding product reliability in the field. When this was established, changing markets pushed our customers into offering new services at a rapid pace, so we cut cycle time. Changing business objectives redirected process and product improvement activities. Such a shift of priorities in a consistent and sustainable way is only achieved with a strong organizational process focus. Alcatel would not have achieved it without high process maturity in that business unit.

Excellence demands a broad perspective on improving the dimensions of processes, products and people for better business performance. For instance, if you are competing on cost, there are several steps to take, such as
- Cost analysis of the end-to-end business processes of the product development in order to find out the cost and value of each activity
- Benchmarking of these activities to identify what has to be improved, scrapped or reworked
- Reengineering those portions of your product which are not anymore competitive and yield overly high development cost.

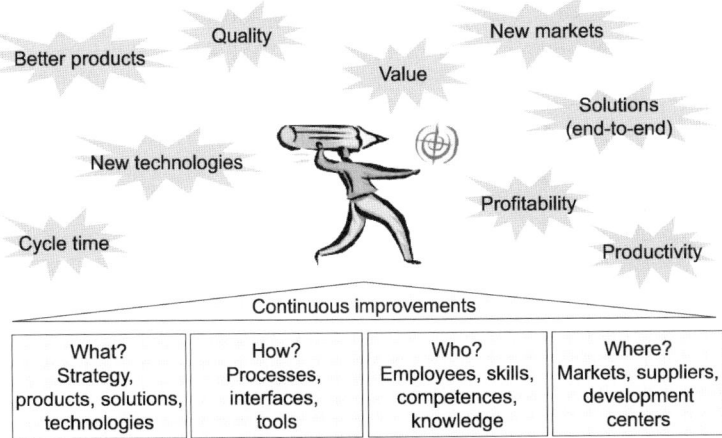

Fig. 11.2. Process improvement must address business needs

How does this relate to measurement? Improvements are directed by business objectives and need to be measured continuously in order to ensure focus, speed, and effectiveness. Emphasis is given to setting and dealing with quantitative objectives and thus making progress of the improvement initiative visible. To survive in today's global competition with extremely low entry barriers in the software industry is important to continuously stretch the targets and thus never stop pushing for improvements.

This chapter is organized as follows. Section 2 provides an overview on process improvement and summarizes the fundamental background. It looks very much to change management, because processes are about people and cultures. Section 3 provides an overview how state of the practice process frameworks (i.e., ISO9001, CMMI, SPICE, Six Sigma) are connected to measurement and what they expect in terms of measurement. Section 4 introduces to productivity measurement and improvement. Quantitative management techniques and statistical process control are elaborated in Section 5. Section 6 explains experimental and empirical techniques as they are used in software engineering. The following Section 7 looks on the business perspective and underlines what rewards to expect from process improvement. Emphasis is given to calculating and presenting the ROI. Section 8 provides practical hints for practitioners and Section 9 summarizes the major lessons from process management and improvement.

11.2. Objective-Driven Process Improvement

11.2.1 Usable and Useful Processes

Processes must be usable by and useful to both practitioners and managers. They must integrate seamlessly, and they must not disturb or create overheads. Process improvement will fail if we do not consider these basic requirements. Process improvement will also fail if we try to make the development processes completely uniform across large organizations. By focusing on the essence of the processes, integrating processes elements with each other and providing complete tools solutions, organizations can tailor processes to meet specific needs and allow localized and problem- or skill-specific software practices, while still ensuring that the basic objectives of the organization are achieved.

> We have introduced the concept of objective-driven process improvement (ODPI) in order to focus processes on the objectives they must achieve. Processes are a means to an end and need to be lean, pragmatic, efficient and effective – or they will ultimately fail, despite all push one can imagine.

Are processes and engineering tools related? Processes without adequate tool support remain theoretical. The objective is to improve visibility in engineering and master a variety of workflows and external interfaces related to R&D. Being able not only to reuse information but also to embed the respective processes in more integrated workflows for specific tasks generates immediate returns by making engineers more flexible, and it reduces friction caused by manual overhead at the boundaries of those tools and processes. A simple business case could be constructed by taking the time and effort necessary to move engineers from one project to another. Having standard workflow management around a standard product life-cycle reduces the learning effort to real technical challenges, instead of organizational overheads.

These workflows together describe how software engineering work products are gradually generated and later on embedded in products or services. They indicate the link to corporate business processes and specific tools environments. Some workflows are entirely internal to engineering, while others are at the boundaries of other functions. Service request management exemplifies such a workflow and related interfaces. Service requests result from field operations and are treated within R&D for corrections that are deployed to the field.

Practitioners do not look for heavy processes, but rather for process support, that exactly describes what they have to do at the moment they have to do it. Different products or components and various parameters such as system size or type of development paradigm ask for a carefully balanced approach of process documentation and maintenance. Modular process elements must be combined according to a specific role or work product to be delivered. Aligning procedures or tools on the organizational level increases synergies. Scalability applies to license cost of tools as well as to training. Managed process diversity, for instance, allows for easier moving of engineers from one product to another, as long as the role descriptions and the procedures are aligned.

After having the concepts for managing process diversity within development activities, the next step is to seamlessly integrate respective R&D workflows, such as software development or software maintenance with their (e-)business counterparts, such as customer relationship management or service request management. Product life-cycle management (PLM) specifically from an end-to-end perspective, will help that engineering processes integrate with the interfacing business processes. Examples include configuration management for software artifacts, and how they relate to the overall product data management. or software defect corrections and how they relate to overall service request management as part of the enterprise CRM solution. Product life-cycles, though necessary as a foundation, are insufficient if not integrated well with non-SW-related business processes.

Fig. 11.3 details how such factors not only characterize the project complexity and thus the management challenges, but also how they determine the level of process integration and workflow management. Various project factors determine different approaches to manage the involved software processes. Workflow management systems offer different perspectives to allow for instance navigation based on work products, roles or processes.

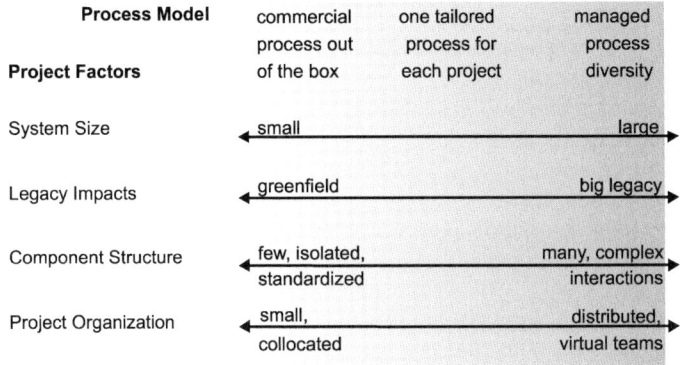

Fig. 11.3. Different solutions for different processes

Usability of any workflow support system is determined by the degree to which it can be adapted or tailored to the project's needs. There are organizational and project-specific environmental constraints which make it virtually impossible to apply the workflow system out of the box. Adaptation is achieved by offering a set of standard workflows which are selected (e.g., incremental delivery versus grand design; parallel versus sequential development; development versus maintenance). On a lower level, work products are defined or selected out of a predefined catalogue. The process models should distinguish between mandatory and optional components.

Tailoring and assembling process elements is outlined in Fig. 11.4. Project parameters (horizontal axis) drive the applicability and assembly of process characteristics (vertical axis). By relating the elements to criteria on a generic level, individual adaptation is far easier than doing this repeatedly for each project. Both the elements and their links are subject to change which is controlled and managed by a process control board. Many process elements are related by their inherent semantics that already predefine many internal relationships. For instance, depending on the permission to allow or to prohibit late requirements changes, the workflow is impacted at many places. This should not be identified for each single project again and again. Instead the hooks are foreseen in the respective estimation, planning or design processes to integrated requirement changes or late requirements which in one case are activated and in the other case are not visible.

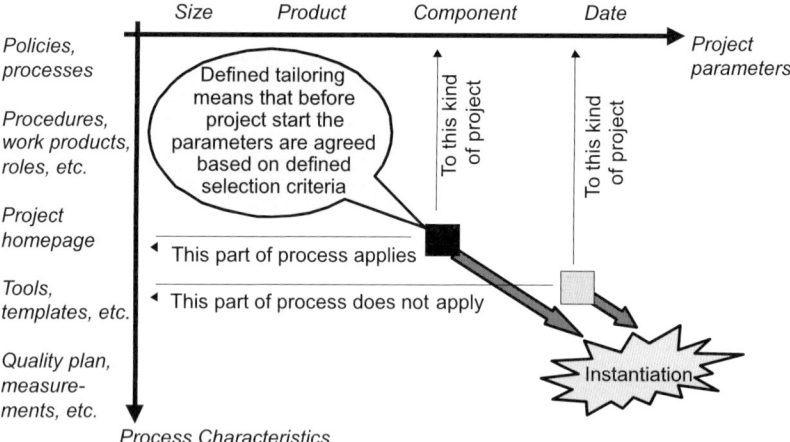

Fig. 11.4. Assembling a specific process instance based on building blocks and project parameters

The perceived conflict between organizational process and individual tailoring can be resolved by a tailorable process framework [Eber03b]. Such a framework should be fully graphically accessible and allow the selection of a process applicable to components as well as an entire product based on selecting the appropriate parameters that characterize the project. The framework allows for automatic instantiation of the respective development process and product life-cycle, a project quality plan or specific applicable measurements, based on modular process elements such as role descriptions, templates, procedures or check lists which hyperlink with each other.

Processes are supported by adequate tools or they will not be consistently implemented. To ease usage, processes and project artifacts should be online accessible as shown in Fig. 11.5. A life-cycle picture shows the global overview of the processes, and many embedded hyperlinks allow navigating with a few clicks to the final element in which the reader is interested. Compared with static process models of the 1980s which typically used standard data modeling languages, the currently available workflow systems provide nicely visualized flows that hide as much as possible anything that is not relevant for a specific view. Usability is key and not formalism.

Process management happens at various levels. A small example shows this approach. To successfully deliver a product with a heterogeneous architecture and a mixture of legacy components built in various languages, certain processes must be aligned on the project level. This holds for project management, configuration management and requirements management. Otherwise, it would, for instance, be impossible to trace customer requirements that might impact several components through the project life-cycle. On the other hand, design processes and validation strategies are so close to the individual components' architecture and development paradigms that any standard would fail as well as all standards for one design or programming methodology have failed in the past. To make the puzzle complete, for efficiency reasons, the manager of that heterogeneous project or product line surely would not like it if within each small team the work product templates or tool-based workflows were redefined. Many workflow systems for unified processes fail on such low-level process change management. They do not allow integrating process needs on different levels into a hierarchy with guided selection.

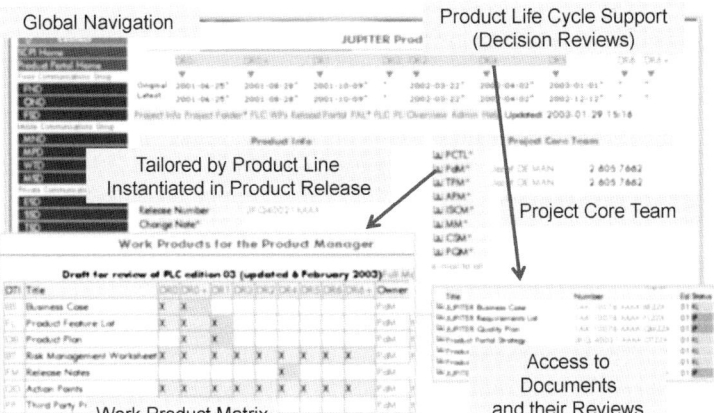

Fig. 11.5. Hyperlinks facilitate integration with other tools and processes. This instance shows the project dashboard that is automatically set up and pre-populated upon approved project

11.2.2 Managing Change

Process improvement has primarily to do with implementing changes. Successful process improvement is successful change management. Success is what is visible in the top and bottom lines. We look here primarily at what can be influenced directly within R&D process improvement which impacts the bottom line more than the top line. Inefficiencies can be attacked, rework can be reduced, customer satisfaction can be improved, and effectiveness and productivity can be enhanced.

Successful change management impacts the "people side" of business. Technology typically can be changed with a new product or at project start, or can be facilitated with dedicated training and tools. However, it is more difficult to overcome obstacles that result from people working with this technology, who might have been working for years in a specific way. Suddenly these previously successful ways of working (i.e., what we call processes) prove obsolete. These changes are difficult in many dimensions. From an individual perspective, engineers fear that with defined processes they can be replaced easier or their work could be outsourced. Managers realize that they not only need to understand new ways of working but they also need to learn new ways of managing people and innovation.

> To be successful and sustainable process improvement must blend a set of changes. On an individual level, behaviors have to change. On a corporate level, culture has to change.

Cultural change is still a phenomenon dealt with mostly within businesses outside the software engineering and IT world [Harv93, Pete88, Binn95]. In particular, the latter study outlines with lots of practical insight from several organizations (among them none with software as their core business) that the more successful leaders are in giving clear direction and being forthright, the more they encourage people to take responsibility and to express their true thoughts and feelings.

> Change is implemented in four consecutive steps which repeat for each new change. It consists of commitment to the change, diagnosis of specific problems, preparation of adequate solutions and implementation of the solutions.

Fig. 11.6 shows these four steps and their iteration.

1. **Commitment**. Business needs and concrete changes are committed by senior management. Concrete business objectives are named to set up improvement objectives. The improvement initiative and strategy are tasked to a dedicated person who will be measured on its success. Successful improvement is considered by senior management as part of their own strategy and vision.
2. **Diagnosis**. Current processes and behaviors are analyzed against the business objectives which are named in the first step. Typically this diagnosis uses established frameworks such as CMMI. It is important that the diagnosis goes be-

yond mere analysis of strengths and weaknesses towards pointing on concrete improvements and priorities.
3. **Preparation**. Following the first two steps a plan is prepared and agreed to achieve the specified improvement objectives starting from the present situation. Concrete improvement objectives are defined and agreed. Milestones are set when which improvement objective must be achieved and how this will be done. Dedicated resources are identified to lead improvement initiatives. A roadmap of changes and expected results is communicated.
4. **Implementation**. Individual change initiatives are executed following the previously agreed upon plan. Detailed process improvements build upon best practices which are evaluated, scaled, automated, piloted, trained, communicated and institutionalized. Focus in this last step is towards understanding which changes have the best yield and measuring progress against agreed targets.

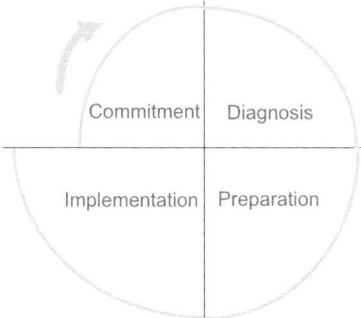

Fig. 11.6. Successful process change management consists of four steps which are performed iteratively

Leaving out one of those steps derails the improvement program towards a point where sustainable change is impossible. However, changes should be done incrementally to avoid too much load in a single step and overly long lead-time until a change is effective and yields benefits. Typically the cycle time should be in between six and 12 months. Individual change projects should take few months only.

Successful process improvement means that results are tangible, are in line with expectations, provide business value and are sustainable – even if management's attention is reduced (Fig. 11.7). At the top of the picture we summarize the starting point of any change program, namely knowing what one's own situation is (by means of an assessment) and what the objectives are for the changes. This has often been summarized as the combination of a map (i.e., knowing one's own position) and a goal (i.e., knowing where you want to go to). The two belong together like two sides of that one coin of successful process improvement.

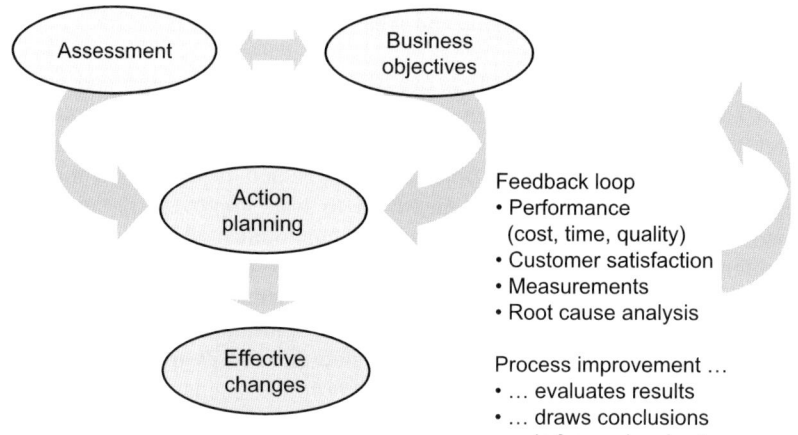

Fig. 11.7. Effective and sustainable changes result from knowing the objectives and the current situation

Process improvement is a journey – typically without an end. It is a journey because there are many intermediate targets. It has no clearly defined end, since there are always companies eagerly waiting to take your business. It is not just a few months of effort and then comes the next wave of new things. In fact, process improvement is the commitment to continuous changes, as it is expected from all doing business in the software arena. To wait and rest on one's achievements too long typically means to see a new competitor entering the picture. The entry barriers are so low that success and loss are only a few months (and sometimes mouse clicks) apart.

This journey is best portrayed by a cyclical endeavor of iterative improvements (see Fig. 11.8 which is detailing Fig. 11.6) [Eber99b]. We start at the top with establishing sponsorship and obtaining an initial commitment. This is key to any change, as it means that the responsible highest management makes a personal commitment to making the change happen. From this executive sponsorship stem the business objectives that the changes should achieve. The next step is the diagnosis. Typically such diagnosis follows a well-defined formalized scheme (e.g., CMMI SCAMPI method [Chri06]).

The assessment generates a snapshot of the current situation, and how that relates to the agreed-upon improvement objectives. Gaps are identified as are next steps. From those gaps a concrete action plan is derived that serves as the basis for making the change initiative into a concrete project. The action plan must be implemented in the form of a regular project, or there will be a continuous lack of resources and insufficient management follow-up. The last piece in this iteration is the continuous tracking of actual improvement performance against original objectives and against project milestones. Here is where measurements come very much into the picture to make changes tangible and to identify what works and what needs still more effort and focus.

11.2 Objective-Driven Process Improvement 339

Fig. 11.8. The detailed loop of a successful change with commitment, diagnosis, preparation and implementation

---

It is important that any change initiative generates tangible value within short-term! Give a change 3-6 months to show value and at most 12 months to generate a tangible ROI. Don't dream of longer timeframes to implement any so-called improvement as it is only a waste of capacity and energy. Change needs time because people need to adjust, but if they get too much time they will not feel the urgency.

Not only your management which pours trust and money into it need convincing arguments to continue, but also colleagues and co-workers want to see benefits for their own day-to-day work. The evolution during a change project can be characterized by several phases with different degree of motivation in the organization and thus probability of success. Fig. 11.9 shows this path from a medium motivation during the launch (when management is committed and understands the need for change) towards the valley of frustration (when changes cost money and create lots of pain) up to the first measurable results (this is where this chapter comes into the picture) and finally tangible external feedback and the preparation of next moves (because now everybody is convinced that it was the right thing to do).

Many change programs fail to reach that point of measurable, tangible results. They take too long and after a while buy-in is lost and the program is doomed. This is why we strongly push towards short cycles from initial planning towards delivering value. Results must be available after few months – even if the change initiative takes several years. The author lead a few years ago a major change program at Alcatel involving over 6000 engineers. The move was from a waterfall-like development cycle towards a feature-driven more agile development process. It was considered impossible – though the needs were critical to survive in a shrinking market. It took almost three years to get it all implemented and was only achieved because of small tangible results in each step. Needless to say, that in the aftermath (almost) everybody was satisfied because cycle-time was reduced to half for all types of products, but certainly they were not during the change initiative. Change management needs guts and leadership. Measurements along the way help to succeed and to sell results.

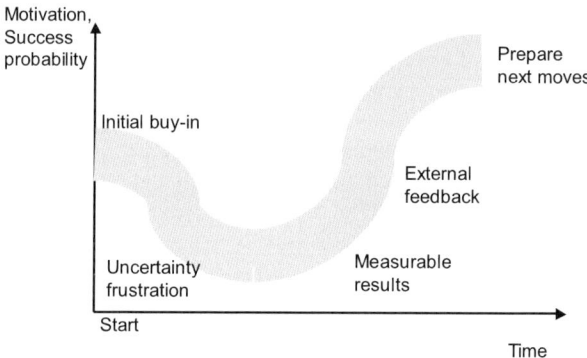

Fig. 11.9. Change projects take time and focus to achieve tangible results

Successful change management needs commitment and push from the top.

While bottom-up initiatives ensure sound technical understanding and avoid jumping on too many fads, it's only the orchestrated behaviors across an organization that make change initiatives consistent and with this consistency show sustainable results across the diversity of products, services, projects and engineers of that organization.

To underline this effect, we studied in Alcatel during the past years the impact of push to success. Fig. 11.10 shows the results of the biggest such study.

The horizontal axis ranks "process push" along four categories from none (which means that management either actively prohibited change or did not at all walk the talk) to minimum (messages from the top but inconsistencies in day-to-day behaviors), medium (management aligned with the change needs) and maximum (management demanding strong commitment towards the intended changes – independently of excuses in their staff). The dependent variable we tested was the improvement objective of that time, namely field defect reduction. We could have taken any other related measurement (e.g., cost of non-quality or early defect removal), but this measurement had the closest link to customer satisfaction – which was at stake.

The trend line shows that increasing push means better field quality as indicated by a reduced number of normalized field defects. Removing outliers would shift the line to the bottom but not really change the direction. Senior management, project managers and line managers must be the change they want to see in the company. Launching a change initiative solely from the bottom and not having management support will be watered down by the many nay-sayers who try to protect their own turf and not really care for performance improvement.

Process change management is typically an activity of the organization, however it is practically happening within individual projects, especially in higher maturity organizations. To facilitate change, any process element should refer to a process owner who typically serves as focal point for change proposals and change decisions. A process owner is the expert for a specific process and guides any type of evaluation, improvement or coaching. Of course, he should delegate authorship or dedicated coaching to experts with more detailed knowledge and experience, but it is helpful to identify a single person with overall responsibility to whom people can ask questions and suggest improvements. Any single instance of a process element should be placed under configuration control which allows managing change in the context of several parallel projects. The latter is particularly relevant to avoid uncontrolled mushrooming of variants, thereby creating situations where an engineer would suddenly have to deal with two versions of the same process. It is for this reason that quality audits always ask for defined time stamps related to process selection.

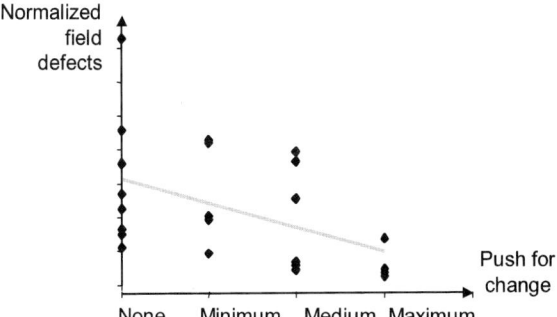

Data Source: Own data of Alcatel from Switching and Routing Businesses between 1998 and 2001. Each data point represents a single project. Reconfirmed in 2004 for all Alcatel business units for performance average.

Fig. 11.10. Change needs a strong push to be successful

The biggest error management can make is to continue asking for unrealistic commitments or not walking the talk. Expectations and responsibilities for successful change management can be summarized as follows:
- Executive management (giving the direction and ensuring focus on concrete business needs, setting and directing strategy, taking action in support of the strategy, establishing a steering committee, reviewing education policy)
- Middle management and engineering process group (translating business needs into concrete improvement objectives, assigning resources, revising existing

and planned resource strategies, preparing training in the spirit of continuous improvement)
- First line supervisors and engineers (working on technical committees, introducing new technologies, thinking about how they build systems, providing feedback on new approaches used

With process change management becoming a management function and process improvement as a project receiving high priority in the context of all engineering projects, real authority is given to the change program. For the same reason, engineering process groups (EPGs) are typically rather small, while at the same time part-time contribution of experts in various areas fosters buy-in and sustainable culture change. To avoid the prevailing attitude that nothing is worse than a six-month old slogan, senior management should make explicit that any change needs within engineering (e.g., efficiency improvement, elapse time reduction, and so on) would be covered under one process improvement (project) umbrella. All this is the life insurance for your process improvement initiative.

> Lessons learned from successful change management:
> 1. Set clear goals on quarterly basis. Avoid too many initiatives in parallel. Get something done, then next.
> 2. Walk the talk. Do not deviate in critical situations. People look at YOU. You are the signal. YOU must be the change you want to see in the world!
> 3. Assign personal responsibilities. Treat improvement as a project (single project manager, plan, tracking, management reviews). If process improvement fails, it is a management failure which is not considered acceptable.
> 4. Measure early and continuously. Take action before the scorecard turns red. Focus on the ROI. Are your projects doing better? Use performance measurements and the customer's voice.
> 5. Improvement is not free. Depending on speed and reengineering needs, it costs around 1-3% of software engineering. This is investment that later pays back (ROI: >5).
> 6. Never be satisfied. Competition is catching up fast. Are you staying competitive? Do you set the roadblocks for the others or run into them?

11.2.3 CMMI for Process Improvement

If you do not know where you are and where you want to go, change will never lead to improvement. To continuously improve and thus stay ahead of competition organizations need to change in a deterministic and results-oriented way. They need to know and improve their process maturity.

The concept of process maturity is not new. Many of the established quality models in manufacturing use the same concept. This was summarized by Philip Crosby in his bestselling book "Quality is Free" in 1979 [Cros79]. He found from his broad experiences as a senior manager in different industries that business success depends on quality. With practical insight and many concrete case studies he could empirically link process performance to quality. His credo was stated as: "*Quality is measured by the cost of quality which is the expense of nonconformance – the cost of doing things wrong.*"

First organizations must know where they are, they need to assess their processes. The more detailed the results from such an assessment, the easier and more straightforward it is to establish a solid improvement plan. That was the basic idea with the "maturity path" concept proposed by Crosby in the 1970s. He distinguishes five maturity stages, namely

- Stage 1: Uncertainty
- Stage 2: Awakening
- Stage 3: Enlightening
- Stage 4: Wisdom
- Stage 5: Certainty

These five stages were linked to process measurements. Crosby looked into the following categories of process measurement: Management understanding and attitude, quality organization status, problem handling, cost of quality as percentage of sales, quality improvement actions with progress and overall organizational quality posture.

The concept of five maturity stages further evolved in the software engineering domain under the lead of Watts Humphrey and his colleagues in the 1980s to eventually build the Capability Maturity Model [Hump89]. Based on mentioned structuring elements of maturity levels, goals and practices, the CMMI offers a well-defined appraisal technique to assess your own or your suppliers' processes and to benchmark performance.

> It is all about business: Your competitors are at least at this same place (or ahead of you). The goal is to further improve planning and decision making, lower costs, increase adherence to schedule and improve product quality.

Process improvement frameworks can provide useful help if introduced and orchestrated well. Effective process improvement can be achieved by using the widely-used **Capability Maturity Model Integration (CMMI)**, originally issued by the Software Engineering Institute [Chri06, SEI06a]. It extends the "classical" CMM and ISO 9000 to an *improvement view* integrating the System Engineering CMM (SE-CMM), the Software Acquisition Capability Maturity Model (SA-CMM), the System Engineering Capability Assessment Model (SECAM), the Systems Engineering Capability Model (SECM), and basic ideas of the new versions of the ISO 9001 and 15504.

This model provides a framework for process improvement and is used by many software development organizations. It defines five levels of process maturity plus an improvement framework for process maturity and as a consequence, quality and predictability..

The CMMI is structured into five maturity levels, the considered process areas, the specific goals (SG) and generic goals (GG) and the specific practices (SP) and generic practices (GP). The *process areas* are defined as follows [Kulp03]: *"The Process Area is a group of practices or activities performed collectively to achieve a specific objective."* Fig. 11.11 shows the general relationships between the different components of the CMMI.

A second, very similar but muss less used process improvement framework is the SPICE model. SPICE stands for software process improvement and capability determination. . Both frameworks are fully compatible and based on ISO 15504, which governs capability assessments on a worldwide scale.

Why do software organizations embark on frameworks such as the CMMI or SPICE to improve processes and products? There are several answers to this question. Certainly it is all about competition. Companies have started to realize that momentum is critical: If you stand still, you fall behind! The business climate and the software marketplace have changed in favor of end users and customers. Companies need to fight for new business, and customers expect process excellence.

> An industry-proven process improvement framework such as the CMMI offers the benefit to improve on a determined path, to benchmark with other companies and to apply worldwide supplier audits or comparisons on a standardized scale.

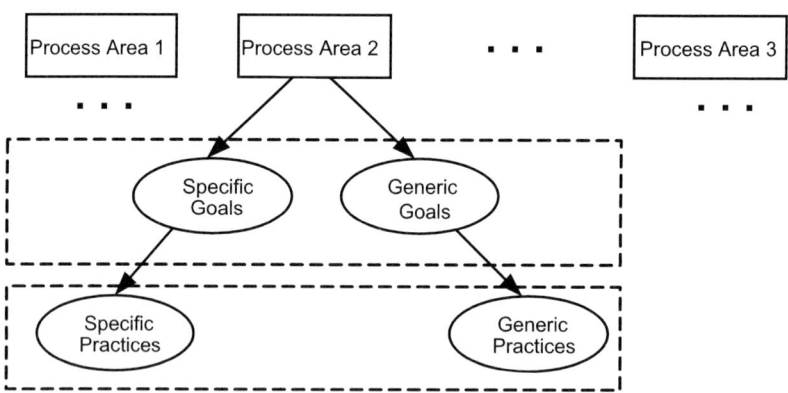

Fig. 11.11. The CMMI model components

We will furtheron look to the CMMI because it is more widely used than SPICE and offers much more concrete guidance *how* to improve. However, what we tell here equally applies to SPICE, for those who have to use that other framework. Both of these frameworks suggest and underline that growing process maturity means better business performance.

The CMMI offers guidance (structured goals to achieve) plus an informative wealth of best practices to embark on (practices to implement the goals). It is structured in five maturity levels that allow to set up a goal-driven roadmap (see

Table 11.1). Each of the process areas is structured into process areas that allow to focus on specific needs (e.g., supplier agreement management or project planning). Each process area can be individually measured by mapping its performance and contents to six capability levels.

Table 11.1. The five maturity levels of the CMMI and their respective impact on performance

CMMI Maturity Level	Title	What it means
5	Optimizing	Continuous process improvement on all levels. Business objectives closely linked to processes. Deterministic change management.
4	Managed	Quantitatively predictable product and process quality. Well-managed, business needs drive results.
3	Defined	Standardized and tailored engineering and management process. Predictable results, good quality, focused improvements, reduced volatility of project results, objectives are reached.
2	Repeatable	Project management and commitment process. Increasingly predictable results, quality improvements.
1	Initial	Ad-hoc, chaotic, poor quality, delays, missed commitments.

The trend in the industry as a whole is growing towards higher maturity levels. In many markets such as government, defense and automotive the clear demand is for a maturity level of 2 or 3. In supplier markets it can well be maturity levels 4 or 5 which is a strong assurance that your supplier not only has processes defined, but that he manages his processes quantitatively and continuously improves.

Fig. 11.12 details the five maturity levels of the CMMI and shows how process areas are mapped to these maturity levels [Chris06]. Each of these process areas follows their respective specific goals which characterize the use of the process areas. In order to see the effectiveness, efficiency and performance of a single process area, specific measurements can be implemented, which we will characterize later.

Using the CMMI and its process areas for an objective-driven improvement increment consists of the following steps:
1. Identify the organization's business goals and global improvement needs.
2. Define and agree on the organization's Key Performance Indicators (KPIs).
3. Identify the organization's areas of weakness or areas where they are feeling the most pain internally or from customers from e.g., root cause analysis, customer surveys, and so on.
4. Commit to concrete and measurable improvement objectives
5. Identify those CMMI Process Areas (PAs) that will best support improvements for the areas identified in Step 3 and provide a return on investment (ROI)

6. Perform an initial "gap analysis" of the PAs identified in Step 5 to identify strengths and weaknesses
7. Develop a plan using the continuous representation for those PAs that you want to focus on first
8. Implement change and measure progress against the committed improvement objectives

Maturity level	Description	Process areas	Productivity, performance
5 Optimizing	Continuous process improvement	Organizational innovation and deployment Causal analysis and resolution	
4 Quantitatively managed	Quantitative management	Organizational process performance Quantitative project management	
3 Defined	Process standardization	Requirements development Technical solution Product integration Verification Validation Organizational process focus Organizational process definition +IPPD Organizational training Integrated project management +IPPD Risk management Decision analysis and resolution	
2 Managed	Basic project management	Requirements management Project planning Project monitoring and control Supplier agreement management Measurement and analysis Process and product quality assurance Configuration management	Poor results, rework
1 Initial			

Fig. 11.12. The CMMI process areas and their mapping to the five maturity levels

The following example shows how this above approach is translated into concrete actions:
1. Identify the organization's business goals and global improvement needs.
   Example: The business objective is to improve the schedule predictability of projects. This is linked to the business objectives of increasing revenues, faster cash flows and fewer delays and cost of non-performance from schedule delays.
2. Define and agree on the organization's Key Performance Indicators (KPI's)
   Example: The performance indicator is schedule predictability and measured as the normalized delays compared to originally agreed deadline. 120% means the project is 20% later than committed. Later changes are not considered in this measurement to avoid that projects would argue that the delay is justified due to changing requirements. This definition is agreed with product managers and business owners to avoid they would challenge engineering teams later.

3. Identify the organization's areas of weakness or areas where they are feeling the most pain internally or from customers from e.g., root cause analysis, customer surveys, and so on.
   Example: A root cause analysis of delays is performed and highlights three areas. 40% of delays result from insufficient project management, 30% of delays come from changing requirements, 20% from supplier delays and 10% from other causes. Customer surveys underline that requirements are often included to the project which is perceived as higher flexibility but in fact these are to all experience not critical requirements but rather nice-to-have features.
4. Commit to concrete and measurable improvement objectives
   Example: Concrete focus is agreed on two domains, namely improving estimations and improving requirements development. The respective performance targets are agreed in a management seminar as follows: each project must have two estimates where the first is allowed to deviate by 20% and the second to deviate by 10%. Requirements change rate after project start has to be below 20% – except that customers pay a dedicated fee calculated to at least double the margins. Time-boxing and incremental development with prioritized requirements is introduced to achieve those objectives. Requirements priorities must be agreed before project start.
5. Identify those CMMI Process Areas (PAs) that will best support improvements for the areas identified in Step 3 and provide a return on investment (ROI)
   Example: Focus will be on requirements development, requirements management, technical solution, project planning and project monitoring and control. Project managers will be educated in project management techniques and negotiation skills.
6. Perform an initial "gap analysis" of the PAs identified in Step 5 to identify strengths and weaknesses
   Example: requirements development is nowhere, requirements management satisfies basic needs for change management, technical solution is too much engineering-oriented and must be extended to capture business reasoning, project planning shows severe weaknesses in estimation and feasibility analysis techniques, project monitoring and control has weaknesses in getting stakeholder agreement on changes. During the gap analysis weaknesses in measurement and analysis PA are detected, so this PA is added to the above list from step 5.
7. Develop a plan using the continuous representation for those PAs that you want to focus on first
   Example: The most urgent need is project planning. A dedicated one-month initiative is launched right away to install a suitable estimation method and train people on it. A tool for feasibility analysis is introduced in parallel because not much own history data was available. A history database is installed for a set of key project measurements. In a second phase, earned value analysis will be introduced. After three months requirements development is launched under the leadership of product management.
8. Implement change and measure progress against the committed improvement objectives

Example: Performance measurements are collected from all ongoing projects as of first day of this initiative. Insufficient performance is not punished but carefully analyzed Mostly it is found that still too many changes appear out of no reason. In consequence a strong focus is given towards change management and change review boards. A weekly project review is introduced and after a few weeks enhanced with daily Scrum meetings of development teams. Requirements changes passing the change review board must have their proper business case or are not accepted. Marketer and sales are unhappy – but the results prove valid. It is them who will not take ownership and do not be held accountable for changes. This reduces changes within the first three months dramatically. The first few projects suddenly reach 20% schedule overrun and two of them are close to 10%. The latter two are further evaluated to identify best practices. As it turns out, the project manager introduced requirements reviews by product managers and testers before the change review board meeting. The quality of requirements substantially improved. This change is immediately pushed forward by senior manager to all projects. This time testers are unhappy because they have not the time for doing the reviews. Rather than demanding overtime, they are budgeted with 5% slots each week for reviews. These are two hours which are sufficient to review 1-3 requirements I sufficient depth.

And on it goes ...

Managing process changes of course depends on process maturity. On lower maturity levels, it is centrally governed, while on higher maturity levels, tailoring and change management – within a defined scope – increasingly is going back into the projects and teams.

We talk a lot about the different maturity levels of the CMMI. Let us briefly and informally characterize them since they impact the way we address change management in this chapter (see Table 11.1). There are five maturity levels, of which maturity level 2 is the most difficult to reach with respect to culture changes in the organization. The major cultural change from an ad hoc behavior on maturity level 1 to the controlled behaviors per project on maturity level 2 is as follows:
- joint commitments are made within the scope of a project
- project plans become increasingly realistic
- the whole project team reviews and has input to the plan
- estimates are made by teams of developers
- schedules are made by project managers comprehend real work time

At maturity level 3 we see another pattern, that of generalizing changes so that they impact the entire organization. This means:
- the organization adopts a standardized process framework
- a common professional culture emerges
- the culture is carried by all engineers and driven by increased pride in the organization
- development and training is achieved through using process assets
- focus on performance improvement with clear business perspective

- customers feel with each contact a coherent and focused way of working
- less rework and cost of non-quality allows the organization to focus on new development
- motivated personnel stay with the organization

At the maturity level 4 we see again a substantial change in culture, this time from the organization back to projects and directly linking performance improvement targets to process improvement. This is where profound process knowledge is consistently visible on all maturity levels and in all functions and roles. Maturity level 5 finally looks into continuous improvements that are driven by empowered teams and individuals.

> The CMMI (and similar frameworks) is a tool to improve projects, product and system development performance but should never be seen as an end in itself.

However, just as a map does not help without a destination, the CMMI needs to be built around your business objectives. Established practices proved for decades in industry that maturity and performance can be effectively improved. It is not rocket science. However, you get what you are asking for. It does not compensate for bad management and wrong roadmap decisions. The CMMI is not a certification and does not prescribe a process. It allows benchmarking due to its wide usage in industry.

11.2.4 Setting Improvement Objectives

Process improvement needs software measurement. Fig. 11.13 shows the dependencies between the execution of a process, its definition and the improvements. The circle follows the **E4-measurement process** starting with objectives (establish), through executing the process and measuring results (extract), evaluating results (evaluate) and deriving and implementing concrete improvements (execute).

Obviously if there is no process, some initial definition has to happen in order to have a baseline. Improvements are only feasible if they relate to measurement. Processes must be judged whether they are good or bad, or whether they are better or worse than before. To make change sustainable, it is based on realistic improvement objectives.

The interaction of objectives and feedback is obvious in day-to-day decision-making. Different groups typically work towards individually controlled targets that build up to business division-level goals and corporate goals.

Let us look at a specific example to better understand these dependencies. A department or business division-level goal could be to improve maintainability within legacy systems, as it is strategically important for all telecommunication suppliers. Design managers might break that down further to redesigning exactly those components that are at the edge of being maintainable. Project managers, on the other hand, face a trade-off with time to market and might emphasize on incremental builds instead. Clearly both need appropriate indicators to support their selection processes that define the way towards the needed quantitative targets related to these goals. Obviously, one of the key success criteria for process improvement is to understand the context and potentially hidden agendas within the organization in order to find the right compromises or weigh alternatives.

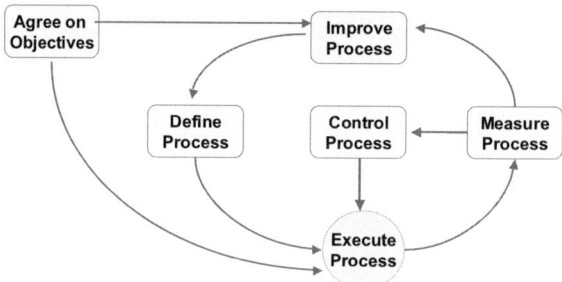

Fig. 11.13. Process improvement is based on upon process measurement

Objectives related to individual processes must be unambiguous and agreed upon by their respective stakeholders. Stakeholders are those who use the process or who benefit from it. These are not just management, but could comprise engineers, suppliers, amongst others. This is obvious for test and design groups. While the first are reinforced for finding defects and thus focus on writing and executing effective test suites, design groups are targeted to delivering code that can be executed without defects. Defects must be corrected efficiently which allows for setting up a quantitative objective for a design group, that is, the backlog of faults it has to resolve. This may uncover one of the many inherent conflict situations embedded in an improvement program. Setting an overall target of reducing defects found by the customer of course triggers immediate activities in design, such as improved coding rules, establishing code inspections, and so on. Finding such defects up front means better input quality to integration test that as a result might not be able to still accomplish efficiency targets, such as a distinct rate of faults per test case. Besides maybe enhancing test coverage, a successfully running test case has little worth from a cost reduction perspective which shows the inherent dilemma of conflicting goals.

A goal-oriented measurement approach (see Chap. 3) ensures that process improvement is embedded in a closed feedback loop (see Fig. 11.14). Goals are business-driven and are translated into annual targets or key performance indicators. They are reflected in and tracked with scorecards. A history database captures process, product and project information. It helps with tailoring processes and with setting specific process and project targets. It also facilitates setting control limits for statistical process control. The feedback loop is built upon measurements from processes that are analyzed against control limits and compared with targets.

11.2 Objective-Driven Process Improvement

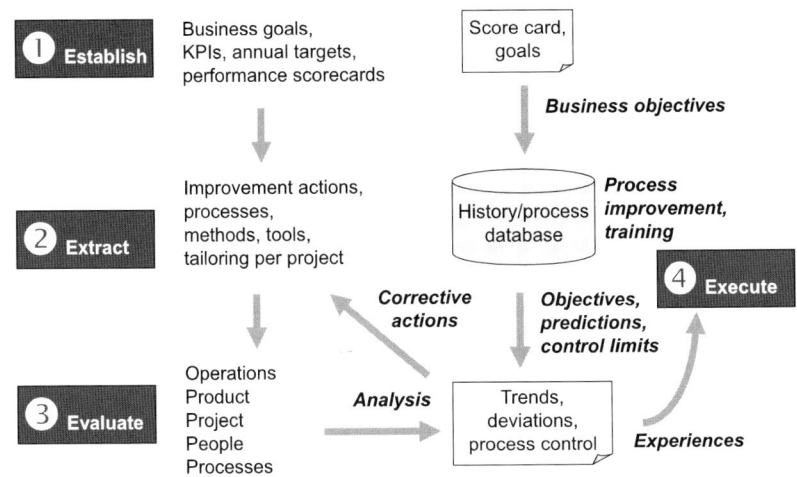

Fig. 11.14. Goal-oriented measurement ensures that process improvement is embedded in a closed feedback loop

Let us look at concrete examples to better understand the usage of a goal-oriented measurement for process improvement. Fig. 11.15 shows the usage of goal-oriented measurement in order to derive a concrete improvement approach from a business goal and then to furtheron measure its implementation (a similar example is already provided in Fig. 2.5). The first column shows some typical business goals as they appear this minute on dozens of board meetings and related presentations of thousands of department managers. What is often missing though is the content in columns two and three. The second column details the business goal into more tangible improvement objectives. Improvement is not achieved by slogans but by understanding what could be done better. This must be self-explanatory to ensure sustainable change. If these improvement objectives are clear, detailed measurements as presented in the third column are used to baseline and monitor progress. Typically these measurements are necessary already to derive useful improvement objectives.

> Always baseline your status quo before starting the improvement program.

This not only ensures you bet on the right horse but is also safeguards your program because you have at all times progress indicators and the possibility to present the value and results of this improvement program.

For instance, if the goal is to reduce cost or to improve productivity, the first step naturally is to analyze cost structure. We therefore need the respective measurements. A result could be that we realize that cost of non-quality is too high. This is by the way almost natural in most IT and software organizations. Defects are often detected by brute force in test rather than by a variety of verification techniques close to the activity where these defects originate. This is overhead due to the rather long correction and feedback loop between test and design. A concrete action could be to invest in more reviews and in static code analysis. This change is measured from here on to see effects and maybe see deficiencies in due time to react.

Business objective	Improvement approach, objectives	Measurements
Reduce cost. Increase productivity	Reduce cost of non-quality by x% y% defect removal effectiveness Introduce product line approach Reengineer processes a, b, c	Effort spent per activity, cost structure, project size, cost of non-quality, cost of rework, productivity
Reduce development elapse time. Improve schedule adherence	x months for generic platform y months for application project z weeks for new service < x% delay on schedule	Elapse time, delivery accuracy and predictability, feature completeness, budget adherence, earned value
Improve quality	Reduce field failure rate by x% Use different verification methods Remove causes of top-3 defects	Number of failures, fault flow, reliability, availability, efficiency during validations
Improve innovation	New technology insertion rate: x% Share of innovative products: y% New patents filed per engineer: z%	Usage degree of new technology, average age of products, patents and license income

Fig. 11.15. Improvements are driven by business objectives and monitored with suitable measurements

It is important to consider different perspectives and their individual goals related to promotion, projects and the business. Most organizations have at least four such perspectives: those of the practitioner, the project manager, the department head and senior management/executives. Their motivation and typical activities differ greatly and often create confusing goals. Generally senior management and practitioners support improvement programs because they feel the needs on a daily basis. This is less true for middle management that has to make improvements happen within conflicting goals and commitments. Projects are still running with agreed-upon deadlines and available resources, while impetus for change might require specific additional resources at a given moment. The yield of any improvement initiative can be substantially lowered if preconditions are not satisfied in the day-to-day project work. For instance, asking for inspections before estimation and planning are adapted might result in superficial preparation and document reading, thus not detecting all defects that could have been found and provoking review findings that are never closed.

Lack of buy-in of middle management to our experience has two crucial effects. First, they definitely put medium-term improvement at a lower priority because they are measured according to short-term project results. Second, they might even send conflicting signals to engineers. Often the traditional reward systems stem from hierarchical organizations that disempower teams charged with executing cross-functional processes. Reuse is an example that continuously creates such discussions. When a project incurs expenses in order to keep components maintainable and to promote their reusability, who pays for it and where is this trade-off recorded in a history database that compares efficiency of projects and thus of their management? Obviously, another critical success factor is to make existing management processes compatible with redesigned business processes. This includes measuring middle management towards achieving realistic and quantified improvements objectives – in other words to leave the classic functional line- or project-oriented merit rating.

Before moving to the next part of effective change, namely feedback, we should say something on planning change. Change should be undertaken in a timely way. It should not be forced so fast that it is obvious to engineers that the targets cannot be reached. There should, however, never be a situation where people wait and wonder what will happen next. This situation typically occurs during the initial period when an assessment has just been finished and workgroups struggle to implement process changes. After having achieved some first benefits, again the risk is high to lose momentum because, after all, change is painful – as it runs in parallel with regular work – and having achieved some goals signals to many involved parties to concentrate more on project work.

Knowing that accurate planning is necessary to make change happen, it is somewhat of a relief to also realize that planning is a motivating activity. Doing the planning makes the targets more concrete, and accomplishing them is suddenly seen as possible, and even inevitable. Planning is the translation of the scorecard principle to reachable individual targets. The vehicle is working groups for operational change management and task forces for macro changes, which based on some high-level business goals establish the plan and later follow it. Seldom are people more motivated to work than just after they have finished their own planning.

11.2.5 Implementing Process Improvement

Process improvement relates to business needs. These needs are very much the same across our competitive markets. They are about cost reduction, better schedule predictability, shorter cycle time and more innovation (see Chap. 2). While the first two translate into the bottom line, the last two improve the top line due to better business. We will address here some improvement proposals in given scenarios. Table 11.2 shows process improvement solutions in typical scenarios as found in many enterprises.

Table 11.2. Process improvement solutions in typical scenarios

Improvement objective	Typical issues	Improvement solutions
Efficiency improvement and cost reduction	Design and product components need to be reworked or redone due to misunderstood or changing requirements.	Requirements development and requirements elicitation. Reviews and inspections of requirements with specific checklists and done by a mixture of stakeholders. Ensure that product managers and sales representatives sign off requirements and that stability is on their KPI's.
	Too many variants cause overheads with consistency and feature implementation	Set priorities for requirements based on the underlying life-cycle business case. Synchronize variants by strict roadmapping. Introduce product line engineering (PLE) to derive variants from a stable platform in defined steps. Emphasize product management to have a clear decision point for feature decisions. Do not allow a project manager, department head or team lead to decide on content.
	Correction overheads due to late defect detection. Overly high cost of non-quality from test and field.	Strengthen verification activities. Measure defect phase containment and early defect removal. Ensure that 60-80% of defects are found in the activity where they are created. Train engineers in all fields on reviews. Deploy dedicated verification tools, such as static code analysis or modern debuggers. Start initiatives for defect prevention, specifically root cause analysis and removing special causes of defects by means of checklists, training, tools, methodology, and so on.
	Insufficient staff morale and motivation.	Train engineers on current topics to give them the understanding that their skills are needed. In case that outsourcing or major staff reductions are ongoing or are envisaged, communicate clearly the reasoning and the implications for the different local teams. Create a feeling of competition and mutual understanding. Include staff into target setting. Make the annual performance rating process a standard process for each person in the company. Ask that as a first step targets be set by the incumbents – rather than their management. Review performance periodically based on reaching agreed targets and personal evolution plans. Ensure each engineer has his own evolution plan agreed and established.

Better schedule predictability	New technologies cause schedule overruns	Train engineers in new technologies so that introduction causes less rework. Initiate dedicated knowledge sharing and knowledge management. Launch dedicated initiatives to promote that results are shared without frictions.
	Delays due to rework	See above in the cause of rework overheads.
	Delays due to insufficient estimation and project management	Determine a best estimation method and train engineers on estimation techniques. Build a history database to evaluate current estimations. Train project managers to better execute. Improve negotiation skills to avoid creeping requirements without a real rationale. Introduce techniques for time-boxing (e.g., agile development, incremental development).
	Requirements change continuously. Changes are not well managed	Establish a requirements development and roadmapping process. Ensure requirements are signed off by critical stakeholders before start of project. Ensure engineers work only on committed and approved requirements. Prioritize requirements and select (triage) those with highest value or best cost-benefit ratio. Revisit the change rate of requirements and causes for change. Improve your process by addressing major root causes. Perform a risk management for each project and address requirements uncertainties explicitly. Agree in each project plan a freeze point for various work products to ensure the critical path can be maintained without delays.
	Delays from bad supplier performance	Establish a process for supplier monitoring and management. Agree upfront dedicated service level agreements to ensure suppliers buy into the needs Review suppliers periodically Demand CMMI-based appraisals from suppliers
Shorter cycle time	Insufficient processes cause overheads and long duration	Analyze processes end-to-end and determine critical path. Evaluate what could be removed or changed on the critical path. Investigate the possibility of using agile methodologies, specifically stable build, time boxing and incremental development. Question for each process and work product whether it is really needed. Investigate the benefits. Ask customers on needs. Instrument processes with suitable tools. Federate tools so that work products can be effectively shared and process steps can be triggered from status of work products.

	Unnecessary functionality is developed	Establish processes for requirements verification Ensure that requirements are linked to an individual business case. Sell solutions rather than trying to deploy functionality. Improve marketing to understand the customer business case before developing a solution.
More innovation, better product	Insufficient earnings from new products. Loosing market share to competitors	Introduce portfolio management to evaluate and decide on portfolio changes in a systematic way. Segment the budget to ensure a defined portion is available for innovative products. Set a distinct amount of budget and space in the portfolio aside for innovative products. Reduce systematically the amount of old products and their maintenance effort. Establish portfolio management techniques to evaluate where to spend money (i.e., the stars) and where to reduce investments (i.e., the cash cows or the dogs). Carefully evaluate your problem children and occasionally remove some to avoid you have too many.

11.2.6 Measuring Process Improvement

Managing and tracking process improvement happens at different levels of abstraction. Senior management is interested in the achievements compared to business goals and in light of what has been invested in the program. Related objectives include the effectiveness of fault detection because the obvious relationship to cost of quality is directly related to the common business goal of cost reduction. Lead-time reduction and effort reduction is related to reduced rework and as such is also related to fewer defects and early fault detection. On the project level, managing process improvements asks for specific process measurements that compare efficiencies and thus relate on the operational level to achieving the business goals. Several achievements of our improvement program can be attributed to increasing the visibility of project status, improved awareness of work product quality and setting of result-oriented improvement targets for each major process. Thorough technical control satisfies all these different needs for effective feedback.

> Questions such as "are we doing better or worse?" will provide feedback from the currently running engineering projects where changes should be institutionalized to the workgroups responsible for making such changes happen.

The feedback loop within a process improvement initiative which we already know from Fig. 11.7 and Fig. 11.13, is detailed in Fig. 11.16. On the left side we have the classic improvement activities, such as periodic assessments and dedicated working groups that would implement specific changes. They certainly influence the way requirements are managed (e.g., CMMI Maturity level 2), how development and engineering processes are improved, what quality objectives could be set and to which degree technology and infrastructure need to be addressed. This is all input to the functional organization that is responsible for implementing the regular engineering projects. They are continuously tracked by means of project tracking and oversight measurements which are not only used to monitor and manage projects, but also to provide feedback to the working groups on the progress of change institutionalization. Root cause analysis of defects or in-process quality checks provide further information on what is going right and what is going wrong.

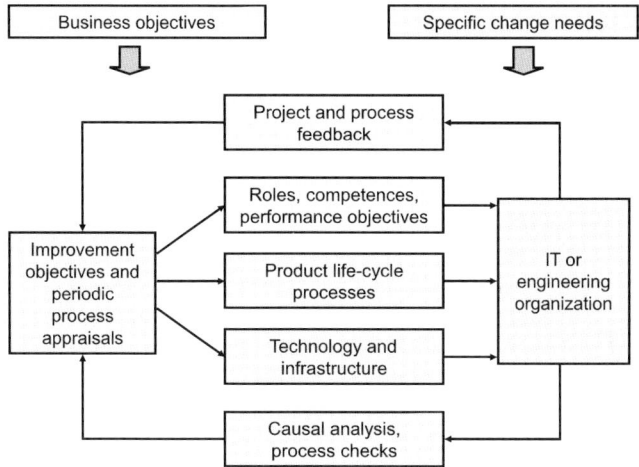

Fig. 11.16. Process improvement activities need feedback loops from actual project and process performance

Unfortunately, many organizations that consider software development as their core business strictly separate business performance monitoring and evaluation on one hand and what is labeled software measurements on the other hand [Pfle97]. As a result, engineering and IT are perceived a cost factor only by the finance people, while engineering never understands markets and business. What is missing is a clear value-orientation on both sides. The result is one-dimensional short-sighted cost reduction programs (i.e., the often-heard "let's do it in India") on the management level and Dilbert cartoons in the engineering cubicles (i.e., the often-heard "management does not understand what we are doing"). This gap has to be closed (and not by bringing Dilbert to finance).

Our motivation while building up a corporate performance improvement program was to link it with the corporate technical control in order to align the different levels of target setting and tracking activities. Only the close link of corporate strategy with clearly specified business goals and with the operational project management helps in achieving overall improvements. We therefore linked the operational measurement program for development and project management with our process improvement initiative to ensure that objectives on all levels correspond with each other.

> Measurements need to make sense to everybody within the organization who will be in contact with them. Therefore the measurements should first be piloted and then evaluated after some time. Potential evaluation questions include:
> - Are the selected measurements consistent with the original improvement targets? Do the measurements provide added value? Do they make sense from different angles and can that meaning be communicated without many slides?
> - Do the chosen measurements send the right message about what the organization considers relevant? Measurements should spotlight by default and without cumbersome investigations of what might be behind. Are the right things being spotlighted?
> - Do the measurements clearly follow a perspective that allows comparisons? Do they avoid ambiguities or heterogeneous viewpoints, thus allowing to be used as historical data?

With such premises it is feasible to set up not only release-oriented phase end targets but also phase entry criteria that allow for rejection to validation activities (such as reviews or integration) if the system quality is inadequate.

There are two major reasons for project failure that can be observed in many organizations. First and most important is the fact that we commit to inadequate estimates prematurely, stick to original budgets and schedules even if requirements change, let requirements change until well into integration, and still rarely update the estimates to match reality. The other major reason is insufficient navigation of managers in the sea of data that modern communication and reporting tools produce. Without navigation and adequate measurements managers invariably veer off in wrong directions.

11.2.7 Critical Success Factors to Process Improvement

The approach of critical success factors allows you to keep your focus on resolving concrete issues by decomposing goals into activities. It also ensures that within complex decision processes, such as in regular project reviews, the relations between day-to-day tasks and the process improvement program and its objectives are not lost.

How do we know whether an improvement program is working? There are several qualitative indicators which are easily visible:
- Improved productivity, product quality and customer feedback
- Better project performance – independently of whether the project had defined targets or if there were changes along the way
- Improved insight into organization performance
- Increased predictability of results
- Better staff morale (and maybe less Dilbert cartoons on the walls)
- Increased ability to manage complexity

- Concrete visibility of business value from each single process
- Engineers and managers improve process performance where necessary without waiting for orders or committees.

> We identified several critical success factors related to a process improvement program.
> - Commitment and motivation from the senior management to the engineers;
> - Treating process improvement as a project;
> - Short-term results that immediately show measurable achievements in running projects;
> - Sustainable results even if pressure were to be decreased;
> - Continuous change within and across processes.

What does it mean that there is a push and concrete commitments behind changes? It is definitely not what we faced in a change initiative in one of our development centers some years ago. An improvement program with heavy emphasis on quality improvement was installed. Both external and in-house consultants were hired for coaching. Management said that it "empowered" team leaders and gave priority to quality. The initiative, however, never flew as the push was lacking, and all management cared about was output and preserving own stakes. Senior management never walked their talk and in critical situations made the same wrong decisions as before.

"Push" means that management plays an active role in setting overall targets and then continuously reviews results. Tom Peters specified such reviews as "during each staff meeting, go around the table posing the questions: What have you changed lately? How fast are you changing? Are you pursuing bold enough change goals? to each colleague. Do it ritualistically. Make these simple questions a prime element in your performance appraisal system, as well as in your informal monthly sit-down appraisal" [Pete88]. In our case such reviews are carried out on a monthly base with the respective vice president, the institutionalization or deviations are questioned in the respective project reviews, and customers are part of the feedback loop.

11.3. Measurement within Process Frameworks

11.3.1 Measurement Processes in CMMI, SPICE and ISO9000

Expert Box. Author: Luigi Buglione

In this book, improvement frameworks such as CMMI and SPICE (Software Process Improvement Capability dEtermination, underlying that it is an instantiation of the meta-model defined in the ISO/IEC 15504 standard) have been mentioned several times. Coming back to their roots in TQM (Total Quality Management), process improvement should be the overarching goal for any mature organization, no matter the reference models taken into account.

Many ISO certified organizations miss (or are weak) in accomplishing clause 8 (*Measurement, Analysis and Improvement*), issues that are – respectively – the "arms & goals" of whatever management system. In order to constantly increase the awareness of those organizations towards a real continuous process improvement and be successful, the journey to higher maturity levels pass through an evolutionary path, not a big-bang. A relevant issue on this path is to apply more granular appraisals rules, as process improvement models do. Mappings between models (e.g., [Muta03b] for CMMI and ISO 9001:2000) put in evidence "*what*" and is requested to do and "*how*", but not the way to appraise it. In fact, a proper comprehension and knowledge of the appraisal process and its results is fundamental to detect the right corrective/improvement actions to include in the improvement plan.

What about measurement in improvement frameworks and in ISO 9001:2000? First of all, measurement has to be thought not only on the *process* dimension, but also on the *capability* dimension which is another level of measurement, a *meta*-measurement. Table 11.3 proposes a comparison among CMMI, SPICE (being the most widely used process improvement models worldwide) and ISO 9001:2000 through a series of possible measurement-related attributes.

Table 11.3. Measurement-related attributes in CMMI, SPICE and ISO 9001:2000

	CMMI v1.2	SPICE	ISO 9001:2000
Nature of the model	Process (how)	Process (how)	Requirements (what)
Domain	Software & Systems Eng.	Software Engineering	General Purpose
Appraisal Requirements	ARC v1.2	ISO/IEC IS 15504-5:2004	ISO 19011:2002
Appraisal Method	SCAMPI (Class A, B, C) v1.2	ISO/IEC 15504-2:2003 ISO/IEC 15504-3:2004	Application of ISO 19011:2002 criteria
Appraisal Criteria	Appraisal by Process Area	Appraisal by Process Area	Efficiency and effectiveness by clause 8 quality principles (ISO 9000:2000)
Rating Scale	N/P/L/F (Not achieved / Partially / Largely / Fully) %NPLF distribution by quartiles	N/P/L/F (Not achieved / Partially / Largely / Fully) %NPLF distribution: 0-15 (N) / 16-50 (P) / 51-85 (L) / 86-100 (F)	Yes / No (eventual non-conformities, rated by severity)
Appraisal Output / Outcomes	Capability Levels Maturity Level	Capability Level	(Non) Conformance to 9001:2000 requirements

| Measurement-related process/clause | Process dimension: MA – Measurement & Analysis (ML2) PMC – Project Monitoring & Control (ML2) OPP – Organizational Process Performance (ML4) QPM – Quantitative Project Management (ML4) Capability dimension: General Practice: GP2.8 | Process dimension: MAN.2 – Project Management ORG.3 – Process Assessment ORG.5 – Measurement Capability dimension: Process Attribute: PA 4.1 | Clause: §4.1: Monitor and Analyze processes §8.2: Monitoring and Measurement (Customer Satisfaction, Processes, Product) |

Thus, on the *process* side improvement models establish a specific measurement process (MA in CMMI; ORG.5 in SPICE) and heavily stress the relevance of gathering historical data for estimation purposes, also for achieving higher maturity levels (in particular as a foundation for ML4), while ISO 9001 in Clause 8.1 simply states that "*The organization shall plan and implement the monitoring, measurement, analysis and improvement processes needed (…)*" with the "*determination of applicable methods, including statistical techniques, and the extent of their use.*" It must be noted that MA and ORG.5 are not the only measurement-related processes in those models, even if they represent the foundation for the other ones (for instance CMMI in its staged representation puts MA at maturity level 2, stressing the relevance of MA as a priority process, providing a transversal help to all the other processes), as also visible in the "Framework interactions" section of the CMMI model document.

On the *capability* side, improvement models propose a four-level rating scale with a list of process attributes, as shown in Table 11.4, while ISO proposes two high-level rating criteria (efficiency and effectiveness), as stated in ISO 19011:2002 norm [ISO02b] in each clause. In particular,
- The first two columns propose a simple comparison – not a mapping – by maturity levels between SPICE PA and CMMI GP. Two issues should be taken into account: first, the distribution of process attributes by ML; measurement for instance is used in different levels in CMMI (maturity level 2, GP2.8) and SPICE (level 4, PA4.1). Second, the level of granularity in defining process attributes. SPICE Process Attributes own more detailed elements contributing to the PA rating, more than visible in the table: GPI (Generic Practice Indicators), GRI (Generic Resource Indicators), GWI (Generic Work Product Indicators) and RPI (Related Processes Indicators). Both issues can have a relevant influence on process ratings and improvement actions taken on the basis of such appraisals results and should be carefully evaluated when choosing an process improvement model.
- The second and third columns propose instead the mapping between CMMI GP and ISO clauses [Muta03b], referring only to the "*All*" value. In this case it is

interesting to note that the cited mapping covers only ML2 and ML3, reflecting the common perception that an ISO 9001:2000 certified organization should be equivalent to a CMMI-SPICE ML2-3 one, not considering ML4 and ML5 issues.

Table 11.4. Comparing SPICE Process Attribute, CMMI Generic Practice, and ISO 9001 Clauses

ML	SPICE (ISO/IEC 15504-5:2006)	CMMI	ISO 9001:2000
	PA – Process Attribute	GP – Generic Practice	Clauses
5	PA5.2 – Process optimization attribute	GP 5.2 – Correct Root Causes of Problems	None
	PA5.1 – Process innovation attribute	GP 5.1 – Ensure Continuous Process Improvements	None
4	PA4.2 – Process control attribute	GP 4.2 – Stabilize Subprocess Performance	None
	PA4.1 – Process measurement attribute	GP 4.1 – Establish Quantitatively Objectives for the Process	None
3	PA3.2 – Process deployment attribute	GP 3.2 – Collect Improvement Information	8.4
	PA3.1 – Process definition attribute	GP 3.1 – Establish a Defined Process	5.4.2, 7.1
		GP 2.10 – Review Status with H/L Management	5.6.1, 5.6.2, 5.6.3
		GP 2.9 – Objectively Evaluate Adherence	4.1
		GP 2.8 – Monitor and Control the Process	4.1, 8.2.3
		GP 2.7 – Identify and Involve Relevant Stakeholders	5.1
		GP 2.6 – Manage Configuration	4.1, 4.2.3, 4.2.4
		GP 2.5 – Train People	6.2.1
		GP 2.4 – Assign Responsibilities	5.5.1
		GP 2.3 – Provide Resources	4.1, 6.1
2	PA2.2 – Work product management attribute	GP 2.2 – Plan the Process	4.1, 4.2.2, 5.4.2, 7.1
	PA2.1 – Performance management attribute	GP 2.1 – Establish an Organizational policy	4.1, 4.2.1, 5.1
1	PA1.1 – Process performance attribute	GP1.1 – Perform Base Practices	None

The typical output expected from an appraisal using an process improvement model is the maturity level (ML) of the organization appraised, as the expression of a *staged* representation. But when using the *continuous* representation, the minimum entity is *each single process area* included in the scope of the appraisal, returning a capability level (CL) on a 0-5 scale, assigned according the accomplishment (or not) of the general practices (GP, in CMMI) or process attributes (PA, in SPICE) defined for the target capability level. The rating results will strongly depend on the distribution of those process attributes by maturity level. So, the contribution of Measurement in process improvement models will be determined by a combination of the two dimensions: process (by rating the first process attribute, GP/PA 1.1, executing the process practices) and capability, from Level 2 on (by rating the GP/PA and – according to the process improvement model, there is one or more attributes related to measurement influencing the final process rating, whatever the kind of representation chosen).

In the middle, there is enough room for several improvements, in particular for those organizations applying ISO 9001:2000 but not an process improvement model, therefore having in return less granular appraisal results and less information about for improving their own processes. The goal is to find strategies for successfully introduce mitigation paths for moving in an evolutionary way from ISO 19011:2002 audit rules towards those proposed in main process improvement models, taking care at the same time to minimize the resistance to change, that's the real drawback to avoid in the implementation of a process improvement program. In fact, one of the main causes for change management initiatives is the overall implementation costs within a short timeframe. But introducing an evolutionary path towards a higher knowledge of our processes by their attributes can minimize the risk for an unsuccessful initiative. Supposing to detect non-conformities in an ISO 19011-based appraisal, the results in the appraisal report will be expressed by qualitative, textual descriptions more than quantitative-based ratings using the N/P/L/F scale. In this case, it will be fundamental the ability of appraisers in properly addressing the non-conformity to a corrective/improvement action. But what about the "intensity" of this action from a technical and economical viewpoint?

Let us look at an example (Table 11.5). Analyzing this example, taken from a real SCAMPI Class B appraisal in the ISO 19011-based report the solely textual-based report based on a few appraisal criteria hides some interesting aspects for improvement: the ability of an appraiser to properly communicate results with the right words is highly critical for the determination of the improvement plan. Again, it could be difficult to briefly express what a picture can easily do in terms of correlations among practices for keeping the better solutions. On the other side, using a whatever PI appraisal method within a *continuous* representation (e.g., SCAMPI), it is possible to quickly observe that in "Project Planning" process area, 5 out of 6 projects had GP2.9 (*Objectively Evaluate Adherence*) rated "P – Partially implemented", showing a diffused situation across projects to solve. In this way, it is possible to have detailed appraisal ratings project by project before detecting eventual non-conformities, classified on more well-specified issues, valuable for determining overall evaluation and provide inputs for the improvement plan. But these advantages in obtaining a better continuous improvement process need necessarily more refined skills on "Measurement and Analysis" at the organization level, and not only at the project level, before starting the journey and it could have much higher costs than budgeted.

Table 11.5. SCAMPI-based appraisal results with generic practices from six projects for the "Project Planning" process area

GP	Prj #1	Prj #2	Prj #3	Prj #4	Prj #5	Prj #6
GP 2.10 – Review Status with H/L Management	L	L	L	L	P	L
GP 2.9 – Objectively Evaluate Adherence	P	P	P	P	L	P
GP 2.8 – Monitor and Control the Process	F	L	F	L	L	L
GP 2.7 – Identify and Involve Relevant Stakeholders	L	L	L	L	L	L
GP 2.6 – Manage Configuration	P	F	L	F	F	F
GP 2.5 – Train People	F	L	F	F	P	L
GP 2.4 – Assign Responsibilities	F	L	L	F	L	L
GP 2.3 – Provide Resources	L	L	F	L	L	L
GP 2.2 – Plan the Process	L	L	P	P	P	L
GP 2.1 – Establish an Organizational policy	L	L	L	L	L	L
GP1.1 – Perform Base Practices	L	L	L	L	L	L

Thus, economically speaking, the trade-off could be between determining the right number of process attributes to take into account for performing a process assessment and the depth for those controls (number of possible states), while from a technical viewpoint, the issue will be to choose the proper process attributes (not necessarily those ones proposed in most known PI models) and rating scales, having in mind the best possible fitness with the characteristics of such organization(s). For instance, for ML2 an SME could choose to adopt 5 process attributes and a three-level rating scale (i.e., High, Medium, Low) and so on. But it could represent in any case a step beyond the simple application of two assessment criteria in the 19011 logic (efficiency and effectiveness) with a two-level rating scale (yes/no), where non-conformities are still a quite subjective mechanism for driving improvements.

The major advantages in applying this approach are
- We introduce (or reinforce, if yet partially present) a more quantitative approach for rating processes, based on a reasoned gathering of evidences (i.e., the D/I/A (Direct / Indirect / Affirmation) taxonomy used with Practice Implementation Indicator Document (PIID) in SCAMPI for CMMI appraisals) shared among practices and processes. Thus, the adaptation will be done customizing the list of GP/PA in terms of
  - proper number of GP/PA per maturity level
  - process attributes relevant but feasible in a certain timeframe: in particular, due to the high number of withdrawn ISO 9001:2000 certificates during last years, it is strongly suggested to apply the CMMI GP2.8 (Monitor and Control the Process), matching with ISO 9001:2000 clauses 8.2.3 (monitoring and measurement of processes) and 8.2.4 (monitoring and measurement of products).
  - distribution of GP/PA according to the proper progression path established by the organization
- to have in return a series of "traffic lights" maps, showing in detail for each process (and also by project-activity) which are the issues to be included in an improvement plan, increasing at the same time the Analysis ability of the organization's personnel at different levels (from the project one, running periodical internal project audits, to the corporate level).
- to improve the organizational Change Management ability.

Concluding this expert box, the invitation for ICT organizations – no matter their size, if they are large companies or SMEs – is to rate their processes in a more quantitative way, taking care to be more granular as possible in the assessment in order to have more information for driving improvements, by choosing the right and proper attributes according to their shape, characteristics, history. And it must be never forget that a model should be a representative picture of a certain reality and be updated according to its changes, not the opposite.

11.3.2 CMMI: Practical Measurements for each Process Area

The selection of measurements needs to be goal-driven. This holds for all type of measurements. However, at times it is helpful to have some idea what others are measuring. This section will briefly dive into the CMMI with its various process areas and propose some measurements suitable for each of the process areas. Fig. 11.11 shows the five maturity levels of the CMMI and how process areas are mapped to these maturity levels [Chris06]. Each of these process areas follows their respective specific goals which characterize the use of the process areas. In order to see the effectiveness, efficiency and performance of a single process area, specific measurements can be implemented, which we will briefly characterize.

Table 11.6 provides a set of measurements mapped to each single process area of the CMMI. Note that this is our selection of what we think is useful. It is neither necessary to use exactly this list nor is it beneficial to have many measurements in parallel – especially if the process area does not create any difficulties. From maturity level four onwards, measurements are selected according to dedicated process and performance needs. On maturity level four the measurements are used to stabilize the process and its sub processes. On maturity level 5 they are used to ensure the process is capable to achieve changing business needs. They are temporary and highly specific.

Further suggestions on deriving measurements from the CMMI are portrayed in Chap. 4.

We will only touch some ideas which you will enhance depending on your needs at hand. The measurements include process and performance measurements. We always have a set of one to three process measurements mapped at the top of each process area (e.g., effort for using the process, number of projects using the process) that focus on use of the process. Afterwards we have such measurements that look to the effects of using the process (e.g., defects detected by the verification processes) and their efficiency (e.g., effort to detect and correct a defect by verification activities).

Table 11.6. Measurements for the CMMI Process Areas

Maturity level	Process area	Measurements
2 Managed		
	Configuration Management (CM)	Number of projects that are using the configuration management process
		Effort and cost for configuration management activities
		Number of changes to an initially agreed baseline
		Cost of changes to the initially agreed baseline
		Amount of change requests processed per week
		Number of CM audits
		Number of changes per document category
		Number of changes according to change category (e.g., defects, misunderstandings, wrong input)
	Measurement and Analysis (MA)	Number of projects that are using the measurement process
		Number of projects that deliver the measurements as requested
		Effort and cost for measurement and analysis activities
		Percentage distribution for causes of variance of actuals against initial plan (e.g., quality, schedule, content, effort, budget, supplier cost, supplier quality)
	Project Monitoring and Control (PMC)	Number of projects that are using the project monitoring and control process
		Effort and cost for project monitoring and control activities

	Project Planning (PP)	Number of milestones achieved compared to planned milestones
Earned value achieved
Variance of actuals against initial plan (e.g., quality, schedule, content, effort, budget)
Number of projects that are using the project planning process
Effort and cost for project planning activities
Effort for planning activities compared to planned effort
Estimation accuracy
Number of revisions to the initial plan
Percentage distribution for reasons of changes to the plan
	Process and Product Quality Assurance (PPQA)	Number of projects that are using the process and product quality assurance process
Effort and cost for process and product quality assurance activities
Number of product and process audits per project
Effort and cost spent for rework
Cost of non-quality
Cost of quality
Number of defects according to category
Number of deficiencies per audit
Percentage of resolved deficiencies within the same project
Number of escalations
	Requirements Management (REQM)	Number of projects that are using the requirements management process
Effort and cost for requirements management activities
Volatility of requirements (percentage of new and changed requirements compared to the project's initial baseline)
Number of requirements in a certain state (e.g., elicited, defined, specified, committed, tested, delivered)
Cycle time per requirements between relevant states (e.g., duration from first notice to delivery)
Number of trace-points per requirements (e.g., requirements to project plan or to test cases)
	Supplier Agreement Management (SAM)	Number of projects that are using the supplier agreement management process
Effort and cost for supplier agreement management activities
Number of changes compared to initially agreed supplier items
Cost of externally acquired software

		Effort for change management in the supply chain
		Percentage of externally acquired items or work packages that are within acceptable limits (cost, quality, schedule, content)
		Percentage of suppliers not delivering according to SLA
		Percentage of failures categories to deliver according to SLA
		Number of contract changes driven by receiving company.
3 Defined	Decision Analysis and Resolution (DAR)	Usage degree of the decision analysis and resolution process (e.g., percentage of major processes, percentage of projects, percentage of organizational entities)
		Effort, cost and measurable benefits for decision analysis and resolution activities
		Percentage of complex decisions with DAR support (e.g., life-cycle decisions, investment decisions, make/buy decisions) compared to those decisions taken without DAR
	Integrated Project Management + IPPD (IPM+IPPD)	Usage degree of the integrated project management process (e.g., percentage of major processes, percentage of projects, percentage of organizational entities)
		Effort, cost and measurable benefits for integrated project management activities
		Percentage of processes that are tailored for a specific project (overall and per major process)
		Reasons for tailoring according to category with percentage rating
		Trend analysis and correlation of process usage with performance
	Organizational Process Definition + IPPD (OPD+IPPD)	Effort, cost and measurable benefits for organizational process definition activities
		Number of defects in standard processes per period
		Number of change requests per process per period
	Organizational Process Focus (OPF)	Usage degree of the standard processes used in different categories (e.g., percentage of major processes, percentage of projects, percentage of organizational entities)
		Effort, cost and measurable benefits for organizational process focus activities
		Maturity and capability levels
		Number of critical issues reported from process audits
		ROI from process improvement activities

Organizational Training (OT)	Effort, cost and measurable benefits for organizational training activities Number of actually delivered courses Average course rating from participants Usage of courses compared to who should be there
Product Integration (PI)	Usage degree of the product integration process (e.g., percentage of major processes, percentage of projects, percentage of organizational entities) Effort, cost and measurable benefits for product integration activities Percentage of actually integrated product components compared to designed product components Defects found during product integration according to cause Trend and forecast of defects until release Forecast of defects post release
Requirements Development (RD)	Usage degree of the requirements development process (e.g., percentage of major processes, percentage of projects, percentage of organizational entities) Effort, cost and measurable benefits for requirements development activities Effort, cost and time spent for requirements rework Changes according to change category per requirement Defects according to defect category per requirement Number of requirements allocated to a release compared to open requirements
Risk Management (RSKM)	Usage degree of the risk management process (e.g., percentage of major processes, percentage of projects, percentage of organizational entities) Effort, cost and measurable benefits for risk management and resolution activities Number of risks sorted according to status (e.g., new, mitigated, pending) Number of risks sorted according to category (i.e., risk class) Number and percentage of risks that materialize per product line Percentage of project budget spent for risk analysis and mitigation Percentage of project or mitigation budget (across product lines or organizational entities) not spent for risk mitigation (because risks didn't materialize).

	Technical Solution (TS)	Usage degree of the technical solution process (e.g., percentage of major processes, percentage of projects, percentage of organizational entities)
		Effort, cost and measurable benefits for technical solution activities
		Effort, cost and time spent for design and development work products rework
		Size and complexity of work products (especially code)
		Defects per work product according to category
		Duration to close a code defect from arrival to closure and regression test
		Number of requirements changes during project execution
		Number of changes according to change category (e.g., reuse, interfaces, security, performance, usability, safety)
		Value of current software progress of the release
		Cost versus value of the currently available content
		Performance measurements for components and software build (e.g., reaction time, load tests)
	Validation (VAL)	Usage degree of the validation process (e.g., percentage of major processes, percentage of projects, percentage of organizational entities)
		Effort, cost and measurable benefits for validation activities
		Number of defects detected per validation activity
		Effort per defect during validation (from detection to correction and re-delivery)
		Average lead time to correct a defect during validation
		Percentage of test cases compared to plan
		Percentage of tested work products compared to plan
		Percentage of defects from corrections
		Percentage of customer or field failures that could have been found in test
	Verification (VER)	Usage degree of the verification process (e.g., percentage of major processes, percentage of projects, percentage of organizational entities)
		Effort, cost and measurable benefits for verification activities
		Number of defects detected per verification activity
		Effort per defect during verification (from detection to correction and re-delivery)

		Average lead time to correct a defect during verification
		Percentage of formal reviews compared to plan
		Percentage of reviewed work products compared to plan
4 Quantitatively managed		
	Organizational Process Performance (OPP)	Effort, cost and measurable benefits for organizational process performance activities
		Effort and time from a process change to the point where it is institutionalized
		Reaction time between a process deviation and implementation of the corrective action
		Success rate of process improvements and change initiative
		Trend measurements per project in terms of productivity, efficiency, cost, cycle time or other organizational improvement objectives
		Trend measurements on organizational level in terms of productivity, efficiency, cost, cycle time or other organizational improvement objectives
		Number of global quality issues compared to process changes
		Indicators for process performance on organizational level (e.g., customer satisfaction)
	Quantitative Project Management (QPM)	Usage degree of the quantitative project management process (e.g., percentage of major processes, percentage of projects, percentage of organizational entities)
		Number and percentage of processes that are statistically managed
		Progress of introducing quantitative project management compared to initially agreed milestones
		Number and percentage of process variations due to special cause of variations
		Effort, cost and measurable benefits for quantitative project management activities
		Number and impact of defects in delivered software
		Number and severity of critical customer requests
		Critical field failures during first year of operation
		Cycle time for projects and project tasks
		Effort for rework due to non achieving the right quality level (cost of non-quality)
		Effort for achieving the necessary quality level without rework (cost of quality)
		Number of changes to requirements

		Coverage, effectiveness and efficiency of reviews
		Coverage, effectiveness and efficiency of test activities
		Ratio of estimated process parameters to the actual effort spent on those (e.g., project duration, project effort, test activities, defects)
		Effectiveness of trainings on specific improvement objectives
		Number and percentage distribution of defects per insertion activity according to category
		Effort and percentage distribution of activities during the project life-cycle and during the product life-cycle
5 Optimizing	Causal Analysis and Resolution (CAR)	Usage degree of the causal analysis and resolution process (e.g., percentage of major processes, percentage of projects, percentage of organizational entities)
		Effort, cost and measurable benefits for causal analysis and resolution activities
		Number and percentage of defects for which a causal analysis is implemented
		Percentage of root causes to defects that are removed compared to all known root causes
		Number of inserted defects to software and work products across phases and their corresponding removal.
	Organizational Innovation and Deployment (OID)	Effort, cost and measurable benefits for organizational innovation and deployment activities
		Effectiveness of process improvement activities (e.g., percentage of individual change projects that reach their targets)
		Effectiveness of technology innovation activities (e.g., percentage of individual innovation projects that reach their targets)
		Number and percentage distribution of change requests for major process areas

11.4. Productivity, Efficiency and Effectiveness

Imagine that, at the start of the year, your senior management establishes an organizational objective to improve development or IT productivity by 10% by year end. Or, they might push to cut cost in your department by 10%. Do not get cynical here. This is a normal way of working since your management is measured on improving the organization and its performance.

However, without cost and productivity measurements in place, how do you know where to start? How would you know whether you can commit to such objective? How will you respond to management when they ask how you are progressing against this objective? How would you avoid that it is agreed and actions are taken that later proof pointless. Your management wants to see the 10%. Let us look into what is productivity, how it can be improved in software and IT and how we can measure where we are and where we need to move (for ROI and business case related information, see also Chap. 12).

> Productivity in software development and IT is difficult to measure. In consequence it is often not measured at all. By not measuring it, it is not improved to the levels that are necessary and feasible. In turn software expenses are outsourced or arbitrarily cut, as this is the only remaining choice for senior management.

Some schools of thought have argued for long that software productivity improvement is impossible due to "natural laws." They claim software inherent difficulties as not solvable:
- Complexity. Not two parts are alike, large number of states and interactions, nonlinearities, communication difficulties.
- Conformity. Software is embedded into other systems to which it has to conform with complex and ever-changing interfaces.
- Changeability. Software can be changed easily but with unknown ripple effects.
- Invisibility. Software is not structured, impossible to draw, difficult to communicate.

But, instead of blaming "natural laws" let us rather learn from "natural intelligence" how to deal with complexity. Examples would be the distributed intelligence of termites which build huge settlements without the central architect and planning; the conformance requirements in swarms which interact and interface in multiple dimensions; the change management of viruses, such as cholera which adapts to all type of environmental conditions. All these examples show that productivity can be mastered. Trying to approach it with some of the established engineering practices must fail because accidents are proliferated and essential needs – or perceived value – disappear in a cloud of unnecessary complexity in our products, projects and processes.

Still many companies in the ICT industry spend huge amounts of resources for developing software while not knowing whether the effort is spent on doing the right things (i.e., effectiveness), or whether the effort is spent on doing things right (i.e., efficiency). Shirley Dox, professor of longitudinal social research of London University claims that "industry has a widespread lack of databases, bad data that is not kept up to date and no culture of measuring things" [FT05]. She continues, "most companies can't say what effect changes in working practices have on productivity because they could not measure productivity at all." Nick Jones a vice president and fellow at Gartner seconds and claims that organizations are bad at measuring performance and often do not know even the cost of time. However "if you do not know that, you are not well placed to measure productivity" [FT05].

Let us therefore work in four steps which will guarantee that you will get a grip on productivity. Fig. 11.17 shows this stepwise approach based on our E4–measurement process (see Chap. 2).

1. **Agree objectives.** The first step is to set a business-driven objective. This implies that you understand what you mean with productivity (establish)
2. **Determine where you are**. The next step is to determine where you are and what should be improved (extract)
3. **Determine how to improve**. Then you analyze in detail how you are doing, compare with others, evaluate how specific industry best practices might help, and agree concrete actions for productivity improvement (evaluate)
4. **Implement improvements**. With this basis you will systematically improve and subsequently repeat the previous steps (execute).

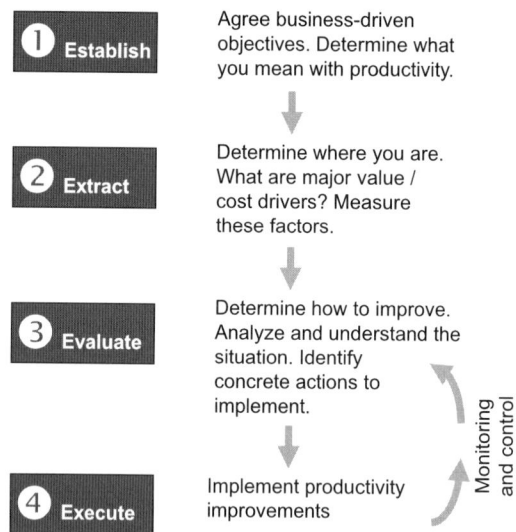

Fig. 11.17. A four-step process towards productivity improvement

Step 1: Agree objectives

It is vital in today business climate to understand and improve your productivity. The objective typically is clear to your management, however often badly articulated. Too often operational activities (our step 4) is already put on the stage during this initial step. Be clear that we need to start top-down here, and keep in mind that it is business what matters in setting objectives. If your competition can offer the same value for less, you need to move – either by offering more value for more or similar value in the same range. Do not jump too fast to cost reduction. It is a red ocean, with lots of fights and shrinking market share or margins. Do not engage in simple cost reductions in order to reduce prize, but think beyond the current offers and how you currently work.

> Productivity is defined as output over input.
> Output in business terminology relates to delivering value and doing the right things. It has to do with perception of your stakeholders. It is about being effective.
> Input is the way you create this output. It relates how well you are working. It is about efficiency.

In order to understand your current level of productivity and to improve it, you first have to figure out what productivity means to your management, to engineering, or to a project manager.

Note that in above definition productivity is improved either by improving effectiveness or by improving efficiency. Do not jump too fast to efficiency as long as you can also impact the top line, that is value delivered.

Assuming that this is understood you can agree a concrete objective, such as reduce normalized project cost within the development activities by 30% within two years.

Do not get lost into details. You need to combine development productivity, test productivity and project productivity towards an "organizational productivity" measurement which is understandable to your senior management. You need to determine how to extract, store, and analyze the respective base measurements that support these productivity measurements. Finally, you have to agree how (and how often) to report the data to ensure that it meets senior management's needs.

> We strongly advocate to take a value-oriented perspective for productivity measurement and improvement.

Fig. 11.18 shows this approach starting with a true systems engineering perspective. The "beholder" is the customer who has certain needs and wants to see a solution. If his needs are satisfied, he attributes a value to that solution. He typically will not care which type of software or mixture of different components achieves this value as long as the solution in his hands has the demanded functionality. This is where the lower level tiers come into the picture. The system we sell might be part of the system that the customer has in his hands. And in the system we build and sell there are components that contribute to our product. Recursion applies to this three-tier-abstraction. What we use as a component to build our product is in itself a product of which we are the customer.

Productivity on each of the three tiers is seen differently:
- Top tier: Productivity the customer pays for. Relates to solution and tangible value. Independent of influences of lower levels.
- Middle tier: Productivity of the supplier. This relates to product development, thus defined as functional size over engineering effort.

- Bottom tier: Productivity of subsystems for which the supplier pays. We decide make, reuse, buy to improve productivity at the next higher level.

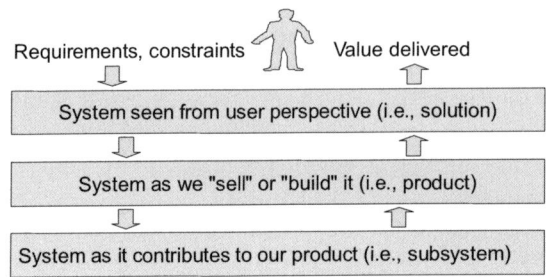

Fig. 11.18. A value-oriented perspective on productivity: Productivity exists only in the eyes of the beholder

Productivity is defined for each of the three abstraction tiers, therefore avoiding that we trap ourselves defining productivity on a level that for the external beholder has no impact. We ought to avoid getting too fast into measurements such as code size per person year or function points per person year which is not a productivity measurement per se.

So what is productivity concretely? How do objectives look like? Here are some examples for guidance:
- Reduce cost, e.g., develop more valuable products for lower costs
- Support estimation, e.g., provide consolidated and parameterized history data
- Benchmark / assess a design center or supplier capability, e.g., Rationalize higher capital-to-staff investments
- Optimize performance and processes, e.g., remove defects at the time they are created
- Streamline software operations, e.g., identify production bottlenecks or underutilized resources

Each can be valid depending where you are and where you need to go. Be specific in this step, because it determines whether you will be successful in your productivity improvement efforts.

Step 2: Determine where you are
Based on above basic understanding of productivity you can now start to extract where you are and what to improve. We will here look into how productivity is measured and how it can be analyzed.

As we have seen, productivity is defined as output over input. Output is the value delivered. Input is both the resources (e.g., effort) consumed to generate the output and the impact of environmental factors (e.g., complexity, quality constraints, time constraints, process capability, team distribution, interrupts, feature churn, tools, design).

11.4 Productivity, Efficiency and Effectiveness

In goal-driven measurement, the following questions could be derived from objectives determined in step 1:
- Objective: Reduce cost
  Question: How can we improve productivity? What is the value-add of getting to higher maturity levels?
- Objective: Support estimation
  Question: Are there simple rules of thumb estimation mechanisms? Project schedules: do we overcommit? Outsourcing contracts: will we get what we ask for?
- Objective: Benchmark / assess design center or supplier capability
  Questions: What can we learn from those who are best in class? How to select a supplier on more than initial contract offer?

Productivity is impacted by external factors, such as pressure, outsourcing, requirements changes, and so on. Avoid comparing or benchmarking things which are different! As an organization, you must seek to build up a normalized expertise in productivity analysis. Effectively work with productivity benchmarks to scrutinize project plans and assess subcontracting offers. Own development and sourcing can be optimized by first understanding your own productivity and then evaluating productivity and costs of external / internal projects.

Let us now move on to some concrete and practically useful measurements of productivity. Based on what we learned so far, we deduct that productivity is a derived measurement, namely a function of output, input and environment.

Input is easy to measure if appropriate cost control mechanisms are in place. We recommend a cost break-down according to the major cost-drivers in order to find out where a cost driver would not create much of the value that we expect on the output side. Cost structure analysis and activity-based controlling are the techniques to use in order to get insight on the input side. Be aware that not all reported cost or effort reflect actual cost or effort! Software development is highly impacted by the effort in person hours spent. This effort is rarely reported in a way useful to make any analyses. Sometimes it is only the nominal hours per day which are considered, while overtime is not reported. Or people work from home or from clients' sides and won't report all hours. Ensure therefore that effort measurements are precisely defined and accurately reported.

Output and environment are difficult to describe and measure. We define output as delivered value. Value exists only in the beholder's perspective. Examples for output and environment related base measurements are as follows:
- delivered source statements, function points, components, documents, artifacts, and so on
- with a certain quality, complexity, and so on
- in a certain environmental setting such as skills, pressure, tool support, computing platform, frequency of requirements changes, and so on
- having created application-domain and technical knowledge.

With input and output being understood we can start to measure both dimensions. Actually we do not recommend combining the two into one single productivity indicator, except that it makes sense for benchmarking in a domain where we can compare items because environmental factors are similar. This implies that they are fairly detailed to ensure that no unintended external effects would pollute the figures. Normally they would take the product and its structure or features as the output, not the revenues created by selling it. Let us look to the software productivity indicators that are used in industry.

> Thorough cost analysis is the starting point of any productivity and efficiency improvement.

The first and most important measurement is a careful analysis of cost, where they occur, how they can be influenced and how they contribute to value creation. In a software organization, engineering and marketing account for the biggest contribution to operating expenses. A careful look to the cost drivers in the product life-cycle (idea to product) and market launch (pricing and selling) is most critical. Cost can be broken down to a variety of factors, such as cost of design, cost of quality, cost of non-quality, repeat cycles due to changing requirements, and so on. Make sure that you rigorously collect cost data from the entire business process – end to end. Often some parts are forgotten, such as the impact of a design decision on life-cycle cost due to high operational cost during maintenance and evolution. Or, cost of sales and marketing is overlooked during strategy and opportunity assessment. In order to internally benchmark, sales, margins and operational cost can be normalized with engineering headcount.

Fig. 11.19 provides an example of cost break-down of software product development. Note that we only look to those elements of cost structure that can be influenced by development. This excludes cost of sales as well as allocated cost, such as a business unit's support infrastructure. Managers ought to look to such cost that they can influence – and then reduce them where appropriate.

Such a cost tree allows to investigate how cost contributes to value and what are the major cost drivers. In our picture, we distinguish during development anything that relates to performance, i.e., implementing features with a value. A second basket is the cost of non-performance (for details, see Fig. 9.20). You will find several cost elements that are directly related to product development and do not create value. The entire share of this second basket in regular development cost is equal or more than cost of performance! Defect correction activities in a regular development project contribute to at least 40% of total project cost, and in most cases it is up to 60-70%. Mostly the figure is unknown, and therefore inefficiency will continue. Gold plating is an interesting example how development might destroy value. We all know the feature overheads in desktop applications or in cars. What is not known is the overhead these additional functions create due to their inherent complexity and dependencies to – relevant – features. For instance, a major car manufacturer was working on features related to rain, such as automatic windows closing or starting the wipers. What sounded appealing at the beginning yielded software complexities that could not be managed anymore. And, worst of all, it was a feature rarely anybody was looking for.

11.4 Productivity, Efficiency and Effectiveness

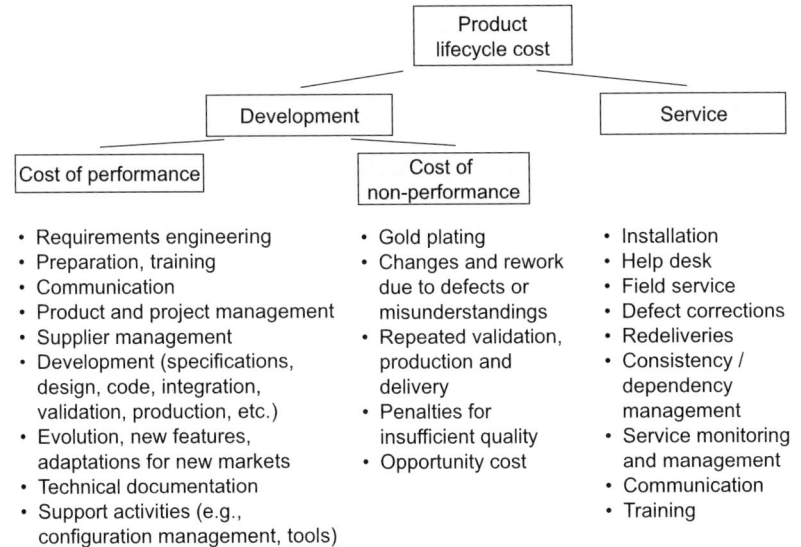

Fig. 11.19. Internal cost tree for software development

The cost tree will help in considering effort and skill needs during project and service planning. It will also point to cost drivers that undermine efficiency. Be careful however when deriving measurements in order to improve efficiency. For instance, when looking to service cost you might want to reduce defect closure time. A consequence could be that your staff would create more defect reports or that defects would be closed only partially and later reopened with a new defect. Both would improve your initial target of reducing defect closure time but negatively impact service cost.

> Cost trees provide insight how to improve performance and how changes in one area might influence another area.

Cost breakdown structures and cost trees should be sufficiently detailed to indicate efficiency problems but broad enough to allow for benchmarking and comparing across organizations. At a given moment you might need to broaden the scope of the cost tree. For instance, your number of variants and related cost of variant management might explode (which is typical for many software products). While there are excellent technical solutions, such as introducing product line engineering, this won't solve the problem because sales will still try to sell customer-specific variants. This means that successful variant reduction and management mostly have to start with sales and marketing.

> The same business case template must be used throughout the product lifecycle. It should be reviewed on both value and cost at the major decision gates. After the market launch and again after one year in operation it needs to be reviewed in terms of validity of assumptions and what can be learned for future products and releases.

Responsibility for the business case lies with the product manager. When comparing margins, market share or sales contributions of engineering, ensure that you look to the same portfolio quadrant (see also Chap. 12). There is no use comparing a cash cow (which needs to deliver) with a growing star (which needs investment). To facilitate cross portfolio evaluations, discounted cash flows can be used in the business cases. The risk here is that assumptions are often severely wrong when it comes to market forecasts and sales expectations.

We will now look to specific software productivity measurements. They are all used currently in industry and play a dominant role in productivity benchmarks. They measure the development process and do not look to sales or market shares. Before jumping on one of those, note that they all miss one key point, namely how effective a company is in understanding its customers' needs and translate them into product strategies, product requirements, technology decisions and product innovations.

> When using one of the following measurements, do not get lost in judging only code-writing efficiency. It will not help to improve your productivity. Instead use them as a benchmark and determine improvement objectives year over year.

Code-oriented output over effort is the single most popular software productivity measurement. Output typically is measured as design or code volume, such as new and changed statements in the product release. Effort is typically the net effort spent on engineering this product release. It is not the best measurement because it entirely leaves out environmental factors, but it can be measured consistently and used as a simple benchmark. This is the reason why – despite all the attacks towards this measurement – it remains after three decades still the one which is used across almost all software industry. Users should be aware on its problems. The more verbose the programmer, the more productive she seems. The lower the programming language, the higher is productivity because more code is written to solve the same problem. This means that using the measurement allows only a benchmarking within exactly the same constraints, i.e., product, company, processes. These conditions considered equal, it is simple yet effective to see how projects are doing. Alternative sizing measurements include unadjusted function points, requirements and use cases. All those can also be used as an output measurement, but should also be benchmarked only in one environment. IEEE Std 1045 Standard for Software Productivity Metrics provides a framework for measuring and reporting software productivity [IEEE92] on the basis of size and effort. It is meant for those who want to measure the productivity of the software process in support of their software product.

Function points over effort is the second most relevant productivity measurement. It is better than mere code-oriented measurements because it looks to the functionality of the delivered output. Aside that it considers environmental parameters and thus allows tuning to specific environments, such as real-time development or embedded systems. The motivation for function points as we saw already in Chap. 7 is that a functionality-based output captures "value delivered" much better than size. Function points do not count requirements but their implementation. They are based on a combination of program characteristics, each associated with a weight, namely external inputs and outputs, user interactions, external interfaces and files used by the system. The advantage compared to size measurements is that complexity of the project and other environmental parameters are considered. The problem around function point counting is that they are more subjective than LOC. Productivity is measured as the ratio of function points to effort. It can also be predicted on the basis of function points to the power of a number (see Chap. 14 for examples).

Embedded techniques where the environmental factors dominate the calculation create a third category of productivity measurements. Delivered size or functionality is just one driver amongst many. Examples are

- Productivity = adjusted size / effort. Adjusted size is the estimated effort based on history and constraints. Productivity is a normalization comparing estimated to actual effort.
- Productivity can be measured as a dimensionless indicator generated by an estimation method and tool, such as QSM SLIM, COCOMO or SPR Knowledge-Plan. These tools relate size to effort and expand this to a "Productivity Index" that encompasses the general development environment and time pressure.
- Productivity can also be measured by comparing earned value with actual effort spent. It is defined as the weighted effort of completed work products against actual or planned effort. This technique is very helpful if earned value based techniques are used for project planning and tracking (see Chap. 8).

Any of the output measurements based on size or function points are sensitive to programming style. Fig. 11.25 provides an example with two different code segments hat deliver exactly the same functionality. Their size however varies substantially.

```
BSP1: PROC;                                    BSP2: PROC;
TAKE [X,Y] FROM INTERFACE;                     DCL QUADRANT BIT(2);
IF (X > 0)                                     TAKE [X,Y] FROM INTERFACE;
 THEN                                          IF (X*Y == 0)
  IF (Y > 0)                                    THEN /* X=0 oder Y=0: DEFAULT */
   THEN                                          QUADRANT:= '00'B1;
    SEND '00'B1 TO LENKUNG;                    ELSE
   ELSE                                         IF (X > 0) /* Bit 1 setzen */
    IF (Y < 0)                                   THEN
     THEN                                         QUADRANT.BIT(1):= '0'B1;
      SEND '01'B1 TO LENKUNG;                   ELSE
     ELSE /* Y = 0: DEFAULT */                   QUADRANT.BIT(1):= '1'B1;
      SEND '00'B1 TO LENKUNG;                  FIN;
    FIN;                                       IF (Y > 0) /* Bit 2 setzen */
   FIN;                                         THEN
 ELSE                                            QUADRANT.BIT(2):= '0'B1;
  IF (X < 0)                                   ELSE
   THEN                                         QUADRANT.BIT(2):= '1'B1;
    IF (Y > 0)                                 FIN;
     THEN                                     FIN;
      SEND '10'B1 TO LENKUNG;                 SEND QUADRANT TO LENKUNG;
     ELSE                                     END; /*BSP2*/
      IF (Y < 0)
       THEN
        SEND '11'B1 TO LENKUNG;
       ELSE /* Y = 0: DEFAULT */
        SEND '00'B1 TO LENKUNG;
      FIN;
    FIN;
   ELSE/*X = 0: DEFAULT */
    SEND '00'B1 TO LENKUNG;
  FIN;
FIN;
END; /*BSP1*/
```

Fig. 11.20. Example: Embedded controller with sonar system. Two different programs with exactly the same functionality

The effects depend on the productivity measurement selected. With the assumption that the same effort and duration is spent to design these two programs we can see:
- LOC based sizing. Counting the executable source code lines.
  Effect: Left code segment has 50% higher productivity.
- Function points, earned value. Functionality of both program segments is equal.
  Effect: Productivity of both program segments is equal (assuming that the outputs are always combined).
- Feature Points. Twice the number of decisions in left code segment means higher algorithmic complexity.
  Effect: Left code segment has higher productivity.
- Project productivity. Twice the number of decisions in left code segment means higher test effort to achieve same C1 coverage.
  Effect: Left code segment has lower productivity.

Measurement impacts what you will be able to control and to improve. Therefore ensure that your selected productivity measurement covers several dimensions. Do not get trapped in providing just one figure, such as function points per person year. Rather measure both the top-line of our equation (i.e., some effectiveness figure) and the bottom line (i.e., the efficiency).

Step 3: Determine how to improve

How can software engineering productivity be effectively improved? Based upon an understanding of what is productivity (step 1) and where we are (step 2) it is a simple step to move forward and determine what must be changed. Fig. 11.21 shows the different levers to improve productivity.

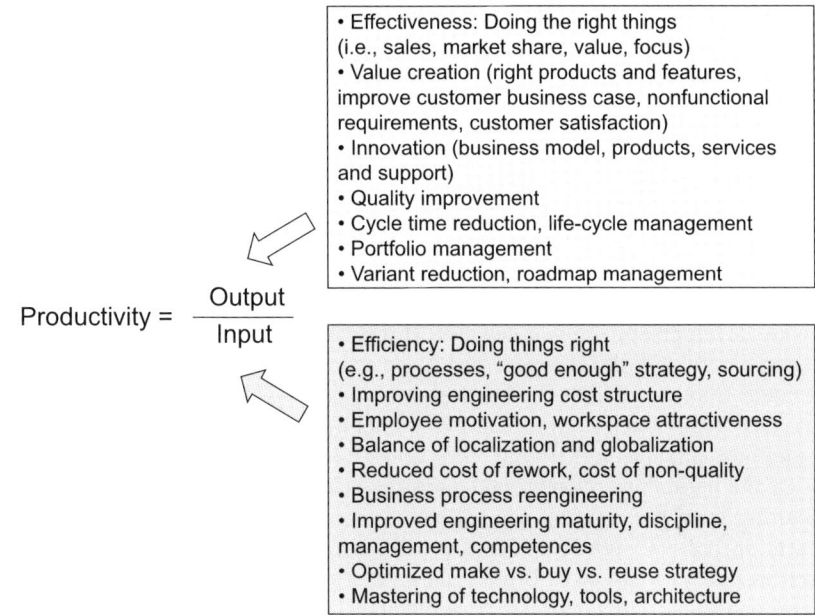

Fig. 11.21. Levers for productivity improvement

The first thing we realize is that in order to improve productivity it is wrong to simply talk about cost reductions. Often the one and only mechanism that is triggered when it comes to R&D or IT productivity is to reduce cost, which is done mostly by cutting out what does not matter at present or by outsourcing. Both has detrimental effects on overall enterprise performance and long-term stability. Reducing investments to new products will create short-term yields but will equally reduce market attractiveness. Productivity improvement means to look to both numerator and denominator.

> In improving productivity start always on the output side and reflect whether you are truly delivering value to your customers – inside or outside the company.

Do you sufficiently manage product content and roadmaps? Are the business case and needs of your customers understood and considered in the product portfolio? Do you have too many variants for different markets and waste efforts on customization that is not paid for? Which of your products have highest market share and market growth? Analyze and manage your portfolio to ensure that scarce resources are spent on critical portfolio elements (i.e., cash cows for today cash flow and stars for new technologies). Reduce the number of versions and rather spend more term on strategic management together with your product managers, marketers and sales. Are you doing the right thing? Note that cost reduction along doing the wrong things will reduce expenses but will not improve performance!

Then look to the input side. It is about efficiency, but certainly not only about cost of labor, although this matters most in software engineering. Evaluate for what you are spending which effort. Embark on a rigorous activity-based accounting to determine which processes consume effort and how much they contribute to value creation. Look to your rework along the entire product life-cycle. Rework is not only created with changing requirements, insufficient variant management or defect corrections. Rework also comes from insufficient processes and lack of automation. Investigate which of your processes need more guidance or management control. Focus on cost of non-quality, because it typically is a huge share in software development and maintenance. If test consumes 40% of resources, this is the process to look into, because test is no value creation. Are there techniques that could improve quality during design and development and thus reduce test overheads? How much of your test is redundant? How do you determine what to test and how much to test. Rarely companies have rules to find out what is good enough and build this notion around a business case.

Starting from the eighties, several studies were performed to understand what impacts on productivity in a software or IT project. The general finding by researchers like C. Jones or F. Brooks shows that there are productivity factors that can be controlled (process-related: accidental) and factors that cannot be controlled (product-related: essential) [Broo87, Jone86]. Jones found that product-related and process-related factors account for approximately the same amount - roughly one third - of productivity variance.

 Often hardware productivity improvement is used as benchmark to raise demands on the software side. Admittedly hardware productivity had been exploding over several decades – but this was above any other industry experience ever. The anomaly is not that software progress is so slow, but that computer hardware progress is so fast. No other technology since civilization began has seen seven orders of magnitude price-performance gain in just fifty years. In hardly any technology can one choose to blend the gains from improved performance and reduced costs. We cannot expect to see two-fold productivity gains every two years in other engineering fields. Or summarized in the words of F. Brooks: "There is no single development, in either technology or management technique which by itself promises even one order-of-magnitude improvement within a decade in productivity, in reliability, in simplicity." [Broo87].

By applying this basic insight we identified two basic approaches towards improving productivity in software projects, namely:
- Reduce accidental barriers (e.g., improve engineering and management discipline, processes and tools; apply standards – from cradle to grave (languages, templates, IDE's, and so on; design to quality, change, cost, and so on; intro-

duce lean and agile concepts such as smaller teams, components, iterations, and so on)
- Control essential barriers (e.g., understand what are the real needs and implement those in the product; do not implement each single change request; evaluate carefully the customer's business case behind a feature and do not implement for where there is no clear business case; improve domain understanding; use suitable modeling languages to achieve a "unified" understanding; develop self-generating and self-updating software; reuse components)

Fig. 11.22 shows the impacts of these two major levers to improving productivity in software product development. Productivity is improved by reducing accidents and controlling essence. This simple yet effective law was derived and detailed from the author's investigation of hundreds of software projects and many empirical studies in process improvement (see also Chaps. 9, 14) where most ROI related results were created either by reducing accidents (e.g., defects found too late and thus creating extra rework) or doing the wrong things (e.g., too many variants of a product and overheads in managing all those over time, or too many requirements that won't create tangible customer value). It is also called Ebert's law of productivity improvement:

Productivity is improved by reducing accidents and controlling essence.

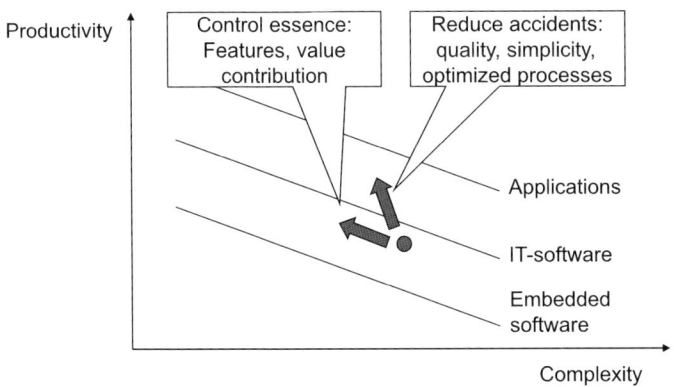

Fig. 11.22. Productivity improvements means to reduce accidents and to control essence

Productivity can be controlled and improved. Here are some concrete guidelines to use in your own environment:
- Reduce essential and accidental complexity. Manage risks and reduce surprises. Deliver added value with increments. Stop firefighting and replace it with accountability. Ask for the value of a requirements change before rushing to implement it.

- Understand value creation. Talk with product management and marketing to understand your markets and customers. Build cross-functional teams during the upstream activities in order to evaluate requirements and features on the basis of customer value. Prioritize requirements to allow time-boxing and budget commitments.
- Follow where the money goes. The biggest impact on productivity improvement has a profound process analysis. Look on cost distribution. Reduce your cost of non-quality.
- Carefully determine what is worth being done. Many platform components can be bought outside. Reuse along product families will help to reduce variant proliferation.
- Reengineer your architecture and technologies if they are impacting efficiency. Often legacy architectures have grown to a point where they are very difficult to further maintain. While the new design might be expensive and risky, keeping the legacy might kick you out of a market because others without that burden will deliver faster and cheaper.
- Buy into the feasible schedule compression if necessary for your markets. Schedule can be reduced – to a point – by adding people and putting more pressure.
- Improve performance with better technology and processes. Any project can excel if engineered and managed intelligently. Using the CMMI with good insight has direct productivity impact as it was proven in several studies. Automate your processes with engineering and management tools.
- Focus on what customers pay for and value-creation. Avoid gold plating. Work tends to expand to fill the available volume. Plan and track earned value. Do not put too much extra buffers on the critical path. (i.e., Parkinson's Law).
- Optimize staffing. Small collocated teams cross-fertilize and boost the productivity of each individual person (i.e., agile development)
- Set concrete objectives to continuously improve engineering productivity by 5-10% per year. This is done by means of techniques such as described by the CMMI by focusing on people and their environments and infrastructures, including the right tools. These improvements must be disciplined and systematic to show value. More improvement in one year needs specific actions, such as reengineering the product, introduction of new organization models or changing the development paradigms.

Let us look at a simple example which we evaluated at Alcatel (see Fig. 11.23). We analyzed requirements instability (i.e., changes of requirements after project start). Typically requirements change and those changes impact delivery dates and productivity as we saw already in Chap. 8. There is a range with stable productivity up to 20% change rate (normalized to project effort and measured after start of the project). With more than 20% changing requirements, productivity starts declining. Admittedly the number of projects on the right side is not big, but that is due to realizing rather early in the field study that this is the "forbidden zone", so no product manager wanted to end up there. The more requirements change – independent what caused those changes – the lower the achieved productivity level.

The changes are caused by either essence (i.e., needs of the client) or by accidents during development (e.g., requirements were not sufficiently analyzed before project start, they were not well specified, roadmap for introducing and delivering requirements was not formally agreed). Often it is a combination of both, essence and accidents.

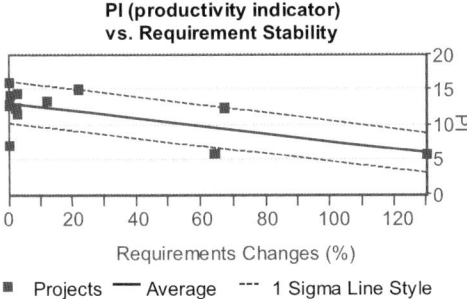

Fig. 11.23. Example: Impact of requirements changes on the productivity of software development

When embarking on productivity measurement you will find many such relationships in your own environment. Just ensure that you compare yourself against your own performance measurements rather than against poorly defined and collected external data, which you cannot trust.

We applied above principle and reduced these accidents while controlling the essential needs from outside. We found that changes could be managed within the allowed tolerance by working with customers on roadmaps, by better integrating sales, outbound marketing and product management, by empowering product management and by prioritizing requirements [Eber06a]. In fact, customers and markets expect that essential complexity is controlled. At times we thought that flexibility would be honored by customers until we realized that it creates an environment where stakeholders would think that changes are always feasible and thus won't prepare at the beginning. A lot of unfinished and not thoroughly analyzed requirements drop into development to be changed later on, or to be removed. Customers need a certain flexibility but much less than what many of us think. What they really need is a profound understanding of their own business, and how they can improve it by using our delivered product. The same holds for domains such as automotive that struggled with delivering far too many functions with insufficient quality, rather than delivering only half and look to nonfunctional requirements, such as reliability or performance. With these mechanisms to reduce accidents and to control essence we could improve performance of the product lines where this was applied.

Step 4: Implement improvements
Implementing productivity improvement is difficult. Compared to other changes it takes longer, is much more comprehensive in scope and needs more guts to con-

vince various stakeholders along the improvement journey – throughout the hierarchy. And, unlike focused changes, such as introducing a measurement program or improving project management techniques, it is a journey that will never end. In fact, the IT and software sector long did not need specific productivity improvement because more productivity came from better hardware and technology innovations. Focus on productivity for decades was entirely on the output side. With increasing global competition and decreasing entry barriers for newcomers to the software world, the focus had to switch to the input side. Suddenly process improvement programs with CMMI and Six Sigma, reduction of defect rates or reuse of components are managerial instruments to effectively control engineering cost.

A major lesson in the new century is that software has finally lost its nimbus of high-performance high-margins and has to look how low-margin sectors are improving. In these more mature sectors, companies must continuously improve productivity and innovate their product portfolios. They relentlessly identify and close gaps with industry best practices in process efficiency. Rather than relying on a single silver bullet (as was often sold and never achieved with technologies such as object orientation, code generation, and so on), productivity leaders in this century work on many topics in parallel, such as portfolio innovation, process improvement, tools support, better modeling techniques, offshoring, quantitative management, to name a few.

Fig. 11.21 has showed a variety of approaches to improve productivity. We looked to both the output and the input. Note that different techniques have different lead-time until they deliver results.

- Short-term impact: Improved sourcing strategy, killing products with too low contribution, improving basic project management, early defect removal, requirements management.
- Medium-term impact: Outsourcing, offshoring, portfolio management, moving to CMMI maturity level 3, introducing adequate engineering and management tools.
- Long-term: Modeling and code generation, moving to CMMI maturity level 5, embarking on Six Sigma, architecture and design reengineering.

Due to these different durations until a tangible ROI is reached you need to embark on several improvements in parallel – and in a well-orchestrated approach. Orchestration is necessary because changes influence each other, and you do not want to engage into so-called improvement programs which won't deliver because whatever one achieved is eaten by the other. As an example take the company which is in severe trouble because its sales erode. Obviously they need to control cost in order to stabilize cash flow. They start with process improvement to reduce cost of non-quality. In parallel they launch a second initiative to cut cost from any engineering activity. Then they start with outsourcing to an Indian supplier. And on top they would revisit the portfolio and kill several products. This all makes sense. However, if run independently the projects might "cannibalize" each other. For instance the cost reduction program will look to the process improvement program as an unnecessary formalism which creates extra effort. Outsourcing might

11.4 Productivity, Efficiency and Effectiveness

look to sourcing processes and not consider the needs from an overall process architecture as it would get from cooperating with the CMMI program. The portfolio management might derive wrong decisions because the measurements and business cases or forecasts are not valid due to insufficient processes or lack of discipline. Better productivity with lasting results is feasible but needs strong change management and clear directions.

Fig. 11.24 shows how a productivity improvement project was launched and implemented in a company with which we worked. Our starting point is the business objective to reduce cost of engineering by 20%. We will not discuss the story behind as it might reveal the situation of the client. Needless to say that senior management immediately suggested to outsource parts of development to India. Our proposal was to first look into what drives productivity before embarking on a mechanism which in fact might not create the benefits that are hoped for. Outsourcing is such example. It is often demanded by senior management because it looks attractive. However what is missed in this proposal is the long learning curve of two years until tangible results are achieved, and the relatively low – compared to expectations – savings potential of 15-20% if executed well (see Chap. 14 for such benchmark numbers).

Fig. 11.24. Case study: Implementing productivity improvement

In company X we found two major cost drivers, namely an overly high amount of small customization projects which did not create much value. Some had been simply started because sales claimed that they would otherwise loose that market. What was missing however was a sound business case and valuation that could proof this statement. A second observation was a high cost of non-quality created by finding defects too late. We proposed and evaluated a set of potential improvements, where we agreed three concrete actions after careful analysis of cost, impacts, duration and feasibility in the specific contact of our client. The first was to install portfolio management with a clear decision making and execution process. This meant that all projects and products were screened based on their contribution and strategic adherence. Within six months we could remove projects with an effort contribution of over 20% compared to overall engineering cost. But this is a one-time effect.

We therefore also embarked on early defect removal and a dedicated "first time right" initiative in engineering. Unexpectedly this latter initiative got very good buy-in from engineering because they realized that many changes and thus rework was introduced from outside. Controlling it and having clear criteria which changes to implement based on portfolio management decision-making was a strong support to focus on value-creation in engineering rather than defect corrections. Some concrete actions will show how we achieved early defect removal and first time right. A key change was to establish a strong requirements management process with reviews of requirements and their changes by a defined expert group of product management, systems engineering, testers and the project manager. Requirements without the customer business case and clear internal business forecast were not accepted and had to pass a monthly steering board under the lead of the business unit vice president. Test-driven development (TDD) was installed to ensure that requirements were consistently broken down to the design specifications and finally code. We used TDD specifically to create and unit test cases that could be reused with each iteration where code was changed and redelivered. This caused strong reduction of defects found by integration and system test and therefore helped after some 10-12 months to gradually reduce these late testing activities. Another action was to use automatic code analysis tools that would be used by the engineer before delivering her code complete milestone in the current increment. While it took a while to tailor and adjust the screening rules to the most relevant defects, it helped to give ownership of defect removal to designers, rather than testers.

With this case study it is obvious that productivity improvement needs several actions that are carefully implemented. There is no silver bullet, despite all the promises by tools vendors and others. Broad experience in engineering and product life-cycle management helps in selecting the right actions with most value in a certain environment. Excellent change management is key to introduce such changes.

Productivity directly influences the feasibility and the layout of a project. For instance, productivity impacts quantitative planning inputs:
- Productivity expectation affects estimates of new projects
- Actual performance validates estimates (or not)
- Own experiences help refine productivity expectations

Productivity also impacts the project feasibility and project set-up
- Project size and productivity. We might ask ourselves what is the optimal size and volume of a project or product release.
- Project complexity and productivity. We might ask at the time of setting up the project which environmental factors (maturity, time pressure, and so on) affect performance.

11.4 Productivity, Efficiency and Effectiveness

- Percentage outsourced and productivity. Here the question could be at which level of outsourcing do we see optimal project performance.

A small example will underline the impact of productivity on the project set-up. Assume for a software project the following parameters (estimated as it was introduced in Chaps. 7 and 8). New and changed volume of code is 4500 LOC, the effort estimated on previous experiences is 16 person months, the estimated duration is 6.1 months calendar time, there are roughly 70 defects to remove after code complete, and the average full-time equivalent staffing is 2.6 per month which translates into a cost of roughly 200 K€. Now we assume that our senior management or sales department cannot accept the duration and needs it three weeks earlier. This translates into a duration of 5.3 months calendar time. With unchanged internal productivity, the effort will increase towards 19.9 person months which translates into 250 K€. A reduction of schedule of three weeks costs 50 K€ more. This could be charged to the customer who would see the same value as with the original estimate but as a higher cost. His perception of productivity would be that it was reduced because he does not understand the impact of duration. However, part of the work could be outsourced at a much lower cost, therefore keeping the total cost flat at 200 K€. This would mean that we deliver the value at a fixed cost even with reduced schedule. If we happened to explain the schedule reduction as a cost driver to the customer, he would see a productivity improvement in this outsourced approach. To conclude, depending on what parameters matter for the customer this project can be set up in different ways with different externally visible productivity impacts. It would be of no sense to start explaining here the function points of lines of code per person month since they will drop in both cases – although for the customer productivity is flat or even increasing.

This example again shows that productivity improvement must always consider output, inputs and environmental factors.

Productivity will be improved based on such principles. Fig. 11.25 shows the evolution of function points per person year for IT systems on the basis of raw data collected by D. Longstreet [Long06].

What we say here is not theory, but practically used. And if you don't improve actively and continuously, your competitors will certainly do. The productivity measured in delivered function points per person year of software development has increased over three times since 1970. As one would expect this increase it exponential. The reasons behind are that more application software is developed, modern design and programming languages allow to deliver more function points per time than ever before, programming libraries are used and more effective tools for software development and testing are deployed. However, this improvement is not much, given other productivity improvements. The major reason is the fast growing complexity which – again – is not considered in this measurement. The average size of programs has grown by a factor of thousand and more since 1970 which naturally eats some of the achieved productivity improvement.

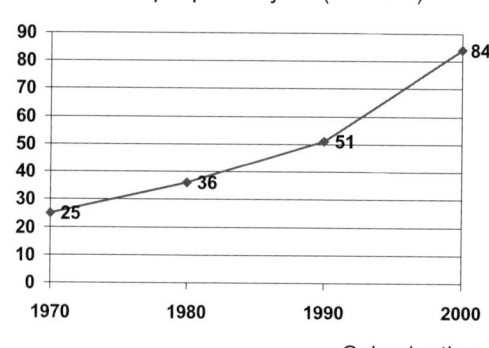

Fig. 11.25. Productivity evolution with function points

A last word on improving efficiency, effectiveness and productivity. It is feasible and it needs continuous improvement. An old Japanese saying is the analogy with the towel: "*Efficiency improvement is like wringing out a wet towel. The biggest reaction is obtained first, but we must keep wringing. Even when the towel appears dry to the touch we must wring it to extract more.*" It's attributed to Toyota and reflects that any improvement is a long road. Once you stand still, others will take the lead. Toyota has succeeded to keep the lead or take it from others over decades by continuously questioning how things can be done better and then improving .

11.5. Quantitative Process Management

11.5.1 Process Excellence

What is it that makes organizations better than others? Why do we prefer some companies and their services and products to others? Mostly it is about performance and the capability of these outstanding organizations to continuously innovate and improve. While the vast majority of companies is glad if the product gets out of the door in time and with the right quality, these excelling organizations would think with each product, customer contact or service, how they could do better. They are not at a standstill. They try hard to do better. We will look here into techniques which distinguish these outstanding companies from the mass.

The concept of maturity will be again used here. Old wisdom from around the world has it that only high maturity makes humans invulnerable to the evil of mediocrity. It is the same as with each one of us during our childhood. Our parents and good teachers helped us to advance to higher maturity and to strive for excellence. Continuous improvement is initially part of each person's genes as we would otherwise not learn and advance after birth, but for laziness and many other factors eventually many give it up. Improvement means to continuously reflect how to do better and how to innovate what we are doing and how we are doing it.

Predictability is a good indicator for the process maturity of an organization. While on lower maturity levels the objective is to get the projects done in time and budget – but with substantial variances, it evolves towards maturity level three to the ability to predict cost, schedule, and defects based on past performance. Improvement information is available and some use this information to advance. On higher maturity levels, boundaries are defined for the expected performance. These boundaries are lined up with business needs and might be different depending on markets, customers or environmental constraints. Estimates actively deal with uncertainties and acknowledge this by intervals instead of point estimates. Commitments will still be aggressive, but the various stakeholders know how to cope with it.

Low maturity organizations often collect measurements just to show data. These measurements can be characterized as follows:
- Unclearly linked business objectives to the measurements being collected and the processes used in the organization
- Centrally defined with huge effort to collect and analyze centrally
- Not widely accepted because people argue that the measurements can be misinterpreted
- Introduced because the CMMI or management demands measurements
- Not used for the day-to-day operational management in teams
- Not used for decision-making on a corporate level because data quality is not trusted

In such organizations, we then face situations where neither practitioners nor their management really use the data. They would bring their reports and when asked questions had no idea how the data points relate to each other and what to do next. This is a waste of effort. Deciding to measure implies the effort to evaluate and execute from what is measured. The analysis techniques include gap analysis between estimates and actual performance, correlations within the quantitative data, trends analysis, classification, partitioning, identification of outliers, and analysis of rationale of such outliers, various process control techniques, including process stability analysis and various analysis techniques related to statistical models for product/service characteristics. This altogether ensures that processes can be managed and can be executed to meet external demands.

Quantitative process management integrates process tailoring, software measurement, thorough performance analysis and knowledge management with causal analysis and resolution and organizational innovation. Quantitative process management involves establishing goals for the performance of the process, measuring process performance, analyzing the resulting measurements, and making process adjustments to maintain process performance within acceptable limits. This means that the software organization collects process performance data from the software projects and uses these data to characterize the process capability of its processes. It is understood that not only processes are variable, but that understanding variation is the basis for management by fact and systematic improvement. It means quantitatively understanding the past, controlling the present and predicting the future.

High maturity organizations have a fully different usage and approach to measurement:
- Measurements are derived from business needs and business objectives
- The measurement process is part of the operational development and management processes
- Data quality is ensured from the collection onwards because engineers doing the work also recognize the need for measurement.
- The culture is one of trust and accountability. Visibility is not a threat but a necessity to achieve teamwork.
- Measurements are used for informed decision-making on all levels of the organization.
- Managers sit down with staff to discuss progress, risks and issues on the basis of facts and measurements.

W. Edwards Deming summarized 14 principles that create a culture of continuous improvement [Demi86]. They are necessary to achieve quantitative process management because they build team-sprit and engage each single person in an organization towards continuous improvement.

1. Create a constancy of purpose toward improvement of product or service with the aim to become competitive, to stay in business, and to provide jobs.

2. Adopt the new philosophy. Management must awaken to the challenge, must learn their responsibilities, and take on leadership for change.

3. Cease dependence on inspection to improve quality. Eliminate the need for inspection on a mass basis by building quality into the product (service) in the first place.

4. End the practice of awarding business on the basis of low bids. Instead, minimize total costs. Move toward long-term relationship of loyalty and trust with your suppliers.

5. Improve the system continuously to improve quality and thus constantly reduce costs.

6. Institute training on the job. Workers and managers must know the difference between common cause and special cause variation

7. Institute leadership. The aim of leadership should be to help people to do a better job.

8. Drive out fear so that everyone may work effectively for the company.

9. Break down barriers between departments. People in research, design, sales, and production must work as a team to foresee problems of production and use that may be encountered with the product or service.

10. Eliminate slogans for the workforce. They can create adversarial relationships.

11. Eliminate management by only numbers or numerical goals. Substitute with leadership.

12. Remove barriers to the pride of workers.

| 13. Institute a vigorous program of education and self-improvement. |
| 14. Make transformation and change everybody's job. |

Note that these principles relate to each other. Selecting few will have adverse effects (e.g., stopping management by objective without leadership and empowered self-improvement will result in chaos). Translated to the CMMI with its five maturity levels, it shows the underlying control elements and their impact:

1. On maturity level 1 the processes are ad-hoc and the sole instrument for control is motivation. Often it is demotivation which explains why in countries with some share of high-maturity companies it is difficult for maturity level 1 organizations to keep good engineers.
2. Maturity level 2 organizations start using measurements and objectives. Their major control instruments are project objectives, such as milestones, budgets, quality or functionality.
3. A maturity level 3 organization with defined processes controls with a set of measurements and organization-wide benchmarks. They use thresholds which are set up centrally to control performance. Change happens but it is slow and not economically viable. Companies on maturity level 3 (and below of course) tend to be overly expensive compared to their high-maturity counterparts.
4. For high-maturity organizations on maturity levels 4 and 5 performance is continuously improving by means of empowered engineers that are in control.

11.5.2 Techniques for Quantitative Process Management

Quantitative process management builds upon statistical techniques to identify process anomalies, to eliminate them and to ensure the processes will deliver what is asked by business needs.

First we must understand some simple statistical terms before we can apply statistical techniques to process improvement. Fig. 11.26 characterizes a distribution of observations from a process behavior. For simplicity we have taken a normal distribution which is characterized by a mean value μ which describes the expected value of an observation and the standard deviation σ which describes the probability that the observation is within a certain range. The curve itself is a probability density. Integrating it up to a certain value would provide the probability that an observation would fall into that range. For instance, the probability that an observation is within one standard deviation (symmetric to the mean value) is 69%. We can see that for a normal distribution 99% of all observations are within the range of 3 standard deviations. This means that for practical reasons, we can treat the range of 3 standard deviations left and right of the mean as the set of expected values. This range of 3 standard deviations will get important when we talk furtheron about expected process variance for setting process control limits. With such normal distribution we can use the set of simple statistical techniques which we learned in school, for instance regression analysis and Pearson correlations when testing hypotheses (see Chap. 3).

396   11 Improving Processes and Products

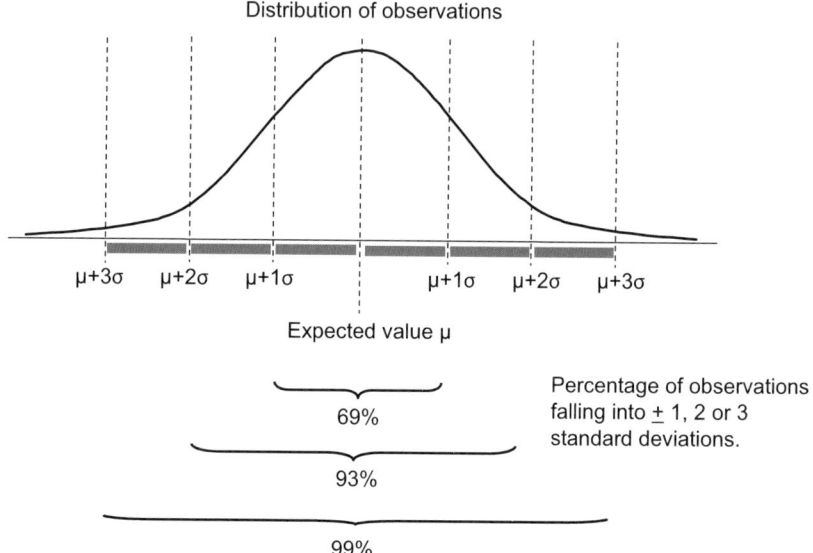

Fig. 11.26. Normal distribution with central tendency (mean), dispersion (standard deviation) and probabilities of observations

Note with this simple example that most observations we have in software engineering are not normally distributed! Often the distributions are asymmetric. They can be single sided (e.g., if we have a natural limit such as zero for the mount of defects found in any piece of code or document), they can have long "tails" on one side (e.g., defect distribution across all modules of a software system), or they can have more than one peak. For those cases we cannot use the common statistical techniques but have to look to non-parametric techniques, such as rank correlation. These non-parametric statistical techniques are described in [Wads90, Gibb76, Whee92, Flor99, Sing99].

Fig. 11.27 gives a short overview of what quantitative process management really means. The dots represent process behaviors over time, for instance, defect detection rates in different test cycles. The business needs determine specification limits, such as a maximum of defects released to the field. Often these specification limits are asymmetric. In our example of field defects, a lower specification limit could be impacted by time to market, thus indicating that the product must have the right quality. The internal process behaviors determine control limits. Control limits are determined by the way the process is defined, trained, automated, and executed. They represent the "natural" behavior of the process if executed as specified. For instance if we have a life-cycle with six different quality gates and respective verification and validation steps, we might end up with a remaining defect level of around 5% (assuming a defect removing effectiveness of 60%). Depending on the volatility of the process, these control limits are inside the specification limits and allow adjustments, if for instance a higher quality level is asked. The 5% of residual defects might be good enough if evaluated with a reliability prediction model based on operational usage schemes and having a support and service organization in place that can provide the necessary assistance to customers as it might be demanded by service level agreements.

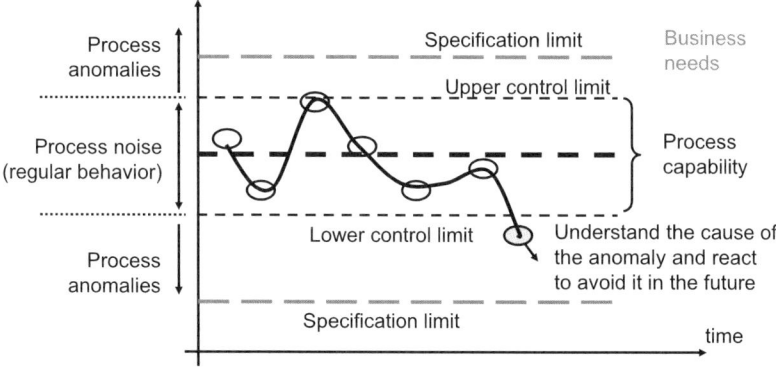

Internal view: A process is stable when "anomalies" have been eliminated.

External view: A process is capable when it lays within the business needs.

Fig. 11.27. Quantitative process management

We call this natural behavior of the process the "voice of the process" (VOP). If this natural, build-in process behavior is consistently reached and outliers would be immediately cured to prevent any trend escaping the control limits, we call the process stable. It is good enough to fit to what we have designed it for. If the voice of the process is within the specification needs as determined from business needs or the "voice of the customer" (VOC), the process is called capable.

For immature organizations, the control limits are mostly outside the specification limits. Those organizations are clueless on how to adapt processes towards reaching specification limits. In fact, these organizations do not even think in terms of control limits, they just hope each time a project is started that it reaches the requested target date or quality level. But volatility of processes yields continuous surprises. The process is not capable. This explains why the CMMI has in its name the word capability.

In quantitative process management we distinguish between the voice of the process (VOP) and the voice of the customer (VOC). Improvement objectives are the voice of the customer. Business needs and the customer base determine how good processes need to be. Capability baselines are used to identify the normal process behaviors (VOC) and to compare to the process needs (VOC). A small example will clarify this relationship. We will again take the quality level at release of a product to the customer in terms of residual defects and related field failures. Your customer might have contracted with you a failure rate of 1 per month in a given load and operational scenario. Your reliability prediction model relates this to 2 defects released per 1000 Stmt of new or changed code. At present you are at 3 defects released per 1000 Stmt. The VOC demands a 50% improvement of residual defects at release time. Unfortunately this cannot be directly translated into concrete subprocesses and improvement activities, so you need to do some analytic work. You may derive from this that if your code reviews have to remove 40% more defects, your unit test has to detect 70% more defects and your system test has to improve by 30%. This set of dependencies is derived from your profound understanding of the process behaviors and are retrieved from process performance models with the respective defect detection measurements. The behavior of your current process is what we call the VOP. The improvement objectives of 40%, 70% and 30% are more specific VOC derived from the high-level VOC. They are sufficiently detailed to start improvement actions. They do however not answer how to improve the respective processes. This is your own insight and experience. Often you need external help for this step and to identify appropriate improvement actions.

Several techniques are used to quantitatively manage processes:

- **Scatter plots**. These are the most simple charts just showing observations around two dimensions. They are used to monitor and control process performance and to detect trends or outliers. They are useful in showing unknown relationships or simply showing relationships across a variety of dependent factors. Usually different combinations of values are shown such as effort over functional size, delivered defects over functional size or delivered defects over early defect removal effectiveness.
- **Regression analysis**. A scatter plot usually draws the attention to certain relationships within the data. Statistical techniques are used to analyze relationships and look for instance to correlations and their confidence levels. Simple regression analysis tries to find out approximate relationships and then give the confidence interval that such approximation is good enough for forecasting behaviors. They can be linear or shaped according to mathematical functions (e.g., polynomic, exponential, logarithmic). It is however not given that such relationships are causal. They might be accidental or caused by a common third factor. Therefore, statistical analyses should not stop at regression analysis. This is just the starting.
- **Fishbone analysis**. The fishbone or Ishikawa diagrams are used to investigate causal relationships on a certain measurement. For instance when looking to failures of the product, one might want to see the underlying defects and how they were introduced and why they were not found before. Those different causes would then be evaluated on their impact so that those few with big relative impact could be removed or improved in order to improve the process.
- **Histogram**. Those are used to show distributions and therefore recognize behaviors of the process. To get a first insight into a population they are very useful. Examples include the size distributions across a set of projects or the defect types for all defects found after release.
- **Pareto chart**. Having looked to histograms one often finds relationships of the type that a subset of the data causes a majority of behaviors. For example, a majority of defects is often caused by a small amount of the software. Knowing

such patterns is an extremely powerful managerial instrument as it helps to focus attention and resources where they really matter.
- **Run charts**. Run charts portray a value over time. They help to find anomalies in data that suggest shifts in a process over time. Influencing factors can be determined from run charts looking to unusually long "runs" of data points above or below the average line, the total number of such runs in the data set, and unusually long series of consecutive increases or decreases. They then can be related to external disturbances.
- **Control charts**. Control charts are most popular in process control. They portray a process characteristic over time. Compared to run charts they include some control parameters, such as deviations or boundaries within which the process should stay. They are useful to evaluate the statistical behaviors of processes and to react if trends become visible. Techniques have been brought forward over time to define useful boundaries (control limits) or to diagnose process deviations.

We will look here at control charts as they help in reducing variance and disturbances of processes. **Control Charts** are used to monitor variation in a measured value from a process. They indicate when changes in data are due to:
- Special or assignable causes of process variation (e.g., external disturbances, undesired behaviors, fluctuations not inherent to a process, problems to be corrected, data points outside control limits, trends in a wrong direction)
- Common causes of process variation (e.g., inherent random variations due to the layout of the process)

Total process variation is the sum of special causes of variation and common causes of variation. Such variation is natural and inherent in the world around us. No two products or service experiences are the same and it is always possible with a fine enough scale to see differences. Good engineering with quantitatively managed processes ensures that the total variation is within the specified limits and deviations are investigated.

> Deviations are not by definition bad! They can point to errors (e.g., a schedule variance which is getting worse or delivered defects that increase in number or impact). But it can also be a sign of – unexpected – process improvement (e.g., a sudden outlier where schedule was much better then before or a reduced number of defects from configuration issues). That is why you should always have an eye on observed deviations.

Fig. 11.28 shows a sample control chart. Instead of specific data points the distribution is indicated. They show the process behavior (i.e., observed data points) over time or following some sequence along which the data points were collected. Given a homogenous set of data from an observed process performance the following rules of thumb hold – even if the data is not normal distributed
- 60%-75% (68.27% for the normal distribution) of the data will be located within 1 σ (standard deviation) of the process mean value

- 90%-98% (95.45% for the normal distribution) of the data will be located within 2 σ of the mean
- 99%-100% (99.73% for the normal distribution) of the data will be located within 3 σ of the mean

Since practically all data lies within the bandwidth of three standard deviations, three Sigma is considered a normal control limit for processes. Control limits are typically placed at the limits of 3 standard deviations. Note that this simplification which we find in many control charts, assumes that distribution follows a symmetrical normal distribution. For asymmetric distributions, control limits must be adjusted accordingly. The same holds if there are natural process limits. For instance, schedule should be close to what is estimated but not necessarily much shorter. Or defects delivered would never be below zero. More interesting and less obvious is the experience that defect detection effectiveness in a process is normally delimited by a threshold of 30-60%. See also Chap. 14 for more such rules of thumb.

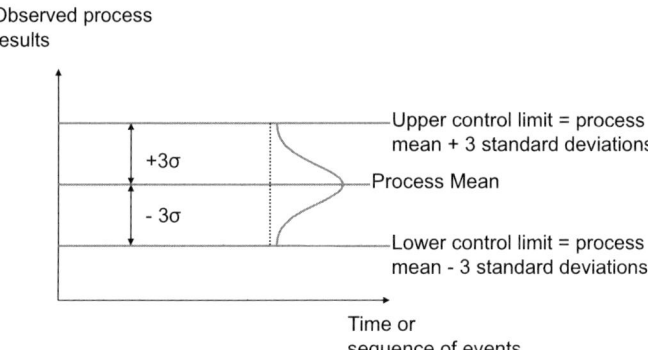

Fig. 11.28. Control charts

For symmetric normal distribution, the probability that observed data points will fall inside the control limits is 0.9973. There is 99.73% confidence that the process is statistically stable.

There are different types of control charts which are used for specific needs to analyze process performance.

p chart. This chart type is used for attribute data segmented into proportions. An example is to count defective software modules or late projects and normalize with the totality of modules or projects. Finding such a defect module or having a late project could be considered a "success." Sample sizes over time can vary which allows using this chart type along different output productivities, as we often face it in software projects.

UCL = p + 3 x square root (p x (1-p) / n))
LCL = p - 3 x square root (p x (1-p) / n)), with a minimum of zero

Fig. 11.29 shows a P chart for regression tests in ten different projects. Each project had a sample size of 200 such tests and a certain amount of those being defective. The defective test case shares all lie between the UCL and LCL thus indicating a controlled process. There are no special causes of variation to be considered. In order to improve the test process or the development process in front of these regression tests must be improved in order to further reduce variation or average values.

Project	# Regression tests	# Defective
1	200	18
2	200	9
3	200	19
4	200	7
5	200	21
6	200	19
7	200	16
8	200	12
9	200	8
10	200	9

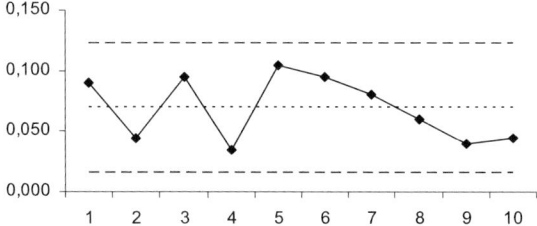

Fig. 11.29. p chart for regression tests

c chart. This chart is used for counting the number of non-conformities in an area of opportunity. It is also a type of attribute chart like the p chart and shows total number of nonconforming items per unit, such as number of defects per customer release or number of defects per requirement being reviewed. It assumes that the size of each sampling unit remains constant.

X chart and R chart. These charts are used for measured numerical data. They start with 20 subgroups of observed values, where each subgroup usually contains 3 to 6 observations. For the process to be in control, both the X chart of mean subgroup mean values and the R chart of mean subgroup ranges must be in control. The X chart is assembled as before showing the mean value of each subgroup and looking to the UCL and LCL. The R chart looks at the ranges of each of the subgroups, thus measuring the dispersion or volatility within each subgroup. The range is calculated as the difference between smallest and largest values in the subgroup. Typically, R is averaged across the time series under observation (also called mR value).

A process is considered to be in control when the control chart does not indicate any out-of-control condition. Such conditions can be the control limits, but also other conditions that are set up based on process observations and understanding.

> Typical criteria for an out of control process are:
> - One data point is outside the control limits and is attributable to a disturbance
> - Five or more points that are still within the control limits are moving in the same direction (trend criteria)
> - Eight or more sequential data points that are still within the control limits are on one side of the center line (mean or median).

The last of these criteria with eight or more sequential data points falling on the same side of the median actually means that R (the range of the process) is out of control.

> Never attempt to interpret the X chart when the R chart is out of control!

A process that is in control contains only common causes of variation. If the common causes of variation are comparatively small, the control chart can be used to monitor the process. If the common causes of variation are bigger than what is acceptable (e.g., the specification limit or the VOC), the process must be changed. Note that deviations beyond the control limit are not necessarily bad. For instance if cycle time of a product development process suddenly is much faster as before, this deviations demands root cause analysis in order to learn how to improve the existing process.

In a Six Sigma process, with "single sided specification", there is a 3.45 per million probability that data points fall outside the specification limit. Single sided specification means "less than a value", or "higher than a value." With double sided specifications, there is a 6.9 per million probability that data points fall outside specification limits. In fact, these probability values actually apply for 4.5 sigma and not Six Sigma. But in setting up Six Sigma it was agreed that one can expect a shift in the process mean to the extent of 1.5 times sigma over long term and therefore assigned the probability values of 4.5 Sigma Process to Six Sigma process. These probability figures are extremely small and software processes are far from this.

A statistically stable process is achieved by analyzing and removing special causes. After doing this systematically, the process should be sufficiently robust to meet its control limits. Typically special causes are removed with root cause analysis and dedicated improvement actions. Using above example would mean to improve the selection of code to be reviewed, provide sufficient time for code reviews and to better train reviewers so that they would find the 40% more defects than in the previous process. Control limits or rules for identifying outliers are heuristic in nature to identify special causes of variation. The basic 3-sigma rule for identifying special causes can be used to explain this reasoning. Just because a point falls outside 3-sigma limit does not mean it is a special cause of variation, as it is natural for a data point to lie outside the 3-sigma limits for a process with normal variation. However, the probability for these outliers is very small.

Common causes of process variance are removed not individually but by reducing their collective impact. A change in testing process from manual testing with big volatility of defect detection effectiveness to automated regression testing done incrementally for each new build with determined coverage and effectiveness could be one such process change.

Fig. 11.30 shows the entire process of process improvement with quantitative process management techniques. It is based on the E4–measurement process which we introduced in Chap. 2. The process has the steps of setting improvement or performance objectives, measuring the process, analyzing the process behaviors and improving the process by first stabilizing it, then keeping it in its specification limits and finally continuously improving it. This goal-driven approach is underlying the maturity level 5 behaviors in the CMMI.

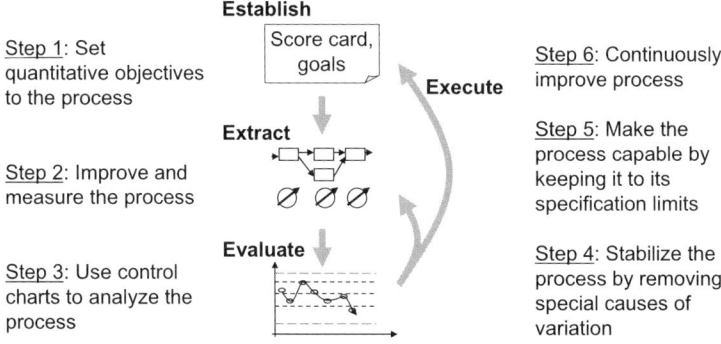

Fig. 11.30. Improving process performance with quantitative process management

11.5.3 Six Sigma in Software Engineering

Six Sigma is a measurement-driven approach to continuous improvement. It is a business philosophy to improve customer satisfaction, reduce cycle time and eliminate rework. Six Sigma emphasizes quality improvement with clear measurable goals. As such, it is part of the objective-driven process improvement paradigm which we introduced earlier in this chapter.

Technically speaking, "Six Sigma" is simply the number of occurrences in a normal distribution that are outside the tolerance band of six standard deviations. Historically Six Sigma had been used to improve the quality by removing defects as early and as thorough as possible [Harr03, McCa04, Pyzd03].

The real benefit came from not only removing defects but designing a system to be capable to deal with errors – knowing that some variance is inherent to any process. This approach of improving quality by knowing the underlying production process and improving the design process to continuously reduce unnecessary variance and to cope with necessary variance has become a guiding paradigm for continuous improvement since the nineties when companies such as Motorola, GE and others had introduced it. Today it is a method that must be mastered by any manager in a business that cares for quality and customer satisfaction.

A Six Sigma software development process is characterized by
- the application of statistical tools to process and product measurements
- quantitative management of process and product quality (e.g., delivery of a high quality product, improving cost and cycle time by reducing rework and time spent in integration and test, reducing process variations to allow better predictability and quality)
- closed loop quantitative process management (i.e., the "execute" step of the E4–measurement process).

It is based on quantitative business goals that are of direct value to the customer. The underlying improvement paradigm is following the objective-driven process improvement paradigm which we introduced earlier in this chapter. It is based on what we introduced at the beginning of this book as the E4–measurement process (see Chap. 2 and also Fig. 11.30).

Six Sigma can be broken down to the four essential steps of quantitative management, namely
- **Establish** concrete business and improvement objectives and the measurement and analysis scope and activities related to these business goals.
- **Extract** measurements for the established needs. Process and product measurements are used to identify specific processes with the greatest leverage to impact achieving the business goals. This can be in either direction, amplifying the business goals or reducing the capability of achieving them.
- **Evaluate** this information in view of a specific background of actual status and goals. The critical drivers for achieving process performance are identified. Improvement goals are related to changes in process outputs.
- **Execute** a decision to reduce the differences between actual status and goals. Improvements are implemented on a pilot basis. If measurements indicate goals have been achieved, improvements are institutionalized. Process performance is controlled to new performance levels by controlling critical input variables.

The specific methodology used in Six Sigma initiatives is called **DMAIC** (design, measure, analyze, improve, control) and translates into the following five steps:
1. **Define** process (i.e., establish a concrete process with expected behaviors)
2. **Measure** the process (i.e., extract goal-oriented measurements that describe the process in order to take appropriate actions)
3. **Analyze** the process (i.e., use the observed process performance to identify causal variables and how they relate to process performance)

4. **Improve** the process (i.e., modify the process, measure the modified process, verify the improvement, define control mechanisms)
5. **Control** the process to sustain improved performance levels (i.e., monitor performance measurements and take designated action when required, perform continuous verification of the stability and capability of the process)

How does the statistical principle of Six Sigma relate to software engineering? Fig. 11.31 shows the DMAIC method applied to a normal review process. The big difference to the review process as it is used by most companies is the embedded feedback loop to process improvement. This can mean to update the review checklist (e.g., removing checks that don't yield results or adding checks that could reveal additional defects not found in the previous approach) or changing the review process (e.g., reducing the review speed, introducing criticality analysis to identify error-prone components or sections) or adjusting process parameters (e.g., adding another reviewer with different expertise).

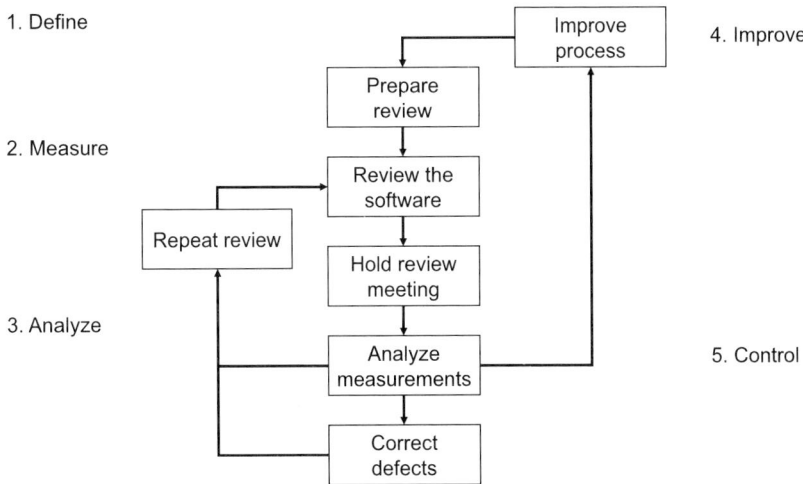

Fig. 11.31. Six Sigma and DMAIC applied to a review process

As a statistical measurement Six Sigma translates into 3.4 defects per million opportunities. Fig. 11.32 shows this statistical relationship assuming a single-sided specification, such as a zero defect target. It shows that with a 3 Sigma distribution the probability of letting a defect slip into the product is much higher than for the 6 Sigma distribution (lower part of Fig. 11.32).

A process that is normally distributed will have 3.4 defective parts per million opportunities beyond a point that is 4.5 standard deviations above or below the mean with a single-sided capability evaluation. This implies that 3.4 defects per million opportunities correspond to 4.5 Sigma, not Six Sigma, as the process name would imply. This can be easily verified by running on a statistical tool like Minitab [Mini06] a process capability analysis on data with a mean of 0, a standard deviation of 1, and an upper specification limit of 4.5. The 1.5 Sigma difference to 6

Sigma (which is the popular naming for this deviation of 3.4 defects per million opportunities) had been added due to the so-called "1.5 sigma shift" [Harr03]. Harry had introduced this 1.5 sigma shift as a measurement to deal with process-inherent variation that he observed as approximately 1.5 Sigma in any of the processes he investigated, and because no other empirical information was available at the time of setting up this Six Sigma approach. Over time, the "Six Sigma" labeling had been used throughout industry, while the underlying statistical distribution actually refers to 4.5 sigma [McCa04]. This should be considered in the following paragraph where we elaborate on the impacts of distributions on cost of quality and residual defects.

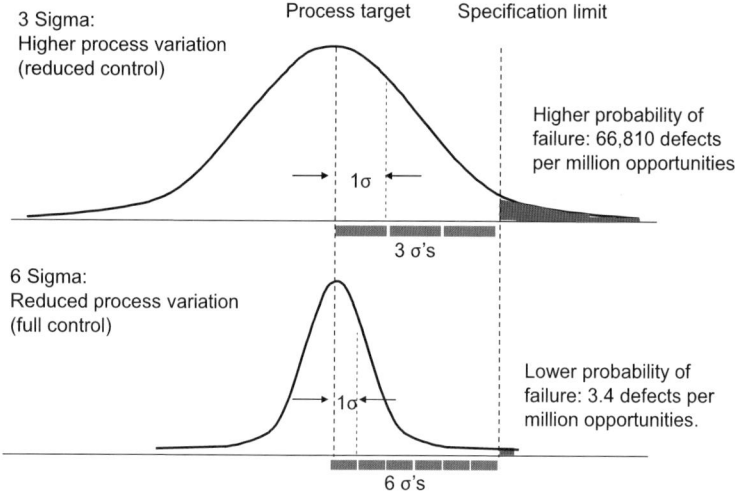

Note: the figures of defects per million opportunities consider the "1.5 sigma shift"

Fig. 11.32. Six Sigma and probabilities for letting a defect slip into the product.

A Three Sigma distribution yields 66,810 defects per million opportunities or 93.3% of opportunities translating into real defects. A Four Sigma distribution yields 6,210 defects being created and delivered with a 99% effectiveness. A Five Sigma distribution delivers 233 defects with a 99.98% effectiveness. Finally, a Six Sigma distribution delivers only 3 defects with a yield of 99.9997% opportunities having not created a defect.

Table 11.7 shows the relationship of Sigma levels, quality and economic impact. The calculation is based on observations from Motorola, Wipro, GE, Alcatel and others. Note that we speak here primarily about defects relating to poor quality. However, defects can as well be other deficiencies being controlled with the Six Sigma method.

Table 11.7. Sigma levels and their impact on defects and cost of quality. Note that they all include the 1.5 sigma shift.

Sigma level	Defects per million opportunities	Yield	Cost of quality
2	308,537	69.1%	20-40% of sales
3	66,807	93.3%	15-30% of sales
4	6,210	99,4%	10-20% of sales
5	233	99,98%	5-10% of sales
6	3.4	99.9997%	1-10% of sales

Six sigma as a performance measurement is not new to software engineering. For instance, telecommunication systems since decades have the target to deliver service for the whole year, 24 hours a day – except an allowed outage of 5 minutes per year. These 5 minutes exactly translate into a Six Sigma performance with 99.999% availability. The means even in the early days of ad-hoc processes were mostly in thorough testing and huge redundancies on all levels of the entire system.

Note that in many other examples we should be careful when speaking about the 3.4 residual defects because often the process target is not zero in a single-sided distribution as it is with defects, but rather some other value with a double-sided distribution. Six Sigma originally assumes a normal distribution as it is the case in most production processes with many repeated process cycles. This is not the case in software engineering where we might have other types of distributions. For simplicity, normal distribution is assumed in the single-sided case of defects delivered in the final product.

There are two important observations with these numbers that affect software and systems development:

- **Six Sigma is focused on opportunities to make a defect**. If the software project with the underlying design and code has one million opportunities to insert a defect, a Six Sigma process is capable to eliminate these opportunities but 3 which escape. An opportunity typically is any manually coded statement in the software as this is the smallest entity of creating a single defect.
- **Six Sigma ensures that defects are not delivered at the end of the process**. If defects are inherent to the selected production process (voice of the process), they cannot be eliminated in this part of the process. They can however be detected by sophisticated defect removal techniques (i.e., verification and validation). They can also be reduced in impact by intelligent design techniques, such as robustness or fail-safe systems.

Both have to be considered when using Six Sigma in software engineering. We are aware that defects are inherent to manual work, and they will not be removed by any formal technique – except that they might be introduced earlier in the lifecycle. Process variation can never be eliminated or even reduced below a distinct level because no two systems or components are the same so process performance always includes some essential complexity and variability and there are very large differences in skills and experience between engineers (and managers). However, software development processes can be fully characterized by simple measurements as we have seen in previous chapters, namely the time required to perform a task, the size or volume of the resulting work products and the number and type of defects, removal time, point of injection and point of removal. Six Sigma for software engineering therefore necessarily implies the suite of techniques to design and to verify and validate towards low defect rate.

Today the average application software company has a Three to Four Sigma performance. Out of 1,000 statements of source code (translating into 1,000 opportunities to make and deliver a defect) roughly 5 to 50 defects are delivered to the customer. Best in class companies are close to delivering 6 Sigma performance.

Six Sigma is not restricted to high-criticality software such as dependable systems in telecommunication or safety-critical systems in transportation and medicine. It is a business decision how to achieve and improve market share and customer satisfaction. Six Sigma will not prescribe dogmatically that defects must be avoided from the beginning. It underlines the need to have the best in class processes to achieve beyond the demands and needs in a market – even if they were not outspoken.

The tools used by Six Sigma are the same as we use in other objective-driven process improvement approaches, namely
- Quality Function Deployment (QFD) for prioritizing functional and non-functional requirements and user needs and relating those to business needs.
- Process and work flow optimization
- Process analysis with scatter plots, regression analysis, fishbone diagrams, histograms, Pareto charts, run charts and control charts
- Analysis of variance
- Failure Modes Effect Analysis (FMEA)
- Statistical Process Control

> Six Sigma is a continuous improvement approach which demands a dedicated organization and leadership from the top of the enterprise.

Unlike many other change initiatives there is no bottom-up approach possible. It is implemented by defined roles, namely:
- Champion. The key stakeholder or business executive who sponsors the process improvement initiative. He sets the improvement objectives and identifies the necessary Green Belts and Black Belts. He kicks off the change initiative and periodically reviews progress.
- Green Belt. A process change expert who is trained in the respective methodology and who executes the process improvement project on behalf of the champion.
- Team members. Functional experts who work collaboratively with a Green Belt
- Black Belt. A process change management and methodology expert and team facilitator who guides the Green Belt and the team in the change initiative, such as problem definition, methodology guidance (e.g., using the CMMI, FMEA, QFD, and so on), statistical tools and change management. Typically there is

one Black Belt for each four Green Belts. Responsibility, compensation and visibility increases.
- Master Black Belt. A specialist in several methodologies who is mentoring the Black Belts.

A strong case study is GE where Six Sigma had been introduced as a general management principle [Welc05]. In his second decade, Welch focused on four basic initiatives: Globalization, Services, Six-Sigma, and e-business. The Six Sigma program at GE was launched in 1996 in response to employee surveys that cited quality as a growing concern. The business objective was stated as delivering perfect products while reducing costs. The scope was seen from the beginning as encompassing GE, not just manufacturing. Six Sigma was translated into software engineering as well as financial services. It is embraced today at all levels at GE and is used for everything from improving call center performance to meeting customer specs for power plants.

Six Sigma delivers value if applied correctly. Globally the logic is that defects delivered cost additional money or reduce competitiveness. M. Harry pointed out that "each sigma shift provides a 10% net income improvement" [Harr03]. Since that figure originally resulted from production processes where insufficient quality means expensive rework and materials loss, our own rule of thumb is as follows:

> For software engineering a sigma shift translates in improved net income of 5-10%.

For instance, Motorola showed that the total cost of software quality has improved on the way from maturity level 1 to 5 from 60% of development cost to 20% of development cost [Eick04]. This translates into a 40% development cost reduction on Motorola's way to high maturity. Assuming that they started from a maturity level 1 behavior, this means a typical Two Sigma or Three Sigma behavior as can be expected from a normal process (i.e., 7-30% of opportunities cause defects). They are today one of the leading Six Sigma protagonists which means that on their journey to high maturity they improved by 2-3 sigma shifts. Cost of quality in this business typically contributes to 50% of total revenue. A 40% reduction therefore means at least 20% overall cost reduction which directly translates into a lower limit of improved net income (it could be higher if there is a lot of rework or loss of opportunity with insufficient software in the delivered products). This fully supports the rule of 10% net income improvement per sigma shift.

A similar observation was done in Alcatel with early defect removal [Eber99a]. The target during the nineties was improved field quality with less software defects. Verification activities were introduced and strengthened to a point where 50-60% of all original defects in design and code were removed before start of test. This introduction of early defect removal meant a shift of 1-2 Sigma. It was not as high as in the previous case because in this early period we only targeted verification activities and not yet reengineered products and defect avoidance. As a conservative assumption we took a factor of ten in cost of defect removal when found with verification (e.g., peer reviews, static code analysis) versus removing defects in validation activities and later. Test amounts 50-60% of total development cost and can be reduced in effort (e.g., number of test cases, regression testing, rework) by at least 10 percentage points for 10% less defects to be found. Removing ten additional percent of all defects directly in the design phase by means of verification activities reduces total development cost by 3 percentage points. We increased the number of defects found in verification from around 10-20% to 50-60%, a yield of 40 percentage points which translates into 10-20 percent less development cost. Using our previous formula of 50% contribution of development to total expenses, we find a net income improvement of 5-10%

Again we can see that a sigma shift translates into 5-10% of net income improvement for software and IT product development. Note that both calculations are conservative and leave out cost of non-quality after release of a product to the customer, such as warranties, lost opportunities, penalties or update releases that have to be developed, distributed and maintained.

11.5.4 Case Study: Quantitative Process Management

We have used the quantitative process management approach in several business units recently and observed that it is a natural and almost deterministic process which improves in defined phases. Fig. 11.33 shows this relationship for a business unit which had embarked on CMM and CMMI for several years in order to control and improve processes. The business unit operates in the telecommunication field and develops software for a variety of networking systems, including test and field support. It has around 300 engineers in two locations.

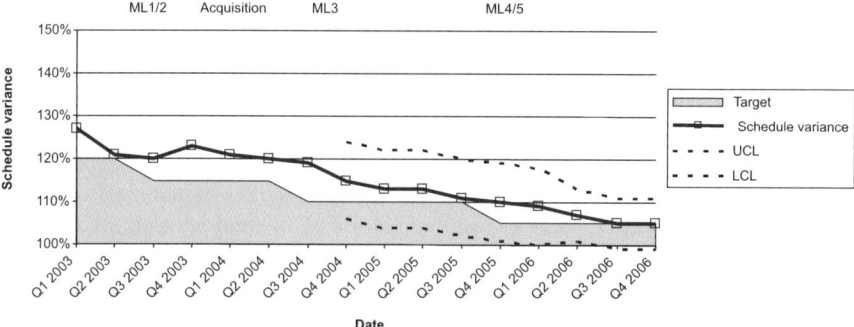

Fig. 11.33. Schedule variance in a product line embarking on the CMMI and using quantitative process management to control variance and achieve improvement objectives

The diagram shows time on the horizontal axis and mean schedule performance on the vertical axis. On the left side, we can see the initial status of ad-hoc processes which are at best repeatable. Schedule performance is in the range of 120-125% which means that the average deviation from committed schedule is 20-25%. That, of course, was not acceptable, specifically in the communications sector where this business operates. Customers build their own business models on specific milestones, where marketing and other activities are accurately timed. Delivering a solution late to such customer immediately means business impacts for the customer.

Understanding the voice of the customer was the very initial step and objectives had been put forward to reach reduced schedule variance. These objectives are shoed in the figure with the shaded area on the bottom. Obviously the objective was not to deliver too early. In fact, management together with their process consultants were smart enough to put a schedule target around 110% in order to prevent people from putting too much effort in uncertainty management and risk management. For instance, time buffers were not allowed as they tend to be eaten with gold plating. Rather time boxing-approaches and feature-driven development were introduced based on the maturity level 3 defined processes. Therefore the shaded area clearly flags a delivery earlier than planned as negative result with performance impact.

The CMM and later CMMI were used to orchestrate the improvement activities in this business unit. Just before maturity level 3 was reached, there were some reorganizations in that business unit that resulted from acquisitions and repositioning in certain markets. As a consequence, the schedule performance dropped immediately. The entire process improvement program was at stake because management had to be retrained, and a start-up culture (in its not-so-good meaning) took hold for a while. Fortunately, this could be cured rather fast by strong management push for discipline and process performance. A clear target was brought forward to reach first maturity level 3 and then after a given period maturity level 4 and 5. Short after reaching maturity level 3 in 2004, the quantitative process management got to speed. The figures show from this time-frame onwards the UCL and LCL which were calculated by using the standard deviations times three. Before that date the curves are not showed due to rather high standard deviations which made quantitative process management pointless. The final stage for this process improvement activity was reached with a solid performance within the 5% band.

What were the different approaches to move forward towards better schedule predictability and thus improved customer satisfaction and earlier cash flow? It was a set of improvement activities which depended on the maturity level. Let us summarize:

- **Maturity levels 1 and 2**. First of all some estimation techniques were brought forward. This included a recording of effort, a break-down into effort drivers, a template (spreadsheet) to calculate effort and to relate it to impact factors, such as requirements or work packages. Project managers were trained on that and a small group was formed to overlook all estimates and check their approaches. This helped to contain deviations within 20-25% but that was not sufficient due to the variety of approaches and too many reinvented methods in each single project.
- **Acquisition and process disturbance**. The first step was to acknowledge that the processes were insufficient to handle any disturbances. The engineering group together with consultants worked with senior management to reduce the risk of complete start-up approach in a market that expected professional be-

haviors and rock-solid products and services. This was from the outset the biggest challenge because agility was hot at the time, and the pressure to get innovative products out of door (which caused the acquisition and subsequent organizational changes) was high. The driver at that time was a strong need for disciplined project management, configuration management, quality control during the development process and the right set of tool support for the routine activities, These all were aspects which the start-up mode could not provide, but which were introduced at fast pace thereafter.

- **Maturity level 3**. Processes were defined and both engineers and managers received continuous training. To avoid high training load project managers were asked to plan training and coaching within their projects at the right moments. An organization-wide training plan and tracking was installed to allow each individual to foresee and plan the necessary training. It was made explicit that training and competence growth were the responsibilities of each engineer, rather than a mysterious "manager" or "training organization." Estimation techniques were refined and mostly done by experienced engineers together with the project manager. Planning happened iteratively and time boxing was introduced to meet deadlines even in uncertain situations. The biggest challenge here was to introduce concepts like requirements prioritization to product managers, marketers and salespeople.
- **Maturity levels 4 and 5**. Once the benefits of defined processes were understood, the challenge was to keep the momentum. Some people argued that defined processes would be enough, and indeed a move towards the 10% schedule variance objective was visible. However, it became obvious that the risk was high to have processes engraved in stone and loose competitiveness. Processes need to change and adapt to ever-changing business situations. And process change should be done by the community rather than a central team. That much of start-up culture was considered helpful. Quantitative process management was introduced and coached from the engineering process group to senior management (what is the benefit? What does it mean?) and to department leaders and their engineers. Initially some errors occurred such as introducing SPC for processes which do not need it. Only a clear relationship from the business need and improvement objective towards the biggest root causes of schedule variance helped to move forward. In this phase it became evident that process improvement will not achieve results if it stayed within engineering. Efforts were extended first to product management and later to product marketing and regional sales. Product managers had to manage their products and to decide on the uncertainty management of changing needs in various markets. Once this was done, estimation accuracy reached the 5%-threshold – without wasting effort for buffers and other activities that a maturity level 2 or 3 organization would introduce to improve schedule variance.

Having observed this evolution over the years we concluded that quantitative management is beneficial but needs clear management and lots of training. We also realized that in order to be effective a big portion of the organization must be part of the process improvement effort. In some of the organizations we worked with, more than half of engineering were actively involved in process change. It was not a chaotic behavior but self-organized by using defined processes and measurements.

11.5.5 Challenges in Applying SPC to Software

Expert Box. Author: David N. Card

Recent industry trends are promoting the use of statistical methods, especially Statistical Process Control (SPC), to software processes. These include the Capability Maturity Model Integration (CMMI) [SEI06a, Chri06], Six Sigma [Harr03], and ISO 9001:2000 [ISO00]. The concepts of SPC were developed in the 1930's for application to manufacturing processes [Shew31]. Initial efforts to apply SPC to software were made during the 1980's [Gard87, Card89]. This expert box discusses some of the common problems encountered in applying SPC to software. These observations are based on the author's 15 years of practical experience in working with these techniques in the software and systems engineering domains.

SPC is a problem-solving approach and a set of supporting techniques. It focuses on managing the variation inherent in all processes. Controlling variation results in processes that are stable and predictable. Many good textbooks (e.g., [Whee92]) explain the principles and techniques of SPC. Recently, textbooks have appeared that discuss the application of these techniques to software specifically (e.g., [Flor99]). The SPC toolkit includes run charts, control charts, histograms, Pareto charts and scatter diagrams. The SPC problem-solving approach involves four steps:
1. Develop a "control" plan
2. Perform a process as defined
3. Measure the results
4. Use the results to control and improve the process.

Stability is the result of control. Achieving control requires real-time feedback on process performance. This means that the performance of the process must be evaluated as it is being executed, not just at the end. For example, controlling software or systems design means recognizing whether or not that design subprocess (or key process elements within it) is performing as expected before all executions of the subprocess or process element(s) have been completed, so that appropriate action can be taken. Put in other words, process control requires in-phase monitoring of the performance of design activities, not just an end-of-phase review of design performance.

Software and systems engineering processes are composed of many subprocesses and process elements. It is impractical to attempt to control all those components. However, the stability of the overall end-to-end process can be promoted by focusing attention on key process elements.

When modeling a complex system, the analyst has a choice between two approaches:

- Developing a comprehensive multi-factor model that encompasses all the important performance parameters.
- Isolating individual factors for studying separately.

The first choice may be implemented via analysis of variance or regression. The second choice may be accomplished via rational sub-grouping and control charting (i.e., SPC). The SPC approach has the advantages of conceptual and mathematical simplicity. However, that does not mean that SPC is the best approach to all process analysis problems. Some critics have argued that the appropriate conditions for applying SPC never occur in software, especially due to the small quantities and human factors involved. Nevertheless, there are many examples of success (e.g., [Gard87, Card89]). Pyzdek explains the situation as follows: "Another example of a single-piece run is software development. The "part" is this case is the working copy of the software delivered to the customer. Only a single unit of product is involved.

How can we use SPC here? Again, the answer comes when we direct our attention to the underlying process. Any marketable software product will consist of thousands, perhaps millions of bytes of finished machine code. This code will be compiled from thousands of lines of source code. The source code will be arranged in modules; the modules will contain procedures; the procedures will contain functions; and so on. Computer science has developed a number of ways of measuring the quality of computer code. The resulting numbers, called computer measurements, can be analyzed using SPC tools just like any other numbers. The processes that produced the code can thus be measured, controlled, and improved. If the process is in statistical control, the process elements, such as programmer selection and training, coding style, planning, procedures, and so on, must be examined. If the process is not in statistical control, the special cause of the problem must be identified" ([Pyzd03] pg. 660).

Clearly, SPC can be applied effectively to some software processes, even if it is not appropriate for analyzing all software process problems. Given that, let us consider the kinds of things that often go wrong in implementing SPC for software. Enough experience has accumulated in applying SPC to software that some common problems and mistakes can be identified. This section discusses six typical areas of misunderstanding.

Process and project measurements
Many practitioners have difficulty distinguishing between project management indicators and process management indicators, since indicators for both purposes may be constructed with the same base measurements. Project management indicators attempt to monitor the accomplishment of work. Process measurement indicators attempt to assess the efficiency and effectiveness of the processes used to perform the work.

For example, the actual number of units completed each week may be compared to the plan to determine if work is proceeding according to the plan. This is a project management indicator. The plan for the number of units to be completed each month depends on assumptions about the productivity of the project team.

This is an assumption about process performance. Whether or not the work gets accomplished on schedule depends on the productivity of the process, and also on other factors such as overtime. Applying more overtime to a project may enable more work to be accomplished faster, but does not necessarily change the productivity of the process. SPC focuses on measurements of process performance (such as productivity) rather than on measurements of work accomplishment. Fig. 11.34 illustrates the difference between the project management and the process management views of performance.

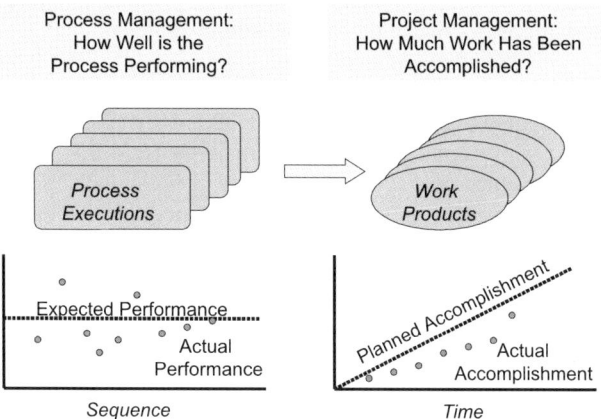

Fig. 11.34. Comparison of process management and project management viewpoints

Control charts at the organizational level
The term "organizational baseline" in the CMMI frequently is misunderstood to imply that data from multiple projects should be combined into one control chart to establish a common organizational process-performance baseline (OPPB). The real intent is to develop a process-performance summary, not to control process execution. Typically, this includes project process-performance baselines, as well as other summary statistics. The OPPB is intended to support planning, not control of processes. Naively combining data from disparate projects does not facilitate effective planning.

Do not try to apply control charts to multi-project data at the organizational level when they have unrelated data points. Some of the reasons why this is not appropriate are as follows:
- This data is not available in real time so it cannot really be used to "control" anything. Communicating data from the projects to the organization and then returning the analysis results typically involves a substantial delay.
- If there is an out-of-control signal, it is difficult to identify its source because each project's process may be tailored and instantiated uniquely.
- Projects are not comparable to the degree that successive executions of a process element within a project are comparable. Different types of projects may exhibit substantial differences in performance in terms of productivity and

quality, for example. A result that is unusual for one project may not be unusual for another project.
- Changes in the process of one project do not affect the results of other projects. Thus, signals may be hidden by project results that cancel each other out or created by accidentally re-enforcing trends among different projects.
- The order of execution of activities among projects often cannot be determined unambiguously (a basic assumption of control charting) because they often overlap in time. Moreover, there often is little communication among the processes of different projects, so changes in one subprocess do not affect the coincident observations (a criteria for rational sub-grouping).

The use of control charts to establish organizational process baselines for project processes is misleading and should be discouraged. However, there are two situations in which organizational control charts make sense. First, organization-wide processes (e.g., training, quality assurance, and process definition maintenance) may be candidates for SPC; these are individual processes that are applied across multiple projects. Second, an organization that consists of many small projects working in the same application domain, and using the same personnel, methods, and tools often may be treated as one large project.

Mixing different instantiations of a process
Process instantiations often are not distinguished from process descriptions. Only the performance of executing processes (instantiations) can be controlled and improved. "Improving" the clarity and consistency of the process definition may be a means of improving the performance of its instantiations. However, each different instantiation may lead to a different level of performance. Do not combine different instantiations of process elements into one control chart. When performing optimization studies, use an analysis technique that allows for multiple instantiations (or levels of factors), for example, analysis of variance. Fig. 11.35 illustrates the factors that contribute to a process instantiation (or to executing a process).

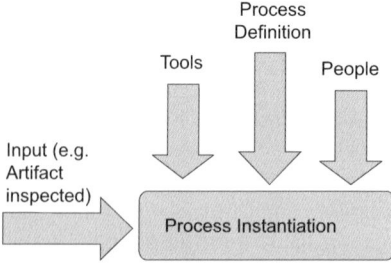

Fig. 11.35. Factors in a Process Instantiation

A common mistake involves combining data from multiple types of inspections onto one control chart, even if all the inspections pertain to the same project. (Combining data from multiple projects only compounds the problem, as discussed earlier.) All these inspections may follow the same process definition (e.g., documented procedure). However, their performance may be very different because of differences in the teams (e.g., systems engineers, software engineers), artifacts inspected (e.g., requirements, design diagrams, code) and practices of inspection (e.g., amount of preparation, degree of training). Analyze each instantiation of the inspection process separately, unless the data indicates otherwise.

Confusing correlation with causality
Process improvement studies often focus on establishing a relationship between an outcome (that the process manager seeks to optimize but may have limited ability to control directly) and a more easily manipulated factor. For example, additional peer review training might be provided to staff if increased training could be shown to result in increased rates of defect discovery (the desired outcome). These studies often employ correlation and regression. The existence of a significant correlation often is mistaken for proof of a cause-effect relationship.

Changes in process performance that occur over time may result from changes in the mix of work or other factors than improvement. For example, the business base of an organization might change from mostly new development to mostly enhancement of existing systems. Depending on how productivity is measured, a regression analysis could show a significant increase or decrease in productivity. This might be assumed to be due to the effect of improvement efforts over time. However, closer examination of the data would reveal that the change is due to differences in productivity levels between enhancement and development projects. In this case, mixing different types of projects together in the same regression analysis contributes to the false assumption of causality.

Reliance on a single technique
Mastering the "basic" statistical techniques introduced above requires a substantial amount of effort. Consequently, organizations (and individuals) may be tempted to learn one technique and then apply that single technique to all problems. This behavior often leads to spurious results (especially when the technique is not appropriate for the scale of the data) or loss of sensitivity (especially, when observations are combined or variances are overestimated).

The *XmR* chart often becomes the subject of misuse. It is the easiest control chart pair to compute and graph. By combining concurrent observations into a single observation, most data can be converted to a sequence of individual values. Failure to check the normality of the underlying data with a statistical test or visual examination of a histogram before control charting often contributes to overuse of the *XmR* charts. The consequences of this mistake include:
- Reduction in the number of observations, thus reducing confidence in the results
- Overestimation of the variance (especially when the underlying data follows a skewed distribution such as the Poisson), leading to wide control limits that do not detect special causes

- Further exacerbating the situation, abusers of the *XmR* charts often focus on the X chart, ignoring the variation in the process. Variance reduction, of course, is a key objective of process control.

This problem may be compounded by using the *X chart* to address issues that are not appropriate for control charting. For example, samples or observations may be plotted in other than chronological order (e.g., alphabetical order or large to small) on a graph that is treated like an *X chart*. The result is that patterns and trends that are entirely accidental are identified and acted upon.

Lack of expert advice
Many organizations adopting CMM and CMMI-based process improvement programs rely on their lead appraiser for most (if not all) training and coaching in preparation for an appraisal. No one can be an expert in everything. These appraisers may be experts in the CMM or CMMI, but neither of these documents is a text on SPC[Card00a]. Six Sigma programs typically do include substantial training in SPC.

> The Six Sigma and CMMI approaches to process improvement are complementary. After having successfully worked on process improvement for some years, SPC will further boost the organization. But, SPC involves concepts and techniques that are fundamentally new to most software organizations and go well beyond what CMMI describes. Real expertise is needed to ensure real success.

Statistical methods are an essential part of high maturity behavior. SPC is one of the conceptually and arithmetically simplest such approaches. While the benefits of adopting these techniques have been demonstrated, they also offer many opportunities for error. Careful attention to the issues raised in this article help to ensure a successful outcome.

11.6. Empirical and Experimental Software Engineering

To monitor impacts of process change and focus on business objectives, dedicated measurements must be available that compare the performance over time with the original baseline before the change. Focus of these process measurements must be on the major improvement goal. If cost is to be reduced, this measurement must show cost. If productivity is to be improved or quality is to be improved, this is what the measurement has to show.

To ensure reproducible and determined handling of process changes and related measurements, several empirical and experimental techniques have been introduced to software engineering [Basi86], Myrvold [Myrv90] and Zelkowitz [Zelk98]. They mostly come from social sciences where since long experiments had to be designed coping with a variety of circumstances, such as insufficient groups size, too many unexplored variables, insufficient possibility to prove by

11.6 Empirical and Experimental Software Engineering

means of hard numbers in one's own environment, or translating best practices and experiences from one setting to another.

> Process improvements typically follow the inductive approach of developing a hypothesis from observations which is then validated or falsified from practical observations.

The approach is inductive because there are no natural laws of software engineering from which we can deduce concrete behaviors or rules. Science theory only has these two approaches: Either we define an environment such as in mathematics and then deduce corollaries and consequences within this closed environment where the law applies. You might recall from Gödel's theorem the difficulties (or impossibility) of even this approach when it comes to verifying certain laws within such closed environment. The other approach which is used in almost all empirical sciences is to observe nature and then deduce hypotheses which are furtheron coined to laws – as long as these hypotheses are not falsified. A verification is basically impossible in the deductive approach, because you can always imagine a certain situation where the law just does not work. Imagine your hypothesis is that theoretically all defects of a software system can be removed by means of formal verification. This is obviously wrong because certain behaviors would not be described formally in the specification and thus will not be subject to formal verification based on that specification. It is therefore only possible to repeatedly validate the hypothesis because there are no counter examples. A single counter example would mean to revisit the hypothesis and maybe restate it to be more precise. Above example on formal verification could be restated towards: "all differences between a formal verification and its implementation in a (semantically complete) programming language can be detected." Let us conclude on this short intermezzo of science theory:

> Software measurement is an important part of science building in software engineering because measurement is the approach towards validating hypotheses and in doing so helping define laws that ensure advance of software engineering.

When a process is considered insufficient, some changes are assumed that would help to improve that process. They are introduced in a controlled and limited environment. Effects are measured to determine the degree and environment to which this solution would justify the change. If the effects are supporting the underlying hypothesis, the change is further deployed. Otherwise new changes are proposed and tested. This is not about trial and error, but about determining a potential solution based on experiences, benchmarks or other insight into the existing processes. It is important to first formally determine what is to be changed and what not and then implement the change in a controlled environment. Anything beyond that is indeed trial or error and will waste resources and disappoint the work teams due to the unprofessional handling.

An example will illustrate this approach. Starting with a business objective of cost reduction, the focus is on early defect removal. Measurements indicate a high variation of defects found during design. Sometimes up to 60% of defects are removed during the activity where they are introduced, and sometimes as much as 60% are removed in test and later. Data points from several projects illustrate this behavior. The cost would be lower if less test is conducted. This however means to ensure defects are removed before test. The proposed solution is to install a series of review and code analysis activities combined with an exit gate at which the defect rate must be below a certain range. The hypothesis (although rarely explicitly stated) is: "If reviews and additional static analysis are conducted systematically and a quality exit criteria is practiced to ensure that delivered code has a certain quality level, then the number of defects found in test will be at 40% or lower." This sounds formal, but is the only approach to avoid ad-hoc changes which will work sometimes and not deliver according to expectations at other times. It is certainly not overhead because at a given moment management and impacted project managers is interested in seeing justification for these additional reviews and quality gates!

The different approaches in software engineering validation are summarized in Table 11.8.

Table 11.8. Validation methods used in software engineering

Validation Method	Description	Usefulness
Assertion	Observational method where data is collected from own experiences.	Typically ad-hoc approach to draw report conclusions from own experiences of using a process or tool. Inexpensive and fast approach to set the stage for more in-depth experiments. Often there are no specific goals set and the environment is too small and not sufficiently stable to deduce valid observations. Impacted heavily by bias and Hawthorne effect, because the observer is part of the study. This is the mostly used method in software engineering despite its many weaknesses.
Project monitoring	Observational method where data is collected from ongoing or finished projects.	Inexpensive and fast approach to set the stage for more in-depth experiments. Often there are no specific goals set and the environment is not sufficiently stable to deduce valid observations. If the number of projects is big enough, it can be an observational field study.
Case study	Observational method where a specific project or setting is monitored in detail.	Unlike the other methods the case study looks into a single case which is described. It is insufficient for validation because the settings are highly specific. Many case studies build the basis for an observational field study – with the advantage of having lots of environmental aspects at hand. It is an excellent educational method for showing what went wrong at a given moment.

Observational field study	Observational method to observe multiple objects.	Amongst the observational methods this is the one with best ground for replicated settings. Objects are observed in their actual setting. Parameters might be controlled to restrict variability. It allows drawing conclusions that are rather robust. Statistical guidance is necessary to determine how many objects are needed to achieve validity. Tests like chi-square and correlations provide the necessary reliability data of the results. Although not all environmental parameters can be frozen, observational field studies with big number of projects within a rather consistent setting (e.g., one product line or one company) give sufficient validity.
Literature search	Historical method where previously published studies are examined.	An inexpensive format for scientific studies based on previous research. Inputs are basically all types of validation methods which are then condensed towards evaluating a specific hypothesis. Looking to a variety of previous studies allows to judge on parameter impacts before starting a new experiment or field study. The clear advantage is the huge available data basis in software engineering literature. The weakness is that the published basis is not always valid and reasonable.
Historical experiences	Historical method to examine completed projects or products	Inexpensive format that builds upon projects experiences as they are covered in lesson learned reports and history databases. Often the quantitative data basis is insufficient thus restricting the scope of such study. The impacting factors are difficult to determine and impossible to constrain. If databases with measurements are available, such analysis can be automated. The risk is that accidental relationship is found because not all measurements are valid or even published.
Replicated experiment	Controlled method where multiple variants of a product or process are compared	Clearly one of the best methods towards constraining influencing factors and determining the effects of one specific change. If such an experiment is well-designed it will find evidences almost ready-to-use in a broad context. Any experiment is however subject to the Hawthorne effect which means that subjectivity will be present amongst those being measured – except it would be done as a blind study which is rarely feasible in software engineering. Due to the constrained environment experiments and their results are rarely accepted in industry (so-called toy examples).
Simulation	Controlled method where processes or projects are executed with artificial data	Simulations are used in software engineering primarily to compare tools or to measure performance and quality data of products. Sometimes simulations are used to try processes and evaluate the impact of environmental changes, such as project simulation games. Simulations can be automated. They are used to remove and determine constraints in a safe environment. The latter is relevant for performance studies of products where tests are too expensive or dangerous. Where people are part of the study the Hawthorne effect must be considered.

While assertions are mostly used in software engineering research [Zelk98], they are certainly not the best method to validate hypotheses. Often this error is also present in process changes. A new methodology or tool is introduced because the users or manager are convinced of their benefits. From the beginning this setting is impacted that a goal must be achieved with exactly this method and that the experimenter is part of the study (e.g., an engineering process group leader or line manager who are accountable for the improvement objective and responsible for the change initiative). It is much better to combine two of these methods and then conclude on the results. For instance if the need is for a better development tool, the firs step could be to investigate experiences that had been published by different sources (i.e., not only the tool vendor). In a second step a replicated experiment could be conducted by using two tools in similar settings. Results are compared, specific additional questions are explored and then a decision is taken. This approach will have much more credibility than simply using a tool for a while because it looked nice in the sales prospects of the vendor and then conclude that this is the right tool. Many paradigms such as extreme programming or object-oriented development were – despite their merits in certain settings – used simply because they were fashionable at a moment, and some time later they proved not to be of that much help in the given setting.

> Guidelines for measuring process changes:
> - State the objectives clearly at the outset of any experiment or study.
> - State as a hypothesis what you expect from the process change. Ensure the hypothesis can be validated or falsified. It must be precise, constrained and measurable.
> - Determine the approach to validate the hypothesis. Do not jump upon using a new tool or process before knowing how the environment and people will influence the effects.
> - Execute the selected methods thoroughly and collect the underlying data for later verification by other persons. Specifically if the data is used for publication or to share in different parts of the company it is important to have it archived in a self-contained format with environmental aspects, project data, measurement definitions, tools and skills participating in that study.
> - Imagine disturbances and external effects on the study which could invalidate the results. For instance the new tool might be introduced in parallel to a process change. Are both coupled or independent? How can effects be isolated?

11.7. The Return on Investment from Better Processes

In this section we will show how the return on investment (ROI) can be calculated from changes, process improvement and process measurement (for ROI and business case related information, see also Chap. 12). Several studies investigated the benefit of process and product improvement from a quantitative perspective

[SEI06b, Gali06, Eber06a, Eick04, McGa03, Dekl97]. They all set up a return on investment (ROI) calculation using measurements collected before and after a change had been implemented. The studies show that the Capability Maturity Model is an effective roadmap for achieving sustainable improvements. A typical short-term ROI of a CMMI-based change yields a fourfold win over the investment [SEI06b] – which of course increases year after year, depending on the timeframe taken because investment is once and savings occur each year. Or in the words of John Mayor a former executive of Motorola: *"from our perspective, level 1 organizations are mostly running into walls, level 2 and 3 organizations are learning where the walls are, and level 4 and 5 organizations are building walls for the other guys to run into."*

The single most important contribution of process improvement to business success is highlighted by the periodic evaluations of project success by the Standish Group [Stand06]. Fig. 11.36 shows this trend of project success rate since the first such reports were published in 1994. While in 1994 only 16% of all IT projects could be considered successful, for those projects finished in 2006 it was already a success rate of 35%. The average cost overrun in 1994 was more than 100%, while today it is less than 40%. Within 12 years a strong momentum is visible which was initiated and driven by a much stronger process focus than ever before. **Process improvement increases project success rate.** We will now look go to the details.

Published results of improvement initiatives such as within Boeing Defense and Space Group [Wigl97] or Motorola [Eick03] help us to understand the value of moving on the long path towards high maturity (see also Fig. 11.39). As one senior manager from a maturity level-5 company said in a workshop the author attended: *"The most valuable asset in our process improvement initiative is that all these engineers still remember how awful it was when we were still at maturity level 1."*

The ROI of process improvement is calculated and illustrated with one or more of the following measurements:
- Productivity: Output over cost (e.g., function points / person weeks); value of delivered work (e.g., revenues per product release, revenues per feature); reuse degree (e.g., effort per variant, effort per feature sold)
- Cycle time: Output over duration (e.g., function points / month); increased revenues due to earlier market entry
- Quality: Defects over output (e.g., delivered defects / Stmt, delivered defects / function point, total defects introduced / Stmt); cost of non quality (e.g., cost of rework, cost of defects detection and removal, cost of defects in the field, penalties)
- Schedule predictability: Estimation accuracy (e.g., difference between committed schedule against achieved delivery date, volatility of estimates); delays (e.g., days of delay until market entry, cost due to late delivery, penalties)

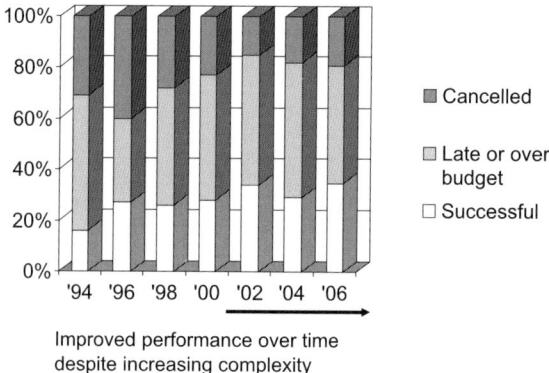

Fig. 11.36. Continuous process improvement means project success on top of growing complexity as shown in the periodic IT-surveys of the Standish Group

To be more concrete about how ROI of process improvement is calculated, let us take practical examples from Alcatel. The business unit that we selected for the detailed ROI-calculation was the first to introduce consistent process improvement in a defined way. It operates in North America, Europe and Asia, thus ensuring representative results independent of geography. Specific and dedicated solutions for customers have been provided in this market for many years. The challenge today is to build upon technology platforms, while offering tailored solutions.

The products of that business unit are components used in communication networks. Examples of usage include switching systems and voice over IP. They comprise platform products that are developed typically every few years and then customized for contract projects. The approach behind is product-line driven, so that platform products would have the basic functionality and customer products are enhancements (or changes) to those platforms. There are also network management systems included which help to configure and operate these products. Data was collected during the late 1990s [Eber99a, Eber01b].

The technology used is real-time and embedded software running on a mixture of own and commercial off-the-shelf hardware components. Middleware (e.g., stacks, operating systems, databases) is commercial off the shelf and might include open source software components where appropriate. Network management systems include user interface frameworks adapted to a variety of customer-specific needs. With the exception of few platform products all projects were linked to a traceably customer contract. The projects evaluated in this study, though primarily in the domains of embedded systems or software applications cover a wide range of the entire world of software dominated projects. Results therefore apply to other industries than communication.

At the beginning of the software process improvement program the focus was on four areas closely related to our overall business goals:
1. improving the customer-perceived quality
2. improving schedule predictability

3. reducing the total cost of non-quality
4. reducing the cycle time

Although these four objectives are somehow related, it is clear that priorities must be given to ensure reproducible decisions in case of conflicts. The order given above reflects these priorities at the start of the process improvement program.

Some results of this software process improvement program can be seen in the following figures. Note that we follow the principles indicated earlier, such as starting to measure *before* changes are implemented. Increasing design defect detection effectiveness over a three-year timeframe is indicated in Fig. 11.37. Design defect detection effectiveness is the percentage of all defects that are detected before the start of integration test. Before starting the improvement program 17% of all faults were detected before the start integration testing, while after three years almost two thirds of all faults are detected up front.

As a consequence, we could reduce defects in the field (after handover to the customer) by more than 20% year after year during this initiative! Besides better overall quality, this of course directly impacts productivity and predictability. Schedule predictability (i.e., achieving the planned delivery date) improved (Fig. 11.38) dramatically. These are typical achievements that you obtain when moving from a maturity level 1 to maturity level 3. But differently from a theoretical lecture, we have shown in this chapter *how* such improvements are implemented to achieve the results.

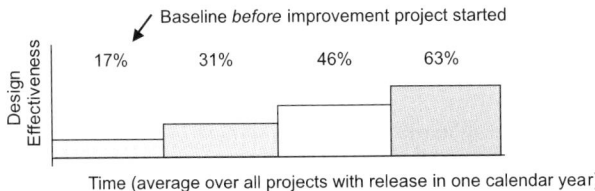

Fig. 11.37. Design defect detection effectiveness over four years

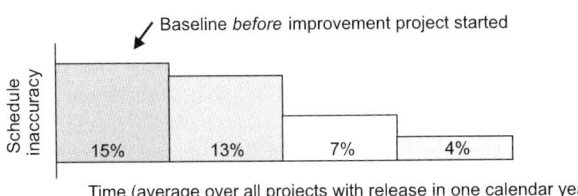

Fig. 11.38. Schedule inaccuracy (in terms of achieved delivery date against plan) over four years

Fig. 11.39 shows a typical evolution of cost of quality with increasing process maturity [Eick04]. The data comes from Motorola's longitudinal study on impacts of process maturity on quality and business. Impacts are measured in cost of quality and its factors (see Chap. 9). The data is mapped to the respective CMM(I) maturity level. Lower process maturity translates into more rework and later defect detection. With increasing process maturity (which means a higher CMM or CMMI maturity level), the share of internal and external failures decreases. Defects are found in the activity where they are created or they are avoided from the beginning. Techniques such as verification (a maturity level 3 process area) and requirements development or technical solution (also on maturity level 3) help in focusing towards reduced cost of quality.

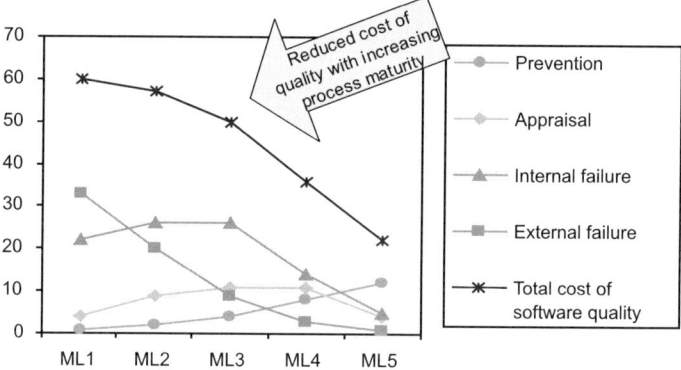

Fig. 11.39. Improving process maturity at Motorola reduced the total cost of quality

Processes can be individually sufficient and perfectly fitting in some overall objectives related to process maturity, while still not positively impacting productivity and throughput of the entire organization. We found, for instance, that at a given time frame a state-of-the-art commercial configuration management system was introduced for more than five components within several business divisions in parallel without knowledge of each other. The process objectives which were long-since agreed upon, were always guiding the introduction, but the set up, the definition of procedures, roles or delivery mechanisms and even the link to standard measurements and standard problem management was reinvented in each single case. Synergy as it is intended within most companies cannot grow with such lack of organizational learning.

Later we used these results to drive as of 2001 across Alcatel a broad engineering process improvement program, called Jupiter [Harv02]. One of the business objectives was to improve overall schedule predictability. As a framework for change and to share experiences and best practices the CMM and later CMMI were used. With increasing capability maturity within an organization, schedule predictability improved.

Fig. 11.40 shows the results of a five-year longitudinal field-study where business units were measured on an annual basis with respect to average schedule predictability and maturity level. Project delays (or schedule performance) are measured by comparing the project end milestone as committed at project start with the actually achieved project end milestone. This absolute difference in calendar days is normalized by the originally committed project duration in calendar days. If a project has been initially agreed to run for 100 calendar days and is actually finished after 120 calendar days, it has a (project) delay of 20%. The line in Fig. 11.40 is the average (not weighted, automatically extrapolated by Excel) with all the individual data points of business units over the five-year timeframe. A business unit in this graph is often represented several times if it moved towards higher maturity during the sample timeframe. In average there are three dots per business units within the five years totaling to some 40 data points contributing to this graph.

Objective-driven, continuous improvement was established because it helped an organization stay competitive and satisfy market and customer demands. The speed to high maturity was different for different organizations due to many environmental (and managerial) factors, and not all made it in three to five years to high maturity.

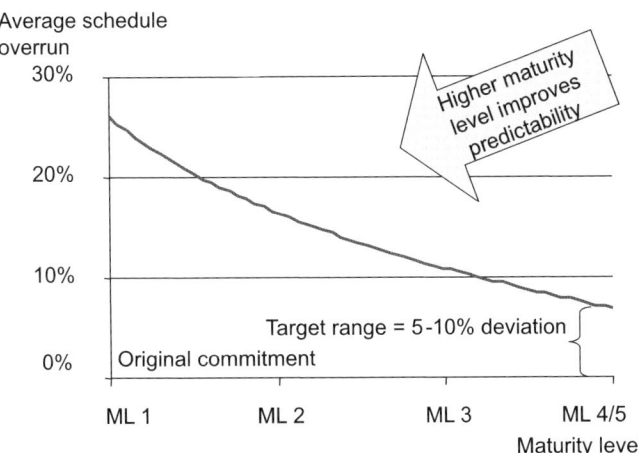

Fig. 11.40. Project performance improves with growing capability maturity

Across the various organizations using objective-driven process improvement statistically we could prove (on the significance level of 5%) that higher maturity yields better performance. It is worth going for high maturity and not stagnating in the low maturity areas where you will be overrun by the growing number of players that know and continuously improve their processes.

11.8. Hints for the Practitioner

A key question that any process improvement activity must answer is, whether the organization can demonstrate actual business benefit. An improvement that after some months does not show sustainable value is badly managed. As the Baldrige award suggests, if the business results are not measurably visible as improvement trends, it signals an approach or deployment problem, perhaps resulting from a focus on getting a "maturity level" or "certificate" rather than achieving business objectives.

Successful process management and process improvement is based upon a few principles:

- Process improvement must always be driven from clear business objectives. Never start a process improvement activity with unclear objectives, or by simply saying that a certain CMMI maturity level must be achieved. It will fail and deliver mediocre results. Improve project performance based on specified criteria of predictability, quality and productivity. These criteria must be derived from your business goals and should be approved or reviewed with your upper management.
- Reinforce accountability through usage of concrete planning and progress tracking instruments. Progress is what is measurable. Objectives will be reached if they are considered meaningful and important. Engineers immediately know if slogans are brought forward which are not considered in day-to-day operational business and decision-making. Ensure that the objectives which are agreed, are used to rate success.
- Keep your processes lean and easy to use. Line up processes with business needs and reinforce continuous learning and improvement driven by the ever-changing business environment. Improve efficiency by using standard processes and the technology and tools that best support these processes. Introduce lean processes that can easily be implemented and followed through, such as a "checklist" concept for determining completeness of milestones. Automate and support processes as much as possible and economically meaningful. Do not rely on specific tools and vendors. Decouple processes from tools to be able to make changes without much overheads. The time of integrated and heavy CASE suites is over. Pushing for processes that cause overheads will not achieve objectives and will frustrate engineers. Facilitate virtual teams across your projects that communicate and interact with an increasingly integrated workflow system. Projects get smaller and teams will be more distributed and mobile than ever. Allow tailoring of processes and workflows depending on business needs. Prepare for such flexibility. Integrate and interface with heterogeneous R&D tool suites.
- Processes are business, too. Your processes are part of the bigger picture of business processes. Organize your process architecture to always observe and measure the value and cost of a process. Align your processes vertically (why do you need that specific engineering process?) and horizontally (what are the interfaces of that process?). Integrate workflows by using standard interfaces

and the same configuration management for process elements and work products. Web services can facilitate the development of simple interfaces. Interface with other critical business processes and workflows based on a general e-business strategy and quality management system (e.g., operations, services, supply chain management, procurement, and so on).
- Continuously challenge existing behaviors. Use external benchmarks to stimulate better performance. Do not let your processes rust on the bookshelf. Processes are here to be used and what is used will change over time. Stimulate organizational learning and avoid architecture- or project-dependent isolation. Processes must be innovated at the speed your products and services are innovated. Treat any improvement or innovation initiative as a project on its own with allocated resources, committed milestones, a project plan and periodic follow-up. Change is not for free, and to assume that it somehow will get done means nothing else than that management is not committed. Do not engrave anything in stone. Ease change management in order to stimulate bottom-up improvements. Engineers know much better how to improve their own work than their management.
- Investigate underlying causes if performance objectives are not reached. Do not simply accept that goals are not reached. Find always out what are the one or two major drivers fro any suboptimal performance. Example: If too many defects slip into release, identify the two major causes for these defects. Then work on those constructively. Each quarter year attack one of the causes and close it based on further defect measurements.
- Be cautious with quantitative process management. Quantitative process management can bring lots of value to an organization but this is not a given. It needs very good insight into the business needs, business processes, and dependencies in the organization. Simply measuring somewhere and trying to stabilize an isolated process is of no use. The first thing to do is to identify which process should be managed quantitatively. Think twice and ask for help if you do not feel secure in your selection. Use run charts to get an understanding of the process and scatter plots to understand influencing factors. Apply special cause analysis to reduce variations and apply common cause analysis for continuous improvement. Do not overreact to common cause variation in process performance. Avoid taking special cause action, designed as a single event to correct an isolated incident, on a common cause problem that is inherent to the process. Optimizing the inspection process is a good place for an organization to start with quantitative management.
- Performance improvement and process change is a professional business. Change will not happen if the change process is not mastered. People will get cynical about "management" because they feel as if they were left alone with not reachable targets. Half of all improvement programs fail due to not managing them adequately. We strongly recommend demanding professional help from outside if these skills are not available in the enterprise. It is worth it given the high ROI of successful performance improvement. Such help can mean support to managers to launch a change initiative, training and coaching to engineers and management or leading a change program.

Before and during process improvement you should step back and ask yourself business-related questions, such as:
- What determines your business success?
- What do your customers demand?
- What are your major pain points in daily operations?
- What are others doing better? How can you find out?
- Has the process considered these success factors?
- Is the process stable?
- How is the process performing now?
- Are you doing better or worse compared to your baseline?
- What are the limits of your capability?
- How is quality determined?
- What are the major cost drivers?
- What are the key influences on process performance?
- Which process elements and tasks mostly contribute to the critical path?
- Are these cost, schedule, performance and quality drivers adequately addressed?
- What could go wrong in this new process?
- What are the signals and early warnings? What trigger events did you consider?

Before changing a process you must understand it. This can be done in different ways, such as benchmarking or process appraisal. A simple yet effective way is to draw a picture of the process considering the following elements. This fast track assessment can be done with a group of persons and a flip-chart. There is no preparation necessary if the people know what they are talking about. Do not work with persons who would only guess.
1. What is the goal of the process? Why is there this process?
2. Who are the major stakeholders?
3. What is the customer of the process? What value is he interested in? If here is no paying external customer, draw a picture of effects from this process until the external and paying customer. What counts is the person who pays for a product or service. Your process has to serve this person.
4. What products are delivered?
5. Are they all relevant? How do you know? Eliminate work products which are done because they had always been done.
6. Draw a simple picture of activity flow, interfaces, work products and involved persons.
7. Add elapsed time and effort to these activities. Relate cost and time to value creation. If effort or time is not known, measure it right away. Never ever change a process without knowing effort and time behind it.

There are several rules for quantitative management which we want to summarize briefly for the practitioner (either getting started or going ahead):
- Processes must be understood before they can be improved. Measurements and statistical techniques provide a solid basis for understanding. A first step is to

baseline the current behaviors in order to compare with the effects of changes and to observe evolution over time.
- Ask these questions to understand process behaviors: What is the normal process variation? What are anomalous behaviors? What differentiates inherent (i.e., common causes, voice of the process) from anomalous variation (i.e., disturbances, errors)?
- Stabilize process performance before trying to achieve performance improvements. Eliminate disturbances and build into the process sufficient robustness to cope with those disturbances that cannot be eliminated. For instance, requirements will change during a project. So the requirements management processes must be able to cope with some degree of change and they must eliminate unnecessary changes.
- Statistics provide a set of useful methods and tools to measure and analyze process behavior, state and verify hypotheses, draw conclusions, and drive improvement.
- A change is worthless if it is not measured in its effects and focused on what matters to the organization and its engineers.

Measuring results of process improvement and thus making the business cases for your own improvement projects should build upon the following insights:

Improved quality. We can directly address customer needs by linking dedicated improvement objectives, such as return rate, via the CMMI to process changes in R&D. This is actually the strength of CMMI maturity levels two and three. Two-digit quality improvements year over year are feasible if the CMMI is applied and closely followed up in engineering projects.

Reduced cycle time. The efficiency and effectiveness of engineering processes directly impact engineering cycle time. For instance, earlier defect detection means faster and more comprehensive defect correction. A defect found during development costs less than 10% to correct compared to detection during testing. Your focus here should be on defect phase containment. Build the necessary checks to ensure that work products have the right quality level before being passed on to the next process step. Cycle time reduction builds upon a consistent product life-cycle and process repository which allows instrumenting and tuning processes to needs.

Improved engineering flexibility. With decreasing size and duration of projects, engineers need to be flexible to quickly start working in new environments. While technical challenges cannot be reduced, the organizational and administrative overhead must be managed and limited. Agreeing and reinforcing one consistent and overarching product life-cycle across the company ensures that you can deliver solutions independently of where the components come from. Increasingly components come from various suppliers, including freely available software. The life-cycle offers the framework for all projects to have a minimum set of decision gates. Engineers can faster move to new projects or other departments if some basic process framework applies to the entire company.

Reduced overhead. Linked to the management system with its process and role descriptions, document templates are embedded in the workflow support system, presenting engineers with immediate process support when and where they need it. Long process descriptions are replaced by pictorial overviews and automated interfaces. For example, clicking on a work product name can activate an interface to a document management system, and administrative data such as the document number are automatically derived from the project context. Less overheads facilitate that work products are kept consistent when changes occur.

Improved communication. Information is presented in a consistent way for all projects, preventing replication of data and reducing search time. A standardized workflow and product life-cycle management system can easily offer a dashboard with immediate visibility on key data and responsibilities contributing to an increase awareness of accountability. If you do not have such workflow system at hand, build nevertheless the project dashboard. Standardizing one management part of the process (such as project measurements) and automating it will increasingly grow towards alignments and standardization of other tools and processes.

Improved alignment of process and tools. With process asset libraries linked to tools, we are able to filter out and evaluate scenarios of how process change impacts tools, or where tool changes would impact processes. So-called "best-practices" can be communicated with related tools and procedures to move up engineering effectiveness and learn from the best in class in your company. Interfaces to tools and their user guides can now be embedded in the process support environment.

Easier generation of training plans. With the advent of managed process diversity, aligned training plans and closer follow-up of skill evolution has been achieved. Increasingly, project roles and specific work product templates or process-related roles are standardized and can be reused, facilitating more consistent skill and human resource management.

Process improvement – if done professionally – yields a positive business case. Typical ROI values are in the range of four times what had been invested – for the first year. This accumulates to bigger savings in following years, because the investment can be reduced once the change had been successfully mastered. For software engineering a sigma shift in defect reduction translates in improved net income of 5-10%.

11.9. 1Summary

In striving for better performance, a simple equation applies:

> Business performance = f (products, processes, people).

Obviously our performance depends on our products and people. But both is very closely liked to the performance of our processes. Controlling and achieving business objectives requires controlling and continuously improving the performance of underlying processes. Process improvement drives productivity improvement and thus frees resources for innovation. This chapter provided a comprehensive view of process improvement, starting from the basics of culture change towards more accountability and building upon a number of integration mechanisms to ensure that technology effectiveness keeps pace with process maturity.

Process management is necessary to ensure having the right processes. Depending on market requirements and technology change, processes need to continuously improve. Process definition and process reinforcement should be as high as necessary to ensure quality, predictability and productivity, and as low as feasible to preserve flexibility and agility. Each single process must be judged on the cost it creates versus the benefit it yields. Processes need commercial justification which is impossible if they are not even defined. Too narrow an implementation of ISO 9000 or CMMI bears the risk that processes specify in all detail what needs to be done. Some organizations believe that with processes everything will be controlled. They loose flexibility and will be overrun by entrepreneurs with much more agility. Also, we have observed organizations that would treat the certifications as the goal, rather as a step in achieving real goals. They will not gain much and frustrate employees. Process improvement frameworks like CMMI are always and only tools to an end. Used well, they are important tools to deliver improvement results. The goal is better performance in projects and products.

> Processes exist whether we acknowledge it or not. The major question is: Do we allow them to develop organically and drive our organizations with uncontrolled results – or do we take a systematic approach to manage their evolution according to our needs and goals.

Software measurement is necessary to gradually build upon observations and their validation in a defined environment. From measurements we can identify what is working and what is not working. We can focus our performance improvement activities on what matters and where it matters. Effectiveness and efficiency of changes are determined and used to justify a change and state its business case. Software measurement is the approach towards validating hypotheses and in doing so helping to define laws that ensure advance in software engineering.

> Productivity is improved by reducing accidents and by controlling essence (Ebert's law).

Accidents result from having defects which could have been avoided or detecting defects too late. Such defects cause rework which reduces productivity. Reducing accidents means efficiency improvement. There are many accidents along the product life-cycle starting with insufficient reviews on requirements and insufficient analysis before project start to having too much test effort up to insufficient quality after delivery with lots of rework. Essence is the real delivered value of what we are doing. Often we do not control value thus wasting time and effort on things which the market won't pay for. Controlling essence means improving effectiveness. Examples include variant proliferation in a product line or unnecessary requirements and features being developed without a business case. We have to control this essence as it directly impacts productivity. Work is not offshored to low-cost countries because of direct labor cost of excellent engineers (which is equaling gradually across the world), but because many of those offshoring companies or countries high focus on creating value at a low cost by reduced rework and focus on what matters.

Quantitative management will help to distinguish special from common causes of variation. It provides methods and a sound foundation to achieve determined improvements in stability (eliminating special causes of variation) and capability (delivering according to business needs). We recall the "prayer" of the seasoned process manager: *Oh Lord give me the power to change what I can change (i.e., eliminate special causes), accept what I cannot change i.e., (the common causes) and the wisdom (i.e., statistical techniques) to distinguish the one from the other.* We would add to this statement that we wish the *power* to also change common causes in order to stay innovative and competitive.

> Three elements are critical to making a change successful, namely objectives, direction and feedback.

Setting objectives – defining what specific change should occur and setting targets for attaining that change ensures that the change will move you in the right direction. Providing *guidance* and direction ensures that you use the right approaches, methods, tools and the like. It means literally doing things right and not derailing during the change. *Feedback* is necessary as the effort to change is underway. Those orchestrating the change must receive concrete information about their progress in achieving the objectives. Often we realize too late that we took the right direction, worked well – but unfortunately got lost in the wrong debates or details.

> Where there are concrete objectives, direction and feedback, both the commitment to change and the likelihood for successful change will increase.

12. Controlling for IT and Software

> *When the smoke clears,*
> *the thing that really matters*
> *to senior management*
> *is the numbers.*
> Donald J. Reifer

12.1. Managing Software as a Business

Business executives, senior management, project and product managers, software engineers, quality engineers and controllers all need to quantify and prioritize objectives, measure progress, control product quality and manage cost. Every morning you should ask yourself some questions:
- Are you and your teams operating at your peak capability?
- How do you know?
- Where are the competitors?
- How will you improve?
- What opportunities come with changing technology or processes?
- What experiences and best practices from other companies might help you?

Once I walked into the office of a senior manager and asked him on some of his previous projects. We were preparing a presentation for a key customer and wanted to explain behaviors and how we manage performance. The manager – without much thinking – shot an immediate answer: "7% of our defects are detected by the customer." The only difficulty with that rapid answer was that he was clueless about the total number of defects and not even knew how much defects as a percentage of pre-release were found in different defect removal activities. Managers need numbers. They are educated to set objectives and somehow achieve them. But not often they know how good their data really is. It seems as if it is for some managers only relevant to have quantitative facts and then decide – not to judge on data quality, validity of explanations or even trends and outliers.

A while ago in a meeting with product line managers in one of Alcatel's business groups the executive VP was asking around his senior managers who would remove below 30% of defects before start of test. Nobody raised his hands. They all knew that this would be a not so good message to pass to their VP. Then he asked who would remove more than 50% of the defects. Again nobody raised his hands. Finally he asked who actually knew the numbers. Well, as a matter of fact again they were all quiet. Such unawareness drove him nuts and he immediately triggered some actions towards improved early defect removal – knowing from our own experiences from another business group that 10% more defects found before start of test had a direct bottom line impact of several percentage points. He knew what matters and had a clear vision that early defect removal would reduce his product development cost. However, his managers with all their colorful presentations and bold statements on productivity and quality had not a clue about where they actually stood.

This chapter looks into management techniques on levels beyond the individual project. It has the organizational perspective and should help you to place software measurements for the success of your overall business. It applies to small and bigger enterprises – so do not worry that this is only for the very big and complex organizations. We take the stance to abstract from organization size and consistently apply the E4–measurement process (see Chap. 2).

The chapter looks into technical and IT controlling, technology management, release management and portfolio management techniques. We have selected areas with very different underlying management objectives to underline the broad scope where measurements are used. First we look into the business case. Then we introduce to portfolio management which is a methodology of increasing relevance to simultaneously manage a set of different products or projects. We will look into managing technology change and disruptive technology introduction. We also show how product and release planning are guided by measurements. These few examples should indicate the necessity of good measurements to manage the software business.

This chapter applies to all those who need a perspective on the business side of software.

12.2. The Business Case

A business case presents a business idea or proposal to a decision maker. It should essentially prove that the proposal is sufficiently solid and that it fits economically and technically into the company's strategy. It is part of a more general business plan and emphasizes on costs and benefits, financing the endeavor, technical needs, feasibility, market situation and environment and the competition. It is created early in the product life-cycle and serves as the major input *before* a decision for investment is taken.

Many projects and products fail simply because the business case was never done or it was not done correctly. The key to a successful business case is that it connects well the value proposition with the technical and marketing concept and with the market evolution and the company's potential. Lacking on one of these four dimensions invalidates the entire business case. A business case is more than only the cost-benefit calculation – which obviously is part of it.

The full business case consists of the following elements:
- Summary (product vision and value in one sentence, summary of entire business case including the major assumptions and the cost-benefit evolution)
- Introduction (motivation of the business proposal, market value, relationship to existing products, solutions or services, own capabilities and capacity)
- Market analysis (market assumptions, industry trends, target market and customers, volume of the target market, competitors, own positioning, evaluation of these assumptions by strengths, weaknesses, opportunities and threats)

- Valuation and cost-benefit analysis (sales forecasts, profit and loss calculation, cash flow, financing the expenses, business risk management, securities, present value of investments, evaluation of assumptions). This part is the core of the business case and often the major focus during review of the business case. It must prove the financial health of the proposed product.
- Summary of operations (organization, responsibilities, customer interfaces, production planning, supply chain, suppliers, make versus reuse versus buy, platforms and components to be used, service needs, management control, quality objectives and quality management)
- Summary of project and release plan (key features mapped to releases, dedicated services, resources, skills, milestones, dependencies, risk management)
- Feasibility study (are the requirements in terms of cost, schedule, quality and content realistically feasible with the current planning assumptions?)

The financial calculation within the business case must as a bare minimum summarize the assumed cost and value both in a quantitative way which allows a sound judgment on short-term risk and long-term value. Typically both cost and income are summarized over the accounting periods (could be quarters or years) and discounted to a net present value which indicates how much would be necessary to invest today to achieve the annual values as described by the business case.

Fig. 12.1 provides a small example that shows this presentation over annual periods. The underlying assumption for the example is that a server would be necessary which costs 20,000 Euro per period. The expected income from this investment will be 30,000 Euro per period. Total amortization should be calculated for five periods. The assumed internal discount is 5% (note that this rate is typically higher and fixed by the CFO for specific investment types in your company). With a simple calculation you find a ROI of 50% per year: An investment of 20 K€ generates a net income of 10 K€ before subtracting other expenses. To achieve these periodic benefits over the 5 year duration you would have to put 43,294 Euro on the bank with the 5% interest rate.

Period	Expenses	Income	Value	Discounting: 5% $1/(1+i)^N$	Present value
1	20000	30000	10000	0.9524	9524
2	20000	30000	10000	0,9070	9070
3	20000	30000	10000	0,8638	8638
4	20000	30000	10000	0,8227	8227
5	20000	30000	10000	0,7835	7835
	100000		50000		43294

Fig. 12.1. Financial calculation within a business case

Note that the **cash flow is not necessarily aligned with the calendar time** (e.g., cost of sales would be compensated in the same period by the respective

sales revenues). While generally it is aligned with product phases (e.g., expenses during the initial phases and income from the deployment onwards), the picture looks different on the next lower level:
- Monthly expenses and payment. The expenses for utilized resources are typically incurred on monthly basis in an internal accounting scheme. Payment can be contracted on a monthly basis for the directly attributable expenses, such as labor or rent.
- Purchased services such as consulting or outsourcing are paid for typically after their delivery. Other payment schemes can be contracted.
- Upfront payment at time of contract signature. This is advantageous for the business case because it ensures an initial budget from the customer. It is typically done in customer-specific projects to ensure that investments would be launched in due time.
- Staged payments for activities with long duration. Typically such stage payments are linked with deliverables, such as increments of the product.
- Payment at purchase. This is the standard situation for product development. First the supplier has to invest and afterwards the clients would pay for the product.
- Payment at completion of critical milestones. This can be an intermediate payment for work completed before the product is completely finished. It is however also possible that this means a delayed payment with credit to the customer, such as if the product would have to pass acceptance tests at the customer site and would only be paid if they run all successfully. This model is dangerous because it is mostly under control of the customer – except that the acceptance process is precisely defined and contracted including the acceptance criteria.
- Delayed payment based on fulfilled customer business case assumptions. This approach is mostly used in consulting projects but will grow into the software solution and service domain. It creates a high interdependency of supplier and customer, where the supplier determines his customer's business case and has to deliver success on the basis of these measurements. While this approach certainly improves trust, it is of high risk, especially if the customer is small or not well established.

A business case has to prove that the proposed concept fits both technically and commercially in the enterprise. It is part of the business plan and is created before the launch of a product development. **Preparing the software business case consists of several steps**:
1. **Coin a vision and focus**. What is the message you want to get across? What will be different with the proposed product or solution? Use language that is understood by decision-makers and stakeholders which means being concise and talking about financial and marketing aspects more than technology. Focus on what you are really able to do.
2. **Analyze the market environment and commercial situation**. How will you sell? How much? To whom? With what effect? For improvement projects identify the symptoms of poor practice and what they mean for your company (e.g.,

cost of non-quality, productivity, cycle time, predictability). Quantify the costs and benefits, the threats and opportunities. For IT projects you should consider that the IT direct cost is only the tip of the iceberg. The true value proposition is in the operational business processes.
3. **Plan the proposed project to the level of details that allows judging risks and cost**. Show how it will be operationally conducted, with what resources, organization, skills and budgets. What are the risks and their mitigation? Who are the suppliers? Perform a reality check on your project. Does the combined information make sense? Can you deliver the value proposed in step 1? How will you track the earned value? Which measurements and dashboard will be utilized?
4. **Validate the business case**. This step is often neglected, however crucial to close the loop between assumptions and a learning organization. The problem lies not in invalid assumptions but in not learning from errors. Therefore at critical life-cycle milestones and afterwards at delivery and during service, the cost and revenues must be reassessed with the perspective to revisit the entire planning (up to the level where a product might be killed for not proving its assumptions), but also to learn towards risk management, uncertainty management and accountability. Specifically in a globally distributed project this step ensures learning from obstacles in people management, turnover rates or insufficient quality levels.

How does the business case relate to software measurement? The business case is quantitative by nature. It builds upon assumptions and propositions which must be evaluated from different perspectives on the validity, consistency and completeness. This is where software measurements come into the picture. They provide for instance the guidance for performing a feasibility study. They relate expected volume or size of the project to effort and schedule needs and thus indicate whether the proposed plan and delivery dates are viable. Fig. 12.2 shows an example for such a feasibility study.

Different project scenarios are portrayed for a given size and productivity. The curves represent respective time and cost for a size and productivity following the Raleigh equation provided in the picture [Putn03]. The example indicates that for a given (estimated) size, the target cost and dates are not feasible. Setting up the project to reach either the schedule or budget limitations is presented by circles 1 and 2, respectively. It is impossible with the given productivity and constraints to achieve both schedule and budget targets. Obviously one solution would be to "improve productivity" (circle number 4). However, this is not something that can be done over night. It would only indicate poor management if such unrealistic assumptions are taken. Only by adjusting project contents, thus reducing size, allows to stay in the allowed targets, while having a feasible project (circle number 3).

Software measurements guide in the risk analysis and later in risk management. They indicate uncertainties and together with software engineering techniques guide the risk mitigation. For instance, knowing that requirements change with 1-3% per month is a starting point for planning releases and incremental deliveries.

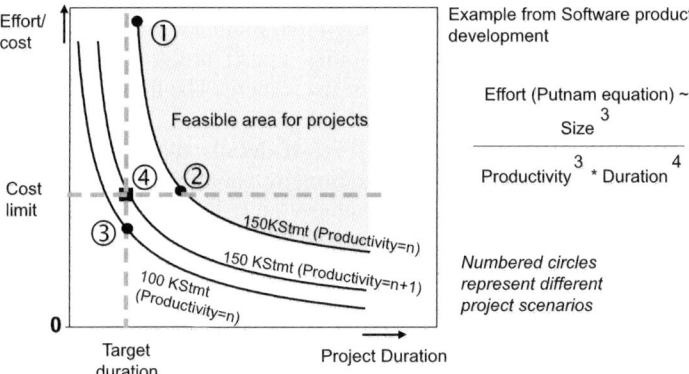

Fig. 12.2. Example for a project feasibility study with different scenarios related to allowed cost and time (duration) limits following the Raleigh relationship

Not all benefits can be quantified the same way. There are also internal benefits of a project which are more difficult to consider in a business case. Such opportunities include:
- Reduced time to market
- Reuse of platform elements or introduction of product line elements
- Decrease of rework due to new and improved verification methods
- Increase of customer basis
- Reduced overheads on both customer side and thus an improved customer business case
- Reduced dependencies on external or internal suppliers; streamlined business
- Improved customer satisfaction
- Reduced training cost

All those elements can be quantified! They are not of the type like "improved employee morale" which indeed makes it very difficult to be considered adequately in a business case. Missing those opportunities in the business case however could not only reduce chances to get the investment approved but might also result in insufficient valuation for the company – simply because nobody pushed for these additional values. Not all benefits (or cost factors) must be considered. A business case also creates cost. Just be sure that your business case is good enough during preparation to consider what is most relevant in the proposed endeavor. Priorities amongst benefits and cost help to stay focused.

The business case is the tool to state and relate assumptions on cost, value and sales. It is rarely perceived as part of software measurement. However good measurement links business objectives to individual performance. Here are some impacts that software measurement has on the business case:
- What are the business case assumptions? Do they suffice?
- Do business case assumptions satisfy as a rule or exceptionally? What trends are visible?

- What is the quality and preciseness of business case assumptions (value, sales, cost, ROI)?
- Are the right financial indicators used to justify investments? Is it a simple cost-benefit trade-off or is it more elaborate with analysis of impacting factors and detailed finance values (i.e., cash flow, ROI, ROCE, and so on)?
- Is there sufficient traceability from software technology and project / product requirements to the business case? Are new technologies or changing requirements analyzed according to their marginal value?

12.3. The Return on Investment (ROI)

Return on investment (ROI) is a measurement how effectively an organization is using its capital to generate profits. In accounting it is the annual income or profit divided by the sum of shareholder's equity and long-term debt. On the level of operational activities the ROI is the tangible outcome or profitability of an investment measured in business measurements (e.g., money).

ROI is defined as the ratio of returns (i.e., result from an investment) to the directly related effort (i.e., the investment).

Often the investments are visible right from the beginning while the value is not so obvious. Nobody wants to burn fingers with claiming an improvement or ROI. This has caused the "software productivity paradox", which began in early 1986 when economist Stephen Roach demonstrated that the huge increase in organizational expenditures on IT (computers, peripheral devices, software, and related services) between 1975 and 1985 was accompanied by virtually no gains in organizational productivity [Bowe96]. Clearly, investing in software and information technology is not a sufficient condition to see tangible productivity improvements. This has stimulated even Nobel laureate Robert Solow to emphasize that "we see computers everywhere except in the productivity statistics." Past growth had been achieved mostly by hardware evolution, while software is still a craft industry and hardly measured on its impact. Often these productivity impacts are consumed by increasingly complex products and processes so that from an external perspective nothing has changed and improved with the IT-investments.

This "productivity paradox" of missing payoffs from investments in software engineering and information technology has been put to rest with using appropriate measures for business case and ROI. The key to achieving payoffs from IT investments lies in changing the nature of work processes to exploit what IT offers. Software products and solutions have been and will be a major driver of productivity growth across almost all business. Yet the difficulty in IT services and software development is still that productivity is not measured consistently – if at all.

ROI is difficult to calculate in software related activities and in IT [Reif02]. The difficulty arises from several aspects:

- The investment in effort is often not directly available. Reporting might be more coarse than what really matters. For instance, effort figures might be available on the project level, while the ROI should be accounted for a tool being used in that project.
- The effects of an investment are not known. Often money is pumped into a new IT service or software product release, while the valuation from a user or customer perspective is missing or inaccurate. This holds specifically for unnecessary features in such service or product, which are produced without knowing their justification.
- The mapping of effort figures that relate to a specific investment (that would have otherwise not been done) and the direct returns from this investment (as a difference to what would have happened if it had not been invested) is not feasible.

Many companies in the ICT industry are almost clueless on what they spend IT money and whether it is spent on the right things. They talk about cost savings and do not measure which activities consume what resources. Generally speaking most companies cannot say what effect changes in working practices would have on productivity because they do not even know the cost of time and resources and the value they are creating.

In practice return on investment (ROI) is critical to justify and control an investment. Too often heterogeneous cost elements with different meaning and unclear accounting relationships are combined into one figure that is then optimized. For instance, reducing the "cost of quality" that includes appraisal cost and prevention cost is misleading when compared with cost of nonconformance because certain appraisal costs (e.g., unit test) are components of regular development. Cost of nonconformance (cost of non-quality) on the other hand is incomplete if we only consider internal cost for fault detection, correction and redelivery because we must include opportunity cost due to rework at the customer site, late deliveries or simply binding resources that otherwise might have been used for a new project.

The following rules should be considered for calculating ROI effects:
- Samples should consider projects before and after the start of the improvement program to be evaluated with ROI.
- Controlling should be able to provide history data (e.g., effort).
- Aggregated or combined effort or cost figures must be separated (i.e., prevention, appraisal cost, cost of nonperformance, cost of performance – which are typically spent in any case).
- Include only those effects that trace back to root causes that were part of the original improvement planning.
- Check cost data for consistency within one project and across projects.
- Obvious management and software engineering practices are typically not ROI topics. For instance, if most of your project managers is already in earned value analysis, it is pointless to convince the remaining project managers with a ROI

of that specific analysis. Rather they need to understand that it is just common project management sense to apply and use it.
- There are many "hidden" ROI potentials that are often difficult to quantify (e.g., customer satisfaction; improved market share because of better quality, delivery accuracy and lower per feature costs; opportunity costs; reduced maintenance costs in follow-on projects; improved reusability; employee satisfaction; resources are available for new projects instead of wasting them for firefighting).
- There are hidden investments that must be accounted (e.g., training, infrastructure, coaching, additional measurements, additional management activities, process maintenance).

ROI is most effectively presented according to the following flow:
1. Current results (these are the potentials, i.e., problems, cost; causes)
2. Known effects in other (competing) companies (i.e., improvement programs in other companies, benchmarking data, cost-benefit estimation for these companies)
3. ROI calculation (calculate cost of quality per month for several sample projects; calculate the savings since start of the improvement program; extrapolate these savings for all affected projects which is benefit; compare the benefit with the cost of the improvement program which is ROI; never include the cost of performance since this is regular effort)

> A last word: Whatever you are doing, be prepared to present the ROI. Have necessary calculations and potential impacts of changes readily in your pocket (literally speaking) and use it for decision-making.

Especially use it when there are changes to your project imposed on your project from senior management, because this is the language they readily understand. As long as you fiddle around claiming that the value of what you are doing is not easy to calculate, you are subject to unpleasant changes. Money and value is what matters. But not all ROI calculations need to be based on monetary benefits. Depending on the business goals, they can as well be directly presented in terms of improved delivery accuracy, reduced lead time or higher efficiency and productivity.

12.4. Cost Controlling

12.4.1 Cost Controlling in Software Projects

It is rare to find practical cost control besides deadline- or priority-driven resource allocation and shifting. An obvious reason is that costs in software projects are predominantly related to labor (i.e., effort), which is therefore often the only factor being controlled – if at all. The benefits of cost control, however, are manifold and must exceed simple headcount follow-up. In decision-making cost information is used to determine relevant costs (e.g., sunk costs, avoidable versus unavoidable costs, variable versus fixed costs) in a given project or process, while in management control the focus is on controllable costs versus non-controllable costs.

A major step towards decision support is an accounting that moves from headcount-based effort models to activity-based costing. Functional cost analysis and even target-costing approaches are increasingly relevant because customers tend to pay for features instead of entire packages as before. Not surprisingly, cost reduction can only be achieved if it is clear how activities relate to costs. The difference is to assign costs to activities or processes instead of to departments.

Activity-based models allow for more accurate estimates and tracking than using holistic models which only focus on size and effort for the project as one unit. Effects of processes and their changes, resources and their skill distribution or factors related to each of the development activities can be considered, depending on the breakdown granularity.

An example is given in Table 12.1 which includes a first breakdown to major development phases. The percentages and costs per thousand lines of code (KLOC) are for real-time embedded systems and should not be taken as fixed quantities [McGa01, Jone01]. Typically both columns for percentages and productivity are based on a project history database that is continuously improved and tailored to the specific project situation. Even process allocation might vary; projects with reuse have a different distribution with more emphasis towards integration and less effort for top-level design. Unit cost values are likely to decrease in the long-term as the cumulative effects of technological and process changes become visible.

Table 12.1. Example for activity-based effort allocation

Activity	Percent	Person months per KLOC
Project management	7%	0.7
Analysis, specification	17%	1.7
Design	22%	2.2
Coding	22%	2.2
Integration, configuration management	16%	1.6
Transition, deployment	16%	1.6
Total	100%	10

All activities that form the development process must be considered to avoid uncontrollable overhead costs. Cost estimation is derived from the size of new or reused software related to the overall productivity and the cost per activity. The recommended sequence of estimation activities is first to estimate the size of the software product, then to estimate the cost, and finally to estimate the development schedule based on the size and the cost estimates. These estimates should be revised towards the end of architecture and top level design and again towards end of unit test or when the first increment is integrated.

12.4 Cost Controlling

Although activity-based accounting means more detailed effort reporting throughout each project, it allows for a clear separation between value adding and non-value adding activities, process value analysis, and improved performance measurements and incentive schemes. Once process related costs are obvious, it is easy to assign all overhead costs, such as integration test support or tools, related to the processes where they are necessary and again to the respective projects. Instead of allocating such overhead to projects based on overall development effort per project, it is allocated related to activities relevant in the projects. For instance, up-front design activities should not contribute to allocation of expensive test equipment.

While dealing with controlling cost, often the question comes up of which tracking system is to be used. Most companies have rather independent financial tracking systems in place that provide monthly reports on cost per project and sometimes even on an activity base. The reports are often integrated with timesheet systems and relate effort to other kinds of cost. Unfortunately, such financial systems are in many cases so independent from engineering that neither the activities clusters nor the reporting frequencies are helpful for making any short-term decisions.

Variance analysis is applied to control cost evolution and lead-time over time. It is based on standard costs that are estimated (or known) costs to perform a single activity within a process under efficient operating conditions. Typically such standard costs are based on well-defined outputs of the activity, for instance, test cases performed and errors found in testing. Knowing the effort per test case during integration test and the effort to detect an error (which includes regression testing but not correction), a standard effort can be estimated for the whole project. Functionality, size, reuse degree, stability and complexity of the project determine the two input parameters, namely test cases and estimated number of faults to be detected in the specific test process. Variances are then calculated as a relative figure: variance = (standard cost − actual cost) / standard cost.

Variance analysis serves to find practical reasons for causes of off-standard performance so that project management or department heads can improve operations and increase efficiency. It is, however, not an end in itself because variances might be caused by other variances or be related to a different target. Predictors should thus be self-contained, such as in the given example. Test cases alone are insufficient because an unstable product due to insufficient design causes more effort in testing.

A major use of cost control measurements combined with actual performance feedback is the tracking of earned value (see also Fig. 8.4). **Earned value** compares achieved results with the invested effort and time. For simplification let us assume that we have an incremental approach in the project with customer requirements allocated to increments. Let us further assume that we deliver increments on a frequent basis which are integrated into a continuous build. Only if such increment is fully integrated into the build and tested, it is accepted. Upon acceptance of an increment, the status of the respective requirements within this increment is set to "tested." The build, though only internally available, could at any time with low overhead be finalized and delivered to a customer. The value measurements then increases by the relative share of these tested requirements compared to the sum of all project requirements. If, for instance, 70% of all customer requirements are available and tested, the earned value is 70%. Weighting is possible by allocating effort to these requirements. Compared with the traditional progress tracking, earned value does not show the "90% complete syndrome", where lots of code and documents are available, but no value is created from an external perspective, because nothing could be delivered to the customer as is.

We can allocate effort to each requirement based on up-front effort estimation. With each requirement that is delivered within an increment the value of the project deliveries would increase by the amount of effort originally allocated to the requirement. The reasoning here is that the effort should correlate with our pricing. This certainly is not reality, however a good predictor for value generated. Why, after all, should one spend a large part of project effort on a small marginal value to the customer? If the value of delivered requirements is bigger than what was supposed to be invested in terms of engineering effort, the project is ahead. If it is less it is behind. The same approach is taken for schedule. Both parameters combined give an excellent predictor for time and cost to complete a project.

Return on investment (ROI) is important when it comes to justifying new development or introduction of new technologies or change of processes (see Chaps. 2 and 10). However, heterogeneous cost elements with different meaning and unclear accounting relationships are often combined into one figure that is then optimized. For instance, reducing "cost of quality" that includes appraisal cost and prevention cost is misleading when compared with cost of nonconformance because certain appraisal cost (e.g., module test) are components of regular development. Cost of nonconformance, on the other hand, is incomplete if we are only considering internal cost for fault detection, correction and redelivery because we must include opportunity cost due to rework at the customer site, late deliveries or simply binding resources that otherwise might have been used for a new project.

12.4.2 Cost Controlling in IT Services

Expert Box. Authors: Falk Uebernickel, Rüdiger Zarnekow, Jochen Scheeg

Concepts for measuring and controlling IT services costs are becoming progressively more important for IT service providers. Due to cost pressure, the need for business-process innovation and IT production-process improvement, service providers face the difficulty of measuring, calculating and controlling IT service costs at a fine-grained level. Traditionally, IT costs are treated like overhead costs or charged in terms of technical services as with CPU-time or network bandwidth consumed. However, managers who use IT services generally work with output units such as payroll transactions, credit risk rankings or invoices. In other words, IT cost accounting and measuring systems need to be redesigned to satisfy managerial requirements and to improve the use of IT technology in business processes.

In order to develop a service-oriented cost accounting and controlling methodology, a service provider must achieve the following:
- design transparent IT production processes and service catalogues
- build up capabilities for calculating both standardized and individualized customer services
- implement flexible profitability analysis by market segment, customer group and services
- integrate measurement, cost accounting and service-level management systems
- design and introduce service-based demand, capacity and cost planning systems

IT service costing
This contribution illustrates how a service-oriented cost measurement and accounting system was applied to a legal entity of a German telecommunication provider during 2006. The portfolio offered consists of services for business-to-business relationships. Examples are bill calculation, presentation, fulfillment and payment processing, as well as treatment and collection processing. The total service volume is about 450 million transactions per year. To ensure an IT service-oriented cost accounting methodology, the company identified two main service categories that are subject to standardization and require a customer orientation:
- *Standard Service Elements*: SSEs are highly standardized IT services that can be produced for a wide range of customers. Such an IT service is characterized by standardized production flows and output units. For each SSE unit, the same applications and infrastructure components are used.
- *Service Elements*: SEs are combinations of application and infrastructure outputs that have been individualized for specific customers. The degree of automation and reuse for other customers is limited.

Due to high overhead or indirect costs, the service provider decided to use an ABC-approach (**activity-based costing**) to allocate incurred costs to IT services. Fig. 12.3 depicts the complete steering logic. During the first stage of ABC, all costs must be allocated to resource centers which represent the basic elements of a cost accounting system. The resources include labor, equipment, telephone, licenses, hardware and software. The separate collection of resource costs enables capacity and cost management at the resource level.

In the second step, all resource costs must be allocated to activity centers, SSEs and SEs or production orders. The ability to assign costs directly to SSEs / SEs depends on different influence factors. For example, labor costs for SSE-managers are directly assignable to single SSEs. However, application licenses are used to produce manifold SSEs and SEs which is why an assignment to activity centers is necessary. Cost drivers are the link between resource and activity centers. Cost drivers mathematically model the allocation rate with respect to how the activity center uses different resources. For instance, the personnel time spent on maintaining and monitoring applications is used to distribute labor costs to activity centers. For this purpose, the centralized time-recording system Tick@ was used. Regardless, the whole assignment process is extremely complex. Other resource costs

448   12 Controlling for IT and Software

such as selling and administration costs must also be assigned, so that other cost drivers have to be identified as well.

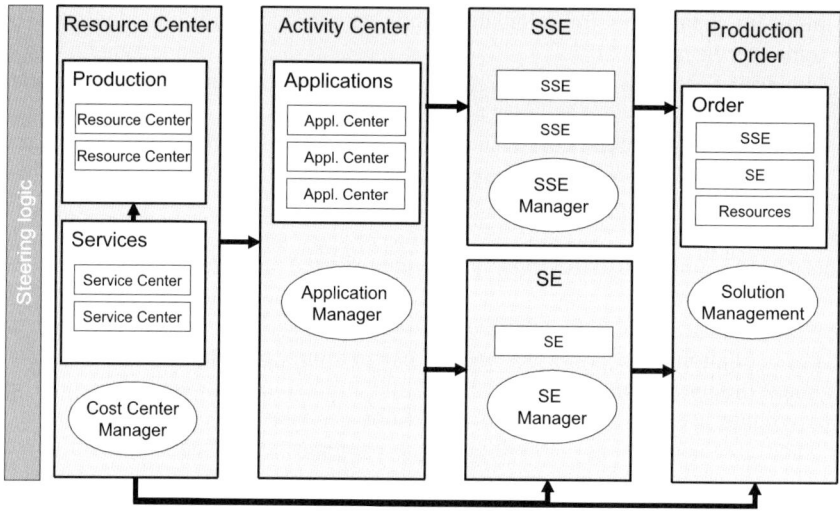

Fig. 12.3. Steering logic for IT service cost controlling

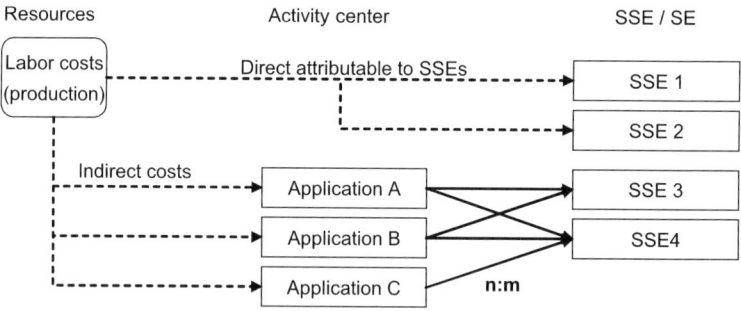

Fig. 12.4. Cost assignment relationships between activity centers and (S)SEs (IT-Services)

In this case, activity centers describe the application landscape of the IT service provider. This point was particularly important, because the granularity level of activity centers determine calculation accuracy and measurement precision. In terms of management aspects, the application manager is responsible for the efficient use of resources.

The third step of the distribution process is to assign activity center costs to (standard) service elements, such as bill fulfillment or payment processing. SSEs are handled as cost elements. Activity drivers are the mathematical rate for distributing all activity center costs to cost elements. Because there are n:m relationships between (S)SEs and applications – one SSE can use multiple applications and one application can support multiple SSEs – a special activity driver was developed (see Fig. 12.4). The driver is based on transaction volumes and the aggregated capacity of the utilized activity center. Table 12.2 shows the calculation of five activity drivers.

Table 12.2. Calculation of activity drivers

Activity center	SSE / SE	Transaction volume (T)	Activity driver (D)
Application A	SSE 1	100.000	33,3
	SSE 2	200.000	66,6
Application B	SSE 1	100.000	16,6
	SSE 2	200.000	33,3
	SSE 3	300.000	50,0

For example, if an application A is utilized by two standard service elements – one and two – the activity driver D for SSE 1 is calculated as follows:

$$D_{A,SSE1} = \frac{T_{SSE1}}{\sum_{i=1}^{n} T_n} * 100$$

The final step is to calculate the dedicated production orders. Production orders are bundles of SSEs and SEs that are individualized for customers. In the end, production orders reflect the total cost of production and development processes for a bundle of IT services. The calculation contains all costs incurred by the affected application systems, personnel, facilities, electricity etc. – such as licenses costs, monitoring and maintenance costs (in the form of labor costs).

Project costs
Another challenge was to distribute project costs to resource and activity centers, as well as to service elements and production orders. The company decided to collect and distribute project costs at four different levels:
- resource-center level: all project costs for training employees or for designing and implementing a new steering logic are collected. Projects at this level affect more than one activity center or SSE.
- activity-center level: here, projects have a direct reference to one application. A link to one customer or SSE is not possible. Software development projects are a good example.
- (standard) service-element level: projects have a link to one IT service. For example, project costs for IT service engineering tasks.
- production-order level: project costs are attributable to one customer.

Results
The new IT controlling system, based on the ABC methodology, enables the management of the service provider to view the IT operations in terms of how IT resources are consumed in sourcing, production and delivery processes. This infor-

mation helps the responsible managers to monitor and control different aspects of management, such as capacity utilization, optimization of production and marketing activities, as well as the emendation of sales activities and unit cost calculations. Another interesting "add-on" is that the budgeting process could be improved, because of the increase in the traceability and precision of information at the IT services level. In, addition customer demands for IT services can be incorporated in the budgeting process.

12.4.3 Financial Analysis and Business Analysis

There are several techniques around for evaluating health of software engineering projects and portfolios. We will briefly characterize both financial and **business analyses** as well as more technical assessments. For more details we refer to [Reif02].
- **Break-even analysis**. When will accumulated costs and benefits or returns match each other? From when onwards will there be positive cash flow?
- **Investment analysis**. Which investment will provide most returns in the short-term? Common techniques include ROI, ROA and ROCE.
- **Value analysis**. Which benefits will occur in the future and what is their net present value compared to outstanding investments? Which of several alternative decisions will generate the most value? This technique is often used to assess the risk level of technology decisions.
- **Sensitiveness**. What are the effects of project- and product-related parameters that are under your control (e.g., resource allocation to projects, technologies to be utilized, content of projects, make versus reuse versus buy decisions for components and platforms)?
- **Trend analysis**. What is the evolution of impacts over time? Are there cyclic effects that with some delay change the entire picture? Portraying current decisions and their future impacts over time is necessary prior to platform or product-line decisions.

12.5. Strategic and Operational Management

12.5.1 Portfolio Management

Portfolio management is the collection and evaluation of product or project information and the decision based on the totality of all these products or projects in order to maximize their value for the enterprise. This includes the following aspects (Fig. 12.5):
- building an inventory of the overall software engineering assets in terms of products, reusable software, ongoing projects and their opportunities, employees, and so on

12.5 Strategic and Operational Management

- continuous evaluation of new opportunities in comparison with ongoing activities
- combined evaluation of static and dynamic assets (e.g., platforms, tools versus skills and customers)
- deciding which resources will be allocated in the (near) future to which assets and opportunities

Portfolio management in software projects means assessing all projects continuously and in totality. It is not a project review and should, in fact, not be mixed with regular tracking and oversight. It means that costs and benefits, contents and roadmaps, threats, risks and opportunities are evaluated comprehensively in order to implement a coherent strategy. It is independent of the size of the enterprise. To simplify the definition: Portfolio management is the project management of the totality of all projects, services or product releases.

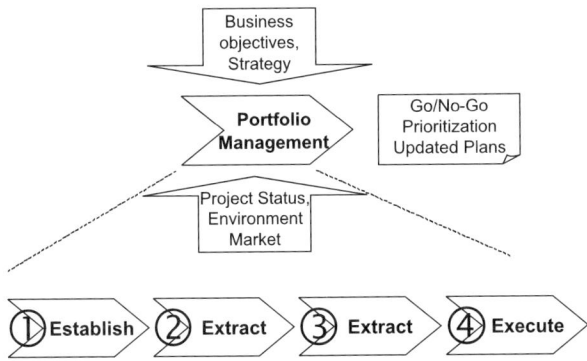

Fig. 12.5. Four steps towards portfolio management following the E4–measurement process as introduced in Chap. 2

Good portfolio management will help to allocate resources in the best possible way, to reduce the number of projects to what is effective and to improve the communication between projects, departments, and functional areas in the company. It also allows management to pull the emergency brake earlier, if necessary. It will normally save around 5-10% of the software engineering budget as the people working on the projects that provide the biggest yield [Meta02, CIO03].

What is the difference between portfolio management and project management? Project management means doing the project the right way. Portfolio management means doing the right projects.

The major bridge from portfolio management to projects and vice versa is the business case. It summarizes – before the launch of the project – the technical, marketing and commercial inputs to make a decision on a business proposal and to later follow up against key assumptions. A business case combines three elements, a business vision or concept of a solution, a concrete and quantitative value proposition and a commercial or marketing positioning.

Is there a difference between managing an IT portfolio (e.g., internal applications and business processes) and managing the portfolio of software engineering projects and products? The questions one asks and the applied techniques are definitely the same. Are scarce resources allocated to the right activities? Are the short- and medium-term targets well balanced? Do they line up with the strategy and with the way the enterprise now earns and will make money in the future? What could engineering or IT do to make the enterprise more profitable? These questions apply across the entire scope of software engineering activities.

Typical evaluation criteria in portfolio management include:
- Risk (probability of success) vs. reward (NPV, benefits after years of launch, market value)
- Innovativeness (technical vs. market)
- Ease (technical feasibility) vs. attractiveness (growth potential, consumer appeal, general attractiveness, life-cycle)
- Strengths (competitive position) vs. attractiveness (market growth, technical maturity, years to implementation)
- Cost (cost to implement) vs. timing (time to impact)
- Strategy (strategic focus or fit) vs. benefits (business intent, NPV, financial fit, attractiveness)
- Cost (cumulative development cost) vs. benefit (cumulative reward)

A small example will show how such evaluations work in practice (see Fig. 12.6). The objective in that example is to evaluate all ongoing projects (i.e., new product introduction, maintenance, service) in one context by the same committee.

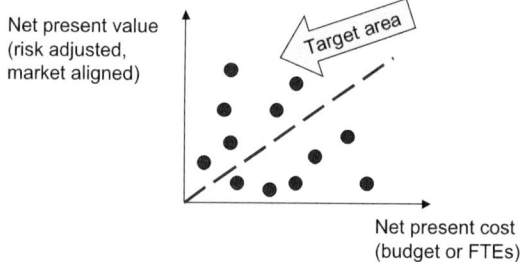

Fig. 12.6. Example for software project portfolio evaluation according to the two criteria of value and cost

The process consists of several steps you can easily introduce into your own portfolio management process:
1. Define the objectives to be achieved (here to optimize the value, such as margin, compared to cost)
2. Extract the information from all your projects. Build in repeatability by using standard indicators
3. Enter all your projects in a two-dimensional system, relating objectives to each other (e.g., net present value over net present cost)

4. Evaluate the projects according to the objective. The same questions are asked for each below-target area project: Is project strategically relevant? Does it bring different value proposition than NPV?
5. Execute according to the results of the evaluation. If above question is answered negatively: Relocate resources to accelerate projects in target area. Keep projects as a reserve for overruns or buffer for cost cuts.

We will look at an example with only five software projects in the portfolio that can be influenced (Fig. 12.7). We will first use the classic picture of a portfolio [Benk03] which is very easy to utilize for software engineering projects. Obviously we need to consider market information to avoid the case in which engineering projects are judged by an engineering perspective only. The matrix shows the projects in three dimensions, namely the relative market share, the market growth and the internal – still expected – net present value of the investment (the size of the bubbles). The idiomatic "stars" and "cash cows" represent the standard vocabulary and relate to the perceived potential of certain matrix elements.

Fig. 12.7 suggests that projects 4 and 5 need more support while project 1 should be stopped. It is also evident that this portfolio is not healthy: it is not sustainable because in no area there is a benefit from high market share and high market growth. In the case of smaller companies who do not know their exact market position, other indicators could be used to indicate their position. Market growth should be used in any case, as it provides an external view on the business evolution.

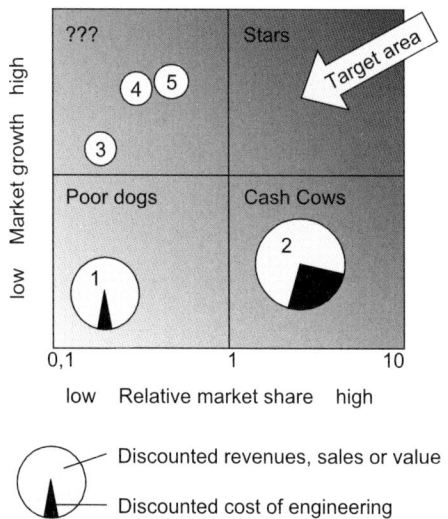

Fig. 12.7. A simple set-up of a portfolio layout for different software products

Often, it is necessary to derive from several of the above-mentioned analysis techniques and the resulting timelines even-more-distant representations of the portfolio matrix just to play with the impact of different alternatives. This holds not only when deciding on technology frameworks or product-line content but also if the company serves and depends on a few customers (or suppliers) whose future one might want to assess in order to make more informed project and portfolio analyses for the company's future.

Evaluating software engineering projects is only valid if all projects and possible decisions around those projects are portrayed in the same larger picture. The prominent review approach is still that project reviews are done in isolation for each project. This is necessary to judge whether the project will deliver what were the agreed assumptions at project start. But they must be accompanied by a look to the totality of the projects. Often there are ripple effects caused by shared resources, suppliers, technology or platforms. A good way to relate such dependent management decisions in multi-project constraints is to hierarchically cluster the projects based on mutual dependencies or synergies. Such cluster analysis takes away the risk of overly fast aggregation and the comparison of apples to pears.

We will look at another example to see how software engineering decisions depend on market evolution (Fig. 12.8). We portray five different product lines or clusters of related products and product releases. The matrix in Fig. 12.8 shows all five product-lines in three dimensions, namely revenue growth, market growth, and net present value of investments (size of circles). The picture shows that product line 1 should be cashed in with a reduced budget, product line 2 needs to be reduced, product line 3 needs increased investments, product line 4 can stay as it is, and product line 5 should be sold or killed.

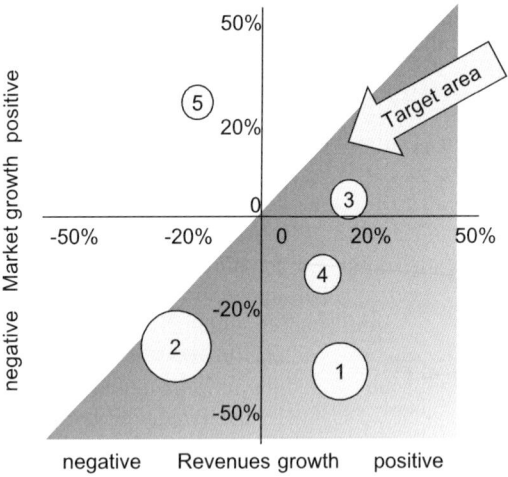

Fig. 12.8. A portfolio map to help in deciding to which software engineering projects to allocate scarce resources

The environment and scenarios under evaluation determine the ways one can interfere and impact decisions. The interfaces are certainly different as is the proximity to the customers and markets. If you are engaged in the engineering of products (e.g., embedded systems, applications, solutions, and so on), one will influence the product strategy, the feature roadmap, the technology mix, the software

12.5 Strategic and Operational Management

processes and their interfaces to business processes. For internal applications and services (i.e., IT activities) you influence business processes and their automation, integration, cost or service levels.

> Portfolio management looks on today's decisions and their impact on the evolution and value of the portfolio in the future. Previous investment is only considered to learn from results, not to judge because of the amount of money that has been invested.

Many errors in making assumptions and decisions can be avoided when looking into previous similar situations and scenarios. However, the investment decisions of today consider only the required further investment and effects in future. What is already paid is "sunk" cost.

> Portfolios must be aligned with strategy and business needs. It is of no use having many projects with most of them delivering sub-optimal margins.

Portfolio management ensures focus and thus helps to move to the top. Alignment varies depending on how much senior management walks the talk. Here some indicators for your own assessment:

- **Weak alignment**: Various initiatives and goals are managed and owned by different organizations. There is little or no coordination of progress, budget or projects between them. The corporate level is basically clueless and just refers to vague intentions.
- **Medium alignment**: The company has agreed a set of common and shared goals that are broken down per department. However, departments are not synchronized and do not have implementation plans. Managers are not measured on results that they control.
- **Strong alignment**: The company has set concrete and hierarchically consistent objectives (e.g., cost reduction by a defined number per year). Plans and technology roadmaps are integrated with these goals and periodically followed ensemble. Managers and staff share KPI's around these objectives.

If challenged with deciding to discontinue a software engineering project, look into what is still required for completion and compare this with the returns from sales once the project is finished. Compare this project with other projects in the software portfolio and evaluate their individual costs and benefits as of today to see which is underperforming. Future investment and returns are always discounted into "present value" to allow for comparison from today's perspective.

> Portfolio management needs measurements that go beyond the single project. They must emphasize the overall assets of the enterprise, its strategy and the business assumptions and reality of all these assets.
> A few checks help to diagnose your portfolio:

> - Is the portfolio aligned with my strategy? How do you measure?
> - How well is the portfolio performing? According to which measurements?
> - What is the overall risk exposure of products and projects? Is it in line with the strategic and operational assumptions? Can the enterprise cope with the risk level? Are there measurements in place that flag risk and how it relates to value?
> - In which projects should you invest and why? For how long?
> - What amount of the budget is spent on new and innovative products, how much on legacy? Is this good or bad?
> - What are the priority projects? Are there any priorities?
> - What are the top three portfolio risks? Do they always come back?
> - How many customers come back to buy more?

12.5.2 Technology Management

How can software measurements be effectively used for technology management? We will apply the above-mentioned steps of extraction, evaluation and execution to the decision-making process of introducing new or even disruptive technologies.

First, you need to extract data that describes what the technology means for you and your business. Running with each new technology because of its hype is certainly not the answer. Moreover, it is expensive too. The major question to ask in this first step is what the new or disruptive technologies are. Many enterprises or R&D departments have only vague answers. A good indicator to identify such "hot" technologies is to simply check what provides the most confrontations and disputes inside the company. Do the software people dispute on a technology with marketing? Do customers challenge the sales or technology people with proposals that were not yet included in the roadmap?

The second step naturally is the evaluation. What are the impacts of this specific technology? Are there alternative technologies to which it should be compared?

Similar to the case with the product portfolio, you also need to picture the products and markets that are addressed in a spectrum of different technologies. Questions are rarely as simple as asking whether one would introduce Java or a specific framework or tool, and they should not be asked in such isolated mode. It is better to identify what the technologies mean in a specific environment and in the context of other technologies. At what speed do they evolve? How much energy do other companies or leading players put into it?

For instance, open source development and especially Linux or Eclipse became a major effort with companies like Sun and IBM engaging hundreds of people in it, and educating their sales forces what that means for the future of software engineering. What will such new technologies substitute? Are there examples from one's own past or that are externally available that indicate how a similar technology change came up and evolved? Such questions need to be addressed in technology management to evaluate scenarios before engaging into one.

12.5 Strategic and Operational Management

Finally, the third step is to decide on the technologies. What will be the answer to this new technology? One possible answer which might be the safe side regarding risk and cost, is to decide firmly to wait for one period or one year. This is legitimate to avoid being consumed by continuous fads. Or one might decide for a very small and limited pilot project to see how a dedicated service might relate to the application development.

Consider for example Web services which initially were exaggerated. However, after a two-year period with shaping of major standardization bodies and industrial groups, it re-emerged as a more solid technology, with early applications being available for trial and for linking to one's own infrastructure. Which market or customer or user needs the technology first? How much would they be willing to pay for it? How is a new feature positioned? Which investments are devoted to it? Which type of pilots or experiments? When do you expect concrete results or further decision points?

We have summarized in Fig. 12.9 how different points within the life-cycle trajectory of a technology would yield different evaluations and decisions. We distinguish the typical four distinct phases that characterize the technology life-cycle [Bowe95]. For each of these phases we apply a different strategy.

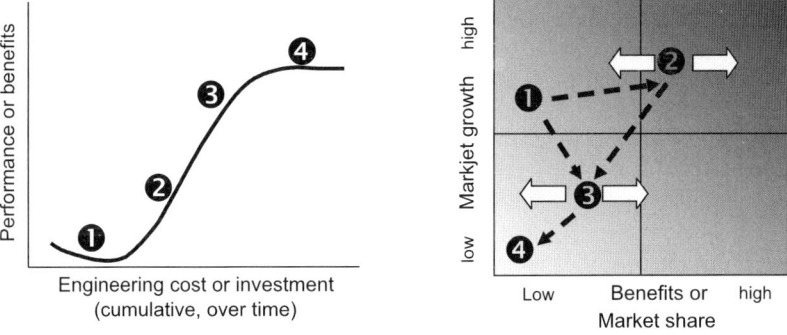

1. experimentation (learning curve, investment, low pay-off => decide next steps)
2. growth (benefits grow fast, market positioning happens => invest if in favor)
3. saturation (technology applied by many players, efficiency improvements
   => reduce investments depending on market position, get out returns)
4. end of life (technology becomes a legacy => manage maintenance, phase-out)

Fig. 12.9. Portfolio management and technology management

Starting from the experimental or "hype" phase (point 1), the technology can evolve on different tracks. If it appears with many open questions or unresolved constraints (e.g., Web services; points 1 and 2), one should take enough time to not bet on the wrong horse. This is at times difficult, because the engineers might be very excited. However, one can spend the engineering money only once, and do not want to engage into the war of the big companies who only drive their proprietary formats. If the technology change and its impact are very fast and determined (e.g., embedded mobile applications), one should find the own position before the market and the customers conclude that the company is not in this field (points 2 and 3).

Often such legacy behavior affects leaders in a technology because all their focus is on improving the existing technology and fine-tuning its application, rather than on questioning it in favor of newer technology. Finally, each technology will reach the point where retreat is in order (point 4). To miss this exit point is also expensive because one must provide skills and resources for maintenance, thereby taking them from innovations. Product lines that are in such situation have too many old products and lots of branches in their roadmaps. That is how the different techniques of portfolio management will help. An evaluation of where you are with respect to market position, market growth, revenues or age of products gives a good indicator of how much priority to give for a new technology.

> Managing technologies and their evolution needs a combination of business related measurements and technology or infrastructure measurement.
> The following checks provide guidance for selecting the right measurements:
> - How does the technology portfolio look like? How do different used technologies relate to the "hype cycle"? Are there sufficient new technologies to fill the pipeline for modern products?
> - How is technology translated into business success?
> - How is technology value measured? Do you simply accumulate technologies and select arbitrarily? Or is there a valuation based on patents or product age?
> - Which technologies contribute mostly to product success – today and next year?
> - What are the technology assumptions? Do they fulfill? Do they fulfill as a rule or exceptionally?
> - In which technologies should you invest and why? For how long?
> - What percentage of technologies misses the initial assumptions? Why?
> - Are engineering skills mapping to the technology needs of new products or projects?
> - What is the customer perception on the technology skills in the company?

12.5.3 Product and Release Management

In today's competitive markets it is of utmost interest to have winning products. The success of any product depends on product and release management. Projects do not run independently; they influence each other in various dimensions. For instance, they share skills from the same resource pool and they compete for the best skills with all other projects. They might build on each other, especially in product-line architectures or in multi-release contracts. They might reuse common components or frameworks, or they simply address the same customers, both internally and externally. Fig. 12.10. shows such dependencies for a single product line where there are releases for markets or customers but also technologies that

12.5 Strategic and Operational Management

are developed in parallel to drive innovative features. These dependencies must be carefully planned and managed to avoid fragmentation and cost overruns.

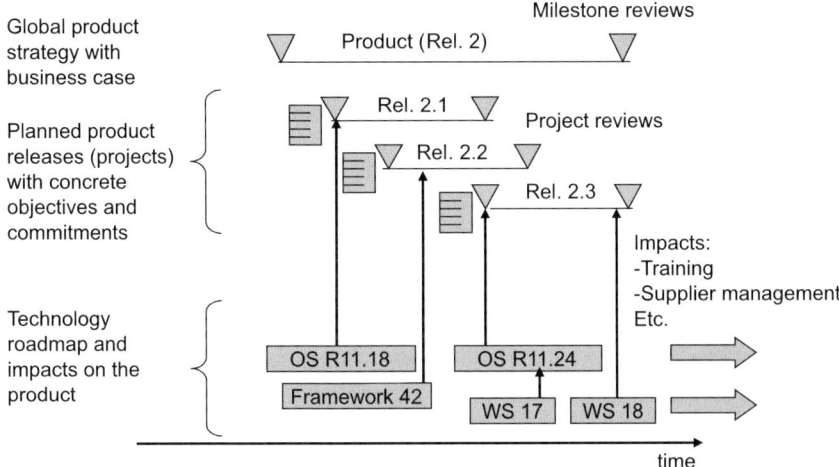

Fig. 12.10. Planning releases, dependencies and roadmaps

Too often projects or product releases fail due to misunderstanding or misinterpreting customer needs and later on coping with associated changes. In a recent meeting with Chinese product managers they claimed that there are continuous changes because of European interference on the requirements. Back in Europe local product managers in another product line asserted that it is impossible to closely follow the variety of politics and relationships in China. An American senior manager pointed out that his unit could do very well – if only the European and Asian regional sales would follow his roadmap and not continuously disturb it. These attitudes relate to the title of this study, because a successful product manager has to balance projects, people and politics. His primary tools are requirements, gate reviews and the business case. Looking only to technical aspects, like many product managers are doing might help to master technical projects and interact well with engineering staff. However, these product managers will continuously blame "politics" for not achieving their missions.

In particular, product lines and multi-release dependencies ask for transparent and consistent roadmap management of the overarching evolution of all products and projects in the enterprise. We can consider this yet another interface between project and business management. We already explained the hierarchical dependencies between portfolio, product line, product release and individual project. A dependable release roadmap and excellent project management are critical success factors for good portfolio management.

> Dependable or accountable means that agreed-upon milestones, contents or quality targets are maintained as committed.

For instance, within a product-line architecture the underlying generic product, platform or components, upon which many customization products build, must be on time and provide the agreed contents. Otherwise, there will be numerous ripple effects. Naturally, project management techniques differ between a generic and an application product. While the platform has to build in resource buffers, the application product can easily work with feature prioritization and time boxing. Measurement will ensure that the milestones, content and quality are quantitatively planned and their accuracy is monitored.

> Do not try to be overly perfect in planning! It will cost a lot of extra money.

If the target is zero overruns, projects will take much longer to get started because managers (who are measured on such success) will try to perfectly analyze the requirements. They also will build in extra buffers. Both concepts are costly and dangerous – except that the contract date at hand is mission-critical such as in some military or service business (e.g., installing a service in due time for a specific event). Having broad empirical data on project success available we evaluated this question quantitatively. Business case validity seems to be optimal with 5-10% delays. Zero is overly expensive and beyond 10% decreases customer satisfaction. A common trade-off in this picture is contract or requirements changes demanded by the customer (or by sales / marketing) which will make projects a bit late but add marginal value for the customer. Engineering and product development performance targets must be set realistically in order to be accepted and show business value.

The following steps during setting up a release roadmap will help to improve its performance and predictability:
- Identify key needs across markets and technologies. Demand from stakeholders the valuation of key requirements.
- Coin a product vision with essential features mapped to releases. Set up and evaluate the business case and the major business drivers.
- Evaluate requirements depending on customer value, cost structure, complexity in development and maintenance, dependencies across releases or technologies, extendibility, or internal life-cycle cost.
- Define releases by mapping key features to releases.
- Describe and maintain a more detailed technology and skills roadmap. Determine dependencies, cost / investment, priorities and major milestones. Indicate which skills are relevant to be created or enhanced in order to master technology needs. Consider technologies demanded by customers.
- Decide and communicate within the entire company which products, platforms, features or even markets are active which are on their phase-out and for which you have effectively stopped support.
- Use time-boxing, incremental and agile techniques to focus on major requirements and stay predictable. Track progress with earned value based on integrated requirements.
- Set concrete time-to-profit targets for increments and releases. Trigger re-evaluation if they are not met.

- Use clean change management for the release roadmap. Never agree to changes without a formal decision process.

Organizations on the capability maturity model's (CMMI) initial maturity level 1 (or simply not using it) will mostly fail with keeping release commitments (see also Chap. 10). Most of their projects run in firefighting mode, and predictability is not known. With each project being managed ad-hoc and without learning effects, scalability between projects does not exist. What exists are dependencies of the form that resources are taken away from a project to satisfy more urgent needs in another projects. This, however, is done in a rather chaotic way. Such organizations first need to improve their project management before moving to release management. But, some of the mentioned principles will help – in the smaller context of single projects – to become reliably and to learn to say yes or no only after the business impacts are known.

Effective product and release management benefits from the techniques described before in project, portfolio and technology management.
Specifically the following questions should be addressed with measurements:
- What are the business case assumptions? Do they suffice? Do they satisfy as a rule or exceptionally?
- What percentage of products misses deadlines? Why?
- How productive are engineering and research resources? Is productivity improving?
- How much overtime is spent relative to total headcount?
- What is the field performance and quality of the products? Are critical defects closed in due time?
- Do the products contribute to business success or risks of customers?
- What is the customer satisfaction? What trend is visible for key accounts and new accounts?
- Is marketing or sales promoting unavailable products? How are they synchronized with engineering?

12.5.4 Distributed Teams and Global Software Engineering

Increasingly software is developed by distributed teams – often in different continents and occupied by different companies. It is hard to find software that is genuinely developed by a single company at one place, except start-up situations but even then, they typically source components from partners or use open source software. Mostly it is components that are sourced from external suppliers. But often it is engineers that are sourced into the development, such as outsourcing or global engineering teams. Basic concepts of global software engineering and lessons learned are detailed and discussed in [Eber06b].

Global software engineering (GSE) is the consequence of the rather friction-free economic principles of the entire software industry. Basically any code can be developed at any place in the world and made visible and accessible to any other place in the world at virtually the same time. There are not many overheads in distribution or industrialization as long as source code is shared. Many companies start global development due to perceived cost differences. Achieved cost reductions are furtheron delivered to customers which means competitive pressure for those enterprises not yet embarking on global development. Further advantages appear when intensifying GSE, such as more flexible work hours of engineers and a demand-oriented provisioning of skills. Starting with smaller chunks of work, GSE intensifies towards globalizing the execution of entire business processes or products. Innovative products are created due to having more capacity and more efficient workflows. Product life-cycles and technology growth will further accelerate due to this increasing innovation driven by GSE. The principle as such is amplified and will not allow any enterprise to exit.

Looking to pure labor cost for comparable skills of educated IT-engineers, several Asian countries offer a rate of 10-40% of what is paid for the same work time in Western Europe or USA. On top, they offer such a huge number of skilled and highly motivated engineers that it is impossible to not consider such potential for project planning. The 2006 ACM Job Migration Task Force report on globalization and software offshoring [Aspr06] underlines that globalization of the software industry will further increase driven by both information technology itself (e.g., sills and technology demands, market evolutions in emerging economies), by government actions (e.g., moving into IT sectors to reduce dependencies from raw materials such as in China) and by economic factors (e.g., labor cost differences). With labor cost contributing to software development cost with two thirds and more, the savings should be in the range of 50%. That is at least what you can read in the newspapers. Reality has it that the savings are much lower, and this is where measurements and controlling come into the picture.

Many global software projects fail. Global development projects do not fail because of incompetent suppliers, project managers or engineers working on these projects; neither do they fail because of insufficient methods or tools. Primarily they fail because of the use of insufficient processes and wrong management techniques [Eber06b]. Processes and management techniques derived and built on experience from small collocated projects are inadequate for monitoring global software development. As a result, service level agreements are not met and the delivered software is late, of low quality and of much higher cost than originally estimated.

Global development projects fail if tasks are broken down too much, such as asking a remote engineer doing the verification for software develop concurrently in another site [Carm99, Carm01]. Here distance effects and lack of direct communication slow down development rather than helping it. The single biggest source of difficulties in GSE is related to communication across sites, bad communication hindering both coordination and insufficient management processes [Cram05, Kris04]. For instance, continuous integration of insufficiently verified and encapsulated software components fails if done remote to the parallel ongoing software development. Distributed teams working on exactly the same topic (e.g., the famous follow-the-sun pattern of developing a piece of software in different time zones) pose highest challenges for coordination and often resulted in severe overheads that would be measurable or tangible only later (e.g., features misinterpreted, insufficient quality, lack of ownership and responsibility, and so on).

Fig. 12.11 gives an example how different global development scenarios impact the project cost drivers. The first scenario (top) shows cost for a fully collocated development. Evidently, there are no interface overheads because the team is sitting at one place. With an assumed total effort of 10.000 person hours for a standard project we find the distribution as depicted in the top part of the diagram. Total cost is the 10.000 cost entities (assuming that one person hour equally one cost entity). With a globally distributed development in two sites, the picture changes. We assume here a cost ratio of 30% per net person hour if work is done in a low cost country. While absolute effort (for simplicity) is kept unchanged and primarily design, project management and interface management are handled in the two sites, we face a total of 11.500 person hours (due to the overheads of working at two sites), however a cost reduction of 18% towards 8.200 cost entities. With a fully offshored development (design and test) that preserves only the upstream activities in the high cost country, the total effort further stabilizes at 10.500 person hours, but with a total cost of only half the original cost, namely 4.800 cost entities.

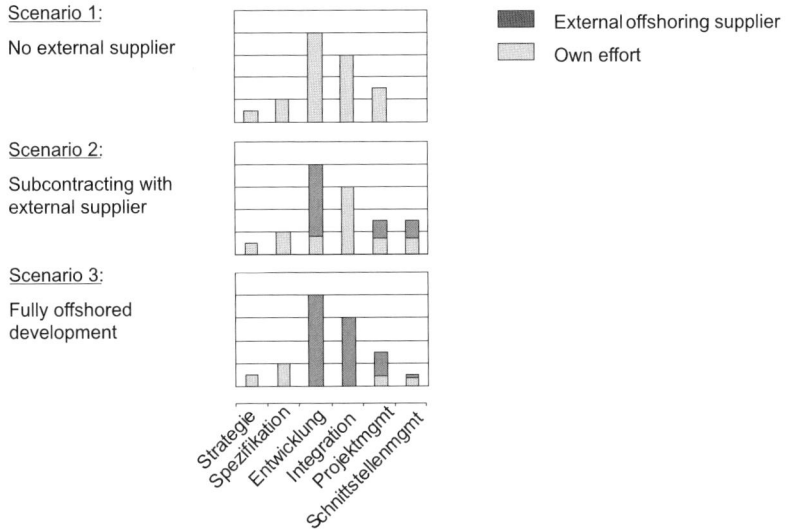

Fig. 12.11. Cost structure of different global development modes with same underlying project

The worst scenario in terms of performance is the scenario 2 with split work across sites or subcontracting of labor to an external supplier with unclear work split. We had done a study of projects at Alcatel where we could distinguish according to the factor of collocation and allocation degree [Eber01b]. Collocated teams achieve an efficiency improvement during initial validation activities of over 50 percent. With the same number of initial defects after code complete they would need half the effort for removing residual defects for a defined quality level at the exit gate. Small projects with highly scattered resources show less than half the productivity compared to projects with fully allocated staff. Similar effects can be observed for quality, schedule accuracy or cycle time.

Monitoring cost, progress and performance of global software projects is a control activity concerned with identifying, measuring, accumulating, analyzing and interpreting project information for planning and tracking activities, decision-making, and cost accounting. Project (or supplier) monitoring and control is the basic tool for gaining insight into project performance and is more than only ensuring the overall technical correctness of a project. Global projects or supplier sourcing is typically done with two different methods for the project level and for the contract level.

Project level: Project monitoring and tracking is done with techniques such as earned value, budget adherence, schedule adherence, project reviews, and so on. Traditional project tracking looked to actual results against plans, where the plans would be adjusted after the facts indicate that they are not reachable. This method creates too many delays and is not sufficiently precise to drive concrete corrective actions on the spot. For global development projects, such monitoring often means that difficulties accumulate too long. Therefore, continuous predictions should be used to relate actual constraints and performance to historical performance results. Good forecasts allow adjusting plans and mitigating risks long before the actual performance tracking measurements would visualize such results. For instance, knowing about average mean time to defect allows planning for maintenance staff, help desk and support centers, or service level agreements.

Contract level: Contracts are absolutely crucial for managing external suppliers. The must include Service Level Agreements (SLA) with defined targets, threshold values, and so on for deliverables, schedules, reaction time of services, quality levels and expenses. Quality criteria are defined by outages, downtime, number of service requests, residual defects in the subsequent phase or by phase-end or hand-over criteria. These targets must be measurable. Independently of the global collaboration model or contract model is established with suppliers, it is key to set the right targets and set them as performance indicators for R&D the management in each location. SLAs are set up at the beginning of a contract (or even for a long-term frame contract) and controlled continuously on the supplier side and periodically on the buyer side. For internally hosted GSE it might be wise (depending on organization structure) to govern by means of internal contracts and SLAs. They have the big advantage that targets and measurements are agreed upfront and would not need continuous debates with senior management if some delivery is late. Certainly such internal contracts and SLAs together with a culture of accountability and clearly assigned responsibility also avoid the political game of finger pointing to "the others" that did not do their job well.

A final word on work allocation and ownership. Shifting coherent activities (e.g., design and verification of related work products) to low-cost countries is highly inefficient. Often tasks are overly fragmented and the quality control activities are handled with poor results due to lack of knowledge. In the end each delivery has to be checked twice, at the time it is shipped to a low-cost country and then again backwards. All this costs time and money – and it demotivates engineers on both sides, as it always ends up in ping-pong. As said before, we strongly recommend building teams preferably in one place and assigning them ownership for a work product including functionality and quality. Such teams should operate globally according to needs and skills availability, but not be internally split into first and second-class engineering tasks.

> Global software engineering and sourcing need the traditional project monitoring activities combined with contract level supervision.
> Measurements include the following dimensions:
> - Project launch: feasibility analysis, requirements quality, process capability (own and that of external or offshore organizations).
> - Results against plan: earned value, budget adherence, schedule adherence, global development teams performance, site productivity.
> - Quality: detected defects per activity, residual defects, reliability forecasts.
> - Forecasts: cost to complete, time to complete.
> - Supplier contracts: service level agreements, cost evolution, productivity and quality of suppliers, performance evolution, supplier rating.
> These different dimensions should be considered when setting up contracts and SLAs (be it internally with distributed development or externally with suppliers).

12.5.5 Supplier Management

With an increasing amount of software components and resources acquired from an external supplier, professional supplier agreement management is a core activity of any project manager and controller. We will here look at supplier management from the perspective of controlling activities that ensure visibility throughout a project. Fig. 12.12 shows the relevant phases along the product life-cycle and the respective activities related to supplier management. Four major phases are distinguished, namely supplier strategy, supplier selection, contract management, and relationship management. The figure shows typical work products that must be available at these phases.

Initially an individual client or customer organization must provide a realistic and precise expectation of functional and nonfunctional requirements (e.g., reliability). They should clearly state that payment will be provided only for systems that meet the agreed upon functionality (e.g., requirements, acceptance tests, SLA conditions). They should demand require milestone presentations of progress for continued funding.

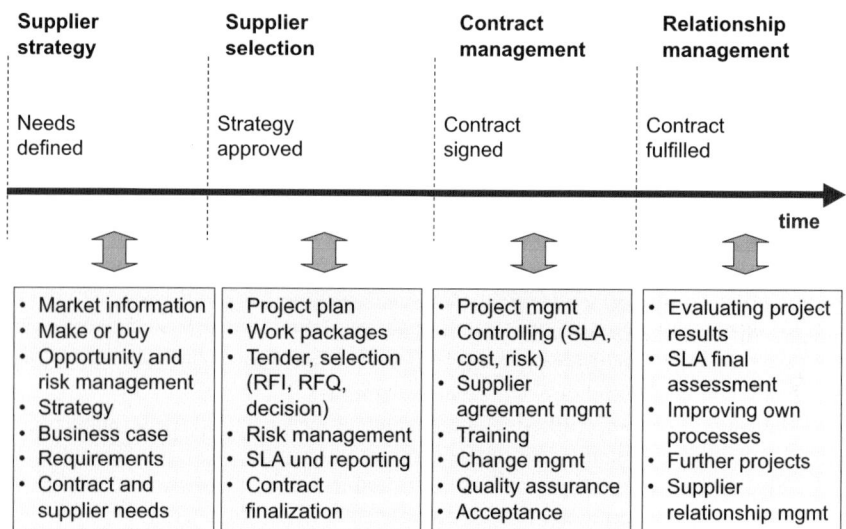

Fig. 12.12. Supplier agreement management across the entire sourcing cycle

Supplier organizations on the other hand must insist on a signed contract with requirements. They must agree before contract execution on clear and reasonable acceptance criteria. The contract must be explicit that the supplier owns the software until final payment. They must clearly agree on liabilities and support after handover. They have to express disagreement and unrealistic conditions openly and not continue with diverging assumptions. They should always strive for win-win results and therefore offer compromise approaches, once needs are understood. In case of component delivery they should include a software key that will operate after the date of contracted software acceptance.

Supplier monitoring is done similarly to what we described in the chapter on global software engineering and sourcing, namely on project and on contract levels. Responsibilities might be split in your company so that the project manager observes the contract execution in his own project and scope (e.g., deliverables, cost control, quality levels, schedule), while a procurement and sourcing manager holds responsible for the overall contract execution and observing that conditions from the frame contract are fulfilled.

As a supplier you should strive for high maturity, for several reasons, primarily:
- The market attractiveness in software-driven industries is extremely high, due to low entry barriers and continuous push for innovative products. You are in strong global competition for excellence.
- Suppliers have recognized that better process maturity ensures better schedule and SLA performance, productivity and quality. Why should not they demand it along their supply chain.
- High market attractiveness continues to push to cost reduction and efficiency improvement. Many new entries start each day with similar business ideas that drive your own company. If you do not continuously improve both products

and processes, they will do it. The best example is the move of high-technology products to Asia, as there is a much higher competitive pressure for high process maturity than in North America or Europe.

Fig. 12.13 summarizes these dependencies between supplier and client process maturity. The win-win situation within a supply chain is driven by moving to high maturity in both dimensions. A low maturity supplier will eventually be replaced for the reasons given before. A low maturity client working with a high-maturity supplier will face extra cost and overheads and thus try to move upwards at fast pace. This move is fueled by the client's own market pressure from competitors that are already optimizing their product development processes. The upper left and lower right quadrants therefore are no stable plateau but will always create forces and momentum towards the upper right quadrant – thus sustaining a win-win relationship between supplier and client.

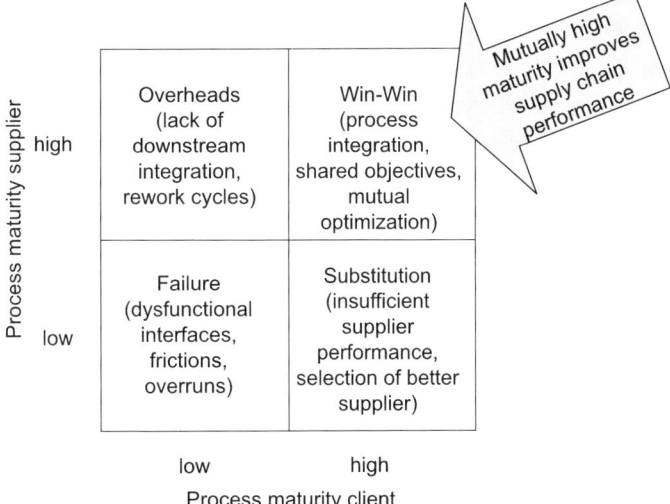

Fig. 12.13. The supplier-client relationship benefits from high maturity on both sides.

As a client you should always consider the golden rule of supplier management: You pay for what you get. Do not get trapped into contracts that look "cheap" and later bring tons of extra cost due to lousy processes and insufficient delivery quality. Preconditions of any successful supplier management are good processes on both sides, i.e., for the client and the supplier. Insufficient client processes cannot be externalized. They will not scale up from a single site to several sites. Often those low-maturity processes can be handled in localized development without many overheads due to collocated teams, but will fail with globalization.

If your own processes (as a client) are on a CMMI maturity level 1 or 2 you better ask for a consultant who can help you in installing effective engineering and management processes. Most suppliers offer such support, but this is not necessarily a sustainable solution, as they have different interest and business models. Independent how your processes look like, it is relevant to review them carefully with your suppliers and agree interfaces on work product, engineering and tools level. The exchange of information must be carefully planned. A change management tool is not enough. It needs rules for documentation, design reviews, change management boards, and so on. Install workflow management and online accessible project, work product and process information to ensure proper knowledge management. Interactive process models, such as RUP and others have proven very helpful to communicate and install processes [Eber03a, Royc98].

Effective supplier management is very much depending on the measurement capabilities of an organization. Too often suppliers are believed to deliver according to specifications and SLA, and suddenly the client realizes that this was mere wishful thinking.

Here some concrete measurement-oriented hints:
- Set up clear and measurable service level agreements. Ensure that this SLA contains all that matters for you in the contract.
- Insist on periodic reporting according to the SLA.
- From the beginning define thresholds that establish when and how insufficient performance will be escalated.
- Measure supplier capability or demand such measurement based on industry standards, such as CMMI.
- As a supplier or customer move towards high maturity product development by using the CMMI and its maturity level 3-5 concepts of process excellence and quantitative management. Do not stagnate on maturity levels 1-3 as you will be eventually replaced.
- Relate value you receive from suppliers to the risk and cost of the delivered services or components. Manage the risk of lock-in and dependencies that could create extra risk and cost.
- Implement contract evaluation after each single project. Go beyond the qualitative checklist and report into measurements and fact-based lessons-learned.

12.6. Hints for the Practitioner

Let us summarize some of the relevant experiences with controlling in IT and software projects and portfolios:
- Plan what you are doing and compare the plan with the actual performance. Controlling is a tool to ensure you reach what you have planned. Start with a vision and clear objectives of what to expect. Define appropriate measurement to sere at any time how your activities contribute to progress and how progress means value. Progress that is not linked to upfront objectives and a clear vision is no progress. It is like the workers that cut tree after tree in a forest to build a new road up to the point where their boss would shout: "wrong direction."

- Let the money talk. Whatever you are doing, be prepared to present the ROI. Have necessary calculations and potential impacts of changes readily in your pocket (literally speaking) and use it for decision-making. Especially use it when there are changes to your project imposed on your project from senior management, because this is the language they readily understand.
- It is more accurate and far easier to collect necessary effort figures during a project than afterwards. Cost and effort should not be estimated for such analyses, but rather collected in comparable past projects. Avoid such after the facts estimations because typically the inputs to any such estimation would be questioned until the entire calculation is no longer acceptable.
- Activity-based costing helps a lot to understand value contribution, cost drivers and causal effects. Activities related to distinct effort figures must be defined upfront.
- Detailed quality costs are helpful for root cause analyses and related defect prevention activities.
- Tangible cost savings are the single best support for a starting and running an improvement program.
- Cost of nonperformance is a perfect trigger for a process improvement program.

> Performance measurement is crucial for managing an effective and efficient software or IT organization. Without measurements there is no control and certainly no way to improve. Always start with building your measurement database with past data and evaluate it from various viewpoints before engaging into new investments. Take risk based on assumptions and validate your assumptions periodically. Don't let yourself get trapped with having no or insufficient data, while having this book on your bookshelf. Pass the book to managers and colleagues that need insight and education.

12.7. Summary

Introducing a complete and hierarchically consistent control program is not easy and often takes several years. It asks for training, communication, shared beliefs and values, and accountable engineering processes. Though there is no immediate need of heavy tools and methods, the effort to continuously manage a complex portfolio requires the intensive and sustainable cooperation of the different stakeholders, such as engineering, product management and marketing.

It is unrealistic to assume that all these methods and approaches would be introduced to the company or department on a "push-button" approach. It is therefore better to introduce controlling in steps. "First things first" could for instance mean that thorough controlling should be applied first to the top 20% of the projects or products that are most critical for your overall business success. A good question to ask is which are the products or projects on which one would bet the future of the company?

Utilize the measurements and evaluation processes first "in vitro." That is, introduce necessary changes stepwise and do not confuse and overload the project managers with too much new reporting and assessments at one time. Many indicators might look interesting, however, maybe just a few standard tracking elements combined with market data will help to get transparency across the portfolio.

> Be prepared *at any time* to present your numbers and how they relate to your business. Have them literally in your pocket.

Have necessary calculations and potential impacts of changes readily in your pocket (literally speaking) and use it for decision-making. Especially use it when there are changes to your project imposed on your project from senior management, because this is the language they readily understand. As long as you fiddle around claiming that the value of what you are doing is not easy to calculate, you are subject to unpleasant changes. Value is what matters – to you, your business, your management and your customers.

13. Measurement Repositories

In God we trust.
All others bring data.
W. Edwards Deming

13.1. Access to Measurement Results

The use of measurements in the development of industrial software is gaining importance. Measurements are particularly suited to qualitative and quantitative assessment of the software development process, of the resources used in development and of the software product itself. However, software measurements can only be used effectively if the requisite measurements are integrated into the software development process and if these measurement values are taken at regular intervals. An effective software measurement process produces an extensive series of measurements and thus the need for efficient measurement data management which must include the contexts to enable discourse on the measurements that are taken as well as to provide extensive evaluation options.

It should also be possible to store the results of validation of a measurement as a new experience within the database. In this context it is possible to use a simple structure based on a file system, a standard portal solution, an explicitly developed measurement database system or, finally, an experience factory. After a short introduction of the International Software Benchmarking Standards Group (ISBSG) approach we show possible sources of measurements, requirements of a measurement database and an implementation of a real system of a measurement database (called metricDB). The metricDB project focuses on an application measurements in object-oriented software development.

13.2. Building the Measurement Database

13.2.1 Motivation and Requirements

One important activity in the context of software measurement access is benchmarking. Benchmarking is used by a company internally for comparing projects and externally for comparing best practices. There are several databases that allow open access to benchmarking data, such as the ISBSG International Repository (http://www.isbsg.org). The goal of the ISBSG is to provide a multi-organizational repository of software project data. The ISBSG grows, maintains and exploits two repositories of software project measurement:
1. Software Development and Enhancement
2. Software Maintenance and Support

The ISBSG approach considers different project data, such as the functional size of a specific software solution, information about the development project itself (elapsed time, team size, required resources) or information about the used technologies for implementation.

Today, this benchmarking repository contains several thousand projects. The repository can be used for a minimal fee and provides the following services:
- The repository can be used as an alternative to an internal measurement database.
- The repository can be used to post realized project benchmarks
- The repository can be used to compare submitted projects with others of the same class within the repository
- The repository can be used to obtain benchmark and other reports about the content of the repository.

Measurement tools mostly address the original source of software measurement data. These tools support different kinds of software modeling, measurement and evaluation. We can establish the following storage techniques and structures for the measurement values:
- Some tools present the measurement only during the evaluation moment.
- Most tools produce a measurement file with some explanations or in a simple value-divided-by-delimiter form.
- The measurements are stored for two evaluations for some tools to compare two variants (an old and a new/modified one).
- Some tools support a file hierarchy for the project-related storage of the code measurement data; an append technique helps to combine different measurements of different project parts to compare the different evaluated aspects.
- Some tools provide facilities for the presentation and analysis of the measurement data, but the final values are hidden from the user.
- In some tool classes there exists a data-handling tool with the capability of detailed analysis of the measurement data.

The examples above demonstrate some interesting aspects of software measurement data storage and handling but are mainly oriented to a special measurement area (process or code evaluation) or to a special environment (platform or language related). Fig. 13.1 shows the possible sources of software measurements according to [Evan94a]. Fig. 13.1 summarizes possible aspects of the design and implementation of a measurement database ([Folt98]).

Industrially acceptable measurement databases are constructed based on some aspects chosen from every dimension of the above model.

The starting point of such measurement repository are derived from the future users of the information system. Additional requirements relate to the adaptability of the application to new situations, the use of different procedural models for software development and possibly also the use of different measurement sources. The target of the measurement database is to cater to the needs of different users and, in particular, to make it easier to control the quality and cost of software projects (independently from the used procedure). In a workshop with potential cus-

13.2 Building the Measurement Database

tomers (e.g., project managers) of the measurement database, requirements were identified and used as a starting point for data and function modeling. These requirements are summarized below ([Abra06, Brau05]).

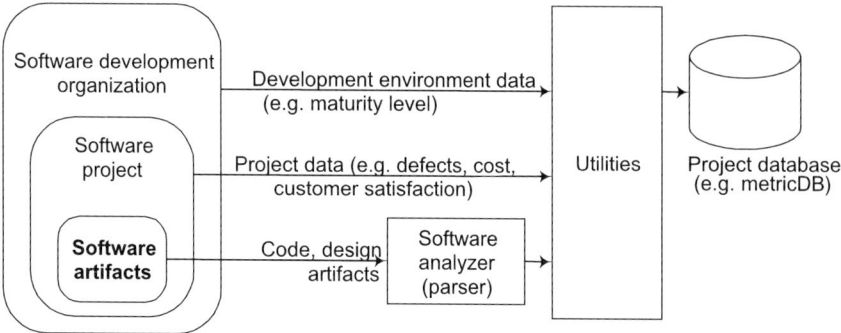

Fig. 13.1. Sources for a measurement database (adapted from [Evan94a])

- The effort involved in using and maintaining or administrating of a measurement database must be kept to a minimum which results in the need for extensive automation.
- It should be possible to map the procedure (e.g., functional or object-oriented development) that is selected for a concrete software development project in the measurement database. It must also be possible to configure the created software artifacts (diagrams, documents, source texts) and to assign measurements that are taken of them.
- Different user types must be served with project-specific rights. Planning currently involves application administrators (creation of new projects), the project manager/developer (use of prefabricated evaluations) or academic staff who can subject the measurements to statistical analysis using external tools such as SPSS.
- The measurement system should include automatic problem detection in software development on the basis of exceeded, configurable threshold values in addition to offers of solution alternatives.
- The measurement system should allow storing different threshold values (external, company- and project-specific experiences). It should allow presenting project measurements and comparing projects by means of various reports, graphs and control diagrams.
- It should include an "experience database" for project development and control, effort estimation, productivity/efficiency and (indirect) cost control.
- It should incorporate automation of part of effort estimation (as in the present version, e.g., the object point method according to Sneed) in order to estimate effort and perform historical costing at different phases of the project.
- It should allow users to check qualitative modeling or implementation criteria by using validated measurements, for example, maintainability, compliance

with the object-oriented paradigm and stability of an object model in the face of change.
- The system must be able to incorporate new measurements and their interpretations into the database relatively easily. To this end, an internal adaptable measurements catalogue should be defined to which it must be possible to interactively map the results produced by measuring tools.
- It should allow to integrate evaluations that are not implemented on the basis of the standard functions offered by the application, such as an Excel or SPSS analysis.
- It should be possible for users to transfer analyses to their specific documents (e.g., OpenOffice) via file referencing or file embedding mechanisms (e.g., DotGNU, Web services, clipboard).
- It must offer easy yet secured access through the intranet.

13.2.2 Architecture of a Measurement database

Architectures of measurement databases naturally depend of their application field. We will characterize very briefly three approaches of measurement repositories described in [Brau05, Will06].

Measurement data warehouse
This approach is based on the data integration including data consolidation by using different kinds of technologies like *extract transform loading (ETL)* and *analytical processing database storage*. The main characteristics are described in Fig. 13.2.

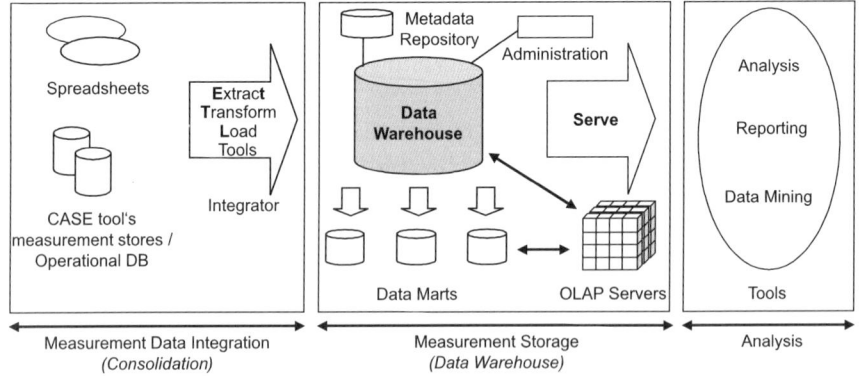

Fig. 13.2. The measurement data warehouse approach

Mediated measurement repository
The mediated-based approach supports data federation and uses an enterprise information integration (EII) methodology. The mediated schema provides access to

measurement data sources (type does not matter). Essential characteristics are shown in Fig. 13.3.

Service-bus-oriented measurement repository
This approach is based on data propagation and involves enterprise application integration (EAI) and Web service technologies for interaction. The propagation from measurement application via service bus to storage or analysis service is one of the typical application of this kind of measurement database. Fig. 13.4 demonstrates the kinds of interactions in this approach.

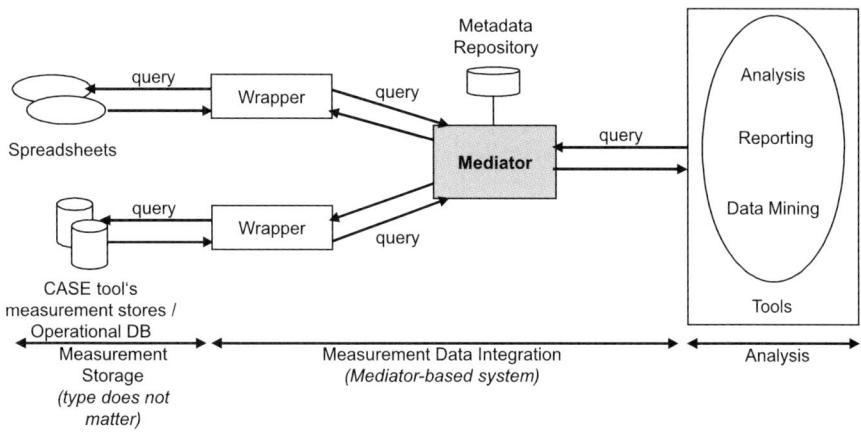

Fig. 13.3. The mediated measurement repository

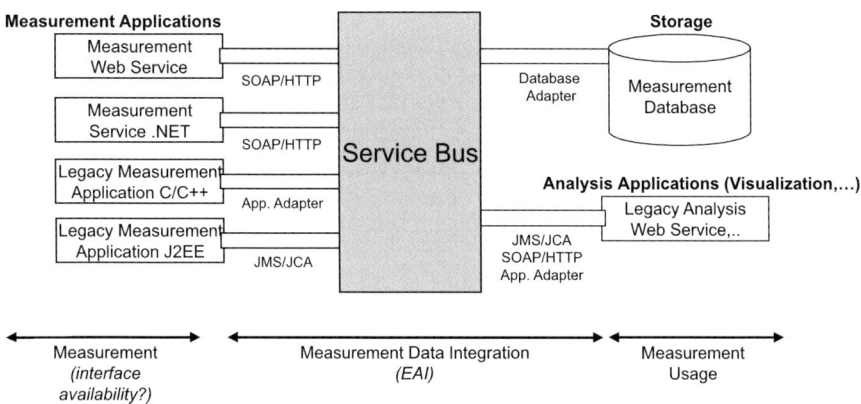

Fig. 13.4. The service bus-oriented measurement repository

The main components of the application are the database server (MS SQL Server or MySQL), a Web server (e.g., Apache or Internet Information Server), a Windows-based administration client and a Web client based on a standard browser (e.g., Mozilla).

Fig. 13.5 shows the software architecture of the measurement DB application. The Web server contains the HTML files and the relevant Java applets from the application which are downloaded to the Web client via HTTP. The database is accessed from the Java applet via the JDBC driver which runs as middleware on the Web server. At the core of the application is the database, set up as a relational database management system.

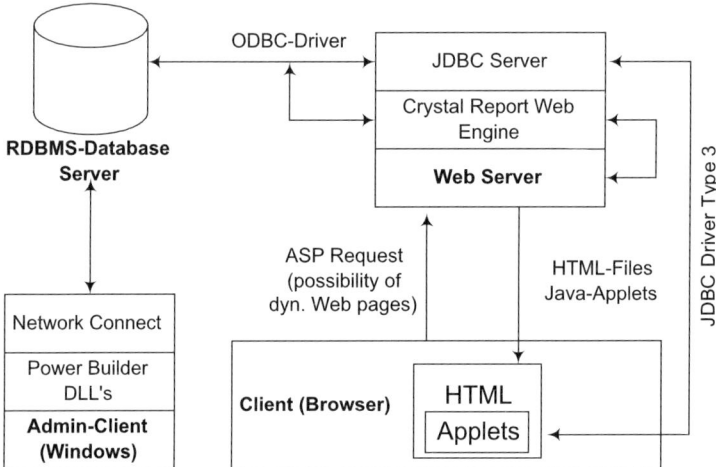

Fig. 13.5. Software architecture of the application

Despite the resulting paradigm inconsistency between the object-oriented application and database management based on the relational model, the following factors influenced the choice of the system:
- Proven database management technology with extensive tool support and offering standard interfaces such as Open Database Connectivity (ODBC) and Java Database Connectivity (JDBC).
- Possibility of using the database contents under standard tools such as Excel and SPSS for statistical data analysis via the ODBC interface.
- The availability of infrastructure, for example, for software distribution or appropriate centralized backup procedures in the company.
- To a high degree the administration client under Windows and the Web clients both execute update-intensive operations which make the use of Online Analytical Processing (OLAP) or data warehouse technologies doubtful.

Use of the type-3 JDBC driver permitted a three level client/server architecture to be implemented in the application on the Internet site. The administration client was linked directly to the database. Despite producing some disadvantages in terms of possible scalability, this is acceptable, as it requires very few administrators in relation to Web-based users. The architecture we have implemented enables all application components to be executed on one system or, alternatively, the use of dedicated computer systems as database and Web servers. The number of administration and Web clients that can be used depends on the performance of the server systems and the load profiles caused by users.

The application, in particular the database component, was modeled using Rational Rose. Fig. 13.8 shows the packages that are currently used and that contain the actual classes or entities. As most packages were described and implemented through parameterizable classes, this resulted in a highly generic data model, permitting various adjustments to be made within the application. For example, metadata is used to describe the structural elements (software artifacts) of a project, the hierarchical levels (mapping of the concrete procedural model) with, for example, cycles, phases, segments, activities and the milestones in the temporal project flow (management view).

On the one hand, this procedure safeguards the option of adapting to various procedural models in software development, on the other, it allows us to consider various sources of measurements, related to the defined structural elements. Inherent in a generic concept of this type is the disadvantage of increased administration effort for application operations. For this reason, the template technology was used several times, storing basic administration work, such as mapping a procedural model for object-oriented development, in the system.

13.2.3 Details of the Implementation

The computation of aggregate measurements refers at present to effort estimation according to the object point method [Snee96]. The measurements that were imported via Computer Aided Measurement and Evaluation (CAME) tools and those that had to be input into the system manually (not measurable) were both used in the computation. This is implemented technically via "store procedures", on the database server. Using these technologies offers performance advantages but has the disadvantage that it is dependent on the actual database system that is in use, here MS SQL Server.

Within the stored procedures the computation formulae for determining object points are mapped using variables so that the application administrator can assign the concrete measurements that are to be used from the measurement catalogue stored in the system. This enables the computation rule to be adapted to whatever measurements the system offers, thereby achieving the independence of the concrete measurement tool in use. For other aggregate measurements, it is possible to define new store procedures. Full disclosure of these program parts which are written in Standard SQL92 (approximately 80 effective LOC), makes this task relatively easy without the need for changes to the application itself.

Templates in the application support the transfer of measurements performed using CAME tools. The functionality of the templates includes parsing the output file created by the CAME tools and writing the measurement values it reads to a temporary file. It is then possible to interactively assign (mapping) the imported measurement values to the measurements that were mapped to the database via the defined measurement catalogue. In this way, the basic output format of the CAME tools can be retained while new versions are adapted to the measurement database by the application administrator.

Typically, a comma-separated output file is created. That is also a common default for spreadsheet export/import mechanisms. This consists of a specification of the type of element (package, class, operation, use case) that was measured, the name of the measurement and the actual measurement value. The sequence of datasets may vary, depending on the measurement tool settings, as it is possible, for example, to not display certain measurements. This is taken into account by the parser. The parser works on the basis of the defined keywords.

It would only be possible to import data fully automatically if the definition of the elements administered in the measurement database were mapped to the output format of the measurement tool. The necessity of defining a standard interface for measurement tools became particularly apparent during processing. This standard should contain a generic measurement description, as well as define the grammar used inside the output file.

13.3. Benchmarking Based on the ISBSG Repository

Expert Box. Author: Ton Dekkers

Performance and outsourcing has become issues in projects and service contracts. Main drivers for this are increasing business value (and often shareholder value), cutting cost and earlier time-to-market. Knowing your performance is the best way to validate the expectations and benefits of improvements and outsourcing deals. Benchmarked repository data is objective reference for decision-making. To be able to benchmark the performance, some basic questions have to be answered:
- What is (software) benchmarking?
- Which performance indicators should be measured?
- What reference is available?

Benchmarking is the process of continuously measuring and comparing activities or products with each other. The areas and conditions for comparison should be defined properly and unambiguously. Another essential precondition is a repeatable measurement process. The availability of internal measurement data will make the benchmarking process more valuable.

Software benchmarking can be regarded as a specific domain. Internal benchmarking is relevant for detecting improvement possibilities and for the outsourcing discussion. External benchmarking will help to set goals for improvement, could lead to organizational restructuring or decision on outsourcing and supplier.

At the moment the most benchmarking data available is on new development of tailor-made software. For 'run and maintain' activities the data is limited. A benchmark repository for business process packages acquisition and implementation is under construction.

For manufacturing, the input-process-output model is quite common in business economics. Why not apply this model to software economics? Fig. 13.6 shows this approach which is often used in benchmarking.

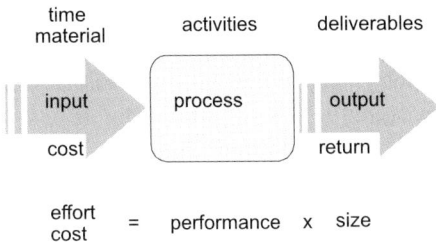

Fig. 13.6. The input / process / output model

In this case, the IT staff (effort) develops (process) the tailor-made software (deliverables). When the variables are defined, the performance can be measured. The model can be used for evaluation (with input and output known, the actual process performance can be determined) and prediction (with output and process performance, the input can be estimated).

Of course, everybody agrees upon business or project managers that will mention that this project has some specific conditions that make it different. Identify with the project manager the specific differences with the nominal situation and quantify the impact of these variances on the performance. A proper discussion is now possible.

The International Software Benchmarking Standards Group (ISBSG) provides a set of clearly defined performance indicators (see Table 13.1).

Table 13.1. Definitions of the performance indicators

Performance Indicator	"Formula" Definition
Project Delivery Rate (Hours per unit)	Effort spent / size of the application
	Measures the rate at which a project delivers software functionality to the end user as a factor of the effort required to do so. It is defined as Project Work Effort (measured in hours), over Functional Size of the delivered software (measured in size units). Project delivery rate is used regardless of how the software is produced.
Speed of Delivery (Units per period)	Size of the application / elapsed time needed for delivery.
	Measures the ability of a team to deliver a quantity of software over a period of time. It is defined as the Functional Size of the delivered software (measured in size units) over the Project Elapsed Time (measured in months).

When measuring performance, size matters. This requires proper size measurement. Fortunately, the IEC/ISO standard 14143-1 [ISO98] defines the principles of a functional size measurement method. At the moment following methods are compliant (certified by IEC/ISO): function points analysis according IFPUG (ISO 20926 [ISO03b]), function points analysis according NESMA (ISO 24570 [ISO05]), Mark II Function Points (ISO 20968 [ISO02c]) and COSMIC Full Function Points (ISO 19761 [ISO03a]). All mentioned is valid for these standards.

The ISBSG is an International 'not-for-profit' organization with 13 members. Members are software measurement associations like IFPUG (USA, Brazil etc.), ASMA (Australia), GIFPU (Italy), NESMA (Netherlands), NASSCOM (India), CSPIU (China) and JFPUG (Japan).

Based on a questionnaire, data is collected from all over the world to fill the benchmarking repositories. Data available is almost completely related to tailor-made software. The "New & Enhancement Projects" repository contains data of over 3,000 projects. The "Maintenance & Support" repository comprises 115 applications or programs. The data can be acquired directly by ISBSG or by the members associations. Under construction are repositories for "business systems software package acquisition and implementation." With this benchmark data it is possible to validate performance, estimates and proposals.

The validation with the use of ISBSG benchmarking data is shown in this real-life case. A request for proposal is sent out to the various suppliers. In the table the main project characteristics. The base for the size calculation is provided as part of the information package (see Table 13.2).

Table 13.2. Case characteristics

Project size	540 function points
Domain	Business application
Language	Cobol
Platform	Mainframe
Constraints	Duration: 10 months
	Cost: 1,000,000 Euro
An average hourly rate of 100 € is used.	

For a quick assessment of the characteristics, the reality checker is used (included in the ISBSG repository package [ISBS06]). The screenshot in Fig. 13.7 shows the results based on the matching repository data.

A summary is given in Table 13.3. The assessment uses the nominal measurement model. The expected cost (effort * hourly rate) are in range with the bandwidth of the repository selection. The duration however is less in balance. Next steps are assessing the expectations with the private data set and verifying data sets used for the benchmark with the project specific circumstances. Applying the identified variances in the enhanced measurement model will give calibrated results to validate the expectations and constraints.

Commercial tools can give similar support. Parametric estimating tools like the SLIM suite (QSM), KnowledgePlan (SPR), the SEER suite (Galorath) and Experience Pro (STTF) are based on similar benchmarking data sets. Their advantage is a more professional approach on estimating where ISBSG focuses on the data set. The advantage of the ISBSG data set is the possibility of creating your own peer group and having access to all underlying data elements. The professional tools only provide a 'black box' external peer group benchmarking. When an internal data set is available, then the underlying data is available.

Whatever solution is chosen, using internal or external benchmark repositories for validating performance will validate the business expectations.

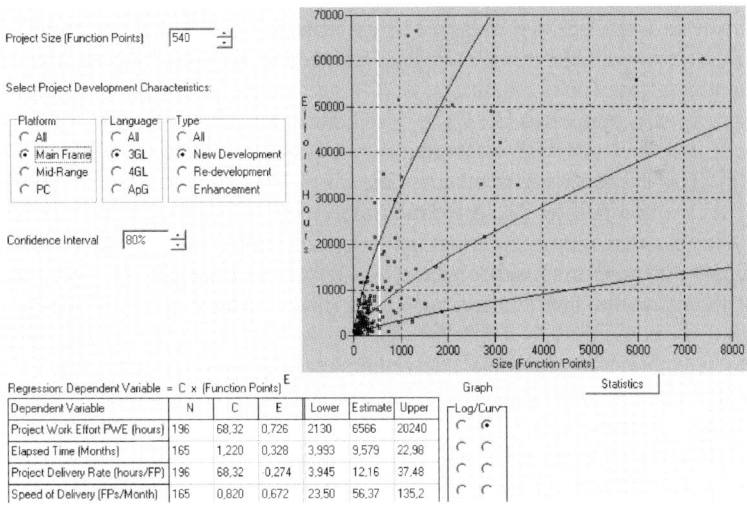

Fig. 13.7. Reality Checker v3.0 – Release 9

Table 13.3. Example project – Reality Checker v3.0, Release 9

	Estimate	Reality Checker v3.0 – R9
Project size	540 function points	540 function points
Domain	Business application	-
Language	Cobol	3 GL
Platform	Mainframe	Mainframe
Constraints	Duration: 10 months	Duration: 9.5–23.0 months
	Cost: 1,000,000 Euro	Cost: 656,000–2,024,000 Euro

13.4. Measurement Database Services for COTS Software

The *Object-Oriented Measurements of Java Technologies (OOMJ)* [Faro05, Faro06] is a Web service and simultaneously a Web application envisaged to provide an approach to evaluate Java components. It also serves as an object-oriented measurement repository containing measurement evaluations for several Java libraries as well as provides numerous ways to analyze these results to highlight various trends and other design aspects of the measured products.

Several object-oriented design measurements have been proposed by experts ([Abre94, Cart00, Chid94, Hend96a]). These measurements describe diverse aspects of an object-oriented design. OOMJ supports the Chidamber-Kemerer measurement suite and MOOD measurement set.

The six structural design measurements proposed by Chidamber and Kemerer in [Chid98] are outlined in following: Weighted method per class (WMC), depth of inheritance tree (DIT), number of children (NOC), coupling between objects (CBO), response for a class (RFC), lack of cohesion between methods (LCOM).

Abreu proposed MOOD measurements in [Abre94] and were later revised in [Abre96] This set of six measurements measures four main structural mechanisms of object-oriented design i.e., encapsulation, inheritance, polymorphism and message-passing. Measurements from the MOOD measurement set supported by OOMJ are: Attribute inheritance factor (AIF), method inheritance factor (MIF), attribute hiding factor (AHF), method hiding factor (MHF), polymorphism factor (POF).

OOMJ maintains measurement evaluation results for several standard Java libraries and open source projects and this list is growing as new projects are being submitted to it for evaluation and analysis.

Below we briefly present measurement evaluation results for all the above mentioned libraries based on Chidamber-Kemerer and MOOD measurements sets. Table 13.4 and Table 13.5 show some basic statistics applied over these measurement results. A confidence interval is an estimate of a population parameter that consists of a range of values bounded by statistics called upper and lower confidence limits, within which the value of the parameter is expected to be located. It is usually calculated at 90%, 95% and 99% levels. We calculated a 95% confidence interval for both Chidamber-Kemerer and MOOD measurements.

Table 13.4. 95% Confidence Interval: Mean of Chidamber-Kemerer Measurements

	Lower Limit	Upper Limit
Depth of inheritance tree : DIT	0.57	0.61
Number of children: NOC	0.14	0.16
Weighted method per class: WMC	8.54	8.85
Coupling between objects: CBO	2.92	3.09
Response for a class: RFC	14.45	15.10
Lack of cohesion between methods: LCOM	35.88	39.14

Table 13.5. 95% Confidence Interval: Mean of MOOD Measurements

	Lower Limit	Upper Limit
Method hiding factor: MHF	98.30	99.25
Attribute hiding factor: AHF	98.09	99.32
Method inheritance factor: MIF	21.73	28.98
Attribute inheritance factor: AIF	20.58	28.92
Polymorphism factor: POF	3.39	5.81

There have been many empirical validations of these measurements which have investigated a possible relationship between value of the measurement and the complexity or other internal quality attribute of the underlying code or software design. Below we discuss each of these measurements individually and derive some inferences about complexity and other such aspects about the measured Java technologies.

First considering the Chidamber-Kemerer measurement evaluation results as shown in Table 13.4, we observe that *depth of inheritance tree* (DIT) is quite small for most of the classes. Inheritance depth has been found to be correlated to maintainability. Deeper classes tend to increase complexity and are thus avoided. *Number of children* (NOC) also shows similar distribution as compared to DIT, most probably majority of classes tend to have a zero NOC value. A higher number of children mean a higher reuse but on the other hand it also shows an improper class abstraction. Classes having higher NOC value are more critical to the design and need rigorous testing. Small values for both of these measurements (DIT and NOC) indicate that class design for most of Java standard libraries reflects simple hierarchy making these libraries simple to use and less complex to understand. On the other hand, it also shows very little use of inheritance.

Chidamber et al. [Chid98] also had a similar observation and they have the opinion that the lack of inheritance could reflect a conscious decision not to use a feature for which some believe that costs, in terms of complexity and maintainability, are deemed to outweigh the benefits. *Weighted method per class* (WMC) affects class complexity and this effect is transferred to inheriting classes. Consequently, more effort and time are needed for maintenance and testing. Extremely high number of methods should trigger designer's attention for rework. Most classes in the Java libraries tend to have a small WMC (close to 9) again indicating small class size enabling easy understanding of the class structures. *Coupling between objects* (CBO) affects change proneness and higher inter-object class coupling calls for rigorous testing. Therefore, a smaller CBO is advocated. It is observed to be close to 3 in our case study. *Response for a class* (RFC) is similar kind of coupling measurement which focuses on coupling between classes. A higher class coupling reduces its testability and understandability. Our results show RFC in the range of 20 to 30 in most cases. Figure 3 shows average value of RFC for some selected libraries and projects. Weka (http://sourceforge.net/projects/weka) and Tomcat 5.5.9 show a relatively high value of this measurement which might possibly increase complexity of these projects.

LCOM is a measurement of *lack of cohesion in methods* inside a class. Chidamber et al. found that high LCOM value was associated with lower productivity, greater rework and greater design effort. Observation of a small LCOM value shows tight cohesion within Java standard classes which is a typical characteristic that a class should be combination of attributes and related methods which manipulate these attributes to perform some action as an independent object.

Now we discuss design characteristics and resulting quality aspects of Java libraries based on MOOD measurements results given in table 13.10. *Method hiding factor* (MHF) and *attribute hiding factor* (AHF), part of MOOD measurement set, measure the level of encapsulation implemented by a system. Encapsulation copes with complexity and helps develop maintainable and reusable software. We observe very high values for both these measurements. Ideally, all attributes should be hidden and AHF in this case is close to the optimal value. However, a very high value of MHF indicates little functionality. Inheritance is measured by *method inheritance factor* (MIF) and *attribute inheritance factor* (AIF). Inheritance on one hand results in reuse but on the other hand may add to complexity of design. Both MIF & AIF fall approximately between 20 and 30% for these libraries. This small use of inheritance by Java libraries has also been discussed in previous paragraph. Values of about 60 to 70% for these measurements were observed by Abreu et al. for some Eiffel [Abre94] and C++ [Abre96] libraries. *Polymorphism factor* (POF) is a measurement of the level of polymorphism implemented by a system. Polymorphism should be used very carefully. It allows simplicity by providing dynamic binding but may also complicate tracing control flow within classes. A small POF of around 4 to 6% is observed for these libraries. A very cautious use of inheritance, encapsulation and polymorphism as reflected by measurements discussed above probably indicates a lack of confidence about usefulness of these features or sacrifices sophisticated design for the sake of simplicity and cost effectiveness.

Measurement threshold analysis: According to Ebert et al. (see [Eber04, Lanz06]) a step in planning a measurement process is measurement adjustment which involves determination of the favorable values and tuning of the thresholds as approximation during the software development from other project components. Here we present few examples using threshold analysis for the concerned measurements. Considering these measurements and assuming these values as desirable measurements ranges exercised by industry, we can perform a comparative analysis of the libraries and software of our interest to spot a deviation from a common industry practice. The attribute inheritance factor (AIF, parts of MOOD measurement suite) has a typical value in the range of 20 to 30%.

Measurement trend analysis: The next two examples briefly discuss changing design trends in different versions of various Java standard libraries. Earlier versions show a less-than-common use of this feature while later versions exhibit a relatively increased use. Although the shift is not so significant and the value for in case of latest version is just close to most commonly found value of 6, this increase may cause complexity issues if it goes much higher.

Fig. 13.8 shows an example with highlighting class size trends (weighted per class measurement, WMC, from C-K measurement suite) in different versions of J2EE standard libraries. We observe fewer number of methods (0-5) in most of classes of a selected package from J2EE 1.2.1 but in newer versions class size is increasing and in version J2EE 1.4.1 a significant percentage (about 30%) of classes have 11-15 methods per class. Despite the fact that this is still not an extraordinarily high value for WMC, it may make the classes error-prone and difficult to maintain.

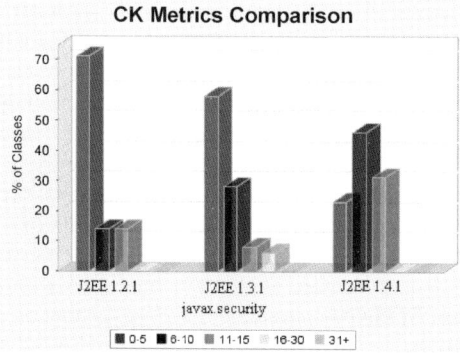

Fig. 13.8. Weighted method per class (WMC) for javax.security package from three versions of J2EE

13.5. Hints for the Practitioner

Before an organization starts with the implementation of a measurement database it is necessary to improve the maturity of the corresponding development process. Otherwise it is difficult to associate measurements to life-cycle iterations, project activities, and so on. Therefore, we recommend starting with simple solutions for the storage of measurements. The following makes this possible:

1. Individualized storage of software measurements by applying standard office/spreadsheet tools. Each user stores his respective measurements. This fragmented and ad-hoc approach is not recommended as huge overheads and inconsistencies are created.
2. Use of externally provided repositories, like the ISBSG approach. Storage of project data like functional size, work effort, error statistics, and so on.
3. Use of a simple storage structure based on a shared file system. We strongly recommend using a configuration management system on top of such file system.
4. Use of a Web-based portal (e.g., Microsoft Share Portal Services or Microsoft Share Point Team Services) and application of a simple visualization. This type of access is especially useful for distributed development organizations or in context of offshore activities. Typically the portal links into operational databases and aggregation mechanisms.
5. Use of a dedicated centralized measurement database, like the proposed solution within this chapter. The solution should be adaptable to different development methods, to different development tools and also usable for process, resource and product measurements. Measuring data should be adopted as automated as possible into the database. Manual interfaces are to be avoided. The output forms should be simple evaluations (bar diagrams, value tables etc.) and are used as input for the statistical tools. The characteristics of the stored

measurement data should be different in the scale type and of a different lifecycle phase. The measurement database should be distributed and stand-alone, and should allow an interactive use. The platform should be server-based by the use of an application server and a relational database management system (e.g., Oracle or Microsoft SQL-Server). Furthermore, we recommend the use of Web-based technologies as user interface. The measurement database should keep the goals of the measurement tool and controlled experiment evaluation and should deliver experience in distributed application of measurements based process and product controlling. It should also be possible to store the results of the validation of a measurement as a new experience within the database; this also implies the use of the measurement database system as discussion forum.

In principle, every type of a storage should offer the possibility to further use the measurement data with external tools like statistical analysis or reporting tools.

13.6. Summary

We have introduced to the needs for software measurement infrastructures. A common usage scheme for such infrastructures is benchmarking or portfolio management. We showed with a case study how T-Systems has built such measurement database. The approach is visible and can be extended to your own environment. The current version of the measurement database primarily considers software artifacts. Planning foresees extending this in the future to include measurements of software development organization, e.g., importing measurements for maturity valuation in accordance with the CMMI model. To summarize the results of the current version, it is a highly adaptable information system that is able to take into consideration the continually changing conditions in software development, such as new procedural models, new measurement tools and a successive increase in experiences, and thus meets the needs of investment protection. The easy-to-use Web interface makes evaluations available to a wide range of users, helping them to gain experience in the use of measurements and, implicitly, in measurement validation.

14. Empirical Laws and Rules of Thumb

*Practicing principles
matters more
than proving them.
Epictetus*

14.1. Applying Software Rules of Thumb

This chapter will summarize the quantifiable experiences and wisdom that the two authors collected in their (combined) over fifty years of practical software engineering. Believe it or not: We have measured all the way over these fifty years!. Knowing that it is often difficult to just use plain numbers to characterize a situation, we are also aware that beginners and practitioners need some numbers to build upon – even if their applicability is somewhat limited. We will therefore provide in this chapter concrete and fact-based guidance with numbers from our own experiences so you can use it as a baselines in your projects.

At many places in this book we advocate to build your own history database. However, everybody initially is at the point where bootstrapping a certain initiative needs some concrete data – before even building a history database. Clearly, this is not a substitute for your own measurement database. You need to build over time your own history database with baselines for estimation, quality planning and the like. However, you might not yet have this data available, or it is not yet scaleable for new products, methodologies or projects. Maybe you have a supplier and want to follow his plan.

Where do you get such initial data? We started with looking into our own project lessons learned and enriched it with experiences from books and conference proceedings, cost estimation tools. Over time, this lead us to some simple rules of thumb (heuristics) that we could use even in situations where no historic information was accessible. The list is far from complete and certainly is not as scientific as one would like – but it is a start. The data stems from our own history databases as mentioned in previous chapters of this book. It is supported by a number of external sources, such as estimation tools, project management literature, and so on [Eber06b, Endr03, IFPU03, ISBS06, Jone97, Jone01, Lyu95, McCo98, Royc98, Shul02].

14.2. Project Planning

Project planning is based on size, schedule and productivity. A good predictor is the **Putnam formula** that states that effort in a project is proportional to size to

the power of 3 divided by duration to the power of 4 and again divided by productivity to the power of 3.
For embedded software, this effort multiplies by a factor of 2-4.
For maintenance projects, this effort multiplies by a factor of 2-5.

High-dependability software costs 3-10 times more per source instruction than low-dependability software [Shul02].

Estimation accuracy of a single person is around 30%. The accuracy improves if the person is a regular development engineer and not an expert who tends to assume his own capability for each and everyone and thus underestimates effort and time. Estimations are best calculated by having several persons look to the task at hand and then building a weighted average according to the following formula:
Estimated value = (lower limit + 4 x most realistic value + upper limit) / 6

Effort distribution on project activities and the overhead for project management depend on the project life-cycle model. Table 14.1 provides the effort distribution as percentages of total effort for two types of project life-cycle models, namely sequential and incremental. Note that this distribution does not explain any effort reduction due to incremental development. Such impact on absolute numbers depends on a variety of factors and is thus not explained as a rule of thumb.

Table 14.1. Effort distribution if projects following sequential and incremental paradigms

Project activities	Sequential approach (e.g., conventional waterfall, big iterations)	Incremental approach (e.g., agile, small features being continuously integrated)
Management activities (project management, quality management)	5%	10%
Infrastructure management	5%	10%
Requirements management	5%	10%
Design	10%	15%
Construction (incl. reviews and unit test)	30%	25%
Test	40%	25%
Transition, deployment	5%	5%
Total	100%	100%

Team size is roughly the square root of effort in person months. This means that a task with 10 person months estimated effort should be done with 3 persons to achieve optimal load balance. Obviously high independencies inside the task allow for more persons and thus shorter duration. However, then most probably the task was specified overly broad and should first be broken down in more and smaller tasks, such as 10 tasks with 1 person month effort, done by ten persons.

14.2 Project Planning

Allocating engineers to several projects in parallel reduces productivity. Experience shows that productivity is reduced in steps depending on the amount of context switching due to the different assignments (e.g., phone calls from the second project while doing design in the first). As a rule of thumb consider some 30% productivity decrease if working on several independent assignments.

The minimum **project duration** in months is 2.5 times effort in person years to the power of 1/3.

The Duration of a task or project (given all other factors are known) can be improved by up to 25% in one shot by improving productivity. This implies excellent team building and teamwork, strong planning and monitoring on the critical path, strong method and tools sup-port, high parallelism and early defect removal. Such mechanisms are not sustainable and demand strong follow-up. They bear the risk of high stress levels and attrition of team members if pressure is maintained too long.

Business case validity seems to be optimal with 5-10% **delays**. Zero is overly expensive and beyond 10% decreases customer satisfaction. A common trade-off in this picture is contract or requirements changes demanded by the customer (or by sales / marketing) which will make projects a bit late but add marginal value for the customer.

Documentation should be planned with roughly 2-3 logical pages per function point. It includes all types of project-related documentation, such as specifications, feature lists, and test strategies. This documentation is typically assembled from a variety of pieces and does not cover automatically generated views on software code or design (which to all experience should be done as online documentation anyway).

Test effort can be planned by estimating the necessary test cases. This is done by a target quality level and coverage criteria to be achieved based on operational scenarios and use cases. Starting during the requirements analysis phase test effort can be estimated by functionality and translates roughly into 0.3-1 test cases per function point. For procedural languages such as C, this translates into 3-7 test cases per KStmt. This is a very rough formula and should be handled with care.

Test effort reduction. Across projects at least 30% of all test cases are redundant. Such an average holds for legacy and new projects, because engineers have the tendency adding test cases "to be on the safe side" but do not control them by means of coverage or related effectiveness criteria. This is an excellent business case in itself towards applying better test management and test coverage tools. Orthogonal test case arrays help in reducing test redundancies.

Maintenance effort for the last level (engineering effort related to defect removal after the welcome desk has done its job) amounts to 5-15% of project effort per year. The Us Air Force has studies hundreds of projects and found that a vast majority of overall cost is spent on defining, designing and testing changes. The total range is 49-80% of total life-cycle cost spent on maintenance related activities [Lech06]. Make sure that this effort is budgeted and staffed before release or you might end up in difficult times with your customers who expect proper SLA management. New and changed functionality (on top of defect corrections) account for 5-8% of new functionality per year and 10% of functionality being changed per year. Altogether, this translates to one third of project cost being budgeted for maintenance especially in the first year after release. It will decrease typically thereafter.

14.3. Global Software Engineering

Working in several locations as we do in global development, costs extra effort. We found in many studies including own experience that with 2 locations you should budget some 20-30% overhead and for 3-4 locations some 30-40% overhead [Eber06b]. This overhead is due to additional interfaces, management, team effort, collaboration support, quality control, reviews, and so on.

Reported **cost reduction from GSE** is much less than the hype figure of 50-70% savings if only labor cost are compared – as often done by media. Dividing a single business process across the world with shared responsibilities costs money and rework effort. Several highly distributed software engineering projects reported a 10-15% cost reduction after a 2-3 year learning curve. Initially outsourcing demands up to 20% additional effort. For India the effective savings after a three-year period is 15-20% as for instance reported in communication and automotive supplier companies.

Cancellation rate of outsourcing contracts during the first year is 20%. Overall success rate is below 50%.

Externalizing insufficient engineering processes creates extra cost and learning curve driven delays – on both sides. These additional cost sum up to 20-40% of regular cost of engineering. The learning curve for transferring an entire software package to a new team (e.g., location) takes 12 months [Eber06b]. Our own experiences and research [Eber01a, Eber01b] show that the effectiveness for software design and coding grows in a learning curve with 50% effectiveness reached after 1-3 months and 80% after 3-5 months. This obviously depends on process maturity and technology complexity. Each of the following bullets accounts for a 5-10% increase to project cost:
- Supplier and contract management
- Coordination and interface management, especially with fragmented / distributed processes
- Project management and progress control

- Training, knowledge management, communication
- IT infrastructure, global tools licenses
- Liability coverage, legal support

14.4. Requirements Engineering

Only half of all requirements that are agreed upon before project start are finally delivered to the client.

Half of all functionality in a software system is never or very rarely used in practice. This means that the list of value-add functionality which can be effectively sold is smaller than the list of requirements. Knowing this factor and eliminating unnecessary requirements allows to save effort and shorten cycle time.

80% of all defects found during test result from missing (30%) or wrong (50%) requirements.

40% of all software defects in embedded systems result from insufficient requirements and analysis activities.

The typical **effort allocated to requirements engineering** is 3-7% of total project cost. It is 5-10% for all requirements management related activities during the life-cycle which includes for instance change management during the project. Doubling this effort has the potential to reduce life-cycle cost by 20%, thus yielding an immediate ROI of 4. The cost reduction mostly stems from reduced error rate during elicitation and analysis, earlier defect removal during specification and requirements verification, and improved consistency across work products.

Requirements change at 1-3% per month normalized to the effort originally estimated. For instance if the requirements are estimated with 1 person year, you would expect an additional effort or change impact of 1-2 person weeks per month. This is not peanuts and needs to be considered in building change review boards and clear rules for change management. Target a freeze point of your requirements in due time by backward planning from project (or task) end.

Requirements changes beyond 20% (normalized to project effort) after the start of the project typically impact productivity (and other project parameters) dramatically. Up to 20% change rate which translates into 3% per month in a six month project, can be digested without negative impacts.

14.5. Quality

The **number of defects at code completion** (i.e., after coding has been finished for a specific component and has passed compilation) can be estimated in different ways. If size in KStmt or KLOC is known, this can be translated into residual defects. We found some 10-50 defects per KStmt depending on the maturity level of the respective organization.

IFPUG uses the predictor of 1.2 defects per function point which translates for C-language into 20 defects per KStmt [IFPU03]. Alternatively it is recommended for bigger projects to calculate defects as $FP^{1.2}$. This is based only on new or changed code, not including any code that is reused or automatically generated. For such code, the initial formula has to be extended with percentage of defects found by the already completed verification (or validation) steps. An alternative formula for new projects takes estimated function points of a project to the power of 1.25.

Verification pays off. Peer reviews and inspections are the least expensive of all manual defect detection techniques. You need some 1-3 person hours per defect for inspections and peer reviews. Before starting peer reviews or inspections, all tool-supported techniques should be fully exploited, such as static and dynamic checking of source code. Fully instrumented unit test should preferably be done before peer reviews. Unit test, static code analysis and peer reviews are orthogonal techniques that detect different defect classes. Often cost per defect in unit test is the highest amongst the three techniques due to the manual handling of test stubs, test environments, test cases, and so on.

Defect phase containment has clear business impact. Detecting 10% more defects in design or code reviews and therefore reducing test effort and long rework cycles yields a savings potential of 3% of engineering cost.

Cost of non-quality (i.e., defect detection and correction after the activity where the defect was introduced) is around 30-50% of total engineering (project) effort. A significant percentage of the effort on current software projects is typically spent on avoidable rework [Shul02]. It is by far the biggest chunk in any project that can be reduced to directly and immediately save cost! Especially for global software engineering projects, this cost rather increases due to inter-face overheads where code or design would be shipped back and forth until defects are retrieved and removed. The amount of effort spent on avoidable rework decreases as process maturity increases [Shul02].

Typically **testing** consumes more than 40% of the resources and – depending on the project life-cycle (sequential or incremental) – a lead-time of 15-50% compared to total project duration. The minimum 15% lead-time is achieved when test strongly overlaps with development, such as in incremental development with a stable build which is continuously regression tested. In such case, there is only the system test at the end contributing to lead-time on the critical project path. On the other hand 50% (and more) stem from testing practiced in a classic waterfall approach with lots of overheads due to components that won't integrate.

Cost of defects after delivery. Finding and fixing a severe software problem after delivery is often 100 times more expensive than finding and fixing it during the requirements and design phase [Shul02]. This relates to the cost of rework and correction which increases fast once the software system is built and delivered.

Each **verification or validation step** as a rule of thumb will detect and remove around 30% of the then residual defects. This means that 30% of defects remaining at a certain point of time can be found with a distinct defect detection technique. This is a cascading approach, where each cascade (e.g., static checking, peer review, unit test, integration test, system test, beta test) removes each 30% of defects. It is possible to exceed this number slightly towards 40-50% but at steeply increasing cost per defect. Reviews of work products can catch more than half of a product's defects regardless of the domain, level of maturity of the organization, or life-cycle phase during which they were applied [Shul02]. It is however important to realize that each such activity has an efficiency optimum (see Table 14.2). Going beyond that optimum often means an increasing cost per defect removed. It could still be valid doing so, especially for critical software, but a careful planning is required to optimize total cost of non-quality.

Table 14.2. Defect detection rate per activity compared to the total number of defects

Project activities	Maximum	Typical defect detection effectiveness	Insufficient
Requirements reviews	10-15%	5-10%	0%
Design reviews	10%	5-10%	0%
Code: static code analysis	20%	10-20%	<10%
Code: peer reviews and inspections	40%	20-30%	<10%
Code: code analysis and unit test	30%	10-30%	<10%
Integration test	20%	5-20%	>20%
Qualification / release test	5%	1-5%	>5%
Total percentage removed	100%	95-98%	<90%

Residual defects are estimated from estimated total defects and the different detected defects. This allows the planning of verification and validation and of allocating necessary time and budget according to quality needs. If 30% of the defects are removed per detection activity then 70% will remain. Residual defects at the end of the project thus equal the number of defects at code completion times 70%

to the power of independent detection activities (e.g., code inspection, module test, integration test, system test, and so on).

Release quality of software shows that typically 10% of the initial defects at code completion will reach the customer. Depending on the maturity of the software organization, the following number of defects at release time can be observed:
- CMMI maturity level 1: 5-60 defects/KStmt
- Maturity level 2: 3-12 defects/KStmt
- Maturity level 3: 2-7 defects/KStmt
- Maturity level 4: 1-5 defects/KStmt
- Maturity level 5: 0.05-1 defects/KStmt.

Quality of external components from suppliers on low process maturity levels is typically poor. Suppliers with high maturity (i.e., on or above CMMI maturity level 3) will have acceptable defect rates, but only if they own the entire product or component and manage their own suppliers. Virtual (globally distributed) development demands more quality control and thus cost of quality to achieve the same release quality.

Improving release quality needs time: 5% more defects detected before release time translates into 10-15% more duration of the project.

New defects are inserted with changes and corrections, specifically those late in a project and done under pressure. Corrections create some 5-30% new defects depending on time pressure and underlying tool support. Especially late defect removal while being on the project's critical path to release causes many new defects with any change or correction because quality assurance activities are reduced and engineers are stressed. This must be considered when planning testing, validation or maintenance activities.

14.6. Software Pareto Laws

The Pareto principle also holds for software engineering.
- 10% of all code account for 90% of outage time
- As a rule of thumb, 20% of all components (subsystems, modules, classes) consume 60-80% of all resources.
- 60% of a system's defects come from 20% of its components (modules, classes, units). However, the distribution varies based on environment characteristics such as processes used and quality goals.
- Post-release, about 40% of modules may be defect-free [Shul02].
- 20% of all defects need 60-80% of correction effort. Most of the avoidable rework comes from a small number of software defects, where avoidable rework is defined as work done to mitigate the effects of errors or to improve system performance [Shul02].

- 20% of all enhancements require 60-80% of all maintenance effort.

This looks a bit theoretical because obviously Pareto distributions rule our world – not only that of software engineering. It is always the few relevant members in any set which govern the set's behaviors. However, there are concrete, practically useful benefits you can utilize to save on effort. For instance, critical components can be identified in the design by static code analysis and verification activities then can be focused on those critical components.

14.7. Productivity and Process Improvement

Project performance: Only 35% of all software and IT-projects achieve the originally committed objectives. 46% miss their objectives and are finished with insufficient benefits. 19% of all projects are cancelled due to not reaching objectives [Stan04]. Consider these numbers when estimating risk and mitigation. This trend typically worsens in times of severe cost reduction, as we could see in 1994-1996 and again in 2003-2005. "Blind" cost reduction with reduced value-add investments typically has the adverse effect. It might be the only help to survive which is a legitimate reasoning. But in many of the observed cases cost reduction was done without much reasoning about any short or mid-term impacts. The best 20% of all enterprises deliver 80% of their projects in time – as it was committed at project start. The average however achieves only a rate of 50% success rate [Coop04]. This means that in the average company half of all projects are late with all consequences from markets and customers.

Engineering productivity can be improved by 5-10% per year for long timeframes. This is done by means of professional engineering and management techniques such as described by the CMMI. For instance when using the CMMI, engineering productivity is improved from maturity level 1 to 2 by having less defects in the field. Moving to maturity level 3 reduces cost of non-quality by enhanced defect phase containment. Moving on to maturity level 4 and 5 further boost productivity by applying statistical process control and thus reacting immediately if processes won't achieve their stated targets. The CMMI is not a necessary precondition for productivity improvement but it provides guidance in a stepwise approach. Improvements "trials" or "projects" must be disciplined and systematic to show value. Beyond CMMI and process-driven productivity improvement, even more than mentioned 10% is achieved with dedicated programs, such as reengineering the product, introducing new organization models or changing the development paradigms. Note that any productivity improvement will only arrive if concrete improvement objectives are set and followed up to capitalization.

Process improvement pays off. The SEI has collected lots of process improvement data over the years. They come from using the CMM or CMMI in a controlled way with data collection before and after a change initiative. This allows benchmarking the impact of process improvement initiatives. The following data had been assembled by the SEI in its benchmarking study [SEI06b] and also validated by independent other studies [Gali06]. They all signal one message: Well-orchestrated and managed process improvements yield a significant ROI!

- Cost reduction. There were 29 industry studies evaluated by the SEI with a mean improvement of 34% across these studies. The distribution was between 3% and 87%.
- Schedule predictability. There were 22 industry studies evaluated by the SEI with a mean improvement of 50% across these studies. The distribution was between 2% and 95%.
- Productivity improvement. There were 20 industry studies evaluated by the SEI with a mean improvement of 61% across these studies. The distribution was between 11% and 329%. The independent second study published by IEEE Software evaluated 16 further industry studies are found an average improvement of 52% with a distribution in the range of 9% to 187%.
- Cycle-time reduction. A study published by IEEE Software evaluated 13 industry studies and found an average improvement of 38% with a distribution in the range of 26% to 83%.
- Quality improvement. There were 34 industry studies evaluated by the SEI with a mean improvement of 48% across these studies. The distribution was between 2% and 132%.
- Return on investment (ROI) from process improvement. There were 22 industry studies evaluated by the SEI with a mean ROI of 4.0 across these studies. The distribution was between 1.7 and 27.7.

This altogether means that process improvement – if done professionally – yields a positive business case. Typical ROI values are in the range of four times what had been invested – for the first year. This accumulates to bigger savings in subsequent years, because the investment can be reduced once the change had been successfully mastered.

For software engineering a sigma shift in defect reduction translates in improved net income of 5-10%. Table 14.3 shows the relationship between Sigma levels, quality and cost of quality (details see Chap. 11).

Table 14.3. Sigma levels and their impact on defects and cost of quality. Note that they all include the 1.5 sigma shift.

Sigma level	Defects per million opportunities	Yield	Quality related cost
2	308,537	69.1%	20-40% of sales
3	66,807	93.3%	15-30% of sales
4	6,210	99,4%	10-20% of sales
5	233	99,98%	5-10% of sales
6	3.4	99.9997%	1-10% of sales

Productivity is improved by reducing accidents and by controlling essence. Accidents result from having defects which could have been avoided or detecting defects too late. Such defects cause rework which reduces productivity. Reducing accidents means efficiency improvement. There are many accidents along the product life-cycle starting with insufficient reviews on requirements and insufficient analysis before project start to having too much test effort up to insufficient quality after delivery with lots of rework. Essence is the real delivered value of what we are doing. Often we do not control value thus wasting time and effort on things which the market won't pay for. Controlling essence means improving effectiveness. Examples include variant proliferation in a product line or unnecessary requirements and features being developed without a business case. We have to control this essence as it directly impacts productivity. For instance, detecting 10% more defects in design or code reviews and therefore reducing test effort and long rework cycles yields a savings potential of 3% of engineering cost. Work is not offshored to low-cost countries because of direct labor cost of excellent engineers (which is equaling gradually across the world), but because many of those offshoring companies or countries high focus on creating value at a low cost by reduced rework and attention to what matters.

14.8. Hints for the Practitioner and Summary

Ensure that your analyses, actions and action proposals all base on significant and meaningful measurements. Whenever you need to evaluate measurements and draw conclusions, be sure that sample sizes of your measurements are sufficiently big. Significance or confidence can be estimated by Sackett's rule of thumb:

$$\text{confidence} = \text{signal} / \text{noise} \times \text{sample size}^{1/2}$$

The signal is typically the changes in values that are observed. It could be the arithmetic difference between values under investigation. The noise level is all type of errors that are introduced from other influences which are not observed in the study. The sample size is the number of data points being investigated.

A last rule should serve as a challenge and incentive at the same time. It is what we call the **Heisenberg-Principle for Software**:

Accurate estimating and measurement change the project.

It is a truism and relates to the Hawthorne effect. The more you know the more you can influence and change. Measurements have impact, and with more impact their usage and benefits will grow.

15. Getting yet more Information

The only Zen you find
on the tops of mountains
is the Zen you bring up there.
Robert Pirsig

15.1. Access to Information Beyond this Book

Software measurement is not easy. Many measurement programs fail to deliver actual performance improvements – for numerous reasons, as we showed in this book. You might have further questions on software measurement that go beyond the book or request specific insight.

The first thing to do is contact our Internet-site that had been established for the book: http://metrics.cs.uni-magdeburg.de/ Aside that you can contact the authors who both are very active in measurement consulting. Both have helped numerous companies around the world to establish and use software measurements.

This chapter will provide further resources, both in print and Internet media. We start with some books on software measurement that detail specific aspects which are covered in this book.

To help with introduction, to ensure useful international standards, and to guide with benchmarking and consulting, there exist many software measurement communities across the world. We provide a selection of those communities with which we have cooperated and thus gained insight in the previous years. The list is far from being complete and we apologize for this obviously subjective selection. All mentioned communities are internationally active and publish on their English Internet Web sites. The authors appreciate update proposals which we will include in the Web page of this book and also the next edition (see Chap. 1). The selection is sorted alphabetically.

Obviously, any such listing is incomplete. On the other hand, it would be of not much help to readers if the list grows to a size that is impossible to process and that has tons of invalid links. Therefore, we tried to cover those where the authors have direct access and know about the activity and its value.

All URLs in this chapter have been checked for validity and appropriateness on 25. December 2006. We invite those that detect gaps or errors to send a short mail to the lead author (mailto: christofebert@ieee.org) in order to keep the list updated for next edition.

All these references (and much more) are also electronically accessible from this book's homepage at: http://metrics.cs.uni-magdeburg.de/.

15.2. Further Reading

No single book is able to cope with all needs of a heterogeneous and international readership. We therefore recommend a few other books which highlight specific topics that might be interesting to some of you:
- Norman Fenton [Fent97] has written the classic textbook on software measurement. It can serve as an introduction providing the mathematical and statistical background of software measurement.
- ISO 15939 [ISO02a] is the international standard for software measurement and should not be missing on any bookshelf in our domain.
- John McGarry et al [McGa01] explain the usage of this ISO 15939 standard in practical terms with several insightful examples.
- Bob Grady [Grad92] in his case-oriented textbook summarizes what HP did in terms of practical software measurement with focus on managing projects.
- Steve McConnell [McCo98] has tons of insight on how to make your software projects a success. We highly recommend it.
- Mary Beth Chrissis et al [Chri06] edited the baseline of the CMMI and precisely elaborate what it demands to systematically improve your processes.
- Capers Jones [Jone01], though a little bit dated, provides a huge set of experience data that you can relate to your own measurements to have some initial benchmarking. It is still a major data reference.
- Rini Van Solingen [VanS00] has eloquently summarized what GQM stands for and how to use it in practice.
- Horst Zuse [Zuse98] provides solid expert materials on the scientific background of software measurement. We recommend it for those who want to engage in empirical research.

15.3. Measurement Communities

CMG
The Computer Measurement Group (CMG) is a globally acting non-profit organization of data processing professionals committed to the measurement and management of computer systems (hardware and software). CMG members are concerned with performance evaluation of existing systems to improve performance (e.g., response time, throughput, and so on) and with capacity management. National chapters of the CMG are active in Australia, Austria, Canada, Germany (as CECMG), Italy, South Africa, the UK (as UKCMG) and the USA. Its home page is http://www.cmg.org/.

COSMIC
The Common Software Measurement International Consortium (COSMIC) was founded in late 1998 by a group of experienced software measurers from industry and science with the aim to design and promote the second generation of software

measurement methods. A short overview of the COSMIC Full Function Points is documented in the Chap. 7.

The COSMIC-FFP method [ISO03a] is based on the strengths of the IFPUG [ISO03b], Mark II [ISO02c] and the NESMA Function Point Method [ISO05]. It uses only four base functional components: Entry, Exit, Read and Write. In developing the method there was a 14-month field trial period starting March 1999 in order to verify in industry the practicability of this new measurement method.

The tests were performed with 18 development projects from 5 organizations (16 new developments and 2 enhancements) on multiple platforms and with 21 maintenance requests of small functional enhancements in a single organization. There was consistent positive feedback about all the test requirements, with the additional benefit of a database of historical data.

The COSMIC-FFP method is the first functional sizing method to be:
- designed by an international group of experts on a sound theoretical basis;
- drawn on the practical experience of all the main existing FP methods;
- designed to conform to ISO 14143 Part 1;
- designed to work across MIS and real-time domains, for software in any layer or peer item;
- widely tested in field trials before being finalized.

The Measurement Manual is available in English, Japanese, French and Spanish. Translation into Italian and German are in progress. Furthermore, the COSMIC-FFP method was approved as an ISO standard in March 2003: ISO 19761. In addition, the COSMIC group has published the COSMIC Guide to the Implementation of ISO 19761. This guide can be downloaded from the Web at no cost at http://www.lrgl.uqam.ca/cosmic-ffp.

The International Software Benchmarking Standards Group (ISBSG) has also approved COSMIC-FFP as a data collection standard. There are several worldwide research activities under way for further improvement and dissemination of the COSMIC-FFP method (ISO 19761).

The COSMIC home page is http://www.cosmicon.com; the standard and publications are hosted at http://www.lrgl.uqam.ca/cosmic-ffp. Publications include case studies as well as a large number of research publications on COSMIC-FFP.

German GI interest group on software measurements
The German GI Fachgruppe Software 2.1.10 Software-Messung and -Bewertung. It is concerned with theoretical foundations of software measurement and evaluation as well as with practical implementation and the requirements arising with the integration in the software development process, as e.g., certifications, measurement databases or experience factories. It also fosters and stimulates research programs. Thus there is cooperation with organizations in industry (e.g., the continuing International Workshop on Software Measurement, IWSM) and international cooperation, especially with the École de Technologie Supérieure, Université du Québec (Montreal, Canada) and the CIM (Center d'Interet sur les Metriques, a Canadian measurement association). The IWSM is organized every year alternately in Montreal, Canada and Magdeburg, Germany. The proceedings of the IWSM are published on the Internet at http://www.lrgl.uqam.ca.

The GI Interest Group on Software Measurement maintains the Software Measurement Laboratory (SML@b) at University of Magdeburg which is a prototype of a software measurement database in the Internet. It allows Java based interactive entry of measurement data of popular CAME tools such as Logiscope, Datrix or OOM and delivers respective reports.

The GI Interest Group also hosts one to two meetings per year with an international audience. The home page is http://ivs.cs.uni-magdeburg.de/sw-eng/us/. It presents rich information about software measurements, experiments and literature.

IFPUG
The International Function Point User Group (IFPUG) in the USA, founded 1984, has developed a standardized function point method [ISO03] with rules for the counting of function points. The measurement of IT projects should be in line with this standard in order to be comparable between different organizations.

Furthermore, the IFPUG offers a certification (Certified Function Point Specialist, CFPS), organizes annual conferences for knowledge transfer and has working groups for the further development of the IFPUG method. Thus in 1998, as an enhancement to the existing detailed two case studies, a third one was published, covering function point counting in object-oriented projects and environments.

Many people from more than 14 countries are IFPUG members and the number grows every year. The home page of the IFPUG, http://www.ifpug.org, delivers plenty of information about software measurements and estimation as well as links to other IT measurement organizations and IFPUG member services.

The book *Measuring the Software Process*, written by David Garmus and David Herron [Garm95], contains an example of a function point examination with two sets 45 multiple choice questions (instead of two sets of 50 questions as in the official examination) and a case study that is a little bit smaller than in the official examination. The solutions are documented as well. Preparation for the CFPS examination by practicing this prototype examination five to six times has been proved to be sufficient, since there are typical questions in this example. Candidates who have counted more than 16,000 function points during practical work have a fair chance to pass the examination. The examination itself consists of three parts with a total score of 150:
- Part 1 with 50 questions about IFPUG rules (definitions)
- Part 2 with 50 questions concerning the usage of IFPUG rules (implementations), but more complicated than part 1.
- Part 3 with a case study for a complete function point count with about 15 transactions and data entities. The case study is formulated verbally and normally follows the transactions and data, with screens and reports to be counted.

For parts 1 and 2 of the examination one should plan to spend the first two hours (about 1 min. per question) in order to have enough time to understand and count the function points of the case study.

At least 90% of the answers must be correct in each of the three parts in order to pass the examination. If any one of the three parts has less than 90% correct answers, the candidate has failed. About 65% of the candidates normally pass the examination.

ISBSG

The International Software Benchmarking Standards Group (ISBSG) started as a loose cooperation of national measurement organizations. These IT measurement organizations mostly used the IFPUG function point method for the sizing of projects. They collected data about software projects with the goal to achieve improvements in software development. The indicators in the ISBSG database are closely connected to the function point sizing method. It is useful for an organization that wants to participate in an ISBSG benchmark to have historical project data sized using function points.

The mission of the ISBSG is the support of international software developers in order to improve global software engineering practices and business management of IT resources through the provision of project data that are standardized, verified, most recent and representative for current technologies.

The primary goal of the ISBSG was the development of an international repository of software project data. The collection of the data and the establishment of the ISBSG database in organizations allow software organizations to use a service that is a true alternative to its own analyses. The ISBSG database lets the organization save the effort of developing their own measurement database and additionally allows it to compare its data with the data of a network that consists of the best performers worldwide. That is benchmarking in its true sense.

The ISBSG offers the following services:

- **IT project benchmarking service**. The procedure allows the members of a national measurement organization or ISBSG to deliver their project data free of charge and with a minimal effort to the ISBSG database. The projects are quality approved and compared with similar projects in the database. A report with graphical results is delivered free of charge.
- **Best practice network**. Everybody who has contributed to the database and who is registered in the ISBSG can participate in the network.
- **"The Benchmark."** A general benchmarking report that is published about every 18 months, containing about 200 analyses and documentation of the collected data. The report has a high benefit for software developers, project leaders, consultants and organizations as well as academics. Organizations that contribute to the ISBSG database can order the report at a reduced charge.
- **Customer-specific analyses and reports**. On special demand of a participating organization the standardized report as well as a customized report according to the organization's data can be delivered. The repository data can also be bought on a disc for independent analyses.
- **Research requests**: Interested parties (e.g., academic institutes) can get the repository data for research projects on special application free of charge.
- **The ISBSG repository**: The number of projects in the ISBSG database rises continually. Release 9 of 2006 [ISBS06] contains several thousands of IT projects from more than 20 countries. The home page of the ISBSG, http://www.isbsg.org, provides information about its services.

SPEC
The Standard Performance Evaluation Corporation (SPEC) is a nonprofit organization formed to establish, maintain and endorse a standardized set of computer performance benchmarks. SPEC develops suites of benchmarks and also reviews and publishes submitted results from member organizations and other benchmark licensees. The SPEC organization is well known for processor benchmarks, but nowadays provides benchmarks for graphical systems, application servers, Web servers, mail servers or different Java implementations. Information about the SPEC can be found at its home page: http://www.spec.org/.

The MAIN Network
The Metrics Association's International Network (MAIN) was founded 2002 in Brussels, Belgium with the goal to promote, coordinate and exchange experiences among software measurements user groups worldwide. It was decided to exchange information about the activities and results of the national IT measurement organizations and to cooperate with the ISO, ISBSG and other international IT measurement organizations.

MAIN is an international network of autonomous software measurement associations. Its goals are:
- Exchange of experience among associated organizations
- Influence in international standard definition processes
- Support for the foundation of new national measurement associations
- Contribution to the organization of software measurement conferences in cooperation with any other entity
- Initiation and control common projects and working groups
- Development of a common knowledge-base of documents such as measurement papers, case studies, training materials, measurement guidelines, research initiatives database, benchmark database

Furthermore, the MAIN network supports and fosters the development of IT measurement organizations in countries that do not have national measurement organizations. The MAIN URL is http://www.mai-net.org.

The MAIN network cooperates with non-European IT measurement organizations IFPUG and ASMA (Australia). The JFPUG (Japan) is an associate member, as is the COSMIC consortium on full function points. The MAIN Network cooperates with the ISO standardization process.

The following national measurement organizations are MAIN members:
- AEMES (Association Espanola de Metricas del Software)
- DANMET (Danish Software Metrics Association)
- DASMA (Deutschsprachige Anwendergruppe für Softwaremetrik and Aufwandschätzung)
- FISMA (Finnish Software Metrics Association)
- FPUGA (Function Point User Group Austria)

- GUFPI-ISMA (Gruppo Utenti Funzioni Punti Italiana). Italy is a spearhead for functional size measurements in Europe since legal restrictions for proposals to government bodies demand the declaration of size in function points.
- IT/KVIV (Genootschap Software Metrics Belgium)
- NESMA (Netherlands Software Metrieken Gebruikers Associatie)
- SwiSMA (Swiss Software & Service Metrics Association)
- UKSMA (United Kingdom Software Metrics Association)
- JFPUG (Japanese Function Point User Group)
- An interested party is the CIM (Center d'Interet sur les Metriques – Canadian measurement association).
- A Russian measurement association is in the starting phase with the support of the FISMA.

TPC

The Transaction Processing Performance Council (TPC) is a nonprofit organization founded to define transaction processing and database benchmarks and to communicate objective, verifiable TPC performance data to the industry. Information about the TPC can be found at its home page: http://www.tpc.org/. Currently TPC provides benchmarks such as TPC-C to simulate a complete computing environment where a population of users executes transactions against a database or TPC Benchmark W (TPC-W) which is a transactional Web benchmark. The workload is performed in a controlled Internet commerce environment that simulates the activities of a business-oriented transactional Web server.

15.4. Internet Resources

To further help in building the global network on software measurement we have summarized here the most relevant links to measurement resources and communities.

15.4.1 Internet URLs for Software Measurement

Introductions, Overviews	
General overview. This the book's homepage (continuously maintained by R. Dumke)	http://metrics.cs.uni-magdeburg.de/
History of Software Measurement by H.Zuse (Univ. of Berlin):	http://irb.cs.tu-berlin.de/~zuse/metrics/3-hist.html
Empirical software engineering	http://www.cebase.org
Experimental software engineering	http://www.iese.fhg.de
List of metrics, examples: Process-product metrics in the PSM Guide:	http://www.psmsc.com/PSMGuide.asp

Standards

ISO/IEC 15939 (measurement process). PSM Guide: (guide from the US DoD, with more than 60 standard measurements and indicators (Part 5) and the measurement process used for deriving the ISO/IEC 15939 standard	http://www.psmsc.com/PSMGuide.asp
CMMI – Measurement & Analysis PA (ML2; excerpt from the CMMI v1.1 model)	http://seir.sei.cmu.edu/GDMforCMMI/CMMI_HTM_Files%5CMA.htm
ISO/IEC 19761 (full function points)	http://www.gelog.etsmtl.ca/cosmic-ffp/index.html
COSMIC and ISO/IEC 19761	http://www.cosmicon.com

Goal-driven measurement

GQM Method Web site	http://www.gqm.nl/
SEI GQM Guidebook	http://www.sei.cmu.edu/publications/documents/96.reports/96.hb.002.html
GQM: The classic article of V. Basili et al	http://www.cs.umd.edu/~mvz/handouts/gqm.pdf

Best Practices in Software Measurement

Books, papers and introductions	http://metrics.cs.uni-magdeburg.de/
IT measurement and productivity improvement. Interviews with all measurement gurus.	http://www.itmpi.org
GELOG (ETS – Univ. of Montréal, Canada) Publications – more than 1000 free publications on Software Measurement, COSMIC-FFP and other FSM methods:	http://www.gelog.etsmtl.ca/publications.html
Measurements for supplier management	http://www.sei.cmu.edu/ttp/publications/tool-kit/LinkedDocuments/Enterprise_wideindicators.ppt
Size measurement	http://www.sei.cmu.edu/publications/documents/92.reports/92.tr.020.html
Metrics for requirements engineering	http://www.cs.umu.se/~int04amd/m.pdf
Software Eng. Body of Knowledge (SWEBOK) which includes in each chapter measurement examples	http://www.swebok.org/ironman/pdf/SWEBOK_Guide_2004.pdf
Portfolio Management and all types of IT management	www.cio.com

Measurement consulting and training (world-wide)

Vector Consulting (consulting and training)	http://www.vector-consulting.de
GELOG (estimation training)	http://www.gelog.etsmtl.ca/
SEI (training on GQM, SPC and quantitative management)	http://www.sei.cmu.edu/sema/

15.4 Internet Resources

Estimation	
Project estimation overview, tools and templates (NASA)	http://software.gsfc.nasa.gov/AssetsApproved/PA1.2.1.doc
Function point calculation in all its variety.	http://www.ifpug.org
Functional size measurement	http://www.geocities.com/lbu_measure/fpa/fpa.htm
Overview on estimation methods	http://www.SoftwareMetrics.com
Effort estimation overview	http://www.geocities.com/lbu_measure/estim/effort.htm
Estimation methods based on SLIM	http://www.qsm.com
Full function points, The Common Software Metrics International Consortium	http://www.cosmicon.com/
Use case points	http://freeback.com/whitepapers/1035194512861.pdf
Requirements points and use case points	http://www.webparation.org/2006/06/16/requirement-points-in-software-engineering/
Parametric Cost Estimation, COCOMO (NASA)	http://www.jsc.nasa.gov/bu2/
Estimation Models for Software Maintenance Based on Functional Size	https://www.softwaretechnews.com/stn9-3/abran.html
Estimation and Software Maintenance Maturity Model	http://selab.netlab.uky.edu/homepage/April%20Huffman%20Abran%20Dumke%20Journal%202005.pdf
Estimating maintenance projects	http://www.cs.jyu.fi/~koskinen/smcems.pdf

Quantitative Management, Statistical Process Control, Six Sigma	
Tutorials	http://deming.eng.clemson.edu/pub/tutorials/qctools/stdntndx.htm
Statistical quality control	http://deming.eng.clemson.edu/pub/tutorials/qctools/ccmain1.htm
Explanations, training, handbook	http://www.au.af.mil/au/awc/awcgate/navy/bpi_manual/handbook.htm
Control Charts usage	http://www.au.af.mil/au/awc/awcgate/navy/bpi_manual/mod10-control.pdf
Six Sigma and CMMI. SEI/Lockheed Martin course.	http://www.sei.cmu.edu/sema/pdf/SixSigma_SiviyPenn_SEPG2003.pdf
SEI presentation and course on measurement in Six Sigma and the CMMI PA Measurement & Analysis	www.sei.cmu.edu/sema/pdf/SixSigma_Siviy_2003.pdf
CMMI Mappings and Comparisons to other frameworks	http://www.sei.cmu.edu/cmmi/adoption/comparisons.html
Statistical Process Control by NASA	www.hq.nasa.gov/office/hqlibrary/ppm/ppm31.htm
Gartner on Six Sigma	http://www.gartner.com/4_decision_tools/measurement/measure_it_articles/2002_10/six_sig.jsp

Northrop Grumman industry experiences	www.dtic.mil/ndia/2003CMMI/Hefner2.ppt
Northrop Grumman industry experiences	www.dtic.mil/ndia/2003CMMI/Facemire.ppt
Raytheon industry experiences	www.dtic.mil/ndia/2003CMMI/Kovar.ppt
Comparing CMMI and Six Sigma	www.stsc.hill.af.mil/crosstalk/2003/09/0309shere.html
Combining CMMI®, PSP, TSP, and Six Sigma for Software	http://www.software.isixsigma.com/library/content/c030502a.asp
Software Six Sigma	http://www.softwaresixsigma.com/CMM_A_SixSigma.htm

Benchmarking

ISBSG (International Software Benchmarking Standards Group) with a huge benchmarking database and online access	http://www.isbsg.org/
Access to ISBSG benchmarking data	http://www.isbsg.org/isbsg.nsf/weben/Repository%20info
APQC industry benchmarks	http://www.apqc.org
Don Reifer: Industry Software Cost, Quality and Productivity Benchmarks	http://www.softwaretechnews.com/stn7-2/reifer.html

Balanced Scorecard

Balanced scorecard and CMMI	http://www.dtic.mil/ndia/2001cmmi/castro.pdf
GQM and balanced scorecard	http://www.sei.cmu.edu/publications/documents/03.reports/03tn024.html
Strategic Planning	http://www.balancedscorecard.org/resources/wpapers.html
Business case calculation for process improvement	http://www.dtic.mil/ndia/2002cmmi/walden2a3.pdf
Raytheon industry experiences	http://www.psmsc.com/UG2003/Presentations/20SilverFinal.pdf

IT Systems Performance Measurement

SPEC, Standard Performance Evaluation - Corporation	http://www.spec.org/
TPC, Transaction Processing Performance Council	http://www.tpc.org

Tools for Estimation and Measurements

Measurement tools overview (Software Measurements Lab at Univ. of Magdeburg	http://www.smlab.de/
PSM Insight (free tool to automate the PSM process)	http://www.psmsc.com/PSMI.asp
eASEE (PLM, workflow, project and multi-project management, project tracking and dashboard, measurements, and so on)	http://www.vector-consulting.de/vc_easee_en.html

Process Dashboard. Open source initiative for a personal and lean measurement tool for the engineer's usage in PSP and for her development activities	http://processdash.sourceforge.net/
Software engineering simulation games	http://www.geocities.com/lbu_measure/games/games.htm
Project-o-poly: Monopoly and software projects	http://www.geocities.com/lbu_measure/games/pop.htm
McCabe tools for quality assessments	http://www.mccabe.com/
Software Productivity Research. KnowledgePlan estimation tools suite	http://www.spr.com
Quantitative Software Management (QSM) : SLIM estimation tools suite	http://www.qsm.com
Dataplot (free, public-domain, multi-platform statistical tool for scientific visualization, statistical analysis, and non-linear modeling)	http://www.itl.nist.gov/div898/software/dataplot/
Minitab (statistical analysis, free 30-day version)	http://www.minitab.com/downloads/
Klocwork static code analysis	http://www.klocwork.com/
Logiscope static code analysis	http://www.telelogic.com
Verifysoft static code analysis	http:// www.verifysoft.com
COCOMO II.2000 estimation tools suite	http://sunset.usc.edu/research/COCOMOII

Measurement Newsletter

IT Metrics and Productivity Journal	http://www.compaid.com/subscribe

15.4.2 Internet URLs of Measurement Communities

Measurement Communities	
AEMES, Spanish metrics organization	http://www.aemes.org/
ASQF, Arbeitskreis Software-Qualität Franken, Germany	http://www.asqf.de
BFPUG, Brazilian metrics organization	http://www.bfpug.com.br
CMG, Computer Measurement Group	http://www.cmg.org
COSMIC, The Common Software Metrics International Consortium (Full Function Points)	http://www.cosmicon.com
DASMA, Deutschsprachiger Anwenderverband für Softwaremetriken und Aufwandschätzung e.V., Germany	http://www.dasma.org
ESI, The European Software Institute, Spain	http://www.esi.es
FISMA, Finnish metrics organization	http://www.sttf.fi
Fraunhofer Institut (IESE) in Kaiserslautern	http://www.iese.fhg.de
GI Fachgruppe 2.1.10 Software-Measurement and -Bewertung, University Magdeburg	http://ivs.cs.uni-magdeburg.de/sw-eng/us/giak/

Gruppo Utenti Function Point Italia – Italian Software Metrics Association (GUFPI-ISMA)	http://www.gufpi-isma.org
IFPUG, International Function Point User Group, USA	http://www.ifpug.org
ISBSG, International Software Benchmarking Standards Group	http://isbsg.org
ISO home page	http://www.iso.org/
IT/KVIV, Genootschap Software Metrics - Belgium, Belgian metrics organization	http://www.ti.kviv.be
MAIN – Metrics Associations International Network, European metrics organization	http://www.mai-net.org
NESMA, Dutch metrics organization	http://www.nesma.org
PSM, The Practical Software and Systems Measurement Support Center, DoD	http://www.psmsc.com
Research Laboratory of the Université du - Québec, Canada	http://www.lrgl.uqam.ca
SEI, Software Engineering Institute, CMMI	http://www.sei.cmu.edu
SwiSMA, Swiss Software & Service Metrics Association	http://www.swisma.ch
UKSMA, British metrics organization	http://uksma.co.uk

15.5. Hints for the Practitioner and Summary

A lot of measurement communities and resources across the world provide expertise and consultancy for the novice and the practitioner. They are concerned with practical research, building up standards and organization of knowledge transfer, e.g., by organization of congresses. They are fostering benchmarking, networking and awareness for software measurement. Do not hesitate to contact these experts in case you have any questions. All these measurement organizations are networked and linked. The list of Internet URLs is your guide to their know how.

> Do not hesitate to contact either of the authors for your remaining questions. We have been working with many companies and individuals to improve software measurement. So far we have been training thousands of persons in getting better with measurement and improvement.

Glossary

The Glossary has been compiled based on entries from various international standards, such as IEEE Std 610 (Standard Glossary of Software Engineering Terminology) [IEEE90], ISO 15504 (Information Technology; Software Process Assessment; Vocabulary) [ISO04], ISO 15939 (Standard for Software Measurement Process) [ISO02a], the CMMI (Capability Maturity Model Integration) [SEI06a, Chri06], the SWEBOK (Software Engineering Body of Knowledge) [SWEB01], and the PMBOK (Project Management Body of Knowledge) [PMI04]. Entries are compiled and adjusted to serve the needs of this particular book. The authors acknowledge the usage of these standards and take all responsibility for deviations within the text below.

Absolute Scale. A → scale with an absolute zero (e.g., the counting of a set of objects, such as defects). See → scale.
AC. See → Actual Cost.
Acceptance Criteria. The criteria that a system or component must satisfy in order to be accepted by a user, customer, or other authorized entity.
Acceptance Test. Test activities for sample checks to verify that a system (or product, solution) has the right quality for deployment and usage. Often acceptance test is done by the customer.
Accreditation. Process used by an authorized body to formally acknowledge that a person or organization is sufficiently competent of doing specific tasks (e.g., leading a CMMI appraisal).
ACM. Association for Computing Machinery. American assembly of computer scientists.
Acquisition. The process of obtaining products (goods and services) through contract.
Activity. An element of work performed during the course of a project. An activity normally has an expected duration, expected cost, and expected resource requirements. Activities are often subdivided into tasks.
Actual Cost (AC). Total costs actually incurred and recorded in accomplishing work performed during a given time period for a defined schedule activity or work breakdown structure component. Actual cost can sometimes be direct labor hours alone, direct costs alone, or all costs including indirect costs. Also referred to as the actual cost of work performed (ACWP). See also → Earned Value Analysis.
Agile Development. Development paradigm to support efficient software engineering for typically small collocated projects. Captures well-known best practices and bundles them towards a style which avoids what is perceived as "unnecessary." Examples for agile methods include → extreme programming, → feature-driven development, → TDD.
Allocate. Assign → requirements to a project, function, process, behavior, or other logical element of the system.
Analogous Estimation. An → estimation technique that uses the values of parameters, such as scope, cost, budget, and duration or measurements of scale such as size, weight, and complexity from a previous, similar activity as the basis for estimating the same parameter or measurement for a future activity.
Application Service Provider (ASP). A company that provides servers and services to host and run applications.

Application Software. Software that is specific to the solution of an application problem (as opposed to → embedded software or a software platform).

Appraisal. Examination (sometimes called assessment) of one or more processes by a trained team of professionals using an appraisal reference model as the basis for determining at a minimum strengths and weaknesses. Mostly used in context of → CMMI (Capability Maturity Model Integration). See also → SCAMPI.

Appraisal cost. A factor of the → cost of quality consisting of the defect detection in the phase in which it is introduced. Examples include code reviews or unit test.

AQAP. Allied Quality Assurance Publication. Series of quality standards.

Architecture. A high-level design that provides decisions made about the problem that the product will solve, component descriptions, relationships between → components, and dynamic operation description.

Assessment. See → Appraisal.

Audit. Systematic, independent and documented process for obtaining evidence and evaluating it objectively to determine the extent to which audit criteria are fulfilled

Auditor. Person qualified and competent to conduct audits. See → Accreditation.

B2B. Business to Business.

B2C. Business to Customer.

B2E. Business to Employee.

Balanced Scorecard (BSC). A set of well-defined performance measurement balanced to capture different dimensions, such as finance, customers, innovation and people. Compared to one-dimensional sets of measurements, a BSC allows comparing multiple dimensions at the same time thus reducing the risk of local optimization (e.g., short-term financial gains at the cost of long-term survival).

Base Measurement. An attribute and the method for quantifying it. A base measurement is functionally independent of other → measurements and should be orthogonal (or independent) of other measurements. See also → derived measurement.

Baseline. See → Configuration Baseline.

Bathtub Curve. Distribution of maintenance effort or defects in a product over time with a U-shape function. For software the decrease at the beginning comes from removing defects, while the increase at the end comes from exploding complexity and changes. Software without changes after release will not show the increasing branch at the end.

Benchmarking. (1) The continuous process of measuring products, services and practices against competitors or those companies recognized as industry leaders. (2) An improvement paradigm with a structured and systematic learning from the best in class. Benchmarking is difficult to implement without highly effective and fast industry networks and therefore offered as a consulting product (contact C. Ebert for details).

Black Box Test. A test strategy which validates a product (or product component) based on its specified functionality. For a module these are the functions of that module, while for a complete system these are the requirements. See also → verification, → white box test, → test coverage, → system test.

BSC. See → Balanced Scorecard

Bug. A defect in a computer program. Synonymous with → defect and → fault.

Business Case. Consolidated information summarizing and explaining a business proposal from different perspectives (cost, benefit, and so on) for a decision maker. Often used for assessing the value of a product or requirements to a project. As opposed to a mere profit-loss calculation the business case is a "case" which is owned by the product manager and used for achieving the objectives.

Business Plan. Plan that details the strategy of a product or an entire enterprise. It describes the execution of a → product vision in a defined operational scenario. The business plan includes the → business case.

Business Process. A partially ordered set of enterprise activities that can be executed to realize a given objective of an enterprise or a part of an enterprise to achieve some desired end result.

Calibration. Transformation of a → measurement to another numeric system while maintaining the empirical meaning. Example: An estimation tool is calibrated before being introduced to a new enterprise.

CAME-Tool. Computer Assisted Measurement and Evaluation Tool. Software tool to prepare, execute and evaluate → measurements.

Capability. A measurement of the system's ability to achieve the mission objectives, given that the system is dependable and suitable.

Capability Maturity Model (CMM). See → CMM.

Capability Maturity Model Integration (CMMI). See → CMMI.

Cardinality. Describes the constraint on the number of entity instances that are related to the subject entity through a relationship. Cardinality is represented for each entity participating in a relationship by indicating the minimum and maximum number of its instances that may be associated with one particular instance of the related entity.

CASE. Computer-Aided (Assisted) Software / Systems Engineering. An engineering tool environment that is used to support systems or software development. See also → IDE.

Cash Flow. Cash flow is a controlling and accounting instrument and refers to the money being received and spent by a business during a defined period. Cash flow analysis is used to determine the state or performance of a business or project as it indicates liquidity. A company can fail because of a shortage of cash, even while profitable. Cash flow is also used to evaluate project rate of returns, such as the internal rate of return and → net present value.

Causal Analysis. The analysis of defects (generally, not only for software defects) to determine their underlying root cause.

CDR. Critical Design Review. A formal review process which is mostly used in a sequential life-cycle and used especially for integration or system projects with close customer-supplier interaction or several contractors involved. For the different participants it assures mutually aligned understanding of architecture and interfaces.

Certification. Acknowledgement based on a formal demonstration that a system, process or person complies with specified objectives or requirements. Example: ISO 9001 certification.

Change Agent. An individual or group that has sponsorship and is responsible for implementing or facilitating change. An example of a change agent is the systems engineering process group. Contrast with change advocate.

Change Control. An element of → configuration management, consisting of the evaluation, coordination, approval or disapproval, and implementation of changes to work products.

Change Control Board (CCB). A formally constituted group of stakeholders responsible for evaluating, approving or rejecting changes to a → configuration baseline.

Change Density. Number of changes normalized with the volume of the changed entity (e.g., changes / LOC).

Change Management. The objectives, processes and actions that are used to change an organization (e.g., introduction of a new culture, strategy implementation, process usage). See also → organizational development, → process improvement.

Change Rate. The share of changed → requirements to the totality of all requirements. Changes are new or deleted requirements or changed content. To see the project impact the changes can be based on the estimated effort. This allows to better considering the greater effort for complex changes. A change rate of 1% per month in a project with 100 person months means that on monthly basis requirements with a total estimated effort of one person month are changed. The actual effort for implementing the change is not considered, as it varies based on the time at which it is introduced.

Change Request. Formalized → requirement to expand or reduce the project scope, modify policies, processes, plans, or procedures, modify costs or budgets, or revise schedules. A change request often ripples into many items of a → configuration baseline.

Class. Classes are used in → object-oriented development to generalize the definition of attributes, operations and the semantics of a set of similar → objects. All objects of one class hold to the same definition.

Class Complexity. (1) The → complexity of a class in an → object-oriented software system. Example: many methods or a lot of method overriding increases class complexity. → Indicator for the → maintainability. (2) → Software measurement for the design and source code. The class structure (e.g., size, methods) is evaluated.

CM. See → Configuration Management.

CMM. A Capability Maturity Model (CMM) contains the essential elements of effective processes for one or more disciplines. It also describes an evolutionary improvement path from ad hoc, immature processes to disciplined, mature processes with improved quality and effectiveness. It describes the stages through which organizations evolve as they define, implement, measure, control, and improve their processes. The originator of the CMM is the → Software Engineering Institute. See also → CMMI.

CMMI. The Capability Maturity Model Integration. It is a → CMM-based concept used for process and performance improvement that is represented by products that include a set of models, appraisal methods, and a training program. It covers systems, software and hardware engineering and procurement activities. The CMMI is fully based on ISO 15504. The CMMI and its predecessor, the Software-CMM, have been used since 1990 successfully for evaluating and improving engineering processes in the IT, software and systems industries. Created and owned by the → Software Engineering Institute. Using the CMMI with fast ROI and avoiding overheads is difficult to implement without guidance and therefore offered as a consulting product (contact C. Ebert for details).

Cockpit. See → Project Dashboard.

COCOMO. Constructive Cost Model. Effort → estimation model created by B. Boehm based on a → size estimate and other environmental factors of the product to be developed.

Cognition. The human processing of information, applying knowledge and changing preferences. Cognition or cognitive processes can be natural and artificial, conscious and not conscious. Cognition depends on many factors (formation, social environment, our objectives), and so does our perception of reality.

Collaborative Product Commerce (CPC). Used synonymously with → product life-cycle management.

Commercial Off-the-Shelf (COTS). See → Standard Software.

Commitment. An agreement that is freely assumed, visible, and expected to be kept by all parties.

Common Cause of Process Variation. The variation of a → process that exists because of normal and expected interactions among the components of a process. Example: the number of defects left after code complete depends on the design and coding process and is the same across different projects in an enterprise. See also → Specific cause of process variation, → quantitative management, → SPC.

Complexity. (1) The degree to which a system or component has a design or implementation that is difficult to understand and verify. (2) Pertaining to any of a set of structure-based measurements that measure the attribute in (1). Not to be confused with → complicated.

Complexity Measurement. A → measurement to evaluate the → complexity of a software component in different development phases. Typically product attributes (e.g., size, nesting depth) are used as → indicators for the later, subjectively perceived difficulty in testing or maintenance activities. Example: → cyclomatic complexity.
Compliance. Meeting the requirements of a standard or meeting specified requirements.
Complicated. Difficult or entangled (following the Latin root of "complicare" = confusing). A system is complicated if it is difficult to understand, to analyze or to use. Complicated thus looks to the interaction of a system as an object and its observer as a subject. It depends on the person using or observing it. Not to be confused with the neutral → complex.
Component. A constituent part, element, or piece of a → complex whole. Product components are parts of the product and help to structure the development and manufacturing processes. They are integrated to "build" the product. There may be multiple levels of product components.
Concept. An abstraction to → model a defined entity from one or several points of view. Concepts are universal in that they apply equally to everything in their extension. They build the elements used by → methods.
Concurrent Engineering. An approach to project staffing that, in its most general form, calls for implementers to be involved in the design phase.
Configuration Baseline. The configuration information formally designated at a specific time during a → product's, product component's or → work product's life. Configuration baselines, plus approved changes from those baselines, constitute the current configuration information.
Configuration Management. A discipline applying technical and administrative direction and surveillance to (1) identify and document the functional and physical characteristics of a → configuration baseline and its items, (2) control changes to those characteristics, (3) record and report change processing and implementation status, and (4) verify compliance with specified requirements.
Confirmatory Data Analysis. A → data analysis used to statistically evaluate raw data to detect relationships and patterns.
Conformity. Fulfilling a requirement.
Contingency Plan. Management plan that identifies alternative strategies to be used to ensure project success if specified risk events occur. See also → risk management, → emergency plan.
Contract. A mutually binding agreement, which obligates the seller to provide the specified product, and obligates the buyer to take it and to pay for it.
Control Flow Measurement. A → software measurement for the design and source code. The control flow (e.g., number of decisions, nesting depth) is evaluated.
Corrective Action. Action taken to eliminate the cause of a detected nonconformity or other undesirable situation
Correlation Analysis. Statistical technique for analyzing the similarity of sets of different → measurements. → Parametric correlation (based on parametric distributions) and → non-parametric correlations (based on the order or ranking of objects) are distinguished.
Cost. Expenses for engineering, producing, selling, and so on, of a product or service. For software systems these are mostly labor cost plus marketing and sales expenses. Costs are typically expensed in the year they are incurred with direct impact on cash and profitability. For long-term investments they can be capitalized, with positive impact on cash but not on profit.
Cost Budgeting. Allocating the cost estimates to individual project components.

Cost Control. Controlling expenses and changes to the allocated project budget. See → Earned Value Analysis.

Cost Estimating. See → Estimation.

Cost of Non-Quality (CNQ). The cost incurred of not having the right level of quality at a given moment. The cost of non-quality includes activities from that moment onwards related to insufficient quality, such as rework, inventory cost, scrap, or quality control.

Cost of Quality. The cost incurred to ensure quality. The cost of quality includes quality planning, quality control, quality assurance, and rework.

Cost Performance Index (CPI). A measurement of cost efficiency on a project. It is the ratio of → earned value (EV) to → actual costs (AC). CPI = EV / AC. A value equal to or greater than one indicates a favorable condition (actual cost lower than planned) and a value less than one indicates an unfavorable condition (cost overrun). See also → Earned Value Analysis.

Cost Variance (CV). A measurement of cost performance on a project. It is the algebraic difference between → earned value (EV) and → actual cost (AC). CV = EV - AC. A positive value indicates a favorable condition and a negative value indicates an unfavorable condition. See also → Earned Value Analysis.

COTS. Commercial off the shelf. See → Standard Software.

CPI. See → Cost Performance Index.

Critical Path. In a project network diagram, the series of activities which determines the earliest completion of the project.

Criticality analysis. Identification of critical software components (e.g., by using → complexity measurements) during their development to focus verification activities.

Customer. Organization or person receiving a solution, service or product. Specified precisely by the contract between supplier and customer. The customer is not always the → user.

Customer Requirements Specification. See → Requirements specification.

Customer Satisfaction. The → customer's opinion of the degree to which a transaction has met the customer's needs and expectations

CV. See → Cost Variance.

Cycle Time. The time needed for getting through a product life-cycle, from inception to release of a product or solution. Often it is the duration of a commercial contract until delivery.

Cyclomatic complexity. A direct → software measurement for the number of linearly independent paths through a program's source code. Typically (and in combination with other → complexity measurements) used as an indirect measurement for complexity, criticality, understandability, testability, and so on.

Dashboard. See → Project Dashboard.

Data. Data is a precision and abstraction to reflect reality. Such abstractions may comprise numbers, words, or images. Measurements or observations of a variable are prominent examples for data. In computer science, data is often distinguished from more static, instructive programs.

Data Analysis. Methods and techniques for the statistical analysis of measurement data. See also → explorative data analysis, → confirmatory data analysis

Data Flow Measurement. A → software measurement for the design and source code. The data flow (e.g., data definitions, data references, usage of data) is evaluated.

Data Model. Abstract and formal model that describes how data is represented and used. It explains three major views namely (1) the data structure(s) which represent the entities or objects modeled, (2) data integrity rules which govern the constraints placed on the data structures to ensure structural integrity, and (3) the processes or operators which can be applied to the data structures, to update and query the data contained in the database. For instance, in the relational model, the structural part is based on mathematical relations; the integrity part is expressed in first-order logic and the manipulation part is expressed using the relational algebra, tuple calculus and domain calculus. See also → information model.

Data Quality. Data Quality refers to the quality of data. Data are deemed of high quality if they correctly represent the mapping from the empirical system (i.e., the real world where we operate) to the numeric system. It is the totality of features and characteristics of data that bears on their ability to satisfy a given need or objective. Such characteristics include availability, completeness, validity, consistency, repeatability, timeliness and accuracy.

Defect. An imperfection or deficiency in a system or component where that component does not meet its requirements or specifications which could yield a → failure. Causal relationship distinguishes the failure caused by a defect which itself is caused by a human) error.

Defect Cost. Cost of resolving a → defect (e.g., corrections, regression test, penalties of the customer). See → cost of non-quality.

Defect Density. The number of → defects identified in a product divided by the size of the product component (expressed in standard measurement terms for that product).

Defect Record. Description of a → defect (e.g., causes, effects, failures, test cases).

Delphi Method. Different experts estimate or forecast and then exchange their results with each other. In a second step they revisit their own estimates based on the group results. See → estimate. Often used for → effort estimation in unknown terrain.

Derived Measurement. A → measurement of an attribute that cannot be measured directly and thus is derived from one or several other direct measurements. Typically used to predict or forecast quality or performance attributes early in the life-cycle before they are directly measurable. See also → Base Measurement, → Indicator.

Design for Change. → Non-functional requirement that directs a solution optimized for maintainability. The entire → life-cycle is considered because most changes in a system occur after the first release. See → maintenance.

Design to Cost. → Non-functional requirement that directs a solution optimized to low → cost. The entire → life-cycle is considered depending which type of cost is put into focus (e.g., cost of production, cost of ownership, reduced pricing to the customer, and so on).

Development. See → R&D.

Development Project. Something new or enhanced (e.g., software technology, changed functionalities) are developed as a product for a market or a customer.

Direct Measurement. See → Base Measurement.

DMAIC. DMAIC (design, measure, analyze, improve, control) is a popular improvement method within → Six Sigma, in order to quantitatively evaluate processes and then improve them.

DNLOC. Delivered New Lines of Code. Number of new LOC in a product version.

Document. Information and its tangible transport medium. Documents describe → work products.

DSI. Delivered Source Instruction. See also → Lines of Code.

E4-Measurement Process. E4 (Establish, Extract, Evaluate, Execute) is a paradigm to use measurements with clear objectives. Based upon → GQM, it emphasizes the closed loop ("execute") in order to achieve concrete actions and improvements from using measurements.

Earned Value (EV). The value of completed work expressed in terms of the approved budget assigned to that work for a schedule activity or work breakdown structure component. Also referred to as the budgeted cost of work performed (BCWP). To be more suitable towards perceived value, the earned value can be adjusted to the market value of requirements. See also → Earned Value Analysis.

Earned Value Analysis. Value of the results achieved to date in a project while comparing with the projected budget and the planned schedule progress at a given date. Progress → indicator which relates already consumed resources and achieved results at a given point in time with the respective planned values for the same date.

Ebert's Law on Productivity. Productivity is improved by reducing accidents (e.g., improve engineering and management discipline, processes and tools) and controlling essence (e.g., understand what are the real needs and implement those in the product).

Effectiveness. A → measurement of the extent to which planned activities are realized and planned results achieved. Effectiveness is "doing the right things".

Efficiency. (1) Relationship between the result achieved (→ effectiveness) and the resources used. Efficiency is "doing things right". (2) A → measurement. The set of attributes that bear on the relationship between the level of performance of the software and the amount of resources used, under stated conditions.

Effort. The number of labor units required to complete an activity or other project element. Usually expressed as person hours, person weeks, or person years. Not to be confused with duration.

Effort Estimation. An assessment of the likely effort, cost or duration of a project or task at the time before or during project execution. Should always include some indication of accuracy (e.g., ± x percent). See also → Estimate.

ELOC. Executable → Lines of Code, Effective → Lines of Code. The amount of executable software code which excludes comments, and so on.

Embedded Software. A software system which is embedded to a larger system which main purpose is not computation (e.g., fuel injection in a car). Most embedded systems are → real-time systems.

Embedded System. Computer system that is embedded into another system or a process and which is not visible to the outside as a computer system. Example: Pacemaker.

EN. Euro Norm.

Engineering. (1) The application of science and mathematics by which properties of matter and the sources of energy are made useful to people. (2) An organization in the enterprise that is in charge of product development, applications or software solutions. Can be software engineering, IT or offshore centers.

Engineering Process Group (EPG). A group of specialists who facilitate the definition, maintenance, and improvement of the engineering process used by the organization. In the → CMMI, this group is generically referred to as "the group responsible for the organization's engineering process activities."

Enhancement. See → maintenance.

ENHPP. Exponential Nonhomogeneous Poisson Process. Stochastic model for reliability predictions of software systems. The failure rates decrease following an exponential function due to corrections.

Error. Cause of a defect and ultimatively a failure in a (software) system due to a human error (e.g., wrong interpretation of a requirement). See also → defect, → failure.

Error type 1. False positives. In a prediction or hypothesis verification the irrelevant elements identified as relevant.

Error type 2. False negatives. In a prediction or hypothesis verification the relevant elements identified as irrelevant.

Estimate. A quantitative assessment of the likely amount or outcome. Usually applied to project costs, size, resources, effort, or durations. It should always include some indication of accuracy (e.g., ±x percent). See also → effort estimation.

Estimate At Completion (EAC). The expected total cost of an activity, a group of activities, or of the project when the defined scope of work has been completed. Most techniques for forecasting EAC include some adjustment of the original cost estimate based on project performance to date. Also shown as "estimated at completion." Often shown as EAC = Actuals-to-date + ETC. See also → earned value and → estimate to complete.

Estimate To Complete (ETC). The expected additional cost needed to complete an activity, a group of activities, or the project. Most techniques for forecasting ETC include some adjustment to the original estimate based on project performance to date. Also called "estimated to complete." See also → earned value and → estimate at completion.

EV. See → Earned Value.

Evaluation. A systematic determination of the extent to which an entity meets its specified criteria (e.g., business objectives, quality goals, process needs). See also → verification, → validation.

Execution Time. The accumulated time a system is executed under real usage conditions. Used for → reliability measurement and predictions to relate individual test time and defect occurrence towards the would-be performance under real usage conditions.

Exploratory Data Analysis. A → data analysis used to aggregate and visualize raw data.

Extensible Markup Language (XML). XML is a standard maintained by the World-Wide Web Consortium for creating special-purpose markup languages.

External Attributes. Attributes of a product, a process or a resource, which can only be measured by considering the relationship of that product, process or resource with its environment. See also → measurement, → indicator.

Extreme Programming. An → agile methodology for software development. Underlying principles are to develop only what is needed and is based on → incremental development, refactoring, pair programming, no documentation except the code, and so on.

Failure. (1) The termination of the ability of an item to perform a required function or its inability to perform within previously specified limits. (2) The effect of a defect in a system on its external behavior. Deficient operational behavior of a system or a component due to a product defect, a user error or a hardware/software error. See also → defect, → error.

Fault. → Defect.

FDD. See → Feature Driven Development.

Feature. Transformation of input parameters to output parameters based on a specified algorithm. It describes the functionality of a product in the language of the product. Used for → requirements analysis, design, coding, testing or → maintenance.

Feature Driven Development. Abbreviation: FDD. → Agile methodology for software engineering. FDD based on → incremental development. Increments are closely linked to requirements (here: features) to assure that each increment delivers tangible value.

Field failure. A → failure which appears during operational usage of a product.

FPA. Function Point Analysis. Quantitative method to estimate function points by evaluating the software requirements or design on the number of inputs, outputs, queries, procedural complexity and environmental factors. The derived function points can be related to effort or duration of a project. See also → Estimate.

Full Function Points (FFP). Extension to → Function Points to use this functional size measurement for systems other than software only (e.g., embedded systems).

Function Points (FP). See → FPA.

Functional Requirement. See → Feature.

Functional Size. A size of the software derived by quantifying the functional → requirements. See also → FPA.

Functionality. The set of attributes that bear on the existence of a set of functions and their specified properties. The functions are those that satisfy stated or implied needs.

Gantt Chart. A graphic display of schedule-related information. In the typical bar chart, activities or other project elements are listed down the left side of the chart, dates are shown across the top, and activity durations are shown as date-placed horizontal bars. Gantt chart and bar chart are the same in project management.

Global Software Engineering. Software engineering in globally distributed sites. Different business models and work breakdown schemes are used. → Outsourcing, → Offshoring, → Rightshoring.

Goal Question Metric. Method for the goal-oriented usage of measurements by identifying goals the user wants to achieve, questions how these goals will be achieved and → measurements that show the progress to which these goals are achieved.

GQM. See → Goal Question Metric.

Graph. Formally, a graph, G={V,E}, is composed of a set of vertices, V, and edges, E, connecting the vertices.

GSD. Global Software Development. See → Global Software Engineering.

GSE. See → Global Software Engineering.

Guideline. Operational explanation how a process or tool are used in a specified situation.

Hawthorne Effect. The impacts on a process and its results by only announcing an experiment on that process.

History Database. See → Measurement Repository.

ICT. Information and Communication Technology. See → Information Technology.

IDE. Integrated Development Environment. Tool suite used to develop application software. It typically supports design, coding and verification. Additional tools support → requirements management or → test and are integrated to the IDE by its vendors.

IDEAL. Initiating, Diagnosing, Establishing, Acting, Learning. Stepwise approach to process improvement derived from the Plan-Do-Check-Act paradigm.

IEC. International Electrotechnical Commission

IEEE. Institute for Electrical and Electronics Engineers. Biggest global interest group for engineers of different branches and for computer scientists.

Increment. Internal delivery of a project. Often increments are planned as steps within a project to deliver most relevant (valuable) functionality first. Increments and iterations are used to divide complex projects and thus mitigate the associated risks. Incremental steps are planned from the beginning and allow stepwise stabilization and measurable value of the project as it progresses. → Earned Value.

Incremental Development. Project is developed and stabilized stepwise in executable and usable → increments.

Indicator. An → indirect measurement used to estimate or predict another measurement which is not yet directly measurable. The result of comparing a → measurement with a baseline quantity or expected result. Example: the design complexity is an indicator of the test effort.

Indirect Measurement. See → Derived Measurement.

Information. Information is the result of processing, transmitting, manipulating and organizing data in a way that adds to the value of the person receiving it. Unlike → data, its value is determined by the receiver and its needs.

Information Model. Abstract and formal representation of information entities including attributes, properties, relationships and possible operations that can be performed on them. Essentially the same approach is taken as in the → data model, but at the level of the represented information.

Information Technology (IT). Denomination for all information, communication and data processing technologies, covering industries, markets, and software or hardware systems and components.

Inspection. Conformity evaluation by observation and judgment accompanied as appropriate by measurement, testing or gauging. Part of → verification.

Institutionalization. The building of infrastructure and corporate culture that support methods, practices, and procedures so that they are the normal way of doing business, even after those who originally defined them are gone. "That's the way we are doing things here."

Integration Project. Different components are integrated to a product or solution. Examples: Integration of standard software (adapted to specific customer needs and integrated to his business processes), integration of components (e.g., interfaces are adapted and combined) or the integration of separate legacy systems into one new system.

Integration Test. The progressive linking and testing of software components in order to ensure their proper functioning in the complete system. See also → verification.

Internal Attributes. Attributes of a product, a process or a resource, which can be measured by only looking to that product, process or resource. See also → measurement, → indicator.

Internal Rate of Return (IRR). Return rate in the enterprise calculated from the → present value (of capital) of an investment. It shows the effective returns of an investment on today's basis.

Interval Scale. Scale type in measurement theory. Intervals of the → measurement are comparable (e.g., calendar time, temperature in degrees Celsius). See → Scale.

IPI. Internal process improvement. Often used together with → CMM assessments as CBA IPI (CMM based assessment) for process improvement within an enterprise, as opposed to externally demanded improvements. See also → SCAMPI.

IPQM. Internal Process Quality Measurements. → Measurements used within the → product life-cycle to monitor progress. Often used as release criteria to start the next activity.

ISO. International Standards Organization. UN-sponsored organization to achieve and enforce globally effective standards.

IT. See → Information Technology.

IT Portfolio. IT assets (static and dynamic) and their relationship to enterprise strategy. See also → portfolio management.

Iteration. Internal delivery of a product. Iterations are used if at start of product development not all requirements or constraints are known. They serve like → increments for dividing big projects into manageable parts and risk. Iterations handle especially technical uncertainties, such as emulating unknown hardware.

ITIL. The IT Infrastructure Library (ITIL) is a guidance and set of requirements towards organizations of processes that are necessary for operating an IT infrastructure within an enterprise.

IV&V. Independent verification and validation. A software or system (component) is verified by an organization which is neither economically nor organizationally linked with the organization responsible for development. See also → verification, → validation.

Key Account Manager (KAM). A sales person responsible for a key customer ("key account") which he supports and represents in internal decision-making processes. Key accounts are business critical because they contribute (or should contribute) to a large share of all revenues or profits.

Key Performance Indicator. A quantitative → measurement used in performance management to agree an objective and measure progress during the reporting period. Often linked to bonus payment. See also → balanced scorecard.

Key Rules. See → Policy.

Kiviat Diagram. Multidimensional diagram. A polygon with one center to show several dimensions in one diagram. The sectors represent the attributes or factors, while the polygons represent different entities. Also called spider diagram. See also → multivariate statistics.

KLOC. Kilo (thousand) → Lines of Code.

KPI. See → Key Performance Indicator.

KStmt. Kilo (thousand) statements. See also → KLOC.

Law of Demeter. Rules for the design of → object-oriented software systems with efficient class hierarchies. See also → class complexity.

Lead Time. → Cycle Time.

LI. Largely Implemented. Possible rating outcome of a practice or goal in an appraisal. See also → Appraisal, → SCAMPI.

Life-Cycle. (1) The system or product evolution initiated by a user need or by a perceived customer need through the disposal of consumer products and their life-cycle process products and by-products from inception until retirement. (2) A framework containing the processes, activities, and tasks involved in the development, operation, and maintenance of a software product, spanning the life of the system from the definition of its requirements to the termination of its use. → Product life-cycle (PLC), → product life-cycle management (PLM).

Life-Cycle Cost. The total investment in product development, test, manufacturing, distribution, operation, refining, and disposal. This investment typically is allocated across the anticipated number of units to be produced over the entire → product life-cycle, thus providing a per-unit view of life-cycle cost. See also → business case.

Life-Cycle Model. See → product life-cycle model.

LNHPP. Logarithmic Nonhomogeneous Poisson Process. Stochastical model for reliability predictions of software systems. The failure rates decrease following a logarithmic function due to corrections.

LOC. Lines of Code. The most popular size measurement for software. There are different algorithms for calculating LOC (e.g., executable code, total written lines of source code). LOC is the basis for → effort estimation and defect forecasting. Also used in hardware and firmware development.

Maintainability. The set of attributes that bear on the effort needed to make specified modifications.

Maintenance. The → product life-cycle phase of modifying a product or component after delivery to correct defects, adapt to a changed environment, improve performance or other attributes, or perform line and depot maintenance of hardware components. That is, it includes maintenance that may be corrective, adaptive, or perfective. See → Design for Change, → maintainability.

Maintenance Project. Dedicated project to provide changes to an existing product for correcting defects and for introducing new or changed functionality. See also → maintenance.

Management System. System that describes how to establish and achieve management objectives, → processes, consistent process practice, and governance.

Market. A group of people with an unresolved need and sufficient resources to apply to the satisfaction of that need.

Maturity Level. A well-defined evolutionary plateau toward achieving a mature → process. Used for evaluating process maturity and for → process improvement (→ appraisal) of both own processes and those of a supplier. The five → maturity levels in the → CMMI are labeled: Initial, repeatable, defined, managed, and optimizing.

Maturity Model. Model which maps → process maturity and → process capability in defined categories and thus permits a reliable and repeatable process evaluation. A maturity model provides requirements and expectations to processes but doesn't prescribe processes. It is thus no → product life-cycle model! Typically used for process assessments and for → process improvement (→ appraisal) of both own processes and those of a supplier. See → CMM, → CMMI.

MBO. Management by Objective. Goal-oriented management method setting concrete objectives which are followed through. See also → KPI.

MDA. See → Model Driven Architecture.

MDD. See → Model Driven Development.

Mean. Statistical measurement for a sample of data points. It is the average and the expected value of a random sample. For a data set, the mean is just the sum of all the observations divided by the number of observations. It is useful primarily in symmetrically distributed samples. The mean is the unique value about which the sum of squared deviations is a minimum. A mean without a description of → standard deviation or variance is useless.

Measurement. (1) A formal, precise, reproducible, objective mapping of a number or symbol to an empirical entity for characterizing a specific attribute. (2) Mathematically: A mapping M of an empirical system C and its relations R to a numerical system N. See also → measurement. (3) The use (e.g., extraction, evaluation, analysis, presentation and corrective actions) of a → measurement. Examples: Product measurements (e.g., defects, duration, deviation from plan, performance) or process measurements (e.g., cost of defect correction, → efficiency, → effectiveness).

Measurement Life-Cycle. The life-cycle of a → measurement or a measurement program. It consists of four phases, namely: status assessment, goal orientation, practical measurement, and optimization. This life-cycle applies to both an individual measurement (i.e., introduction, usage, optimization) as well as the entire measurement program (i.e., introduction and continuous improvement of measurement activities).

Measurement Plan. Guideline for focused → measurement during the → product life-cycle.

Measurement Repository. Repository used to collect and make available → measurement data. This repository contains or references actual measurement data and related information needed to understand, analyze and utilize (e.g., for estimations or statistical management) the measurement data.

Measurement Theory. Theoretical basis for measurement and their analysis. A branch of → statistics dealing with the use of → measurements and → scales.

Measurement Vector. Set of → measurements for a comprehensive measurement and evaluation of different (related) properties. Example: → balanced scorecard with different performance measurements.

Median. Statistical measurement for a sample of data points. It is the value where exactly half of all data points would be above and half would be below. The median of a finite list of numbers can be found by arranging all the observations from lowest value to highest value and picking the middle one. For an even number of observations, the mean of the two middle values is taken. Used in non-parametric statistics and for asymmetric distributions to describe populations.

Method. Systematically used, well-founded procedures or techniques for reaching predefined goals by execution of small steps in defined order. Derived from predefined → principles. Example: object-oriented analysis or → GQM.

Metric. (1) Mathematics: A distance vector comparing two → measurements. Aggregation of two or more measurements. (2) Software Engineering: Often used synonymously to → measurement. In line with ISO we are consistently using the term "measurement".

Migration Project. A migration project replaces a product or system at its end of life with another product or system.

Milestone. A significant event in the project, usually completion of a major deliverable. Used to structure a → life-cycle.

MIS. Management Information System. Database system for collecting, aggregating, reporting and analyzing various project and enterprise figures. There are different tools to be used. See also → CAME.

Mitigation. See → Risk Mitigation.

MLOC. Mega (million) → Lines of Code.

MM. Man month (person month). An effort measurement.

Model. An abstract representation of reality in any form (including mathematical, physical, symbolic, graphical, and descriptive form) to present a certain aspect of that reality for answering the questions studied. Example: → solution model.

Model Driven Architecture. A → MDD based method to develop (software) systems based on a strict separation of functionality and implementation. → Models and generators are used to assure continuity of models and consistency between architecture and implementation.

Model Driven Development. Product life-cycle model for development of software and systems. (Software) systems are described with a set of related → models. The models build a continuous hierarchy of abstractions. The level of abstraction is continuously decreasing from the business process to the system definition the design and finally the implementation. Changes are incorporated first to the model and afterwards in its implementation to ensure consistency across all models at all times. See also → MDA.

Modification. See → Variant.

Monte Carlo Analysis. A schedule → risk evaluation technique that performs a project simulation many times in order to calculate a distribution of likely results.

MStmt. Mega (million) statements. See also → MLOC.

MTTF. Mean Time to Failure. Reliability → measurement showing the time between two failures.

MTTR. Mean Time to Repair. Reliability → measurement showing the time a system is on average not working (due to defects or maintenance).

Multi-Project Management. The optimal allocation of resources to different projects. Being different from → portfolio management, multi-project management looks only for the best possible execution of the respective projects.

Multivariate Statistics. Statistical analysis techniques investigating relationships across several dimensions of the data. Example: Factor analysis is used to determine underlying factors describing the behaviors of a set of unknown data.

NA. Not Applicable. (1) Generally used to indicate cases where raw data is not available or a formula is not applicable. (2) Possible rating outcome of a practice or goal in an → appraisal.

NCLOC. Non-Comment Lines of Code. Lines of code that are all executable. See also → NLOC.

Net present value (NPV). See → present value.

Network Plan. Representation of a project plan as a network of activities, their relations, durations and effort.

New Development. Development of a new solution to a defined set of requirements.

NI. Not Implemented. Possible rating outcome of a practice or goal in an appraisal. See also → Appraisal, → SCAMPI.

NLOC. (1) Net Lines of Code. Number of source code lines excluding comments and empty lines. See also → NCLOC, → LOC. (2) New Lines of Code. Number of newly generated source lines of code in a variant or version compared to the baseline.

Nominal Scale. Scale type in measurement theory. Only for qualitative evaluations and abstractions (e.g., colors, class names). See → Scale.

Nonfunctional Requirements. Abilities or constraints of a product or service. They are → requirements like their functional counterparts. Must be considered during requirements analysis, architecture design, system modeling, performance tests, system tests, and so on. Example: maintainability, security, reliability.

Nonparametric Correlation. A correlation between data values not depending on any specific distribution (e.g., Spearman rank correlation).

Notation. A set of symbols that allows representing one or several concepts. Example: → UML.

NYI. Not Yet Implemented. Possible rating outcome of a practice or goal in an appraisal. See also → Appraisal, → SCAMPI.

Object. (1) generally an entity, something. (2) In → object-oriented development an object is a tangible entity with its own identity and defined scope. It possesses a state and a behavior. Its state is represented by data attributes and relationships, its behavior by operations or methods. An object is the instantiation of a → class, which generalizes attributes of objects. The defined structure and behavior of a class applies to all its instantiated objects. Only the values of attributes ("data") are specific for each object of a class.

Objective-Driven Process Improvement. A process improvement paradigm. It demands to first state explicit, business-driven improvement objectives. A dedicated improvement project is launched and executed to achieve exactly those objectives with short cycle time and tangible results. Compared to mere framework-oriented approaches that target a certificate, it uses frameworks, benchmarking and quantitative management as tools to achieve business improvement. ODPI is difficult to implement without guidance and therefore offered as a consulting product (contact C. Ebert for details).

Object-Oriented Development. Object-oriented development describes the relationship of → classes and → objects. This relationship can be static (e.g., refinement, inheritance) or dynamic (e.g., binding, messaging).

Object-Oriented Measurement. A → software measurement for the → object-oriented paradigm. Specific object-oriented attributes are characterized (e.g., method overriding, class hierarchy, → class complexity).

ODC. See → Orthogonal Defect Classification.

ODPI. See → Objective-Driven Process Improvement.

Offshoring. Executing a business activity (beyond sales and marketing) outside the home country of an enterprise. Enterprises have their offshoring branches in low-cost countries or they ask specialized companies abroad to execute the respective activity. Offshoring should therefore not be mixed with → outsourcing. See also → Nearshoring.

OMG. Object Management Group. Standardization group driving the evolution of CORBA or → UML.

OO. Object-orientation. See → object-oriented development.

OOA. Object-oriented analysis. A requirements analysis method based on → object-oriented development. OOA identifies → objects which are brought to a structure.

Open Source Software. Software which is openly (freely) accessible to the public with the right to modify, distribute, and so on. Free does not rule out license agreements, such as copyright. It means free to use.

Opportunity Cost. Additional cost or reduced income due to missed business opportunities. Example: A product has many faults and the customer therefore buys next time from the competitor.

Ordinal Scale. Scale type in measurement theory. The order of the → measurements is comparable (e.g., IQ, hardness of minerals, CMMI maturity level, priorities of requirements, street numbers). See → Scale.

Orthogonal Defect Classification (ODC). A method to classify defects according to symptoms or defect types. Having orthogonal (i.e., independent) types assures that each type has its own attributes and root causes. ODC is used to relate new defects towards previous defects thus allowing causal analysis and resolution.

OSS. See → Open Source Software.

Outsourcing. A lasting and result-oriented relationship with a supplier, who executes business activities for an enterprise which traditionally were executed inside the enterprise. Supplier can reside in direct neighborhood of the enterprise or offshore (outsourced → Offshoring).

PA. See → Process area.

Parametric Correlation. A correlation between data values depending on a specific distribution, typically normal distribution (e.g., linear correlation).

Pareto Analysis. The analysis of data by ranking effects or causes from most significant to least significant. Pareto analysis is based on the observation of the mathematician V. Pareto that most effects come from relatively few causes, i.e., 80% of the effects come from 20% of the possible causes.

Pareto Diagram. A histogram, ordered by frequency of occurrence that shows how many results each generated identified cause.

PD. Person Day. Effort → measurement.

Peer Review. Internal review activity in which experts on the same organizational hierarchy level as the author verify a work product. See → verification.

Percent Complete (PC). Percentage of the amount of work that has been completed on an activity or group of activities. See also → Earned Value.

Performance. A quantitative measurement of a product, process, person or project characterizing a physical or functional attribute relating to achieving a target or executing a mission or function. Performance attributes include quantity (how many or how much), quality (how well), coverage (how much area, how far), timeliness (how responsive, how frequent), and readiness (availability, mean time between failures). See also → efficiency.

PERT. Program Evaluation and Review Technique. Project management method developed during the 1950s in the USA to integrate planning and monitoring specifically for projects with subcontractors. It includes statistical treatment to the possible time durations and uncertainties and thus achieves better accuracy than simple one-value based techniques.

PI. Partially Implemented. Possible rating outcome of a practice or goal in an appraisal. See also → Appraisal, → SCAMPI.

PIID. Practice Implementation Indicator Description. A major work product used for a → SCAMPI → appraisal.

Plan. A documented series of tasks required meeting an objective, typically including the associated schedule, budget, resources, organizational description and work breakdown structure.

Planned Value (PV). The authorized budget assigned to the scheduled work to be accomplished for a schedule activity or work breakdown structure component. Also referred to as the budgeted cost of work scheduled (BCWS). See also → Earned Value Analysis.

PLC. See → Product Life-Cycle.

PLM. See → Product Life-Cycle Management.

PMBOK. See → Project Management Body of Knowledge.

PMI. Project Management Institute. Globally active organization that trains and certifies project managers independent from the application domain.

Policy. Guiding principles designed to influence or to determine decisions or actions. A high-level but concrete commitment that each process has to follow (i.e., applicable to all processes, projects, contracts or customers).

Glossary 527

Portability. The set of attributes that bear on the ability of software to be transferred from one environment.

Portfolio. The sum of all assets and their relationship to the enterprise strategy and its market position. See also → portfolio management.

Portfolio Management. A dynamic decision process aimed at having the right product mix and performing the right projects to implement a given strategy. It evaluates all projects in their entirety with respect to their overall contribution to business success and answers the question: do we have the right projects. It selects projects and allocates limited resources in order to meet business needs.

Practice. A technical or management activity that contributes to the creation of the output (work products) of a process or enhances the capability of a process. Example: requirements specifications are reviewed by a tester.

Precision. A statistical measurement for the quality of information retrieval. It is the ratio of the number of relevant records retrieved to the total number of irrelevant and relevant records retrieved. It is usually expressed as a percentage. It forms a natural pair with a second measurement called → recall.

Present value. Current value of all future expense and income considering a realistic interest rate with the today's ("present") date as a common reference point.

Prevention Cost. A factor of the → cost of quality capturing the effort necessary to actively prevent → defects. This factor is difficult to measure since it includes not only dedicated prevention activities, but also analysis of previous defects, and so on.

Price. The amount a customer is charged for one or more instances of the product. For internal products (e.g., IT services) there is typically an internal pricing scheme based transaction cost and external market prices.

Principle. A principle is a set of → key rules. Identifying or defining a rule as a principle says that, for the purpose at hand, the principle will not be questioned or further derived. A principle reduces the chain of arguments towards agreed axioms. Example: Information hiding is a principle to improve maintainability.

Priority. The degree of importance of a →requirement, event, task, or → project.

Probability. The likelihood of a specific outcome, measured by the ratio of specific outcomes to the total number of possible outcomes. Probability is expressed as a number between 0 and 1, with 0 indicating an impossible outcome and 1 indicating an outcome is certain.

Problem. Unfavorable and difficult to cure result or behavior in a → project or → process. Problems mostly result from not adequately managed → risks. Example: quality problems arise from undetected → defects and surface as → failures.

Process. Set of activities, which uses resources to transform inputs into outputs. A sequence of steps performed for a given purpose. Example: The → product life-cycle.

Process Area (PA). A structuring element of the Capability Maturity Model (→ CMMI). Each PA follows the same template, thus facilitating process understanding and change.

Process Capability. (1) The range of expected results that can be achieved by following a process. (2) The ability of an organization to develop and deliver products or services according to defined processes.

Process Description. A documented expression of a set of activities performed to achieve a given purpose. A process description provides an operational definition of the major components of a process. The description specifies, in a complete, precise, and verifiable manner, the requirements, design, behavior, or other characteristics of a process. It also may include procedures for determining whether these provisions have been satisfied. Process descriptions can be found at the activity, project, or organizational level.

Process Improvement. (1) A project or activities designed to improve the performance and maturity of the organization's processes related to business needs. (2) The results of such a project.

Process Maturity. See → Maturity Level.

Process Measurement. The set of definitions, methods, and activities used to perform → measurements of a → process and its resulting products for the purpose of characterizing and understanding this process.

Process Model. Abstract representation (→ model) of one or more related processes. Example: → product life-cycle model.

Product. A product is a deliverable which creates value. A combination of materials and services that is produced, is tangible and can be either an end item in itself to be used or a component item used for other products. The term "Product" covers products, customer solutions, systems, services (e.g., consulting, installation, operation, maintenance), and variants or versions of those. Products can be intended for general availability, limited deployment, pilots or prototypes. See → software product, → work product.

Product Component. See → component.

Product Data Management (PDM). PDM is a set of applications and capabilities for capturing and maintaining the definition of a product and related data through all phases of a product's life. The four most commonly used PDM applications are library functions (search and file check-in/check-out), management of bills of materials (BOMs), product configuration management (PCM) and engineering change management (ECM).

Product Life-Cycle (PLC). The sum of all activities needed to define, develop, implement, build, operate, service, and phase out a product or solution and its related variants It is subdivided into phases that are separated by dedicated milestones, called decision gates. A new phase can only be started if the previous phase has been completed and the respective phase-end or phase-entry milestones have been successful passed. With the focus on disciplined gate reviews, the PLC fosters risk management and providing auditable decision-making information (e.g., complying with product liability needs, or Sarbanes-Oxley Act section 404).

Product Life-cycle Management (PLM). PLM is the process for guiding products and solutions from inception through retirement. It comprises all processes and requires stakeholders to manage and effectively execute the PLC, including business and technology strategy, product and field marketing, portfolio management and product development. By providing aligned and collaborating processes and tools, PLM facilitates the discipline to implement strategy, planning, management and thus ensures execution through each phase of the life-cycle. PLM facilitates an enterprise's ability to monitor activities, analyze challenges and bottlenecks, make decisions and execute decisions. By lining up goals and processes, it fosters sustainable performance improvements. → Product Life-Cycle Model.

Product Life-cycle Model. Integrated assembly of all development and management → processes that are used in a project or for the lifetime of a product. A product life-cycle model describes how necessary (intermediate) results are developed. It is not a → maturity model! See also → life-cycle. Example: → V-Model.

Product Line. A group of products sharing a common, managed set of features that satisfy needs of a selected market or mission. A product within a product line shares the common basis and exhibits a defined variability to address specific market needs. Such a product line is a platform with platform elements (P1-Pn) and functionalities (F1-Fm), which are selected within a defined scope for the instantiation of a concrete product.

Product Management. Product management is the discipline and business process which governs a → product (incl. solution or service) from its inception to the market/customer delivery and service in order to generate biggest possible value to the business.

Product Measurement. A → measurement for attributes of a → product. Example: size, number of defects.

Productivity. Productivity is defined as Output over Input. Output: the value delivered. Input: the resources (e.g., effort) spent to generate the output, the influence of environmental factors (e.g., complexity, quality, time, process capability, team distribution, interrupts, feature churn, tools, and language).

Program Management. Achieving a shared objective with a set of related projects. Historically related to a set of projects for a single customer.

Project. A temporary endeavor undertaken to create a unique product or service. In software engineering we distinguish different project types (e.g., product development, IT infrastructure, outsourcing, software maintenance, service creation, and so on).

Project Controlling. Comparing actual performance with planned performance, analyzing variances, assessing trends to effect process improvements, evaluating possible alternatives, and recommending appropriate corrective action as needed. Example: → Earned value. See also → Project Dashboard.

Project Dashboard. Aggregation of all relevant → project measurements that are necessary for controlling a project. See also → project controlling.

Project Life-Cycle. The set of sequential project phases determined by the control needs of the organizations involved in the → project. Typically the project life-cycle can be broken down into at least four phases, namely concept, design, implement and closure. The project life-cycle and the → product life-cycle are interdependent, i.e., a product life-cycle can consist of several projects and a project can comprise several → products.

Project Management. The application of knowledge, skills, tools, and techniques to project activities in order to meet or exceed stakeholder needs and expectations from a → project.

Project Management Body of Knowledge (PMBOK). A repository presenting a baseline of → project management knowledge. Serves as a de-facto industry and educational standard and is used for certification. Originated and maintained by the → PMI.

Project Manager. The individual responsible for managing a → project. For technical projects it is called the technical project manager (TPM).

Project Measurement. A → measurement to evaluate attributes of a project. Example: project duration against commitments.

Project Plan. A formal, approved document used to guide both project execution and project control. The primary uses of the project plan are to document planning assumptions and decisions, to facilitate communication among stakeholders, and to document approved scope, cost, and schedule baselines.

Prototyping. Evolutionary development method for stepwise development of a solution if some requirements or constraints are fully unknown (e.g., user interface). Different from → incremental development there are no usable intermediate results. Prototypes should be thrown away as they cover only part of the needed functionality and are not designed to grow.

PSP. Personal Software Process. A → capability maturity model for personal usage. Software and systems engineers use this model to improve their own individual capability to deliver software in time and with good quality. It is fully based on small course work. The assessment is typically done based on self examination.

PV. See → Planned Value.

QFD. See → Quality Function Deployment.
Quality. (1) The ability of a set of inherent characteristics of a product, service, product component, or process to fulfill requirements of customers. (2) The degree to which a set of inherent characteristics fulfills requirements.
Quality Assurance (QA). Part of → quality management, covering the planned and systematic means for assuring management that defined standards, practices, procedures, and methods of the process are applied.
Quality Control (QC). Part of → quality management, covering the operational techniques and activities that are used to fulfill requirements for quality.
Quality Function Deployment. Method applied to → requirements prioritization or → process improvement. An evaluation of work products or project status to ascertain discrepancies from planned results and to recommend improvement.
Quality Management (QM). Sum of all planned systematic activities and processes for creating, controlling and assuring quality. See → quality control, → quality assurance.
Quality Management System (QMS). System to establish a quality policy and quality objectives and to achieve those objectives. See also → management system.
Quality Measurements. Coordinated activities to measure and direct an organization or process towards achieving → quality. Direct quality → measurements evaluate specific quality objectives (e.g., defect density, reliability). Indirect quality measurements are indicators for a direct quality measurement before it can be measured (e.g., code complexity for maintainability).
Quality Model. The set of characteristics and the relationships between them, which provide the basis for specifying quality requirements, and achieving and evaluating → quality objectives.
Quality Objective. Specific objectives, which if met, provide a level of confidence that the quality of a product is satisfactory.
Quality of Service (QoS). A → measurement that describes quality features of a delivered service. Example: Schedule adherence of an outsourcing supplier.
Quantitative Control. Any quantitative or statistical technique appropriate to analyze a process, identify → common and → specific causes of process variations in the performance of a process and bring the performance of the software process within defined limits. Example: → SPC.
Quantitative Management. Management based on quantitative or statistical techniques. It depends on defined and institutionalized processes which are optimized to achieve business goals.
Quantitatively Managed Process. A defined process that is controlled using statistical and other quantitative techniques. The product quality and other relevant process-performance attributes are measurable and controlled throughout the project.
R&D. Research and development. Comprises typically any engineering activity in the → product life-cycle. R&D is not the product management, marketing or operations activities to produce or deliver the product.
Ratio Scale. Scale type in measurement theory. Ratios of the → measurement are comparable (e.g., length, size of a program, cost, effort, time intervals). See → Scale.
RCA. See → Causal Analysis.
R Chart. Statistical control chart that monitors the dispersion or variability of a process. It shows the sample range (i.e., the difference between smallest and largest values in the subgroup) over time. See → X Chart.
Real-time system. A computer system in which not having a result available in exactly the specified timeframe will yield an error or even the loss of the entire mission.
Recall. A statistical measurement for the quality of information retrieval. It is the ratio of the number of relevant records retrieved to the total number of relevant records in the

database. It is usually expressed as a percentage. It forms a natural pair with a second measurement called → precision.

Release. Delivered → version or → variant of a product.

Reliability. The ability of a component or system to perform a required function under stated conditions for a stated period of time.

Requirement. (1) A condition or capability needed by a user to solve a problem or achieve an objective. (2) A condition or capability that must be met or possessed by a system or system component to satisfy a contract, standard, specification, or other formally imposed document. (3) A documented representation of a condition or capability as in definition (1) or (2). In simple terms a requested need not yet implemented. Explaining what needs to be done. Different types of requirements are distinguished, following a refinement from external perspective to concrete product requirements, namely a) Customer, business or solution requirements, b) product, system or marketing requirements, c) component requirements. Requirements are part of contracts, orders, project plans, test strategies, and so on. They serve as a base for defining, estimating, planning, executing, and monitoring projects.

Requirements Analysis. A systematic investigation of user → requirements (→ requirements model) to arrive at a definition of a product or system (→ solution model). All requirements are analyzed to consider their dependencies on each other and to derive on an overall impact and effort estimate. Typically several alternative designs are compared during the requirements analysis before one solution is selected and described in the → solution specification.

Requirements Engineering. The structured engineering approach in handling → requirements. See also → requirements management.

Requirements Management. The disciplined and systematic approach to elicit, structure, specify, verify, analyze, evolve and control → requirements while considering economic and business-oriented targets.

Requirements Specification. Specification which summarizes in a document all → requirements to the product to be developed. A requirements specification is not a solution description and must not mix the requirement (what is to be done?) with the solution (how is it implemented?).

Resource. Impacting or used input of a process. Examples: Human resources, equipment, services, supplies, commodities, materiel, budgets, or funds.

Return On Investment (ROI). (1) A → measurement how effectively an organization is using its capital to generate profits. In accounting it is the annual income (profit) divided by the sum of shareholder's equity and long-term debt. (2) The tangible outcome or profitability of an investment measured in business measurements (e.g., money). Defined as the ratio of returns (result from an investment) to the directly related effort (investment). See also → Return on Assets (ROA), → Return on Capital Employed (ROCE).

Reuse. The use of an existing asset (e.g., product, product component) in engineering or integration of a different product.

Review. A review of a work product, following defined procedures, typically by peers of the product's producer for the purpose of identifying defects and improvements. See also → verification, → validation.

Review Measurements. Dedicated → measurements to quantify the review process and its results. Example: review efficiency (time per defect) or review effectiveness (defects found as percentage).

Rework. Action taken on a nonconforming product to make it conform to the requirements

Risk. An uncertain event or condition that, if it occurs, has a positive or negative effect on a project's objectives. It is a function of the probability of occurrence of a given threat and the potential adverse consequences of that threat's occurrence. See also → risk management.

Risk Management. The systematic application of management policies, procedures and practices to the tasks of identifying, analyzing, evaluating, treating and monitoring → risk. Risk management evaluates the effects of today's decisions on the future. Is used in project management, product management and portfolio management. It is NOT → problem management after a risk had materialized.

Risk Mitigation. Part of → risk management. Taking steps to lessen a → risk by lowering the probability of a risk event's occurrence or reducing its effect should it occur. There are four techniques for risk mitigation: avoiding, delimiting, handling, ignoring.

ROA. See → Return on Assets.

ROCE. See → Return on Capital Employed.

ROI. See → Return On Investment.

Role. A task and responsibility within a process or workflow. Roles are not limited to a single concrete person. A person can have several roles.

Scale. (1) A vector (M,C,R,N) of a mapping M from an empirical system C with given relations R to a numerical system N. Scales are not given by nature or behaviors, but depend on the mapping of the empirical system and the transformation allowed in the numeric system. (2) Attribute of the measurement data of a → measurement with respect to nominal, ordinal, interval, ratio or absolute empirical relationships. The scale type determines the usefulness and usability of statistical techniques. For instance an average makes sense with an absolute or ratio scale, but not with a nominal or ordinary scale.

SCAMPI. Standard CMMI Appraisal Method for Process Improvement. Assessment method used for the CMMI.

SCCB. Software Change Control Board. See → configuration management, → change control.

Schedule Performance Index (SPI). A measurement of schedule efficiency on a project. It is the ratio of → earned value (EV) to → planned value (PV). SPI = EV / PV. An SPI equal to or greater than one indicates a favorable condition (earlier delivery than planned) and a value of less than one indicates an unfavorable condition (delay). See also → Earned Value Analysis.

Schedule Variance (SV). A measurement of schedule performance on a project. It is the algebraic difference between the → earned value (EV) and the → planned value (PV). SV = EV - PV. See also → Earned Value Analysis.

S-Curve. Progress of a project or process considering the availability of results over time.

SEI. See → Software Engineering Institute.

SEPG. Software Engineering Process Group. Team responsible for process improvement activities. Often called → EPG.

Service. (1) Intangible product that is the result of at least one activity performed at the interface between the supplier and customer. Service provision is defined as an activity that does not result in ownership. (2) Phase of the → product life cycle, covering all types of maintenance as well as activities that maintain or enhance the value of a product.

Service Level Agreement (SLA). Contracted agreement on a certain service level for services. The SLA defines the expected quality of a service and describes how it will be measured (e.g., cost, defects, flexibility to changes). Its limits are part of a contract and serve continuous quality improvement. A SLA has three elements: the measurement description, the objective and the pricing scheme which relates degree of fulfillment of the objective to the price to be paid.

Service-Oriented Architecture. IT infrastructure oriented at demanded business processes. The system architecture offers application- and usage-specific services and functions as IT services. Driven by usage demands and rapid adaptation to requirements and changes within the business environment.

Significance. A result from an evaluation is called significant if it is unlikely to have occurred by chance. A statistically significant result means that there is statistical evidence that there is a difference between the observed data sets. The significance level α of a test is the probability, assuming the null hypothesis, that the result would be observed in reality. The significance level is therefore also the probability that the null hypothesis will be rejected in error when it is true (a decision known as a Type I error, or "false positive").

Six Sigma. A process improvement paradigm using → statistical process control that governs processes with sufficient accuracy and control to stay with its standard deviation of outputs (sigma) within a range allowing that six times that standard deviation just reaches the allowed control interval. Six sigma is difficult to implement without guidance and therefore offered as a consulting product (contact C. Ebert for details).

SLA. See → Service Level Agreement.

SMART. Attributes of → objectives. Objectives or goals should be SMART which stands for Specific (precise to identify a clear focus), Measurable (with an underlying definition), Accountable (towards a person or activity), Realistic (achievable in the given scope), Timely (show results in a short time-frame).

SOA. See → Service-Oriented Architecture.

Socio-Technical System. A → system with technical and human components. Example: A software system which is embedded into a technical process and operated by a human.

Software. Computer programs and associated documentation and data pertaining to operation of a computer system.

Software Engineering. (1) The application of a systematic, disciplined, quantifiable approach to the development, operation, and maintenance of software; that is the application of engineering to software. (2) The study of approaches for (1).

Software Engineering Body of Knowledge (SWEBOK). A repository presenting a baseline of software engineering knowledge. Serves as a de-facto industry and educational standard.

Software Engineering Institute (SEI). An organization at the Carnegie Mellon University in Pittsburgh, USA, established to drive software process improvement. The SEI has created and owns the Capability Maturity Model. See → CMM, → CMMI.

Software Measurement. Quantified attribute of a characteristic of a software product or the software process. See also → measurement.

Software Measurement Tool. See → CAME-Tool.

Software Metric. See → Software Measurement.

Software Product. A → product which consists primarily of software. This includes software applications, services around software engineering, installation and maintenance and products in which software is embedded. It is a matter of perception whether a product is software. Example: E-Banking is a bank product within the banking industry but also a software product within a bank's IT department.

Software Reliability. The ability of a software product to run according to its specification for a defined duration. See also → reliability, → quality objective.

Software System. Part of a physical or conceptual → system consisting of software elements and a structure in which the software elements are arranged.

Software Tool. A software product providing automatic support for software life-cycle tasks. See → CASE.

SPC. See → Statistical Process Control.

Special Cause of Process Variation. The variation of a → process that exists because of temporary circumstances and not an inherent part of a process. Example: the number of defects found during test decreases due to hiring inexperienced testers. See also → common cause of process variation, → quantitative management, → statistical process control.

Specification. Precise description of an activity or a work product which serves as basis or input for further activities or work products. A specification can comprise → requirements to a product and how they will be solved. Different parts of a specification (e.g., what is to be done, how it will be done) must not be mixed.

SPI. (1) Software → Process Improvement. (2) See → Schedule Performance Index.

SPICE. (1) Software Process Improvement and Capability Determination. ISO 15504 Standard which assures globally comparable process appraisals. The → CMMI is based on this ISO standard. (2) Methodology for process improvement, similar to CMMI, but rarely used.

SPIN. Software Process Improvement Network

SRE. Software Reliability Engineering.

Stakeholder. Persons and organizations such as customers, sponsors, performing organization and the public, actively involved in the project, or whose interests may be positively or negatively affected by execution or completion of the project. They may also exert influence over the project and its deliverables.

Standard. Guidelines that reflect agreements on products, processes or operations, by nationally or internationally recognized industrial, professional, trade or governmental bodies - or accepted de facto by industry or society.

Standard Deviation. Statistical measurement to describe how observations of a set of data points differ. The standard deviation is the square root of the average of squared deviations from the → mean. Typically the standard deviation is used to further describe the mean.

Standard Software. Items that can be purchased from a commercial vendor. Commercially available components or tools that are supplied from outside. They are reused as they are (out of the box) and typically only adjusted by parameter setting or interface adjustments. Also called commercial off-the-shelf (COTS). Examples: SAP system or Linux OS. → Components can be standard software if they are offered to different customers in a standardized way.

Start-Up. New company built around an innovative product concept, but yet before the first release.

Statement of Work (SOW). The Statement of Work (SOW) is part of the project contract and describes the general → requirements to the product or service.

Statistical Process Control (SPC). The strategies, techniques and actions taken by an organization to ensure they are delivering a product or service within quantitatively defined objectives of quality, cost or time. It identifies → common and → special causes of variation in the process performance, and maintains process performance within limits. SPC is part of → quantitative management.

Statistics. The science of data. It involves collecting, organizing, analyzing, reporting and interpreting data.

Strategy. The plan for reaching an → objective while considering complex situations, given one's environment, strengths and weaknesses.

Sunk Cost. All expenses incurred before the decision at stake will be made. A paradigm that prevents the bias of decisions due to past expenses, which are of no future value.

SV. See → Schedule Variance.

SWEBOK. See: → Software Engineering Body of Knowledge.

SWOT Analysis. Analysis of strengths, weaknesses, opportunities and threats to understand and analyze one's own profile in a market and to identify potential attack or defense plans towards successful strategy execution.

System. An integrated composite consisting of one or more of the processes, hardware, software, facilities and people, that provides a capability to satisfy a stated need or objective.

System Test. Test activities to → validate an entire system (or product, solution) against product / customer → requirements.

Systems Analysis. → Requirements Analysis.

Tailoring. The adaptation of a given norm (e.g., process, contract, industry standard, design model) for an endeavor or project by excluding or adapting parts of the norm within predefined limits.

TCO. See → Total Cost of Ownership.

TDD. See → Test-driven Development.

Test. An activity in which a system or component is executed under specified conditions, the results are observed or recorded, and an evaluation is made of some aspect of the system or component. Part of → quality control. See →validation, → verification, → black box test, → white box test, → integration test, → system test, → acceptance test.

Test Coverage. A → measurement of the coverage of a program or a software system during the execution of test cases. The most often used test coverage measurements are C0 and C1 coverage. Test coverage measurements are used as → indicators for test progress and test quality.

Test Planning. Selection of test methods and test cases for a test process following defined objectives, constraints (e.g., infrastructure) and with progress → measurements. See also → test.

Test-Driven Development. → Agile method for software development where tests are designed before the development of the respective component. This ensures coverage of relevant functionality, which can be regression tested in case of changes and updates.

Time Boxing. Method for project management to finalize project in due time. Requirements are prioritized and the most important requirements are implemented first. If time or effort had been underestimated, some less relevant requirements are removed at the end for keeping schedule commitments. See also → incremental development.

Tool. Instrumented and (semi-)automated support for practically applying methods, concepts and notations in engineering tasks. See also → CASE, → CAME, → IDE.

Total Cost of Ownership (TCO). Real cost of a purchase, all impacts and contributions considered. This includes capital and operational expenses even if not included to the balance sheet, as well as process savings resulting from doing the investment. Future cost and savings are discounted to NPV. See also → business case.

Traceability. The ability to trace the history, application or location of an item or activity, or → work products or activities, by means of recorded identification. The establishment and maintenance of relationships between such items. Horizontal traceability describes the relationship between work products of same type (e.g., customer requirements). Vertical traceability describes the relationship between work products which build upon each other or are derived from each other (e.g., from customer requirements to qualification test cases). Bidirectional traceability allows to directly following relationships in both directions.

Tracing. The process of following the content of → work products amongst different work products. See → traceability.

Trend. A trend in an observation (e.g., → control chart) is any upward or downward movement of five or more consecutive points.

UML. See → Unified Modeling Language.

Unified Modeling Language (UML). Standardized → notation for modeling design descriptions, architectures or scenarios. Not depending on a specific → method. Issued and maintained by the → Object Management Group (OMG). See also → model, → use case.

Unit test. A test of individual programs or modules in order to remove design or programming errors. See also → Verification.

Usability. The set of attributes that bear on the effort needed for use, and on the individual assessment of such use, by a stated or implied set of users.

Use Case. (1) Concept to describe a system based on usage of system resources by its environment. Characterized by an objective-driven set of interactions within and at the borders of that system. (2) Notation from → UML for describing a scenario (usage approach, operational scenario) from the perspective of its user. See also → requirement.

User. Person or organization that will use the system during later operation to achieve a goal. User is not necessarily the → customer (e.g., a software application is bought by the procurement organization and used by the engineering team).

Validation. Confirmation by examination and provision of objective evidence that the particular requirements for a specific intended use are fulfilled ("doing the right thing"). Part of → quality control. See also → validation.

Variant. A precisely defined instance of a product or product component, which is different from others. A variant is derived from a product → version by defined changes. Variants are typically used if different markets or customers have heavily overlapping requirements which differ only in some details (e.g., different languages in user interface). See also → configuration management, → version.

Verification. Confirmation at the end of a process by examination and provision of objective evidence that specified requirements to the process have been fulfilled ("doing things right"). Part of → quality control. See also → verification.

Version. An instance of a product or product component with defined content which differs from others. A version is often one part in a chain of related versions building upon each other. Not all versions are necessarily delivered to all customers. See also → configuration management, → variant.

Virtual Team. A group of persons with a shared objective who fulfill their roles with little or no time spent meeting face to face. Virtual teams can be comprised of persons separated by great distances (e.g., offshoring) or separated by organizational limits (e.g., different suppliers). Various forms of technology are used to facilitate communication among team members.

V-Model. Sequential → product life-cycle model, with the right side moved upwards to a V-shape to show that each conceptual (design) step on the left side has its respective verification or validation step on the right side. (2) De facto product life-cycle standard for government projects in Germany.

VOC. See → Voice of the Customer.

Voice of the Customer. The demanded behavior of a → quantitatively managed process. Such demand arises from markets or customers and includes cost performance or number of defects delivered by the process. See → quantitative management, → statistical process control.

Voice of the Process. The regular behavior of a → quantitatively managed process. A capable process aligns the voice of the process with the → voice of the customer. See → quantitative management, → statistical process control.

VOP. See → Voice of the Process.

WBS. Work Breakdown Structure. The hierarchical refinement of a project into work packages.

White Box Test. A test strategy which validates a product (or product component) based on its known internal structure. This could be the control flow which is tested by following different paths through the code. See also → verification, → black box test, → test coverage.

Wiki. A Wiki is a collaborative work environment in the internet or intranet whose contents can be accessed and changed by its users. The name is derived from wikiwiki, the Hawaiian word for "fast." There many Wiki-based tools to easily implement collaborative workflows (e.g., requirements specification, test management).

Win Win Method. A negotiation strategy to reach the maximum result from diverging opinions of the various stakeholders. The goal is to achieve that all parties leave the concluded negotiation with the perception that they have gained something.

Work Package. A deliverable at the lowest level of the work breakdown structure. A work package may be divided into activities.

Work Product. An artifact associated with the execution of a process (e.g., requirements specification, test case).

X Chart. Statistical control chart that monitors the process means of successive subgroups over time. It is calculated by first computing the means for each subgroup and then showing them over time. Typically the X charts and → R charts are monitored together (so-called → XR Chart)

XP. See → Extreme Programming.

XR chart. Two statistical control charts showing the → X chart for process means and → R chart for process variance.

Literature

[Abra01a] Abran, A.: COSMIC – Deployment of the second generation of FSM methods. Presentation at JFPUG 2001. www.gelog.etsmtl.ca (2001). Cited 25. December 2006

[Abra01b] Abran, A., Desharnais, J., Oligny, S., Symons, C.: COSMIC FFP Measurement Manual Version 2.1. Common Software Measurement International Consortium, 2001. www.gelog.etsmtl.ca (2001). Cited 25. December 2006

[Abra02] Abran, A., Dumke, R., Desharnais, J., Ndyaje, I., Kolbe, C.: A strategy for a credible & auditable estimation process using the ISBSG International Data Repository. In: IWSM'02: Software Measurement and Estimation. Dumke, R., Abran, A., Bundschuh, M., Symons, C., 12th International Workshop on Software Measurement, Magdeburg, October 2002, Shaker, Aachen (2002) pp. 246-258

[Abra03] Abran A., J. M. Desharnais, S. Oligny, D. St-Pierre, and C. Symons, "COSMIC-FFP Measurement Manual – Version 2.2, The COSMIC Implementation Guide for ISO/IEC 19761:2003", École de technologie supérieure- ETS, Montreal (Canada) 2003. Available free at: www.gelog.etsmtl.ca/cosmic-ffp. Cited 25. December 2006

[Abra04] Abran, A.; Khelifi, A.; Buglione, L.: A System of Reference for Software Measurement with ISO 19761 (COSMIC FFP). In: Abran et al.: Software Measurement – Research and Application, Shaker Publ., Aachen, 2004, pp. 89-108

[Abra05] Abran, A.; Dumke, R. (Eds.): Innovations in Software Measurement. Shaker Publ., Aache, Germany (2005)

[Abra06] Abran,A.; Bundschuh, M.; Büren, G.; Dumke, R. (Eds.): Applied Software Measurement. Shaker ubl., Aachen, Germany, (2006)

[Abre94] Abreu, F. B., and Carapuça, R. Object-oriented software engineering: Measuring and controlling the development process. In Proceedings of the 4th International Conference on Software Quality, ASQC, McLean, VA, USA (October 1994)

[Abre96] Abreu, F. B., and Melo, W. Evaluating the impact of object-oriented design on software quality. In METRICS '96: Proceedings of the 3rd International Symposium on Software Metrics (Washington, DC, USA, 1996), IEEE Computer Society, pg. 90.

[Adam79] Adams, D. N.: The Hitchhiker's Guide to the Galaxy. Harmony Books, New York, 1979.

[Adam95] Adams, D. N.: The Ultimate Hitchhiker's Guide to the Galaxy, A Trilogy in Five Parts. Heinemann, London, 1995.

[Agle06] Aglet website. Available at http://www.trl.ibm.com/aglets . Cited 25. December 2006

[Albr83] Albrecht, A. J., Gaffney, J. E.: Software function, source lines of code and development effort prediction: a software science validation. IEEE Transactions on Software Engineering, 9: pp. 639-647 (1983)

[Armo04] Armour, P. G.: The Laws of Software Process – A New Model for the Production and Management of Software. CRC Press, 2004

[Aspr06] Aspray, W., F.Mayadas, M.Y. Vardi (ed.): Globalization and Offshoring of Software – A Report of the ACM Job Migration Task Force, Association for Computing Machinery, 2006, online at www.acm.org/globalizationreport/

[Auru03] Aurum, A. et al. (eds.): Managing Software Engineering Knowledge. Springer, Berlin Heidelberg New York, ISBN: 3-540-00370-3 (2003)

[Bach94] Bache, R.; Bazzana, G.: Software Metrics for Product Assessment. McGraw Hill Publ., 1994

[Basi01] Basili, V. R.; Boehm, B. W.: COTS-Based Systems Top 10 List. IEEE Computer, May 2001, pp. 91-95

[Basi84] Basili V. R., Perricone B. T., Software Errors and Complexity: An Empirical Investigation, Communications of the ACM, Vol. 27, No. 1, January 1984, pp. 42-52.
[Basi86] Basili, V. R., R. W. Selby, and D. H. Hutchens: Experimentation in Software Engineering. IEEE Transactions on Software Engineering. Vol. SE-12, No. 7, pp. 733-743, Jul. 1986
[Basi94] Basili, V., G. Caldiera, and H.D. Rombach, The Goal Question Metric Approach, Encyclopedia of Software Engineering, pp. 528-532, John Wiley & Sons, Inc., 1994.
[Basi96] Basili V., Briand L.C., Melo W.L., A Validation of Object-Oriented Design Metrics as Quality Indicators, IEEE Transactions on Software Engineering, Vol. 22, No. 10, October 1996, pp. 751-761
[Beck00] Beck, K.: eXtreme Programming eXplained: Embrace Change. Addison Wesley, Reading, USA (2000)
[Benk03] Benko, C.A., McFarlan, W.: Connecting the Dots. Aligning Your Project Portfolio With Corporate Objectives. McGraw-Hill, New York (2003)
[Bert03] Berthold, M.; Hand, D. J.: Intelligent Data Analysis. Springer Publ., 2003
[Biel00] Bielak, J.: Improving Size Estimate Using Historical Data. IEEE Software, Nov./December 2000, pp. 27-35
[Biff00] Biffl, S.: Using Inspection Data for Defect Estimation. IEEE Software, Nov./December 2000, pp. 36-43
[Binn95] Binney, G. and C. Williams: Leaning into the Future. Nicholas Brealey Publishing, London (1995)
[Boeh00] Boehm, B. W.: Software Cost Estimation with COCOMO II. Prentice Hall, Englewood Cliffs, USA (2000)
[Boeh88] Boehm, B.: A Spiral Model of Software Development and Enhancement, IEEE Computer, 21: 61-72, (1988)
[Boeh99] Boehm, B.: Software Cost Estimation with COCOMO II, Prentice Hall, Upper Saddle River, NJ., (1999)
[Bowe95] Bower, J.L. and C.M.Christensen: Disruption Technologies – Catching the Wave. Harvard Business Review, Jan-Feb (1995)
[Bowe96] Bowen, D.: The puny payoff from office computers. Fortune, 26. May 1986, pp. 22-26. (1986)
[Brau05] Braungarten, R.; Kunz, M.; Dumke, R.: An Approach to Classify Software Measurement Storage Facilities. Preprint No 2, Dept. of Computer Science, University of Magdeburg (2005)
[Broo87] Brooks, F. P.: No Silver Bullet, Essence and Accidents of Software Engineering. IEEE Computer, Vol. 20, No. 4, April 1987, p. 10-19 (1987)
[Bugl06] Buglione L. and Abran A., ODC and CMMI: Introducing the Root-Cause Analysis at Lower Maturity Levels, Proceedings of MENSURA2006, 1st International Conference on Software Process and Product Measurement, 6-8 November 2006, Cadiz, Spain. (2006)
[Bund00a] Bundschuh, M., Fabry, A.: Aufwandschätzung von IT-Projekten. MITP Bonn (2000) p. 331
[Bund00b] Bundschuh, M.: Function Point Approximation with the five Logical Components, FESMA 00, Madrid, Spain, October 18-20, (2000)
[Bund02b] Bundschuh, M., Estimation of Maintenance Tasks, in: Dumke, R. et al. (eds.) Software Measurement and Estimation – Proceedings of the 12th International Workshop on Software Measurement, 2002, Shaker Aachen (2002) ISBN 3-8322-0765-1, pp. 125-136
[Bund99] Bundschuh, M.: Function Point Prognosis Revisited, FESMA 99, Amsterdam, Netherlands, October 4-7, 1999, pp. 287-297

[Burk03] Burke, Rory: Project Management. 4. Edition. John Wiley & Sons, Chichester, UK, 2003
[Buzz87] Buzzel, R. D. and B. T. Gale: The PIMS Principles – Linking Strategy to Performance. The Free Press, New York (1987)
[Cai98] Cai, K.: On Estimating the Number of Defects Remaining in Software. The Journal of Systems and Software. Vol. 40, No. 2, pp. 93-114 (1998)
[Card00a] Card, D. N.: Sorting Out Six Sigma and the CMM. IEEE Software, Vol. 17, No. 4, Jul/Aug 2000
[Card00b] Card, D. N.: Making Measurement Understandable. IEEE Software, January/February 2000, pp. 95-96
[Card89] Card, D. N. and R. A. Berg: An Industrial Engineering Approach to Software Development. Journal of Systems and Software, October 1989 (1989)
[Carl92] Carleton, A.D. et al.: Software Measurement for DoD Systems: Recommendations for Initial Core Measures. Technical Report CMU/SEI-92-TR-19. (1992), Pittsburgh, USA.
[Carm01] Carmel, E. and R. Agarwal: Tactical Approaches for Alleviating Distance in Global Software Development. IEEE Software, Vol. 18, No. 2, pp. 22-29, Mrc./Apr. 2001
[Carm99] Carmel, E.: Global Software Teams. Prentice Hall, Upper Saddle River, USA, 1999.
[Cart00] Cartwright, M., and Shepperd, M. An empirical investigation of an object-oriented software system. IEEE Trans. Softw. Eng. 26, 8 (2000), 786–796.
[Chap03] Chapman, C. and Ward, S.: Project Risk Management: Processes, Techniques and Insights. Wiley, New York, USA, 2003
[Char05] Charette, R. N.: Why Software Fails. IEEE Spectrum, Vol. 42, No. 9, pp. 42-49., Sep. 2005
[Chid94] Chidamber, Shyam. R. and Kemerer, Chris F.: A Metrics Suite for Object Oriented Design. IEEE Transactions on Software Engineering, 20(6), pages 476–493, 1994
[Chid98] Chidamber, Shyam R.; Darcy, David P. and Kemerer, Chris F.: Managerial use of metrics for object-oriented software: An exploratory analysis. IEEE Transactions Software Engineering, 24(8), pages 629–639, 1998
[Chil02] James Chiles: Inviting Disaster: Lessons from the Edge of Technology. HarperCollins, New York, USA (2002)
[Chil92] Chillarege, R. et al: Orthogonal Defect Classification – A Concept for In-Process Measurements, IEEE Transactions on Software Engineering, Vol. 18, No. 11, pp. 943-956, Nov 1992.
[Chri06] Chrissis, M.B., M.Konrad and S.Shrum: CMMI. Guidelines for Process Integration and Product Improvement, ed. 2. Addison-Wesley, Reading, USA (2006)
[CIO03] The CIO newsletter: Portfolio Management. How to Do It Right. http://www.cio.com/archive/050103/portfolio.html all cases: http://www.cio.com/research/itvalue/cases.html. Cited 25. December 2006
[Clar02] Clark, B.: Eight Secrets of Software Measurement. IEEE Software, September/October 2002, pp. 12-14
[Cock02] Cockburn, A.: Agile Software Development. Addison-Wesley, Reading, USA (2002)
[Cons95] Constantine, Larry: Constantine on Peopleware. Yourdon Press Computing Series, Prentice Hall, Englewood Cliffs, USA, 1995.
[Coop04] Cooper, R. G. et al: Benchmarking Best NPD Practices: Research – Technology Management; Part I: Jan. 2004, pg. 31, Part II: May 2004, pg. 43; Part III: Nov. 2004, pg. 43. Accessible via: http://www.apqc.org . Cited 25. December 2006

[Cour93] Courtney, R. E. and D. A. Gustafson, "Shotgun Correlations in Software Measures", Software Engineering Journal, Jan 93 pp 5-13 (1993)
[Cram05] Cramton, C. D. and S. S. Webber: Relationships among geographic dispersion, team processes, and effectiveness in software development work teams. Journal of Business Research, vol. 58, pp. 758-765, 2005
[Cros79] Crosby, Philip: Quality is Free. New American Library, New York, 1979.
[Davi95] Davis, A. M.: 201 Principles of Software Development. McGraw Hill Publ., 1995
[Dekl97] Dekleva, S. and D.Drehmer: Measuring Software Engineering Evolution: A Rasch Calibration. Information Systems Research. Vol. 8, No. 1, pp. 95-105 (1997)
[DeMa82].DeMarco, Tom: Controlling Software Projects – Management, Measurement & Estimation. Yourdon Press, New York, NY, USA (1982)
[DeMa95] DeMarco, Tom: Mad About Measurement. Essay in Why Does Software Cost So Much?, Dorset House Publishing, USA (1995)
[Demi86] Deming, W. E.: Out of crisis. Cambridge, MA: MIT Center for Advanced Engineering (1986)
[Denv92] Denvir, T.; Herman, R.; Whitty, R. W.: Formal Aspects of Measurement. Springer Publ., 1992
[Deva02] Devaraj, S. and R. Kohli: The IT Payoff. Financial Times/Prentice Hall, Englewood Cliffs, USA (2002)
[Dill84] Dillon, W. R. and M. Goldstein: Multivariate Analysis – Methods and Applications. John Wiley & Sons, NY, NY, USA, 1984.
[Dreg89] Dreger, J. B.: Function Point Analysis. Prentice Hall, 1989
[Druc73] Drucker, Peter: Management: Tasks, Responsibilities, Practices, Harper & Row, New York, 1973.
[Dumk00] Dumke, R., Abran, A. (eds.): New Approaches in Software Measurement. Proc. of the 10th IWSM'00. Lecture Notes on Computer Science. LNCS 2006, Springer, Berlin Heidelberg New York (2001) p. 245
[Dumk01] Dumke, R., Abran, A. (eds.): Current Trends in Software Measurement. Proc. of the 11th IWSM'01, Shaker, Aachen (2001) p. 325
[Dumk02a] Dumke, R., Rombach, D. (eds): Software-Messung and –Bewertung. Deutscher Universitätsverlag, Wiesbaden (2002) p. 254
[Dumk02b] Dumke, R., Abran, A., Bundschuh, M., Symons, C. (eds.): Software Measurement and Estimation. Proc. of the 12th IWSM'02, Shaker, Aachen (2002) p. 315
[Dumk02c] Dumke, R.; Lother, M.; Wille, C.: Situation and Trends in Software Measurement – A Statistical Analysis of the SML@b Metrics Bibliography. In: Dumke/Abran: Software Measurement and Estimation, Shaker Publ., 2002, pp. 298-314
[Dumk03a] Dumke, R., Lother, M., Wille, C., Zbrog, F.: Web Engineering (Pearson Education, Boca Raton (2003) p. 465
[Dumk03b] Dumke, R., Abran, A. (eds): Investigations in Software Measurement. Proc. of the 13th IWSM'03. Shaker, Aachen (2003) p. 326
[Dumk04] Dumke, R.; Cotè, I.; Andruschak, O.: Statistical Process Control (SPC) – A Metrics-Based Point of View of Software Processes Achieving the CMMI Level Four. Preprint No. 7, University of Magdeburg, Fakultät für Informatik, 2004
[Dumk05a] Dumke, R.: Software Measurement Frameworks. Proc. of the 3rd World Congress for Software Quality, Vol. III, Munich, Sept. 2005, pp. 75-84
[Dumk05b] Dumke, R.; Kunz, M.; Hegewald, H.; Yazbek, H.: An Agent-Based Measurement Infrastructure. Proc. of the IWSM 2005, Shaker Publ., pp. 415-434
[Dumk05c] Dumke, R.; Richter, K.; Fetcke, T.: FSM Influences and Requirements in CMMI-Based Software Processes. In: Abran et al.: Innovations in Software Measurement. Shaker Publ., 2005, pp. 179-194

[Dumk06] Dumke, R.; Braungarten, R.; Blazey, M.; Hegewald, H.; Reitz, D.; Richter, K.: Structuring Software Process Metrics – A semantic network based overview. In. Abran et al.: Applied Software Measurement, Shaker Publ., 206, pp. 483-498
[Dumk96a] Dumke, R., Foltin, E., Koeppe, R., Winkler, A.: Softwarequalität durch Meßtools – Assessment, Messung and instrumentierte ISO 9000. Vieweg Braunschweig Wiesbaden (1996) p. 223
[Dumk96b] Dumke, R., Winkler, A.: Object-Oriented Software Measurement in an OOSE Paradigm. Proc. of the Spring IFPUG'96, February 7-9, Rome, Italy (1996)
[Dumk96c] Dumke, R.: CAME Tools – Lessons Learned. Proc. of the Fourth International Symposium on Assessment of Software Tools, May 22-24, Toronto (1996) pp. 113-114
[Dumk97] R. Dumke, H. Grigoleit, Efficiency of CAME Tools in Software Quality Assurance. Software Quality Journal, 6: pp. 157-169 (1997)
[Dumk99a] Dumke, R., E. Foltin: An Object-Oriented Software Measurement and Evaluation Framework. Proc. of the FESMA, October 4-8, 1999, Amsterdam, (1999) pp. 59-68
[Dumk99b] Dumke, R., A. Abran (eds): Software Measurement – Current Trends in Research and Practice Proc. of the 9th IWSM'99. Deutscher Universitätsverlag Wiesbaden (1999) p. 269
[eASE06] eASEE Product Lifecycle Management. http://www.vector-consulting.de/vc_easee_en.html Cited 25. December 2006
[Eber01a] Ebert, C. and P. DeNeve: Surviving Global Software Development, IEEE Software, Vol. 18, No. 2 (2001) pp. 62-69.
[Eber01b] Ebert, C.: Improving Validation Activities in a Global Software Development. Proc. Int. Conf. on Software Engineering 2001. IEEE Comp. Soc. Press, Los Alamitos, USA, 2001
[Eber01c] Ebert, C.: Metrics for Identifying Critical Components in Software Projects. In: Handbook of Software Engineering. And Knowledge Engineering. Vol.1. World Scientific Publishing, Singapore, Singapore, ISBN 981-02-4973-X. Ed. S.K.Chang. 2001
[Eber03a] Ebert, C. and M. Smouts: Tricks and Traps of Initiating a Product Line Concept in Existing Products. Proc. Int. Conference on Software Engineering (ICSE 2003), IEEE Comp. Soc. Press, pp. 520-527, Los Alamitos, USA (2003)
[Eber03b] Ebert, C., J. DeMan and F.Schelenz: e-R&D: Effectively Managing and Using R&D Knowledge. In: Managing Sofware Engineering Knowledge. Ed.: A. Aurum et al., pp. 339-359, Springer, Berlin (2003)
[Eber04] Ebert, C., R. Dumke, M. Bundschuh, and A. Schmietendorf: Best Practices in Software Measurement. Springer Verlag, (2004)
[Eber06a] Ebert, C.: Understanding the Product Life-cycle: Four Key Requirements Engineering Techniques. IEEE Software, Vol. 23, No. 3, pp. 19-25, May 2006
[Eber06b] Ebert, C.: Global Software Engineering. IEEE ReadyNote (e-Book), IEEE Computer Society, Los Alamitos, USA, 2006
http://www.computer.org/portal/cms_docs_cs/ieeecs/jsp/ReadyNotes/displayRNCatalog.jsp . Cited 25. December 2006
[Eber92] Ebert, C.: Visualization Techniques for Analyzing and Evaluating Software Measures. IEEE Transactions on Software Engineering, Vol. 18, No. 11, pp. 1029–1034, Nov. 1992.
[Eber95] Ebert, C.: Tracing Complexity through the Software Process. Proc. Int. Conf. on Engineering of Complex Computer Systems ICECCS'95. IEEE Computer Soc. Press., pp. 23-30, Los Alamitos, CA, USA, 1995.
[Eber96] Ebert, C., Dumke, R.: Software-Metriken in der Praxis, Springer, Berlin, (1996), ISBN 3-540-60372-7

[Eber97a] Ebert, C.: Experiences with Criticality Predictions in Software Development. In: Proc. Europ. Software Eng. Conf. ESEC / FSE '97, Eds. M. Jazayeri and H.Schauer, pp. 278-293, Springer, Berlin Heidelberg New York (1997)

[Eber97b] Ebert, C.: Dealing with Nonfunctional Requirements in Large Software Systems. N.R.Mead, ed.: Annals of Software Engineering, 3: pp. 367-395, (1997)

[Eber99a] Ebert, C., T.Liedtke, E.Baisch: Improving Reliability of Large Software Systems. In: A.L.Goel, ed.: Annals of Software Engineering. 8: pp. 3-51 (1999)

[Eber99b] Ebert, C. and C. Hernandez Parro: Lessons Learned from Process Change Management. Alcatel Internal White Paper. Used for invited lectures: Process Change Management in Large Organizations, Proc. FESMA '99, The European Software Measurement Conference, Amsterdam, Netherlands, Oct. 4.-8., 1999 and for tutorials on change management.

[Eick03] Eickelmann, N.: An Insider's View of CMM Level 5. IEEE Software, Vol. 20, No. 4, pg.79-81 (2003)

[Eick04] Eickelmann, N.: Measuring Maturity Goes beyond Process. IEEE Software, Vol. 21, No. 4, pg. 12-13 (2004)

[Emam05] Emam, K. E.: The ROI from Software Quality. Auerbach Publ., 2005

[Emam98] Emam, K. E.; Drouin, J. N.; Melo, W.: SPICE – The Theory and Practice of Software Process Improvement and Capability Determination IEEE Computer Society Press (1998)

[Endr03] Endres, A., Rombach, D.: A Handbook of Software and Systems Engineering – Empirical Observation, Laws and Theories. (Addison-Wesley, Reading, USA (2003) p. 327

[Erdo02] Erdogmus, H., Tanir, O.: Advances in Software Engineering – Comprehension, Evaluation, and Evolution. Springer, Berlin Heidelberg New York (2002) p. 467

[Erl05] Erl, T. Service-Oriented Architecture Concepts, Technology, and Design. Prentice Hall, 2005

[Evan94a] Evanco W. M., Lacovara R.: A model-based framework for the integration of software metrics. Journal of Systems and Software 26, 77-86 (1994)

[Evan94b] Evanco, W. M. and W. W, Agresti: A composite complexity approach for software defect modeling. Software Quality Journal, 3: pp. 27-44 (1994)

[Faro05] Farooq, A.: Conception and Prototypical Implementation of a Web Service as an Empirical-based Consulting about Java Technologies. Master thesis, University of Magdeburg, 2005

[Faro06] Farooq, A., Braungarten, R., Kunz, M., Dumke, R., and Schmietendorf, A. Towards SOA-based approaches for IT quality assurance. In CONQUEST 2006: Proceedings of 9th International Conference on Quality Engineering in Software Technology (Berlin, Germany, September 2006)

[Fent00] Fenton N., Ohlsson N., Quantitative Analysis of Faults and Failures in a Complex Software System, IEEE Transactions on Software Engineering, Vol. 26, No. 8, August 2000, pp. 797-814

[Fent02] Fenton, N.; Krause, P.; Neil, M.: Software Measurement: Uncertainty and Causal Modeling. IEEE Software, July/August 2002, pp. 116-122

[Fent93] Fenton, N.E.; Hill, G.: Systems Construction and Analysis – A Mathematical and Logical Framework. McGraw-Hill, 1993

[Fent97] Fenton, N. E., Pfleeger, S. L.: Software Metrics – A Rigorous & Practical Approach. Thomson, London (1997) p. 236

[Fetc99] Fetcke, T.: A Generalized Structure for Function Point Analysis. Proceedings of the International Workshop on Software Measurement, Lac Superieur, Mon Tremblant, Canada (1999) pp 1-25.

[FIPA06] FIPA (Foundation for Intelligent Physical Agents) website. Available at http://www.fipa.org . Cited 25. December 2006

[Flor99] Florac, W. and A. Carleton: Measuring the Software Process: Statistical Process Control for Software Process Improvement, Addison-Wesley, Reading, USA, 1999

[Folt98] Foltin, E., Dumke, R. R.: Aspects of Software Measurement database Design. Software Process – Improvement and Practice, 4: pp. 33-42 (1998)

[FT05] Financial Times: It's hard to measure the efficiency of moving targets. Financial Times, 23. Feb. 2005, pg. 4 (2005)

[Gaff94] Gaffney, J. E. Jr.: A Simplified Function Point Measure. In the Proceedings of the IFPUG 1994 Fall Conference, Oct. 19-21, 1994, Salt Lake City, Utah

[Gali06] Are CMM Program Investments Beneficial? Analyzing Past Studies. IEEE Software, Vol. 23, No. 6, pp. 81-87, Nov. 2006

[Garc05] Garcia, S.: How Standards Enable Adoption of Project Management Practice. IEEE Software, Sept./Oct. 2005, pp. 22-29

[Gard87] Gardiner, J. S. and D.C. Montgomery: Using Statistical Control Charts for Software Quality Control. Quality and Reliability Engineering International (1987)

[Garm95] Garmus, D., Herron, D.: Measuring the Software Process, Yourdon Press Computing Series, Prentice Hall PTR, Englewood Cliffs, New Jersey (1995)

[Gart02] Gartner Research Notes #TU-11-0029 (A Project Checklist) and #SPA-13-5755 (IT Portfolio Management and Survey Results). Similar survey results in: Vanderwicken Financial Digest, Standish Group, http://www.iqpc.com. Cited 25. December 2006

[GEIA02] GEIA EIA-731-1. Systems Engineering Capability Model. Government Electronics and Information Technology Association. 01. August 2002. Accessible at http://www.eia.org . Cited 25. December 2006

[Gero03] Geroimenko, V.; Chen, C.: Visualizing the Semantic Web – XML-based Internet and Information Visualization. Springer Publ. 2003

[Gibb76] Gibbons, J. D.: Nonparametric Methods for Quantitative Analysis. Holt, Rinehart and Winston, New York, NY, USA, 1976.

[Gome04] Gomez-Perez, A.; Fernandez-Lopez, M.; Corcho, O.: Ontological Engineering. Springer Publ., 2004

[Grad92] Grady, R. B.: Practical Software Metrics for Project Management and Process Improvement. Prentice Hall, Englewood Cliffs, NJ (1992)

[Hale00] Hale, J.; Parrish, A.; Dixon, B.; Smith, R. K.: Enhancing the Cocomo Estimation Models. IEEE Software, Nov./December 2000, pp. 45-49

[Hall01] Hall, T., Baddoo, N., Wilson, D.: Measurement in Software Process Improvement Programmes: An Empirical Study, in: Reiner Dumke, Alain Abran (eds.) New Approaches in Software Measurement, Proceedings of the 10th International Workshop, IWSM 2000, Berlin, October 2000, Springer, Berlin Heidelberg New York (2001) pp.73–82, ISBN 3-540-41727-3

[Hals77] Halstead, M. H.: Elements of Software Science. Prentice Hall, New York, 1977

[Hane03] Hanebutte, N.; Taylor, C.; Dumke, R. R.: Techniques of successful application of factor analysis in software measurement. Empirical Software Engineering, 8(2003)1, pp. 43-57

[Hans06] Hansson, C. et al: How agile are industrial software development practices? Journal of Systems and Software, Vol. 79, pp. 1295-1311 (2006)

[Harr03] Harry, M. and W. Schroeder: Six Sigma. Random House, New York (2000)

[Harv02] Harvey, F.: Bright stars in the Jupiter project. Financial Times, pg. 38, 18. Sep. 2002

[Harv93] Harvey-Jones, J.: Managing to Survive. Heinemann, London (1993)

[Hend96a] Henderson-Sellers, B. Object-oriented Metrics: Measures of Complexity. Prentice-Hall, Inc., Upper Saddle River, NJ, USA, 1996.
[Hend96b] Henderson-Seller, B.: The Mathematical Validity of Software Metrics. Software Engineering Notes, 21(1996)5, pp. 89-94
[Herb03] Herbsleb, J. D.; Mockus, A.: Formulation and Preliminary Test of an Empirical Theory of Coordination in Software Engineering. Software Engineering Notes, , pp. 138-147
[Hitt95] Hitt, L. and E. Brynjolfsson: Productivity, Business Profitability, and Consumer Surplus: Three Different Measures of Information Technology Value. MIS Quarterly, 20: pp. 121-142 (1995)
[Hump00] Humphrey, W. S.: Introduction to the Team Software Process. Addison-Wesley Reading, USA, 2000
[Hump89] Humphrey, W. S.: Managing the Software Process. Addison-Wesley, Reading, USA (1989)
[Hump97] Humphrey, W. S.: Introduction to the Personal Software Process. Addison-Wesley, Reading, USA (1997)
[Idea00] IDEAS International, Übersicht zu ausgewählten Benchmarkergebnissen (TPC, SPEC, SAP, BAPCo, AIM), http://www.ideasinternational.com/benchmark/bench.html. Cited 25. December 2006
[IEEE06] IEEE Standard for Developing Software Life-cycle Processes. IEEE Std 1074:2006, IEEE, Piscataway, USA. ISBN: ISBN 0-7381-4956-X (2006)
[IEEE05] IEEE Standard Dictionary of Measures of the Software Aspects of Dependability. IEEE Std 982.1:2005, IEEE, Piscataway, USA. (2005)
[IEEE90] IEEE Standard 610.12-1990. IEEE Standard Glossary of Software Engineering Terminology. IEEE, New York, NY, USA. ISBN 1-55937-067-X (1990)
[IEEE92] IEEE Standard 1045-1992. IEEE Standard for Software Productivity Metrics. IEEE, New York, NY, USA. ISBN 1-55937-258-3. (1992)
[IEEE93] IEEE Standard 1044-1993: ANSI / IEEE Standard Classification of Software Anomalies, IEEE Computer Society Press, New York, 1993
[IEEE98] IEEE Standard 1058-1998. IEEE Standard for Software Project Management Plans. IEEE, New York, NY, USA. ISBN ISBN 0-7381-1447-2 (1998)
[IFPU03] Longstreet, D.: Test Cases & Defects. Published at http://www.ifpug.com/Articles/defects.htm. Cited 25. December 2006
[IQPC03] The International Quality & Productivity Center: http://www.iqpc.com/. Cited 25. December 2006
[ISBS02] ISBSG, The Software Metrics Compendium (The Benchmark, Release 7), ISBSG, Warrandyte, Victoria (2002) ISBN 0 9577201 2 2
[ISBS06] ISBSG, The Benchmark, Release 9, ISBSG, Warrandyte, Victoria (2006) accessible at: http://www.isbsg.org/isbsg.nsf/weben/Downloads . Cited 25. December 2006
[ISO00] ISO 9001:2000. Quality management systems – Requirements. ISO, http://www.iso.org (2000)
[ISO01] ISO/IEC 9126-1:2001 – Software engineering – Product quality – Part 1: Quality model. ISO, http://www.iso.org (2001)
[ISO02a] ISO/IEC 15939:2002. Software engineering – Software measurement process. ISO, http://www.iso.org (2002)
[ISO02b] ISO 19011:2002. Guidelines for quality or environmental management systems auditing. ISO, http://www.iso.org (2002)
[ISO02c] ISO/IEC 20968:2002. Software engineering – Mk II Function Point Analysis – Counting Practices Manual. ISO, http://www.iso.org (2002)
[ISO02d] ISO/IEC 15288:2002. Systems engineering – System life-cycle processes. ISO, http://www.iso.org (2002)

[ISO02e] ISO/IEC 16949:2002. Quality management systems – Particular requirements for the application of ISO 9001:2000 for automotive production and relevant service part organizations. ISO, http://www.iso.org (2002)

[ISO03a] ISO/IEC 19761:2003 Software engineering – COSMIC-FFP – A functional size measurement method, ISO, http://www.iso.org (2003)

[ISO03b] ISO/IEC 20926:2003. Software engineering – IFPUG 4.1 Unadjusted functional size measurement method – Counting practices manual. ISO, http://www.iso.org (2003)

[ISO04] ISO/IEC 15504-1:2004. Information technology – Process assessment – Part 1: Concepts and vocabulary. ISO, http://www.iso.org (2004)

[ISO05] ISO/IEC 24570:2005. Software engineering – NESMA functional size measurement method version 2.1 – Definitions and counting guidelines for the application of Function Point Analysis. ISO, http://www.iso.org (2005)

[ISO06a] ISO/IEC 15504-5:2006 Information technology – Process Assessment – Part 5: An exemplar Process Assessment Model. ISO (2006)

[ISO06b] ISO/IEC 16085:2006 Systems and software engineering – Life cycle processes – Risk management. ISO, http://www.iso.org (2006)

[ISO95] ISO/IEC 12207:1995. Information technology – Software life-cycle processes, ISO, http://www.iso.org (1995)

[ISO98] ISO/IEC 14143-1:1998. Information technology – Software measurement – Functional size measurement – Part 1: Definition of concepts. ISO, http://www.iso.org (1998)

[ISO99] ISO/IEC 14756:1999. Information technology – Measurement and rating of performance of computer-based software systems, ISO, http://www.iso.org (1999)

[ITIL06] The ITIL Home Page, http://www.itil.org.uk/what.htm, Cited 25. December 2006

[Jacq97] Jacquet, J. P., Abran, A.: From Software Metrics to Software Measurement Methods: A Process Model, Third International Symposium and Forum on Software Engineering Standards, Walnut Creek, Canada (1997)

[JADE06] JADE website. Available at http://jade.tilab.com . Cited 25. December 2006

[Jeff97] Jeffery, R., Software Models, Metrics, and Improvement. In: Proceedings of the 8th ESCOM Conference, Berlin (1997) pp. 6-11

[JeWo94] Jennings, Nicholas R. and Wooldridge Michael J.: Agent Theories, Architectures, and Languages: A Survey. In ECAI Workshop on Agent Theories, Architectures, and Languages, pages 1–39, 1994

[John05] Johnson, P.M.; Kou, H.; Paulding, M.; Zhang, Q.; Kagawa, A. & Yamashita, T.: Improving Software Development Management through Software Project Telemetry. IEEE Software, 2005

[Jone01] Jones, C.: Software assessments, Benchmarks, and Best Practices. Addison-Wesley, Reading, USA (2001)

[Jone02] Jones, C.: How Software Estimation Tools Work. Technical Report, Software Productivity Research Inc., Burlington, MA (2002)

[Jone86] Jones, C.: Programming Productivity. McGraw-Hill, New York, (1986)

[Jone95x Jones, T. C.: Return on Investment in Software Measurement. In: Proc. 6. Int. Conf. Applications of Software Measurement. Orlando, FL, USA, (1995)

[Jone96] Jones, C., Applied Software Measurement, McGraw-Hill, New York, (1996)

[Jone97] Jones, C., Software Quality, International Thomson Computer Press, Boston, MA, (1997), ISBN 1-85032-867-6

[Jura00] Juran, J. M. and A. Blanton Godfrey: Juran's Quality Handbook. McGraw-Hill, New York, 2000.

[Juri01] Juristo, N., Moreno, A. M.: Basics of Software Engineering Experimentation Kluwer Academic, Boston (2001) p. 395

[Kan95] Kan, S. H.: Metrics and Models in Software Quality Engineering. Addison-Wesley Reading, USA, 1995
[Kapl92] Kaplan, R., Norton, D.: The Balanced Scorecard – Measures that Drive Performance. Harvard Business Review, (Jan. 1992)
[Kapl93] Kaplan, R., Norton, D.: Putting the Balanced Scorecard to Work. Harvard Business Review.(Sept/Oct 1993)
[Kell03] Keller, A., Ludwig, H.: Journal of Network and Systems Management, Special Issue on E-Business Management, Volume 11, Number 1, Plenum Publishing Corporation, March (2003)
[Kene99] Kenett, R. S., Baker, E. R.: Software Process Quality – Management and Control. Marcel Dekker, New York Basel (1999) p. 241
[Kern04] Kernchen, Steffen: Evaluation of ALIVE – Implemented with the Grasshopper Technology (In german). Case study, University of Magdeburg, 2004
[Keye03] Keyes, J.: Software Engineering Handbook Auerbach Publ., (2003)
[Khos96] Khoshgoftaar, T.M. et al: Early Quality Prediction: A Case Study in Telecommunications. IEEE Software, 13: 65-71 (1996)
[Kitc95] Kitchenham, B. A., Pfleeger, S. L., Fenton, N.: Towards a Framework for Software Measurement Validation. IEEE Transactions on Software Engineering, 21(12), 929-944 (1995)
[Kitc96] Kitchenham, B.: Software Metrics – Measurement for Software Process Improvement. NCC Blackwell, London (1996) p. 241
[Kris04] Krishna, S., Sahay, S., and Walsham, G. Managing cross-cultural issues in global software outsourcing. Communications of the ACM, Vol. 47, No. 4, pp. 62-66, 2004.
[Kulp03] Kulpa, M. K.; Johnson, K. A.: Interpreting the CMMI – A Process Improvement Approach. CRC Press Company, 2003
[Kunz06] Kunz, M.; Schmietendorf, A.; Dumke, R.; Wille, C.: Towards a Service-oriented Measurement Infrastructure. Proc. of the SMEF06 May 10-12, 2006, Rome, Italy, pp. 197-207
[Kütz03] Kütz, M. et al: Kennzahlen in der IT. Dpunkt-verlag, heidelberg, Germany, (2003)
[Lair06] Laird, L. M. and Brennan, M. C.: Software Measurement and Estimation: A Practical Approach. IEEE Computer Society Press (2006)
[Lang98] Lange, Danny B. and Oshima, Mitsuru: Programming and Deploying Java Mobile Agents with Aglets. Addison Wesley, Reading, USA, 1998
[Lanz06] Lanza, M. and Marinescu, R.: Object-Oiented Metrics in Practice. Springer Publ. (2006)
[Lech06] Lechner, D.: Software Recapitalization Economics. Crosstalk, Nov. 2006. http://www.stsc.hill.af.mil/crosstalk/2006/11/0611lechner.html, 2006, Cited 25. December 2006
[Lesz00] Leszak M., Perry D. E. and Stoll D., A Case Study in Root Cause Defect Analysis, Proceedings of the 22nd Int. Conf. on Software Engineering (ICSE 2000), Limerick (Ireland), June 4-11 2000, IEEE Comp. Soc. Press. pp. 428-437 (2000)
[Lesz02] Leszak, M., D. E. Perry and D. Stoll: Classification and Evaluation of Defects in a Project Retrospective. Journal of Systems and Software, Vol. 61, pp. 173-187 (2002)
[Lesz04] Leszak, M.: Process Modeling and Quality Control for Embedded Telecommunication Systems. Proc. IEE Workshop on Process Modeling and Simulation (ProSim), Edinburgh, May 2004 (2004)
[Long06] Longstreet, David: Software Productivity since 1970. http://www.ifpug.com/Articles/history.htm. Cited 25. December 2006
[Loth01] Lother, M., Dumke, R.: Points Metrics – Comparison and Analysis. In: Dumke, R., Abran, A. (eds.) IWSM'01: Current Trends in Software Measurement, 11th Inter-

national Workshop on Software Measurement, Montreal 2001. Shaker, Aachen, (2001) pp. 228-267

[Loth02a] Lother, M., Dumke, R.: Efficiency and Maturity of Functional Size Measurement Programs. In: Dumke et al. (eds.) Software-Messung und -Bewertung. Proceedings of the Workshop GI-Fachgruppe 2.1.10, Kaiserslautern 2001, Deutscher Universitätsverlag, (2002) pp. 94-135

[Loth02b] Lother, M., Dumke, R.: Application of eMeasurement in Software Development. Proc. of the IFPUG Annual Conference, San Antonio, Texas, (2002), chap. 5

[Loth03a] Lother, M., Dumke, R., Böhm, T., Herweg, H., Reiss, W.: Applicability of COSMIC Full Function Points for BOSCH specifications. In: IWSM'03: Investigations in Software Measurement, ed by Dumke, R., Abran, A., 13th International Workshop on Software Measurement, Montreal, September 2003, Shaker, Aachen (2003) pp. 204-217

[Loth03b] Lother, M.: Functional Size eMeasurement Portal. http://fsmportal.cs.uni-magdeburg.de/FSMPortal_Start_d.htm (2003). Cited 25. December 2006

[Loth04] Lother, M.; Braungarten, R.; Kunz, M.; Dumke, R.: The Functional Size eMeasurement Portal (FSeMP). In: Abran, A et al.: Software Measurement – Research and Application. Shaker Publ., Aachen (2004), pp. 27-40

[Lyu95] Lyu, M.R.: Handbook of Software Reliability Engineering. McGraw-Hill, New York, (1995)

[MadK06] MadKit website. Available at http://www.madkit.org . Cited 25. December 2006

[Marc94] Marciniak, J. J.: Encyclopedia of Software Engineering. Vol. I and II, John Wiley & Sons Inc., 1994

[Mark06] Marks, E. A.; Bell, M.: Service Oriented Architecture – A Planning and Implementation Guide for Business Technology. John Wiley & Sons, Hoboken/NJ, 2006 (2006)

[Maye99] Mayer, Tobias and Hall, Tracy: Measuring OO Systems: A Critical Analysis of the MOOD Metrics. In TOOLS '99: Proceedings of the Technology of Object-Oriented Languages and Systems, pg. 108, IEEE Computer Society, Washington, DC, USA, 1999

[McCa04] McCarty, T. et al: The Six Sigma Black Belt Handbook. McGraw-Hill, New York, 2004.

[McCa76] McCabe, T.J.: A Complexity Measure. IEEE Trans. on Softw. Eng., Vol. SE-2, No. 4, S. 308–320, December 1976.

[McCo03] McConnell, S.: Professional Software Development. Addison-Wesley, Reading, USA, (2003)

[McCo98] McConnell, S.: Software Project Survival Guide. Microsoft Press. Redmond, USA, (1998)

[McGa01] McGarry, J. et al: Practical Software Measurement. Addison-Wesley Longman, Reading, USA, (2001)

[McGa03] McGarry, F. and B. Decker: Attaining Level 5 in CMM Process Maturity. IEEE Software, Vol. 19, No.6, pp.87-96, (Nov. 2002)

[Meli99] Meli, R., Santillo, L.: Function Point Estimation Methods: A Comparative Overview. In: Proceedings of the FESMA Conference 1999, Amsterdam, (1999) pp. 271–286

[Meta02] Meta Group: The Business of IT Portfolio-Management: Balancing Risk, Innovation and ROI. White Paper. Jan. 2002

[Mill02] Miller, A., Ebert, C.: Software Engineering as a Business. Guest Editor Introduction for Special Issue. IEEE Software, Vol. 19, No.6, pp.18-20, (Nov. 2002)

[Mill72] Mills, H. D.: On the Statistical Validation of Computer Programs. Technical Report FSC-72-6015, Gaithersburg, MD : IBM Federal Systems Division (1972)

[Mini06] Minitab. Minitab Release 14 Statistical Software for Windows http://www.minitab.com . Cited 25. December 2006

[Morr96] Morris, M., Desharnais, J. M.: Validation of the Function Point Counts. In: Metricviews, summer 1996, (1996), p. 30

[Muns03] Munson, J. C.: Software Engineering Measurement. CRC Press Company, Boca Raton London New York, 2003

[Musa87] Musa, J. D., Iannino, A., Okumoto, K.: Software Reliability – Measurement, Prediction, Application. McGraw-Hill, New York, (1987)

[Musa91] Musa, J. D., Iannino, A.: Estimating the Total Number of Software Failures Using an Exponential Model. Software Engineering Notes, Vol. 16, No. 3, pp. 1-10, July 1991 (1991)

[Muta03a] Mutafelija, B. and H. Stromberg: Systematic Process Improvement Using ISO 9001:2000 and CMMI, pg. 300 (Artech House, Boston (2003)

[Muta03b] Mutafelija, B. and H. Stromberg: Mapping of ISO 9001:2000 and CMMI version 1.1, July 2003, URL: http://www.sei.cmu.edu/cmmi/adoption/iso-mapping.html . Cited 25. December 2006

[Myrv90] Myrvold, A.: Data Analysis for Software Metrics. Journal of Systems and Software. Vol. 12, pp. 271-275, 1990.

[NASA95] NASA: Software Measurement Guidebook. Technical Report SEL-94-102. University of Maryland, Maryland, (1995) p 134

[Niel99] Nielson, F.; Nielson, H. R.; Hankin, C.: Principles of Program Analysis. Springer Publ., 1999

[Noel98] Noel, D.: Analyse statistique pour un design plus simple de la methode de mesure de taille fonctionnelle du logiciel dans des contextes homogenes. Doctoral dissertation, UQUAM, Montreal, Canada, 2.8.1998 (1998)

[Nort00] Norton, T. R.: A Practical Approach to Capacity Modeling. Tutorials WOSP 2000, Ottawa, Canada, Sept 17-20, 2000, (2000)

[Offe97] Offen, R. J.; Jefferey, R.: Establishing software measurement programs. IEEE Software, March/April 1997, pp. 45-53

[Oman97] Oman, P., Pfleeger, S. L.: Applying Software Metrics. IEEE Computer Society Press, Los Altimos (1997) pg. 321

[Open06] OpenOffice, http://www.openoffice.org, 2006 Cited 25. December 2006

[Pand04] Pandian, C. R.: Software Metrics – A Guide to Planning, Analysis, and Application. CRC Press Company, 2004

[Paul95] Paulk, M. C. et al., The Capability Maturity Model, Addison Wesley, Reading, USA (1995)

[Pele01] Peled, D. A.: Software Reliability Methods. Springer Publ., 2001

[Pelt03] Peltz, C. Web Services Orchestration and Choreography. Computer, 2003

[Pete88] Peters, T.: Thriving on Chaos. Macmillan, London, (1988)

[Pfle97] Pfleeger, S. L. et al: Status Report on Software Measurement. IEEE Software, Vol. 14, No. 2, pp. 33-43, Mrc. 1997 (1997)

[Pfle98] Pfleeger, S. L.: Software Engineering – Theory and Practice. Prentice-Hall Publ., 1998

[Plat03] Plato: The Republic. Penguin Classics, 2003.
see also in filepedia: http://www.filepedia.org/node/4 Cited 25. December 2006

[PMI04] A Guide to the Project Management Body of Knowledge (PMBOK). 3. Edition. PMI (Project Management Institute). American National Standard ANSI/PMI 99-001-2004, (2004)

[Pott00] Potter, R. W.: The Art of Measurement. Prentice Hall Publ., 2000

[Prec01] Prechelt, L.: Kontrollierte Experimente in der Softwaretechnik – Potenzial and Methodik. Springer Publ., 2001

[Proc06] Process Dashboard Initiative. Sourceforge. http://processdash.sourceforge.net/ (2006) Cited 25. December 2006
[Putn03] Putnam, L. H., Myers, W.: Five Core Metrics – The Intelligence Behind Successful Software Management. Dorset House Publisching, New York (2003)
[Putn92] Putnam, L. H.; Myers, W.: Measures for Excellence – Reliable Software on Time, within Budget. Yourdon Press Comp., 1992
[Pyzd03] Pyzdek, T.: The Six Sigma Handbook, McGraw Hill, New York (2003)
[Radi85] Radice R.A. et al: A Programming Process Architecture, IBM Systems Journal, IBM Corp., Vol. 24, No. 2, 1995, pp. 79-90
[Reif02] Reifer, D.J.: Making the Software Business Case. Addison-Wesley Longman, Reading, USA, (2002)
[Reme00] Remenyi, D. et al.: The Effective Measurement and Management of IT Costs and Benefits (2nd eds.). Butterworth Heinemann, London, (2000)
[Royc98] Royce, W.: Software Project Management. Addison-Wesley. Reading, USA, (1998)
[Ruff06] Ruffler, M. and M. Leszak: Software Quality Assessment – A Tool-Supported Model. Proc. IWSM/Metrikon2006, Potsdam, Germany, Nov. 2006
[Sack01] Sackett D.L.: Why randomized controlled trials fail but needn't: 2. Failure to employ physiological statistics, or the only formula a clinician-trialist is ever likely to need (or understand!). CMAJ. 2001 Oct 30;165(9):1226-37.
URL: http://www.cmaj.ca/cgi/content/full/165/9/1226 . Cited 25. December 2006
[Schm01] Schmietendorf, A., Dumke, R.: Empirical Analysis of the Performance-Related Risks. In Proc. of the International Workshop on Software Measurement IWSM'01, Montreal, Quebec, Canada, August, 2001 (2001)
[Schm02] Schmietendorf, A.; Dimitrov, E.; Dumke, R.: Enterprise JavaBeans. MITP, 2002
[Schm03] Schmietendorf, A., Dumke, R.: Empirical analysis of availabe Web Services, in Dumke, R.; Abran, A. (eds.): Investigations in Software Measurement. pp. 51-69, Shaker Aachen, September 2003 (2003)
[Schm04] Schmietendorf, A.; Dumke, R.; Reitz, D.: SLA Management – Challenges in the Web-Service-Based Infrastructures. Proc. of the ICWS 2004, San Diego (2004) 606-613
[Scho99] Scholz, A., Schmietendorf, A.: A risk-driven performance engineering process approach and its evaluation with a performance engineering maturity model. In: Proceedings of the 15th Annual UK Performance Engineering Workshop. Bristol, UK, (1999)
[Schw04] Schwaber, K.: Agile Project Management with Scrum. Microsoft Press, Redmond, USA, 2004.
[SEI06a] CMMI® for Development, Version 1.2. CMU/SEI-2006-TR-008. August 2006
[SEI06b] Performance Results of CMMI®-Based Process Improvement. CMU/SEI-2006-TR-004. August 2006
[SEI06c] SEMA, Process Maturity Profile – CMMI v1.1 SCAMPI Class A Appraisal Results 2006 Mid-Year Update, Software Engineering Institute, September 2006, URL: http://www.sei.cmu.edu/appraisal-program/profile/pdf/CMMI/2006sepCMMI.pdf Cited 25. December 2006
[Shel97] Sheldrake, R.: Seven Experiments That Could Change The World. (German) Goldman Publ. 1997
[Shew31] Shewhart, W. A.: Economic Control of Manufactured Product, Van Nostrand, London (1931)
[Shul02] Shull, F. et al: What we have learned about fighting defects. Proceedings of the 8th International Symposium on Software Metrics. IEEE, Los Alamitos, USA, pp. 249-258 (2002)

[Sing99] Singpurwalla, N. D., Wilson, S. P.: Statistical Methods in Software Engineering – Reliability and Risk. Springer, Berlin Heidelberg New York (1999) p. 295

[Skyt05] Skyttner, L.: General Systems Theory – Problems, Perspectives, Practice. World Scientific Publ. (2005)

[Smit90] Smith, C.: Performance Engineering of Software Systems. Software Engineering Institute. Addison-Wesley, Reading, USA (1990)

[Smla06] SML@b Web Site: see http://www.smlab.de/ (2006). Cited 25. December 2006

[Snee05] Sneed, H.: Software-Projektkalkulation. Hanser Publ., 2005

[Snee06a] Sneed, H.: Reengineering for Testability, GI Software-Technik Trends, Band 26, Heft 2, May 2006, pg. 8 (2006)

[Snee06b] Sneed, H. and S. Jungmayr.: Product and Process Metrics for the Software Test" InformatikSpektrum, Band 29, Nr. 1, Feb. 2006, pg. 23 (2006)

[Snee96] Sneed, H. M.: Schätzung der Entwicklungskosten von objektorientierter Software. Informatik Spektrum, Springer Berlin Heidelberg New York, (1996) 19: pp. 133-140

[Soft05] IEEE Software: Theme issue on adapting agile approaches. Vol. 22, No. 3, pp. 17-49, May 2005.

[Spil06] Spillner, A., I. Linz, I. and H. Schaefer: Basic Knowledge of Software Testing, dpunkt.verlag, Heidelberg, (2006)

[Stan07] Standish Group, Chaos Reports: http://www.standishgroup.com. Cited 07. Apr. 2007. (2007)

[Star94] Stark, G., Durst, R. C., Vowell, C. W.: Using Metrics in Management Decision Making. IEEE Computer, Vol. 27, No. 9, pp. 42-48, (1994)

[Stoll99] Stoll, D., Leszak, M., Heck, T.: Measuring Process and Product Characteristics of Software Components – a Case Study. Proc. 3rd ASQF Conf. on Quality Engineering in SW Technology, Nuremberg / Germany, Sept. 1999 (1999)

[SWEB01] Guide to the Software Engineering Body of Knowledge (SWEBOK). Prospective Standard ISO TR 19759. See also at http://www.swebok.org. Cited 25. December 2006

[Symo91] Symons, C.: Software Sizing and Estimation – Mark II FPA. John Wiley and Son (1991)

[Tayn03] Tayntor, C. B.: Six Sigma Software Development. CRC Press (2003)

[Tele06] Telelogic Logiscope, Diverse Manuals, http://www.telelogic.com, (2006). Cited 25. December 2006

[QuEST06] QuEST Forum: TL 9000 Measurements Handbook. Rel. 4.0., Nov. 2006. http://www.tl9000.org/tl_hbks.htm. Cited: 03. Feb. 2007

[Ullw06] Ullwer, C.: Konzeption and prototypische Realisierung einer Telemetrie-basierten Mess-Architektur. Diplomarbeit, Otto-von-Guericke Universität Magdeburg, 2006

[VanS00] Van Solingen, R., Berghout, E.: The Goal/Question/Metric Method: A Practical Guide for Quality Improvement of Software Development. McGraw-Hill, London, (2000)

[Wads90] Wadsworth, H. M. (Ed.): Handbook of statistical methods for engineers and scientists. McGraw-Hill, New York, (1990)

[Wall02] Wallin, C. et al.: Integrating Business and Software Development Models. IEEE Software vol. 19, No. 6, pg. 18-33, November/December (2002)

[Wang00] Wang, Y., King, G.: Software Engineering Processes – Principles and Applications. CRC Press, Boca Raton New York London (2000) pg. 708

[Warb94] Warboys, B.C. (eds): Software Process Technology. Proc. of the EWSPT'94, Lecture Notes on Computer Sience, vol 772, Springer, Berlin Heidelberg New York, (1994)

[Wayn93] Wayne, M. Z., Zage, D. M.: Evaluating Design Metrics on Large-Scale Software. IEEE Software, Vol. 10, No. 7, pp. 75–81, Jul. 1993 (1993)

[Wein92] Weinberg, G. M.: Quality Software Management. Vol. I and II, Dorset House Publ., 1992
[Welc05] Welch, Jack et al: Jack: Straight from the Gut. Warner, New York, 2005.
[Whee92] Wheeler, D. HJ. and D.S. Chambers: Understanding Statistical Process Control. SPC Press. (1992)
[Whit97] Whitmire, S.A.: Object Oriented Design Measurement. John Wiley & Sons, 1997
[Wigl97] Wigle, G.B.: Practices of a Successful SEPG. European SEPG Conference 1997. Amsterdam, 1997. More in-depth coverage of most of the Boeing results. In: Schulmeyer G. G., McManus, J. I. (eds.): Handbook of Software Quality Assurance, (3rd edn), Int. Thomsom Computer Press, (1997)
[Will02] Wille, C.; Dumke, R., Stojanov, S.: New Measurement Intentions in Agent-Based System Development. In: Dumke et al.: Software Measurement and Estimation, Shaker Publ., 2002, pp. 203-227
[Will05] Wille, C.: Software Agent Measurement Framework. Shaker Publ., Aachen (2005)
[Will06] Wille, C.; Braungarten, R.; Dumke, R.: Adressing Drawbacks of Measurement Data Integration. Proc. of the SMEF 2006, May 2006, Rome, Italy, (2006)
[Wink03] Winkler, D.: Situation des eMeasurement im WWW. Research Report, University of Magdeburg, March 2003 (2003)
[Wohl00] Wohlin, C., Runeson, P., Höst, M., Ohlson, M., Regnell, B., Wesslen, A.: Experimentation in Software Engineering: An Introduction. Kluwer Academic, Boston (2000) p. 204
[Wool01] Wooldridge, Michael J. and Ciancarini, Paolo: Agent-Oriented Software Engineering: The State of the Art. In: Ciancarini/Wooldridge: Agent-Oriented Software Engineering, Lecture Notes in Computer Science 1957, Springer-Verlag, pages 1–28, 2001
[Xia04] Xia, W.; Lee, G.: Grasping the Complexity of IS Development Projects. Comm. of the ACM, 47(2004)5, pp. 69-74
[Zelk98] Zelkowitz M. V. and D. R. Wallace: Experimental Models for Validating Technology. IEEE Computer, Vol. 31, No. 5, pp. 23-31, May 1998.
[Zuse03] Zuse, H.: What can Practioneers learn from Measurement Theory. In: Dumke et al.: Investigations in Software Measurement, Proc. of the IWSM 2003, Montreal, September 2003, pp. 175-176
[Zuse94] Zuse, H.: Software Complexity Metrics/Analysis. In: Marciniak: Encyclopedia of Software Engineering, Volume I, John Wiley & Sons Inc., 1994, pp. 131-166
[Zuse98] Zuse, H.: A Framework for Software Measurement. DeGruyter, Berlin, (1998), ISBN 3-11-015587-7

Index

acceptance 151
accountability 428
accounting 444
Accuracy 126
activity-based controlling 444
activity-based costing 447
Adams, Douglas 17
additivity 58
adjusted function points 184
agents 317
aggregation 29
agile development 228, 242
aglet 319
analysis techniques 453
ANOVA 70
application counts 184
application systems 183, 184, 187
AS 9100 6
assets 27, 450
Availability 126
average function complexity 184, 185

balanced scorecard 32, 142, 184, 287
basic measurements 28, 33, 35, 200, 201, 208, 241
Basili, Vic 21, 80, 81
benchmarking 331, 471, 478, 503
benchmarking repository 472
benefits 244, 418
Boehm, Barry 168
break-even analysis 450
budget control 207
business 21, 350
business analysis 450
business case 23, 27, 144, 436, 438
business indicators 121
business objectives 26, 141, 352, 418
business success 230
buy-in 352

CAME tools 52, 84, 91, 477, 502
Capability Maturity Model 343
capable process 397
case study 420
causal analysis 284
causal analysis and resolution 286
causality 65

CFPS 502
Challenger 154
change management 336, 341, 342, 352
Chaos Report 20, 200, 423
Checkpoint/KnowledgePlan 193
chi-square test 70, 131, 266
cluster analysis 133
CMG
   Computer Measurement Group 500
CMIP
   Common Management Information Protocol 96
CMISE
   Common Management Information Service Element 96
CMM 81
CMMI 6, 76, 81, 117, 206, 234, 245, 246, 252, 286, 343, 359, 365
COCOMO 168, 193
COCOMO II 92, 168, 191, 279
code inspection 251
code review 260
CodeCheck 93
cognition 133
COMET 95
commitment 359
communication 119, 162
Completeness 126
complexity 51, 94, 264, 271, 272
Computer Aided Measurement and Evaluation (CAME) *See*
configuration management 333
Consistency 126
continuous improvement 394
control 446
control chart 69, 285, 399, 400, 411, 415
controlling 158, 435
core measurements 28, 33, 35, 200, 201, 208, 241
correlation analysis 71, 131, 417
COSAM 95
COSMIC 165, 167, 169, 187, 500, 501, 504
COSMOS 93
cost analysis 331
cost breakdown 26, 28, 32, 378
cost control 443

cost control measurements 445
cost controlling 446
cost estimation 444
cost of appraisal 295
cost of nonconformance 295
cost of non-quality 258, 294, 295, 442
cost of performance 295
cost of prevention 295
cost of quality 294, 295, 442
cost structure 28, 32, 378
cost tree 378
COSTAR 92
COTS software 482
CPM 501
criticality prediction 262, 269
Crow model 292
culture 148, 157, 428
culture change 348
customer 245
customer measurements 143
customer satisfaction 245
cyclomatic complexity 51, 94, 264, 272

dashboard 29, 30, 207
DASMA 153, 504
data quality 126, 130, 146, 157
DATRIX 93
DCF 142
De Marco, Tom 19
deadline 206
defect 246, 251, 283, 350
defect distribution 249
defect estimation 247
defect prediction 269, 272
defect reporting 251, 283
defect tracking 251
defects 288
DeMarco, Tom 138, 158, 283
Deming, William 24, 394
design activities 126
design review 251
Disraeli, Benjamin 136
DMAIC 84, 405
DOCTOR HTML 95
documentation 152
DoD 2167 6
Drucker, Peter 19

E4–measurement process 8, 24, 39, 109, 110, 111, 217, 349, 403, 404, 436

early estimation 183
earned value analysis 212
Ebert's law 299, 385, 497
EBIT 142
e-certification 103
e-experience 103
effectiveness 226, 260
efficiency 260
effort 149, 151, 152, 189, 190, 191, 193, 197
effort estimation methods 119
EFQM 287
EIA 731 6
embedded software 268
e-Measurement 102
e-Measurement communities 102
e-measurement consulting 102
empirical relational system 57
empirical software engineering 418
end user efficiency 152
engineering balance sheet 201
ENHPP 292
e-quality services 102
e-repositories 103
error type 1 250, 266
error type 2 250, 266
estimation 48, 189, 193, 502
estimation crisis 194
estimation tool 185, 189, 193
EVA 212
Excel 95
exchange of experiences 153
experimentation 47, 65, 67, 418, 420

factor analysis 47, 132
failure 246, 288
failure prediction 251
fault tree analysis 272
feasibility study 180, 237, 439
feature churn 221
feedback 149, 150
feedback loop 356
FFP 165, 167, 169
finance indicators 142
financial analysis 450
finite failure model 292
fishbone analysis 398
fishbone diagram 69
forecasting 238
FTA 272
F-test 70

Index

full function points 169, 180
Full Function Points 165, 187, 501
function component proportions 184
function point approximation 183
function point estimation 183, 185
function point method 502
function point proportions 184
Function Point Workbench 93
function points 183, 184, 185, 187
functional size 180
functional size measurement 180, 197
functional user requirement 170
fuzzy classification 266

global software engineering 461, 490
goal 119, 188, 189, 349
goal-oriented 21, 38
goal-oriented measurement 350
Goal-Question-Metric 21, 65, 80, 284
GQM *See Goal-Question-Metric*
GSE 461

Hawthorne effect 19, 497
Heisenberg principle 497
histogram 68, 398
history database 145, 487
hypothesis test 420

IEEE 1044 283
IEEE 982.1 6
IFPUG 166, 184, 502
incremental development 223
indicator 25
infinite failure models 292
information model 2
information theory 18
inspection 260
inspection planning 261
internet resources 505
interval scale 46
Investment analysis 450
ISBSG 184, 187, 471, 479, 503
ISBSG Measurement Repository 471
Ishikawa diagram 284
ISO 4, 5, 504
ISO 12207 6, 35
ISO 14143 6, 501
ISO 15288 6, 35
ISO 15504 5, 343, 344, 359
ISO 15939 6, 83, 118
ISO 16085 6

ISO 19761 6, 165, 169, 501
ISO 20926 6
ISO 9001 5, 245, 343
ISO/TS 16949 6
IT measurement organizations 153
IT measurements 149, 152, 197
IT project 22, 188
IT services 446
ITIL 78
IWSM 501

Kiviat diagram 99
Knowledge PLAN 92
KnowledgePlan 193
KPI 353

law 487
laws
  global software engineering 490
  process improvement 495
  project management 487
  quality 492
  requirements management 491
  Software Pareto laws 494
LCL 285, 400, 411
LDRA 94
lean measurement 228
liability 233
lines of code 180
Littlewood-Verrall model 292
LNHPP 292
LOC counting 120
Logiscope 96
LOGISCOPE 93

MAIN 504
MAIN Network 153
maintainability 245
maintenance projects 242
management support 184, 188
management techniques 205
manipulation 155
Mark II 501
Mark II Function Points 166
McCabe, Thomas 51, 94, 264, 272
measurement
  agent-based systems 317
  analysis 67, 117, 129
  basic measurements 28, 33, 35, 200, 201, 208, 241
  benefits 22

558   Index

CAME 52
CMMI process areas 343, 365
cognitive process 133
collection 124
communication 129
communities 505
complexity 51, 94, 264, 272
core measurements 28, 33, 35, 200, 201, 208, 241
cost 26, 28, 32, 212, 378
cost control 445
COTS software 482
dashboard 30, 147, 207
data quality 126
database 145, 183, 473
definition 58, 120
E4–process 8, 24, 39, 109, 110, 111, 217, 349, 403, 404, 436
e-learning 103
empirical laws 487
empirical relational system 57
failures 3
foundations 41
framework 79
goal orientation 141
goal-driven 21
information model 2
introduction 111, 160, 469
introduction steps 111
life-cycle 109, 111
life-cycle 109
life-cycle 111
manipulation 155
methods 44
misuse 154
model 55
numerical relational system 57
objectives 25, 42
performance 301
plan 121
process 23, 39, 44, 115
process improvement 349, 356
process measurement 343
productivity 372, 381
program 111, 113, 188, 243
quick start 18
reliability 247
requirements management 217, 220
responsible 114
risks 3, 25, 39, 128, 196
ROI 158, 294, 422, 441

roles and responsibilities 113
scale 46, 49
service 311
SOA 309
stakeholders 113
standards 4
storage 472
success factors 2, 156, 196
suite 28, 33, 35, 200, 201, 208, 241
system 42
template 121
theory 54, 62
tool 52
tools 91, 472
training 157
units 50
usage 2, 11, 111
validation 43, 54
viewpoint 170, 175
METKIT 96
Metrics One 93
MIL 498 6
minimum measurements 28, 33, 35, 200, 201, 208, 241
misuse 154
module test 260
MOOD 93
MOOD measurements 324
motivation 151
motivational system 151
multi-agent system 317
multivariate statistics 132

NESMA 501, 505
nominal scale 46
non-cost of quality 295
non-parametric statistical techniques 396
NPV 142
numerical relational system 57

objective-driven process improvement 332, 345, 427
objectives 22
observational field study 421
ODPI 332
offshoring 461
OOMJ 94
Open Office 106
operational profile 251
ordinal scale 46

organizational baseline 415
orthogonal defect classification 286
outlier 130
outsourcing 461, 478

P&L statement 22
parameters 193, 194
Pareto analysis 131, 398
Pareto chart 68
Pareto rule 262
PC-METRIC 94
PD *See* person day
people 148
percentage method 189
performance 89, 206, 245
performance engineering 301
performance improvement 356
person day 189
person hour 189, 246
person month 189
person year 246
Philip Crosby 342
Plan, Do Check, Act 24
planning 149, 151, 193
PLM 35
PM *See* person month
PMBOK 6, 212, 254
PMT 94
Poisson process 291
policy 6, 142
portfolio management 25, 33, 147, 450
precision 249
prediction 239, 249
   error type 1 250, 266
   error type 2 250, 266
   precision 249
   recall 249
prediction system 48
presentation 129
probability 64
process change management 341
process deviation 399
process improvement 193, 227, 329, 338, 428
   benefits 418, 422, 431
   laws 495
   measurement 356, 359, 418
   measurements 343, 365
   model 87
   solutions 353
   success factors 358, 394

process management 335, 428
process measurement 343, 349
process owner 341
product data management 333
product liability 233
product life-cycle 32, 35, 159, 202, 333
product life-cycle 27, 28
product life-cycle 33
product life-cycle 35
product life-cycle management 252, 333
product line 459
product management 459
product quality 153
productivity 29, 141, 193, 381, 444
productivity improvement 351, 372
productivity measurements 183
productivity paradox 441
project complexity 193
project control 201, 204, 205, 243
project dashboard 30, 207
project duration 190, 193
project estimation 183
project life-cycle 201
project management 189, 199, 460, 487
project manager 205
project measurement 28, 33, 35, 200, 201, 208, 241
project register database 184, 187
project review 203
project size 191
project team 119
project tracking 230
project tracking measurements 207
Putnam 168

QSM 193
quality 152, 188, 189, 193, 492
quality assurance 188, 189
quality assurance measurements 189
quality control 189, 251
quality features 189
quality gates 252
quality goals 189
quality management 207, 245
quality measurement 230
quality measurements 188, 189
quality of service 311
quality planning 188
QUALMS 93

quantitative process management 392, 393, 410
quick estimation 185

ratio scale 46
RATplus 269
recall 249
reengineering 331
regression analysis 47, 187, 188, 398
release management 459
release timing 225
reliability 246
reliability engineering 269
reliability growth model 291
reliability improvement 247
reliability model 247, 269, 290
reliability prediction 247, 291
Repeatability 127
replicated experiment 421
reporting 38
repository 474
requirements 188
requirements creep 193
requirements management 217, 491
requirements quality 220
resistance 151, 152
resource planning 191
risk 152
risk analysis 235
risk management 34, 232, 243, 266
RMS 93
ROA 34, 142, 450
ROCE 34, 450
ROI 32, 142, 144, 158, 246, 294, 423, 441, 446, 450
ROI calculation 294, 422, 431, 441
rule of thumb 52, 185, 187, 487
RuleChecker 97
run chart 68, 399

safety 268, 272, 408
Sarbanes-Oxley Act 6, 142, 233
scale 46
SCAMPI 6, 338, 363
scatter diagram 69
scatterplot 398
scorecard 32
security 78, 89, 144, 245, 268, 315, 320
SEI core measurements 25
sensitiveness 450
sensitivity analysis 193, 194

service control 479
service measurement 309
shotgun approach 71
sigma distribution 406
significance 131, 137, 191, 256, 325, 427
simulation 421
simulations 193, 194
six sigma 6, 84, 402, 403, 413
size measurement 120
SLA 311, 465
SLIM 92, 168, 191, 193
SMART 38, 254
SOA 104, 309
SOA reference model 310
SOAP 106
SOFT-CALC 93
SOFT-ORG 92
software crisis 194
software development 188
software development process 189
software engineering 17, 63
software law 52
software measurement 150
software measurement program 244
software measurements 502
Software Process Dashboard tool 124
software process measurement model 87
software product 188
software project management 200
software reliability engineering 287
software system 188
Space Shuttle Challenger 154
SPC 395, 413
SPEC 504
SPICE 81, 344, 359
SPR function points 185
stakeholder 22, 29
standard measurements 28, 33, 35, 200, 201, 208, 241
standards 5, 504
Standish Group 20, 200, 423
statistical process control 67, 395, 413
statistical test methods 70
statistical tests 131
statistical verification 420
statistics 56, 67, 395
   non-parametric techniques 396
   normal distribution 395
   standard deviation 395

STW-METRIC 94
success factors 151, 359
supplier management 465
SWEBOK 6

tailoring 334
TCO 142
team size 189
technology management 456
template 121
test 222
test coverage 251
test defect detection effectiveness 259
test measurements 273
test progress 226, 279
test tracking 212
TestChecker 97
time series 130
time to profit 34
Timeliness 127
TL 9000 6
TPC 505
tracking 207
tracking system 445
Trend analysis 450
trigger event 234
t-test 70

UCL 285, 400, 411

UCP 167
UKSMA 505
UML
    Unified Modeling Language 303
unadjusted function points 184
UQAM 187
usability 89, 245
usage specification 251
use case points 167

VAF 184
validation 273
Validity 127
value analysis 450
variance analysis 445
visibility 119
voice of the customer 397
voice of the process 397

warehouse 474
Watts Humphrey 343
Web services 309
Weibull process model 292
work breakdown structure (WBS) 193
workflow management 332

Yamada-Osaki model 292

ZD-MIS 96

Printing: Krips bv, Meppel
Binding: Stürtz, Würzburg